Clarence Darrow
FOR THE DEFENSE

CLARENCE DARROW

Clarence Darrow
FOR THE DEFENSE

A BIOGRAPHY BY

Irving Stone

DOUBLEDAY & COMPANY, INC.

Garden City, New York

For

JEAN STONE

(*my good right arm*)

Foreword

THE READER will find six hundred and thirty source notes at the back of the book. All notes are designated by page reference and subject matter, thus making them readily available to the student without constantly interrupting the reading mood of the more general reader.

The main sources of this biography were Clarence Darrow's private correspondence, family documents, manuscripts, legal briefs, notebooks and unpublished memoirs, sold to me by Mrs Darrow; the back files of court reports, congressional reports, newspapers, magazines and privately printed pamphlets; the personal contributions of more than two hundred of Darrow's lifelong friends, partners, associates, and the untiring efforts of the Darrow family, in particular Mrs Clarence (Ruby) Darrow and Paul Darrow, to enrich and authenticate every phase of Clarence Darrow's life. No restrictions were imposed upon me by the Darrows as to what I might write or publish.

The names of those who contributed so liberally to this biography are published at the back of the book, but it would be ingratitude indeed if I did not acknowledge at this point that A. Kroch is the godfather of the project; that Justice Francis S. Wilson has worked indefatigably to document it; that Maurice Berkson has read every line of manuscript in an effort to keep it free from legal errors.

The entire collection of Clarence Darrow's private papers, as well as all correspondence with the author, is in the possession of Leo M. Cherne, of the Research Institute of America, 292 Madison Avenue, New York City, where it may be seen or studied by anyone who is interested.

IRVING STONE

February 27, 1941

Contents

I may hate the sin, but never the sinner.

CLARENCE DARROW

PROLOGUE

A Lawyer Comes of Age

Hɪs ᴅᴇᴄɪsɪᴏɴ ᴍᴀᴅᴇ, he stretched out his fingers before him on the mahogany desk, pushed upward and rose. It was only a short distance down the hall from the legal department, with the roar of the elevated trains pouring in on a level keel from the open third-story windows, and up two flights of stairs to the office of the president, but if he traveled those few steps they must prove the longest journey he had undertaken in his thirty-seven years. He could cite few sustaining precedents in the casebook of lawyers: he knew he was not the stuff of which martyrs are made; he was not even the possessor of a cause to lend him the courage of fanaticism. Yet his father had served as the Kinsman, Ohio, link of the Underground Railroad, and many a midnight the boy had been awakened to ride to the next village on top of a load of hay that concealed an escaping Negro slave.

As he opened the door of his office and stood with the knob in his hand, his head down, his mind re-created the picture and impact of all he had learned about his employers in the two years since he had come to work for them as general attorney. If he had been seeking affiliation with bigness and power, not even a position at the right hand of the Roman emperors could have offered him such an opportunity. The railroads and their contributing industries gave employment to two million workers; their capitalization was easily a tenth of the estimated wealth of the nation. By masterful management the railroads determined the price manufacturers should receive for their machines and farmers for their fruit, wheat or hogs; decreed which towns should flourish and which decay; which states should remain agricultural and which become industrial; which companies should be wiped out and which converted into gigantic trusts.

He closed the door firmly behind him and strode down the hall, his massive shoulders hunched forward, musing that he would make a mighty poor opponent for an industry that attempted to control the national Congress and the courts, to elect governors and mayors, to buy state legislators and city councilmen. True, he owned the modest home in which he lived, but aside from that he had only a few hundred dollars in the bank; he was a quiet, bookish fellow who loathed discord; what business had he in this mess?

Without waiting for an answer to his knock he thrust open a door and entered a large plain room. Marvin Hughitt, president of the Chicago and North Western Railway, was seated behind his desk at the far end, in front of a row of windows that gave a commanding view of the Chicago River and the passenger station on its opposite bank. Though it was a hot July day, Hughitt was dressed in a heavy dark suit, his iron-gray hair and long beard giving him the appearance of an Old Testament prophet. A man who rarely smiled, Hughitt's eyes twinkled slightly when Darrow came in, coatless, his broad black suspenders holding shapeless blue trousers, the black satin necktie wiggling down his white shirt front like a corkscrew, his big head telescoped into wide shoulders, his fine brown hair falling from a part on the left side over a high, rounded brow.

Clarence Darrow admired Marvin Hughitt because he had a sense of justice; only the year before he had risked his position and reputation by joining with Darrow in a plea to Governor Altgeld to pardon the four anarchists convicted of a conspiracy to throw the fatal Haymarket bomb. On his part, Hughitt was fond of the younger man; he had been responsible for bringing him into the company after following Governor Altgeld's suggestion to watch the work his protégé was doing in the law department of the city of Chicago.

Though the job of counsel for the Chicago and North Western Railway was several steps up the legal ladder, Darrow had accepted it with misgivings, sensing that the main body of his work would consist in defending the railroad against workmen or passengers who had been injured. By a stroke of good fortune the claim agent, Ralph Richards, was fair-minded; together they were able to "help a great many people without serious cost to the road." Hughitt liked Darrow's simple manner of handling and settling what other lawyers might have turned into complicated cases; if he cost the company a few extra dollars he justified the expenditures by earning good will and keeping them out of the courts. Hughitt and the other officials of the Chicago and North Western knew Clarence Darrow to be an intellectual liberal, sympathetic to the underdog, but he made no attempt to proselytize within the offices of the company, and he did his job better than anyone else they could find.

"You look hot, Clarence," ventured Hughitt.

"I am, under the collar—even if it isn't buttoned."

"Tomorrow's the Fourth; you'll be able to cool off."

Darrow towered to his full six feet; he weighed only a hundred and eighty pounds, but when he wasn't contracted into a slouch he seemed enormous.

"Nobody's going to be cool in Chicago tomorrow," he said in a tight voice. "I just finished reading the injunction the Circuit Court served against the strikers this morning. It not only makes it a criminal act for a man to go out on strike, but it becomes a prison offense for one man to suggest to another that he strike."

"That injunction will save bloodshed and the destruction of property," replied Hughitt soberly.

"I thought this was supposed to be a free country? I thought men had a right to stop work when they didn't find conditions satisfactory? If their own elected government tells them it's illegal to strike, that they must work under any terms the employers see fit to grant them or go to jail, then they're no better than slaves. If this is really a democracy we live under, that injunction is illegal."

Marvin Hughitt was a self-made man in the most robust American tradition: he had begun as a telegrapher in the Civil War and by sheer force and conviction had become one of the railway leaders of the country. Though he was autocratic in his methods, his employees respected him for his ability to fill a tough job.

"It's perfectly legal, Clarence, under both the Interstate Commerce Act and the Sherman Anti-Trust Law."

"Now there's a sweet piece of irony!" exploded Darrow. "The Interstate Commerce Act was directed against the monopolistic practices of the railroads, and the Sherman Anti-Trust Act was passed to control corporations like the Pullman Company. You know as well as I that neither act contains any references to labor organizations."

"We made our injunction stick in 1877," replied Hughitt doggedly, "when we broke the first big railroad strike."

"You had a technical excuse then: the railroads were in receivership; you could claim that put them in the custody of the Federal courts."

"We have a technical justification this time too. No body of men can obstruct the United States mails."

Darrow shook his head brusquely at Hughitt, as though to say, "You'll have to do better than that!" Aloud he commented, "You'd have the devil's own time proving the mails are being obstructed. Only three days ago the Chicago superintendent of mails wired Washington that no mails have accumulated here and that with a few exceptions all regular trains are moving nearly on time—except those carrying Pullmans."

"But surely, Clarence," replied Hughitt, "you can see that this strike should never have been called. The railroad men have no grievance against us. They went out only because they were sympathetic to the striking Pullman shop employees."

"Eugene Debs and the other American Railway Union officials are certainly not going to obey this highhanded injunction and send their men back to work defeated. If they did they would set a precedent for crushing every strike that arose. Mr Hughitt, I've learned something about conspiracy since I've been with you. I've watched your General Managers' Association control wages on the twenty-four lines operating out of Chicago; I've watched you depress wages uniformly on all the lines, so the men couldn't quit and find better jobs elsewhere; I've watched you use black lists against good workmen whose only offense was that they thought labor should have better hours and wages; I've watched your agency supply men to member lines on which there were strikes, to break those strikes; I've watched you pool your millions to keep your workmen powerless. Why do you think Debs formed the American Railway Union? To fight your conspiracy. Within a few days Debs and the boys will be in jail with contempt and conspiracy charges against them. Don't you think that in the spirit of fair play the heads of your General Managers' Association should keep them company in jail?"

There was silence in the sun-filled room. Darrow's usually soft and merry blue eyes were dark and brooding.

"I'm giving up my job here, Mr Hughitt, to defend Eugene Debs and the American Railway Union."

Hughitt regarded Darrow sternly: how to make out this unorthodox behavior? The traditional role of the lawyer was to serve big business against any and all comers, to accomplish its purposes by any and all means. This chap Darrow was a freak, a renegade, but he was a good man even if he was a misguided sentimentalist.

"They haven't a chance, Clarence; this injunction is a Gatling gun on paper. Why give up a good position for a hopeless cause?

Don Quixote only tilted at windmills; you're going to run into a high-powered locomotive under full steam."

"Without even the benefit of a horse or a lance," grunted Darrow.

"I know seven thousand dollars a year isn't a great deal of money, Clarence, but it 'll be ten thousand by the end of another year and twenty thousand at the end of three or four. These unions can't pay you anything; when the case is over you'll be stranded, without clients or a future, and every businessman in Chicago avoiding you as a radical. Stay with us; we can put you on top, make you governor of Illinois or United States senator, get you a post in the Cabinet——"

"Like Attorney General Olney," commented Darrow bitingly.

"Yes, like Olney. There's fame and fortune for the asking——"

"Then I guess those are not the things I'm asking for," broke in Darrow. "I guess I got the wrong background. I believe in the right of people to better themselves, and I'm going to throw in my ten cents' worth to help them."

"You're determined?"

"I'm determined. When a member of the United States Cabinet like Olney, who is an old-line railroad lawyer, appoints Edwin Walker special assistant attorney general at Chicago, knowing that Walker is at the very same time the lawyer for the General Managers' Association, and Walker as a representative of the United States government persuades two Federal judges in a Chicago Circuit Court to enjoin the workers from striking, that's too much of a conspiracy for my weak stomach. I gotta get up and fight."

Hughitt leaned across the desk, his hand extended.

"After we've broken the strike, Clarence, and wiped out the American Railway Union we want you to come back."

Darrow stared at his boss in astonishment. "You want me to come back!"

"Well, not full time—if you don't want to. Say half time: handle our cases that don't involve labor or personal injury."

Darrow grinned his broad, boyish grin and shook hands with Hughitt. He then went back to his office, stuffed some papers into a brief case, threw his coat over his arm and walked out on his job as counsel for the Chicago and North Western Railway.

CHAPTER I

What Goes into the Making of an American?

A FEW DAYS before his son had given up his job, Amirus Darrow had decided to spend a week in Kinsman visiting old friends. Clarence had slipped several greenbacks into his father's pocket, and Jessie put up a lunch for her father-in-law for the train. Amirus left early in the morning, riding the streetcar downtown from 4219 Vincennes Avenue. When he found that he had a half-hour before train time he descended a flight of stairs into a basement secondhand bookstore.

At ten o'clock that night the bell rang at the Darrow home. Clarence opened the door to find his father glaze-eyed, hugging a huge bundle under each arm. Amirus had found so many books for which he had always yearned that he had not emerged from the bookshop until twelve hours later, his railroad and vacation money spent. He had come home to read his precious literary treasures, all desire to visit Kinsman gone. Seeing his father standing before him on the porch, his eyes dreamy and withdrawn and beautiful, the son realized that the older man had always missed his train because he had found something more interesting in a book than would be waiting for him at the end of a journey.

Amirus Darrow was the son of a New England farmer who had emigrated to the pioneer country of Ohio around 1830 in an effort to improve himself. He did not better himself materially; no Darrow was ever blessed with the special gift of making or retaining money. But, poor as the Darrows may have been, they gave their children the best available education. Amirus went to a good school in Amboy. In one of his classes he met Emily Eddy, whose parents

6

had also emigrated from Connecticut and whose father had likewise served as a station for the Underground Railway. The couple fell in love, married very young and moved to Meadville, Pennsylvania, where Amirus, athirst for knowledge, attended Allegheny College. Here Clarence's parents acted out their prologue to poverty, living in austere simplicity on whatever coins Amirus could earn in his spare hours. They were happy because they both loved the world of books and ideas and learning.

Amirus soon realized that his greatest joy would always be in contemplation and that he must manage to earn his living from the spoken word and the printed page. Theology being the only apparent field in which one could subsist on the earnings of a scholar, Amirus entered the new Unitarian school in Meadville. He was the first to be graduated. The Unitarian Church was prepared to find him a parish. With a comfortable life assured him, with innumerable hours of the day and night available for his reading and thinking and learning, Amirus abandoned theology because his studies led him to doubt. "The end of wisdom is the fear of God; the beginning of wisdom is doubt." He was equipped neither by training nor temperament to do anything else; already knowing the privations of poverty, the young couple walked fearlessly into a dark uncharted world rather than be dishonest to their convictions and beliefs.

Amirus and Emily Darrow were evidence that everyone is capable of his own peculiar heroism. He may not recognize it under that imposing title, for he is merely doing what his instincts tell him he must do to set his life straight; yet it is, in fact, so great a heroism that his neighbor, living out his own unrecognizable heroism, is awe-stricken at the other man's courage: and that is what holds the world together.

As a result of their decision Amirus and Emily lived lives of quiet desperation. They returned to Farmdale, just two miles from Kinsman, where they found themselves persecuted because they were always the opposition and always the minority: the lone free-thinkers against rock-ribbed religionists, the lone Democrats against Ohio's solid Republicans, the lone free traders against the high-tariff tradition, the lone intellectuals in a tiny valley of farmers. Amirus Darrow enjoyed this role of the opposition, not only because it kept his mind alert, kept him studying, gave him serious subjects to think about and discuss, kept him ever searching for fresh knowledge and wisdom, but because it enabled him to be a teacher, to bring ideas from the world beyond the mountains, to plead for open-mindedness, variety in thought, tolerance, the love of the naked truth.

There were difficult days during which the parents of Amirus and Emily must have helped, for the young Darrows earned more children than money from their early efforts. Amirus fumbled dreamily from one job to another; finding carpentry the least to his disliking, he began building hard wooden furniture for the farmers. That he ultimately trained himself to become a tolerable craftsman is attested by the fact that some of the beds, tables and chairs he built seventy years ago are still in use around Kinsman; but his heart was never in his work. Clarence said that all his life his father was a visionary and a dreamer; even when he sorely needed money he would neglect his work to read some book. Amirus loved knowledge for its own sake; the pure scholar, he had no thought of turning it either to use or profit. Though the family sometimes lacked for the necessities of life, the house was always filled with hundreds upon hundreds of books: Latin, Greek, Hebrew; history, law, metaphysics, literature; strewn about the floor, on the tables, mantelpieces, chairs, underfoot no matter where one stepped.

"In all the country round," said Clarence, "no man knew so much of books as he, and no man knew less of life. The old parson and the doctor were the only neighbors who seemed able to understand the language he spoke. I remember when his work was done how religiously he went to his little study with his marvelous books. My bedroom opened directly from his study door, and no matter how often I wakened in the night I could see a streak of lamplight at the bottom of the door which showed me that he was still dwelling in the fairylands of which his old volumes told. Often, too, he wrote, sometimes night after night for weeks together, no doubt his hopes and dreams and doubts and loves and fears."

To her everlasting glory, Emily Darrow, who had to bear eight children and raise seven of them, cook for them, wash their dishes, scrub their clothes and necks and feet, nurse them when they were ill and train them when they were well, who had to see that the thin stream of dollars continued to trickle into the house and then make each dollar fulfill the obligations of its two missing companions, never reproached her husband for his impracticality or tried to change his nature or way of life. Nor did her privations turn her against books; she continued to read whenever she could find five unoccupied minutes, was active in the woman's-suffrage movement, campaigned for Democratic candidates in a Republican fortress and could be counted on to work for the liberal movements in religion, education and politics. She was an open-faced, wide-eyed, attractively unbeautiful gentlewoman with a high forehead, robust oval, strong mouth and chin and hair that she parted in the center to comb tightly downward, concealing all but the lobes of her ears. If she was not demonstrative with the children it was because demonstrations of affection were thought to be signs of weakness rather than love.

The first Darrow to come to America, around 1680, sharing a grant from the king of England for the town of New London, Connecticut, was an undertaker, and Amirus Darrow continued to carry on that trade in conjunction with his small furniture factory in back of the house in Kinsman. The main difference between the original Darrow and Amirus was that the poverty-stricken Amirus had somehow contrived to buy a hearse. When it wasn't being used for funerals the Darrow hearse was pressed into service as a delivery truck and farm wagon, delivering the beds, tables and chairs ordered from the carpenter shop or transporting chickens, pigs, grain. Amirus' fifth child, Clarence, carried on the family tradition: a good part of his life was devoted to burying economic and social corpses that insisted on coming up after every storm.

2

Clarence Seward Darrow was born on April 18, 1857, in a white frame building in Farmdale, an attractive one-and-a-half-story cottage shaded by huge trees. In 1864, when he was seven and just beginning to understand why so many Trumbull County lads were being brought home for burial in the graveyard behind the church, his family managed to buy a house just a half mile from the town square of Kinsman, "and he called this place home until he was twenty-one years of age."

Kinsman was a valley town planted alongside a small river on whose banks the original settlers, after they had felled the trees and driven off the wild animals, built white frame houses and planted corn, potatoes, hay. There was little reason for the town to grow big; there was little reason for anyone to grow rich or poor: the settlers remained within the citadel formed by the two flanking ranges. Neither their legs nor their thoughts roamed past the protecting wall of hills, for life was primitively ample in Kinsman. The settlers were content, and their children remained after them, content. All except the Darrows, whose father "looked to the high hills to the east and to the high hills to the west and up and down the narrow country road that led to the outside world. He knew that beyond the high hills was a broad inviting plain, with opportunity and plenty, with fortune and fame, but as he looked at the hills he could see no way to pass beyond. It is possible that he could have walked over them or even around them if he had been alone, but there was the ever-growing brood that held him in the narrow place."

There is an old saying that "every pot finds its cover." The non-conformist Darrows, who served as the town agnostics and intellectuals, stumbled onto the one eccentric and nonconformist house in the countryside, an octagonal-shaped structure with a wide wooden pavilion running around seven of its eight sides. There was a hill in the back yard down which Clarence would sled when there was snow on the ground, a creek at the bottom of the hill where he could wade in warm weather and apple, spruce and maple trees in the yard to climb. There were chickens, horses, dogs, a cow, also roaming the back yard with the Darrow progeny. For his first pet Clarence was given a baby chick to raise. One day he returned home to find his pet being served for supper. The boy fled from the table in tears, for seventy-five years steadfastly refusing to swallow one morsel of chicken! When he was defending Big Bill Haywood, secretary of the Western Federation of Miners, in Boise, Idaho, Mrs Wilson, the wife of his assistant counsel, invited him to dinner for the following day. That midnight, when the Wilsons were asleep, there was a knocking on the door. There stood Darrow, without a necktie, his hair falling over one eye.

"I forgot to tell you," he murmured apologetically, "I don't eat chicken. When people invite me to dinner they invariably serve me chicken."

"That's just too bad about you," replied Mrs Wilson. "I've already bought my chickens, and you'll eat what the rest eat."

The next evening Darrow sat resignedly at the Wilson table, watching everyone in turn being helped liberally to roast chicken with giblet stuffing. When it came time for him to be served Mrs Wilson emerged triumphantly from the kitchen with a two-inch sizzling steak.

For Clarence the most fascinating part of Kinsman was the town commons, where he played baseball and stored up the richest memories of his childhood. On Saturday afternoons the entire population assembled to watch Kinsman play Berg Hill, Warren or Andover, the games lasting from one o'clock until dark, with the girls of the town serving an out-of-doors supper when the contest ended.

"Clarence was the star first baseman," proudly boasted his younger sister Jenny, "and all the girls vied for the honor of making his uniforms."

The climax of his youth occurred on the afternoon when, coming to bat in the last half of the ninth inning, their opponents leading them by one run, with two men out and two on base, he hit a home run over the grocery store. Through the years, as he would sit in the bleachers on Saturday afternoons eating peanuts and rooting for the Chicago Cubs, he would remember his sweetest triumph and chuckle.

In the town square was located the wagon shop, with its stacks of lumber and piles of long shavings, where he played "I Spy"; the blacksmith shop with its white-hot fire, anvil and hammers and the mighty-muscled smith—who was also the town's bellows-lunged lawyer—hammering Fourth of July sparks into the air. He knew that the shoeshop was by far the biggest factory in the country, for in busy seasons it employed as many as four men. There was the tavern, into which he never dared to venture even though his father had built most of its furniture, "for the owner, it was darkly rumored, kept a barrel of whisky in a secret corner of his cellar." And then there was the general store, where he wandered among the shelves, marveling that people could think of so many different things to make, wondering for what they could all be used. Lastly, across the river, was the most enchanting place of all, the gristmill with its water wheel, the dam and pond with its frogs and the millrace where the big wooden gate was lifted and the water came over the wooden flume to turn the groaning wheel.

At the long-anticipated age of six he was entered in the one-room district school. "Every morning we children were given a dinner pail packed full of pie and cake, and now and then a piece of bread and butter, and sent off to school. Almost as soon as the snow was off the ground in the spring, we boys took off our shoes. No matter how early we left home it was nearly always past the hour of nine when we reached the door. For there were birds in the trees and stones in the road, and no child ever knew any pain except his own. There were little fishes in the creek over which we slid in winter and through which we waded in the summertime; then there were chipmunks on the fences and woodchucks in the fields, and no boy could ever go straight to school or straight back home after the day was done. The procession of barefoot urchins laughed and joked and fought and ran and bragged and gave no thought to study or to books until the bell was rung. Then we watched and waited eagerly for the recess, and after that still more anxiously for the hour of noon, which was always the best time of all the day because of the games."

In Clarence's McGuffey readers every manifestation of virtue earned its immediate and grandiose reward, but not one story told that any profit "might come from willfulness or selfishness or greed."

By observing the savage conduct of their playmates and the business ethics of their elders, the children rejected their teachers and books. In most of their minds was destroyed the faith in the printed word, the truth to be found between book covers, the value of an education.

After passing six years in the district school his first pair of long trousers was given to him, and he was sent up the hill to the public academy. His estimate of his high-school years is best delineated by the consternation he caused when he was invited to address the 1918 graduating class of the Nicholas Senn High School in Chicago. The story is told by one of the students.

"Our glassy-eyed, pompous principal had us five hundred graduates thoroughly numbed and awed by the recital of our great responsibilities. Darrow patiently sat it out, playing with a watch chain and looking up at the ceiling as he sprawled in his dinky folding chair. Finally he was lavishly introduced with the usual long hot-air harangue of noble phraseology. Darrow ambled over to the big rostrum and leaned against it comfortably in that stooping way he had. He looked like a big easygoing janitor in the wrong place with all those ramrod stuffed shirts around. He looked us over, turning his head in dead silence, and finally he began to chuckle.

" 'Look—let's you fellows down there relax now. That was as fine a lot of bunk as I ever heard in my life, and I know darned well you youngsters didn't believe a word of it. You're no more fit to "go forth and serve" than the man in the moon. You're just a bunch of ignorant kids full of the devil, and you've learned practically nothing to show for the four years you spent here. You can't fool me, because I once spent four years in just such a place!' "

"The parents were shocked; the faculty was purple with rage, but naturally we students were ecstatic. It was the only good sense we had heard in months."

3

At home easygoing Amirus was a tyrant when it came to studies. He was going to train his children to live cultivated and intelligent lives, to fill important places in the world, whether they liked it or not.

"John Stuart Mill began studying Greek when he was only three years old," he drummed into each of his seven children in turn. Clarence wailed when he had to leave a game of leapfrog or abandon a berrying in the woods to study the lesson in Greek mythology his father had set for him.

"Father was pretty strict," said Jenny. "Books and study were all important; play and fun didn't count. Every night we sat around the kerosene lamp and studied our lessons. When we thought we had learned them we had to recite them aloud to Father."

Everett, the eldest, intervened for Mary to gain her special privileges. Mary, in her turn, interceded for Clarence when he just had to get out to baseball practice. "If I wanted a favor," said Jenny, "Clarence was the first one I turned to."

From his father Clarence learned that tolerance is something more than an opportunistic demand made on other people to persuade them to endure one's views. As an agnostic, Amirus would have no part of the commanding church on the hill, with its square white belfry; yet every Sunday morning the seven young Darrows were scrubbed with soap and brushes in iron tubs heated on a wood-burning stove, dressed in their best clothes and shoes and led up the hill to services—by Mother—while Father retired to the sanctity of his study. Amirus contended that merely because he was unreligious was no justification for forcing his opinions on his defenseless children. After they had participated in the ritual of the church and been grounded in the history of world religions at home, they would be free to form their own preferences to fit their particular natures. The contest was doubtless not an even one, for the church strove to stifle any joyful religious impulses of the young.

"The Sabbath, the Church and religion were serious and solemn matters to the band of pilgrims who every Sunday drove up the hill," wrote Clarence. "All our neighbors and acquaintances were members of the United Presbyterian Church, and to them their religion seemed a gloomy thing. Their Sabbath began at sundown on Saturday and lasted until Monday morning, and the gloom seemed to grow and deepen on their faces as the light faded into twilight and the darkness of the evening came. I could not understand then, nor do I today, why we were made to go to church; surely our good parents did not know how we suffered, or they would not have been so cruel or unkind. I could not have sat through the interminable prayers but for the fact that I learned to find landmarks as the minister, his white face circled with a fringe of white whiskers, went along. At a certain point I knew it was well under way; at another point it was about half done, and when he began asking for guidance for the President of the United States it was three quarters over, and I felt like a shipwrecked mariner sighting land."

When Clarence was fourteen his mother died. Emily Eddy Darrow was only forty-four, but she had already done the work of two lifetimes. Despite the brood of children growing up at her feet, she was often lonely, for she had no companions among the orthodox women of the town, and her husband spent his spare hours with his books. No one was able to compute how many thousands of meals she had cooked, beds she had made, floors she had swept, necks, dishes and shirts she had scrubbed, breads and pies baked, colds treated, fevers fought. Yet as she staggered along without sufficient funds or hours in the day to do her unending job, no one found time or thought to thank her. The husband and children took her for granted; not until she was gone did they realize how important the mother had been to the home, how empty and forlorn it was without her. Not until he reached his full maturity did her son Clarence understand how kind and strong and good his mother had been; how overworked and harassed and unappreciated.

At sixteen, lanky and gangling, he was sent off to Allegheny College to follow in the footsteps of his father, even though his father's education, to all external appearances, had seemed to do him more harm than good. He lived with the family of Professor Williams, doing chores to earn his board and lodging. His visage was as plain and open as an alarm clock. His eyes were already deep set; like his mother and father, he had an enormous forehead, a forward-looking nose, contradictory mouth with its ascetic upper lip and sensual under lip and a smooth, granitelike ball chin with an indentation low down toward the jawbone. It was what lawyers call an affidavit face; one that did not lie; broad beamed, broad across the heavy eyebrows to the close-fitting ears, broad across the cheekbones, mouth and chin; not handsome, but big, honest, affable.

Young Darrow did not know why he was going to Meadville to college. He had not the faintest notion what he wanted to do. Yet his father and his older brother Everett and older sister Mary, who had already graduated from college and were teaching, believed passionately in the magic charm and potency of education. If only Clarence would subject himself to education all obstacles would be removed, all uncertainty vanish; an open, shining road would be revealed. Nor was this mouthy talk with the three older Darrows: they scrimped and saved and denied themselves the ordinary comforts that they might garner the few dollars to send Clarence to college. Here he majored in baseball, added to his dislike of Latin and Greek, stonily refused his father's plea to study Hebrew, "got by" in geometry and scratched his first spark of interest in the natural sciences. On Decoration Day he visited home because he had been invited to speak a piece in the Presbyterian Church, a great honor for the son of the town agnostic.

At the end of his freshman year he returned to Kinsman torn between apathy and disgust with higher education. And here, in 1873, the railroads made a change in his life, just as they would later in 1894. Jay Cooke and Company, the banking house that had floated loans for the government during the Civil War, gathered in capital from small investors all over the country to push the building of the Northern Pacific Railroad. The money was used extravagantly, the road built beyond the needs of the times; when the interest payments could not be met on the bonds Jay Cooke and Company went into bankruptcy, dragging the rest of the country into a severe depression.

If not for the panic of 1873, Darrow might have completed his studies at Allegheny; how that would have altered his course was something he liked to speculate about when he was pondering the imponderables of life.

<h2 style="text-align:center">4</h2>

That summer he did his first consistent work, helping in the little furniture factory behind the octagonal-shaped house, though he still refused to go near the shop when his father was measuring a corpse for a coffin. He never became a good carpenter, but his father finally came to trust him with a turning lathe or a paintbrush. What Amirus did not know was that Clarence was refusing to paint the bottom side of the seat of chairs, on the grounds that it was a waste of time and paint. To this day the people of Trumbull County in Ohio turn over Darrow chairs to see whether it was Clarence who wielded the paintbrush.

Charles A. Beard relates, "Once a bright reporter asked Darrow to what he owed his success. Gently protesting against the use of the word 'success' in connection with his life, Darrow replied: 'To hard work.' When the reporter looked pained at this chamber-of-commerce reply, Darrow explained, 'When I was a boy my father set me to work on a hot summer day, hoeing potatoes, and after I had worked hard for a few hours I ran away from that hard work, went into the practice of law and have not done any work since.' That was truly Darrowesque. He punctured a conventional sham with a shot. Everyone who knew him knew that he was, in fact, a hard worker all his life, but he simply could not endure the conventional lies of civilization."

At the beginning of the fall, to his astonishment, Clarence was offered the job of teacher in the district school at Vernon, three miles from Kinsman. He was not the first Darrow to be offered this job. His sister Mary had some time before been given a year's contract by the school board, only to be ousted by indignant parents who were horrified at the thought of "the daughter of a freethinker teaching our youngsters!" Mary had taken her contract to a lawyer, who had assured her that it was unbreakable; that all she had to do was hold herself in readiness to teach. At the end of the year Mary had sued and recovered the contractual salary.

Opposition to his appointment arose on the ground that he had been subjected to unfortunate influences which he might communicate to the children; but by now a number of years had passed, and because of their exemplary life folks thereabouts had come to the charitable conclusion that the Darrows were almost as good Christians as they would have been if they had attended church. Clarence had a gentle disposition; he came from a bookish (albeit the wrong kind of books) home, and he had spent a whole year at college. Besides, the wage was so low that no full-grown man would take the job.

The fears of the trepidatious proved to be well founded: he promptly set out to revolutionize district-school teaching. Having been slapped by his teacher the first day he had entered school, he abolished corporal punishment. The McGuffey readers were thrown out, as was the system of teaching in terms of moral precepts; he taught from books borrowed from his father's study. Resolving to make his pupils happy instead of wise, he utilized the teaching tools of humor and sympathy, lengthened the noon hour and recesses, joined in their sports, coached their baseball team, tried to make them understand that as their teacher he was a friend and not an enemy. For his efforts he was paid thirty dollars a month, most of which he turned over to the family, and was received as a guest in the home of a different pupil each school night.

"I was company. Only the best was set before me. I had pie and cake three times a day."

Now that he was freed from the discipline and restraint of devoting his days to courses in which he was not interested, now that he had the leisure to think and the right to choose his own fields, the heritage of Emily and Amirus Darrow made itself felt. His brain began to clear from the miasma of adolescence; he found himself leaving home on Monday morning with a package of books under his arm, the novels of Balzac, the poetry of Pushkin or Baudelaire, the political satire of Voltaire, the *Odyssey* of Homer or the *Republic* of Plato. He spent his late afternoons and evenings reading with the eager gusto of the awakening mind that is beginning to question, search, evaluate.

Children brought up in book-loving homes rarely get the dream out of their eyes; the exultation in clear, philosophic thinking, the joy in the pure line of poetry, the delight in a character come to life, a story well told, the music of the lyrical passage swelling across the page in vivid black notes, these add a third dimension of understanding and beauty to the two-dimensional eat-and-work-a-day world. In his father's home he had been taught, "The truth is your friend; it shall set you free."

The favorite form of entertainment in Trumbull County was the Saturday-night debate, which was held in the schoolhouse or the largest barn in the district. Everyone from Kinsman came, as did the farmer families for miles around. The subject being debated mattered not at all; the folks, smelling slightly soapy from their Saturday-night scrub in the big wooden or iron tubs, came for the sport, to enjoy the clash of wits and personalities, to hear language spoken more literarily than it could be heard anywhere else.

Clarence debated nearly every Saturday night; throughout his school years it had been the only academic activity he enjoyed wholeheartedly. He was lackadaisical about preparing other lessons, but if he had been given "a piece to speak" there was no limit to the number of hours he would spend in writing it down, committing it to memory. His sister Mary had trained him to speak pieces from the time he was two; the child had taken pleasure in the vocal activity and the limelight provided by an audience; he had spoken naturally, without shyness or hesitation; as he learned to think swiftly on his feet he earned the reputation of being "the best young speaker in these here parts." On the Fourth of July he was again invited to give an oration in Kinsman Square.

The Darrows were always anti. As the newest member of the tradition to grow up, Clarence could be relied upon to take the unpopular side of a subject, the side with which almost everyone in the audience disagreed and knew in advance he would be wrong about. He liked the tart sensation of getting to his feet, after his opponent had received an ovation which shook the kerosene lamps hanging on nails in the walls, and facing a solidly hostile pattern of faces, four or five hundred people whose expressions were compounded of aversion, incredulity, disbelief. There was no exhilaration equal to that of standing alone against the field, beaten before he started, fighting for a hopeless cause. He loved the danger and excitement of flailing against minds that were as sprung and shut as an iron trap over the broken leg of an animal. These good people liked young Clarence, but while he was on the platform fighting against the things they believed in, he became the enemy, the infidel, the apostate, the turncoat. Though he never succeeded in winning a debate, occasionally he had the pleasure of puncturing one of their ideological bubbles with a pinprick of satire or good sense.

After the debate had been settled to the satisfaction of the audience, the benches were cleared away, fiddles and gee-tars made their appearance, and the square dances and Virginia reels began.

"Circle eight! Break trail and form a line!
Corner by the left, partner right. Once and a half, first couple out!
Corner to and swing, partner do the same. Do see do."

Clarence was fond of dancing, but most of all he liked to dance with Jessie Ohl, who was the best dancer in the crowd, an expert at calling the reels. Jessie had a trim figure, amply curved for a sixteen-year-old girl, and an honest, forthright face with the glowing skin of youth. They made a pleasant couple.

5

After a year of teaching the eighteen-year-old boy found his interest turning more and more to the lawbooks in his father's study.

"Every Monday morning, as I started off to teach my school, I took a lawbook with me and, having a good deal of time, improved it fairly well."

He was drifting, not knowing that he wanted to become a lawyer. The only thing he knew for sure was that he did not care for physical labor, that like his father he wanted to earn his living by the spoken word, the formulated idea, the expressed thought. Since the Church was out of the question, there remained only two fields: teaching and the law. He sensed that working with young minds in classrooms would not satisfy him long, though it had proved to be a fine life for Everett, who was much the dreamy scholar his father had been. He saw by now that he enjoyed conflict, the clash of mind against mind in the fight for what each conceived to be the right and the truth. His temperament was gratified by the system of logic manifest in both Roman and English law; he was stimulated by the play of human story and drama in the cases he read, and often he was fired by thinking of the cases in which he would battle to help justice triumph. But of what the practice of law actually involved he knew little; he had opportunity to know but little.

"The law is a bum profession, as generally practiced," he was to write many years later to a young man who contemplated entering law school. "It is utterly devoid of idealism and almost poverty stricken as to any real ideas."

This was knowledge after the fact, which he could not have had before. Like all the other boys, he had seen the county lawyers make a big splash at the Fourth of July picnics, and he had been impressed.

"When Squire Allen got through reading the Declaration of Independence, which we thought he had written because he always read it, he introduced the speaker of the day. This was always some lawyer who came from Warren, the county seat, twenty miles away. I had seen the lawyer's horse and buggy at the hotel in the morning, and I thought how nice they were and how much money a lawyer must make and what a great man he was and how I should like to be a lawyer and how long it took and how much brains. The lawyer never seemed to be a bit afraid to stand up on the platform before the audience, and I remember that he wore nice clothes, and his boots looked shiny, as though they had just been greased. He talked very loud and seemed to be mad about something, especially when he spoke of the war and the 'Bridhish,' and he waved his hands and arms a great deal. The old farmers clapped and nodded their heads and said he was a mighty smart man and a great man."

When Clarence was twenty and had been teaching for three years, it was obvious that he could no longer continue at the district school at thirty dollars a month. It was also obvious that he had all the prerequisites of a lawyer: he liked books; he had a natural fluency of speech, was able to think clearly and to the point; he had a pleasant, bland personality which inspired confidence, and the law was surely the open sesame to the world beyond the encircling hills, to politics and a lucrative profession. The family put its loyal head together in consultation. Everett, who was teaching high school in Chicago, and Mary, who was teaching grade school in Champaign, insisted that he go to the law college at Ann Arbor, Michigan; they would send him enough money for his keep.

Once again he spent an undistinguished year in college. Though he enjoyed mildly the companionship of his classmates, he made few friends, and no one influenced him. His grades were mediocre; if his instructors thought about him at all, which is unlikely, they would have had reason to decide that he would become another pettifogging country lawyer, ranting speeches at Fourth of July celebrations so that his farmer constituents would elect him to some minor political office. He was not impressed by his teachers, their method of instruction or the books in the library to which he was assigned to brief cases. He liked to teach himself, to work alone, to stumble along by himself, to ferret, accept, reject, come to his own conclusions.

He did not return to Ann Arbor for the second year of his course. Instead he found a job in a law office in Youngstown, twenty miles from his home, where he did odd jobs around the office, earned enough to pay for his keep and read the lawbooks, interesting himself in the various subjects as he came upon them or as they arose in practical cases in the office. A few weeks after his twenty-first birthday he presented himself to "a committee of lawyers who were chosen to examine applicants. They were all good fellows and wanted to help us through." He passed the simple test and was embarked upon a legal career which was to cover six decades and implicate him in nearly every conflict at the core of expanding American life.

In the meanwhile his friendship with Jessie Ohl had deepened. He had liked her since he was seventeen and had apparently been attracted by no other girl—though in the innocence of his youth and the innocence of the age he seems to have done no experimenting to test his emotion. They were well suited to each other; they were both kindly, easygoing, forthright and simple in their tastes. There could be little doubt but that Jessie would make a good wife and mother.

Jessie's family was one of the best in the valley and owned the gristmill where he had played as a boy. He had a tremendous admiration for Mrs Ohl, who spent the major portion of her time in Minnesota, where she managed a wheat farm of many hundred acres, took care of all the business details, cooked for a large crew of Swedish and Norwegian hands and on Sunday mornings preached evangelical sermons to the farmers of the county: a woman of courage, strength and sound education. When he began riding the six miles from Kinsman to Berg Hill, Jessie's mother had commented: "Seems an awful long ways to come acourting!"

The legend that Clarence took up with Jessie out of his boundless sympathy, because she was a wallflower with whom no other man would bother, is blasted by the long trip he made to the Ohl farm in Minnesota, just after he turned twenty-one, to spend his summer vacation with her. He had no source of income, but that did not deter young people from marrying in 1880; there was little possibility that a man couldn't find work and earn a living in the uncrowded West. He asked Jessie to marry him, and Jessie agreed most heartily.

It was a better match for Clarence than it was for Jessie; the Ohl family was solidly entrenched, while he was penniless. And there was always the danger that he would be too much his father's son, that he would spend his life in genteel poverty, his nose in a musty book.

6

They were married in the home of Jessie's brother in Sharon, Pennsylvania, and went directly to Andover, Ohio, a sleepy but prosperous farming center of about four hundred people, ten miles from Kinsman. Here they rented a flat above a shoestore, with a bedroom, parlor and bath. The bedroom faced the long flight of stairs and was turned into an office, Jessie spending part of her wedding money to buy lawbooks with which to impress the potential clients. When the first couple of months passed and the young lawyer took in less than the thirty-dollar wage he had earned as a schoolteacher, Jessie decided they would have to retrench.

The Darrows took in a boarder. James Roberts was a young lawyer who, under the terms of the agreement, became not only Clarence's table companion, but his law partner as well. The records fail to reveal where Roberts slept, since Jessie had already converted the parlor into their bedroom, but the question is an academic one at best, for within a few weeks young Roberts acquired some poker debts and absconded with the lawbooks Jessie had bought her husband.

Very much of an unawakened country boy, Clarence had been unimpressed by the world beyond the Kinsman hills when he had gone to Ann Arbor, and he had rejected the idea of beginning his practice of law in Youngstown, where he had worked and passed the Bar and acquired a few friends, because it was a metropolis of twenty thousand people. Its bigness frightened him. In spite of his father's rigorous insistence upon study, he was sketchily educated, had only a meager training in the law and was not overly industrious or ambitious. Nor could anything happen in Andover to bring him to maturity, for the most exciting events in the passing days were the falling down of a horse in Main Street or the lowering of a safe from a second story. His business consisted of drawing up papers for horse trades, for which he would receive fifty cents from each participant, or suing one farmer in the name of another for fraudulent representation over the matter of livestock or seed, in which instances there might be as much as two dollars. For the satisfactory settlement of a boundary dispute he felt entitled to charge three dollars. There was now and then an action in replevin in which he went into court to secure the return of goods or chattels for his client, and for trying the case he received five dollars. Occasionally he defended a farmer accused of selling hard cider, in return for which he got more cider than cash.

After a year of practice he found that he was taking in as much as fifty and sixty dollars a month, which provided a modest living and even enabled the frugal Jessie to save a few pennies. The climax of his practice was reached on the night he dashed into the kitchen, slapped his knee excitedly and exclaimed to his wife:

"I made twenty dollars today!"

The Darrows spent a pleasant three years in Andover. Jessie was an enthusiastic cook and a spotless housekeeper. In addition she washed and ironed Clarence's linen, pressed his suits so that he would look well groomed and made friends with the townspeople and farmers so they would bring her husband business. The young couple loved each other; they got along well, and Jessie never interfered in Clarence's way of life. On December 10, 1883, a son was born to them, named Paul; this event stirred Clarence sufficiently to get him to move to Ashtabula, a town of five thousand people, the largest in the surrounding country.

He was no stranger in this village of modest cottages on tree-lined streets. The people remembered him from his baseball and debating days; besides, he had journeyed here several times to try cases for Andover folk and had come off pretty well. He was now approaching twenty-six, had achieved his full growth and was a responsible family man. He had a fund of what the farmers called horse sense; he grasped situations quickly, thought through them logically in terms of right and justice, rather than codified law, and could always be relied upon to be honest. In discussing cases he talked the simplest English, never attempting to hide his ignorance behind a barrage of legal phraseology. He rarely took a case in which he did not believe his client to be right and, having thus convinced himself, fought with an emotional intensity that transcended the small fees or properties involved.

When Farmer Jones hired Darrow to regain title to a cow from Farmer Brown and succeeded in regaining the cow, Farmer Brown might cuss Darrow for a week of Sundays, but when next he had a suit over the title to a horse or a harness he did not go back to the lawyer who had lost his cow for him. He went instead to young Darrow.

"A lawsuit then," wrote Darrow, "before a justice of the peace, was filled with color and life and wits. Everyone for miles around had heard of the case and taken sides between the contending parties or their lawyers. Neighborhoods, churches, lodges and entire communities were divided as if in war. Often the cases were tried in town halls, and audiences assembled from far and near. An old-time lawsuit was like a great tournament, as described by Walter Scott.

The combatants on both sides were seeking the weakest spot in the enemy's armor and doing their utmost to unhorse him or draw blood."

It was Darrow's technique to unhorse his adversaries rather than to shout them down. When the opposing attorney tore off reams of bombast he made the rhetoric sound silly by stating quietly and simply the point at issue; when they wandered far afield he poked gentle fun at their meanderings; when they took shelter in abstruse technicalities he appealed to the common sense of the judge and jurors. All his life he remained a country boy at heart; his understanding of the farmer's psychology served him well, as is illustrated in his appeal to the jury in a famous arson-perjury case a number of years later.

"You folks think we city people are all crooked, and maybe we are, but we city people think you farmers are all crooked. There isn't a one of you I'd trust in a horse trade, because you'd be sure to skin me. But when it comes to having sympathy with a person in trouble, I'd sooner trust you folks than city folk, because you come to know people better and get to be closer friends. Here's a case where a girl lied to save a friend. I don't doubt but that all of you have done that in the past or would do it if you had a friend in trouble. Of course if you wouldn't tell a lie to save a friend in trouble there's only one thing for you to do, and that's to vote for conviction. But if any of you ever have told a lie to save a friend I don't see how you can vote to send this girl to the penitentiary."

The girl was acquitted.

Darrow had been in Ashtabula only a short time when he was taken into the office of Judge Sherman, with whose young sons he had become friends. With the judge's backing Darrow ran for the office of city solicitor. Remembering the shouting and arm waving of the Fourth of July orators, Darrow took the opposite tack, making only a few quiet talks. He was elected hands down. The salary was seventy-five dollars a month, in addition to which he could take his own cases, which now became fairly numerous because clients liked the idea of having the city attorney handle their business.

He remained in Ashtabula for four years. He made a comfortable living, was well liked and was on his way to becoming one of the leading lawyers of the county. During the evenings he played poker with his cronies, the game he loved best next to baseball; over a few bottles of beer or highballs the men would tell tall tales, play for low stakes and high excitement. For the first time Darrow had fun. He did only a little reading; his love of books and knowledge for its own sake lay dormant. For two hundred years no Darrow had distinguished himself, and it did not appear that Clarence would ruffle the family tradition.

He had already passed thirty before the role of country lawyer played itself out. Having saved five hundred dollars, he and Jessie decided to buy a home. They found a suitable one for sale for thirty-five hundred dollars. Darrow drew up a deed with the owner which provided for the payment of five hundred in cash and the balance in monthly payments. The next day the owner turned up without his wife's signature on the deed, saying that she refused to sign—the implication being that she did not think young Darrow could meet the monthly payments.

"All right," fumed Darrow, "I don't want your house because —because—I'm moving away from here."

The following afternoon he met a woman of whom he was not specially fond.

"And how is our prominent lawyer today?" asked the woman.

"Oh, fine, fine," replied Darrow. "I just got a big case."

"How nice. Here in Ashtabula?"

"No-o-o-o," stuttered Darrow, "in—in Chicago."

"That's just lovely. When are you going to try it?"

"Why—as a matter of fact—tomorrow."

He took the early-morning train into Chicago. "The next day I had to go to Chicago, because if the woman saw me on the streets of Ashtabula she would have told the whole town I was a liar—which I was."

Having nothing better to do, he went to see his brother Everett. Everett had been working on his younger brother, whom he loved and admired, to move to Chicago.

"You have too big a brain for a small town," he told Clarence. "You belong in a big city, where important things are happening and where you can play your part."

"But it's an awful big jump, Everett, and I have only five hundred dollars in the bank. I don't know a soul here. I'd have to start from scratch again."

"It won't take you long to catch on. Besides, I have a steady job and I can lend you whatever money you need until you become established. You owe it to yourself, Clarence."

Darrow maintained that if the deed he had drawn had been signed he would have spent the rest of his life in Ashtabula, worrying about meeting the overdue payments. But there are indications that he was tiring of the pleasures of small-town comradery and of small-town life, where, he wrote, "Protestantism is inspired, the Republican party and all its doctrines came as a divine revelation, where farmers were the backbone of the country and the most intelligent people in the world, where all pleasure was sinful and all suffering righteous, where the cities were evil and the country good."

His nature drew him back to the books. A banker of Ashtabula introduced him to Henry George's *Progress and Poverty*, which excited both his imagination and his critical faculties, starting him on the jagged, boundless road toward economic justice. A police judge by the name of Richards gave him a copy of *Our Penal Machinery and Its Victims*, by John P. Altgeld, which turned his mind to thinking about crime and prisons. His intellectual vigor renewed, he again began reading in history and political economy and the verses of the *Rubáiyát* and hungered for someone with whom to discuss them. He consumed the works of Walt Whitman, who was anathema in Ashtabula, as were the European novelists with whom he felt a kinship of spirit: Flaubert, Turgenev, Zola. He wanted to discuss free trade and free thought, states' rights and single tax, socialism, paganism; he wanted to hear theories built up or torn apart by educated and trained minds. He wanted to meet people who knew the outside world, who could lead him to new books and philosophies, who argued from the premises of logic rather than prejudice.

He was slowly, awkwardly, painfully, coming of age. As he did so, the son of Emily and Amirus Darrow began to feel the constricted life of Trumbull County confining. If he had been content in Ashtabula he would have found another house to buy with his five hundred dollars down.

7

The Chicago into which Darrow took his wife and son was rough, crude and vital, the fastest-growing city in America. "Even in its early days," said Darrow, "Chicago had that wonderful power which clings to it still—that power of inspiring everyone who touches it with absolute confidence in its greatness and strength." It was the nerve center of a vast railroad system which sent thousands of cars daily into every nook of the nation and received them back. Carl Sandburg was to write, "Three overland trains arriving the same hour, one from Memphis and the cotton belt, one from Omaha and the corn belt, one from Duluth, the lumberjack-and-iron range." It was the slaughterhouse of America, with the never-ending flow of animal blood. "A carload of shorthorns taken off the valleys of Wyoming last week, arriving yesterday, knocked in the head, stripped, quartered, hung in iceboxes today." It was becoming one of the great industrial centers, with its open-hearth furnaces roaring by night and day to furnish the young country with resilient fibers of steel, its chimneys belching soft black smoke to become ingrown under eyelids and fingernails. "The city is a tool chest opened every day, a time clock punched every morning, a shop door, bunkers and overalls."

A million people had crowded into this stretch of prairie at the end of Lake Michigan, the most amazing polyglot of tongues since the Tower of Babel: Polacks, Croats, Serbs, Rumanians, Russians, Norwegians, Swedes, Germans, Irish, Sicilians, Greeks, Bulgarians, Finns. And Americans, too, second- and third- and fourth-generation Americans, reaped off the farms and from the hamlets of a dozen neighboring states by the suction of a tumultuous new metropolis in the building.

Darrow went into Chicago in a confused state of mind. He wanted intellectual and literary companionship; he wanted the company of intelligent people with whom he might discuss the problems of the modern world; he wanted access to bookstores, to honest newspapers and penetrating magazines; he wanted to see a great city in action, but what he wanted for himself he did not know. He hoped to do a good job and an important job—in that respect he was ambitious—but his ambition did not include the making of large sums of money. He simply wanted to find his place in the world, do his share of its work, think his share of its thoughts, feel his share of its feelings, know his share of its knowledge. He could not guess into what fields his activities would lead him, nor did he care, except that they be tied up with the interesting and important movements of the day.

He installed his family in a modest apartment on the south side near his brother Everett, was admitted to practice in the state of Illinois, then rented desk space in a law office. Like his father before him, he wore stiff white collars with a black bow tucked in under the wings, a lapeled vest and heavy dark suits. His face was slowly maturing, though his eyes were still childlike in their candor. Coming from a small town, dressing like a country lawyer, talking in a lazy drawl, almost naïve in the open simplicity and sweetness of his manner, he made no impression on the train-shunting, skyscraper-building, hog-killing, steel-blasting city. He knew no one, and in a big city, where one cannot hang out his shingle on a Madison Avenue or a State Street, clients do not stumble into the office of strangers with their legal problems. The weeks passed; several months passed; the savings dwindled; Darrow became homesick for his friendly Ohio villages and contemplated going back.

He started on a new tack: since clients could not find their way to him, he would find his way to the clients. His first step was to join the Henry George Single Tax Club. After he had attended a few of the weekly meetings and gotten the general tenor of the debates, he ventured to speak. His personality was warm and lovable, his voice low, musical, rich in tonal contrasts, and he did not rise to his feet until he had formulated precisely what he had to say. His combination of logic and good-natured humor helped the group accept his arguments even when he disagreed with certain of their theories. After the meeting he joined in the informal discussion; introductions were exchanged, strong hands shaken in hearty, rough masculine fellowship, and at midnight the group adjourned to Mme. Gali's Italian restaurant for a steak and a bottle of beer, for many pipefuls of tobacco and many mouthfuls of spirited, intelligent talk.

He also joined the Sunset Club, whose hundred members formed the rallying point of the literary renaissance in Chicago. Here he was even more at home than at the Henry George Club, where he could not help but be critical of their economic panaceas. In the Sunset Club he could read aloud from Omar Khayyam and Robert Burns, hear lectures by visiting authors, discuss Tolstoy's *War and Peace* or Dickens' *Hard Times*, debate the literary values of the realism of *L'Assommoir, Germinal, Crime and Punishment*, the short stories of Guy de Maupassant, as against the romanticism of Stevenson's *Treasure Island* or Daudet's *Tartarin of Tarascon*. His first lecture before the Sunset Club was on "Realism in Literature and Art." Since there are no faster or firmer friendships than those formed between people who love the same books, Darrow was heartily accepted by the writers, teachers, librarians, clergymen, journalists and professional men who were eager to participate in the robust new cultural movement sweeping the Western world.

He had been in Chicago only a few months when he was asked by the Democratic committeemen he had met at the Henry George Club to campaign in the 1888 election. He accepted with alacrity, hopeful that some crumb of what he said might find its way into the newspapers or that someone in the hall would be impressed and bring him a case the next day. But he always found himself just one of an interminable string of ambitious young lawyers striving to make an impression. His five hundred dollars gone, living off Everett's savings, able to find only an occasional real-estate abstract to examine, he became increasingly discouraged and sorry he had left his practice in Ashtabula.

Then suddenly, but naturally, his opportunity came.

The Henry George Club staged a Free Trade Convention in Chicago which attracted speakers from all over the country, including Henry George himself. Because Darrow had been a faithful worker for the club and was conceded to be one of its best speakers, he was put on the program of the mammoth closing session to be held in the Central Music Hall. Having little law business to distract him, he worked for days on his paper, sound in its economics, constructively critical of the single tax in its weaker links and written with a lyrical lucidity. The paper finished, he committed it to memory and set out for the meeting.

Alas! Henry George was scheduled to speak first. His long, strongly idealistic talk was so good it not only gripped and thrilled the assemblage but also left them completely satisfied. When the applause died down the audience rose and began to leave the hall. Darrow begged the chairman to introduce him quickly; his few friends clapped as loudly as they could when he came forward. The departing throng turned its head momentarily in the aisles to see what was going on. Leaning on the years since he was two and Mary had taught him to "speak pieces," on the years in Kinsman of debating before hostile and indifferent groups, Darrow struck out boldly, thinking hard and fast and clear as he adapted his speech to supplement what Henry George had said, stimulated, as always, by the presence of an audience. People began slipping back into their seats; soon the aisles were clear, and for the first time in his life Darrow felt that he had his listeners entrapped in his words and thoughts, that he could move them to any emotion or conviction he willed.

When he had finished he received an ovation. Henry George wrung his hand and assured him that he had a brilliant future. Newspaper reporters crowded about to ask further questions and scribble hurriedly in their notebooks. Friends pounded him on the back; strangers came up to shake his hand, suggested that they have lunch together, get better acquainted.

The next morning his name and opinions were on the front pages of the Chicago newspapers. His old acquaintances dropped in to congratulate him—"and use his telephone." But no new business or cases arrived on the flood of publicity. However, in a few days new friends came into the office to urge him to speak in favor of DeWitt Cregier for mayor. Having learned something of political tactics, Darrow picked his own hall, the best in town, and spoke alone. Newspaper reporters took down what he said, quoted him with moderate accuracy in the morning papers.

By this token Darrow knew that he had arrived, that he was

established in Chicago life. Though his first year of practice had brought him only three hundred dollars in cash, the prospects for the next year looked good. He moved out of his small apartment and rented a house, the upper floor of which canny Jessie sublet, thus earning back the better part of their rent.

8

During his first year in Chicago the most important thing to happen to him had been his meeting with another lawyer, John Peter Altgeld, author of the book *Our Penal Machinery and Its Victims*, which the police judge had handed him in Ashtabula. John P. Altgeld had had ten thousand copies printed at his own expense and sent out inscribed to every legislator, judge, warden, minister, educator, writer, lecturer, social-service worker and club president he could find on a mailing list. He had attempted to show in his book that poverty, slums and the lack of opportunity which resulted from the unequal distribution of wealth lie at the base of the major portion of crime; that the brutal treatment afforded to the merely accused, and later to the imprisoned, was a second crime committed by society against the individual whose obsolescent surroundings had been one of the contributing causes of his original criminality. Published in 1884, five years before Lombroso's *L'Uomo Delinquente*, supposedly the first scientific investigation into criminality, was released in Italy, this book puts Altgeld in line for the title of father of modern criminology. It was not until 1899, fifteen years after the publication of *Our Penal Machinery*, that Lombroso abandoned his theory that "the criminal is a special type, standing midway between the lunatic and the savage" and reached Altgeld's conclusions on the economic base of crime.

To Darrow, who had been spending sleepy days defending farmers accused by their neighbors of stealing fifteen-dollar harnesses, reading this pioneering effort was like being plunged into a cold, clear mountain stream, giving him a clue to the kind of independent thinking being done in the metropolitan world and quickening his desire to get out of the small farming community. One of his first acts upon reaching Chicago was to go to Altgeld's law office with a copy of *Our Penal Machinery and Its Victims* under his arm and tell him what a courageous and penetrating piece of work it was. Altgeld had been so delighted to find his book reaching young lawyers, he had forgotten his restraint in meeting people, his difficulty in making friends, and had welcomed Clarence with warm affection.

The two men found they were kindred spirits, and a deep friendship developed: both had come from small farming communities; both were plain, down to earth, detesting pretension, hypocrisy and deceit. Both had an intuitively passionate sympathy for the underdog, were gentle-souled, desirous of avoiding discord, yet so intensely stirred by injustice and human suffering, they were willing to endure strife, contumely and ostracism to fight against them. Both were students, bookish men, intellectuals in the days before it was fashionable to be intellectuals; both read constantly in Tolstoy, Dostoevski, Dickens, Zola, drawn by the love of these authors for humanity.

The forty-year-old Altgeld was the profoundest influence in Darrow's life. He helped educate the younger man, buttressed in him his love of study, of acquiring all the facts no matter how distasteful they might appear, of clinging steadfastly to the truth even in the face of such devastating tempests as were nearly to destroy both men before their lives were finished. In return Darrow was able to bring to the childless Altgeld some of the good things brought to a father by a son: love, filial respect, an eagerness to learn, an hour spent in the warmth of confidence.

During his second year in Chicago Darrow managed to clear expenses by carrying on the general run of minor law business. His evenings he spent at the various clubs and homes of members, debating socialism, discussing modern poetry, formulating plans to help young labor unions to earn recognition. He wrote articles for the liberal and labor press, the most trenchant of which was his attack on the McKinley high-tariff bill for which *Current Topics* gave him the lead space and a full-page picture as a frontispiece, thus launching him as a professional journalist. He called the tariff "the work of the monopolists and the strong, the narrowest and most reactionary of any law passed by an American Congress. Probably no civilized nation in this century ever so deliberately turned its face to the past, so ignored and derided the growing sentiment of peace and universal brotherhood which is the hope of all the progressive people and countries of the earth." But mostly he liked to lecture on literary subjects. He would go to any amount of work to prepare a paper and be happy to give it to as few or as many as cared to listen. A member of one of his early audiences gives an amusing picture of young Darrow on the lecture platform.

"I first saw Clarence Darrow when he lectured at a Sunday-afternoon meeting of the Chicago Single Tax Club in Handel Hall on Randolph Street. He was dressed in a cutaway and had on a white boiled shirt, a low starched collar and a narrow, black bow tie. His subject was Tolstoy's novel *Anna Karenina*. He was in entire accord with the philosophy of the novel and its sympathy for the oppressed and outcast. Every little while during the address he hunched his wide shoulders forward and ran his hand through the long, straight, stringy, dark brown hair, which fell away from the part on the left side of his head, toward and almost into his right eye, so as to smooth it back. The lecture was full of striking, original statements, in simple language, punctuated with shafts of wit and sarcasm, which brought titters and laughter from his audience, but it was apparent he did not utter them to wisecrack; they were relevant to a serious argument, and his face was earnest as he made them. He read a passage from the novel with deep feeling and emotion. This talk made a strong impression on me and, I believe, on the audience."

Peter Sissman, who was later to save him for the legal profession after Darrow had barely escaped ending his life in San Quentin Penitentiary, gives the earliest picture of Darrow on the lecture platform:

"I first met Darrow in February of 1893, when he gave a Sunday-night lecture in Jefferson Hall for the Secular Union, a group of Ingersoll freethinkers and rationalists. His subject was 'Some Fundamental Errors.' The charm of his speaking was in his voice and manner and logic. He was analytical and scientific toward socialism. Morally it was a weakness, that realistic view of his, which made him always doubtful; he could never be carried away by the enthusiasm that the average radical is inspired by."

Darrow made a profound impression on his audiences because he had that rare and most beautiful gift, a golden personality. His magnetism leaped out and engulfed people, made them feel warm inside, made them feel good, made them feel happy, made them feel soft and friendly, sympathetic and generous and clearminded, brought out the best in them. He became one of the leaders of the young and vigorous cultural life in Chicago because he was so gentle and genuine and honest, because his love for books and thinking shone through everything he said, because he had the gift of the bold, striking phrase, the delicious chuckle, because he could dramatize literature and knowledge, bring them to life with tenderness and a wallop. He had passed the point of hoping to find business through this kind of activity; it was self-expression for him and gratified the inherent Darrow love of teaching, of communicating to others the joys he had found.

Like a legal Lochinvar he dashed out to break a lance for every good social cause. He passed the hat at a mass meeting to collect funds for the Boers. He drew an ovation from the Fenians, who were also seeking their freedom from England, when he told them that " . . . the men who made the world wiser, better and holier were ever battling with the laws and customs and institutions of the world." "The Chicago *Evening Mail* started a crusade to compel the streetcar companies to supply seats to passengers. Darrow spoke at mass meetings, chiefly downtown in Central Music Hall at the corner of State and Randolph streets. Then, as ever after, an unruly forelock would come down over his brow, caused by the heat and emotions generated in his great dome. He convinced the city that the people were unjustly treated, that something must be done about it. Blue-ribbon badges were distributed, inscribed with letters of gold: N.S.N.F. at the top and 'No Seat, No Fare' below. Everybody was wearing them, and on a given date if a fare of five cents was accepted, the conductor MUST furnish a seat. On 'der Tag' the traffic was completely upset. Everywhere the police were called to help eject passengers, and many were arrested. It was a short-lived 'revolution.' The company promised more cars at rush hours and a strap for every passenger."

9

He had been in Chicago two years when he received a note from Mayor Cregier, asking him to call. He promptly ran to the mayor's office, where he was astounded to be offered the position of special-assessment attorney for the city.

"But, Mr Mayor, how do you happen to send for me and ask me to be special-assessment attorney when you never met me before?"

"Don't you know? Why, I heard you make that speech that night with Henry George."

Since the salary was three thousand dollars a year, Darrow accepted the offer and was on the pay roll before he stumbled down the steps of the city hall. He trotted all the way to Altgeld's office.

"But I haven't sufficient experience in big-town law," he protested, afraid that he had been rash.

"I'll see that you get the proper instruction," replied Altgeld with his quiet smile. Darrow did not know it was his friend's recommendation to the mayor that had helped secure his appointment. "A year from now you'll be laughing at your hesitancy."

He was given an office in the city hall, with a big desk, a library, a secretary and a law clerk, and without preliminaries was plunged into work. His duties were to pass on matters of assessments, taxes.

condemnations, licenses; to advise city officials who wanted legal justification before they went ahead. Because the city officials wanted opinions right away, right now, without waiting for him to look up the law, Darrow found himself swimming in the middle of a wide, wide ocean. With Altgeld's help he evolved a *modus operandi* which was to serve him all his professional life: he thought through a problem on the basis of its facts, then came to the conclusions which he thought to be right, logical and just. If upon looking up the matter in the casebooks he found precedent against him, he did not abandon his stand.

"This is the sensible and honest way for such a matter to be decided," he would exclaim. "Somewhere, in some lawbook, there must be a precedent to sustain me."

And he would continue his search. Nearly always he found a decision that upheld his point of view.

Three months after Darrow had been serving, the assistant corporation counsel of the city got into a party row and was forced to resign. The politicians had found Darrow easily met, accessible, ready to give them the best opinion he could conjure up on a moment's notice, an opinion that had not yet led any of them seriously astray. They liked him—a sentiment he did not always return—so he was promoted to the office of assistant corporation counsel, at five thousand dollars a year. His job was to represent the city in court in all contested cases. Here he acquired his first experience in court procedure, sharpening his knowledge of technique, the relation of the law and the client to the judge and jury. In addition he was in constant conference with the mayor and aldermen and came to know all the judges.

He had held office only ten months when the corporation counsel became ill. The thirty-three-year-old Darrow was promoted to be corporation counsel of the most tumultuous city in America. One of his assistants writes, "During the period when Mr Darrow and I were connected with the law department, two events occurred which increased its importance: first, the annexation of adjacent municipalities; second, the preparation for the Columbian Exposition, which was to open in 1893." Here Darrow first crossed swords with two of his future opponents: the railroads—and prohibition. "The annexation of the villages of Hyde Park and Lake gave rise to many legal complications; for example, whether the absorption of Hyde Park annulled that village's prohibition policy. As to the Columbian Exposition, the interests of the city and the railroads came into sharp conflict. The railroads opposed the city's efforts to open streets across their rights of way to offer greater access to the Exposition grounds, and efforts were made to block condemnation proceedings and to enjoin the opening of streets. The railroad employed many of the leading lawyers of the Chicago Bar, but Darrow won the litigation and the streets were opened."

He was honest; he was industrious, and he was clearheaded; though there was little else to distinguish his tenure of office, these three virtues enabled him to carry on his work satisfactorily. He was well liked and became entrenched in the Chicago legal world.

After four years of working for the city the offer had come from the Chicago and North Western Railway, inspired in part by the trouncing he had given their "leading attorneys of the Chicago Bar" in the right-of-way litigations. On the advice of Altgeld, against his own inclinations, he had accepted. The months and years had passed quickly enough; he had repaid his debt to Everett, bought a comfortable home for himself and Jessie on the north side, had continued to read and lecture and debate, making friends with socialists, labor leaders, anarchists, skeptics, freethinkers of all breeds. He remained ambidextrous, serving the railroad with his right hand and the liberals with his left. A few lines appeared in his boyish face; the hair began to disappear at the left temple where he made his part; the eyelids were not open quite so wide in wonder at the world. Life was interesting. He had no conception of what the future held for him.

Then the workers of the Pullman Palace Car Company had struck; the American Railway Union had gone out in sympathy, and an injunction had been issued, for defiance of which Eugene Debs would be thrown into jail.

CHAPTER II

A Liberal Gets a Liberal Education

THE NEXT MORNING, July Fourth, he rose at six-thirty, had break-fast with his wife and son Paul and rode downtown on the street-car. The business district was holiday deserted; he liked the city in this quiescent mood, without the scurryings of people to confuse it. He checked the satchel he was taking with him to Springfield, where he had been invited to take supper *en famille* with John Peter Altgeld, who had been elected governor of Illinois two years be-fore; this done, he walked toward Lake Michigan, which he could see sparkling and blue through the stubby cavern of Randolph Street, then strolled a couple of blocks south on Michigan Avenue with the sun on his face.

Suddenly his attention was caught by the sound of marching feet. In the distance, coming north on the boulevard, he could see troops swinging along, four abreast, the guns on their shoulders glistening. As they came closer he saw they were Federal troops, Companies A and C from Fort Sheridan. Then as he heard the commanding officer bark, "Column right," and watched the soldiers march onto the bare lake-front property next to Convention Hall, where Abraham Lincoln had been nominated for President only thirty-four years before, break ranks and pitch their tents, he realized they had not been ordered into Chicago for anything so innocent as a Fourth of July parade. They had been sent here by the secretary of war to carry out the injunction against the strikers; they were the enforcing half of what Marvin Hughitt had so neatly termed "a gatling gun on paper."

Just the day before Eugene Debs, president of the American

35

Railway Union, had confided to him, "I do not believe in socialism, but I am forced to the conclusion that government ownership of railroads is decidedly better for the people than railroad ownership of government." Darrow smiled ruefully as there flashed through his mind the symptomatic joke coined by the people of Pennsylvania to satirize their plight: "The legislature will now stand adjourned—that is, if the Pennsylvania Railroad has no further business to transact."

He had looked up the law; he knew that the order to send troops into Chicago violated the Constitution, which guaranteed states' rights. No divisions of the Federal army could be sent into a state until the governor of that state had officially asked for them. Not only had Governor Altgeld not asked for military aid, but Mayor Hopkins of Chicago, without whose specific request no state militia could be sent into the city, had made no request of Governor Altgeld for troops. There had been no trouble in Chicago, no hostile gatherings, no violence, no attacks on property, for the American Railway Union had pledged itself to keep the strike peaceful, to protect the Pullman shops and railroad property and to turn malefactors over to the law. They had kept that pledge faithfully: from May eleventh, the day they had gone on strike, three hundred strikers had guarded the Pullman shops so constantly that the Pullman executives themselves had never asked for police protection. The Chicago police had patrolled the many miles of railroad track without clashes or disturbances; Superintendent of Police Brennan had reported only the night before that everything remained peaceable. Nor was there the slightest reason to assume that Governor Altgeld would not send state militia when requested to do so by Mayor Hopkins, for he had instantly dispatched regiments to Cairo and other railroad centers when requested by the local authorities.

Yet this was the United States Army, organized to defend the country, permitting itself to be cast in the role of strikebreaker. Clarence crossed Michigan Avenue and watched the soldiers make camp. Resting on one leg, following the movements of the uniformed men, some of them husky sunburned boys, sons of farmers or immigrants, others older men with flowing mustaches, he ruminated on the irony of Federal troops being sent to break a people's strike on Independence day! It was a bare hundred and eighteen years since the colonial farmers and merchants, craftsmen and mechanics, laborers and clerks, had formed the first American army to rid themselves of the economic and political yoke of the English monarchy. Men had suffered the miseries of starvation, dysentery, fever and cold that they might think of themselves as free men, that they might name their own taxes and governors, run their farms and shops and offices, their homes and churches and government. They had torn themselves from their homes and families, died with their own blood strangling them in their throats that they and their children and their children's children might not be forever strangled by an economic despotism that controlled their lives without giving them a voice or a hearing. Freedom, even so material a concept as economic freedom, had been worth fighting for and dying for.

Now they were ruled at home, where they could be ruled more efficiently and comprehensively. Where the General Managers' Association, an illegal organization, could unlegally use its influence on the attorney general of the United States to extralegally appoint the General Managers' Association's attorney as assistant attorney general in Chicago and then illegally order that assistant attorney general to demand an injunction be issued, no matter how peaceful conditions might be in that city. Two Chicago Federal Circuit Court judges, Grosscup and Woods, would then meet with the newly appointed Assistant Attorney General Walker and assist him in the drawing up of an airtight injunction—with no representative of labor allowed to be present to defend the interests of the workers. To complete the cycle the United States Army would then illegally be ordered into Chicago to smash the strike.

2

Riding out to gather data in the town of Pullman, where all the trouble had begun, Darrow reflected that George Pullman was the living proof that in America a man needed but one good idea to make millions. When Pullman had been only twenty, working in his brother's cabinet shop in upstate New York, he had taken his first overnight ride in a sleeping car. He was given a wooden bunk at one side of a converted coach, where he stretched out fully dressed on a rough mattress and covered himself with his overcoat, for no bedding was provided. Above and below him were other businessmen reclining uneasily in their street clothes. There was dim candlelight; heat was provided by a wood stove on the opposite side of the car, and no fresh air could be had because none of the windows could be opened. The car was noisy and filthy, filled with coal smoke; sleep was next to impossible. A night on such a car was to be dreaded by even the most stouthearted, and women rarely entered them. For twenty years these horrendous bunk cars were carried without improvement; for twenty years passengers rode them; conductors and brakemen passed through them; railroad officials and managers inspected them, yet no one saw the imperative of making them habitable.

Young George Pullman made only one trip in the so-called sleeping car, yet immediately he saw the need for a beautiful and comfortable bedroom on wheels; this son of a mechanic, this trained cabinetmaker, was able to formulate overnight and reveal to his closest friend, Ben Field, of Albion, his plan for a genuine sleeping car which was, in effect, the very one now being produced by the Pullman Palace Car Company, toward which Darrow's Illinois Central train was at this moment carrying him.

For four years Pullman had continued to work in his brother's cabinet shop, taking occasional contracts, such as the removing of shacks from the bank of the Erie Canal, which was being widened to accommodate heavier traffic. At the age of twenty-four he had decided he could make his way in a big city; he rejected the close-by New York for the younger and more romantic frontier Chicago, which was growing at the foot of Lake Michigan as fast as the wild onion for which it had been named and which he saw must ultimately become the railroad center of the continent. Personable, bold, enormously resourceful, George Pullman soon established a solid place for himself in Chicago, taking contracts which had frightened off more seasoned men to raise the level of streets and subsequently of whole blocks of brick and stone buildings which were suffering from a lack of drainage because the city had sprung up haphazardly on low lands behind the sand dunes.

In his spare hours he worked on his plans for the new sleeping car, the dominating passion of his life. In 1858, when Cyrus McCormick completed his reaper factory on the bank of the Chicago River, when the stockyards were beginning to take business away from such porkopolises as Debs' Terre Haute and Marshall Field was watching his general-merchandise mart boom into a department store, Pullman persuaded the Chicago and Alton Railroad to let him try his experiments on two of their old coaches. There were no blueprints for the remodeling, Pullman figuring out the measurements and details as he came to them. He hinged the backs of seats so they could be folded down to make a bed, hung the upper berths on pulleys so they could be closed during the daytime and hold the bedding. The cars were upholstered in plush and lighted by oil lamps, with a washroom at each end. The brakeman made up the beds; on the first run the conductor had to compel the passengers to take off their boots before they got into the berths.

Though the new sleeping cars were popular with travelers, the railroad companies refused to become excited about them. For his part, Pullman knew that remodeling old coaches was a make-shift, that he would have to build his sleeping cars from the tracks up. The following year he went to the Colorado mining fields where he opened a store, spent many hours each day drawing blueprints for the first complete Pullman car. The task took him four years; he then returned to Chicago, joined with his friend Ben Field, secured patents on his numerous inventions and poured his entire working capital of twenty thousand dollars into the Pioneer. The car took a year to build and was indeed a pioneer: it was a foot wider and two and a half feet higher than any car then in service; the beauty and artistry of its furnishings were unprecedented, for Pull-man had spent as much to decorate his car as other men spent to fur-nish their parlors. The Pioneer also gave an immeasurably smoother ride, making sleep possible, for among Pullman's inventions was an improved truck with springs reinforced by blocks of solid rubber.

The astounding part of this new car was not only its mechanical ingenuity, which revolutionized car building, but the fact that Pullman, in order to take care of his necessities, had built his car so large that it could not be used on any existing railroad because it was too high to pass under bridges and too wide to be used at station platforms. Pullman, in his strength and daring, had said, "This is what a sleeping car must have; the entire railroad system of America will be changed to fit its needs." Shortly after the car was completed Abraham Lincoln was assassinated. There was a demand that the Pioneer be attached to the funeral train which conveyed his body from Chicago to Springfield for burial. The Chicago and Alton Railroad promptly adapted itself to the needs of the Pioneer, and the Pullman Palace Car Company was launched.

The Pullman palace car helped to contract space and annihilate time; states would be joined more closely together, virgin territories made habitable; commerce would be quickened; mails and mer-chandise would be carried more swiftly, the separation of families made sufferable. Businessmen, engineers, builders, teachers, pro-fessional practitioners, would move about the country, harnessing its resources, opening mines, felling forests, laying out farms, build-ing factories, rearing cities. In the growing power and strength of America George Pullman had made as outstanding a contribution as Fulton or Whitney.

3

When the train stopped at the Fifty-ninth Street station, where only a year before it had disgorged crowds to see the World's Fair on the Midway, Darrow took from his pocket a pamphlet he had picked off his desk before leaving home that morning. It was called *The Story of Pullman* and had been distributed by the Pullman Company to visitors to the World's Fair. He read, "Imagine a perfectly equipped town of twelve thousand inhabitants, built out from one central thought to a beautiful and harmonious whole. A town that is bordered by bright beds of flowers and green velvety stretches of lawn; that is shaded with trees and dotted with parks and pretty water vistas and glimpses of artistic sweeps of landscape gardening; a town where the homes, even to the most modest, are bright and wholesome and filled with pure air and light; a town, in a word, where all that is ugly and discordant and demoralizing is eliminated and all that inspires to self-respect, to thrift and to cleanliness of person and of thought is generously provided."

When the conductor called out his destination Darrow descended from the train and struck out for the village that Pullman had created from five hundred acres of unused prairie land. He walked down the main street with its bright red flower beds in the center and rows of tall green trees lining the walks, the houses of neat red brick with trim lawns in front. Why should any workman privileged to live in this utopia want to strike against his benevolent employer?

By way of answering his own question he dropped into the library that Pullman had erected for his workers. A few discreet questions asked of the librarian revealed that the annual dues to borrow the books Mr Pullman had circumspectly selected for his employees to read were so high that only two hundred and fifty families out of the five thousand families living in the town availed themselves of its privileges. Yet the deserted library was well peopled compared with the padlocked parsonage alongside of the imposing church edifice, where Darrow stopped next; the parsonage had never known human occupation because the sixty-five-dollar rent Mr Pullman asked for the cottage made it unobtainable for any of the Protestant clergymen who had been called to preach in the church.

Knocking at random at the doors of several of the red brick houses, Darrow introduced himself as the attorney for the American Railway Union. Some of the men were at the shops on guard duty; the others talked to him freely, their wives standing behind them, to one side, the youngest child in their arms, the older ones clinging to their skirts. It took only a tour of inspection to convince him that the town of Pullman was a false front, designed to impress the casual visitor: the houses were of the cheapest construction, the rooms small and dark and airless, the equipment of the most rudimentary type. Each house had only one faucet, generally in the basement, where it cost the least to bring in pipes, from which water had to be lugged in pails to other parts of the house. In spite of Pullman's protestation that in his town "everything that inspires to cleanliness of person is generously provided," there was not one house that had a bathtub.

For these dwellings the Pullman employees paid twenty-five per cent more rent than had to be paid for similar housing in neighboring communities, but no man could have a job in the Pullman shops unless he rented a Pullman house. The rent was deducted from his check by the Pullman bank before he was handed his wage. If any repairs had to be made to the house before the worker moved in, the Pullman Company advanced the money to repair it, and the total sum was taken out of the worker's wages. In the lease which the worker had to sign before he could get his job there were provisions that he must pay for all repairs but that he could be evicted upon two weeks' notice. Every family Darrow visited told him they had to take in roomers.

Realizing that the deeper he penetrated the closer he would get to hard-rock truth, Darrow left the main street and walked into the back part of town where visitors were never taken. Here he found lawnless tenements with four and five families crowded into each railroad flat, all the families using one toilet. Again the rent of seventeen dollars and a half paid by each family was from twenty-five to thirty-three per cent higher than they would have had to pay for single dwelling accommodations in the neighboring districts, where they could have had privacy, sunlight, a lawn, flowers and a back yard for their children. Behind the tenements he found genuine slums, wooden shanties that had cost only one hundred dollars to erect, occupied by marginal families who had eight dollars a month taken out of their wages, a return of from forty to fifty per cent to the Pullman Company on its investment.

Going from family to family, most of whom he found to be second-generation Americans, Darrow became profoundly dejected as he pieced together the story of life in Pullman, where "all that is ugly and discordant and demoralizing is eliminated and all that inspires to self-respect is generously provided." The inhabitants were constantly spied upon, everything they said being reported back to the company. When the men went out of town their every move was watched; with the first attempt of a man to join a union he was fired, his family turned out of their home, his name entered on a black list and sent to every railroad in the country. Any at-

tempt to discuss, protest or better any condition brought immediate
dismissal. The company gave free medical care to men injured in
the shops, but only in return for a liability release signed by the
injured workman; if he were misguided enough to bring suit the
company doctor testified against him. All savings had to be de-
posited in the Pullman bank; no saloons or resorts were allowed so
that the men might enjoy an hour of fun or escape. The workmen
complained that even in the sanctity of their own homes they
couldn't go to the toilet without Mr Pullman knowing about it.

George Pullman, proclaiming to the world that he had built a
"perfectly equipped town, built out from one central thought to a
beautiful and harmonious whole," had created for himself a feudal
village where he could be the lord and his workmen the serfs;
where he could control their every reflex, and where he could
take back in rent the better part of the wages he paid them. The
families lived under a reign of terror, afraid to trust their neighbors
or friends, afraid to think or talk or show their feelings except in
the dark, behind shuttered windows and locked doors.

4

But all of this had not caused the strike of May 11, 1894, now
almost two months old. A depression following the panic of 1893
had seized the country, and business had fallen off severely. Pullman had found it difficult to secure contracts for his shops to build
new passenger or freight cars and, in order to keep his plant working, had accepted, at an estimated loss of fifty thousand dollars,
building contracts to cover the first few months in 1894.

He had then cut wages. When he saw that these cuts were not
going to be sufficient to absorb the fifty-thousand-dollar loss that
the thirty-six-million-dollar Pullman Company would sustain on
these contracts, he changed the wage scale from a day wage to a
piece wage, at the same time cutting the piece rates to speed up
production. By February expert workmen who had been with the
company for years and who had been earning $3.20 a day, were
down to $2.60 a day, then $2.20 a day, then $1.80 and $1.20 a day,
and were forced to turn out more work by the piece scale to earn
their $1.20 than they had had to turn out to earn their $3.20. By
March skilled mechanics were drawing for two weeks' work, after
their rent had been deducted, sums ranging from eight cents to one
dollar, on which they had to feed families of four and five and six
for the following two weeks. After their meager savings were gone
able-bodied but starved men had to stop work every hour and sit

down for a few minutes to gain enough strength to carry on. Conscientious workmen fainted at their machines and were carried out by their fellows. In the homes the mothers beat their skulls against empty larders to know how to keep little children from becoming ill, developing rickets.

Yet George Pullman refused to lower his rents by one single penny. "The Pullman Land Company has to earn its three-and-a-half per cent," he said. "The Pullman Land Company has no connection with the Pullman Palace Car Company, so I can do nothing about rents." When it was pointed out that Mr Pullman also owned the Pullman Land Company, that his rents had always been twenty-five per cent above prosperity prices, that these were now depression times and that rents in surrounding towns, like Kensington, had been reduced twenty and thirty per cent, Pullman replied by so distributing work that every inhabitant of a Pullman house was enabled to earn just enough to cover his rent debt to the company: a pattern for starvation so ingeniously contrived that only the mechanical brain of George Pullman could have invented it.

There is a starvation level below which not even the most abject laborer will permit his family to sink, for it will do him no good: they will be destroyed in either event. The Pullman employees organized; they sent word to the company to ask if a delegation would be received to present their grievances and if the company would promise not to discharge their delegates. The company promised. Forty-three delegates were elected. They told their story to Mr Wickes, the vice-president, after which George Pullman stormed into the room and informed the men that he had nothing to discuss with them. The following morning all forty-three of the delegates were discharged, their families given dispossess notices.

That was when the workers struck. They walked peacefully out of the shops. They sent delegates to Mr Pullman, asking him to arbitrate. Pullman declared that he had nothing to arbitrate. "The workers have nothing to do with the amount of wages they shall receive; that is solely the business of the company." Mayor Hopkins of Chicago investigated conditions at Pullman and announced his sympathies with the strikers; Jane Addams of Hull House investigated and urged Pullman to meet his workers; the mayors of fifty-six American cities telegraphed Pullman, urging him to arbitrate. Pullman folded his arms on his chest and stood like a colossus above his shops and his village and his workers, a medieval king who ruled by divine right and whose omnipotent will was not to be questioned.

It was, thought Darrow, walking to the train with the background material he needed for the preparation of this case, an almost unparalleled instance of brutal greed and callousness. From the train window he watched the model town of Pullman until it disappeared from sight. In building that town George Pullman had had one of the greatest opportunities of the modern age. The hopeful eyes of the world had been upon him, waiting to see if, with his magnificent talent, foresight and courage, he was going to create the beginnings of a new social order, help build a stronger and wiser breed of man, generations of skilled craftsmen who would live vigorously and well, who would work in loyal and intelligent co-operation, whose families would grow up strong of body and alert of mind, educated, independent, robust citizens of an industrial democracy which would become ever richer and stronger in its arts and crafts and sciences and humanities. If Pullman had been as farsighted, courageous and resourceful in building his town as he had been in building the Pioneer he would have been revered as one of the greatest pioneers of the ages; the designer, not merely of a railroad car and a railroad system, but of a humane civilization.

Sitting in his train seat with his eyes closed, the powerful sun beating through the windowpane onto his face, Darrow speculated on why it was that America was bringing forth the greatest mechanical geniuses in history. Was it the historical imperatives that had developed them? Then why had not those historical imperatives brought forth men of equal talent and fortitude to invent social machines, to erect a human society which would be the equivalent in its workings to the superb mechanical structure? Why was it that the mechanical and executive geniuses of the times were rarely interested in the welfare of humanity? Did interest in the machine preclude interest in people? Did the mind come to consider the machine as the ultimate goal, with mankind serving only as a tool? Why had America developed so few men whose rich, resourceful and inventive minds conceived of the machine as the liberator of all men, rather than the producer of wealth for the initiate?

Was it too soon yet? Darrow asked himself. Had we of necessity to create our industrial machine first, before we could turn our peculiarly inverted gifts to using that machine for the benefit of the people who manned it?

5

He picked up his valise and walked quickly to the Chicago and Alton station, where he bought half a dozen Chicago and Eastern newspapers before boarding the train. In several of them were pictures of George Pullman, his hands stretched out in front of his chest in clerical gesture, all five finger tips touching; under the photographs were encomiums of the patriot and benefactor who was being attacked and undermined by the striking "anarchists." Within the same pages were cartoons of Governor Altgeld, standing on the supine bodies of President Cleveland and the Democratic donkey, an incendiary torch in one hand, the flag of anarchy in the other: Altgeld, the "fomenter of lawlessness, the apologist for murder, the encourager of anarchy, rapine and the overthrow of civilization, the lunatic, the mysterious fragment of jetsam from Lord knows where, an alien by birth, temperament and sympathies who has not one drop of true American blood in his veins."

Darrow had pronounced publicly when Altgeld had been elected a Superior Court judge, "What ought to be done now is to take a man like Judge Altgeld, first elect him mayor of Chicago, then governor of Illinois."

He had been laughed at for his gratuitous counsel, yet John Peter Altgeld, one of the least attractive-looking men in public life ("If I had to depend on my looks I'd have been hung long ago!"), with a harelip, an impediment of speech, coarse hair that grew forward on his skull like a mat, with heavy features and a thick torso on stubby legs; the man who had risen from the most abject poverty, from the enslavement of a brutish peasant father, who had been badly fed, badly clothed, worked into exhaustion as a child, who was without formal education, who had been despised and ridiculed by his playmates and had endured the humiliations and sufferings of the underdog, had fulfilled Darrow's rash prediction and become the first Democratic governor of the state of Illinois.

Altgeld was uncommunicative about his background, but he had told the story to his friend Clarence: brought from Germany at the age of three months, he had had to flee his unsympathetic home in Ohio to escape his father, who had insisted that he stay away from books and study and work on the land from dawn to dark. The young boy had wandered on the road like a derelict, working now as a farmhand, now as a section hand on the Mississippi, Kansas and Texas Railroad, now as a laborer in a chemical plant in St Louis, half the time without work, hungry, destitute, cold, friendless, ill, without hope. Yet within him had flamed a resolve not to remain homeless and despised, ignorant and unwanted. Through his hunger to learn he had read enough to qualify as a rural schoolteacher, then a rural lawyer, at length making his way to Chicago, the dream and hope of the Middle West. In Chicago there had been years of grubbing, making a friend here, a dollar there, but always impressing people by his honesty and thoroughness. Finally he managed to save five hundred dollars, which he invested in real estate in outlying parts of Chicago, subdividing and building with such an accurate eye for the growth of the city that within a few years he was handling single deals amounting to two hundred thousand dollars and was on his way to becoming a millionaire.

He had been elected by the working people of Illinois because he had worked for their rights and protection in the form of industrial legislation. Altgeld believed in capitalism, not the kind that Pullman practiced, but the kind which would bring to actuality the promise of industrial democracy implicit in the line of the Declaration of Independence which says that "every man is entitled to life, liberty and the pursuit of happiness." Pullman, in refusing to recognize or deal with a union, said, "We deal with our men individually as a corporation, and we expect them to deal with us individually as workmen." Altgeld felt that if it had been true politically for the thirteen colonies that "In Union there is strength" and that Union had made it possible for the colonies to turn themselves into an independent nation, then it was also true economically for the tens of millions of workers that "In Union there is strength," and the more their union brought them strength, the more would it enstrengthen the nation.

At dusk the train reached Springfield, and Darrow walked briskly to the imposing brick edifice that had been built in 1854 to serve as the governor's mansion. Mrs Altgeld, who was a lovely and sedate woman, came herself to open the door for Clarence, bid him a warm welcome and led him upstairs to the governor. From the open door of the library he had time to observe that the older man's face was drawn and tense as he wrote hurriedly at his desk, his full-bearded face framed against low shelves of leather-bound books. Clarence walked across the heavily rugged room; Altgeld looked up disturbedly, then relaxed, rose and gripped his hand.

"Well, Clarence, I hear you resigned from your job with the Chicago and North Western to defend Debs. I trust it isn't misguided idealism, son; there's little but grief in this martyr business."

Darrow's blue eyes twinkled slightly as he thought, "No one knows that better than you." Aloud he answered, "You know, Governor, most men do things through a desire to escape pain. Did you ever stop and watch a blind man begging on a street corner? A man passes by hurriedly and suddenly stops still; he looks hurt, annoyed. He goes back and drops a coin in the blind man's cup. Well—maybe he couldn't afford the dime. But the sight of the helpless man standing forlornly at a corner hurts him, makes him feel a sense of social responsibility, and so he buys ten cents' worth of relief from social pain. It hurts me too much to see Debs and men like him faced with the possibility of spending years in prison, so I am buying relief too."

Altgeld smiled, put his hand on Darrow's shoulder for an instant, then returned wearily to his desk, waving Darrow to a near-by chair. Darrow hitched up close.

"I watched Federal troops pitch camp in Chicago this morning."

"Yes," replied Altgeld. "I'm just drawing up my protest to President Cleveland. Right this very moment I have stationed in Chicago three regiments of infantry, one battery and one troop of cavalry, but neither Mayor Hopkins nor the superintendent of police, nor the sheriff of Cook County has felt there was any need for them. In the light of these facts, how can the United States Army move in?"

"It's pure railroad politics: the railroads make it appear that you refuse to protect private property, then have Attorney General Olney misrepresent to President Cleveland and get the Federal troops in here. That gets you out of the way, and they have complete control."

"There's more to it than that, son. By remaining peaceful, by merely refusing to move trains carrying Pullmans, the strikers are on their way to victory; their demands are just, and the public is with them. The only thing that can defeat the strike now is violence. The railroads know that by bringing Federal troops in here they can outrage the workers and start them fighting. If the fights don't start spontaneously the railroads will start them. As soon as one soldier is killed or one train wrecked the strikers will be defeated, no matter who is responsible, for the newspapers will blame it on the workers, and the people of the country will turn against them. Even now the press is carrying on a vitriolic campaign to convince the country that anarchy prevails in Chicago, that the strike is a revolution and that the issue is not the Pullman workers' wage question but a contest between law and order on one hand and lawlessness and anarchy on the other."

Darrow nodded his head.

"This day has been heavily interlarded with ironies for me, Governor, but coming up on the train I was struck by the most profound irony of them all: our independent American press, with its untrammeled freedom to twist and misrepresent the news, is one of the barriers in the way of the American people achieving their freedom."

"Yes, but we have to keep them free to misrepresent now in the hopes that one day they will use that freedom to tell the truth for the whole people." He picked up the sheets on which he had been writing, carried them to the north window and stood reading in the failing light, his lips moving silently as his mind rehearsed the sentences. Mrs Altgeld came in to tell them that supper was ready. Seeing her husband silhouetted against the window, his expression somber and harassed, she crossed to him, slipped an arm gently through his.

"Clarence," asked Altgeld, "would you perhaps like to hear the protest I am sending to President Cleveland? . . . 'Waiving all questions of courtesy, I will say that the state of Illinois is able to take care of itself. Our military force is ample and consists of as good soldiers as can be found anywhere in the country. They have been ordered promptly whenever and wherever they were needed. So far as I have been advised, the local officials have been able to handle the situation. But if any assistance were needed, the state stood ready to furnish one hundred men for every one man required and stood ready to do so at a moment's notice. In two instances the United States marshal applied for assistance of the state to enable him to enforce the processes of the United States Court, and troops were promptly furnished him. To ignore a local government in matters of this kind, when the local government is ready to furnish the assistance needed and is amply able to enforce the law, not only insults the people of this state by imputing to them an inability to govern themselves, but is a violation of a basic principle of our institutions. I ask the immediate withdrawal of the Federal troops from active duty in the state.' "

Darrow took the paper from the governor's hand and scanned it quickly. "If Cleveland has any regard for the laws under which he is supposed to rule——"

Altgeld shook his head sadly. "He won't withdraw the troops. The Eastern papers are screaming that a state of insurrection exists in Chicago. Olney is showing him frantic telegrams from Edwin Walker crying for more troops to quell the riots. Clarence, if you want to get a clear picture of what will happen to you if you defend labor leaders and fight for social justice, just watch the flood of invective that will be poured on my head in tomorrow's papers for protesting this clear and inexcusable violation of the Constitution. . . . It's their final insult because I pardoned the anarchists; they want to repudiate me as a Democrat so the Republicans won't have the chance to say to the country, 'We told you the Democrats are radicals, that they favor anarchy and the destruction of property.'"

As Darrow bade him good-by to catch the midnight train back to Chicago, Governor Altgeld murmured, "Watch developments closely and keep me informed. We are partners now, son, and there are going to be bad days ahead for both of us."

6

The next morning Darrow alighted cramped and stiff from the coach in which he had sat up all night, had breakfast and rode a streetcar into South Chicago. When he reached the point where the tracks of the Illinois Central and the Rock Island, the two lines at the center of the trouble, paralleled each other, he found the tracks heavily guarded by men with revolver holsters strapped about their waists, thirty-six hundred of them having been sworn in as deputy marshals. Rich men would not do the rough work of deputies for a few dollars a day; professional men were too busy to serve; men with jobs could not give up those jobs for a few days of work; unemployed workers did not take police jobs against their fellows. Who, then, was left? Walking among the newly sworn deputies, stopping here to share a cigarette and there for a chat, he saw that they had been recruited from the dregs of the Chicago tenderloin, swollen by the influx of adventurers to the World's Fair the year before: gangsters, hoodlums, toughs, petty criminals, sharpers, loafers, dope addicts, alcoholics. These were the men who now wore the badge of the United States government, who were going to enforce law and order, defend society against the revolutionary strikers. The headlines of the newspapers that had alleged Chicago to be in control of incendiary anarchists had indeed come true; these deputized representatives of the Federal government, armed and paid for by the railroads, fitted neatly into what the terrorized public had been bludgeoned into believing the anarchists were: miscreants who had nothing to lose, who would burn and destroy a city for the pleasure and pillage involved.

By midmorning he had made his way to the stockyards. He halted abruptly as he saw United States soldiers attempting to move a cattle train out of the yard, astounded at the boldness of the General Managers' Association in committing this most obvious illegality of them all: Federal troops had been sent into Chicago by President Cleveland to protect property, and here they were acting as strikebreakers. The assembled workers and their sympathizers, as had been expected, were not liking this idea; each time the soldiers

tried to move the train the track ahead was blocked by the overturning of empty freight cars and the spiking of switches. Darrow
watched the contest all day; by nightfall the army had been able to
move the train six blocks.

Learning that the General Managers' Association was determined
to prove they could bring a Pullman train into Chicago over the
Rock Island road, early the following morning Clarence hurried
south to Fifty-first Street. A through train was coming slowly down
the track, United States soldiers stationed on its cowcatcher. A protesting crowd collected; the engine slowed; the soldiers jumped
down, charged into the men and dispersed them. There was jeering;
a few stones were thrown. When the train reached Fortieth Street
it was blockaded by overturned freight cars; only through the combined efforts of Mayor Hopkins, Superintendent of Police Brennan and a railroad superintendent with a crack crew which righted
the freight cars was the Pullman able to move the next thirty blocks
by the end of the day. The railroads were paralyzed; foodstuffs and
machinery could be moved neither in nor out of the city; the
workers had won. Nevertheless, the overturning of the strike was
implicit in the overturning of the cars, for contrary to the orders
of Eugene Debs, the first railroad property had been manhandled.

That night violence broke loose. Standing above the yards,
Darrow watched a number of freight cars—and the strike with
them—burst into flame and vanish in smoke. The next morning
the newspapers of the country informed their readers that Chicago
was in a state of insurrection. The railroads demanded further protection; Mayor Hopkins wired Governor Altgeld, who promptly
provided six companies of state militia.

Human blood once again flowed in the streets of Chicago, the
slaughterhouse of the nation. The police spent a considerable portion of their efforts restraining the newly appointed United States
railroad deputies from slugging and shooting into the crowds,
arresting numbers of them for drunkenness and thievery. Mayor
Hopkins, fearing that the railroads might sue the city to collect
damages on the grounds of inadequate protection to property,
gathered forty depositions to prove that agents of the railroad companies had set fire to the cars. By afternoon huge crowds collected
along the tracks and in the yards: some few hotheaded strikers
who could not be restrained by Debs's orders, thousands of sympathizers, the interested and the curious, the wild boys, the foreign-
speaking population, which inhabited those sections, and the entire
underworld of Chicago came out to watch the sport, to enjoy the
excitement, to see what they could get out of it.

They milled about; the excitement rose; angry names were called; fists flew. At three-thirty in the afternoon they charged into the police and militiamen who were trying to disperse them. The soldiers fired. Three men fell dead of bullet wounds. Many others, including women, were bayoneted and clubbed.

By dinnertime Debs had been arrested on charges of criminal conspiracy and of violating the Federal injunction and was lodged in the Cook County jail. Darrow's four-day observation period of America in the making was over. He was now just a lawyer whose one and only client was behind prison bars.

7

The guard led him down a "long hall with iron floor, ceiling and walls," then unlocked a cell door. Darrow stepped inside; the iron clanged sharply behind him. A tall sinewy man with a long, plain face stepped forward to clasp his hand. In the cell were five strangers, waiting to be tried on petty criminal charges. Some were "stripped to the waist, scratching the bites inflicted by all manner of nameless vermin, the blood trickling down their bare bodies in tiny red rivulets. Sewer rats as big as cats scurried back and forth over the floor."

"Better sit on the bench and keep your feet off the floor," said Debs; "the rats are vicious. Though I guess I'm lucky at that; the guard showed me the cells down the line where they kept those anarchists who were hanged."

Darrow sprawled onto the hard bench, crossed one leg over the other and said ruminatively, "You know, Gene, finding you in the same cell block leads me to think maybe there's something to this anarchism business. Men like Parsons, Spies, Fischer and Engel believed that in America the capitalist monopoly was maintained by the state. That forced them to the conclusion that government was in enemy of the people. The events of the past few days would seem to bear them out."

A moment of quiet followed in which the two men could hear the voices of the newsboys shouting their extras. "Railroad strike broken; read all about the Debs Rebellion!"

"Debs Rebellion," murmured Darrow acidly. "You're in rebellion against the existing form of government and are out to burn civilization to the ground."

"I broke into railroading as a fireman," replied Debs, nodding his head. "I'm used to handling the stormy end of a scoop."

"Did you know that a schoolteacher in New York City had her

class debate on 'Why Eugene Debs is the most dangerous man in America'?"

Debs was aghast. "Just think of it: poisoning the minds of little children."

In the dimly lighted cell Darrow studied the face opposite him: the wide, ascetic mouth and stubborn chin, the long Alsatian nose, the clear, honest blue eyes, the enormous forehead doming back to meet the few straggling hairs left on his head. "There may have lived sometime, somewhere, a kindlier, gentler, more generous man than Eugene V. Debs," Darrow always said, "but I have never known him. Nor have I ever read or heard of another."

Darrow and Eugene Victor Debs were enough alike to be blood brothers. Debs had come out of the hard-boiled pioneer community of Terre Haute, Indiana, where his father had conducted a small grocery store in the parlor of their home. The mothers of both were hard-working, practical women, the fathers bookworms, scholars, idealists, dreamers; Eugene's middle name of Victor had been given him to honor the Debs's household god, Victor Hugo, while Darrow had had Cicero and Virgil rammed down his throat from the time he was six. Debs, too, had joyously dug his knowledge from books, from Hugo, Voltaire, Paine. Both men were intuitively non-sectarian; when Debs led his class in spelling for an entire term at the Old Seminary School in Terre Haute his teacher gave him a Bible with "Read and Obey" written on the flyleaf. "I did neither," remarked Debs fifty years later. At the age of seventy-eight Darrow was still preaching the virtues of skepticism and agnosticism to capacity audiences in the Midwest. Both were soft spoken, uncorrupted by a love of money. No two men in American history were to earn more bitter enemies than these two sitting side by side on a prison bench, their legs hitched under them to avoid the rats scampering beneath their feet; few would be more vilified in the press, from the pulpits and school platforms; few would have more splenetic hatred heaped upon them—and always for identical reasons. Both would suffer endless persecution, overwork, illness, ingratitude, and both would live long and fruitful lives.

"Go get a good night's sleep, Clarence, and don't worry about me," said Debs, the client comforting his lawyer. "We'll come out all right. If not this time—next time."

During the following days Darrow worked frantically to have Debs released on bail while the battle continued to be waged on both the political and economic fronts. After a sharp interchange of letters President Cleveland silenced Governor Altgeld with a curt and final note: "While I am still persuaded that I have neither transcended my authority nor duty in the emergency that confronts us, it seems to me that in this hour of danger and public distress discussion may well give way to active efforts on the part of all in authority to restore obedience to law and protect life and property."

Cleveland was greeted with salvos of praise; the attacks on Governor Altgeld for fighting for the principles of states' rights and local self-government, to which his and Cleveland's Democratic party were pledged, grew increasingly bitter. *Harper's Weekly* reflected the tone of the daily press when it called Altgeld "the most dangerous enemy to American institutions of all the ruffianly gang which has broken out of the forecastle of the ship of state and attempted to seize the helm."

On the labor front the pattern of violence entirely replaced the pattern of peaceful strike. Everywhere Darrow went he found freight cars overturned or burning in their yards. Several of the remaining Exposition buildings were set afire; three hundred thousand dollars' worth of railroad property was destroyed by young boys, vandals, the unemployed, a portion of the railroad men who, knowing they had been beaten, wanted to get in their blows of retaliation. Names were called; fists flew; rocks were thrown; clubs were swung; rifles were fired. Seven men lost their lives. No accurate count was taken of the injured. Then the violence had run its course; the crowds dispersed, and the last manifestations of the strike were over. Only then was Eugene Debs granted bail and released from his cell. Attending the last bitter meeting of his industrial union, he asked, "Has anyone ever heard of soldiers being called out to guard the rights of workingmen?"

The following day a communication was sent to the General Managers' Association by the American Railway Union, asking if they would negotiate. The association refused to receive the communication. Disorganized, whipped, humiliated, without funds and with serious charges against their leader, abused by the press, the pulpit and the government, men and women began drifting back to work: to the Pullman shops on the same wage scale against which they had struck—but not until they had turned in their A.R.U. cards; to the railroad yards on any terms. Anyone who had had any voice in the strike was refused work and black-listed; for the next decade derelicts of this industrial war drifted over the face of the continent, seeking a chance to work at their trades, in disguise, using false names, torn from their wives and children and homes; wounded veterans of internecine strife, with no government hospitals or veteran bureaus to which they might turn for help.

While they were in the depths of defeat and despair President Cleveland appointed a Senate Investigating Committee to get at the truth underlying the strike. Since his client would soon be called to trial for conspiracy, Darrow attended the sessions, gathering material for his case. Before this committee, under the leadership of Carroll Wright, scientific economist and first head of the United States Labor Bureau, paraded hundreds of witnesses: Pullman officials testifying that "three hundred strikers were thrown around the closed Pullman shops to protect them, and that from May 11 to July 3 there was not the slightest disorder or destruction of property"; police officials testifying that there had been no disorder in Chicago and no need for Federal troops; newspaper reporters affirming they had seen almost no strikers in the violence mobs; Debs and other union officials revealing why organization was needed to combat the General Managers, and lastly, George Pullman, who avowed that "we recognize that the working people are the most important element which enters into the successful operation of any manufacturing enterprise" and was then forced into the staggering disclosure that for the depression year of August 1893 to July 1894, when he had slashed wages below the subsistence level and refused to lower rents, his company declared a profit dividend of two million, eight hundred thousand dollars!

In addition to the thirty-six millions of capital invested in the company, which over a period of years had paid dividends of twenty-five million dollars at rates ranging from eight to twelve per cent, there was at that very instant in the treasury of the Pullman Company, in available cash, earned but undistributed profits of another twenty-six million dollars! A hundred thousand dollars taken off the almost-three-million-dollar stock dividend, a bare one twenty-eighth of the depression year's profits left in workingmen's wages, would have completely avoided the starvation, illness, desperation, strikes and industrial warfare, with its subsequent stabbings, stonings, clubbings, beatings and shootings, the destruction of life and property, the destruction of faith in the American law, the American courts and the American way of life.

But George Pullman had known that you can't give in to your workingmen. When asked by the commission whether he didn't think that workmen who had been with him for so many years, who had helped build his shops, his prestige and his fortune, were not entitled to some consideration—in this case a reduction of a dollar or two of dividends on each share of stock—Pullman had replied publicly: "My duty is to my stockholders and to my company. There was no reason to give those workingmen a gift of money."

The reading portion of the public was profoundly shocked at these revelations. The industrialists of America were sore at Pullman for letting himself get caught with his corporate pants down.

8

The hearing concluded, Darrow threw himself into the history of criminal conspiracy, the law which says that if two people agree to do something together which either of them could legally do alone, then both may be deemed guilty of an illegal act; the law against which he would fight for the next forty years. The Senate Investigating Committee had observed, "Some of our courts are still poring over the law reports of antiquity in order to construe conspiracy out of labor unions." This, Darrow knew, was precisely what his clients were up against.

He found that prior to the seventeenth century in England there had been no mention of any combination or confederacy having been held criminal under the common law. Although in 1611 a judge in the Poulterers' Case established that if the gist of a crime is conspiracy, no other overt act is necessary, "there was not a single case in the seventeenth century where the courts allowed a conspiracy conviction for a combination to commit an act not in itself criminal."

However, as early as 1721, with the Industrial Revolution beginning to show that the small, personally owned handicraft way of production and way of life had to yield to large concentrations of workers under one employer roof, there was a statute in force in England which expressly made it criminal for journeyman tailors to enter into any agreement "for advancing their wages or lessening their usual hours of work." In this year came the first application of the conspiracy laws to labor. Certain journeyman tailors were indicted and found guilty of a conspiracy to raise their wages. The court said, "A conspiracy of any kind is illegal, although the matter about which they conspired might have been lawful for them to do if they had not conspired to do it."

This type of legal reasoning, Darrow decided, made the judge the law. "Under any such principle everyone who acts in co-operation with another may someday find his liberty dependent upon the innate prejudices or social bias of an unknown judge. There would be a very real danger of courts being invoked, especially during periods of reaction, to punish, as criminal, associations which for the time being are unpopular or stir up the prejudices of the social class in which the judges have for the most part been bred." The Senate Investigating Committee commented, "In England, prior to 1824, it was conspiracy and a felony for labor to unite for purposes now regarded there by all classes as desirable for the safety of the government, of capital, and for the protection of the rights of labor."

Coming down to the American scene, Darrow discovered that in 1806 a group of Philadelphia cordwainers were "tried on an indictment for criminal conspiracy for having agreed together not to work except for higher wages. There prevailed at that time among the upper classes a bitter feeling of hostility against the working classes; the generally accepted view was that any concerted action by the workers against their employers must be by the very nature of things inherently criminal. The defendants who had been bold enough to organize a strike for higher wages were found guilty and branded as criminals." However, in *The Commonwealth* vs. *Carlisle*, 1821, "where a journeyman sought to convict certain master shoemakers for combining to depress wages, the courts held that the defendants were not guilty of criminal conspiracy."

In Chicago seventy-three years later history was repeating itself with an identical pattern: the General Managers' Association's concerted efforts to depress wages was not a criminal conspiracy; the attempts on the part of the American Railway Union to prevent those wages from being depressed was actionable at law.

During the fall months of 1894 Darrow rented a small office, surrounded himself with lawbooks, history and economics books and mapped his defense of Debs and the A.R.U. Slowly he evolved a plan. He would not stand on the defensive; he would not go into court as the counsel for the wrongdoer and the guilty, pleading for justice or, at best, mercy. No, he would go in and attack. He would indict the General Managers' Association for criminal conspiracy, revealing to the country their illegal agreements to control rates and service as well as wages, thus eliminating the benefits of the competitive system. He would indict and try George Pullman for antisocial conduct, inimical to the well-being of his country, dangerous to democratic principles. But most important of all, he would place on trial in that Chicago courtroom the industrial oligarchy under which twenty per cent of the people enjoyed comfort and security while the other eighty per cent suffered uncertainty, intermittent unemployment and want, with no discernible share in the democracy which Andrew Jackson and Abraham Lincoln had imagined was created for the betterment of all.

True, he could not convict George Pullman. He could not send the General Managers' Association to jail, nor could he persuade the judge to reconstruct the economic machinery even if he proved it guilty. He realized that in cases of this nature he could not be a trial lawyer. He would have to be a teacher, an educator. His clients might be convicted and sent to prison, but in the meanwhile he would be making every effort to damn the convictors in the mind of the general public, that inert, formless, seemingly power-less mass which, if ever sufficiently educated and aroused, might rise up in its wrath to reshape its civilization.

Words were wax bullets; dollars were dumdums. But words were the only weapons he had at hand.

9

On the morning of January 26, 1895, Darrow led his eight clients into the courtroom of Judge Grosscup, one of the two Federal judges who had issued an ex-parte injunction to Edwin Walker, with no representative of labor present because labor had not been informed by the court that the hearing was to be held. The eight accused were Eugene V. Debs, George W. Howard and Sylvester Keliher, officers of the A.R.U.; L. W. Rogers, editor of the A.R.U. newspaper; William E. Burns, Martin J. Elliot, Roy M. Goodwin and James Hogan, directors of the organization.

At the defense table with Darrow sat S. S. Gregory, one of the best lawyers Darrow had ever known. "He was emotional and sympathetic; he was devoted to the principles of liberty and always fought for the poor and oppressed. In spite of all this, he had a fine practice, and his ability and learning were thoroughly recog-nized." The country, already upset by the idea that a railroad lawyer had resigned his position to defend the obviously guilty Debs, was even more confused to find Gregory, a former president of the American Bar Association, also working for the accused. The presence of these two men, coupled with the findings of the Senate Investigating Committee, provoked certain portions of the public to ask, "Is there more to this case than we are permitted to read in our morning paper?"

Nearly every pair of eyes and ears in America was turned toward that courtroom in Chicago. The courtroom itself was jammed with spectators who wanted to see the murderous beast Debs, who, like Altgeld, had been portrayed by the press as the most dangerous anarchist and ruffian of his times. "They sat back in frank dis-appointment when Gene was pointed out to them. This was no long-haired fire-eater; on the contrary, Debs was nearly bald, mild appearing, with candid blue eyes behind gold-rimmed spectacles. He wore a high white collar, a black-and-white scarf, a gray tweed suit, a boutonniere."

The prosecution opened the case with a searing indictment against Debs. He was guilty of murdering the seven men who had been shot by the troops; he was guilty of inciting riots; he was guilty of destroying three hundred thousand dollars' worth of railroad property; he was guilty of a conspiracy to starve the country, paralyze its industries, wreck its economic structure. He was also guilty, parenthetically, of the charge on which he had been brought into court: persuading railroad workers to remain on strike.

Darrow, "who always sat slumped far down in a chair, as though sitting on the back of his neck," slowly pulled himself upward, walked toward the jury box and stood facing the twelve men. The twelve men could feel him thinking; they could see from his plain, lined farmer's face that this was an honest man, mistaken doubtless, but honest. They thought his case a hopeless one and they wondered what he could possibly say to defend these men who had so palpably broken the law. But the veteran Kinsman debator was accustomed to facing groups who thought him whipped before he started. When he began speaking in his low, musical drawl, as though really wanting to find true words for true thoughts, they were astounded to find that by some curious twist of reasoning he had become the prosecutor.

"This is a historic case which will count much for liberty or against liberty. Conspiracy, from the days of tyranny in England down to the day the General Managers' Association used it as a club, has been the favorite weapon of every tyrant. It is an effort to punish the crime of thought. If the government does not, we shall try to get the General Managers here to tell you what they know about conspiracy. These defendants published to all the world what they were doing and in the midst of a widespread strike were never so busy but that they found time to counsel against violence. For this they are brought into court by an organization which uses the government as a cloak to conceal its infamous purposes."

For a solid month, backed and advised by Gregory, he reviewed the history of labor unions and conspiracy laws. He exposed the conditions at the Pullman plant, revealed the activities of the General Managers' Association and finally presented to the nation Eugene Victor Debs. In order that the American people might learn how so base and villainous a character could be produced under such a salutary economic system, he led Debs through the story of his life. Aware that the imprisonment or freedom of Debs and unionism depended upon how thoroughly he could convince this jury, sitting in supreme judgment, that Eugene Debs was a man of integrity and of incalculable value to the permanent well-being of his country, he drew out that story with such skill, he converted biography into an art form. The judge leaned forward across his big desk, listening intently; the jurors craned on the edge of their chairs, disturbed and anxious; the spectators sat breathless, their faces turned upward to the accused man in the witness box.

10

Eugene V. Debs was born in Terre Haute, Indiana, on November 5, 1855, of Jean Daniel Debs and Marguerite Marie Betterich, both recently arrived from Alsace. His father collected fine books and prints; his mother, who managed the parlor grocery store and raised a large brood of children, was a woman of indomitable character with a gentle soul. "There is not a page of our memory," wrote Debs on his parents' fiftieth anniversay, "that is not adorned and beautified by acts of her loving care."

At the age of fourteen he went to work for fifty cents a day, scraping paint off the sides of old railroad cars. A romantic, with a roving energetic mind, there was no way for him to read any fun or adventure into this work. "I worked there for a year, and it almost killed me." Then one day he was picked out of the shop by an engineer whose fireman was drunk, and put on a freight engine, shoveling coal into a ravenous and roaring firebox as the train sped through the dark night. As a stripling of fifteen he had been chosen as one who could handle "the stormy end of a scoop." Romantically he enjoyed every detail of the railroad business and soon found himself a steady job on the Terre Haute and Indianapolis Railroad at a dollar a night; during the day he robbed himself of sleep by attending a private school and burrowing in the encyclopedia a book agent had sold him on the installment plan. He was an eager student; he wanted to be intelligent, to understand the times he lived in: the problems of San Domingo and Cuba, the corruption of the Grant administration and the reconstruction of the South. By the time he reached eighteen he was not only well educated for his day, he was "six feet of wiry muscles, hard as a spike maul, accepted by the veteran railroad men as a first-class 'rail.' "

A year later, realizing the apprehension and fear his mother suffered over the constant railroad wrecks and killing of crews, he reluctantly gave up his job as fireman and went to work in a wholesale grocery house. But he never ceased to think of himself as a railroad man; he attended meetings of the union, did their clerical work and, when the Terre Haute lodge of the newly formed Brotherhood of Locomotive Firemen was formed, was chosen secretary. "I have put a towheaded kid in at Terre Haute," said Joshua Leach, the organizer, "and someday he will be at the head of the order." For the next seventeen years Gene Debs *was* the Brotherhood of Locomotive Firemen. He drew no pay for his work; he wanted none. In his spare hours he prepared meticulous reports to national headquarters, edited the *Locomotive Firemen's Magazine* and wrote articles for it; in bad years he contributed as much as nine hundred dollars, out of the fifteen hundred he earned, to keep the union and the magazine going. When the national organization was on the brink of bankruptcy and annihilation, six thousand dollars in debt, he was made secretary-treasurer. When strikes and depressions depleted the membership he "opened the hall, sat for an hour alone, staring somberly at empty chairs, then went back home depressed but determined to meet the challenge." At the age of twenty-five he met the challenge by working all night writing hundreds of letters to members who had fallen off, telling them that they must come back into their union; organizing meetings throughout the Midwest, addressing groups no matter how small or indifferent, trying to infuse courage and unity, shunting from one railroad system to another, teaching the workmen how and why they must present a solid front—a man possessed, a man inspired. "My grip was always packed; to tramp through a railroad yard in the rain, snow or sleet half the night, to be ordered out of the roundhouse for being an agitator or to be put off a train were all in the program."

He was elected city clerk of Terre Haute. As president of the Occidental Literary Club he brought to Terre Haute its literary and controversial life in the form of James Whitcomb Riley, the poet; Wendell Phillips, the reformer; Colonel Robert Ingersoll, the agnostic, and Susan B. Anthony, the firebrand of woman's suffrage. He read constantly in economics, politics, history, trying to clarify his thoughts and determinations; he strove hard to become a good speaker so that he might reach the hearts of the workers. He got along on three and four hours' sleep a night; he had no personal life, but with the passage of the years he made himself that rarity among union leaders: an educated man, well equipped to compete with the managers on their own ground. For sixteen years the brotherhood grew under his guidance, securing ever-better wages and hours for its men, safer working conditions on the line.

Then in 1892 Eugene Debs had one of the great social visions of his century: just as Pullman's Pioneer had revolutionized the mechanics of the railroad industry, an American Railway Union would revolutionize the human side. Like the original Pioneer it, too, would be built from the ground up, too high for the bridges and too wide for the platforms of the existing industrial system, but that was the way it had to be built to fulfill its needs, and Debs was as foolhardy and courageous as Pullman in insisting that the entire capitalist roadbed would be renovated so that industrial unionism could run on its tracks. The General Managers' Association had combined all the railroads within the system to control hours, wages and working conditions for the industry. Then, reasoned Debs, we must also organize all labor within the industry to cope with it. It is not enough to have only the highly skilled trades unionized, for they represent only a small portion of the workers within any industry, probably not more than twenty per cent of the working people of the country. What good is it for any one group of workers to strike if the other trades continue to work? No, every last job within an industry, no matter how unimportant or menial, must be organized and joined in a union as big as the industry itself; an injury to one group then would be an injury to all. Trade or craft unions served the small-shop age; the growing industrial machine needed new union structures to house all workers within an industry, just as new plants were being built to house all processes within the manufacture. As soon as the railroads were organized in a great industrial brotherhood they could go to the steel industry, the rubber and oil industries, then the meat-packing and textile and lumber and mining industries, until every workingman in the country belonged to his union as to his industry; a solid wall of labor to confront the solid wall of management.

After a stormy session with the Brotherhoods of Locomotive Engineers, Brakemen and Firemen, which wanted to confine union strength to the skilled trades, fearful lest some of their privileges be dissipated if everyone were organized, Gene Debs resigned and formed the American Railway Union, which would take in all workers within the industry, from the lowliest section hand, track-walker or seamstress who sewed upholstery at the Pullman plant to the most highly skilled mechanic and engineer. In spite of the brotherhood opposition he built his American Railway Union to a membership of a hundred and fifty thousand, with four hundred and sixty-five separate lodges. Then on April 1, 1894, when James J. Hill cut the wage of his common labor from a dollar and a quarter to a dollar a day, the American Railway Union helped organize the Great Northern workers, stopped all service on the line and, with the aid of the St Paul Chamber of Commerce, forced Hill to restore the wage cut. With this unprecedented victory of unskilled labor, his conception of industrial unionism was justified, and the membership soared. The delegates came confident and flushed with success to their first convention in Chicago in June 1894. There they had encountered the Pullman strike.

The A.R.U. had helped organize the Pullman shops. When the Pullman workers had found it impossible to live on the wages being paid them the A.R.U. had urged arbitration and attempted to achieve it. But Pullman had stood firm on the nineteenth-century rock that workers had nothing to say about the wages they received, that he had nothing to arbitrate. Against the advice of the A.R.U. the Pullman workers had struck; their delegates had come into the convention to tell harrowing tales of starvation, oppression, injustice, despair. Debs and the A.R.U. officers had remained firm: their union was too young to stage a sympathetic strike, too inexperienced; they did not have a sufficiently large membership or enough money in the bank. Then in the midst of their denials a girl had come into the convention to tell of how her father had died, owing the Pullman company some sixty dollars in back rent; of how the company was now taking that money out of her wages, letting her work for two weeks, then deducting a portion of her father's debt before handing her a few pennies as wages.

The A.R.U. workers were feeling men; they had known unemployment, uncertainty, hunger, want, despair; it required no exercise of the imagination for them to conjure up these pictures; they had lived with them at their elbows all their lives. All they could do was to vote the sympathetic strike and refuse to move Pullman cars.

They had struck; they had stayed at home and remained peaceable; they had woven for the country a design of industrial unionism. Then the railroads took over the government, and now Eugene V. Debs was a criminal on a witness stand, the strike broken, the workers in disrepute, industrial unionism so effectively smashed it would not raise its head for four full decades.

11

Satisfied by the look and feel of the jury that Debs had gone a long way to acquit himself, Darrow made his next bold move: he would juxtapose George Pullman to Eugene Debs and let the country draw its own conclusions. He subpoenaed Pullman to come into court and reveal the details of the two-million-eight-hundred-thousand-dollar dividend distributed in the preceding depression year and the twenty-six millions in cash of undeclared dividends in the coffers of the company at the same time that the men who had helped him earn this money were fainting at their machines of hunger.

But George Pullman was nowhere to be found. He had fled. The subpoena could not be served. The Chicago *Tribune* declared, "It is not strange that he should not be willing to go on the stand and be questioned by Mr Darrow. It is not pleasant for a person who is at the head of a great corporation, who has many subordinates and no superiors and who is in the habit of giving orders instead of answering questions, to be interrogated by persons who are unfriendly to him and who may put disagreeable inquiries which he has to reply to civilly."

Darrow made the most of this flight, portraying Pullman to the jury and to the world as the true insidious enemy of society. The shoe was neatly on the other foot; the prosecutors were being prosecuted. Pulling his master stroke, Darrow now announced that he was going to subpoena every last member of the General Managers' Association, whom he would then proceed to convict, not only of criminal conspiracy to depress wages, but further, of a criminal conspiracy to take over and use the Federal government for their own conspiratorial purposes.

But Clarence Darrow had planned too well; his first big case promptly blew up under his hand. The next morning only eleven men took their seats in the jury box. Judge Grosscup set forth that, "Owing to the sickness of a juror and the certificate of his physician that he will not be able to get out for two or three days, I think it will be necessary to adjourn the further taking of testimony in this case."

For once he was on his feet like lightning, demanding that another juror be named, that the record of the case be read to him. Judge Grosscup denied the motion; the case was put over until May. The jurors are reported to have come out of the jury box and shaken hands with Debs, ignoring the outstretched hands of the prosecutors, and to have told Darrow that their sentiment had been eleven to one for acquittal.

That Darrow had acquitted his clients of the criminal-conspiracy charges was clear; the government never again called the case for trial. However, Debs and his seven associates were now cited by the Chicago circuit court for "contempt" in having refused to obey the injunction first issued. Darrow was aghast at this move, for in the

Federal Court the defendants would not have the benefit of a trial by jury. Judge Woods, the second of the two Federal judges who had granted the injunction, heard the evidence and sentenced the union officials to six months in jail.

For several days Darrow's thoughts knocked about confusedly in his mind. In the midst of his bitterness he persuaded Lyman Trumbull, one of the small but valiant group of idealistic lawyers to be found in every American city, to join him in his appeal to the United States Supreme Court. It was Lyman Trumbull who, as the senator with the deciding vote to cast in the impeachment trial of President Andrew Johnson, in 1868, with his reputation, his profession, his very life threatened by the political ruffians who were seeking to remove Johnson for their own venal purposes, defied those conspirators, voted to acquit Johnson and thus helped to save his country from an international disgrace. Trumbull had been a judge of the Supreme Court of Illinois and was acknowledged to be Chicago's outstanding attorney. His appearance in the Debs case further confounded the public.

The Darrow-Trumbull brief was simple and direct. It attempted to show that not since 1824 had there been any statute in the United States making it a crime to organize labor unions or go out in peaceable strike. Therefore, the accused were guilty of no crime under the common law, but even if they had been, both the criminal law and the Constitution provided that the trial of all crimes shall be by jury; a court of equity, such as Judge Wood's court, had no jurisdiction over criminal- or common-law cases. Consequently the Grosscup and Woods court of equity had assumed jurisdiction illegally when they issued the injunction, and they were now further assuming jurisdiction illegally by depriving persons of their liberty without a trial by jury.

Darrow was confident the Supreme Court would throw out the contempt conviction. This assumption was his first major error in judgment: he had failed to go back to the beginnings of the Supreme Court, to trace its consistent efforts to defend and entrench property rights over personal rights in the development of American life. Caught thus off guard, he was astounded at the decision of the Supreme Court, and even more at the methods by which it reached that decision.

Ignoring the fact that there had been no obstruction of the mails, the Supreme Court justified the sending of Federal troops into Chicago and the violation of states' rights by claiming that "among the powers expressly given to the national government are the control of interstate commerce and the management of the post office

. . . and the strong arm of the government may be put forth to brush away all obstructions to their freedom. There was in existence a special emergency, one which demanded that the court do all that courts can do; the jurisdiction of the courts of equity to redress the grievance of public nuisances by injunction is clearly established; having this right, the court must also have the right to punish those who disregard its orders." Apparently not attempting to be satiric, the Supreme Court avowed that "the government of the Union is emphatically and truly a government of the people; in form and in substance it emanates from them; its powers are granted by them and are to be exercised directly on them and for their benefit." And thereupon refused to set aside the contempt conviction.

There was nothing more Darrow, Trumbull or anyone else could do. Debs once again packed his bag and with his associates went to jail in Woodstock, Illinois. Governor Altgeld had been defeated by President Cleveland. Eugene Debs and the American Railway Union had been defeated by the General Managers' Association. Clarence Darrow had been defeated in his first big case by the Circuit and Supreme courts. The more he studied the Supreme Court decision the more he became convinced that it was based on class prejudice rather than the Constitution, aimed to further buttress the power of industry and leave the mass of working people without means of protection or redress. He felt deep in his heart that "both sides recognized that Debs had been sent to jail as a victim of the world class struggle, because he had led a great fight to benefit the toilers and the poor." "Debs really got off easy," he commented. "No other offense has ever been visited with such severe penalties as seeking to help the oppressed."

12

With Debs and his companions safely locked behind iron bars, the case was apparently ended, the apotheosis of the struggle of the nineteenth century to build into the structure of American life the insuperable and everlasting law of property. But for Clarence Darrow this was only the beginning of the case. The American corporation was growing to be an ever-greater colossus, absorbing roots and soil and wheat and trees in its onrushing march, until at length there would be nothing left on the continent save this gigantic mechanism, with one leg on the Atlantic Ocean and the other on the Pacific, sucking up materials and men and institutions and rights until there would be no more humans left on earth, until the machine had of necessity consumed the very men who had made it. Was that to be the end of America, the country of the new freedom and the new hopes?

Bitter and cynical as he felt, sitting at his desk in his lonely office, poring over the pages of the decision, he did not think so. When the nineteenth century died its peculiar machine civilization must die with it; upon its broad machine base a new society must be born. Already there were vital voices and forces in the air, in the new books and magazines, in the lectures and debates, questioning, examining, clarifying, demanding to be shown the value of this magnificent industrial machine if, in spite of the great wealth of goods it was producing, it continued to maim and imprison humanity instead of liberating it. The nineteenth century had solidified the law of property to keep pace with the growth of property. The twentieth century, he sensed, must develop the law of persons.

In this development he was ready to play any part which the times and the exigencies demanded of him.

CHAPTER III

Darrow Sprinkles Salt on the Tail of Truth

IF DARROW had wanted to go to a modern law college he could never have passed the entrance examination:

"What is the first thing you must do when a client walks into your office?"

"Get a retainer fee."

The story that Clarence Darrow had given up a lucrative job to defend Eugene Debs spread the legend that a phenomenon, a sport, had arisen within the legal profession: a capable lawyer who would fight for the poor. His modest office in the Reaper Block promptly became a one-man legal clinic. On the hard benches of his waiting room sat endless lines of clients in well-worn, unfashionable clothes: the disinherited who could bring him little but their grief, workingmen who had lost an arm or leg at their job and had been cast off without compensation, wives whose husbands had been killed at their work or in other accidents, unemployed families about to be dispossessed, gullible victims who had been defrauded of their savings, mothers from the slums whose children had run afoul of the law. The faces were lined, thin, harassed, the skins weatherbeaten, the shoulders and knees bent from years of hard labor, the hands rough, gnarled, bruised: the faces, the skins, the shoulders and knees, the hands and the eyes of laborers, all.

When he finished with one client he would walk into the waiting room in his shirt sleeves and say to the next in line, "All right, you can come in now." His office girl was instructed never to turn anyone away; no one was ever told he was too busy; everyone who came could sit and wait his turn. No matter how late it got, he never sent anyone home, to come back again the next day. When people with jobs wanted to see him he let them call after six o'clock. When he went to court he left orders that if anyone needed him to send them to the courtroom. He would talk to these people during recess, and if that were not time enough he would work with them again on his lunch hour. There was always someone waiting for him on the courthouse steps to tell him his troubles as he walked back to the office. He saw even the crackpots, the lunatics, though briefly. He was a sap, a sucker, a sentimentalist, but he was no fool: he could smell an impostor as far away as an outhouse.

With a boundless capacity for feeling the other man's grief, he sat sprawled behind his desk, generally in his white shirt and galluses, absorbing into his sensitivity, his mellowness, the tears of his little corner of the world. He did not seek injustice and suffering because he enjoyed them; they came to him; always they found him out, and when they did he could never refuse them. And so they filed into his office, the old, the halt, the poor, the lowly, the ignorant, the dispossessed, each with his burthen of care. Here was a man who looked at them with the unmistakable glow of brotherhood in his childlike blue eyes, who talked so softly and simply that even the most inarticulate could speak to him easily, pour out their hearts.

So sympathetic was his nature that he couldn't turn anyone down, even when the cause was hopeless. "He hated to tell anybody he didn't have a case and didn't have a chance. He would come out of his office and murmur, 'That poor devil, I don't know what I can tell him.'"

"Darrow was one of the kindliest and best-natured men I have ever known," said one of his future partners. "He was actually unable to say, 'No!' People often thought his silence meant 'Yes,' and if he didn't come through they thought he had broken his promise."

"I did not sit in my office only to wait for someone to bring me a good fee; anyone who came inside my door was welcome; whether he had money or not was of small concern. I did not go after business; I simply took it as it came, and the criminal courts and the jails are always crowded with the poor. . . . A lawyer has to do a great deal of work for which he cannot hope to be compensated; all he can hope is that once in a while he will get a client who can afford to pay. Ability to pay should be the main test of a just fee. A lawyer is justified in charging a higher fee, even for lesser services, to people who can pay."

With personal-injury cases it was the custom of lawyers to charge twenty-five per cent if they settled out of court, thirty-five per cent if they tried the case. They always insisted on contracts. "Darrow never wanted a contract. He would drawl, 'Well, we will see how it comes out.' When the case was over he would say to his client, 'How you fixed? Got a family, haven't you? This kind of money won't last long.' Then he'd take a hundred dollars when he could have taken five hundred."

Later, when he had become the country's most famous trial lawyer, an old attorney who had fallen upon bad times stumbled into his office, tears streaming down his face: his son had just murdered a woman in Humboldt Park. They had loved each other, and when the woman announced she was going to break off the relationship the boy killed her. It would be a long and difficult case; Darrow had little stomach for it, but when he looked at the pain-racked father he could not break a "No!" past his teeth.

"I haven't much money left," cried the father; "how much will you——?"

"Any other lawyer would charge you five thousand. Oh, say a thousand dollars."

"All right, but I can't give it all to you."

"Give me what you can. I have to pay court costs."

Darrow laid out his own money for the costs. On the opening day of the trial the attorney handed him a five-hundred-dollar check. Four days later the check was brought to him in court, marked "Not Sufficient Funds." Darrow gazed at the oblong strip of paper, then said:

"Don't tell the poor fellow his check was returned. He's unhappy enough as it is."

Darrow completed the case, persuading the jury to disagree. Only then did he tell the father about the bad check. The man wept, saying he had hoped the bank would honor it. Darrow replied not to give him another bad check but to wait until he had the money. He then retried the case; the boy was acquitted. Now completely broken, the father never scraped together any part of the thousand-dollar fee, nor did Darrow dun him for the money.

The records reveal that from a third to a half of his professional efforts were devoted to clients from whom he collected nothing. His friends said of him, "He devoted more of his time to widows and orphans than all the other lawyers in Chicago put together."

"Once in Paris, when the American Bar Association there gave him a banquet, a group of lawyers and judges surrounded him, saying they wanted a look at the attorney who did such a lot of work for nothing. One said, 'Why, you don't belong in our profession; you belong in a museum of freaks.' "

2

In 1895 he joined the organization of a new firm, Collins, Goodrich, Darrow and Vincent, with offices in the Rookery Building. Lorin C. Collins, the head, had been a judge of the Circuit Court and former Speaker of the Illinois House of Representatives; Adams A. Goodrich was a former state judge; William A. Vincent had been chief justice of the Supreme Court of the then territory of New Mexico—all of which put him in illustrious company. The new firm was "organized for the distinct purpose of entering the practice of corporation law and representing corporations, including banks and railroads." Almost immediately a sensational murder was committed in Chicago, and Darrow ran afoul of the firm's avowed policy.

"A poor, half-witted, religious zealot" by the name of Pendergast, who earned a meager living by selling newspapers and "whose mentality is disclosed by the fact that in order to come closer to God and nature he used to mingle in the pastures with cattle and browse with them," forced his way into the office of the newly elected mayor, Carter H. Harrison, Senior, and insisted that Harrison had promised to give him an important political appointment in return for the electioneering he had done. When the mayor tried to ease the unbalanced man out of the room Pendergast pulled a gun and assassinated him.

"Mr Darrow volunteered to defend the man, without a fee, paying the costs himself. His so doing was upon his expressed thought that if the law declared that an insane or mentally incompetent person should not be convicted of such a crime, then Pendergast was entitled to the benefit of that law, regardless of the fact that his victim was a man of great prominence." It was Darrow's first murder trial and the only one he ever lost—for Chicago was caught in the grip of one of its recurrent blood lusts and demanded Pendergast's execution.

A junior partner gives a picture of Darrow at the time: "Mr Darrow was greatly beloved by the young men of the organization because of his unfailing consideration of them and his informal, friendly make-up. Within the four walls of the library he was a keenly analytical and conservative lawyer. There was no pose allowed to interfere with his analysis of the law, and such analyses were cold, keen and based upon the law alone. Outside the law, and on public questions, he was beginning to be the Darrow we all knew in later years, and, as I have heard him express it, he was 'generally agin everybody else.' I remember one incident which disclosed some of Mr Darrow's idiosyncrasies. I had handled an attachment case for him and had succeeded in collecting the claim. I asked Mr Darrow how much to charge the client.

" 'How much time did you spend on it?'

" 'Two and a half days; the main thing was that I beat the other creditors to the assets.'

" 'Make a charge of five hundred dollars.'

" 'But, Mr Darrow, that's inconsistent with your idea about correcting the existing evils of compensating people for their labor. The other day you told me that every individual should receive for his work a certificate for each hour of labor, and no matter what kind of work men did, their labor-hour certificates should be of equal value. You illustrated your point by saying that you should receive a certificate for an hour's law work, and the Rookery elevator men should receive an equally valuable certificate for an hour's work. The elevator man gets fifty-five dollars a month, and here you are charging five hundred dollars for two and a half days' work!'

" 'To hell with the elevator men,' grunted Darrow; 'we're practicing law.' "

He based that practice on an intuition for human nature rather than a detailed knowledge of the law. His cryptographical mind penetrated the façade of spoken words, gestures, expressions, protestations. Though his eyes were mild, his voice soft, his manner gentle, his evaluating apparatus was objectively hard, sharp and incisive. He put faith in his own judgments:

A twenty-three-year-old attorney was brought a case in which he had to make a settlement through Darrow. He drew up an agreement and took it to Darrow for his inspection, revision and the usual months of compromise. Darrow sat chatting across the desk with the young man for a quarter of an hour, discussing the affairs of the day. When the man finally drew out his proposed agreement Darrow said:

"Does this seem a fair settlement to you?"

"Yes, it does, Mr Darrow."

"Is it as fair to my client as it is to yours?"

"I leaned over backward to make it so, sir."

"Very well, I accept it."

"You accept—without even reading it!"

"In the few minutes we have spent together I have judged you to be an honest and qualified lawyer. If you say this plan is completely acceptable to both sides, how can I improve it?"

The most valuable use of his ability to get his hands on the core of a man was exercised in the selection of juries. He spent weeks examining prospective jurors, oblivious to the passage of time, his other obligations or the size of the fee involved.

"Darrow always picked common people," said a Chicago lawyer; "he didn't want big businessmen. He had a farmer's way about him that appealed to common jurors. He talked to a plumber as though he, too, were a plumber; to a groceryman as though he, too, were a groceryman. He knew Chicago so well he could divine how the juror would react to his theories by the part of the city he came from. He was a great reasoner. When you opposed him you had to try the case the way he wanted it tried. He would shift his position logically on a moment's notice; we all had to imitate his methods. He was never arrogant or contemptuous with other lawyers and never quarreled with opposing lawyers before a jury. The district attorney's office hated it when Darrow was to defend; he was so resourceful. A marvel as a cross-examiner, he would never give up examining until he got some comfort out of it. No matter how badly the point went against him, he would work on it and turn it to his advantage."

He worked just as carefully on the judge as he did on the jury. "The most important thing to do is to make the judge *want* to decide things your way," Darrow advised one of his younger partners. "They are human beings, moved by the same things that move other human beings. The points of law merely give the judge a *reason* for doing what you have already made him want to do."

3

Injustice or cruelty in any form burned him with a white-hot fury. He jumped in where more discreet men would have feared to tread, and as a consequence he often led with his chin. When he was traveling to the Pacific coast for a vacation with his son Paul, he approached the dining car from the day-coach end and waited his turn behind an old lady who had apparently been there for some time. A few moments later a party came to the diner from the Pullman end, and when a table was available the steward, catering to the first-class passengers, ignored the old lady and went to escort the more prosperous party to the table. Darrow intercepted him.

"This elderly lady was here first," he said. "She is entitled to that table."

"She'll have to wait her turn," replied the steward brusquely.

"This is her turn." He took the woman by the arm and led her to the table, then went back to wait in the vestibule. When it came time to pay his bill he had only a fifty-dollar greenback; the steward, enjoying his revenge, handed him forty-eight cartwheels in change.

"Will you report him to the Chicago and North Western when you get back?" asked Paul.

"No, no, son," exclaimed Darrow. "Never hurt a man who is working for his living."

Another time when he was on a summer vacation at the Belworth farm near Port Jarvis he saw the small-town sheriff manhandle a young boy.

"What's he done?" asked Darrow.

"Been pulled off a freight car by a railroad dick. What business is it of yours?"

"Well, the boy has a right to talk to me."

The sheriff gazed at Darrow's open shirt, black suspenders and dusty pants and said insolently, "Who in hell are you?"

"Oh, just a lawyer from Chicago. Seems to me there's no railroad tracks down in this part of the state. Did you bring that boy across a state line?"

"Well—what if I did?"

"Nothing, except that it's a violation of the Federal law, and I can have you indicted."

The boy was promptly released.

Darrow became known in Chicago as an unfailing source for a "touch." A fellow would come into his office and say:

"Enjoyed your speech very much last night, Mr Darrow."

"That's fine."

"Eh—Mr Darrow—I'm financially embarrassed. Could you—eh—lend me a couple of dollars?"

"Well, I guess the compliment you just paid me is worth it," Darrow would reply with a grin and hand the man a dollar bill.

The disconcerting part of his minor philanthropies was that he rarely had any money with him—because he could never remember to put any in his pockets. His associates complained that they often had to stand the cost of Darrow's charities because they had the cash to shell out. His office boy once ushered in an acquaintance who, after complimenting Darrow on his lecture of the Sunday before, made a touch. A search of Darrow's pockets revealing not a dime, he borrowed fifty cents from the office boy to give to the man. At the end of the week the boy said:

"Mr Darrow—eh—I'm a little broke. Do you think I could—eh—have that fifty cents back?"

"What fifty cents, Willum?"

"Why, the one you borrowed from me to give that man."

"Willum, you heard the fine compliment he paid me, didn't you?"

"Yes, I certainly did."

"And it gave you pleasure?"

"Yes, Mr Darrow, it made me very happy."

"Did it make you fifty cents' worth happy?"

"Why—eh—yes—I suppose so."

"Then if you got your money's worth, Willum, you shouldn't ask for it back."

The first week William Carlin came to work in the office he was sent to the bank with a couple of hundred dollars to deposit. Growing frightened at the thought that he might have lost the money, the boy stopped on the street, opened his buttoned coat and took out the bankbook, a sudden gust of wind blowing away the greenbacks. He could recover only two or three of the smaller denominations. When he had summoned sufficient courage to return to the office he confided in his aunt, who was Darrow's invaluable secretary, and one of the younger associates. All three went to beard the lion in his den.

"Well, Willum," said Darrow without looking up from his papers, "did you get to the bank all right?"

"Mr Darrow, that's a terrible question to ask me!"

Darrow looked around at the unhappy faces and drawled, "What's this committee doing in here?"

After the boy had told his story Darrow asked, "How much are you getting here?"

"Ten dollars a week—but you won't have to pay me any more; I'm quitting on Saturday."

"No, you're not," replied Darrow. "How do you expect me to get my money back? I'll let you have a couple of dollars a week."

Carlin relates, "Of course he never took anything. But every time I went to the bank he would say, 'Now, Willum, don't take that money out of your pocket. Remember the Chicago winds.' Even a few days before his death he was still kidding me about it."

"Darrow had no business sense," commented a lawyer-relative of the Loeb family who had assisted him during the Loeb-Leopold case. "He didn't want to be bothered with money. He trusted everyone. When the expenses of the psychiatrists had to be paid by our office Darrow asked me:

" 'How many checks do you think we will need?'

" 'Oh, fifty or sixty.'

" 'Then why not let me sign them all now?' "

An opposing attorney, having agreed to a settlement, came into the office with four thousand dollars in currency. He handed the roll to Darrow, who stuffed it into his pocket.

"Why, Mr Darrow," exclaimed the attorney, "aren't you going to count that money?"

"You counted it, didn't you?"

"Yes, of course, but I——"

"Then what's the sense in my counting it too?"

He sat behind a large flat-topped desk of black wood, placed at about the center of a large office, the wood trimmings of which were also black. Large prints of Altgeld, Tolstoy, Carlyle, hung on the walls in wide black frames, each carrying a quotation from the subject of the picture. "He never had a harsh word for anyone in the office. If someone made a mistake he would drawl, 'Hell, that's why they make erasers.' " If it were a nice day and he had nothing in particular for her to do, he would tell the secretary to take the afternoon off; "then one of his associates would come out looking for her and be sore as hell."

He was the despair of his office force and his associates, for he refused to keep files, notes or records. He had an encyclopedic memory: he kept the facts in his head, the indictment in his pocket, and that was his whole case. Since his employees were forbidden to clear his desk, which was littered with hundreds of papers, no one could locate anything on it, yet he could put his hand on the right document instantly. A few years later his two partners, Francis Wilson and Edgar Lee Masters, thinking to teach him the virtues of tidiness, spent an entire Saturday afternoon clearing his desk while Darrow was off somewhere lecturing. The exemplary efforts disrupted and almost dissolved their law business, for when Darrow returned on Monday the entire force had to search in wastebaskets, drawers, basements and furnaces to find his cases.

4

Darrow was always the first to reach the office, unlocking the door at eight-thirty on the dot every morning. Bulging in his coat pocket was an apple or a bunch of grapes which he ate at his desk at lunch time while browsing through a new book on anthropology or philosophy. Years later, when crossword puzzles appeared, he became an inveterate fan, working them during his lunch hour, in trains while traveling on cases, standing up in hotel lobbies while waiting for people, while walking the streets from one building to another. The policemen of Chicago would watch for him, take his arm and lead him through traffic while Darrow would ask them, without looking up from the newspaper, for a six-letter word, beginning with "ts," meaning a South African dipterous fly. Once H. G. Wells came into his hotel on the French Riviera to have dinner with him and saw his friend furtively shove something behind the overstuffed cushion of his chair in the lobby.

"What are you trying to hide from me?" demanded Wells.

"Oh—nothing much," muttered Darrow sheepishly, pulling out the paper. "When I got nothing else to do, I kinda like to work crossword puzzles."

"Don't be foolish," exclaimed Wells. "I work two of them every day of my life, one before breakfast and one before dinner."

When his day's work was finally done, around six or seven o'clock, his cronies would throng into his office to argue politics and religion. Nearly every night he went to a debate, a lecture or a meeting, though he still preserved one night a week for his poker game. "He enjoyed poker like a boy," reports a Chicago lawyer with whom he played. "He would laugh and chuckle all through the game. He preferred penny ante and would never go above a twenty-five-cent limit."

His greatest joy came from teaching. He would have preferred to be a teacher, but he knew there was no school or institution that would permit him to spread his heresies. There was no particular set of facts he wanted to convey: for him wisdom did not consist in facts, which altered with every change in the light, but rather in a sharpening of the tools of logic, in an attitude toward truth, in the constant, courageous search for truth. The tragedy of most human minds, he thought, was not so much that they were small as that they were closed. He disliked virginity in any form: if only minds could be opened, they could be impregnated, fertilized, and anything might grow, even—who knows?—tolerance.

"He got pleasure out of logic. He enjoyed it as much as a good meal. An interesting fact tickled his palate as much as a good steak."

He rewrote the adage, "The truth shall set you free," to read, "The pursuit of truth shall set you free—even if you never catch up with it!" It took a bold and vigorous mind to say, "I shall pursue truth even though I can never fully grasp it or settle it for all time; even though truth is such a chameleon that it changes color the moment one manages to pour a little salt on its tail." He was wary of those minds that believed truth could be absolute and unchanging, that accepted one set of doctrines to the exclusion of all others, forever and aye. That made people feel that anybody who didn't believe in their little package of truth was not only wrong but probably evil. A closed mind was a dead mind. Shut minds constipated progress.

"The scientific mind holds opinions tentatively and is always ready to re-examine, modify or discard as new evidence comes to light." It didn't matter so much if people made mistakes, so long as they were eternally searching, challenging, testing, accepting, rejecting, modifying, holding their minds open. For his own part, he wanted to keep his mind alert to every new theory and voice, to try to find if there was anything good or valuable in it; as an eclectic, he wanted to take what was valid from every new philosophy without being shackled to it in its entirety.

Because it took a tremendous force to open anything that had been long closed, he evolved the method of shock to open heavy and dense minds. Electricity was just beginning to show its endless magic; Darrow saw that objects of any weight or density could be opened if the job were wired and a direct contact made. As a congenital anti, nearly everything he believed and could say to an audience would be anathema, and anathema he found to be the supreme shock. If his audience were religious he would speak of the fruits of agnosticism; if the audience were reactionary he would extol the virtues of the planned socialist state; if the audience were socialistic he would plead the virtues of anarchism and the freedom of the individual in an uncontrolled society; if the audience were academic he would laud the imperatives of heresy and incessant mental revolution; if the audience were moralistic he would attack the principles of free will, prove that there was no such thing as sin, crime or individual responsibility; if the audience were sentimental or romantic he would argue the blessings of realism; if the audience were mechanistic he would plead the need for spiritual values.

Wherever he went he voiced the cause of the underdog—sometimes gratuitously. There are rumors that he was once run out of a Southern town by irate white farmers before whom he pleaded for the rights of Negroes. The farmers were in part justified; he had announced that he would speak on some other and innocuous subject. Invited by one of Chicago's multimillionaires to address a group before a dinner party, he went to the house straight from his office, in his wrinkled blue serge suit. He found the women gowned in lace and ermine, wearing many diamonds and pearls, the men in swallowtails and white vests. Standing before his audience in the luxurious drawing room, Darrow slumped on one foot, hunched his shoulders forward, raised one eyebrow quizzically and announced in his most guileless voice:

"Friends, the subject of my little talk tonight will be: 'Down with the Rich!' "

He got away with his system of "teaching by shock" because he did it in such a sweet and gentle fashion, though audiences hearing him for the first time were inclined to mutter, as they stumbled from the hall, "That chap is off his chump!"

5

Amirus Darrow had been a sound scholar; Clarence Darrow was a sound student. Amirus had taught his son that doubt is the beginning of wisdom, and Clarence had grown up with a robust skepticism: accept nothing merely because it exists and hence appears to be true; believe nothing merely because you would like to believe it. Yet he did not consider it sufficient to be a skeptic for the not inconsiderable pleasure of constituting the opposition. Skepticism had to serve its traditional function of puncturing platitudes, spearing shibboleths, illuminating lies, but once the plain had been swept clear one also had to know what materials went into the building of a more intelligent, beautiful and civilized world. For this task one had to think clearly, simply and disinterestedly; one had to find those incisive minds of the age who were contributing their share to a pragmatic utopia; above all, one had to be a fighter: life consisted of change; change met dogged opposition; hence life implied eternal warfare.

He was fortunate to reach his independence during a renaissance of thinking: beneath the static surface the scientist's laboratory had come into being, and from it were emerging methods of analyzing natural phenomena. In England Darwin and Huxley were demonstrating the *Origin of Species*, the evolution of man from a common ancestor with the apes, formulating *The Riddle of the Universe* with which husky minds might grapple. In Germany Nietzsche was glorifying amorality and the superman. Spencer was elucidating his *First Principles* of scientific doubt and the relation of the knowable to the unknowable. Henrik Ibsen in Norway and George Bernard Shaw were revealing in their plays the hypocrisy and cupidity which lie at the base of society. In every country men were documenting an economic interpretation of history. Sociology was testing its fledgling wings as a near science of diagnosing and treating social ills. Economics was being transformed from the dull study of account books to the art of co-operative living.

He took to the revolutionary movements like a monk to prayer. A natural student with a rigorous principle of selection, he doubted constantly, absorbed quickly, correlated easily, discarded the false, the erroneous, the deceptive, no matter how long or ardently his mind had embraced them. "He read a good deal, assimilated thoroughly, then digested the material—and when it came out, it came out pure Darrow."

"The only books he never seemed to care for were textbooks and legal books," said Francis Wilson, his closest friend and most beloved partner. "He had a lazy streak and wouldn't work on a case until the last minute, until he had to. Most of the legal preparation was done by others." However, once he had plunged into a case, "he was endowed with a remarkable memory. He was a quick observer and could retain without outside aids. He hardly ever took a note in a case, yet there was hardly a point that could be used that escaped him." When Darrow went to Tennessee to try the Scopes "monkey case" against William Jennings Bryan, "the scientists had to make out affidavits, telling what they would have testified if the court would have permitted them to. They were amazed to find that he could dictate their affidavits."

Another of his associates reports of him at this time: "The shortcomings of his reasoning lie in the fact that he read only those books which interested and charmed him: history, natural science, anatomy, physiology—these last two he knew as well as most doctors—zoology, but he never liked to read in political economy. Philosophy, yes, but not economics. He had never read Marx, Ricardo, Adam Smith." It was an omission Darrow was soon to amend.

For him study was never work, but the highest of all pleasures. He liked to acquire knowledge not only because it would be useful in his war against prejudice, intolerance and oppression, but because the achievement of any knowledge was sheer intellectual delight and the greatest of all human attainments. Even as an old man, when he no longer had any need for knowledge except the pleasure that thinking gave him, his deepest love was still for books.

"Two or three nights a week he would telephone downstairs to our flat," says Dr Leeming, "and say to my wife, 'Hello, Maggie, what are you doing? Come on up and we'll read.' He would spend about five minutes on the amenities, then pick up a new book, settle into his comfortable rattan chair by the fireplace and begin. When he had read something interesting he would peer over the top of the book and smile. If it were a controversial book he would read a chapter, then start a discussion which would last until midnight. Mostly he liked the short stories of Mark Twain, Bret Harte, Balzac, De Maupassant, which he could read aloud in an evening. He was so interested in the characters that every once in a while he would stop and comment about them. He also loved to read the poets: Housman, Whitman. He was one of the first Americans to discover lots of new writers, for he subscribed to the book catalogues from the London bookstores and publishers."

The one determination he made at this time was that he would remain unfettered. Nearly everybody in America belonged to something: a church, a political party, a fraternal order, an economic clique. He would belong to that rapidly diminishing brotherhood which owed allegiance to no man, creed or program. He feared set and rigid doctrine, no matter how valid it might look at the moment: its followers would too often oppose or close their eyes to change in the external world rather than be forced to make internal modifications. He knew that too often people accepted creeds, philosophies and panaceas because of their imperative need to believe in something, to belong to something, rather than because they had made a searching examination of its tenets and were intellectually convinced; that was why neither reasoning nor facts had much effect upon their emotional allegiances.

Since everyone around him was *for* something so passionately, he would remain free to be *against*. He would be Voltaire's "citizen of the world." It was not only that he saw the need in a swiftly changing society for the nonconformist, the detached critic, the astringent logician, but also that his nature and family heritage demanded this role of him.

"Darrow often debated and spoke for us socialists; he was a drawing card for the intellectuals. Yet we could never count him as one of us. He poked fun at us. He felt that no positive program could succeed in the face of an unpredictable future and lectured us on the need for a fluid program which would allow for modification."

He was in agreement with Kropotkin and the philosophical anarchists who claimed that the growth of government was a social evil because it curtailed the liberties of man and lent itself to manipulation by those interests which seized control; the seizing of the government by the railroads and the General Managers' Association during the A.R.U. strike was proof that the anarchists had a point. However, when he lectured to them or wrote articles for their press he always said: "I think you folks are right—but not altogether right. Your idea of free associations would have worked in a handicraft stage of society, like we had back in Kinsman when I was a boy, but you fail to take into account the growing machine age."

Before the freethinkers of America he committed the heresy of insisting that if they wished to remain freethinkers they had to make constant explorations into the realm of the spirit and that they had to build their freethinking on the hypothesis that they might be wrong. When the Atheists' Society invited him to lecture he dressed them down for being as arrogant and prejudiced as the church: religion insisted that there absolutely was a God, heaven and hell; the atheists insisted there absolutely was no God, no heaven and no hell, and neither could prove their point.

Since 1888 he had been attending the single-tax meetings and was considered one of its stanchest supporters, yet it had been his flailing of Henry George's speech that had won him his spurs—and the admiration of George and Mayor Cregier.

"One day Hamlin Garland lumbered in, threw himself into a roomy chair and from under his bushy eyebrows fixed his inquiring gaze on Clarence and asked, 'Well, Darrow, what's your latest slant?'

"Darrow crouched down into his coat collar, shrugged one shoulder higher than the other, peered across at Garland and said, 'That's what you always ask me.'

" 'Well, that's why I come here,' replied Garland, 'to get your latest slant on things. You know, you're one of the few who changes his mind with the times, and I'm always sure of hearing some new angle—how you've come to completely change your mind about one thing or other according to the turn of world affairs. You're the only man I know who hasn't the least pride—or shame—about admitting that he's been wrong; in fact, you kind of glory in pointing out that you've been fooled.'

" 'There's no such thing as standing still,' nodded Darrow. 'Unless a fellow moves ahead, he's left behind.' "

6

As this growth and change came to dominate his days, so, too, growth and change came into his personal relations—and finally into his home.

Darrow had been in Chicago only a year or two when he began to perceive that the choice of his youth was not the choice of his maturity. Jessie was a homebody. She did not like to go out nights,

in particular, she did not enjoy lectures, debates, forums on social
and political subjects, for she did not understand them very well.
When they first came to Chicago she had accompanied Clarence
to his meetings, but she found it difficult to follow the discussions,
and she could not grasp why people should become so excited over
matters that hardly seemed to concern them directly. Since she
read none of the new novels that were talked about at the literary
gatherings, she found herself uncomfortable and, eventually, unhappy. Clarence's associates tried to persuade her to participate, to
draw her into the discussions, but when they perceived that she
was uninterested, in reality bored with them and their abstract,
endless talk, they began to resent and then to ignore her. As soon
as Jessie saw that these people looked down on her because she
wasn't intellectual, even despised her a little, she flatly refused to
go to any more meetings.

She always had been willing to entertain her husband's friends
in her home, had prepared dinner for them, served coffee and cake
in the evenings, lemonade and cookies when it was warm. As time
went on she asked herself with increasing frequency why she
should go to all the work of entertaining people who thought her
stodgy and dull, who were not always able to conceal that they
did not consider her good enough for Clarence. When she no
longer wanted to entertain Darrow stopped asking people to his
home; since his wife did not care to accompany him to meetings,
he began to see very little of her. Home became a place where he
slept and on Sundays spent a few hours with his son. Jessie had
developed into a plain woman: plain-looking, plain-dressing, plain-
thinking. Yet in spite of her plainness, if she had had an exciting
intellect, if she had been interested and stirred by the movements
of the day, had accompanied her husband on his adventures into
the realms of the spirit and the *societas,* if she had had verve and
laughter and social passion, it is possible that they would still have
had enough in common to hold them together.

As it was, he respected Jessie and was grateful for her goodness,
but there was almost no point at which their minds could touch,
no common ground on which they could be companionable. He
was fun loving, but there was little buoyancy in Jessie, who was
inclined to be lethargic and slow-thinking. He was rarely interested
in eating: he mauled his food around on his plate, lit a cigarette,
smoked it halfway down, then crushed it out in the middle of a
beef stew or steak—the ultimate affront to a housewife. He cared
nothing about sleep: he did not wear himself out with exercise
during the day, and so he was rarely tired; when he came home

from a meeting at twelve or one o'clock there was always a new book or magazine to be read until three. He was oblivious to clothes, never knowing what he had on, and he was indifferent to his home surroundings.

At his clubs, lectures and debates he was meeting the kind of women he enjoyed: social workers studying the causes and cures of poverty; newspaperwomen fighting against heavy odds to create a new profession for their sex; women who were writing novels, composing music, training for the theater and the ballet; women vibrantly alive, in revolt against the restraints and taboos of the puritanical nineteenth century; women who were vividly aware of their times and the important movements within it; the new emancipated woman, no longer a hothouse plant; standing on her own feet, thinking her own thoughts and feeling her own feelings: this was the kind of woman he liked.

Not that was an esthete: he took women for the sheer physical delight of them, waking in the morning to chuckle over the delicious dialogue, the deep-throated laughter, the feel of a slender arm crooked about his neck. Women gravitated to him, attracted by his courage and independence and the feel that here was a man; drawn by the low musical voice that hit them in the stomach, by the kindly eyes that withal unmasked them and looked through them, by the magnetism of his personality that put people at their ease, untied the knots in their souls, made them glow. His physical appetites, like his mental appetites, did not mature until his thirties; once they had matured they remained in full flower.

There is an old saying that a couple no longer well mated will remain together just so long as neither of them meets someone who fires their imagination and brings their discontent into focus. X was one of Chicago's first newspaperwomen and one of the most beautiful in that city or any other. "She was the Irish type, with light brown hair, blue eyes and a magnificent figure." She was bright and well read, with an inexhaustible fund of high spirits and the inimitable Irish genius for repartee. She kept Clarence chuckling, kept his imagination jumping apace, kept his blood tingling as though a million ants were crawling inside his veins. She taught him how little he knew about the feminine mind and constantly delighted him by outsmarting him, by thinking swifter and deeper than his fumbling male mind could carry him. They became inseparable, had luncheon together every day, attended meetings together, criticized each other's work, spent their spare hours in each other's company. Their friends say they were as perfectly matched as a male and female animal can be: in brains, in courage, in physical attractiveness. Darrow loved her very much, and X loved him. He went to Jessie and asked for his freedom.

"I knew that Mr Darrow was a man of the world. He had to be away from home a lot, to travel about, and I said, 'Well, Clarence, if you want to be free I won't put a feather in your way.' Darrow replied, 'I don't know, I may be making a mistake, but I feel I must have my freedom.'

"Clarence was always good to me; he carried me around when I was ill and was always generous. I could never say anything against him in the world; he was good and he was kind. He wanted to be free, to have no ties. It nearly killed me to give him up, but he never knew that; I never let him know."

By this time Darrow, in his unrest, had sold the brick house he had built in 1892 at 4219 Vincennes Avenue and had moved in with his mother's sister's family, a Dr Fisher, who lived at 1321 Michigan Avenue. From here Jessie Darrow packed her possessions and with her son Paul left for Europe. When Darrow asked her to secure the divorce, she answered that it would do him less harm in his profession if he divorced her, an act that was little short of noble. At the final meeting for the property settlement Darrow wept; once, about a year after the divorce, he went to her in an emotional mood, saying he had made a terrible mistake.

He did things to hurt himself many times; on a few regrettable occasions he did things to injure society and the causes for which he was laboring, but his separation and divorce are the only instances in which Darrow, so excruciatingly sensitive to the pain suffered by humans in their harrowed flight across the earth and the years, knowingly inflicted unhappiness on another person.

He moved into the Chicago Athletic Club and divorced Jessie. "This was done without contest or disagreement and without bitterness on either side, and our son has always been attached to both of us, and she and I have always had full confidence and respect toward each other." He gave her a home and a liberal allowance, which he maintained all his life. He always spoke affectionately of Jessie, though in his autobiography he fails to give her credit for her many years of service and in particular was unwilling to reveal that when "I took a little office in the village of Andover, borrowed some money to buy some books and flung my shingle to the breeze," the money had been provided by his bride, Jessie.

After a number of years Jessie married a Judge Brownlee of Ashtabula, before whom Darrow had tried a number of cases. As late as 1940 both Jessie, then eighty-three, and her sister Belicent, then eighty-one, spoke with kindness and love of all the Darrows.

Clarence Darrow had begun courting Jessie Ohl when he was eighteen and had married her when he was twenty-one. There is reason to believe that he was virginal at the time. He loved Jessie for about twelve years; he was faithful to her, and they were happy together. If he had remained a small-town lawyer, if Jessie had not been transplanted from Ashtabula, where she had been thriving, to cosmopolitan Chicago, they might never have separated. Jessie had every virtue as a housewife and a mother: she was hard working, conscientious, frugal, loyal and self-sacrificing. Unfortunately she had inherited none of her mother's intellectual vigor, as had her bright-eyed, fast-thinking younger sister Belicent; she cared nothing for books, ideas, theories or the changing world. That was her husband's job; hers was to keep her house attractive and her family well.

Their slow drifting apart was certainly not Jessie's fault. She had made Clarence no promises, when they had married eighteen years before, that she would keep pace with him mentally; for that matter she could have had no way of knowing that he would develop into a heavyweight. For his part, though there is little that can be said in justification of a man who discards a faithful woman after eighteen years of love and service, Darrow was unfortunate in that Jessie, coming from a brilliant, intellectual heritage, fulfilled none of the promises of the Ohl tradition. He had had no way of knowing that Jessie Ohl, with the gay, sweet sheen of youth on her face, would stop developing the moment she became a wife and mother, any more than Jessie could have foretold that the perfectly normal stripling, whose sole outstanding virtue was "a gift of the gab," would pull ahead of his field like a champion. If they could have known they might both have married somebody else. Such are the dangers of marriage; such, the casualties.

CHAPTER IV

Who's a Criminal?

At forty Darrow was smooth-faced and hard-stomached. He wore a jaunty black derby on the street; in cool weather his meandering black satin tie was kept within the confines of his vest; his clothing had not yet reached that stage of acute dishabille which occasioned his reply to reporters at the Loeb-Leopold trial, who were twitting him about his appearance:

"I can't understand why you chaps look so different from me. I have my suits made at the same tailors you do. I pay as much for them. I go to the same stylish shops to buy my haberdashery. The only thing I can figure is maybe you dudes take off your clothes when you go to sleep at night."

He had spent two summer vacations in Europe, stimulated to venture on his first trip because his friend Judge Barnum was taking his family and invited him to come along. The Barnums had been admirers of Darrow since 1894 when they had heard him cry at a giant Populist meeting, "There never was any discontent among the people except for good and sufficient reason. Under the benign administration of the Republican party the aggregate wealth of this republic increased in the hands of the few at the expense of the many. True patriotism hates injustice in its own land more than anywhere else!" For the first two days he lay flat in his bunk, moaning, "Tell them to stop the boat; I want to get off." Recovering from his seasickness he became friends with Gertrude, the judge's comely young daughter who was soon to "flee a vapid society life" to become one of the pioneer organizers of women workers. In Europe they spent many companionable hours together tramping in the

Alps. He was far more enchanted by the majesties of nature, the mountains, lakes and mellow countryside than by the cities or works of art made by man. After slogging for several days between rows of ecclesiastical Madonnas in the Italian art galleries he exclaimed, "I can't look at any more improbable mothers of impossible children." He sent back a number of mildly interesting travel articles to the Chicago newspapers, though how they managed to decipher his letters remains a mystery, since his handwriting was illegible and his spelling monstrous.

As a country boy who "had a great deal of the frontier attitude, personality and type of mind, who would have been at home in primitive America with his great-great-great-grandfather who settled in New London in 1680," he had even less patience with the man-made elegancies of the Continent. One noon while he and Gertrude were having luncheon high up in a Swiss chalet, the garçons brought in an endless succession of rich and beautiful platters containing tiny, tantalizing appetizers. Hungry, wanting to get on with his outing, Darrow muttered under his breath, "Why not take us out to the pantry and show us all your china closets of dishware? Then we could come back in here and have some food."

Though Collins, Goodrich, Darrow and Vincent had a substantial practice, "it became evident in the early stages of the partnership, because of Darrow's bent on labor, public and political questions, that the life of the firm would not endure—when you took into consideration the purposes for which it was organized." In 1897 it "fell of its own weight—too many great lawyers, perhaps," and Darrow organized the first firm of which he was to be the senior partner and hence the boss. As juniors he took in William O. Thompson, who had been associated with the former firm, and Morris St P. Thomas, who had been his assistant in the office of the corporation counsel. They first occupied offices in the Chicago Title and Trust Building at 100 Washington Street, later moving to the Ashland Block, on the corner of Clark and Randolph streets, where Darrow was to remain for many years. The three men worked well together and enjoyed each other.

"We did a very considerable business from the outset," writes Thomas, "but the office was not a large one, as things go now. The big law offices now are much like department stores. Our office force was small—a bookkeeper, a couple of students and a stenographer or two. Much of our business was strictly of a civil nature; the division of fees was on a percentage basis; Darrow had a half, I a third and Thompson the balance. Darrow was always eager to take chances, and many of our cases were on a contingent basis—

notably personal-injury cases where he was quite successful in obtaining good verdicts. He was a good business getter, and I well remember his telling Thompson and myself not to trouble ourselves about getting business—he said he would attend to that—and he did. Having obtained a good verdict and judgment, he left it largely to us juniors to sustain them in the courts of appeal.

"The principal channel which brought business to Darrow was labor organizations, for he was their principal representative in legal disputes. At the time there was considerable controversy between business and organized labor, and in these controversies Darrow nearly always represented the labor side. Business concerns would seek to enjoin some union from striking or picketing, and these lawsuits were usually bitter and protracted. Members of the several unions were very apt also to resort to him in connection with their individual and personal troubles.

"Another channel of business grew out of our former connection with the corporation counsel's office and the firm's supposed familiarity with municipal questions. When the city sought to condemn property for public purposes, Darrow often appeared for the property owners to secure adequate compensation. When the city adopted an ordinance for the purpose of licensing certain occupations and imposing license fees, the members of the affected interests would often band together and engage us to oppose the enforcement of the ordinances.

"Darrow loved to defend people charged with crime. I do not think he could have ever become a successful prosecutor, for he was definitely for the underdog. Nor do I think he was so constituted as to have become a successful judge; he was more prone to mercy than stern justice. As an advocate and a trial technician he was incomparable. He was often called in by other lawyers, particularly in jury cases where a forceful presentation of intricate facts was demanded."

He had found his niche in life. It is characteristic of Darrow that his was the only niche of its kind, that he had to evolve it for himself. He was against all people who were against people, the broadest beam of his philosophy being that we should be *for* people, not *against* them; that it was sufficiently difficult for the mass of struggling humanity to make its way against the adversities of nature and the implacability of fate without the additional burden of fratricidal hatreds; that intolerance was a greater evil than any evil it set out to destroy.

In this country people were too often judged by whom they were against, not whom they were for. He would have liked to write across the sky, in black ink for the daytime and white ink for the night, "Difference of opinion doesn't make the other fellow wrong." It was too easy to be tolerant of the things one liked and understood; real tolerance applied to those modes of living or thinking that one hated, feared and could not understand. If this put him in the anomalous position of having critics say to him, "You're intolerant of intolerance," he was not enervated by the seeming contradiction.

Though this kind of tolerance might appear visionary, he believed it to be the only kind that could keep a democracy functioning; otherwise the conflicting groups would be forever at one another's throats, attempting to destroy each other, and in the wake of their conflicts would come the destruction of their community. For him America was an experiment in co-operative living of groups of folks who didn't agree with each other on all issues but who were willing to accept these differences with good will.

Inducing people to live at peace with those whose convictions they found repugnant was a thankless and endless task. He was called an atheist when fighting the religionists for wanting the free-thinkers gagged; a medievalist when he opposed the free-thinkers who wanted the churches leveled. When the puritans wanted the pagans suppressed he fought for the pagans; when the pagans wanted the puritans laughed at he fought for the puritans. Beyond such ideological differences lay the more crucial issues: racial tolerance, economic tolerance, sociological tolerance. When the whites were against the Negroes, chaining them to their mops and brooms, their poverty and their ignorance, he fought the whites; when shortsighted employers were against their workers, chaining them to their machines and their starvation wages, he fought those employers; when society was against the sick, the mentally incompetent or unbalanced, the errant, the miscreant or the unfit, he fought society. Racial hatred was the most incendiary form of intolerance; all his life he fought for the rights of the Negro. Low wages and long hours were sheer greed and avarice on the part of the employers and hence the most corrosive form of intolerance; always he fought for those who sweated for their bread. Revenge in the form of criminal trials and penitentiaries was the most brutalizing form of intolerance; always he fought for a humane and scientific form of criminology. Callousness and injustice were the most destructive forms of intolerance; always he strove to secure for the poor and underprivileged the same opportunities for health, education and legal justice as were available to the wealthy. That is what he meant by tolerance.

2

His living he made from his civil cases. Like all hard-working heroes, he would occasionally get fed up with his virtue and exclaim petulantly, "Who's going to feed me, the birds? I'm no Saint Francis!" Yet more and more his interests and sympathies were drawn to the criminal courts, for there, every hour, dramas were being played that had social implications. Crime, as his earliest master, John P. Altgeld, had taught him, was not a cause, but a result; the prisons were the open sores of a diseased social body. Because of his heretical background, because of his almost pathological sensitivity to the suffering of others, the uppermost characteristic of his nature was its organic need to defend: to stand with the quarry against the pack, to fight for the individual against the mob.

"I entered my first criminal case in the attitude of the 'good' lawyer—the lawyer who attends all the Bar Association meetings and so gravitates as rapidly as he can to the defense of Big Business. The tragedies, the sorrow and despair that were present in the criminal court I knew nothing of and did not want to know. A verdict of 'not guilty' or a disagreement had been viewed by me as by the general public as a miscarriage of justice and a reflection on the jury system. The jail was a place spoken of as we sometimes mention a leper colony.

"I grew to like to defend men and women charged with crime. I sought to learn why one man goes one way and another takes an entirely different road. I became vitally interested in the causes of human conduct. This meant more than the quibbling with lawyers and juries, to get or keep money for a client so that I could take part of what I won or saved for him: I was dealing with life, with its hopes and fears, its aspirations and despairs. With me it was going to the foundation of motive and conduct and adjustment for human beings, instead of blindly talking of hatred and vengeance."

Each client became not a legal case but a highly complex mechanism, the result of thousands of years of evolution, molded into its specific form by the environment in which it was immediately conditioned and over which it exercised no power. Since he could not be defending these afflicted ones for the money they did not have, they knew he came to them in compassion: and so they poured out their stories, their griefs, their incoherencies, in their often stumbling fashion telling him more than they realized they were telling about the weaknesses of the human machine that sometimes breaks down on the assembly line. It was from this early conception of man as a machine, which he evolved as an antidote to the conception of man as a spark of the godhead, that he developed into one of the leading proponents of the mechanistic philosophy in America. It was at base a philosophy of love and understanding, but to people who did not grasp its implications—that you cannot blame or punish a human machine that has cracked, any more than you can blame or punish a steel machine that has broken down; that instead you repair it without moral judgment or abuse so that it may carry on with its work—this view of humanity seemed fraught with pessimism and despair.

"When I was a cub lawyer in Chicago, in 1925, I got the idea of trying to write a life of Darrow," says David Lilienthal. "I knew him fairly well, and he co-operated with me very generously. But I found his philosophy of mechanism so at odds with my own ebullience that I finally gave it up, as it was too depressing."

His interest in why individuals came to be what they are drove him inevitably into a study of the forces that make and control contemporary society. First, however, he went back into anthropology and *The Golden Bough*, which shed light on the countless centuries when man was little more than an animal living in the forests, fighting and killing for his food. Once you knew what man came from, once you grasped the thousands of years of painful and not altogether successful struggle to emerge from bestiality into a controlled social order, it was easier to understand why men did the seemingly inexplicable.

"Scientists have so thoroughly established the theory of evolution, there is no longer any room for such a doctrine as freedom of the will. Nothing in the universe is outside the law, whether mineral, animal or vegetable. Free will means that man would live day by day, governed by his transient will, instead of being moved and virtually controlled by every experience of his life. The laws that control human behavior are as fixed and certain as those that control the physical world."

Religion, which was acclaimed to be the approach of love, tolerance and forgiveness, said that man sprang from God, was created whole and responsible; anything he did which was adjudged to be bad was entirely his own fault and his own choosing, arising from the deliberate and conscious evil which he elected of his own free will to exercise. Consequently no one was responsible for him: not society, not the Church, not even God. Since he diabolically chooses to be evil, it is no more than just retribution that he be disgraced, cast out, punished, his life broken forever. Darrow's philosophy of mechanism, which was accused of being a cruel, inhuman and godless approach, insisted that there must be a cause for every antisocial act, and once that cause was found and either removed or eliminated, the *victim of the cause* could be made well and whole again, just as people with diphtheria or typhoid are made whole and well again once the cause of the disease is determined and then wiped out. In his fight for tolerance Darrow went even one step further, and it was his next step which brought down upon him the wrath of organized society: that it is cruel and wasteful to punish further people who are already ill and that no more blame or moral obloquy should be visited upon the victim of a mental or nervous illness than upon a man with a physical illness. Both should be put in hospitals; both should be given the finest treatment that modern science can afford; both should be returned to their families and their jobs.

"Sufficient statistics have been gathered," he wrote, "to warrant the belief that every case of crime could be accounted for on purely scientific grounds if all the facts bearing on the case were known: defective nervous systems, lack of education or technical training, poor heredity, poor early environment, emotional unbalance. The demented, the imbecile and the clearly subnormal constitute more than half of the inmates of prisons, and the great majority of crimes are committed by persons between the ages of seventeen and twenty-five, clearly the most difficult period of mental and emotional adjustment. We no longer put the insane into cages, to amuse the public and be tortured by them; science should be able to do for the mental aberrations of man what it has already done for the physical diseases."

His experience in the criminal courts soon taught Darrow that most illegal acts break, not too neatly, into two categories: crimes against property and crimes against persons. The majority of crimes were crimes against property; an overwhelming number of these were committed by the poor; these crimes increased in direct proportion to unemployment and the rise in the cost of living. On the opposite side of the shield he watched certain businessmen committing countless frauds, manipulations and polite embezzlements and for their efforts taking places of honor in their communities.

"What about those social crimes that are not punishable by law," he demanded; "exaggerated and lying advertisements that bleed millions of their wages for products that are useless; manipulation of stocks that rob the uninitiate of their savings; forestalling markets, controlling prices of consumption goods by monopoly control, misrepresentation of all sorts?"

For the crime of stealing food or money when a man or his family was hungry Darrow thought somebody ought to be convicted, but not the hungry man: rather the legislators, the jurists, the bankers, the industrialists, the clergymen, the educators, all those who permitted their economic system periodically to starve out a portion of its people when there were quantities of food available for consumption. Since he believed that drastic punishments not only destroyed the individual but brutalized society, he spent his days in the criminal courts, trying to explain to juries why these men and women had done what they had done, pleading for tolerance, sympathy, another chance. The tragedy of punishment, when he failed to get his client freed, lay not only in what happened to the person in prison, but in what happened to his family on the outside: the mother forced out of her home, the children taken from school to earn a few pennies, the family life broken up, its innocent victims disgraced, made bitter, antisocial. The state thought its job was done when it sent the miscreants to prison. Darrow, who visited their homes and saw what havoc the convictions wrought, knew better: if the state saw fit to incarcerate the breadwinner to protect itself, then it was also the duty of the state to support the man's family, clothe and feed the children, keep them in school. For no unorthodox theory was more derisive laughter brought down upon him than for this last.

3

In his efforts to keep people out of prison he sometimes went to unconscionable lengths. "An insurance adjuster in Chicago was indicted on a charge of arson and released on bond. During the pendency of the indictment he concluded that his only chance to escape the rap was to prevail upon his stenographer, who was a very fine young woman and had been in his employ many years, to provide an alibi. Mildred Sperry refused to perjure herself, 'but after the pleading of Clark's wife and daughter she gave in and went before the court to testify that Clark was in Chicago on the day of the alleged crime.' Clark was convicted, Miss Sperry indicted for perjury."

Mildred Sperry appealed to Darrow. Moved by her story, he paid the expenses to Springfield, where he took the young woman to see Governor Frank Lowden. Mildred Sperry told her story, and as Governor Lowden listened, "tears rolled down his cheeks."

"You poor girl, I can understand why you did that to save your employer."

"Governor, I had hoped that when you heard her full story you would pardon Miss Sperry."

Governor Lowden hesitated for a few moments.

"How long is her sentence, Clarence?"

"Oh, she hasn't been sentenced yet. The trial doesn't start until next week."

Governor Lowden smiled, then murmured, "Well, Clarence, I can't pardon Miss Sperry until she's been convicted. However, the Parole Board is meeting upstairs. Let's go up and tell them the story. Maybe they can do something for Miss Sperry."

Upstairs went Darrow and the governor, to relate the tale to the attentive Parole Board.

"Then you are making a formal application for parole, Clarence?" asked the chairman.

"Yes."

"How long has Miss Sperry to serve?"

Clarence shifted his weight from one foot to the other.

"Oh, she isn't serving. The trial doesn't start until next week."

There was an embarrassed silence in the board room.

"Well, Clarence, we can't parole the girl if she hasn't yet been convicted. Come back and see us when she goes up."

"That's right," agreed Governor Lowden when they were again in the corridor: "you go back and try the case, and don't let Miss Sperry get into jail until you reach me by telephone."

He couldn't plead Mildred Sperry guilty, because the judge would have to sentence her. He pleaded the girl not guilty, then led her carefully through the story of why she had done it. "The jury was out about thirty minutes and returned a verdict of 'not guilty.' In spite of the admonition of the court to preserve order, a pandemonium of approval reigned." Darrow telephoned Springfield and said, "Thanks, but we won't need your help. She's been acquitted." When he returned to Chicago he told his partner, "I must have made a good speech, because the jury was in tears and even the judge turned his face to the wall so he could hide."

His attitude that no individual was singly responsible for his acts, and hence could not be condemned, often jockeyed him into a difficult situation. In 1933 when participating in a symposium on religion in Jackson, Michigan, an official of the state prison came up to him and invited him to tour that institution.

"Whereupon Mr Darrow delivered himself of a lecture on 'Free Will and Penology,' concluding with these sentences, 'I don't believe in your prisons. Let 'em all out, I say!' Later a small group gathered at a local home to keep Mr Darrow company while he waited for his train. The discussion was continued. In the course of the conversation Mr Darrow expressed the highest regard for Franklin D. Roose velt. When we arrived at the railroad station the newsboys were shouting about the attempt to assassinate Roosevelt.

" 'Mr Darrow,' I said, holding a copy of the paper behind my back, 'do you think it would be good or bad for the country if anything were to happen to Mr Roosevelt?'

" 'It would be a calamity,' he answered, 'a national calamity.'

" 'If someone tried to kill Mr Roosevelt, would you defend him on the same basis as you defended the inmates of the state prison in your remarks this evening?'

" 'Certainly, why not?'

"Then I showed him the headlines.

" 'Poor fellow,' said Darrow in his most sympathetic tones, 'he couldn't help it. He had to do it.'

"He went on to defend the would-be assassin with an appeal that was interrupted only by the arrival of his train."

As a passionate opponent of violence in any form, the brunt of his social indignation was directed against the barbarities of capital punishment. "A killing by the state is more cruel, malicious and premeditated than a killing by an individual. The purpose of state executions is solely to satisfy the vengeance of the populace."

Darrow had unwittingly stumbled into America's theater of violence and bloodletting par excellence. He deemed it more than a geographic accident that the stockyards flourished in Chicago. It seemed inherent in the character of the city that a frenzied cry was raised for the blood of the accused in the Haymarket Riot in 1886 and again for the blood of the Loeb and Leopold boys in 1924; that in 1877 the city police could beat striking railroad workers over the head while assembled in a meeting hall, and that again in 1937 the figuratively identical police could beat the heads of the identical striking workers with the identical clubs for the identical crime of assembly, outside the Republic steel plant.

4

Darrow had arrived in Chicago in 1887 while the sound of four human necks being broken by the noose was still fresh in the ears of the people who had clamored for their deaths. "Hang them first and try them afterward," Chicago had cried out in its psychotic sweat against the anarchists who, so the papers screamed at them, were ready to dynamite Chicago into the middle of Lake Michigan.

Eight men had been tried for the conspiracy to throw a bomb in Haymarket Square on the night of May 4, 1886, which had killed seven police officers. The state had not accused any one of these men

of throwing the bomb; the state had never named anyone as the
thrower of the bomb; the Illinois law said that an accessory could
only be tried after the guilt of the principal had been proved; yet
the eight men had been convicted of "a conspiracy with an unknown" to throw the fatal bomb. Three had been sentenced to fifteen years in the penitentiary; one had blown off his head in prison;
four had been hanged. The people of Chicago not only had wanted
these men executed; they had forced their execution by the weight
of their pressure. Because of this willingness and the legal adage that
"who does through another does himself," Darrow believed that
every last citizen who had demanded the execution of these four
men had been, individually, their executioners.

He had gone frequently to the penitentiary to visit with Fielden,
Neebe and Schwab, the three men who had escaped the hangman's
noose, and had come to love them as good and innocent men,
guilty only of the crime of striving to free mankind from its
economic shackles. The flaming article in which he demonstrated
that the eight men had been railroaded in a corrupt and illegal trial
had been his first brilliant paper on social justice. "Clarence was
invited by H. H. Waldo, a bookseller, to come to Rockford and
read this paper before a select audience of twenty-five people,
among whom was the editor of the *Morning Star*. At the conclusion
of the reading there was a moment of silence, broken by Mr Browne,
the editor, who declared:

" 'Don't you think it was necessary, in order that society be protected, that these men be hanged as an example, even if they were
innocent?'

" 'Why, Mr Browne,' retorted Darrow, 'that would be anarchy.' "

With the passage of the months and the growing realization that
the eight men had been convicted, not of having conspired to have
a bomb thrown, but of having been opposed to the type of capitalism practiced by such industrialists as Pullman and McCormick;
with the ever-spreading knowledge that the sole conspiracy had
been committed by the state—the manufacture of evidence by the
maniacal police captain, Schaack; the arrest of innocent men who
were offered their release to turn state's evidence; the hand-picking
of a jury panel which would be sure to convict, and the refusal to
excuse jurors who swore they could not give the accused a fair
trial; the lynch decisions handed down by Judge Gary—it became
clear that the citizens of Chicago who had cried out for the death of
these men were not merely executioners by proxy, but actually murderers of innocent men in a legal crime far greater in its implications than the heinous crime committed by the irresponsible lunatic

who threw the bomb. The Haymarket bomb had destroyed seven lives; in Darrow's opinion the trial of the anarchists had bombed the Constitution, the Bill of Rights, the structure of legal justice for all men upon which the people of the New World were trying to nurture a free and intelligent social organism.

The philosophy of the four men who had been hanged and the three who went to prison was for the larger part German socialism, mixed with lesser degrees of trade unionism and anarchism; yet they were universally called anarchists by the press, as all his life Darrow was to be called an anarchist, because that was deemed to be the most effective whip with which to beat the dog. Albert Parsons edited the *Alarm,* August Spies the *Arbeiter-Zeitung;* Adolph Fischer was a printer on the *Arbeiter-Zeitung,* in which company Oscar Neebe owned two dollars' worth of stock. George Engel believed that the social revolution would one day grow out of the people; Samuel Fielden and Michael Schwab were socialists who lectured at labor meetings. All seven were family men, hard working, honest. All agreed that private property was the source from which flowed the evils of capitalism: wage slavery, poverty, misery, crime, injustice, war. Since force was used against the workingman whenever he attempted to better himself, force alone could free him. The *Alarm* and *Arbeiter-Zeitung* ran frequent articles on the virtues and values of dynamite.

The year 1886 was to have been the great year of liberation for American labor, which had had to work from sixty to eighty hours a week to earn its living. On May first unions all over the country were going out on strike for the eight-hour day. The movement was strongest in Chicago, where "railroad and gas-company employees, iron-mill workers, meat packers and plumbers were out on strike for shorter hours, eighty thousand participants in all." Police and state militia guarded the streets, but May first passed in perfect quiet. Some employers locked out their employees; others agreed to arbitrate and cut working hours.

On May third the locked-out employees of the McCormick plant, who had been on strike since March, clashed with the men who had replaced them as they came out of the plant, the police killing one striker, shooting five or six others, beating many with clubs. August Spies, who witnessed the battle, rushed back to the *Arbeiter-Zeitung* to write up the conflict and to call for a protest meeting the following night in the Haymarket Square.

The following night proved to be cold and dreary. Instead of the twenty thousand workers expected, only twelve hundred showed up, Parsons, Spies and Fielden addressing them from the seat of a

wagon that had been lᵉft at one end of the huge square. Mayor
Carter Harrison was there to make sure no incendiary talk was indulged in; he heard passionate speeches against the injustices of the
system, the insecurity of the workingman, the evils of the Pinkertons and the deputies being used to slug workers, the misrepresentation of labor by the capitalist press; but the mayor found the
speeches peaceable. At a little after ten, while Fielden was winding
up the meeting, it began to drizzle, and within a few minutes only
a quarter of the people were left. Mayor Harrison went home. Just
as Fielden said, "In conclusion . . ." a hundred and eighty police
dashed into the square, led by the sanguinary Captain Bonfield, who
had been forbidden by the mayor to bring police to the meeting.
Fielden, ordered to break up the already ended meeting, replied,
"We are peaceable," and began to descend from the wagon, when
suddenly a bomb was thrown from one of the buildings above the
square, exploding near the front rank of the police.

That bomb killed not only seven officers, but the socialist and eight-
hour movements as well—even as the burning of railroad property
killed the American Railway Union and industrial unionism under
Debs. Chicago insisted that somebody be prosecuted, and led by
the Chicago *Tribune*, which was owned by the same McCormicks
who owned the harvester plant in front of which the strikers and
scabs had battled the day before, the Haymarket Riot was used to
discredit labor in general and to railroad its outstanding leaders
through "trial by prejudice." When in 1893, by working with thousands of prominent Americans, Darrow helped persuade Governor
Altgeld to pardon the only three survivors, he was able to say
publicly, "The Bar in general throughout the state, and elsewhere,
came to believe that the conviction was brought about through
malice and hatred and that the trial was unfair and the judgment of
the court unsound."

5

The people of Chicago, he knew, did not like the feeling of
being murderers; that was why they now turned upon Governor
Altgeld with fury and venom for pardoning, as innocent of the
crime charged, Fielden, Schwab and Neebe, who had already been
in the penitentiary for seven years. Since that act of justice was now
in process of destroying Atlgeld both as a political leader and a man,
it was the case of the Haymarket Riot that started Darrow on his
lifelong crusade against the conspiracy laws and capital punishment.
There had been no way for Governor Altgeld to reprieve the four
men who had been hanged by the neck, nor the one who had com-

mitted suicide, and there was no way to reprieve the bloodthirsty Chicagoans who had demanded their death. Altgeld had turned them into official murderers? Then destroy Altgeld; make him the foulest human that ever lived, the encourager of lawlessness, the destroyer of civilization.

Because of his love for Altgeld and his distress at the abuse heaped upon his friend, Darrow consented to run for Congress in the 1896 campaign on the same ticket with Altgeld, who was seeking re-election and a vindication of his political and economic liberalism. He had little liking for professional politics, in which he had had a laboratory course while city counsel; he preferred to remain outside the arena so he could choose his own battlefields. But he was over-joyed to see Governor Altgeld rise once again in his full vitality and intelligence, after the eclipse and illness he had suffered for the 1893 Haymarket pardons. The Pullman strike had become one of the issues of the campaign: Altgeld was out to wrest control of the Democratic party from Grover Cleveland, who had defeated the working people by sending Federal troops into Chicago in 1894; Darrow was out to indict "government by injunction." One plank of the Democratic platform read:

"We especially object to government by injunction as a new and highly dangerous form of oppression by which Federal judges, in contempt of the laws of the states and the rights of the citizens, be-come at once legislators, judges and executioners."

However, the major issues were Free Silver and Free Golden Ora-tory. The country was in the grip of one of its recurrent depres-sions. The farmers of the Midwest, in hock to the money interests of the East, believed with the intensity of a religious fervor that if silver were once again made legal tender the value of gold would be brought down, more money would be put into circulation, pros-perity would come back, they would be able to pay their debts. Both Darrow and Altgeld embraced Free Silver, Altgeld because he wanted to use it to defeat gold-standard Cleveland, Darrow be-cause he thought it would be a good vote catcher for a program which was the most progressive ever offered to the American public. But they were neither of them so delighted when they found they had to embrace, along with Free Silver, the gaseous form of William Jennings Bryan, boy orator of the Platte.

Bryan, who was a member of a contested delegation to the Demo-cratic convention, was invited to Chicago by Altgeld, expenses paid, because Altgeld wanted to stop him from splitting the Free Silver candidates and from making a nuisance of himself by begging and conniving for votes. Yet four days after his arrival, when the

Illinois delegation convened at the Sherman House, to Altgeld's disgust there was Bryan, "buttonholing all the delegates."

"Tell Bryan to go home," Altgeld finally snapped; "he stands no more chance of being nominated for President than I, and I was born in Germany." Bryan had no legitimate role to play at the convention, yet once he got his feet onto the platform as chairman of a debate on Free Silver, "among the bearded veterans of the party, glowing with youth, his raven locks gleaming, his face and manner electric," almost the first words of his rehearsed Chautauqua sermon cast the mesmeric spell he had hoped for:

"The humblest citizen in all the land, when clad in the armor of a righteous cause, is stronger than all the hosts of error. I come to speak to you in defense of a cause as holy as the cause of liberty —the cause of humanity." When he finished with: "Having behind us the producing masses of this nation and the toilers everywhere, we will answer demands for a gold standard by saying to them: 'You shall not press down upon the brow of labor this crown of thorns; you shall not crucify mankind upon a cross of gold!'" men went mad with emotional joy, threw their hats in the air, shouted and wept. . . . The election was lost and the Democratic party, which had had an excellent chance of electing the popular "Silver Dick" Bland, went into eclipse and bondage for almost sixteen years; the cause of liberalism and the working people was shackled to an opportunistic demagogue who embarrassed his fellow liberals by being for the right causes for the wrong reasons.

Darrow and Altgeld sat in the Illinois delegation, looking at each other questioningly. The next day, when sonorous-sounding Bryan had swept the convention hall like a typhoon, Altgeld asked Darrow, "I have been thinking over Bryan's speech. What did he say, anyway?"

Darrow didn't get a chance to answer that question fully until 1925, during the "Scopes monkey trial" in Tennessee, when these two bull moose, each representing the faith and convictions of tens of millions of followers, locked horns in one of the most spectacular and fantastic battles over religion ever waged.

Darrow stumped the state, campaigning for Altgeld, Bryan and the Democratic party. He spoke everywhere—except in the district from which he was running for Congress, because that district was alleged to be uncorruptibly Democrat. When the votes were at last counted Bryan had been defeated for President, Altgeld for governor and Darrow for congressman. There were rumors that large sums of money were spent in Darrow's district by the Republicans, that "Democratic leaders had been reached and the organization disrupted." In any event Darrow was kept out of Congress by a margin of a hundred votes.

"I really felt relief when I learned of my defeat. I did not want to be in political life. I realized what sacrifices of independence went with office seeking. Perhaps I would have spent the rest of my life in the pursuit of political place and power and would have surrendered my convictions for a political career." On the other hand, if he had been elected, he might have moved up to the Senate and become, like Robert LaFollette, Senior, an intelligent conscience of the nation.

6

After the campaign Darrow returned to his practice, which had begun to include a large colored clientele. In Chicago at the time it was almost impossible for a Negro, even if he had a little money, to get a white lawyer to defend him. When it came to people, Darrow was color blind: he didn't feel sorry for the Negroes; he didn't pity them; he didn't think of them as a racial problem. He liked them as human beings, probably because they had the same childlike quality with which he had been endowed. When he had lived on Vincennes Avenue a colored tailor named Wheeler, a very bright and able fellow, would call for him regularly on Sunday mornings. Darrow would strap his lunch to the handle bars of his bike, and together they would ride into the country for a day in the woods, to enjoy the foliage and the changing contours of the hills. Every New Year's Eve he went to services in a colored church.

The colored people sitting shoulder to shoulder with the whites on Darrow's undiscriminating benches were nearly always clinic cases. "The wife of a young Negro came to him and told him that her husband had been arrested and charged with murder. She brought humble Negroes to testify to the fact that he was innocent. The family had no money. The woman was pregnant with her third child. She sat in his office, mute, and with her eyes pleaded that he defend her husband. He undertook the case—but it took a long while; witnesses had to be found, detectives employed. Darrow defrayed the expenses of the investigation. The date for the trial was postponed time and again, and the young wife was threatened with eviction. Darrow paid her rent and supported the family—until he got an acquittal for the husband."

For Negroes in trouble he had a special sympathy: they were the underdogs under the underdogs, caught in the complexities of the white man's law and a machine age for which their background had not prepared them.

When the "almost naked and badly mutilated body" of a white Chicago nurse was found in a lonely spot in the country and it was ascertained that she had last been seen walking along the country road with a tall Negro, the police went through their files of ex-convicts and found a picture of Isaac Bond, who had served four years in a Missouri prison on a charge of killing a white man in self-defense. Bond was a Negro, and he was tall; with no further connection than that his picture was printed in the papers. Bond went directly to police headquarters, where he gave a detailed report of the work he had been doing in Gary, Indiana, the night of the murder. The police were in sore need of a conviction; Bond was locked up and brought to trial. His friends went to Darrow and begged him to take the case.

It was the old story: there was no money for expenses, let alone for fees, and it was a foregone conclusion that the man would be convicted. All Darrow could hope for was to save Bond from the gallows and to save the state from a premeditated killing; but that was sufficient. He went to Gary, interviewed the men who had seen Bond at work on the night of the murder, which took place miles away, showed the jury that there was not the slightest scrap of evidence to connect Bond to the killing. The best he could get was a life sentence. The jury brought in a verdict, not against Bond, but against the horrendous crime; Bond happened to be accused of it, and he suffered the repulsion of the jury and the community to the murder itself.

"Some years later I took his case to the pardon board," wrote Darrow, "and am convinced that they thought I was right. One said he was satisfied that I was, but they did not dare touch it unless the proof was complete as to who committed the act, because the killing was so brutal and revolting." Bond served ten years in prison, where he contracted tuberculosis and died.

In the light of such continuous efforts it is small wonder that the Negroes of America loved Clarence Darrow. There was hardly a colored child over five who did not know his name and recognize his face. When he took a driving trip through the South with friends, Mrs McKay noticed that wherever they sat down to a table, in hotel or restaurant, Darrow was always served the largest portions and the choicest cuts of meat. One colored waiter in St Louis, after serving Darrow, murmured:

"You is Mistah Clarence Darrow, ain't you, suh?"

"That's right, I am."

"I'm mighty proud to have the chance to talk to you, suh."

"What time do you finish work here?"

"About nine o'clock, suh."

"Then come on up to my room when you're free, and we'll have a chat."

Shortly after the Loeb-Leopold case Darrow lectured at the psychiatrists' convention in Richmond, Virginia, after which "a small group of attorneys tendered him a dinner at the Commonwealth Club, sitting up and chatting with him until three in the morning." One of the lawyers exclaimed:

"Mr Darrow, I do not understand how a man of your standing could advocate an equality of the races."

"Why, I don't see why that should worry you. I enjoy the company of intelligent Negroes."

"But, Mr Darrow, what about the purity of the Anglo-Saxon race?"

"Purity of the Anglo-Saxon race," snorted Darrow; "the greatest race of sons of bitches that ever infested the earth. Mind you, if there is such a race, I am one of them, because my ancestors lived in this country for nearly three hundred years. But I do not brag about it; I apologize for it."

7

A lawyer's life is like mountainous country. There are occasional peaks, periods in which the advocate climbs to the heights and gains a commanding view of the flatlands below, but most of the time he remains on the plains. Darrow took the routine cases that came to him and did his best with them. Then suddenly a case would flash on the horizon, a case which might prove to be the gateway into the bright future of the twentieth century.

In the town of Oshkosh, Wisconsin, three men were arrested for having organized a strike. The leader of the strike was Thomas I. Kidd, an old friend of Darrow's and general secretary of the Amalgamated Woodworkers' International Union, whose office was in Chicago. Kidd had consulted Darrow frequently on legal matters pertaining to his union and sent other workers to him who wanted to draw up constitutions or arbitrate with their employers. The men were accused of criminal conspiracy; in a very definite sense it was a continuation of the Debs conspiracy case; through his studies in connection with the Debs case Darrow knew more about conspiracy laws than any lawyer in America; the strikers had been woodworkers; Darrow was the son of a woodworker. It was inevitable that he should be asked to defend the case, and it was inevitable that he should have accepted.

George M. Paine owned a lumber company in Oshkosh which distributed sash and doors throughout fourteen states. The plant employed sixteen hundred workers and, in Paine's figures, "was worth a million dollars." The average wage of the sixteen hundred workers for a ten-hour day was ninety-six cents; skilled mechanics, who had been with him from eight to ten years, received for operating dangerous saw machines a dollar and a quarter a day. Contravening the Wisconsin law which made it a crime to employ children under fourteen, Paine had the hunger-driven fathers sign false age affidavits, thus enabling him to employ children from ten years up. Since he could get these children for sixty-five cents a day and women for eighty cents, he was gradually discharging the men and replacing them with their wives and children; each replacement made him an additional profit per worker of from thirty to forty cents a day, and as a good businessman he knew that a profit was a profit. Though the Wisconsin law made weekly wage payments mandatory, he paid his men once a month, thus operating three quarters of the time on their withheld wages.

Each morning when Paine's employees were all inside the factory, the gates were locked behind them. No one could leave his work to go to the toilet without express permission, and no unnecessary talking was allowed. When the workday was over the gates were unlocked so that the workers could go home. Darrow observed that the main difference between the Paine Lumber Company and the Wisconsin penitentiary was that the workers were not allowed to sleep on the premises. The sixteen hundred Paine employees lived in a jungle slum of shacks and tenements beside the Oshkosh railroad tracks. The efforts of the fathers to feed, clothe, house, educate and keep healthy their families of from three to eight were Herculean and had brought a daily toll of hardship, suffering and deprivation. Nor were such early Industrial Revolution conditions made necessary by hard times, decreasing business, financial deficits; Paine admitted that his company was making a considerable and consistent profit.

Sitting with these undisputed facts before him, Darrow asked himself the question:

"Who's a criminal?"

Was a criminal the hungry man who broke into a grocery store? The young desperado whose unbalanced mind had been inflamed by stories of gunmen? The lover who killed out of jealousy? Or was it a responsible man like George M. Paine who daily kept bread from the mouths of some six thousand human beings, who daily committed acts of fraud against the state of Wisconsin? It was possible to measure the amount of damage done by a criminal who held up a bank at the point of a gun, who killed a guard, but where was one to find a yardstick with which to measure the suffering and misery, the illness and deprivation, the hundreds of thousands of hours of fatigue and frustration of the stunted bodies and stunted minds of the people who made it possible for George M. Paine to earn his riches?

"In all social systems there must be a class to do the menial duties, to perform the drudgery of life," said Senator Hammond of South Carolina in 1857; "that is, a class requiring but a lower order of intellect and but little skill. Its requisites are vigor, docility, fidelity. Such a class you must have, or you would not have that other class which leads progress, civilization and refinement. It constitutes the very mudsill of society and of political government, and you might as well attempt to build a house in the air as to build the other except on this mudsill."

To such minds the future of America would rest solely on the totality of their control over the mass of human machines; the greatness of the country would be determined in an inverse ratio to the intelligence and independence of the workers and their families. Thus George Paine could logically employ children of ten years of age, thwart their physical growth, rob them of their education, doom them forever to fractional lives of toil and ignorance, and do so in all virtue because the future of America depended upon developing a docile and faithful labor supply which would enable him to turn out sash and doors and millions in profits, which would in turn create "progress, civilization and refinement."

Darrow did not want to see Thomas I. Kidd, George Zentner and Michael Troiber go to prison, but the issue was bigger than that. He did not want to see labor unions wiped out by the star-chamber conspiracy charges, but the issue was even bigger than that. The issue could be put in a few simple words, words that struck to the vitals of the national problem: was America going to develop into an economic democracy or into an industrial slave state? Were conscienceless men like Pullman and Paine to be permitted to destroy the dream of the New World?

8

He packed his bag, moved to Oshkosh, contacted two local attorneys and selected his jury. By quiet but relentless cross-examination he brought to light the simple and to him familiar facts of the case. When one quarter of the men in the Paine plant had

been replaced by their women and children, the workers had organized and sent a letter to George Paine with four requests: he was
to stop replacing men at the machines with women and children; he
was to obey the Wisconsin law and pay his workers once a week;
he was to grant a raise in wages, and he was to recognize their union.
Paine threw the letter into the wastebasket, called a meeting of the
Oshkosh Manufacturers' Association, of which he had several times
been president. It was agreed that they would fight the union co-
operatively.

When Paine failed to answer the letter sent him a committee of
employees visited him and asked him why. Paine replied, "Because
your letter was unbusinesslike." Notwithstanding the decision of
the Manufacturers' Association to fight the union co-operatively,
Paine told the workmen that he dealt individually with them and expected them in all fairness to deal individually with him. Any
worker who had anything to request was to come to the office,
where his demands would be considered. Two of his oldest workmen took him seriously; the next day they went to his office to ask
for a raise. The first was told:

"You get out of here or I'll give you a raise in the pants!" The
second was told, "Go to hell, God damn you. I can get a damn sight
better man than you are for a dollar and a quarter a day."

The men struck. Paine replaced as many of them as he could
with non-union workers, then appealed to the courts of Oshkosh to
grant him an injunction against the strikers, which would force
them to return to work. The court replied that in America workmen had a right to cease work, even in concert, when they chose.
The workers called upon Kidd to come up from Chicago and show
them how to conduct their strike.

In the fourteen weeks of the strike there was no attempt to injure the Paine property. Only two non-union men were molested.
Paine brought in Pinkerton labor spies, and the mayor asked for state
militia. In the one disorderly scene of the fourteen weeks the strikers clashed with the militia by a gristmill, and one worker was killed.
Winter was coming on; the union's funds were gone; the workers
were penniless; Paine's plant was still operating; the strike was lost,
and the men returned to work under the best conditions they could
get. Determined that there should never again be a strike in his plant,
and encouraged by the fact that Darrow had not been able to set his
precedent against criminal-conspiracy charges in the Debs case,
Paine persuaded the district attorney of Oshkosh to arrest Kidd,
Zentner and Troiber on charges of "conspiracy to injure the business of the Paine Lumber Company." Once again with the eyes of

the industrial world upon him, Darrow was face to face with the greatest potential weapon against the freedom of the American people. This time he was determined to bury it as deep as his father had buried the good folk of Kinsman when their time had come.

He rose to present his closing argument without a paper in his hand, nor did he once in the two days of summary consult a note, yet his address to the jury, in effect a funeral oration on the passing of the nineteenth century, was constructed in so lucid and lyrical a literary style that it stands today, a model of organization, clarity and force. Declared by William Dean Howells, editor of the *Atlantic Monthly*, to be "as interesting as a novel," it is one of the outstanding social documents of its time, enunciating in such logical terms the rights of persons over the rights of property that it helped lead the way toward a new ordering of life in America. Darrow touched greatness for the first time in his appeal; he was to touch it several times more in his long and turbulent life, even though greatness would prove too white-hot to hold constantly in his naked hands.

A few years later in Switzerland he was introduced by a native Swiss to the proprietor of the coffee shop where he went for breakfast. "Darrow?" said the proprietor. "I know a Darrow. An American. I have a book he wrote." The man disappeared into the living quarters behind the shop, to emerge a moment later with a translated copy of the appeal in the woodworkers' conspiracy case. And so his name began its encircling tour of the civilized world.

Darrow's technique in his closing argument was one of the most effective yet evolved by an attorney for the defence. Once again its appeal was educative rather than legal, aimed at the millions of the public rather than the twelve jurors in the box, designed to change the thinking of the nation rather than the mere keeping of his clients out of jail. It is a tribute to the brilliance of his mind that in his every major case, whether it was labor, racial or religious, he succeeded in merging the jury with the rest of the country, in merging the hour of appeal with the centuries of the past and the immediate decades of the future.

His first step was to show that the state of Wisconsin was not the complainant, but that George M. Paine, the wealthiest man in Oshkosh, had prevailed upon the district attorney to file the complaint. "Paine has used almost everything else in Oshkosh, men, women, little children. And now the district attorney has made an assignment of the state to him." He then moved to strip away the pretenses in the case, to bare the real issues and, as in the Debs case, to indict the prosecution.

"Whatever its form, this is not really a criminal case. It is but an episode in the great battle for human liberty, a battle which commenced when the tyranny and oppression of man first caused him to impose upon his fellows and which will not end so long as the children of one father shall be compelled to toil to support the children of another in luxury and ease. Deep in your hearts and mine is the certain knowledge that this drama in which you play such an important part is but a phase of the great social question that moves the world. Malicious as these Paines are, I have no idea that they would prosecute this case simply to put Kidd in jail. These employers are using this court of justice because in their misguided cupidity they believe that they may be able to destroy what little is left of that spirit of independence and manhood which they have been slowly crushing from the breast of those who toil for them. Ordinarily men are brought into a criminal court because they are bad. Thomas I. Kidd is brought into this court because he is good; if he had been mean and selfish and designing, if he had held out his hand to take the paltry bribes that these men pass out whenever they find one so poor and weak as to take their gold, this case would not be here today. Kidd is a defendant in these criminal proceedings because he loved his fellow men, and this is not the first case of the kind in the history of the world, and I am afraid it will not be the last. *It is not the first time that evil men, men who are themselves criminals, have used the law for the purpose of bringing righteous ones to death or to jail.*"

Darrow took the jury through the history of the conspiracy laws as they had developed from the earliest days in England and as he had painstakingly tracked it down for the Debs defense. With this picture clearly outlined, he painted the conspiracy that had been entered into between the Paines and the district attorney. Nathan Paine, son of the owner, had said, "Kidd is the one I want!" but since even in Oshkosh they could not indict Kidd for conspiring with himself, the prosecution had dragged in two obscure men who had been captains of pickets—and had forgotten to prosecute them. Paine had then secured the appointment of a lawyer and Sunday-school teacher by the name of Houghton, at fifteen dollars a day, to act as special prosecutor, and Houghton had sent for employees of the Paine plant, demanding of them as they walked in his door:

"Are you here to convict Kidd?"

In order to strengthen his case, Houghton produced a witness by the name of Jones, who testified that he had heard Kidd say in a public meeting, "If scabs went to work in Chicago as they did in Oshkosh, they would find themselves in the hospital the next day." Not one workman, not even those threatened with the loss

of their jobs, could corroborate this "inciting-to-violence" statement, nor could the secretaries sent by Paine to take records of
everything said at the meetings. Darrow laid the blame for this
manifest perjury on the shoulders of Houghton rather than Mr
Jones.

"There is a conspiracy, dark and damnable, and I want to say
boldly that someone is guilty of one of the foulest conspiracies that
ever disgraced a free nation. If my clients are innocent, other men
are guilty of entering the temple of justice and using the law,
which was made to guard and protect and shelter you and me and
these defendants, for the purpose of hounding innocent men to a
prison pen. It is an ancient law that a man who conspired to use
the courts to destroy his fellow men was guilty of treason to the
state. He had laid his hand upon the state itself; he had touched
the bulwark of human liberty. When George Paine raised a hand
to strike a blow against the liberty of Thomas Kidd he raised a
hand to strike a blow against your freedom and mine, and *he conspired to destroy the institutions under which we live*. There are
criminals in this case, criminals who in the eye of heaven and the
light of justice have not been guilty of the paltry crime of conspiring to save their fellow men, but criminals who have conspired
against the liberty of their fellows and against the country in which
they live."

9

It was Darrow's good fortune that the opposing attorneys made
tactical blunders which outraged the sensibilities of the American
public. The first day Paine appeared in the courtroom Houghton
jumped to his feet and fawningly led the employer inside the
lawyer's enclosure, then shook hands with him warmly before
putting him on the witness stand.

"He would have been glad to lick the dust from Paine's boots,"
commented Darrow dryly, "had he been given the opportunity to
perform this service."

Houghton reached the height of his legal virtuosity when, seeking to establish a precedent for the conviction, he went back a
hundred years to the case of a man who had been convicted for
writing a poem lauding Thomas Paine and his *Rights of Man*.

"How Brother Houghton's mouth would have watered," said
Darrow in mordant sarcasm, "if he had been given a chance to convict Thomas Paine for daring to proclaim the rights of man!"

Houghton should never have been in the case at all, for the
district attorney's office was equipped to handle the case without

special appointments. Darrow rubbed Houghton's nose in the fifteen dollars a day he was getting for this prosecution until the man should have become so housebroken that he would never again wet the penal code in his uncontainable excitement at the prospect of making some extra money.

Then he plunged into the essence of the conflict: shall working-men be allowed to combine to better their conditions or shall they be convicted as criminals for these activities?

"Let me tell you something of labor organizations. I have studied this question because I believe in it, because I love it as I do my very life, because it has been the strongest passion of my years, because in this great battle between the powerful and the weak I have ever been and ever will be with the weak so long as the breath is left in my body to speak. In my own way I wished to do what I could for the thousands, aye, the millions, of people who are yet poorer than myself. I know the history of the labor movement; I know what it has come through. I know the difficulties it is in to-day. I know the past is a dark, dark chapter of infamy and wrong, and yet these lawyers have been groping among the dead ashes of the past to find the blackest pages of history, to ask you to adopt them in the closing years of the nineteenth century.

"There is no man strong enough to subvert the manhood of the workers of the United States, and if the time shall ever come when there is a man so strong, then American liberty is dead."

Darrow's next blow was struck for the future, hoping this time to set a clear and forceful precedent for the obliteration of the black pages of criminal-conspiracy charges against workers and their unions from the book of the twentieth century.

"I take it that in a free country, in a country where George M. Paine does not rule supreme, every person has a right to lay down the tools of his trade if he shall choose. Not only that, but in a free country where liberty of speech is guaranteed, every man has a right to go to his fellow man and say, 'We are out on strike. We are in a great battle for liberty. We are waging war for our fellow men. For God's sake, come with us and help.' Has it come to that point in America, under the guarantee of the freedom of speech and under the Constitution, that a free man cannot go to his neighbor and implore him not to work? If a jury or a court should write a verdict like that, it would be the death knell to human liberty."

Throughout he kept weaving his elemental lesson in economics: "Paine is not supporting these people; these men, women and children are supporting him." All along he kept enunciating the heretical notion that the jury could not convict Kidd, Zentner and Troiber because they were not on trial at all—that the jury system was on trial and that they could convict only the jury system by a verdict of guilty!

Then, for the first time, in this woodworkers' conspiracy case, Darrow utilized the most powerful contradiction of his philosophy: he excoriated the prosecution until they wanted to crawl inside their skins and pull their skins in behind them—after which he pleaded with the jury not to judge them too harshly, in fact, to forgive them, for they, too, were innocent victims of their heredity and environment.

"They cannot make so much money if Kidd is allowed to live They started out by consulting lawyers to see how they could get him out of town, and they have wound up by consulting the district attorney to see how they can keep him here. The malice of George Paine is exceeded only by his avarice. It is not enough that he should take the toil and sweat and the life of these poor men for starvation wages; it is not enough that he should import his spies into this town to dog and incite and destroy them; it is not enough that they should go back to work as best they could; but when all is past and gone, he dares to prostitute the state, to take the law into his polluted hands, the law which should be holy and above suspicion, and use it as a dagger to stab these men in the back.

"However, men do not make events, but events make men. In my heart I have not the slightest, no, not the slightest feeling of bitterness against one of these men. I would not wantonly and cruelly hurt the feelings of any man that lived, because I know, down in the depths of my being, that George M. Paine is what he is, and he knows no other way. I know that Nathan Paine was born as he is, and he sees no other way. I cannot tell what causes there were that induced Brother Houghton to take this case; I know they were enough for him."

Once again Darrow had his jury of businessmen and farmers leaning forward in their seats. In closing his case he brought into focus the historical perspective by showing them the part they were playing in fashioning the future of their people.

"Men do not build for today; they do not build for tomorrow. They build for the centuries, for the ages, and when we look back it is perhaps the despised criminal and outlaw, the man perhaps without home or country or friend, who has lifted the world upward and onward toward the blessed brotherhood which one day will come. Here is Thomas I. Kidd; it is a matter of the smallest consequence to him or to me what you do, and I say it as sincerely as

I ever spoke a word. No man ever entered this struggle for human liberty without measuring the cost, and the jail is one of the costs that must be measured with the rest. I do not appeal for him; that cause is too narrow for me, much as I love him and long as I have worked by his side. I appeal to you not for Thomas Kidd, but I appeal to you for the long line—the long, long line reaching back through the ages and forward to the years to come—the long line of despoiled and downtrodden people of the earth. I appeal to you for those men who rise in the morning before daylight comes and who go home at night when the light has faded from the sky and give their life, their strength, their toil to make others rich and great. I appeal to you in the name of those women who are offering up their lives to this modern god of gold, and I appeal to you in the name of those little children, the living and the unborn.

"It has fallen to your lot to be leading actors in one of the great dramas of human life. For some mysterious reason Providence has placed in your charge for today, aye, for the ages, the helpless toilers, the hopeless men, the despondent women and suffering children of the world. It is a great, a tremendous, trust, and I know you will do your duty bravely, wisely, humanely and well; that you will render a verdict in this case which will be a milestone in the history of the world and an inspiration to the dumb, despairing millions whose fate is in your hands."

The jury brought in a verdict of "not guilty"; with the weight of the centuries on their shoulders they could do no less.

CHAPTER V

"Let Me Speak for the Children of the Poor"

SHORTLY AFTER his return from Oshkosh Darrow began one of the most pleasant periods of his life. He joined forces with Francis S. Wilson, a young cousin of Jessie's who had been born and raised just thirty miles from Darrow's home in Ohio. Wilson was short, husky, handsome, jovial, and made a delightful companion. Together they rented bachelor quarters close to Hull House, furnishing them with pieces that Darrow had left over from his marriage.

"The Langdon Apartments had just been erected as model tenements on the corner of Des Plaines and Bunker streets in the ghetto of Chicago," says Wilson. "We were among the opulent tenants and had two three-room flats made into one, as a result of which we had two bedrooms. In the living room was a small grate for fire, which we adorned with a couple of andirons representing two large cats. When fire came through the glass eyes it made them look animated. We had a lot of fun with them. These were my purchases in the basement of the Fair and my contribution to the interior decorating. Darrow's contribution was the red carpet and red curtains, so you see we were rather artistic in a modest way. We also had one of the original Svendson paintings called The Fire in the Forest.

"Our guests were mostly writers, painters and social-service workers who liked to sit at Darrow's feet. They were bohemianish, inasmuch as they preferred to come in through the windows rather than the door and sit on the floor rather than chairs. Darrow's books were scattered around in a miscellaneous fashion; he was a collector in a nonchalant way of first editions and autographed copies. Frequently of an evening he would read aloud from Nietzsche or Marx or some Russian author, and I would make my exit shortly after for the purpose of seeking younger companionship."

The Langdon Apartments became known as a "Co-operative Living Club. Distinguished artists, writers, professors, scientists, musicians, labor leaders and liberals from Europe and America came to have dinner in the common dining room and discuss public affairs in the common drawing room. The Co-op put on plays by Shaw and Ibsen and gave masquerade dances in neighborhood halls, one of which Darrow attended as a policeman!" His closest neighbors were Gertrude Barnum and Helen Todd, daughter of a wealthy Minnesota miller who, through Darrow's intervention, became Chicago's first factory inspector for child labor. Darrow and Helen Todd, whose high-spirited nature may best be illumined by the rifle she took with her to the University of Wisconsin, firing it from her dormitory window as a salute to the sun after many days of rain, became intimate friends. His most frequently uttered sentiment to her as she wove incessantly from ottoman to chair to sofa, from job to job and social theory to social panacea, ever ready to fire her rifle as a salute to something new, was the epitome of his criticism of most social workers from above:

"Light, Helen, light!"

Gertrude Barnum says of the Langdon Apartments, "Darrow was the center of attraction in our leisure hours. He loved to read aloud from Voltaire. Bobby Burns brought tears streaming down his cheeks. In lighter vein we had Mr Dooley and George Ade. His education in classical music had been neglected, but he doted on Kenneth Harris' spirited rendition of 'The Road to Mandalay' and always responded to simple melodies and folk songs. We celebrated his fortieth birthday there. I had prepared twenty questions with slams on those present. One of the questions was, 'Who is it that resists not evil, neither lets any good thing pass?' and the chorus chanted, 'Darrow, Darrow, Darrow.' After that we made him sing the words of a tune he frequently hummed when weary or depressed:

> The bear went over the mountain
> To see what he could see,
> He came back over the mountain,
> 'Twas all that he could see.

> 'Twas all that he could see-ee-ee,
> 'Twas all that he could see.

Having got him started on this many-versed song, the trick was to make him stop. In thanking us he said, 'It's the best party I ever was to.'

"There is nothing in my life of which I am so proud as of Clarence Darrow's faith and friendship. While there never was any romance between us—I was frightened by his theories of free love and, because of his dirty fingernails and rather greasy hair, found him unattractive physically—he surely made all the men of my set look like pygmies and had much to do with my remaining a spinster. My contributions to labor organization, Americanization and adult education had no more generous or faithful backer; he never once refused my appeals for funds for needy individuals or worthy causes. No matter how small or despised the groups who appealed for his educational talks, he never refused."

The anomalous part of Darrow's leadership at the Langdon Co-operative Living Club was that he was opposed to the work being done at Hull House. "Jane Addams spent forty arduous years appealing to the more fortunate to share wealth and opportunity with the 'underprivileged.' Darrow supported and defended the downtrodden in their own self-help organizations to improve their conditions by collective bargaining and strikes, ever urging them to scorn the stigma of philanthropic aid, to rise in their own strength and take what was rightfully theirs; in short, to cease being underprivileged."

Gertrude Barnum portrays this dramatic conflict of social pragmatisms between Jane Addams and Clarence Darrow. "In the gay nineties, to be a settlement worker was to be a 'radical' in the minds of the pillars of society. But those of us who abandoned frivolity to respond to Jane Addams' appeal were unmoved by jeers and warnings. We viewed with scorn friends and relatives who did not share our fanaticism. In short, we became odious young social-service snobs, who must have been hard to bear with. Clarence Darrow did not bear with us, but upon us. At a dinner party given by him, at which all sorts of bigwigs were present, I was embarrassed to have their attention focused on my young head when my host asked me, across the length of the table, what I was doing at Hull House. I announced:

"'I am helping to furnish legitimate amusement for the people.'

"'Do they like that kind?' Darrow drawled.

"Whereupon I was the butt of hearty laughter from all present. For years it was nip and tuck between Jane Addams and Clarence Darrow in a tug of war for young souls like mine. It seemed a choice we simply had to make between philanthropy and self-help movements in Chicago."

That Darrow may have been right when he observed of Hull House, "It's no good putting cold packs on the brow of a feverish man; find the source of the fever and rout it out of the body," is evidenced by this mordant sentence written forty-five years later by one of Miss Addams' most trusted assistants:

"In the social and academic honors lavishly showered upon Miss Addams she found scant consolation for her utter failure to lessen poverty even in her own settlement neighborhood."

2

Partly because of the confining influences of his first marriage, but mostly because he was a leader of the general revolt of the day, one of whose chief planks was free love as a road to individual liberty, Clarence openly avowed that he wanted no more of marriage. He preached ardently against his young friends allowing themselves to be caught in its mesh—possibly diverting a few. X had also believed in free love; she and Clarence had entered their pact with the clear understanding that they would remain together only as long as they desired, that they would not permit themselves to drift into marriage and that each would be free to terminate whenever he wished, without apologies or explanations. He had rented a room in the home of X and her mother, ostensibly as a boarder, but after a few months he learned that free love was not particularly free when he had to come home every night. He found that X was emotionally incapable of living up to their bargain; she loved him with a terrifying intensity which made her, against her own will and better judgment, jealous and possessive. She insisted that he account for every moment of his time spent away from her, showed up unexpectedly at places where he had gone without her, gave him the feeling that he was being watched and spied upon and ended by causing tearful and hysterical scenes when he went out with other women. For Darrow this possessiveness soon became oppressive.

Though he had moved into the Langdon Apartments to recapture his bachelordom, he and X went to plays and meetings, often had dinner together and on week ends would accidentally meet at the same resorts in the country. He did not feel any necessity of being faithful to her, for if he had to be faithful he might as well have married. While social-service workers were not the most delectable prey, he favored them because he could enjoy a little intelligent conversation before he got around to feeling amorous. He had matured since the days when he took women for their sheer physical pleasure; his friendships were now confined to those in whom he found a gentility, an emotional sympathy. Gertrude Barnum insists there was nothing of the philanderer about him. "People worshiped the ground he walked on, men and women and children alike." With the men he loved he fought for liberal causes, worked and studied and discussed; with the women he loved it seemed only natural that their love should be completely expressed. One of his associates remarks, "There was never any such thing as conscious seduction on his part; the women always showed themselves open and willing."

After he had been indicted in Los Angeles he was greatly depressed by a report that the district attorney was going to introduce into evidence a photograph purported to have been taken of him as he left the house of a beautiful Pasadena widow at dawn. One of his friends consoled him by saying, "Don't be downcast, Clarence; your enemies will believe the worst of you, even without photographs, and your friends will know it is a fake. They will know that if you had spent the night in the home of a beautiful widow you wouldn't leave at dawn. You would stay for breakfast."

3

Each morning the roommates walked the two miles to the office, stopping on the way at Race's Fish House for breakfast. Wilson tells that Darrow was full of boyishness and had a most delicious chuckle. He liked to laugh for the sake of laughter. He was fond of limericks and had the Midwest farmer's zest for bawdy jokes. A woman who was late for a dinner appointment explained that she and her husband had been detained because her son had dropped one of his balls out of the window, and she had had to go out in the dark to hunt for it.

"What a terrible accident," murmured Darrow. Every time he met the woman after that he would inquire solicitously, "And how is the little boy now?"

By this time he had already grown what his friends called "inordinately fond and proud" of his son Paul, an open-faced lanky lad of sixteen who resembled Amirus. He took the boy with him for companionship on many of his business and lecture trips. When the weather was nice they would go for vacations into the Wisconsin woods, tramping as many as fourteen miles a day. It was his greatest hope that Paul would become a lawyer, so that he could

train him and take him in as a partner. During the summer vacations from the private preparatory school to which the democratic
Darrow oddly enough sent his son, Paul sometimes worked on the
books in the office; from these periods he came to the conclusion
that he had no liking for the law. At sixteen, when he had graduated
from high school, he wanted to find a job.

"No, you're too young," said Darrow, disappointed. "You've got
to continue school."

Paul worked for a short time for A. C. McClurg, the publisher,
where most of the men were Dartmouth graduates. They sold the
father the idea of sending his son to Dartmouth. At the opening of
the school year Clarence took the none-too-complaisant Paul to
New Hampshire, saying, "You stay until Christmas, and if you
don't like it you can come home and take a job." When he left
Paul behind he gave him only one piece of advice:

"I never want you to get into a poker game unless there is a
limit."

Like most bits of parental advice, it was precisely the kind the
father himself was unable to follow. His parting shot was, "If you
ever get into any difficulty of any kind whatever, probably you
had better tell me about it, because I don't think you can get into
anything I haven't been in."

Paul enjoyed Dartmouth and stayed there for four years, until
he graduated. "My father was always liberal with his allowance.
When I wanted to tell him what I did with my money he said, 'I
don't want to know what you did with it; it's spent, and that's
enough.' I could spend any amount of money I wanted on books.
Dad was a peach. He never lost his temper, rarely punished me. He
was patient in explaining, even if I had done something wrong.
He always took time to reason things out with me."

4

For a man who has once been married, bachelordom, no matter
how exciting, is an interregnum. One night in the spring of 1899
Darrow went to lecture on Omar Khayyám at the White City
Club, which was made up of artists, writers and musicians. After
the lecture he was introduced by his friend John H. Gregg,
originator of the shorthand system, to a young woman with auburn-
colored hair, a pink-and-white complexion, wearing a wine-colored
jacket trimmed with baby lamb and a pert hat to match.

"Of course you've met Mr Darrow," said Gregg.

"Sorry," replied Ruby Hamerstrom, "but I haven't."

Struck by the sparkle and alertness of the young woman's eyes, by the proud, independent manner in which she carried her head, Darrow asked Miss Hamerstrom to make an appointment for dinner. She declined. He continued to block her way, talking to her; when the caretaker had turned out the lights he held her hand in the dark, refusing to let her go until she agreed to meet him again or at least give him her address. Miss Hamerstrom finally slipped past him to join the Greggs, who were waiting for her on the sidewalk.

Smitten, Darrow sat before the glowing-eyed cats of his fireplace and composed messages to the auburn-haired girl which he sent through the Greggs, begged his friends to get another appointment for him and ended, man-fashion, by accusing Mrs Gregg of not delivering his messages. Ruby Hamerstrom was engaged to a New York stockbroker at the time. She went to her fiancé, who was visiting in Chicago, and said, "If you think I should, I'll go to dinner with him just once at the Greggs, in order to tell him that I have received all his messages and it's not Mrs Gregg's fault that I have made no appointments with him."

"I can't see any harm in going to dinner with him—just once," replied her fiancé.

Ruby Hamerstrom was born in Galesburg, Illinois, where Knox College is located. Her mother was a "Swedish beauty with black hair who wrote nice things for the religious magazines." Her father, who was in charge of the blacksmith shops of the Chicago, Burlington and Quincy Railroad, was studious, keeping volumes of Voltaire and Tom Paine in the house, even though he went to church faithfully, because "he always liked to know both sides of a case." Ruby dropped out of high school at fourteen to take care of her bedridden mother and six younger brothers but found time to read widely in the Knox College library, devouring all the books she could find on "How to Be a Journalist." She did some writing, but her mother burned what she wrote, saying, "Anything that isn't religious is sinful." She wasn't allowed to train herself to do a job because she was needed to "help about the house and raise the six brothers." At eighteen she resigned from the Lutheran Church. When her mother told her that she couldn't work in Galesburg because it would disgrace the family, "she took her small savings out of the bank and left for Chicago to become a newspaper woman . . . two long braids of auburn hair dangling down her back."

In Chicago she found employment as a bookkeeper in the home of a Mr and Mrs Gross, homeopathic doctors. In her spare time she wrote articles. Hearing that Laura Dainty Pelham, Midwest head of the Women's Rights organization, had just returned from

New York, Ruby went to her for an interview; Laura Pelham, wishing to help the aspiring journalist, told her of the new fad in New York called the "Pink Tea," about which the women of Chicago had not yet heard. Ruby wrote up the "Pink Tea" and sold her article to the Chicago *Evening Post,* the first paper to give women space, in a column called "Women and Her Ways." Before long Miss Hamerstrom was by-lining the entire Women's Page for the Sunday edition and doing feature articles on such disparate subjects as the building of the Whaleback for the Fair and Iron Mining in Northern Michigan.

Ruby was twenty-six when she met Darrow, who was then forty-two. She had a fast, well-informed mind, steadfastness of character; though she was not beautiful she had a colorful and charming personality.

"I lived west," said Ruby, "and I planned with Mrs Gregg who was going to have dinner with us, that I should stay over with her so that Darrow wouldn't see me home. When he met us in a Loop restaurant that night he said,

" 'I have to give a lecture out west tonight, and if you don't mind coming to hear me speak I can take you home after the meeting.'

" 'Oh no,' replied Ruby, 'I'm staying with Mrs Gregg tonight.'

" 'I don't see any reason why you shouldn't go to the meeting with Mr Darrow,' said Mrs Gregg. 'You're not afraid to have him take you home, are you?'

" 'Surely you're not afraid?' twitted Darrow.

" 'No, but I have an early appointment . . .'

"Finally I capitulated. We took Mrs Gregg home. Then in the middle of the Rush Street Bridge, with the wind and the rain blowing in our faces, Darrow stopped, took off one of my gloves and stuck my hand with his into his overcoat pocket.

" 'I've never known anyone I liked so much—right from the start,' he said; 'that's why I think I ought to tell you. I've been married. I never intend to marry again.'

" 'That's fine,' answered Ruby, 'because I'm leaving in two weeks to be married myself.'

" 'You're not! Well, we'll have to devise ways to break your engagement. People who like each other as much as we do shouldn't be separated.'

"I had fallen in love with Mr Darrow that first night when he lectured on Khayyám," said Ruby. "That was why I didn't want to see him again. But it was four years before I dared to marry him."

5

In 1900 Darrow persuaded the now ill and nearly destitute Altgeld to join his firm in the place of Morris St P. Thomas, who had retired from the partnership to become a master in chancery. After his defeat in 1896 Altgeld had not wanted to return to the practice of law. "He had come to rather despise that profession; he felt that its strongest men sold themselves to destroy people, to perpetuate and intensify the poverty of the oppressed and enlarge their burdens." To honor his beloved friend, Darrow made him titular head of Altgeld, Darrow and Thompson. This was a gesture of courage and love on Darrow's part, for not only could Altgeld bring the partnership no business, but his name attached to it would keep certain corporation business away. Though Thompson reports flashes of Altgeld's old-time legal brilliance, Wilson says, "Altgeld was a broken man; he used to fall asleep in his office." Darrow's move helped to repatriate the former governor of Illinois, afforded him a living after his wealth had been stripped from him by his political enemies.

The turn of the century was a happy time for Clarence. Frankie Wilson was a gay home companion; he had Altgeld next to him in his office; he was growing ever more enchanted with Ruby Hamerstrom. He spent many delightful evenings discussing the latest revelations of biology at the Sunset Club:

> *Any genial man,*
> *If he chooses, can,*
> *When he pays his dues,*
> *Join, and air his views.*

When the Colonel Robert Ingersoll memorial meeting was held in Studebaker Hall in August 1899, a few weeks after Ingersoll's death, he was called upon to give the main speech because he was fast becoming Ingersoll's most eloquent disciple. He brought down tremendous applause from the Christian audience, which might have been expected to hate Ingersoll for his agnosticism, when he said, "We meet to pay a tribute of love and respect to Robert Ingersoll, not because he was a great orator or a great lawyer, but because he used his matchless powers for the good of man, because he gave his life to human liberty. The man who speaks the truth that is in him, although all the world hisses, is a sight of such moral grandeur that all mankind should bow down and honor him." They were a good deal alike, these two Chicago lawyers who suffered persecution and bitterness in their fight for what they deemed to be the truth.

He lectured to ever-growing audiences on scientific and literary subjects; he would not only lecture without compensation, but he would pay his own expenses to get to an audience in a neighboring city, a type of monetary indifference which made him a plague to professional lecturers. One night Howard Vincent O'Brien found him in a towering rage, composing a fiery letter of protest over the galley proofs of an article that had been written about him and which would appear in the *Atlantic Monthly*—unless he threatened to sue.

"What is it you are protesting about?" asked O'Brien.

"This so-and-so called me a mountebank."

"Well, what is a mountebank? Isn't it a strolling player?"

"Yes."

"You speak and lecture anywhere you can, don't you? You're the worst scab in the lecture business."

"That's true," grinned Darrow.

"You like to play on juries, don't you?"

"Sure, I don't play any musical instrument, but I like to play on people."

"Well, there you are; you're just a damned mountebank."

Darrow laughed as he tore up the letter of protest.

His law business prospered; as always, many of the cases had social implications which enabled him to do a little leveling. The Teachers' Federation engaged him to bring suit against a number of corporations that were defrauding the public on their tax payments, particularly in their scandalously low real-estate-assessment taxes. Frequently he won these cases, thus making available for teachers' salaries additional public funds. He continued to try negligence cases, such as streetcar accidents, in which his percentage might be as high as five to fifteen thousand dollars. His conduct in money matters was still erratic:

"The head of a Polish family was permanently injured in the Illinois Steel mills of South Chicago. I arranged with Darrow to take the case for a contingency fee of fifty per cent, the usual method. Darrow's handling it induced the company to settle for twenty thousand dollars without court action. After the check was sent in I was knocked off my pins when Darrow said that ten dollars was all he could really charge, because most of the work was done over the phone and in a personal conference with one of the mill lawyers. He also saw to it that the victim invested some of his money in a home and arranged to safeguard the balance of his money. I doubt if he ever discussed this matter with anyone. He wanted no backslapping."

There is a saying that in the breast of every lawyer lies buried the wreck of a poet. This was particularly true of Clarence Darrow, son of a writing father, who confided to his roommate Wilson, "The one thing I want most of all to be is a writer." In 1900 William Randolph Hearst invaded Chicago; he hired Darrow to incorporate the *Evening American*. So ardent were the established Chicago newspapers to spread the one and only truth, they sent out men with clubs to beat up and keep off the streets vendors of other papers. As general counsel for Hearst, Darrow soon had his hands full instituting suits. The Hearst account was profitable, but its importance lay in the fact that it at long last afforded Darrow the one further activity necessary for his full expression.

His first essays developed from the preparation of lectures on such topics as "Realism in Literature and Art" and his early writings on Walt Whitman, Robert Burns, Omar Khayyám. These papers, which were later published under the title of *A Persian Pearl, and Other Essays*, are appeals for the realistic and critical approach to life. Written in an age when Whitman and Khayyám were condemned as immoral, unfit for the eyes of innocent youth, they remain to this day lucid, forceful and courageous. In Omar Khayyám he found corroboration for his own fatalism:

"Above man and his works, Khayyám found the heavy hand of destiny, ever guiding and controlling, ever moving its creature forward to the inevitable fate that all the centuries had placed in store for the helpless captive, marching shackled to the block." He was not above using Khayyám for his own purposes, as every artist uses the artists who have gone before him; writing of the philosophy of Khayyám, he was able to state by indirection the essence of his attitude toward the new and scientific criminology. "Every son of man travels an unbeaten path—a road beset with dangers and temptations that no other wanderer met. His footsteps can be judged only in the full knowledge of the strength and light he had, the burden he carried, the obstacles and temptations he met and a thorough knowledge of every open and secret motive that impelled him."

A congenital iconoclast himself, Darrow loved Walt Whitman for being a revolutionary. "He seems one of those old bards, fresh from the hand of nature, untaught in any schools, unfettered by any of the myriad chords which time is ever weaving about the hearts and brains and consciences of men as the world grows gray. To the world with its crowded cities, its diseased bodies, its unnatural desires, its narrow religion and its false morals, he comes like a breeze of the morning from the mountains or the sea."

For many years he had been eager to write stories, novels, poems, but he had been busy, and the provocation had somehow never arisen. Now, through his connection with the Hearst papers, he saw a way of getting his stories into print. Hearst did not pay him for them but indulged his dilettantish attorney by permitting the stories to be published in the Chicago *Evening American*. The series of short sketches called *Easy Lessons in Law* was a searing indictment of the evils within our economic and judicial systems. Darrow was no imaginative writer; each story arose from an actual case he had handled.

The "Doctrine of Fellow Servants" grew out of his railroad experience. Through the negligence of a conductor, who fails to give a "proceed-slowly" order to the engineer, the last car of a Pullman train is thrown off the tracks and wrecked, killing two men: Horace Bartlett who, "within the last month had made two hundred thousand dollars on corn; that is, he had bet it would go up, and it did"; and Robert Hunt, a brakeman who was earning forty-five dollars a month, "having been raised a total of five dollars in the twelve years he had been with the company." The company paid Mrs Bartlett five thousand dollars without a suit; Mrs Hunt was informed that "the road was in no way responsible for her husband's death; however, if she would sign a release they would pay the expenses of his funeral, as he was a faithful employee and a worthy man." Mrs Hunt sued, but the judge told her that "it was plain that Hunt's death was due to the negligence of the conductor in not delivering the message to the engineer; that the conductor and brakeman were fellow servants, and that therefore the company was not responsible." Mrs Bartlett spent the winter in the south of France to assuage her sorrow; Mrs Hunt drowned hers in the washtub in which she scrubbed clothes to support her three children.

In "The Doctrine of Assumed Risk" he tells of Tony, who left his beautiful hillside in sunny Italy to dig dirt and snow from the switches of the Chicago railroad yards; who had his leg cut off by a locomotive, and how the judge instructed the jury to bring in a verdict for the railroads because, "if Tony did not know better than to work in such a dangerous place, he assumed the risk." "The Breaker Boy," which he wrote from his experiences in the coal-mining region, is the finest of the group, for it has an artistic symmetry beyond its burden of ironic injustices. Johnny McCaffery goes to work as a breaker boy at the age of eleven because his father is killed in the mines. Johnny's job was to straddle the chute and, "as the lumps of coal ran swiftly down between his legs, to snatch out the pieces of slate as fast as his hands and arms could move." By the time he is fifty-four Johnny has progressed from doorboy to driver to helper to miner; his face is scarred, and one ear is missing from an exploded fuse; one arm is crippled from a falling rock. Now too old to work in the mines, Johnny is once again sent to straddle the shute, to be a breaker boy; and that is the life of Johnny McCaffery, whose family emigrated from Ireland because they had heard that "America had no English landlords, no rack-rented tenants, no hopeless men and ragged women and hungry boys and girls."

These stories are authentic proletarian literature, written when proletarian literature was in its inception. They have a high if not altogether professional quality of literary excellence, for Darrow wrote almost as well as he talked; he wrote only when he was inflamed, and passion is a purveyor of good ink. He was a teacher and reformer; he would have laughed at art for art's sake. Everything he wrote had its purpose: to correct an evil, to avert an injustice, to assuage a suffering.

6

In 1902 Darrow had his second—and last—success with a voting public. When he had been governor of Illinois Altgeld had vetoed a measure passed by the boughten legislature to hand over the Chicago surface lines to the brigand-financier Yerkes, on a fifty-year franchise; now that Yerkes was once again lobbying to have the legislature bequeath him the streetcar franchise Altgeld consented to run for mayor of Chicago on an Independent ticket. Once again Altgeld, Darrow and their friends from the Democratic party of 1892–96 stumped the city, lecturing—but again Altgeld was defeated. His defeat left him ill and depressed, but he roused himself to make one last valiant fight, lecturing every night to rouse sympathy for the Boers, "because a great nation was trampling a small one into the earth."

On the afternoon of March 12, 1902, Altgeld left the office to go to Joliet for a lecture. Darrow sent the office boy to carry Altgeld's bag to the depot. When they reached the street the boy urged Altgeld to take a taxi to the station, but he replied:

"No, the streetcar is good enough for me."

That night as he stood on the platform in Joliet, his arm and voice raised against the cruelties of the world, he was stricken. By midnight he was dead. Darrow went to Joliet the next morning to bring back the man he loved most. "He lay in state in the public library," wrote Darrow. "All day long the people filed past and lavished their loving looks upon their great and brave champion. It was the same throng that had so often hung upon his courageous words, the same inarticulate mass for whose cause he had given his life."

Darrow had invited two clergymen to conduct the funeral services. Frightened at the thought that they might lose their pulpits if they officiated at the bier of John *Pardon* Altgeld, they refused. Darrow and Jane Addams of Hull House gave the farewell messages. In eulogizing his beloved friend Darrow once again enunciated, as he had at the Ingersoll services, a fundamental tragedy:

"In the great flood of human life that is spawned upon the earth, it is not often that a man is born."

Many horse-drawn carriages followed the hearse, but Darrow walked, alone, by the side of his friend.

Shortly after Altgeld's death Yerkes sent his purchasing lobby to the state capitol. Little stomach as he had for professional politics, but feeling it was his job to carry on Altgeld's fight, Darrow asked the Democrats to put his name on their list of legislators. He was promptly informed by the party for which he had campaigned the past ten years that they wanted no part of Mr Clarence Darrow, "whose very name was anathema to Chicago businessmen." Aroused now, he ran as an Independent on a Municipal Ownership ticket; that he used his own peculiar methods to secure support is attested by a member of one of his audiences:

"He advised the voters that he did not need the job. In his whimsical way he told the audience not much could be done, except that he might be able to unlock the prison doors and set some of the inmates free." When the votes were counted he had received more than all the opposition combined.

By now, having reached forty-five, Darrow began to think of himself as approaching middle age. His hair and face were thinning; the lines in his forehead and cheeks were deepening; his eyes were retreating deeper under their ridges. His accomplishments thus far had been meager: he had published a book of literary essays, a few short stories, a number of controversial pamphlets that had been transcribed from his lectures. He had failed in his efforts to defeat government by injunction and save the American Railway Union from destruction at the hands of his former employers, but in defending the woodworkers' union he had been successful in trying extortionist-capitalism before the bar of public opinion. He had fought numberless tiny battles for intelligence, for justice for the poor, for the release of the human mind from its shackles of the centuries. Yet his efforts were unfocused: aside from his general campaign for tolerance he had consecrated himself to no one task. His enemies among the employer-church-moralist groups called him "a radical, argumentative, opinionated, anarchistic busybody who muddied the waters of everything he touched without doing any good." To those who knew little of his intent he seemed an amiable lunatic who went around saying inexplicable things like, "If you put a gun to a man's head and force him to give you ten cents to buy food, it is robbery. If the coal barons get all the coal in the world and let the people freeze, it is business."

If American history had not been suddenly thrown into sharp and dramatic focus he might have continued to be considered an eccentric lawyer, little known outside the state of Illinois. "The crises in Darrow's life coincided with the crises in our national life." When, of all the attorneys in the United States, he was chosen by John Mitchell, president of the United Mine Workers, to lead the anthracite-coal miners' fight for existence, the fact was announced calmly at the tail end of a long newspaper column. By the time the hearing before President Theodore Roosevelt's commission was in full swing the name of Clarence Darrow was being blazoned in headlines across the continent, and America had set up a new idol to worship—and at whom to fling offal.

7

Darrow was elated at the invitation to take charge of the miners' case in this greatest industrial crisis in American history. This was the first time since the "Debs Rebellion" that the workers of an entire industry had combined to strike. It was the first time that individual unions called for mass co-operation in fighting for their own salvation. It was the first strike in which the entire public participated, for had not coal been proven to be as much of a public utility as water or gas? The strike in the anthracite fields had been called in May 1902; though it was now only October, industry was verging on collapse; railroad schedules had been cut to a basic minimum; the London *Times* predicted "coal riots in all major American cities as soon as the winter weather came on." In spite of the sharp rise in the price of coal, in spite of the imminent misery of a heatless winter, the public was solidly in sympathy with the coal miners and was expressing that sympathy in audible and concrete terms. For some reason the mass of people had understood emotionally what it meant to live year after year on the ragged edges of dread, hunger and illness.

As Darrow read back over the files of the newspapers since the walkout of the hundred and fifty thousand miners, he was astounded to find a change, too, had taken place in American journalism. The newspapers of the country, with the exception of those owned by the Pennsylvania railroads, were bitterly denouncing the practices of the coal operators! Altgeld had been right in saying that "we have to keep the papers free in the hopes that one day they will use that freedom to tell the truth for the whole people." It was a period of intense agitation, led by President Roosevelt, against the industrial combines which were openly flouting the Sherman Anti-Trust Act, defying the national government to call them to account. Here was a magnificent opportunity for Darrow: a public incensed against the coal barons, who had combined to force up the price of coal and force down the price of labor, was in a receptive frame of mind. There was no town or hamlet so small that one of its newspapers would not print every word of the hearing before the commission, and there were few persons within reaching distance of a newspaper who had not been so disturbed that they would not read everything printed.

Yet to Darrow the most hopeful aspect of the upheaval was that for the first time in industrial disputes the operators had agreed to accept the decision handed down by the commission. The Senate committee investigating the railroad strike of 1894 had been empowered only to listen to evidence and submit recommendations to the President. The Coal Commission of 1902–03 had the power, ceded to it by the operators in their last moments of desperation, not only to hand down a decision, but to enforce its awards. This seemed like coming forward eight hundred years in eight; at last industry was to be made responsible to the government.

Not that the operators had ceded with good grace: only four days before their capitulation their spokesman, George Baer, president of the Reading Railroad, of the Philadelphia and Reading Coal and Iron Company, of the Lehigh and Wilkes-Barre Coal and Iron Company, of the Temple Iron Company, etc., etc., had taken the most hostile attitude toward President Theodore Roosevelt, who was attempting to avert a disaster for the public and to send the miners back to work on a settlement satisfactory to both sides.

"The duty of the hour is not to waste time negotiating with the fomenters of this anarchy and insolent defiers of the law," said Mr Baer, "but to do what was done in the war of the Rebellion, restore the majesty of law and re-establish order and peace at any cost. The government is a *contemptible failure* if it can only protect the lives and property and secure the comfort of the people by compromising with the violators of law and the instigators of violence and crime."

Somehow, neither President Roosevelt nor the Congress nor the Supreme Court nor the voting citizens enjoyed hearing themselves called a contemptible failure. Yet this was the mildest of the four immortal phrases minted by George Baer, four phrases which were to do more to bring about industrial democracy in America than the heroic flailing of Darrow and his fellow liberals.

Sitting at his office desk, surrounded by newspaper files and magazines, treatises on mines, labor conditions and immigration, by account books and statistical charts, Darrow saw that although the discovery of the anthracite-coal beds in Pennsylvania had proved a source of great wealth to American industry and a boon to consumers who needed a cheap fuel, it had from the outset been a curse to the miners who drew it like clotted black blood from the veins of the earth. It became the most difficult and dangerous industry in which men could earn their living, for the miners worked with death constantly leering over their shoulders. Six men out of a thousand were killed every year; hundreds were maimed by explosions and cave-ins; few escaped the ravages of asthma, bronchitis, chronic rheumatism, consumption, heart trouble. By the age of fifty the miners were worn out and broken, good for little but the human slag heap.

If a miner were hurt in an accident "the ambulance was of a very crude nature, practically a covered lumber wagon furnished with horse blankets." If he were killed in the mine the company paid nothing to his family, and his neighbors chipped in to pay for his burial. If he were injured in an explosion, his legs or back broken, the company would not provide medical care—unless the injured man signed a company release.

"I notice that you have lost a leg. How did you lose it?"

"Making a coupling one morning."

"Did the company buy you an artificial leg?"

"No."

"Did you ask them to do anything like that for you?"

"We went down, but we got no satisfaction."

Dr Gibbons of Scranton said, "I never expect to get anything from an ordinary miner, not because they are unwilling to pay, but because they are unable to do so. If it is a poor man with a large family I don't ever think of asking him to pay me, and if a little woman lost her husband and had one young man bearing the burden, I would not charge anything."

In spite of their dangers and difficulties, Darrow perceived that miners were known the world over as one of the most courageous and independent craft of men to be found. They were courageous because only courageous men could descend, day after day, into the dust-laden blackness. They were independent because a majority of them were either "contract miners" or worked for contract miners who were paid by the carload of coal delivered to the operators and over whom, in the endless dark labyrinths of a mine, it was impossible to exercise the kind of supervision and discipline maintained over workers in a factory. With these attributes of courage and independence, miners could have made the highest quality of citizenry; instead they were kept in a continuous state of ignorance and inescapable debt which made them a potential source of peril to the continuation of a democracy.

"Why?" Darrow asked himself.

Was it imperative that these hundreds of thousands of people be kept in a state of destitution? Was it economically inescapable? The figures at his elbow did not seem to indicate so. The anthracite mines, which were confined to a small section in Pennsylvania, had been bought up by the competing Pennsylvania railroads who thus made sure of getting their haulage—and a return of as high as forty-five per cent on their investment.

Through his work for the railroads Darrow had learned that combination in industry generally resulted in a combination to control prices. With these railroad-owned mines combination also involved a restraint of labor, for the banks owned the railroads which owned the mines; thus the billions of national wealth could be mustered to keep the mineworkers from wresting some iota of power from the hands of the operators; nor was any distinction drawn between good or responsible unions and bad ones.

"We spent four million dollars breaking the last strike, and the union along with it," publicly boasted a coal-mine owner. "It was the best investment we operators ever made!"

"During the last two generations a slow, stubborn contest has been waged by labor in the anthracite-coal fields against the ever-growing power of monopoly," said John Mitchell. "The strike of 1902 was but the culmination of a development lasting through three quarters of a century."

8

After several days of intensive study Darrow packed his valise and set off for the coal towns, to visit the collieries and the rows of unpainted shacks on the flanks of barren mountains in which the miners and their families lived, their only trees or vegetation the piles of black slate that had been segregated from the coal by breaker boys. Some of the shacks were propped up from either side by poles to be kept from caving in. Though their total valuation could not exceed ten dollars, the miners who had to live in them to get work were charged two dollars and fifty cents a month. Each shack contained two or three iron beds, a bureau, a stove, a wooden table and chairs; these constituted the worldly possessions of the families that worked in the mines year after year. As in the town of Pullman, he was accepted without distrust; people talked their hearts out to him because he was such a plain and simple cuss, looking and feeling like any other mechanic.

The average "composite" wage of a miner was said to be four hundred and eighty dollars a year; Darrow quickly learned that few actually earned this much.

"You paid three hundred outside men, who worked two hundred and forty-four days and over, between three hundred and four hundred dollars a year?"

"Yes. They are the laborers."

"But they are adults, are they not?"

"Yes."

"And you paid three hundred men who worked two hundred and sixteen days a year between two hundred and three hundred dollars a year?"

"Yes."

"Then," exclaimed Darrow, "what in hell is a composite man? Where does he go to draw his pay?"

All miners traded at the supply stores owned by the company or they lost their jobs, yet the company store charged from twelve to a hundred per cent above the sum charged by neighboring stores. What most outraged the miners was the practice of charging them two dollars and fifty cents a unit for the explosives necessary for their work and for which the company paid ninety cents, with a similar profit margin superimposed upon all other work equipment. Thus the operators made a profit not only from the miner's work, but from his wage as well, a practice known as "mining the miners." By such ingenious devices the miners, who were alleged to receive the "composite" wage of four hundred and eighty dollars a year, actually received the equivalent of about two hundred dollars' worth of house, food, clothing, coal and work supplies. This afforded them approximately twelve dollars a month on which to feed, clothe, medicate, educate, cultivate and make happy their families.

The companies had devised other subtle ways of "mining the miners." The contract men were paid a fixed sum for delivering a car of coal, but the companies kept increasing the size of the car without increasing the payment. The companies kept their own dockers to check on the quantity in any one car of slate or other waste, with no miners' inspectors allowed to be on hand and no protest possible; these dockers arbitrarily took as much payment out of the miner's wage as they saw fit. The men were paid once a month instead of the twice which the Pennsylvania law demanded; they were paid in lump sums, with no detailed accounts available. The firemen and pumpmen, who received a dollar seventy-five a day, worked a twelve-hour shift and twenty-four hours in a stretch every other Sunday, when the day and night shifts interchanged. They were not allowed off on the Fourth of July, Thanksgiving or Christmas; each year they worked three hundred and sixty-five days, except in leap year—when they worked three hundred and sixty-six.

Public schools were provided, but by the time the boys were eleven or twelve they had to climb to the breakers to earn their mite.

"As a school director of the city of Wilkes-Barre, what percentage of the school children that went to high school would you say were miners' children?"

"There was no percentage of miners' children," replied Mr Shea. "They got out before they got there."

The little girls could not be used in the mines, but the owners of textile mills, knowing that coal-mining areas were centers of poverty in which they could buy labor for a few pennies a day, set up their mills close to the mines and employed girls from ten years up. In this practice they were encouraged and aided by the railroads that owned the mines, because they could then get the textile business, sell their coal to the mills and, in addition, have the mills feed wages into the miners' families. *The girls were paid from three to seven cents an hour and worked a twelve-hour shift.*

What Darrow found in his researches in the Pennsylvania coal fields was a social philosophy in action. The operators, who wanted a large and docile supply of labor from which to choose their workers, contracted with steamship companies to send agents throughout central Europe to round up families on the promise of a good job and high wages in America, the golden land of opportunity. The eager immigrants were given "free" transportation, the fares being deducted from their subsequent wages, when they reached New York they were loaded onto coal cars and carted like cattle out to Pennsylvania, moved into a company shack and given credit at the "pluck-me" store. From that hour onward a large proportion of them were never out of debt to the company, bound to their jobs as the serfs had been bound to the earth, for any attempt to move on to another locality, another industry, meant imprisonment for skipping these debts. It was not uncommon for families to work from the beginning of the year to the end without ever receiving a dollar in cash.

George Baer proved himself to be a master at *reductio ad absurdum* when he said, "We refuse to submit to arbitration before the Civic Federation, because they are to decide not whether the wages paid are fair, but whether they are sufficient to enable the mine-workers to live, maintain and educate their families in a manner conformable to established American standards and consistent with American citizenship. More impractical suggestion was never formed. It would require many years of examination to determine just what those standards are and to determine whether it meant that a man should earn enough money to send his son to Yale or Harvard or to some modest college like Franklin and Marshall, where we keep down expenses."

To Darrow's emotional nature the crux and symbol of the strike lay in the story of Mrs Kate Burns, whose husband was killed in the mines and who could be given a Christian burial only because her neighbors each contributed a few nickels. Mrs Burns worked for six years as washerwoman and scrubwoman, "night and day," to keep her children in school. When the oldest boy was fourteen he went to work in the breakers.

"Did Mr Markle, the manager, give you any money or aid you in any way?"

"No sir, I never secured a cent, except from the miners."

"When your boy received his first check, how much did he receive?"

"When my boy returned home after receiving his check, like all other women who have met with adverse circumstances, I felt a sense of pride. But to my sorrow, instead of wages, I was notified for the first time that I owed the Markles three hundred and ninety-six dollars. It was stated on this check that the debt was due on back rent and coal. Two years later I placed a second boy at work, and for the last twelve years the little fellows have been trying to pay off the debt."

"Have they succeeded in doing so?"

"Yes sir."

"Did you receive a cent from the Markles during the last twelve years?"

"No sir, not one cent."

"Did Mr Markle ever tell you that you had to pay for the house or coal when you were able?"

"He never said a word. The matter was never mentioned in my presence."

Although the Markle mine had made a profit of one million, one hundred thousand dollars in five years, paying a dividend of forty-five per cent, when the Burns boy lost a leg in an explosion the company did not reduce the family debt by one penny but sent the boy back to the breaker as soon as his stump had healed. Such revelations of the inherent and blindly brutal greed of mankind made Darrow ill to his stomach; they led him to the conviction that it was as impossible to cross political democracy and economic oligarchy as it was to cross a horse with a cow: the result, if it could be brought to life at all, would be a monstrosity which could neither give milk nor pull a cart. Political democracy had to be bred to complete economic democracy so that no man could victimize his neighbor by the avarice and callousness so deeply rooted in human nature.

9

Though a number of the earlier mining families had come from Ireland, Wales and Germany, the greater portion of them now were central Europeans: Poles, Austrians, Hungarians, Slavs, Italians, who had made the difficult wrench from the homeland, from their friends and relatives, and had taken the plunge into the unknown to find a better life for themselves and their children. They were for the most part of good racial stock: hard working, independent; despite the fact that some of them had been at odds with the religious, political and economic structures of the country they had left, they were reverent and law abiding. A questioning of the operators revealed only a few complaints against the miners prior to the strike: they still wanted to take off too many of their European holidays; sometimes their propping was so hastily put up, in their scramble to get out the coal, that the roof collapsed and killed everybody under it. The operators did not appear to believe this negligence to be intentional; in fact, they rarely mentioned it, for it was a custom that the safety engineers never got around to inspection until after the accident had happened.

The hopes of these venturesome Europeans had been rudely blasted in the Pennsylvania coal mines, where life was harder, uglier, more bitter and more enslaved than the life they had come from. They had had no way of knowing that they had been imported for the very reason that they were accustomed to poverty, because they could subsist on the smallest possible quantities of food under the direst living conditions, because they could be worked hard for small wages.

"They don't suffer," cried George Baer indignantly when confronted with their plight; "why, they can't even speak English!"

By this charming *non sequitur*, Darrow ruminated, the basic problem was posed not only for Pennsylvania and its coal fields, but for every state and every industry in the land. Were the millions who poured in from Europe to become an integral and valuable part of our life; were they to enrich the country with their vigor, their independence, their courage, their native cultures, or were they to be kept as a half-starved, half-cowed human mudsill over which those who had pre-empted the status of Americans might walk into the house of civilization?

Darrow had been in Wilkes-Barre and the vicinity for only a few days when he perceived that something more than a wage strike was at issue in the coal fields. He determined to present this "something more" to the eagerly waiting public, to present the issue simply and clearly on its broadest sociological base: was it possible for America to become an authentic democracy, to achieve the hopes and promises of its founders, when millions of powerless ones were kept in bondage, forced backward through the centuries until they cowered on the very periphery of animal life? Was not democracy founded on individual justice, on a consideration of certain inalienable human rights? Could a free state continue to grow and prosper, achieve the national unanimity necessary for a nation to become strong and great, when it had a slave state eating at its vitals? Could cruelty and indifference exist harmlessly in a country whose motivating force had been co-operation and inter-responsibility? Or must it inevitably lead to an industrial-militarist state?

For Clarence Darrow the answer came almost immediately in the form of the Jeddo evictions. Like the docking of the young Pullman girl for the back rent owed by her dead father, which precipitated an unwilling American Railway Union into a sympathetic strike, and the quoting as precedent by Houghton, the prosecutor in the woodworkers' case, of the hundred-year-old instance of the man who had been convicted of the crime of writing a poem lauding

Thomas Paine and his *Rights of Man,* the Jeddo evictions proved a tactical blunder of catastrophic proportions for the perpetuation of this type of rapist capitalism.

Despite the promises of the operators to President Theodore Roosevelt that they would not refuse work during the arbitration to former employees on the grounds of union activities, "twelve men were selected from their fellows by John Markle as men whom he absolutely refused to re-employ at the close of the strike. No definite charge was made against any of these men, whose names sound like a cross cut of all the nations and creeds that helped found America: Nahi, Keenan, Poucun, Polack, Jacquot, Gallagher, Kanyeck, Coll, Dunleavy, Helferty, Demchock, Shovlin. At midnight Sheriff Jacobs was roused from his sleep by an agent of the Markles and told that the evictions must take place the next day.

"A cold drizzle set in early in the morning and continued at intervals until late in the afternoon, when a heavy rainstorm set in. It was almost seven o'clock when seven teams, owned by the Markle Company, set out, carrying non-union men to do the drudgery. They were attended by their armed escort, a company of militia equipped with rifles and a corps of heavily armed Coal and Iron police.

"The stroke was paralyzing in its suddenness. It caught everybody unprepared. To an appeal that was made by a tenant for a few hours' grace there came a curt refusal and an order to the sheriff to proceed immediately with the work. Houses were stripped bare of their poor furnishings. Women and little children, in spite of their pleadings and tears, were hurried out of the places that had been their homes. A bedridden woman, blind and more than ninety years old, was carried out into the storm. The wife of Henry Coll, a woman of fragile frame and of most delicate health, was not exempted from the rudeness of the evictors and the elements. As a direct consequence of the exposure and shock of that day, so says Henry Coll, she died soon after.

"It was evening when the work was done and the belongings of the last household on the list had been hauled from the village and dumped on the highway a quarter of a mile distant.

"Then we drove home with the teams."

"How far was it," asked Darrow, "from the place where these people's goods was dumped to the nearest place where they might rent houses?"

"Only about two and a half miles."

"It rained heavily that evening, did it not?"

"Yes, quite heavily."

"Do you know how many children, infants in arms or how many sick persons were among those you evicted?"

"No. I did not see any."

"Did you think of the people you had made homeless as the storm came up that night?" continued Darrow in a rage of scorn. "Did you think of their entire store of personal possessions exposed to the wind and the rain?"

The man who had helped with the evictions could find no answer, but deep in its heart the people of America found one, an answer compounded of pity and terror. "Suppose I were a man by the name of Coll," said laborers, mechanics, clerks, in every hamlet and every state, "and the people I worked for made me live in one of their houses. Suppose my wife was sick, and one night in a rainstorm they put us out—left my children without their mother . . . " "Suppose my name was Gallagher or Jacquot or Kanyeck," said doctors and teachers and merchants, "and the company I worked for put my old mother out into a storm . . . " "Suppose my name was Mrs Keenan or Mrs Demchock," said the housewives and mothers, "and I was in bad health—soldiers came into my house—put my furniture out in the rain—left me there to die . . . "

10

Side by side in nearly every miner's shack hung two unframed pictures: Jesus Christ, who would help them in the next world, and John Mitchell, who was helping them in this. Darrow was tickled to see how startlingly like himself, in a younger and smoother-faced version, John Mitchell looked: there was the fine hair parted from the left side and growing scant where the comb had left its tracks, the high and rounded brow, the clear, deep-set eyes, the aggressive nose and full-flowered mouth, the rounded slab chin—in all, a face as open as a department-store window display. Mitchell was only of medium height and build but, like most men of indomitable purpose and courage, gave an impression of being big and broad-framed; to an extent unknown to any labor leader before him, he enjoyed the respect and confidence of workers, government officials and the general public.

Standing in the shack of a Polish family, the cracks of its unplastered walls stuffed with newspapers to keep out the cold, Darrow gazed up at the picture of John Mitchell and mused that no man had more fully earned that respect or against more insuperable odds. Mitchell had come out of Braidwood, Illinois, the son of a bituminous-coal miner who himself went down into the mines at the age of thirteen. Like Eugene Debs, he had had a hankering for books and knowledge, had spent his spare hours studying, trying to understand the pattern of the world as he found it. He had joined the feeble and ineffective Knights of Labor; by the time he was seventeen he had so impressed his fellows with his forcefulness and understanding of the potential functions of a labor union that he was elected president of the local Knights. When he was twenty he was involved in the 1889 permanent lockout of striking bituminous miners at Spring Valley, Illinois. The strikers' families had suffered from hunger, cold and disease, a brutal tragedy having been averted only when Henry Demarest Lloyd, author of *Wealth against Commonwealth* and the only man in America brave enough to expose the depredations of Rockefeller's Standard Oil, arrived with carloads of food and medicine that had been subscribed in Chicago.

Heaping abuse on the heads of labor leaders was a popular sport of the day, but John Mitchell, who had three sons and a daughter and a tranquil home life in Spring Valley, escaped the torrent. He was not merely honest; he was incorruptible; he was fearless even in the face of the shocking brutality of the armed Coal and Iron police, and nearly everyone agreed that he was intensely devoted to the cause of the miners. No one accused him of posturing when, invited to become a political power by pledging his union's vote, he replied, "I would rather be able to take the little boys out of the breakers than name the next President of the United States." During the heat of the strike, when the operators were hurling brickbats at everyone from President Roosevelt down, the worst they could find to say against Mitchell was that, having come from the bituminous fields of Illinois to the anthracite fields of Pennsylvania, he was consequently an alien and unauthorized to speak for the anthracite miners; that he encouraged European aliens to violence against scabs and nonstrikers.

Mitchell's greatest asset was that he was a swift-thinking Irishman who could speak and write as forcefully as the lawyers hired by the operators: inestimable virtues in a labor leader. By 1895, when he was only twenty-six, he was elected secretary-treasurer of the Northern Illinois Mine Workers; by 1898 he had been elected national vice-president of the United Mine Workers. The elected president resigning a few months later, Mitchell became acting president until the 1899 convention, at which time he was elected president. When he took over the job his union was in much the same condition as Eugene Debs's Brotherhood of Locomotive Firemen when he had taken over that moribund organization: bankrupt, feeble, discredited. When he finished leading the strike which Clarence Darrow was now preparing to defend before the commission, he had welded a powerful union which was not only to work at peace with the operators, but which was to demonstrate the enduring value of partnership between management and labor.

Mitchell writes, "The spring of 1897 found the total number of members of the United Mine Workers reduced to less than nine thousand, there being practically nothing left of the organization in the anthracite field. The bituminous men again sought relief from their hard and grinding conditions in a general strike. After a stubbornly fought contest a compromise settlement was made which, while giving the miners only a slight advance, lent an impetus to the organization. In the following year joint conferences between miners and operators were re-established and comparative peace and prosperity assured."

Dealing with the railroad-owned anthracite mines was another matter, for the anthracite mines maintained a force of Coal and Iron police, armed and ever present, and so effective a black list that a man merely suspected of being interested in a union could never again find work for himself or his family. Nevertheless, the organizers succeeded in setting up a union structure and in holding a convention. The operators would not meet with the delegates to discuss a new scale of wages, because by so doing they would be acknowledging the existence of a union. Though the union had less than eight thousand members when it called the strike in 1900, over a hundred thousand men walked out. Because a presidential election was coming, Senator Hanna, chairman of the National Republican Committee, prevailed on the mineowners to compromise so that he could tell the country that everything was peaceful and friendly, and consequently another Republican ought to be elected as President.

This was the kind of political reasoning the operators could follow. They posted notices on the bulletin boards announcing a ten-per-cent raise in wages. Suspecting that the raise would be revoked the day after the election, the men refused to return to work. Under pressure from the Republican machine and its allied bankers and industrialists, the operators posted a second set of notices, agreeing to keep the ten-per-cent raise in effect for a year, to obey the law by paying wages semimonthly and to cut their charge for powder. The miners accepted. Though securing only a small fraction of their demands, they believed even this partial victory in the toughest labor field in America would bring into the union every man in the anthracite mines. It did.

The 1900 agreement was renewed in 1901; in 1902 the operators refused to grant any further agreements on the grounds that "there cannot be two masters in the management of business." A thirty-per-cent rise in the cost of living having wiped out the benefits of their raise, the miners now asked for a twenty-per-cent increase, an eight-hour day for outside men, their own dockers, no further extensions of the elastic-coal car, observance of the Pennsylvania law which made it illegal to force workers to buy at a company store, the recognition of their union. Taking a leaf from George Pullman, the operators repeated over and over, while the miners delayed their strike and used every possible means to gain a conference:

"We have nothing to arbitrate!"

John Mitchell called his strike.

With the approach of winter, after five months of rising coal prices for the consumers and relief kitchens for the miners, mass meetings were held throughout the country demanding that the operators yield to President Roosevelt's request for peaceful arbitration; the newspapers waged a brilliant war against the obstinacy of the owners; at length, as the New York *Evening Journal* put it, "The mineowners recognized the fact that coal must be produced to stop, if possible, the public clamor for legislation against the trust." At long last the operators had come to understand that the views of the country had been well expressed by Mrs John Lochner, herself the niece of a coal baron, when she wrote for the same paper:

"If for only a week these stubborn coal barons could be put in the miner's place and see his boy do the work the miner's boys do, he would be willing to give a helping hand to lift children out of such a life of toil and privation. The operators are the cause of a great national disaster brought on the poor of the country by the lightning grasp of monopoly."

The operators sent J. P. Morgan to the President with their acceptance of arbitration. The miners went back to work jubilantly, assured that all decisions of the commission would be retroactive to the day they began work. President Roosevelt named the able Carroll D. Wright, who had been chairman of the Senate Investigating Committee in the railroad strike, as secretary, then appointed a mining engineer, a brigadier general, a judge of the United States Circuit Court, the grand chief of the Order of Railway Conductors, the former owner of a coal mine and a Roman Catholic bishop to make up the committee. The operators named a panel of twenty-three attorneys who would present their case; the miners named

Clarence Darrow, James Lanahan and the O'Neil brothers, "well-equipped lawyers who had worked in the mines and were familiar with all the terminology as well as the method of work."

The commission went into the Pennsylvania coal fields to do some firsthand investigating; so did Darrow, Lanahan and the O'Neil brothers. On their first mine tour of inspection two members of the commission could stay down only an hour and twenty minutes because of the "uncomfortable conditions of the mine and the dampness." The committee reached the Clifford mine a few hours after a Hungarian had been killed by the falling of a roof. They were not told about the accident.

11

Preliminary hearings were held in Scranton, but the commission quickly adjourned to the Federal Courthouse in Philadelphia for the big show. The streets were thronged with visitors; newspapermen assembled from all over the world; the hotels and restaurants were jammed; the telegraph offices had to put on extra men and wires.

The United Mine Workers rented two floors of "a large Philadelphia residence on Vine Street that had been reconstructed for hotel purposes." Here they set to work a large and efficient staff of accountants, bookkeepers and researchers; Darrow was too sound an economist to make his appeal solely on the basis of the humanities. He set out to prove to the commission, and hence to the nation, one of his fundamental convictions, that economics can be not only an exact science, but is also the basic science by which a man's life is conditioned: his health, his longevity, his surroundings, the well-being of his family, his leisure, his education, cultivation, intelligence—the very freedom of his brain and body and spirit. If a "composite" workman cost the industry two hundred dollars a year, and after deducting the prorata cost of material, management and other overhead, this same composite worker returned to his industry a profit of a thousand dollars, where then was the economic necessity of keeping this workman on a subsistence level so low that his children had to be sent into the breakers and the textile mills?

This move to force industry to bring its books into the court of public opinion was for the mass of American working people almost as great a revolution as the one that had taken place in 1776. Up to this moment industry had been responsible to no one; it had been free not only to despoil the health and happiness of millions of its neighbors but also to plunder and squander the natural resources of the country, its timber, minerals, oil, earth. It had been free to mulct public funds, to absorb public savings by fraudulent manipulations and waterings of stock, to sponge up the wages of the eighty per cent of the people who worked for their living by monopoly-rocketing prices.

"God in His infinite wisdom," cried George Baer, when refusing to meet in the same room with union delegates, "has put the control of business into the hands of Christian gentlemen."

Darrow smiled sadly when he recalled another of the wistful little jokes the miners had made up to keep the anarchy of these Christian gentlemen endurable:

"Mother, why can't we buy any coal to heat our house?"

"Because the mines have shut down, dear, and Father is out of work."

"But why have the mines shut down, Mother?"

"Because people have no money to buy coal with."

The newspaper accounts broadcast to every crevice of the nation soon showed the public that this man Darrow was raising startlingly basic questions that they had never heard of before, revolutionary questions, really, going far beyond the immediate question of whether the miners were entitled to a raise. *Could the coal mines pay a living wage and still earn a sufficient profit to justify remaining in business? Which was of greater importance, to maintain a living wage for workers or a dividend for stockholders? When business fell off, which should be cut first, wages or dividends?* The very raising of such questions was anathema; once again vituperation was heaped upon Darrow's head, while the slowly awakening people stood aghast, waiting for the answers.

Management said, "We must maintain dividends or capital will flee the industry. We will then have to shut down, and labor will lose its work. Therefore, it is a natural economic law that wages must be cut to maintain dividends, and we are powerless to change that law. Labor has no risk and no stake. The responsibility is solely ours, and we aim to protect our industry against depression, falling prices, scarcity of money."

Labor replied, "If dividends, bonuses and managerial salaries are kept at a feasible level, if stock is not watered and account books corrupted, then industry can put aside sufficient reserves to protect itself should capital momentarily flee. American industry has earned billions, and billions more have been reinvested; they do not need to scrape their security from the hides of their workers. The life of an industry rarely depends on a ten-per-cent raise in a standard of living; it is not so feeble or sickly as all that, particularly when that ten or twenty per cent is immediately spent for goods and hence returned to industry. The loss of a portion of a dividend on hard-earned and honestly invested savings is unfortunate, but not half so unfortunate as the hunger, cold, illness, suffered by the millions who are deprived of the barest necessities of life. Industry can make good the loss of a dividend when the cycle swings upward again, but what can ever make good those horrible hours of privation and shattering fear, so irretrievably lost and yet so essential to the well-being of a nation?"

Darrow had been able to demonstrate in both the Pullman and Paine cases that a raise in wages would have made but a slight diminution in the profits earned year after year, a diminution which would have been offset by a stronger, healthier, happier and hence more loyal working force. Was this not even more true in the coal fields where supervision was impossible? A secure, healthy labor force must help build a prosperous nation, but the coal barons weren't interested in anything so abstract or unremunerative as a nation. Their job was to get out as much coal as they could at the lowest possible cost and then sell it at the highest possible price.

Mr Baer asked, "Are you going to increase the rate of wages and attract still more people there to sit down and wait in the hope of getting enough money in a day to support them for a year?"

This was a sophistry made to order for Darrow's lampooning humor. Newspapers rang with headlines and streamers: OPERATORS' MISLEADING TABLES RIDDLED BY MINERS' ATTORNEY. DARROW EXPOSES WAGE STATEMENTS. BAD DAY FOR OWNERS.

"Even the most devoted adherents to the cause of the operators at the close of yesterday's session admitted that the miners had scored heavily and often," said the Philadelphia *North American* on January 14, 1903. "To unprejudiced observers the discomfiture of the witnesses for the operators had the appearance of a rout. Under the raking fire of Mr Darrow's cross-examination the general sales agent of the Delaware and Hudson Company was so entangled in his own figures that he finally preferred silence to explanation. This was after he had testified that the company received no more for coal now than it did a year ago; this in the face of his previous testimony that the same-sized coal that a year ago brought two seventy-five a ton at the mines now brings as high as six dollars a ton delivered in the city of Carbondale, which is near some of the Delaware and Hudson mines."

"What average did you put down there that the miners got in Indian Ridge?" Darrow demanded of a company comptroller.

"Five hundred and fifty-six dollars."

"How many miners got above that?"

"Twenty."

"How many got less?"

"Four hundred and seventy-six."

"Then there are only four per cent of the men in Indian Ridge colliery who got as much money as you set down as the average earnings of the whole colliery? And ninety-six per cent got less? Is not that true?"

"I presume it is."

The *North American* again reported on January thirty-first, "From J. P. Jones, chief paymaster of the Philadelphia and Reading Coal and Iron Company, Mr Darrow drew admissions concerning the computations of averages that seriously damaged the cases of all the operators. This much was admitted even by the attorneys for the operators at the close of the session."

"Mr Jones, you were asked specifically by the commission for statistics of seven collieries. Three of those as you understand it were those showing higher wage earnings; two were lower ones, and one was somewhere near the middle. Is not that so?"

"Mr Darrow, I am frank to say to you that I did not take into consideration when the names of the collieries were furnished to me what their averages showed."

"You know about the one that you dropped out?"

"Yes sir."

"I do not mean to insinuate that you dropped it out for that purpose, but the one that you dropped out . . ."

"I believe it shows the less average."

"It is one of the very lowest?"

"Yes sir."

"And the three that you put in its place were three of the very highest wage scales, were they not?"

"Well, that I really do not know. . . ."

Always it had been known that big business corrupted politicians in order to use the resources and processes of government for its own ends; it had been known that big business combined and conspired illegally to wipe out its competitors; it had been known that industries established monopolies in order to control supply, service, quality, price; yet the great body of people had condemned these practices only mildly. They were manifestations of the peculiar American genius, of the shrewdness and cleverness that had built the nation to such grandiose mechanical proportions in so short a time; and withal they were a little proud. But that billion-dollar industry should stoop to such petty trickeries as doctoring wage scales to prevent a possible raise—that was a blow to the pride of the American people.

Darrow succeeded in so incensing the commissioners that Judge Grey flared out at Markle's accountant over the debt of Mrs Kate Burns: "Of all things in the world, the worst is to get hold of a professional accountant who will not see anything unless it is a column of figures with debit and credit at the top. Who does know about this indebtedness? It is obvious this witness does not!" As a gesture of protest, the commissioners sent Christmas baskets to the widows who were still paying on coal and rent debts incurred ten years before.

12

Under Darrow's method of gently leading witnesses as he would a horse to the watering trough, hundreds of persons from every walk of life paraded before the commission. First he brought on the crippled and maimed and sick miners to testify about conditions in the mines, then doctors to verify their plight with evidence on industrial diseases, eliciting trenchant dialogue that projected the listeners into the heart and brain of the stricken.

"Are you a miner?"

"Yes sir."

"How much do you earn every two weeks?"

"I make from five dollars, sometimes ten dollars, maybe once or twice in the year twenty dollars, in two weeks."

"What vein are you working in?"

"The parlor vein."

"How thick is the coal there?"

"Two and one half feet bony coal."

"How is the air there?"

"Pretty bad."

"What do you mean by bad? Do you have headaches?"

"Yes sir, made me sick in the eyes and the head too."

"Now, John, go on and describe what effect the bad air had on you."

"About two weeks ago I had to go down about sixty yards in a gangway without any light, no lamp, no matches to burn."

"How did you work there?"

"I worked in the breast and had to stay home sometimes three days."

"Why did you stay home?"

"Could not work; there was no air."

"Did you ever see a mine inspector?"

"I worked ten years for Pardee, and I never seen the mine in-spector inside."

Aware that the hearing was going against them, the operators made a flanking movement, attacking from a tangent: the unions were organizations of violence and lawlessness, hence the miners didn't need a raise and weren't justified in demanding one. Suddenly the hearing flashed into focus, stripped of its evasions, pretenses and verbiage: the operators were only mildly concerned over a possible raise in wages; their purpose was to destroy the United Mine Workers and unionism.

"We deny," declared T. P. Fowler, president of the Scranton Coal Company and the Elkshill Coal and Iron Company, "that union of workingmen tend to better the discipline of the men and to the improvement of their physical, mental or moral conditions and to the preservation of friendly relations between employer and employee."

A separate group of lawyers was engaged by the operators to represent the non-union men of the coal fields. These men told how they had been beaten up by union men when they tried to go to work, how their families had been intimidated and boycotted, stones thrown through the windows of their homes. Darrow sat with his chin on his chest as he listened to these stories, for in spite of Mitchell's constantly reiterated plea that "the person who violates the law is the worst enemy the strikers could have," hotheads among the hundred and fifty thousand strikers had used their fists, clubs and stones to keep other men from working.

Nor was it the first time that there had been bloodshed in the Pennsylvania coal fields. From 1867 through the bitter strike of 1875, years in which a depression had reduced wages to six dollars a week for a twelve-hour day, the Irish members of the Ancient Order of Hibernians, whose ancestors under the name of the Molly Maguires had fought evictions from the English landlords in Ireland in 1843, founded the American version of the Mollies in the six anthracite counties. A secret organization, their members first worked co-operatively to beat up and run out of the state strikebreakers who had been imported by the Coal and Iron police. Since violence, like a narcotic, must be used in increasingly larger doses to achieve similar results, the Mollies began overturning coal cars, injuring bridges, committing acts of vandalism against collieries where they had been badly treated, beating up mine superintendents who fired or mistreated members of their organization. As the range of their terrorism grew they attracted an element of the illiterate

Irish who loved force for its own sake, often petty criminals rather than workingmen or miners. Several superintendents were found mysteriously slain; the gangsters and terrorists came to control the Ancient Order of Hibernians, whose original purpose had been to "promote friendship, unity and true Christian charity among the members and to raise a fund of money for maintaining the aged, sick, blind and infirm members."

To destroy the Mollies, the president of the Philadelphia and Reading Coal and Iron Company called in Allan Pinkerton, able head of the first private-detective agency in America, which had done good work in capturing criminals who operated across state lines before the days of either Federal or state police. Pinkerton had been instrumental in smuggling Abraham Lincoln through Baltimore when a plot was revealed to assassinate him in that city, prior to his inauguration; had served the Union by supplying a spy service against the South during the Civil War; had helped the city of Chicago organize its first police force. His former functions having been largely absorbed by governmental agencies, Allan Pinkerton was now working for private industry to combat the unions which were springing up throughout the land.

To smash the Mollies, Pinkerton selected a twenty-nine-year-old Irish Catholic by the name of James McParland, whom he currently had working as a streetcar conductor, for McParland had the honor of being one of America's first "labor spies." He had been sent by Pinkerton to join with the streetcar men to secure a list of those active in forming the union, so that they could be fired, and to sabotage any union that might get started in spite of the firings. Disguised as a poor and shabby laborer, McParland now went into the Pennsylvania coal fields, made friends with the Irish miners by his jolly singing and playing of the guitar, his handy manner with his fists, the steady flow of drinks he bought with money which he alleged he got by counterfeiting. He ingratiated himself with the Mollies and after a year was taken into their secret organization, where he worked himself up to the position of general secretary. When he was at last discovered to be a detective he fled, and murder charges were brought against the leading Mollies of the six counties. The leading witnesses against the men were James McParland, who claimed he never knew of the murders in advance but always heard of them immediately afterward, and a self-confessed murderer by the name of Kerrigan, whom McParland persuaded to turn state's evidence on the promise of immunity. With Kerrigan's testimony McParland succeeded in getting four Mollies "of good reputation" hung for the killing of one Yost, a man whom Kerrigan had confessed murdering only a few hours after he had killed the man—and his wife, the mother of his children, so testified in the trials.

In all McParland succeeded in getting fourteen men hanged, some of whom were guilty, some innocent. The only authoritative book in the field says, after a scholarly review of the evidence, "That many of the convicted Molly Maguires were not labor leaders and that some of them were murderers was established by the statements of the prisoners themselves. There is still, however, considerable importance to be attached to the manner in which a militant organization of workingmen, of one nationality and one religion, was dispersed by the execution of its leaders for murder, following prosecutions conducted by lawyers in the employ of the leading corporations in the region." As for McParland, "working for a firm that specialized in spying upon organized labor and in combatting labor in the interests of the employing class, his activities in the Pennsylvania coal fields were partially, if not primarily, devoted to this end."

As a reward for his services, James McParland was promoted to the head of the Pinkerton agency in Denver, Colorado, where the hard-rock miners were making their first efforts to organize. Here McParland remained for thirty years, until he tangled with Clarence Darrow in another murder charge against miners—a charge whose purpose once again was to hang the leaders and hence destroy the Western Federation of Miners.

13

The problem of the scab and non-union worker presented one of America's most nearly insoluble dilemmas: what were the millions of workingmen who were willing to suffer the privations of a strike and risk of black list, to deny their families the necessities of life in order to better their lot for the future, to do about their neighbors who were too timid or too frightened or too brutalized to care about bettering the lot of their families, particularly since these men who continued to work would share equally in the advantages gained by the sacrifices of their fellows? America was a free country; a man had a right to join a union or not, as he saw fit; he had a right to join a strike or not, as he saw fit. It was as bad for a union to use force to make him join their ranks and their strike as it was for the operators to use force to keep men from joining a union or a strike. Yet Darrow felt impelled to agree with John Mitchell that "a man who works during a strike has no moral right to work if his work destroys the hopes and aspirations of his fellow men."

The operators charged union men with rioting against state troops; Darrow countered by putting Mitchell on the stand and dramatizing for the country the now-infamous "Shoot to kill!" order given by General Gobin to stop the small boys from throwing rocks at the troops as they marched through coal towns. "Darrow and Mitchell made a colorful, aggressive combination," commented a newspaper reporter at the hearing. "Both had excellent news sense. Darrow was particularly alive to dramatic opportunities in the presentation of evidence."

"Sheriff," said Mitchell, "isn't it true that whenever you reported any trouble in Lackawanna County to me I sent a committee of mineworkers and officers of the union with you to assist you in restoring order?"

"I believe that is true."

"Did you issue a call for the second contingent of troops that arrived in Lackawanna County?"

"No sir, I did not."

"Who did?"

"I don't know. I guess the governor took it upon himself to send them."

"We have heard repeatedly about the reign of terror in Lackawanna County. Do you consider that such a state of affairs existed? Would you say that there was at any time general lawlessness?"

"No, I can't say that I would."

"Didn't you tell me on several occasions when I asked you about the disturbances that the lawbreakers were few in number and that all the trouble was created by a comparatively small contingency of men?"

"That is true."

Mitchell having shown that since the sheriff had not asked for the troops, they had been sent in illegally, Darrow now made clear how it followed that responsibility for the deaths of the two workmen and two troopers who were killed in the clashes fell directly on the shoulders of the governor and not the workmen. For the first time the public was presented with a graph to clarify the technique of strikebreaking: the history of strikes in America established that when no disorder arose it was a profitable investment for the employers to bring in Pinkertons, scabs and deputies to incite fights, riots and the destruction of a small amount of property in order to alienate the sympathy of the press, the public and the courts and "put down the anarchists."

"Shoot to kill!" General Gobin had ordered his troops.

"Shoot to kill—whom?" asked a badly frightened citizenry. "The people of Pennsylvania? Is this a war?"

Darrow finger-combed the veil of brown hair away from his right eye and patted the cigarette ashes into the gray material of his coat with his other hand before turning to George Baer as his greatest asset in the hearing. Often in the past he had complained that words were only wax bullets; in the mouth of Mr Baer they became stench bombs.

"The unions are corrupting the children of America," cried Baer, "by letting them join their illegal organizations."

Darrow was on his feet like a thunderbolt.

"If the children had not been at work in the mines they could not have joined the union!"

Explaining to the commission that capital could not share its management with labor because "God in His infinite wisdom had bequeathed the management of industry to Christian gentlemen," Baer evolved another phrase which, along with his other two, became for the American workman counterparts of those rallying phrases of the Revolution "No taxation without representation" and "The British are coming."

"We cannot interfere," proclaimed the patriarchal-bearded Baer, "with the divine right of stockholders."

From the clergy arose the cry: "We'll thank you not to drag in the name of the Lord to justify your evil practices," and sermons demanding that "the trusts be busted and the country given back to the people" were preached in edifices from the clapboard shanty to the great stone cathedral.

To Darrow these phrases fell like manna. For centuries the rulers of Europe had built their thrones upon the phrase, "the divine right of kings," persuading their people that God had appointed them their rulers, that any hand raised against a king was a hand raised against God, that all protest was fruitless, for God would protect the kings he had appointed and destroy all those who opposed them. How much innocent blood had been spilled, how many millions of lives destroyed, how many more millions of souls condemned to the chains of ignorance, brutal labor, starvation, before the people had come to learn that the divine right of kings was a fiction designed to keep them in slavery; before they had risen in their might to thrust aside the deceptive phrases and deceptive rulers and given themselves a republican form of government? The nineteenth century had dissipated the divine right of kings. What was to be the fate of the divine right of stockholders in the twentieth?

14

After two months the hearings came to a close; each side girded its loins for the final appeal. Darrow slipped away from his comrades and walked alone to his hotel, but he felt too low even to wash or comb his hair. He wandered the streets aimlessly for an hour before entering a workingman's restaurant, his gorge so high in his throat over the fears, uncertainties and anxieties of the morrow that he sat slumped in the hard wooden chair, unable to swallow a bite of the food before him. He had worked hard; he had worked well; he felt that victory would ultimately come to his cause, yet just before he launched himself on one of the greatest single efforts of his life he was seized by a shattering depression. The hearings had forced him to the heartbreaking conclusion that, left to its own devices and its own conscience, industry's alleviation of the evils it had itself created went forward with the speed of a worm burrowing through a stone wall. It was during this unguarded moment that he engaged in his first conflict with John Mitchell. The publicity adviser for the miners tells the story of a quarrel that night in Darrow's hotel room.

"The publishers of the *North American* had been asked by counsel for the operators to print in full their closing arguments, for which they offered to pay a dollar a line. Darrow and Mitchell agreed to this proposition, providing Darrow's argument would be printed in full without charge to the mine workers. Mitchell then asked Darrow to outline the argument he was going to make to the commission.

"Darrow, with occasional references to brief notes, proceeded with his outline. For about fifteen minutes he spoke, outlining the background of labor's struggles in America. Mitchell became more and more irritated and nervous as the recital proceeded. Finally he interrupted:

" 'Darrow, what you are proposing to do is to make a socialistic speech to the commission.'

"Darrow flared angrily.

" 'I propose, Mr Mitchell, to argue in the manner I believe to be most effective.'

" 'And I tell you, Darrow,' said Mitchell, 'that this whole case must be argued upon the testimony that has been produced. I want an increase in wages and better living and working conditions as

soon as I can get them. I'm not interested in the development of
your private theories which may come into effect many years
hereafter.'

" 'I am attorney for the United Mine Workers,' said Darrow, 'and
I will argue this case according to what I believe to be their best
interests.'

" 'You are wrong, Darrow, about your employer. You are attorney for John Mitchell, because in this case John Mitchell is the
United Mine Workers' organization.'

" 'What do you propose to do if I refuse to argue your way?'

" 'That's easy,' replied Mitchell; 'I will tell the commission that
we have disagreed upon a question of policy in the final argument.
I will argue the case myself.'

"They glared at each other. Then Darrow realized that he had
been wrong and backed down.

" 'Have it your way, John,' he said."

The next morning the final pleas were opened. In honor of the
occasion Darrow donned a long frock coat, a starched white shirt
and a black bow tie whose ends dangled down to the lapelled vest.
News that he was to speak crowded the courtroom to the side walls,
with thousands of disappointed spectators standing in the hallways,
the lobby, on the outside steps and in the street. Millions the world
over waited in anxiety, fear and hope, for his voice became the
voice of every man, woman and child who toiled for his daily
bread. After his death one of his intimates said of him, "He was a
comet but not a star," yet those who heard him make his plea for
struggling humanity declare him to have been as great in these
hours as it is possible for one man to be great, for one man to be a
star. The transcript of this plea bears them out: it is lyrical, profoundly beautiful; it cuts deep; it cuts true; it rings with mordant
wit, with coruscating passion and the revitalizing vision of a better
life. Though each year thousands of volumes are published, Darrow's social document, worthy of the Gettysburg Address tradition,
has never been printed and is nowhere obtainable except in the few
remaining back files of crumbling newspapers.

S. P. Wolverton fired the final salvo for his twenty-two legal
colleagues by a "sand-in-the-eyes technique" of avoiding the consequences of the elicited testimony. "Who demands the shortening
of the hours of labor?" demanded Mr Wolverton. "Is it the strong,
industrious, ambitious young man who desires to succeed in the
race for life, or is it the indolent theorist? The young man who has
his own fortune to make has no time for theory. One who inherits
a fortune or has it thrust upon him by some kind testator has time

to theorize upon sociological problems, but to the young man who has his fortune to make for himself [on the breakers?] life is real. Great care should be taken in making any raise in wages that the laborer himself is not injured. There are limits beyond which wages cannot be increased in any business without injury to the laborers themselves."

George Baer, in closing for the operators, won the sympathy of the commission and of many of the listeners by a well-thought-out statement: "These are problems that the 'antediluvian' captains of industry in these days must consider—how to increase the wealth of the community you are serving by increasing its prosperity—because only in that way can you add to your revenues; how to return to your stockholders a just payment for the money they have invested, and how to give honest wages, fair and full wages to the men you employ. These are burdens. You may think they are light, but to the man who is charged with responsibility they become terrible realities."

Then after a penetrating defense of the historical role of capitalism in which "the individual was given free scope within the sound rule of law to exercise all the powers he possessed to improve his condition and advance himself in life," which earned him further deserved plaudits, Baer launched into the more practical and concrete business of thwarting the miners' demands. "There are some trades where eight hours is enough, but there ought to be no limitation on work in the collieries. Who has ever refused to bargain? Every day in the mines bargains are made with the men. Is there a man incapable of bargaining for himself? It takes two to make a bargain. We offer them work and we tell them what we will give, and they say what they are willing to take for it, and an agreement is made between man and man, and he goes to work and works honestly on that contract. The man works contentedly and receives his pay, and that system, we are told, is one-sided and slavery. Who enslaves the men? There is plenty of work in the country."

15

On the afternoon of the third day Darrow rose to speak for the workers, and a hush fell over the courtroom. He stood in the silence for a moment, his face lined, his eyes somber, the fugitive clump of hair falling over his right eye, fully conscious of the burden he had now to carry. "As he started to speak a young lawyer deferentially handed him a bulky sheaf of notes, but he impatiently waved the man aside. Squaring his hulking shoulders and swinging his long arms before him, he delivered his address." He spoke for about seven hours. Though only a few paragraphs of this all but lost document can be given here, they deserve to be re-created so that the reader may hear them just as they came from the lips and heart of Clarence Darrow on that distant and yet immediately present day in February 1903.

"This hearing, coming after the long and bitter siege, looked to me from afar as though it would be bitter too. I felt as I was coming here that I would do all in my power to make the feeling less bitter than it was. I felt that I did not wish to go away from this region and feel that I had stirred up dissension, instead of bringing closer together the two rival parties so that they might live together in that peace and harmony in which it was meant that all men should dwell together on earth.

"But I find myself at the closing in a position where I have to take very good care that all my good resolutions do not go for nought. I have listened to the arguments of counsel for the operators; much that is vituperation, much that is abuse, much that is bitterness, much that is hatred, much that could not have come from a brain that sees widely and largely and understands fully the acts of man. I have heard my clients, one hundred and forty-seven thousand workmen who toil while other men grow rich, men who have little to hope for, little to think of excepting work—I have heard these men characterized as assassins, as brutes, as criminals, as outlaws, unworthy of the respect of men and fit only for the condemnation of courts.

"I am not here to say that these eminent gentlemen are not as good as other men, are not as kindly as other men, are not as just as other men. I think they have been deceived by their doctors—doctors of figures. It needs nothing to shake down the unsubstantial fabric of our civilization and to make it fall about our heads, except to raise wages in the anthracite region, and then civilization is doomed, for another aeon, at least. A shortening of hours, a raising of wages, a changing of conditions, and all that we have striven for and hoped for and toiled for is lost.

"If the civilization of this country rests upon the necessity of leaving these starvation wages to these miners and laborers, or if it rests upon the labor of these little boys who from twelve to fourteen years of age are picking their way through the dirt, clouds and dust of the anthracite, then the sooner we are done with this civilization and start anew, the better for the humanities. I do not believe that the civilization of this country and the industry of the East depends upon whether you leave these men in the mines nine hours or ten hours, or whether you leave these little children in the breakers. If it is not based on a more substantial basis than that, then it is time that these captains of industry resigned their commission and turned it over to some theorists to see if they cannot bring ruin and havoc a good deal quicker.

"This demand for eight hours is not a demand to shirk work, as is claimed in this case. It is a demand for the individual to have a better life, a fuller life, a completer life. I measure it from the standpoint of the man, from the standpoint that the interests of the government, the interests of society, the interests of law and all social institutions is to make the best man they can. That is the purpose of every lawmaking power. It is the purpose of every church. It is the purpose of every union. It is the purpose of every organization that ever had the right to live since the world began. There is only one standpoint from which you have the right to approach this question, and that is, what will make the best man, the longest life, the strongest man, the most intelligent man, the best American citizen, to build up a nation that we will be proud of. Whenever he has turned his attention to improving his condition man has been able to do it.

"The laborer who asks for shorter hours asks for a breath of life; he asks for a chance to develop the best that is in him. It is no answer to say, 'If you give him shorter hours he will not use them wisely.' Our country, our civilization, our race, is based on the belief that for all his weaknesses there is still in man that divine spark that will make him reach upward for something higher and better than anything he has ever known."

16

When the applause had died down the commission retired to pore over its ten thousand pages of evidence. On Saturday, March 21, 1903, the awards were published. America spent its week end knee-deep in economics. All contract miners were given a ten-per-cent raise and by means of a sliding scale were to benefit from increased coal prices when they went over four dollars and fifty cents a ton. Engineers and pumpmen were put on an eight-hour day, with Sundays off. Company employees were put on a nine-hour day. The miners were permitted to have their own docking bosses and weighmen; the operators had to give a detailed accounting, and any increase in the size of the coal car had to be accompanied by a corresponding increase in wages. Though the commission put no restrictions on the company store, though they soundly castigated the union for the acts of violence on the part of its members and failed to concede that the rate of pay was so low that miners' children were forced into the breakers at a tender age, the decision was an almost solid victory for the United Mine Workers.

To carry out the awards, which were to extend for three years, the commission set up a six-man board of conciliation to handle all disputes. No suspension of work could take place by lockout or strike pending the adjudication of any matters under dispute. President Roosevelt had conceded to the operators that the final award would not include compulsory recognition of the United Mine Workers, but since the union was to be a party to the six-man board, it had received its recognition in fact if not in name. It was a tremendous step forward for unionism, perhaps the greatest in American history.

To no one's astonishment civilization was not destroyed by the award, nor did American industry collapse. Miners and operators worked together in comparative peace for many years; the miners turned out as much or more coal than they had under the longer hours, and the operators made as much and more profit.

Darrow's part in this victory was widely acclaimed. Eager to prove that the prophet was no longer without honor in his own country, Chicago bestowed upon him the greatest honor in its possession: he was asked to become Mayor Darrow!

Spectators and participants in these hearings maintain that Darrow's handling of the case was one of the most magnificent performances they had ever witnessed. When the commissioners, in the midst of some heated argument, wanted figures they could trust they had turned to Darrow who, with no mathematical training, had analyzed and committed to memory hundreds of statistical charts, tables and groups of figures. Francis Wilson, who went to Philadelphia to be with him, reports that "all the attorneys engaged in the trial had a very high opinion of him; there was a feeling of admiration for this man who was dominating the entire proceeding. His memory was so keen that often when questions of fact arose as to what had occurred previously even the commission would refer to Darrow for the answer. In addition to his ability as a cross-examiner and his power as an advocate, he created a friendly atmosphere which was more seductive than antagonistic. He obtained most of his results, both among the lawyers and of the members of that tribunal, by reason of his friendly persuasiveness."

The accolade of supremacy in his field was draped about his shoulders toward the end of the hearing when, telling how the operators had all the advantages, he said, "Their social advantages are better; they speak the English language better; they can hire expert accountants; they have got the advantage of us in almost every particular," and Judge Grey, glancing over at the battery of twenty-three corporation counsels, murmured with a faint smile: "Except the lawyers!"

CHAPTER VI

Can a Lawyer Be an Honest Man?

Chicago was beautiful in early April. The first tight green buds were swelling on the maples and oaks in Lincoln Park, and Lake Michigan lay blue and vast as an ocean, high and white-capped near the shore. The air had been washed clean by the rains and softened by falling snow; it had that brisk yet soft tang that told of a winter just departed. If one chanced to gaze out of a tenth-story window the dark haze of the Michigan horizon could be discerned sixty miles to the east.

South of the city there was a long green sward which had been the Midway of the Exposition of 1893, on one side of which the new University of Chicago was rising in stone piles. Here Clarence and Ruby walked hand in hand while he watched the brittle spring sunlight fire her auburn hair. In Jackson Park along the lake there was a delicate Japanese bridge over a lagoon and a colorful pagoda where they rested and talked of life and love, then sat in comradely quiet with the rejuvenating warmth on their faces. It was good to be home again, to have Ruby near him, to watch her eyes sparkle when he told one of his childish jokes.

He cursed his folly for having allowed himself to be elected to the legislature, but since that august body had already been in session for several weeks he had to content himself with a three-day vacation. He packed a small handbag with some extra shirts and socks and an enormous portmanteau of books and left for Springfield. The town seemed lonely and forlorn to him now that John Altgeld was gone. During those hours when he did not have to be in the assembly chamber he would lie fully dressed on his hotel bed to read Joseph Conrad, Lecky, Westermarck.

"Often when I went down to the assembly room," writes Darrow of his state-legislature days, "I would find an array of letters and telegrams on my desk. Looking at the grist, I could say without opening them, 'Now here's another bill that I must help kill; no bill on behalf of the people could muster so many friends.'"

The confidence games of the professional politician revolted him. Some of the legislators who were passing laws to lengthen the lists of criminal acts were at the same time proposing regulatory measures against the railroads and telegraph companies for the sole purpose of having the corporations buy them off. When legitimate control bills were introduced legislators went to the corporations with their hats in their hands for bribe money, in return for which they would vote against the socially necessary legislation. It was impossible for him to compare the venality of a crime against society, such as the taking of a bribe from industry to enable it to continue its excesses, with the crime against an individual, such as a holdup; the latter injured one person or small group of persons, the former injured the entire state and weakened the fabric of self-government.

"I soon discovered that no independent man who fights for what he thinks is right can succeed in legislation. He can kill bad bills by a vigorous fight and publicity, but he can get nothing passed. Among the bills that I always tried to kill, and with good success, were laws increasing penalties and creating new crimes."

However, he did his bit to help pass the Child Labor and Municipal Ownership bills and did succeed in putting over a few important measures: a law raising the limit of recovery for deaths caused by negligence from five thousand to ten thousand dollars, a blessing to the families of workingmen; one to furnish constructive employment within prisons to inmates who were decaying in their cells after having been rescued from the barbaric custom of being leased out to private contractors.

By April of 1903, having spent three months on the anthracite case and another three months in Springfield, his Chicago law practice had pretty well evaporated. After the death of Governor Altgeld the firm had been foreshortened to Darrow and Thompson; it was further foreshortened when Thompson resigned because "he had married the daughter of the owner of considerable Loop property and desired to devote his time exclusively to the management of that property." Darrow now found himself not only without a business, but without a firm. As a consequence he formed a partnership with Edgar Lee Masters, which was to result in the only tragic relationship of his life.

They met through the accident of having offices on the same
floor in the Ashland Block; Masters was apparently doing badly
in his partnership with Kickham Scanlan, for Mrs Darrow reports
that when she first visited the Masters family they had a "first-floor
apartment in a poor locality; cheaply, scantily furnished." It is
difficult to imagine a sharper contrast between two men: Darrow
despised the human race but loved people; Masters loved humanity
but hated people. Darrow was warm, informal, generous, tolerant,
lovable; Masters was cold, intellectual, brittle, self-centered. Darrow admired Masters' objective legal mind and piercing briefs;
sensing that their natures complemented each other, the two men
agreed to try a partnership. In the breast of the firm of Darrow
and Masters there was now harbored the wrecks of two poets.

2

In July Clarence and Ruby were married by Mayor Dunne in
the home of John Gregg. Darrow's friends were thoroughly
shocked at this apostasy by a man who had been preaching the
virtues of free love and damning the confining influences of marriage; the few who had been deterred from marriage by his eloquence were perhaps justifiably piqued. Many wondered why a man
who loved his freedom so passionately had wanted to marry at all;
others wondered why, if he must marry, he should choose Ruby
Hamerstrom; still others decided that he had made a wise choice.

The couple went to Europe for a two and a half months' honeymoon "through Holland, Germany, France, Switzerland, dawdling
and happy, up and down countless Alps, over mountain passes,
through interminable tunnels and over the Channel back to England." While on this trip he wrote *Farmington*, the recounting of
his childhood in Farmdale and Kinsman. The story is told with
incisive, delicious humor, with a keen but tolerant eye for the foibles
of humanity; it is written with what George Francis calls "his
genius for the precise phrase" and Fay Lewis terms "his natural
poetic rhythms." *Farmington*, now an American classic which has
gone through many editions, is perhaps the only one of his dozen
books which achieves the artistic symmetry and perfection for
which he longed.

Mrs Darrow says, "He was well past the middle when we paused
at Zermatt; he wrote at the window, looking out at the Matterhorn,
but at the same time he would be plying his pencil like lightning
over his paper. He continued to write on it in Geneva, while sight-
seeing, finishing the manuscript in Paris. More than anything else

he dreamed of someday being able to retire, to travel more and to write. He loved writing! He delighted in losing himself and forgetting all the world over some little story like those in *Easy Lessons in Law*, though many of these were spun off in haste, through the weary late hours at home when he should have been resting and sleeping. Often he would reproach himself for having let some article or story go to press without being rewritten, without considering it well done, but he felt that his meaning was more important than correctness of wording, and what he wanted was that his viewpoint reach the public."

The Darrows returned to Chicago in mid-September. Francis Wilson was dispossessed at the Langdon Apartments, so that the couple might have a place to live, but before long Ruby had "found an apartment on Sheridan Road, more suitable and roomy and less embedded in the soot of the west-side manufacturing." Darrow's entertaining had been informal; when he had invited a lot of people to take supper with him he would say to the waiter, "Bring enough beefsteak and potatoes for the crowd, and if anybody doesn't like it they're out of luck."

Ruby changed all this. "We brought home with us the Sheffield steel, ivory-handled knives and forks, bought at the plant, that he had always wanted and the white metal spoons that polished like silver. We served caviar as appetizer, delicious soups, meats, potatoes, desserts, almonds done in olive oil, after-dinner coffee in tea-sized cups. There were daintily colored and arranged bonbons, fine liqueurs in most enticing Old World glasses, exquisitely cut finger bowls on cut-glass saucers, either a low, large bouquet or low, wide bowl of many-colored fruits, usually decorated with glowing cherries or strawberries dotted in among green geranium leaves."

Ruby Hamerstrom had taken to herself no small task when she took on Clarence Darrow as husband, but she was more than equal to the task. "He had a limited taste for foods and an incurable aversion to things that most people consider the choicest. He never ate fowl or lamb or veal or onions or cabbage, while celery, tomato, radish, green beans, were words to make him shudder." His last words to Fay Lewis, who had asked him if he liked shredded-wheat biscuits, were, "No, and I don't like anybody who does." His aversion to vegetables enabled him to originate a line to fortify generations of helpless children: "I don't like spinach, and I'm glad I don't, because if I liked it I'd eat it, and I'd just hate it."

"In all our life together," says Ruby, "I never ordered or ate in his presence any dish other than whatever he wished for himself, at hotels or restaurants at home or abroad, and never indicated that

I liked any of the things he disliked. In all the thirty-six years of
life at home no one ever had a meal at our table that was not considered exceptionally good, and yet never was anything served that
Clarence did not eat, excepting salads as side dishes, for I never
allowed him to sit through a course for others that he did not
share in."

Having rescued her husband from the toils of free love, Ruby
was inclined to be a trifle suspicious of Clarence's former lady
friends, some of whom encountered "a wall of ice" when they were
first invited by Darrow to his new home. Perhaps because he knew
that whatever quarreling he did with Ruby was over externals, he
made no attempt to postpone their arguments until they were
alone; their intimates report spirited clashes, for Ruby could talk
faster and more indefatigably than her husband. Clarence teased
her a good deal by advising other people never to exchange their
freedom for the shackles of matrimony. One of his favorite comments was that "getting married is a good deal like going into a
restaurant with your friends. You order what you want, and then
when you see what the other fellow has got you wish you had
taken that." Though Ruby's love for Clarence rose to planes of the
sheerest idolatry with the passing of the decades, she always fought
back, never taking his guff in public. Before long it became clear to
everyone that they were a good match, that they loved each other
and that their relationship would endure. Darrow was happy to
have a home again to which he could invite his friends; rarely did
an evening pass without half a dozen of his old cronies gathered
about him to read and argufy.

3

A short time after Darrow formed his partnership with Masters,
Francis Wilson was made a partner. They took offices in the Ashland Block, which was the "leading office building in Chicago and
housed among its tenants the leading members of the legal profession." For the next eight years the firm of Darrow, Masters and
Wilson was one of the most successful in Chicago, clearing from
twenty-five to thirty-five thousand dollars a year for each partner,
exploding only when a bomb blew up the Los Angeles Times Building, killing twenty men and wrecking Darrow's career as the country's most brilliant defender of the rights of working people.

Darrow had a large office with a private entrance off the elevator hall, while Masters selected for himself a corner office at
the inner and most inaccessible end of the suite, where he is re-

puted to have spent a considerable portion of his time writing Greek tragedies and other poems. A young lawyer who had offices a few doors down the hall gives a vivid picture of Darrow during this period:

"He always gave me the impression of being slow and deliberate in his movements, relaxed and loose jointed. In this respect and in others, he was as Lincoln has been represented. I do not recall ever having seen him hurry. In conversation especially he was slow of speech and he chuckled with a rapid shrug of the shoulder when something struck him funny. His eyes were bluish gray, kindly and deep-set under a large and very full brow, and I noticed that his ears joined the skin under the jawbones, without the usual lobes. His hands were long, and the fingers were long and tapered. His skin was pale and frequently sallow and muddy. I heard him say in connection with dental work, which he found had to be done, 'Hell, nature never did know how to make teeth.' He had Lincoln's simplicity of statement and argument, his directness and sincerity, and he did not hesitate to present ideas that were unpopular."

He was like Lincoln, too, in that he told simple jokes about serious matters in an attempt to lessen the emotional intensity and bring people to a friendly, even fraternal, basis. His devoted secretary, Ethel Maclaskey, whom he hired because he first met her at a free thinkers' meeting and said, "We free thinkers and liberals should patronize each other," observes of him, "I believe he went on the assumption we were all like children, and jokes made a common meeting ground." In the case of Mrs Simpson, who had shot and killed her husband while he was on the witness stand attempting to secure a surreptitious divorce, the judge who had been sitting in the divorce proceedings was subpoenaed to come into court and testify against the woman. The state's attorney insisted upon calling the testifying judge "Your Honor," to which Darrow objected, saying that no man should be called Your Honor except when he was on the bench.

"Why, Clarence," exclaimed the Dutch judge presiding over the murder hearings, "I took you to lunch once, and you called me 'Your Honor.'"

"Sure," replied Darrow, "but that was because you paid the check."

As an instance of the supreme faith his clients had in him, a year after he had secured an acquittal for Mrs Simpson on the grounds of temporary insanity, the lady came into his office and asked that he now have the charge of insanity expunged from the court records, as it was hurting her position in Chicago.

As soon as it became known that he was back in town to stay business picked up. "The firm was an extremely busy one," says William Carlin, who had now been with Darrow for many years, "and Mr Darrow supplied the principal business." With one notable exception Darrow did all the appearing before judges and juries, for although Masters' organization of a case was logical and forceful, his personality alienated sympathy from his clients. The exception occurred in a personal-injury suit against a railroad, which Darrow and Masters had handled so well together in court that there could be no doubt but that their client would recover damages. Darrow was scheduled to make the final plea to the jury, but when the morning came he failed to appear at the office at his usual eight-thirty. Nine o'clock came, and no Darrow; nine-thirty, and no Darrow. Masters fumed about the office. At a quarter to ten, forced to leave for court, he instructed Carlin to get in touch with him the instant he heard from Darrow. At five minutes to ten a telegram arrived from Cincinnati where Darrow had gone the night before to give a lecture on "Is Man a Machine?" Masters made the final plea to the jury—and the railroad won the case.

It was at this time that Darrow evolved his formula for jury picking that has served succeeding generations of lawyers. "Never take a German; they are bullheaded. Rarely take a Swede; they are stubborn. Always take an Irishman or a Jew; they are the easiest to move to emotional sympathy. Old men are generally more charitable and kindly disposed than young men; they have seen more of the world and understand it."

His rule of never giving up a cross-examination until he had some comfort from it is exemplified by the blowup of the doctor who was used by the streetcar company in personal-injury suits because he could think faster than most lawyers in Chicago. The doctor had a list of twenty hospitals with which his name was associated; when a tiny hospital opening somewhere in the suburbs invited him to put his name on their staff he consented because the addition would make his titles seem more imposing to credulous juries. Darrow in examining him droned through the list of hospitals, asking the doctor where each of them was—a method of questioning apparently without purpose. Finally he came to the bottom of the list and asked where the new hospital was located. The doctor almost bounded out of the witness chair.

"Jesus Christ, Clarence," he exclaimed, "you got me!"

He took pleasure in outwitting medical men. In the world-renowned Massie case in Honolulu "a prosecution witness, a doctor, had a reputation for withholding on direct examination just enough facts so that if on cross-examination the examiner sought to bring out anything favorable to the defendant, the doctor still had some undisclosed fact with which to confound the defense. It was evident that this doctor was pulling his punches and waiting to tangle with Mr Darrow. When Darrow rose he asked amiably:

" 'Did you enjoy your trip from Los Angeles, Doctor?'

" 'Yes, I did.'

" 'Are you being paid for testifying in this case?'

" 'Yes, I am.'

"Mr Darrow turned solemnly to the bench and murmured, 'No further questions.' "

In Chicago at the time, such a large number of massage parlors were being used as fronts for houses of prostitution, the word "massage" had come to be used as a synonym for a four-letter word which could not be bandied about in polite society, while to give someone a "massaging" stood for the present participle of its more vigorous Anglo-Saxon counterpart. As part of a reform movement all massage parlors in the city were closed up, thereby depriving a lot of honest and hard-working masseurs from earning a living. Their association sent a committee to Darrow, asking him to secure an injunction against their closure. Darrow's sarcasm in court was so excoriatingly funny that when he had finished the state's attorney rose and muttered:

"Clarence has a way of 'massaging' all of us." The ordinance was revoked.

George Leisure, a young lawyer whom Darrow took with him to Honolulu on the Massie case in 1932, gives a picture of Darrow's superb technique and power under the glare of the international spotlight: "I was interested in learning how a great lawyer put the steelwork together for making a moving address to a jury," says Leisure. "I had made the opening argument to the jury on behalf of the defense, and Mr Darrow was to follow the next day with the closing argument for the defense. Up to the night before he was to argue the case I had observed that he had not made a single mark on a paper in preparation for his summation. Consequently, when some of the navy men wanted to call on us that night, I was about to tell them on the telephone that Mr Darrow would be busy. He interrupted me, however, and told me to tell them to come on over. We sat and talked until ten o'clock that evening, when Mr Darrow went to bed.

"The court convenes in Honolulu at eight-thirty, so as soon as we had breakfast we went directly to the courtroom. Mr Darrow had made no visible preparation up to that time. During the five

minutes we were in the courtroom before the judge called the court
to order, Mr Darrow made four or five little half-line notes on a
yellow pad, which he proceeded to throw down and leave behind
him on the desk when the court said, 'Very well, you may proceed
now, Mr Darrow.'

"He walked out in front of the jury and delivered his address
until the noon hour. At lunch time, as soon as we had taken lunch,
I walked out of his room, assuming that he would want to jot down
a few thoughts for the remainder of his summation. When I called
for him again in ten minutes I found him asleep. We proceeded
immediately to the courtroom, where he continued his summation
all afternoon without reference to any notes and without the help
of any memoranda of any kind. Just as the long shadows began to
fall in this tropical and beautiful setting Mr Darrow finished his
summation with lines which were almost poetic.

"At the time I felt that my effort in trying to learn how a great
lawyer put together the steelwork of a great summation had been
a total failure, but in thinking the matter over, I realized that I had
learned a great deal. Mr Darrow was an insatiable reader. It was
almost impossible to mention any book that he had not read and
with which he was not thoroughly familiar. His tremendous reading and his tremendous brain power enabled him to dictate these
jury addresses. I say dictate, because that is how I discovered what
it was that Mr Darrow did in the preparation of his speeches. When
I first got out of law school it was necessary for me to write out in
longhand every agreement and every brief before I dictated it from
my own notes to a stenographer. Later, when I became sufficiently
familiar with the subject matter, I always dictated directly to the
stenographer without making notes in advance. I then realized that
that was exactly what Mr Darrow was doing when he summed up
to a jury. He knew all the facts of the case thoroughly when he
started to sum up, and with his knowledge of those facts he drew
upon his tremendous store of knowledge and gave his address just
as the atmosphere and character of the courtroom demanded."

Chicago lawyers who watched him work over a period of years
say it was magnificent to see the slow, mesmeric manner in which
he broke down hostility and aversion, his warmth and love permeat-
ing with kindliness courtrooms in which bitter, acrimonious contests
were being waged. Rarely did he attempt to convert the courtroom
merely to the innocence of his client; rather he converted them to a
mellow and tolerant philosophy of life in which all mankind was
innocent as charged. Before long opposing attorneys, witnesses,
jurymen and judges were sweating in a glow of brotherly love.

In only one recorded instance did he lose patience with a judge. Darrow was concentrating on his defense when "the judge rather suddenly interrupted the proceedings to ask how long he had practiced law in Chicago.

" 'Twenty-one years, Your Honor,' replied Darrow. 'How long have you practiced?'

" 'Twenty-eight years, Mr Darrow,' replied the judge.

"After a lapse of a minute or two Darrow turned to the court:

" 'Now that we have both acquired additional knowledge, may we proceed with the case?' "

Except when he was defending genuine victims of circumstance or gaining money for people injured by the carelessness of industry, he did not care much for his practice of the law. "My life has been misspent in musty courtrooms," he wrote to a friend, "with hair-splitting lawyers and ponderous judges quibbling over nothing. My only consolation is that I have always been for the defense." Though Angus Roy Shannon quotes him as saying, "Everybody is entitled to a defense; it is not only the right, but the duty, of every lawyer to defend," even his attitude toward this conception of defense had matured. He would no longer represent professional criminals. He defended the Yellow Kid in his first trial and got him off, but when the Yellow Kid came back a few years later, offering him any sum of money he named to again defend him, Darrow refused. "I told you if you ever got into trouble again not to come back to me." Of another habitual criminal he said, "I got him off when he was young and gave him his chance, but you can't cure confidence men; it's in their blood."

Though he was modest and plain as an old shoe, he had a vigorous ego and all the innocent vanity necessary to men who do important work. "Even though there might be other good lawyers on his side, he always wangled it so that he closed the case. He never wanted anyone to follow him. He liked to be standing under the spotlight when the final curtain fell." His friends said of him that "he was devoid of obnoxious egotism, yet he loved the limelight—perhaps because he did his best work under its white heat."

4

From eight-thirty in the morning until six at night he worked as a lawyer, but in the evenings he considered himself free, free to write, lecture, debate, study. He had always called himself a lazy man; once when he went back to Kinsman with George Whitehead, his lecture manager, Whitehead commented that the public library was displaying a set of carpenters' tools purported to have belonged to Amirus Darrow and asked Clarence if he wouldn't identify them. "I'd be the last one in the world to be able to do that," replied Darrow; "I kept as far away from those tools and that carpenter shop as I could." Yet his laziness was entirely physical; there were few days in which he worked at his various desks for less than sixteen hours.

He had progressed from the role of the gadfly, which stung people into thinking, to the point where he was now one of the country's most effective antidotes, an antidote to the poisons of stuffiness, moralism, lethargy. Watching his audiences, even as he had watched the expressions of his Kinsman audiences, he found that he had to transpose his adage of "The truth shall make you free" to read, "The truth shall make you mad." But he did not mind making people mad; he was not afraid of their anger, resentment, hatred. He enjoyed wading in where the going was the thickest. Perhaps if he could make them mad enough he might make them mad enough to start thinking for themselves.

"In Miami he was introduced at a public gathering by a chairman who said, 'It gives me great pleasure to present Mr Darrow to such a large and intelligent audience.' Darrow got up, surveyed the six hundred persons before him silently for several seconds and said, 'My friend, the chairman, is mistaken. There are not this many intelligent people in the whole world.'"

He was no respecter of sacred cows: the more sacred the cow, the more he believed it needed to be shot at, for every time a man accepted a sacred cow he closed off still another portion of his brain. To antidote the sanctimonious he took upon himself the role of irreverence, a part for which his nature and background had well fitted him. At a labor meeting one night he was introduced as a friend of the laboring man. "When Clarence arose to speak he said, 'Yes, I have always been a friend of the workingman, and I hope I always will be. I would rather be a friend of the workingman than to be a workingman.' At another meeting in Kansas City, shortly after the death of J. Pierpont Morgan, he had occasion to call his audience's attention to the will of Mr Morgan, which had gained considerable currency in the press. It read something as follows: 'I return my soul to my Saviour who gave it. All the rest, residue and remainder of my estate I give and bequeath to my son John.' Darrow commented, 'So you see, the Saviour got his soul and his son got his money. I should say that was one time at least when the Saviour got the worst of it.'"

When in Washington a few years later Darrow was met on the

street by an acquaintance who was excited because President Taft was going to address a joint session of the Senate and House that afternoon.

"Tickets are at a terrible premium, Clarence, practically impossible to get. By a stroke of good fortune I have an extra one. You must come along."

After a moment of hesitation, during which Darrow recalled that it had been Judge Taft who had issued the first local injunction against the American Railway Union strikers in 1894, establishing a precedent for the Federal Court in Chicago, Darrow agreed to accompany his friend. The House was packed, the galleries jammed. Taft received a tremendous ovation before launching into his message. The friend watched Darrow eagerly for some reaction to Taft's words, but he remained stony faced. Toward the end of the speech Darrow nudged his friend, who thought, "Ah, at last I shall hear a pearl of wisdom," and leaned closer to catch every word.

"Fat son of a bitch, ain't he?" asked Darrow.

He once remarked, "When I was a boy I was told that anybody could become President. I'm beginning to believe it."

Nothing was too trivial or too sacrosanct to escape his biting humor. "On his way home from Europe aboard a Cunard liner he was asked to speak at a concert the night before the ship landed. He began with, 'Well, this voyage is almost completed, and it is a blamed good thing, too, because the cook has run out of fancy names for the same old gravy soup.' The passengers laughed and applauded, but the ship's personnel was furious."

Darrow and a college professor named John had debated frequently, "always kidding each other in a humorous vein on the platform. Darrow knew of the professor's inclination to step out of an evening. After his death Darrow and a friend called to pay their respects to the widow, who had placed her husband's ashes in an urn on the mantelpiece. When she left the living room for an instant Darrow gazed up at the urn.

" 'Poor John,' he murmured, 'you'll have to stay in nights now.' "

A good-looking young man came into Darrow's office and asked Darrow to defend him against a charge of robbery. Darrow inquired when he could get a portion of his fee. "I can get some of the money for you tonight," replied the young man. "No-oo," murmured Darrow, "I don't care to accept money that has been stolen—so recently."

Toward more serious problems he turned an acid irreverence. Invited as a criminologist to address the prisoners of the Cook County jail, he gave them a lecture on Altgeld's revolutionary theory of the economic base of crime. "There is no such thing as crime as the word is generally understood. Nine tenths of you are in jail because you did not have enough money to pay a good lawyer. While some of you men might pick my pocket because that is your trade, when I get outside everybody picks my pocket—by charging me a dollar for something that is worth twenty-five cents. If every man, woman and child in the world had a chance to make a decent, fair, honest living there would be no jails and no lawyers and no courts."

When he had finished a guard asked one of the prisoners what he thought of the speech. "He's too radical," replied the prisoner.

When speaking to a colored audience before the Men's Forum on "The Problem of the Negro" he castigated their white oppressor even as he had flayed their thieving but honored business practices to the incarcerated men. "Probably I do not look at the race problem in as hopeful a way as many of your people do, for I am somewhat pessimistic about the white race. When I see how anxious the white race is to go to war over nothing and to shoot down men in cold blood for the benefit of trade, when I see the injustice everywhere present, the rich people uniting and crowding the poor into inferior positions, I fear the dreams we have indulged in of perfect equality and unlimited opportunity are a long way from realization. The colored race should learn this: if the white race insults you on account of your inferior position they also degrade themselves when they do it. Every time a superior person invades the rights and liberties and dignity of an inferior person he retards and debases his own manhood."

He carried forward his campaign against the maleducation which rendered the mind of each generation in turn incapable of understanding its problems or achieving an intelligent social state. "The university graduate has suffered the fate of the feet of the Chinese girl," he wrote in *Tomorrow* magazine; "he has been so thoroughly molded that he can no more get beyond the little groove in which the four narrow walls so long confined him than he could make a journey to the moon." To his mind one of the most virulent poisons that had been pumped into the vitals of American life was its Pollyannish God's-in-His-heaven, all's-right-with-the-world blind faith. Because of his determination to antidote this creeping paralysis he was accused of being a futilitarian, a pessimist.

"He was a consummate actor; he would go to a banquet where people were talking about the bigger and better life, and he would get up and give one of his pessimistic speeches." Frank P. Walsh said of him:

"Darrow is a wonderful man with a fine mind, a big heart and a great social vision. But, you know, he is never happy except at a funeral, and not then unless it was where the deceased had committed suicide."

What people called his pessimism was the recoiling of a sensitive nature from the unnecessary suffering in the world. The man who sees all this suffering, understands its basic causes and thinks he has a cure that can be readily affected is rarely called a pessimist. But Darrow's discerning logic tore holes in every one of what Bertrand Russell was to call the *Proposed Roads to Freedom*. Taking his stand with no one ideology, but insisting upon scrutinizing with relentless logic and accepting what was valid from each social philosophy, he was the man on the raft in the wide, wide ocean. Yet he could not swallow some ism whole hog merely because a man needs direction if he is to steer a straight course—a straight course to where—to what? He expressed his credo to Abram Adelman, the neighboring attorney in the Ashland Block, in one sentence which might serve as his epitaph:

"I can say with perfect honesty that I have never knowingly catered to anyone's ideas, and I have expressed what was within me, regardless of consequences."

Charles Edward Russell writes of him, "The complement of his intense and boundless sympathy for the individual sufferer was a good-natured contempt for all efforts to raise man in the mass. Man was a monkey, always had been a monkey, always would be a monkey, and all efforts to make him anything else were but lost motion. Because of his prominence and warm generosity he was continually besought to join some reforming enterprise of uplift. With two exceptions, the League to Abolish Capital Punishment and the National Association for the Advancement of Colored People, he invariably declined." Despite his belief that a socialist state might be superior to a predatory capitalist state, "he looked upon socialists as well-meaning, interesting and utterly futile folk who were wasting their time gesticulating at a chimera. He could not see that bloody revolution, which some of his friends believed to be the universal panacea, would help, since men would still be monkeys when they had ceased to blow one another up with dynamite. Yet he was not really the stuff of which ironbound skeptics are made; he was too sensitive to keep out all faith." Corroborating Russell, other of Darrow's friends say, "In spite of his recurrent hopelessness in mankind ever finding a permanent structure of peace and plenty, we never heard a note of bitterness from Darrow; his attitude was one of tolerant amusement."

Taking the negative side in a debate against Rabbi Goldman of Chicago on "Is Life Worth Living?" Darrow saw the sumptuous night-club entertainer, Texas Guinan, enter the auditorium. He nudged the rabbi and murmured, "There's an argument in your favor."

He was a sentimental cynic. He was a gullible skeptic. He was an organized anarchist. He was a happy pessimist. He was a modest egocentric. He was a hopeful defeatist. And was perhaps aware of the various contradictions he was housing under one dome.

A reporter for the Toledo *Blade* commented that "Darrow is a real human being because he wrings the last drop of juice out of his grapefruit." He didn't like life; it was all a silly mess, yet he squeezed the last drop of juice out of it as he squeezed the last drop of juice out of the grapefruit, even though the grapefruit was sour, and what the hell, he didn't like grapefruit anyway!

5

As the business of Darrow, Masters and Wilson became more profitable Darrow spent a larger portion of his time traveling for his lectures and debates. If it had been possible to evangelize on economic rather than religious subjects he would have given up his law practice to become a traveling evangelist. His most consistent pleasure remained in lecturing and debating. Since his primary motivation was to give any and all ideas an airing, he employed the architectural method of batter, or purposeful leaning over backward, to provide correction for the mass of people who were leaning so far forward in obeisance that they were lying on their faces. When debating Rabbi Kornfeld in Toledo on the subject, "Is There Something in Man above the Animal?" he wired his sponsors, "I shall contend that man is simply a machine and that there is nothing in him that cannot be found in a dog, an auto or a tree. I care nothing about winning the debate. I only want to give the ideas a hearing. I'm sure that the great majority of the crowd will be on the rabbi's side. If they are not, I'll be sure I'm on the wrong side."

Newspaper reporters sent to interview him found him to be hot copy, for he had a vivid sense of the theatrical, furnishing them with apostasies that made electrifying banners for their columns. An associate says, "I recall that following the decision in the Scopes evolution case he received a number of reporters at my office and expressed to them very strong opinions in respect to various public questions, such as the treatment of Negroes and defense of criminals, and in every case made strong pronouncements without qualification. After the reporters had left I reminded him that he had discussed those very same questions with me at length and that his views on the subject had been qualified in much the same way as that of other citizens who were not regarded as radical and cynical.

" 'That's quite true,' replied Darrow. 'But when you want to get anything before the public you must decide what is the thing you most wish to emphasize at the time and then state it strongly, forcefully, without qualification, and your view will then attract public attention to the particular thing which you wish to emphasize—it will be news. If you qualify your main point the thing you wish to emphasize loses its news value; it loses its interest to the public.' "

His name was anathema to the gentry of the Midwest, where he was known as an anarchist, an atheist; the reporters who came to him were often frightened, hostile and suspicious, but his dirt-farmer ways, his gentle good humor and lovability converted them. One very correct young man was astonished to be received in the bathroom where Darrow was shaving in his undershirt, suspenders down.

"Make yourself comfortable, son," he drawled through the soapy lather. "Here, sit on the edge of the bathtub or on the toilet."

His informality and friendliness extended to every walk of life because he recognized no difference between walks of life; he liked people alive on the face of the earth, caring little about their titles, position, wealth or other external appurtenances. "He had a kind word for everyone and took time to talk to each, inquiring into their daily life, thereby making them feel that he was an old and very dear friend." A man from Ohio says, "Darrow was scheduled to make a Labor Day speech at Akron. My friend and I decided to make a pilgrimage from Cleveland to hear that speech. After the meeting we walked over to the hotel, and there was Darrow, standing in the lobby talking to another man. My friend, who was a complete stranger to him, dragged me over to Darrow. He accepted our introductions as a matter of course. It wasn't long before the four of us were lined up at the hotel bar having a drink. Then we sat down to a table in the dining room for a thirty-five-cent dinner, Dutch treat."

In debates he was a tough adversary. Will Rogers, who once served as chairman, first introduced Clarence True Wilson; when Wilson had finished his argument Rogers introduced Darrow, saying to Wilson as he did so, "And may the Lord have mercy on you!" Darrow liked to debate against rabbis because "they are good platform men, and in a debate, as in any other contest, the combatants must be well matched for the crowd to get a real play." Rabbi Goldman says, "You couldn't take a manuscript to debate with Darrow because you couldn't tell where he was going." Before one lecture a newspaperman, asking to see a copy of his speech, was handed a blank pad. "This is my speech for tonight," said Darrow.

"Why, Mr Darrow," exclaimed the reporter, "that's the speech I reported last week!"

Because of his Kinsman predilection for taking the weaker side in any debate, "the other fellow won the argument and Darrow won the crowd." A member of one of his audiences says, "His voice was low, musical, his message direct and courageous, his communication such that one could hear a pin drop. Some idol of my cultural thought was being so logically smashed that I had to let it go. Darrow was often unanswerable because he seemed to have thought to finality about many things."

During this period he gave a night course in court procedure for the Illinois College of Law. One of his students recalls that "he was patient in teaching the boys and conveyed the impression that he wanted us to 'get it.' He reminded me of a father talking to his sons. Here is what he told us about preparing a case: 'Before going before the court and jury get the facts, all the facts, every little detail, and get them yourself. Do not delegate this fact getting to an investigator; do it yourself; see it with your own eyes. Then when you are in court your confidence will be communicated to the jury.'

"When a question was asked Mr Darrow would answer immediately, without hem and hawing. His definite, immediate and emphatic answers gave us the impression that he knew every minute detail of procedure." Even in his classrooms he could not help but proselytize. "I am firmly convinced that one purpose dominated his whole life: to defeat the law of capital punishment. He took it for granted that we were studying law with the ultimate purpose of keeping persons from being executed."

Though he loathed professional reformers as hard, intolerant self-seekers, he became something of a reformer himself, for he never turned down the opportunity to lecture on the evils of existing society. His greatest strength as a teacher and humanitarian was that he "hated vile traits, but never the person who displayed them." His greatest weakness was that, serving as a debunker or cathartic which emptied the bowels of the mind, he had no concrete program to offer as strengthening food. He was incapable of giving himself unquestioningly to any one program, for he was "leery of the idea that laws on the statute books would bring love and brotherhood in the land." The more he grew to value his freedom and independence of thought, the more impossible it was for him to become a joiner. If it had not been too patently a contradiction in terms he would have liked to think of himself as an individualist-socialist; that was as close as he could come to categorizing himself. Gertrude Barnum tells that:

"At ever larger and larger meetings he appeared, to challenge the complacency of advocates of the various isms of the day. Never to be forgotten was one such meeting. Knowing that men and women of many minds were present and seeking to emphasize the points upon which all might unite to fight the forces of reaction, Darrow made a speech calculated to encourage all who were working for the cause of the masses. When the meeting was thrown open for questioning the speaker got the floor.

" 'I notice,' he shouted, 'that there are many single taxers in the audience who seemed to like what was said here tonight. No doubt they think Mr Darrow is one of them. I should like to ask, "Mr Darrow, do you believe in the single tax?" '

" 'Why, yes,' was the reply. 'I think there is a lot in that.' (Loud applause from one group.)

" 'Well now,' continued the heckler, 'I also noticed that your speech pleased the anarchists here. I ask, are you perhaps also an anarchist?'

" 'Yes,' admitted Darrow, 'I guess I'm a good deal of an anarchist.' (Loud applause from another group.)

" 'Finally,' continued the chairman with growing intensity, 'I heard you make points for socialists. Are you perhaps also a socialist?'

" 'Why, yes, comrade,' said Darrow. 'I think there is a lot to be said for socialism.'

The little man drew himself up for the final thrust.

" 'Then we want to know why you don't join us in the Socialist party.'

" 'Well, for one thing,' replied Darrow, fixing the chairman with an amused smile, 'because there are so many unsocial people in the Socialist party.' "

Fay Lewis says, "At one time I asked Darrow if he really didn't believe in socialism.

" 'Yes, I do,' he answered.

" 'Well then, why don't you go with the socialists and take part?'

" 'I would,' replied Darrow, 'if it weren't for the socialists; they're so damned cocksure of everything.' "

He had his blind spot: he held a low opinion of the political capacity of women. Charles Edward Russell writes, "For a man of his general breadth and catholicity of vision, he was rather inclined to a low estimate of women, steadily opposed their enfranchisement and spoke with scorn of 'lady suffrage' as a foolish fad and no addition to the state."

He attended the very first votes-for-women meetings in Chicago, and his aversion to suffragettes probably arose from the asexual picture they presented in their mannish clothes and spectacles, waving angular arms as they strode across the platform. Gertrude Barnum reports that this apostle of tolerance laughed at them but that everybody else in the audience laughed uproariously, too, and that when the students at the university heard there was to be a suffragette meeting that night they went en masse for the sport.

George Briggs, the single taxer, met Darrow one Sunday morning at an atheist-science service and accompanied him and three of Darrow's women friends to the Auditorium Hotel for luncheon. Briggs had a five-dollar ticket in his pocket to hear Mary Garden sing but let it lapse because he preferred arguing with Darrow. At the end of an afternoon of intense discussion Darrow turned to Briggs and, indicating his three women admirers who had filled so admirably the role of audience, commented:

"These women have laughed in the right places; they have nodded their heads in the right places; they've asked the right questions—but none of them knows a damn thing of what we've been talking about.

"If you give votes to women," he said, "they will bring prohibition down upon us." Another friend relates, "I remember making some remarks about the desirability of women having the same rights, privileges and duties as men. Darrow replied:

" 'I'm not so sure about that. We notice that nature makes the least differentiation between the sexes in her lowest orders. As we rise in the scale the differences become greater until, when we reach the human animal, it is greatest of all. I think possibly it is better that way.' "

He confided to Gertrude Barnum that "votes for women would put progress back fifty years"—but voted for suffrage anyway.

6

Among his clients was still William Randolph Hearst, who also used him as political adviser. In July of 1904, having contrived to pledge the Illinois delegation to nominate for President the then-liberal Hearst, whose papers had been stoutly on the side of the anthracite miners, Darrow attended the Democratic convention in St Louis. When the convention opened the man nominating Parker spoke so low he couldn't be heard. At the cries of "Louder!" he said, "I'm not talking to the gallery, I'm talking to the delegates."

Darrow got up to nominate Hearst, declaring, "The men who scuttled the Democratic ship in 'ninety-six are in control of this convention. Now let them elect their candidate." The gallery cheered, but the delegates hissed. "I'm not talking to the delegates," called out Darrow; "I'm talking to the gallery."

Hearst was defeated. The next time he wanted to run for political office he again wrote Darrow, asking if he thought it advisable. Darrow replied, "No." Hearst ran anyway, commanding his attorney to stump for him. Darrow refused. He was fired by return telegram.

He stayed in St Louis for three days, visited the Fair and had great fun riding in the gondolas with Paul. He then returned to Chicago to straighten out his affairs and leave with Ruby for the West to spend their summer vacation. During his vacation he wrote his first and only novel, *An Eye for an Eye*. "He wrote it sitting on logs in the Colorado mountains," says Ruby, "while we'd rest from long tramps. He'd write at the foot of some beguiling mountain, scribbling away while he drank in the beauty of the vista. He finished it in two weeks or a little more."

An Eye for an Eye starts out to be a study of how brutalizing poverty drives a man into a crime of violence but breaks uncertainly in the middle and becomes the study of a man in flight after he has committed a murder. The novel served as a receptacle for Darrow's ideas on poverty, social justice, crime and the revenge motive under which society executes those who have been driven to take a human life. Predating such books as Upton Sinclair's *The Jungle*, also laid in Chicago, *An Eye for an Eye* is one of the first novels in American literature to deal with the life of the poor, with their hard, incessant labors, debts, fears and want. The story is portrayed with heart-wringing realism, pervaded with a sense of love and gentleness for those unfortunates caught in the inexorable meshes of the economic system. *An Eye for an Eye* is repetitious and confused in structure but contains magnificently written passages. Though more interested in getting over his ideas than in adhering to an art form, even Darrow realized that if it were better constructed it would have gained a wider public.

From Colorado the Darrows continued to Vancouver. Meeting up with a group of Dartmouth men who were going into the Yoho Valley, Darrow joined them for a three-day camping-and-walking trip to Lake Louise. In September he returned to Chicago, refreshed.

His most pressing problem was not his law business but his son Paul, who had just graduated. Having lunch with him one day at the Jefferson Democratic Club, Darrow met an old friend by the name of Eagle, who was about to leave for a vacation—only he didn't know where.

"Paul, why don't you go along?" asked the father.

"No. I want to go to work."

"Hell, you have all your life to work. Take a boat ride to Europe or something."

Eagle volunteered, "I give you my promise that I won't let him take a drink all the time he's with me."

Darrow, who always said his son was too strait-laced, replied, "Hell, you get him good and drunk, and I'll pay the expenses of your trip."

From his mother, Jessie Ohl, Paul had inherited many solid virtues: emotional stolidity, which his father and grandfather Amirus sometimes lacked; the love of a worth-while routine; the desire for a secure niche, no matter how unpretentious, which he would always know was his and which no force on earth could change. His nature was placid and, unlike his father, his decisions were prompted by cool mental processes rather than hot emotions. He was a good fellow, well met and well liked, equal to any task set before him, but he was not one to spend his life seeking for tasks, causes, chimerical Holy Grails. He liked books, but with him reading was a pleasure rather than a passion. He didn't want to debate, argue, differ, quarrel or fight with anybody; he liked peace and quiet. Nor was he altogether sure he approved of his father's radicalism; perhaps as a part of the perennial revolt of youth against its elders he was a conservative in his economics as well as his politics. A number of years later, when a reform party in Chicago was urging Darrow to run for alderman, he suggested his son in his place. An investigating committee came to the Darrow home to question Paul.

"How do you stand on the utilities?" the chairman asked.

"I think the government is altogether too severe on the utilities," replied Paul.

"What is your stand on the traction problem?"

"I think the rates need raising."

"And what do you think about taxation?"

"I think the income tax is too high."

Darrow turned to the chairman of the group and said smilingly: "Paul must have more money than I thought he had."

Once again Paul went to work for McClurg, but a few months later, when Darrow had to go to Cuba on business, he persuaded his son to join him. "Come on along, Paul; you'll have fun." While in Havana Darrow became interested in the possibilities of building a railroad to the sugar plantations and left his son behind to learn about sugar. Paul went inland, became covered with fleas and boils and escaped on the first boat. Back home he asked his father to get him a job with the Chicago and North Western Railway. Darrow called his friend, the general manager.

"Send him over after lunch," said the manager.

When Paul arrived he asked, "When do you want to start?"

"I'd just as soon start right now."

"Well, no use to start now. Come back Monday morning."

Paul ran all the way to the Ashland Block, burst into his father's office and exclaimed, "I got it!"

"No, you didn't," answered his father. "I changed my mind. I just phoned the manager not to give you the job."

"But, Father, why?" groaned Paul.

"Because I hate the idea of your working for a big corporation."

Shortly thereafter a lawyer by the name of Abner Smith approached Darrow, suggesting that he help finance a bank with a new operating idea: they would sell stock to druggists, in return for which they would make the drugstores depositories or branch banks. His son was to be given an important job in the organization. Darrow, a poor businessman under any circumstances, was at this moment doubly susceptible because he wanted to see Paul well placed; he invested ten thousand dollars, almost the total of his savings. He also persuaded friends to join him in the venture, chief among whom was his partner, Masters. The Bank of America opened its office on the second floor of the Ashland Block, a few doors down the hall from Darrow. His business judgment for once proved sound; within less than three months the bank had three hundred thousand dollars on deposit and was spreading fast.

"Then the officers started grafting and putting in bad loans," said Paul. "I advised Father what was going on. He closed them up."

The next morning Darrow had an early session with the Chicago Clearinghouse, which was anxious to avoid a failure. The clearinghouse offered to lend him twenty-five thousand dollars on his personal note if he would open the bank that morning and pay all depositors who demanded their money. By ten o'clock father and son were established behind separate teller's cages with cash before them, meeting all comers. The clearinghouse money, plus the cash on hand, was sufficient to meet the immediate needs; since a fair portion of the collateral was good, the stockholders got some of their money—all except Darrow and Masters.

7

No one knew better than Darrow that lawyers are janitors who have to clean up all sorts of dirty legal messes. Darrow mopped up his share, for at least half of his time now was devoted to corporation law. He was criticized by the liberal groups of Chicago for consorting with the enemy. Then, as ever afterward, people thought he earned enormous sums of money, a misconception which boiled to a rage of indignation when he was accused of prostituting his talents in defending the Loeb-Leopold murderers to earn a million-dollar fee. Yet it is attested by all his partners that Darrow never knew his worth to his clients. "He charged them five thousand when they were prepared and willing to pay thirty thousand for valuable services rendered." To conduct the defense of the woodworkers in the Paine case, the trial of whom lasted several months, "he received the nominal fee of two hundred and fifty dollars."

Nine years before, in 1895, he had first been attacked with charges of taking corporation gold when he helped an electric company push through an ordinance which the mayor had vetoed. The attack had been made by an estimable woman friend at Hull House, who charged him with betraying the people of Chicago. Darrow's answer to "My dear Miss S." gives a portrait of a confused, tortured young man struggling upward through the darkness of an acquisitive society: possibly the most illuminating letter written during his long lifetime.

"I undertook to serve this company, believing they had an ordinance procured by the aid of boodle. Judged by the ordinary commercial and legal standards of ethics, I did right. I know that in your mind this is no justification; it is no justification in mine. I do not care a cent for all the ordinary rules of ethics or conduct. They are mostly wrong. I am satisfied that, judged by the higher law, in which we both believe, I could not be justified and that I am practically a thief. I am taking money that I did not earn, which comes to me from men who did not earn it but who get it because they have the chance to get it. I take it without performing any useful service to the world."

He then makes an outright statement to Miss S. of the *modus operandi* which was to serve him all his days. When he had come to Chicago in 1887 his attention had been called "to the rights of labor and wrongs of the world" by his friend Swift, with whom he had discussed these questions "not only abstractly, but as applied to our own life and our own conduct." When Swift had been appointed administrator of his father's estate he had taken all the patent-medicine bottles out of the family drugstore and smashed them in the back yard. "He then left town without money, refused to compromise with the world, lived as best he could, was nearly a tramp. He raised a Coxey Army, marched to Washington, is now shunned by most earnest people who cannot follow him. He is no doubt loved by those who know him; he has lived his life as he thought right and best; he has perhaps done some good by refusing to compromise with evil. . . ."

But the hardheaded idealist Darrow thought his friend Swift had taken the wrong methods. "I determined to get what I could out of the system and use it to *destroy* the system. I have since sold my professional services to every corporation or individual who cared to buy; the only exception I have made is that I have never given them aid to oppress the weak or convict the innocent. I have taken their ill-gotten gains and tried to use it to prevent suffering. My preaching and practicing have ever been the same: I have always tried to show a state and a way to reach it where men and women can be honest and tender. I care nothing whatever for money except to use it in this work. I have defended the weak and poor, have done it without pay, will do it again. I cannot defend them without bread; I cannot get this except from those who give it and by giving some measure of conformity to what is."

Thus very early he posed the dilemma at the core of his life, the dilemma on which sits pronged the liberal American lawyer: in order to gain money to relieve suffering, to arm those forces fighting injustice, he lent his talents to strengthen the sinews of the very capitalism which in this same letter he attacks as a "legal fraud and despoiler of the people."

The only way he could conceive of unhorsing himself from the dilemma was to live frugally and put aside enough from his earnings to enable him to retire. He wanted to devote his entire time to writing because he felt he could be of more value as a writer than a lawyer; he would be able to reach a larger audience and educate on a wider ideological front. Twice before he had saved a tidy sum with this dim hope half formulated in his mind, only to lose his money in bad investments. This time he was more cautious: he bought railroad stocks and bank stocks and became partners with the dependable banker Lutz of Gardner, Illinois, in the ownership of the Black Mountain gold mine in Mexico. This Black Mountain mine "was believed to be one of the richest, safest mines ever opened, boasting the most elaborate, expensive and up-to-date equipment of any gold mine." If he sank his money into the mine for a very few years it would make him independent for life. Then he and Ruby could roam the world while he wrote all the beautiful and trenchant stories that were beating at his breast for expression.

Though he consorted with the enemy he had the queasy stomach of the idealist. The first case he gave to George H. Francis, who later became a junior in his office, was a routine foreclosure for a real-estate corporation. A widow had been sold a restaurant in downtown Chicago, in return for which she had given a mortgage on her forty-thousand-dollar home. The night before the matter was to go into court the widow called at Francis' home. He perceived that she was a woman of integrity.

"You are a young man," said the widow. "You cannot be long in the law business."

"As a matter of fact," replied Francis, "this is my first case."

"Then you should not commence your legal career with such a dishonorable affair on your conscience. The real-estate people misrepresented when they sold me the restaurant. My home is the only asset my husband left me, and if you take it away from me I shall be destitute."

"I really know nothing of the background of the case," said Francis. "It was handed to me as an office foreclosure by Mr Darrow. I'll be glad to tell him what you said."

"Then the matter will rest between God and Mr Darrow."

"I'm afraid the connection between the two may be rather remote."

"God will intervene," replied the woman calmly, thanked him and left.

The next morning, when Francis reported the meeting to Darrow, he picked up his telephone, made a few pointed inquiries and learned that the real-estate corporation had twice previously sold the restaurant to professional restaurateurs, both of whom had failed in that location. Darrow did not believe in *caveat emptor,* let the buyer beware; he summoned his client.

"You will return to this woman the deed to her home," he announced, "and call the whole deal off."

"But we can't do that, Clarence," exploded the president of the real-estate concern. "We've paid commissions, incurred other expenses . . ."

"I hate to do your thinking for you, but that's exactly what you're going to do."

The deed was returned to the widow. Darrow submitted no bill to the corporation, nor did they ever again bring him business. God had intervened.

"My study mate," says one of his students at the Illinois College of Law, "was Richard, a preacher's son who rode his bicycle all the way from Denver to Chicago to enter law school. Having a church background, Richard and I used to discuss the question whether one could be a successful lawyer and still maintain the Christian principles. One evening Richard arose and in his deliberate, methodical manner propounded our problem.

" 'Professor Darrow, I respect your ability and I value highly the instruction you give us, and I should like your opinion on the question as to whether or not one can be a successful lawyer—I mean financially successful, make a great deal of money, a million dollars—and do it without resorting to sharp practice, taking advantage of the technicalities of the law or injuring the other fellow.'

"Mr Darrow's answer was given without the least hesitation and in the same definite courtroom manner as he answered questions of law.

" 'No.'

" 'Well, Professor Darrow, you are a successful lawyer and have earned a great deal of money. Then you admit that you are crooked?'

"Mr Darrow did not resent the question. He answered like a father explaining a problem to a child.

" 'They say I am a successful lawyer, but I am not financially successful. The persons I represent are for the most poor people. My clients are not people of money; they are the downtrodden.'

"He then dismissed the class, took his hat from a chair and walked slowly from the room, his head down, thinking—thinking."

Thinking, perhaps, of the cases in which God had not intervened? In which he, Darrow, had unwittingly served as the instrument to injure some defenseless person because he was not in full possession of the facts? Could a lawyer work for corporations and remain an honest man? Could he continue to compromise by giving part of his time to the rich and part to the poor? Were not his powerful clients demanding more and more of his energies; would not he perforce grow away from the poor wretches whose defense was his only justification? When this happened would not the world come to think of him in the sentiment of his young student, "a successful lawyer who had earned a great deal of money and hence must be crooked"? Was he permitting himself to sink ever deeper into the position of the "good lawyer—the lawyer who attends all the Bar Association meetings and so gravitates as rapidly as he can to the defense of Big Business?" What good were his speeches if he himself knew he was not an honest man?

Bouts of introspection were rare with Darrow; this one not only had a salutary effect, but came at a particularly opportune moment. On the sage and dust prairies of far-off Idaho an ex-governor opened the gate to his cottage and was blown up by a bomb that had been connected to its hinges. That explosion was the climactic salvo in one of America's most sanguinary wars. In addition to killing ex-Governor Steunenberg, it also shattered to a thousand fragments Clarence Darrow's dilemma.

CHAPTER VII

Who Will Prosecute the Prosecution?

It was another of life's ambiguous jokes that he who had just published a book called *Resist Not Evil* should be called upon to defend the most militant union in America against charges of murder, a defense which must of necessity include a partial justification of force and violence in the industrial wars of the West.

The trouble with the Western Federation of Miners, those hard-rock drillers of Colorado, Montana and Idaho who went deep into the earth to blast out great fortunes in gold, silver, copper and lead, was that they somehow hadn't gotten around to reading Clarence Darrow's beautiful little book. Or if they had read it they hadn't quite been converted to his doctrine of nonresistance. Many of them were religious men; they were acquainted with the lines from Matthew upon which it had been based, "But I say unto you, that ye resist not evil, but whosoever shall smite ye on thy right cheek, turn to him the other also." They had been told in their simple wooden churches that the meek would inherit the earth, but by some obscure machinations the mineowners had inherited the earth and all the riches within it; the workers had inherited the twelve-hour day, the seven-day week, the marginal-subsistence wage and working conditions so dangerous and so unguarded that hundreds of their comrades perished each year under mountains of rock.

For fifteen years now the miners had fought back: with fists, clubs, bullets, guns, dynamite: those who earn their living from dynamite are acquainted with its uses. In the heat of a strike local unions had shot it out with Pinkertons, deputies and non-union workers; they had used their guns to take possession of mines being operated by scab labor, and they had twice blown up mines and mills in the Coeur d'Alene region of northern Idaho. The last explosion had taken place in 1899, six years before, yet as a direct result the officers of the Western Federation of Miners were now in jail in Idaho, charged with murdering Idaho's ex-Governor Frank Steunenberg during the Christmas holidays of 1905.

Darrow found himself in much the same predicament as the Western miners: even after he had finished his book he had not been able to convince himself that nonresistance could serve any purpose in the machine age which was replacing the pioneer-handicraft economy of nineteenth-century America. "At its best the doctrine of nonresistance can only be held by dreamers and theorists and can have no place in daily life. Every government on earth furnishes proof that there is nothing practical or vital in its preachings; every government on earth is the personification of violence and force." The better to prove him right, the government of Colorado had in effect seceded from the Union in order that they might, in the words of their militia head, General Sherman Bell, "do up this anarchistic federation."

In the open and publicly avowed warfare between the state of Colorado and the Western Federation of Miners from January 1, 1902, until June 30, 1904, forty-two men were killed, a hundred and twelve injured, thirteen hundred and forty-five arrested and seven hundred and seventy-three deported from the state. The tragic part of this warfare was that it had been caused in its entirety by the refusal of the state government to live up to and obey the laws of its state. From his experience in industrial conflicts Darrow had learned the inexorable lesson that hate breeds hate; force breeds force, and violence breeds violence. It was because the unions had fought back that he was now on a fast train from Chicago to Denver at the request of John Mitchell, whose United Mine Workers were then conducting a strike to secure the same conditions for the coal miners of the South and West as had been earned for those of the East; any injury to the hard-rock miners would necessarily injure the cause of the coal miners. He would not merely defend the federation against the killing of Frank Steunenberg, but against allegations of conducting the most fantastic murder ring ever charged to "an inner circle of terrorists" in American history.

He did not have to surround himself with sets of books and newspaper files to recall the defection of Colorado; the bloody details were still too fresh in his mind. The workingmen of Colorado who had long been brutalized and exhausted by the twelve-hour day in the mine, smelter and mill had labored hard to get an eight-hour law passed in the state. By an intensive program of education they had at length succeeded in getting the legislature to pass their law. But the state Supreme Court had promptly declared it unconstitutional. "It is unconstitutional," observed Darrow, "to pass a law which won't permit Guggenheim to take twelve hours out of the hide of his men. If this is true, then what is the constitution for, except to use for the rich to destroy the laws that are made for the poor?"

This blow would have discouraged a less hardy group, but the miners, "men who worked hard, played hard, fought hard," set to work all over again to amend their constitution so that it would permit the eight-hour law. "Their amendment was adopted by a majority of nearly forty-seven thousand, a large one in a state where the vote for President in 1900 was only two hundred and twenty thousand. A legislature pledged and duty bound to enact this amendment was elected." Then the mine- and smelter owners stepped in, exerting such power and force over the legislature that that body refused to pass the amendment which they were legally bound and obliged to pass.

The miners struck, and "certain mining camps in Colorado became little short of hells on earth, owing to the contest of the desperate strikers with the men who had taken their places." Non-union workers were clubbed, shot, run out of the Cripple Creek and Telluride sections: the miners had believed in the efficacy of the vote; they had squandered their years, their strength and their funds to get laws passed; when they found that the owners could make a farce out of a political structure in which the government was pledged to operate according to the will and with the consent of the governed, they saw no way to gain their ends except through force. Force had prevailed; the miners had succeeded in their strikes, had won the eight-hour day and gone back to work under good contracts.

2

But the men who worked in the smelters were still on the twelve-hour shift, with twenty-four hours straight every other Sunday. The miners belonged to a federation, and federation meant all trades within their industry. When the smelterers went on strike and were being defeated because the absentee smelter owners sent in deputies, Pinkertons and scabs, the miners stopped work to keep ore from being provided to the smelters. The mineowners were impelled to call in non-union miners; more blood was shed, and Governor

Peabody, declaring the Cripple Creek section in a state of insurrection, ordered out the militia.

The commander of the militia was General Sherman Bell, who had been a Roughrider in Cuba with Theodore Roosevelt and had been working for one of the mine companies at five thousand dollars a year when Governor Peabody offered him the job of adjutant-general. The Boston *Transcript* reported that since this job paid less than the five thousand he had been earning, the Mine Owners' Association agreed to pay him the difference. In addition, as Ray Stannard Baker wrote in *McClure's*, "The mineowners even advanced money to pay the soldiers." The *Army and Navy Journal* cried out, "That the governor should virtually borrow money from the mineowners to maintain the troops he had assigned to guard their property was a serious reflection upon the authority of the state. That arrangement virtually placed the troops in the relation of hired men to the operators. It was a rank perversion of the whole theory and purpose of the National Guard and was more likely to incite disorder than to prevent it."

General Bell, proclaiming publicly that his purpose was the extermination of the miners' union and its affiliates, now played the role of Roughrider over the citizens of Cripple Creek. He seized a private building to use as his military headquarters, marched his troops on the city hall, where he informed the mayor and chief of police that unless they obeyed military orders their city hall would also be seized. The sheriff, county assessor and treasurer were forced to resign. Every workingman in the vicinity who belonged to a union was arrested, thrown into a military bull pen and held incommunicado for weeks. When the editor of the Victor *Record* dared to criticize his usurpation of power, Bell established a military censorship of the paper, arrested the entire staff and marched them to his prison, where he kept them for twenty-four hours without food. Women and children voicing criticism were also lodged in the bull pen. In answer to the demand of the hundreds of prisoners for their right of habeas corpus, or their right to be charged with a specific crime and given a public hearing in court—the foundation of the American legal system, which Blackstone called "the second Magna Charta"—General Bell declared that the writ of habeas corpus had been suspended! Judge Seeds of Victor, outraged, ordered the general to bring his prisoners into court. Bell surrounded the courthouse with troops, put Gatling guns in the streets, sharpshooters on the roofs of the surrounding buildings and lined up his prisoners in the courtroom. When Judge Seeds handed down a decree that all prisoners be surrendered to the civil courts General Bell laughed at the order and marched his union men back to the bull pen.

General Bell had precedent in Colorado. When Charles H. Moyer, president of the Western Federation of Miners had gone to Telluride to help the miners in their strike and was seized by the military on the grounds that he had desecrated the American flag by printing on it the complaints of the miners held in the bull pens, Judge Stevens had issued a writ of habeas corpus for Moyer. The general had flatly refused to turn him over to the court, and Governor Peabody had sustained his general by publicity proclaiming, "We have suspended the right of habeas corpus." The federation lawyers had appealed the governor's decree to the state Supreme Court, but the Supreme Court had upheld the governor's right to suspend the writ. When told that he was violating the Constitution, Judge McClelland had replied, "To hell with the Constitution; we're not following the Constitution!"

Darrow had sent a shart protest to President Roosevelt when this decree was handed down, but Roosevelt had not wanted to ride rough over his brother Roughrider and had said nothing. Colorado had stepped out of the union. The miners were abandoned. Henry George, Jr., an eyewitness, telegraphed to the New York *American*, "The astounding situation here in Colorado is that instead of bending all their efforts to putting down what they declare to be a state of lawlessness, Governor Peabody and the higher authorities, using the military arm of their government, are devoting practically all their attention to putting down the law. The prime insurrectionist against the constitutional order of things and the chief rebels against the regularly established laws are the governor and his soldiers, acting with various citizens' committees, inspired and influenced by, where they are not directly representative of, the great and all-powerful railroads, mining and smelter interests of Colorado. It is bayonet rule against the rule established by the ballot."

Then on June 4, 1904, a small railroad depot at Independence was blown up, killing fourteen non-union men. The bomb was set off by a smooth, round-faced man named Harry Orchard, who had worked in various mines for a total of eleven months in the previous five years, carried a union card, but for the six months immediately preceding the explosion had been, by his own confession, working for the Mine Owners' Association as an informer, reporting federation meetings to private detectives Scott and Sterling. Five witnesses had seen Orchard climb the back stairs of the boardinghouse in which

Scott and Sterling lived no less than twenty times in the days immediately preceding the explosion. When bloodhounds had picked up Orchard's trail the man who owned the dogs was called off the job by Sterling, who told him, "Never mind, we know who blew up the station."

The federation was instantly charged with the crime. Citizens' Alliances, sponsored by the Mine Owners' Association, seized control of the region. Almost eight hundred men, many of them owning homes and businesses in the Cripple Creek area, were deported from the region at the point of bayonets. "In one instance all the union employees of a certain mine were loaded into a train and under military escort were taken across the line into Kansas and dumped on the prairie like so many cattle."

A howl of protest went up throughout the nation. Ex-Senator John M. Thurston of Nebraska, whom *The Arena* classed as a strong Republican and friend of the corporations, said in the *American*, "The act of the Colorado militia in driving out of the state members of the Western Federation of Miners was purely an exercise of despotic power. In Russia this sort of thing would go unnoticed, but we will not countenance it in the United States. The attempt of the militia to deport miners is a crime against the United States government. Every theory of our government argues against this action; if they have established a precedent there will be no such thing hereafter as a place of justice for anyone against whom a state or an individual sets its seal."

The Colorado operators were not impressed by the outcry. *Harper's Weekly* reported the president of the Citizens' Alliance in Pueblo as saying, "The alliance will not lay down its arms until the federation and the United Mine Workers have left the state." The head of the alliance in Denver said, "Unions should not strike; striking unions are not legitimate; the federation must be destroyed." General Bell arrested greater numbers of workingmen, sent troops to search their homes without warrants, committed unbridled acts of vandalism against the property of the local unions. The Pittsburgh *Dispatch* said of him, "The despotic manner in which, without trial or even definite charge, but upon the mere fact of being union miners, citizens were deported and dumped, starving, upon contiguous states will remain as a disgraceful record for Colorado long after Bell has vanished," while the Cleveland *Leader* excoriated Governor Peabody by saying editorially, "Neither will Colorado shine excused before the country if its accused residents are tried by court-martial and deprived of the right to the due processes of law and the proper opportunity for defense that belongs to civiliza-

tion and should not be alienable by any governor's proclamation."
President Roosevelt maintained a disinterested silence.

Though large sums of money were offered for the arrest of the
culprits, though Orchard could have been picked up by the Pinkertons at any time, no one was ever tried for the Independence Depot
explosion.

This was the setup; these were the men Darrow would have to
meet in the Idaho courts; these the men the billion-dollar mining-
and-smelter interests would employ; these the methods with which
they would try to hang the three union officials. For Governor
Gooding of Idaho had declared, "These men will never leave Idaho
alive!" and Darrow knew that millions would be spent to make good
that threat. He knew that it would be the toughest case of his career,
a knock-'em-down and drag-'em-out brawl with no holds barred.
The Mine Owners' Association had been unable to exterminate the
federation in 1904, but nothing was to be allowed to stop them in
1906. Boise was to be the final battlefield.

3

In Denver Darrow was received by Edmund Richardson, tall,
lean, dark, bald, one of the most forceful and fearless attorneys of
the Northwest. Richardson had long been the attorney for the
federation. He was hard, fast, pyrotechnic, a fierce cross-examiner;
Darrow was gentle, slow, persuasive, a pleader. Richardson had already made one trip to Idaho for the preliminary hearings. As he
detailed the circumstances of the killing and the arrest of the federation officers Darrow shook his head in sadness and consternation.

On the evening of December 30, 1905, Frank Steunenberg conferred until late with the officials of the Caldwell Bank, of which he
was president, then walked over to the Saratoga Hotel to sit in the
lobby, read the paper and chat with friends. Watching him from a
corner of the lobby was Harry Orchard, who had been in and out
of Caldwell for five months, masquerading under the title of Tom
Hogan, sheep buyer. At six o'clock Steunenberg rose to go home
for his supper; Orchard ran up to room nineteen, picked up the
bomb he had prepared there and hurried across the snow-covered
fields by a back route to Steunenberg's house. He attached his bomb
to the gate, stretched a string near ground level which Steunenberg
must kick as he entered his grounds. His work done, he ran as fast as
he could in the direction of the hotel. When he was a block and a
half from the Saratoga there was an explosion "that rocked the supper dishes on the tables of Caldwell and could be heard miles away

at Palma." Orchard hurried into the bar, called upon the bartender for a drink and engaged him in conversation as to the possible cause of the explosion.

The bomb tore a hole in Steunenberg's side and back. He was carried into his home, where he died within the hour. The only words he spoke were, "Who shot me?"

"Who was this man Steunenberg?" Darrow demanded of Richardson. "What was his background? Why should Orchard want to kill him?"

Frank Steunenberg was a big, solidly built man with the face of a Roman senator; by nature he was plain, phlegmatic, unassuming, bluff, a family man; his only idiosyncrasy was that he would never wear a necktie and would never permit anyone to ask him why he wouldn't wear one. He had come out of Iowa where he had served as a printer during the winters on the Des Moines *Register* while working his way through the agricultural college at Ames. By 1886, the year of the Haymarket explosion, he was editing the Knoxville *Express* in Iowa and shortly thereafter joined his brother in Caldwell, Idaho, where they published the Caldwell *Record* with moderate prosperity. In 1896 he was nominated for governor by the Democratic party because they couldn't agree on any one of their professional politicians; since he had been a union printer and had been made an honorary member of the Boise Typographical Union, the labor vote came out for him solidly.

His first term was pleasant, but in 1899 the Coeur d'Alene miners went on strike, with the bitterest friction in the Bunker Hill and Sullivan mines, which had imported strikebreakers from Chicago and other big cities and was using armed Pinkerton operatives out of Denver and Spokane to guard them. Described by one of the union members as "children who, when they got mad, could see no further than the veil of anger before their eyes," the miners had met in their union hall in Burke and, against the counsel of their president and cooler heads, voted to blow up the Bunker Hill mine. They took possession of a freight train standing in the main street of the valley town, rode to Gem, where they picked up more men and dynamite from the depot, and proceeded a thousand strong to Wardner, where they blew up the mine.

The local authorities were few in number; the state militia was fighting in the Philippines; Governor Steunenberg saw no recourse other than to ask President McKinley for Federal troops. It was a difficult decision to make: he had been elected by the labor vote, yet a forbearance of this crime could bring destruction to the state. Within four days troops had occupied the territory and martial

law was in effect. Once again every union man in the region was arrested, without any attempt being made to separate the guilty from
the innocent; more than a thousand men were herded into a bull pen
made up of one barnlike structure and a string of boxcars closed
in by barbed wire. Colored troops were sent in to guard the prisoners. Here they were held for from four to six months, without trial
or any effort made to locate the ringleaders; the sanitary conditions
were excremental, the food bad, the families of the men not permitted to see them. A sign was hung out which read THE AMERICAN
BASTILLE. Some of the conditions of overcrowding were perhaps un-
avoidable; a United States Senate Investigating Committee, which
summoned Steunenberg to Washington to account for his conduct,
gave him a partial exoneration.

It was his next move which had made his name anathema to every
workingman in the Northwest: he decreed that all members of the
federation were equally guilty and equally criminals; as a consequence he set up a "permit system" whereby no man could work
in an Idaho mine or mill unless he were first approved by the general in charge of the troops, by the adjutant general of the state, and
unless he first renounced his allegiance to the federation. Hundreds
of men who had homes in the Coeur d'Alene, who had relatives
and friends and deep roots in northern Idaho, lost their jobs, had
to pack their belongings and, like the veterans of the American
Railway Union strike, tramp the roads and mountains of strange
countries, face an ever-spreading black list, trying to find work to
support their wives and children.

Several years later a Federal court sitting in Boise was to impugn
Governor Steunenberg's motives when charging that Steunenberg
had defrauded the United States government of its lands by bribing
dummy owners, often mendicants picked up on the streets of Boise,
to stake out homesteads and then turn them over to Steunenberg and
his associates. In his opening statement to the jury, in which he was
outlining the case against Senator Borah as counsel for Steunenberg's
land company, Federal Judge Burch, acting as special assistant to
the United States attorney general, declared:

"In 1889 there was some trouble in the Coeur d'Alene district.
Governor Steunenberg had gone there presumably on the patriotic
mission of stopping those troubles. In the course of that transaction
he became acquainted with a wealthy mineowner, A. B. Campbell,
of Spokane. Friendly relations between these two men grew out of
the settlement of, or at least some time during, such trouble up there.
Mr Campbell proffered any kindly offices that he might at any time
show Governor Steunenberg in any way. I say they (the Steunen-

berg land combine) reached the end of their money and needed more, so Steunenberg took himself to Washington to meet his friend Mr Campbell."

Through the good offices of Mr Campbell, Steunenberg was able to secure from certain lumber interests sufficient money to continue his operations and save the money he had already invested. Steunenberg had enjoyed a reputation of being an honest man; he had turned down a twenty-thousand-dollar bribe to pardon a convicted murderer; when "offered a seat in the United States Senate if he would pardon Diamond Field Jack, who had been convicted of killing several men in the bloody sheep-and-cattle wars of the Idaho range, he had brought his fist down so hard on a table in the Palace Hotel in San Francisco that he had cracked its marble top, refusing to become a senator at that price, much as he wanted to be a senator." Considering the evidence which had been gathered by the Federal investigators, if Frank Steunenberg had not been martyrized by Harry Orchard's bomb, he would never have become encased in a bronze statue in front of the Idaho capitol.

4

The townspeople of Caldwell had quickly gathered about Steunenberg's home when the site of the explosion became known. Within two hours Governor Gooding and other state officials arrived on a special train from Boise, thirty miles away. A Citizens' Committee was at once formed which offered a twenty-five-thousand-dollar reward for the capture of the murderer; the governor offered another five thousand dollars. Many were too shocked to wonder who had committed the cowardly crime; others said at once, "It's the miners getting even for what he did to them in the Coeur d'Alene in 1899." "Each fellow had a different theory of what had happened," relates an eyewitness, "but most felt it had been an act of revenge for something he had done as governor." A. B. Campbell, who turned out to be an officer of the Mine Owners' Association, cried, "There is no doubt that Steunenberg's death was the penalty for his activity in doing his duty during the strike. I heard today that the men who were sent to the penitentiary as a result of that strike have been getting out in the past few months." No one suspected Harry Orchard, who was mingling with the crowds at the Saratoga, for the Caldwell men who had become acquainted with him over the five months described him as a "sociable, affable fellow, well liked. The boys enjoyed having him sit in the game of solo or slough. He was a little red-faced, round-faced man with a kindly appearance; he seemed a whole-souled mick who wouldn't hurt anybody—a common-looking, jolly fellow who you wouldn't pick out for any peculiarity." The only criticism made of Orchard was by Sheriff Moseley:

"Orchard can't meet your eye. When he meets your glance his eyes do not waver exactly, but slide away, smoothly, easily and almost imperceptibly."

On the train from Boise had also come Joe Hutchinson, lieutenant governor under Steunenberg during his first uneventful term. Hutchinson found a piece of fish string near the gateway, which he handed to Charles Steunenberg, brother of the murdered man, saying, "This is the string your brother kicked to touch off the bomb." The next morning Charles Steunenberg was passing the Saratoga Hotel with his friend George Froman, who pointed to Harry Orchard sitting complacently in the lobby behind the plate-glass window.

"There's the man that did it," observed Froman.

"Why do you say that?"

"Because he's been hanging around here for months, doing nothing. He's affluent but has no business. A number of times he has asked about your brother, when he was coming back."

Charles Steunenberg told Hutchinson of Froman's suspicions. Hutchinson "asked Lizzie Volberg, a hasher in the hotel, if she could get him into Orchard's room. Lizzie got a key and, while her sister Theresa stood guard at the head of the stairs, let Hutchinson into room nineteen. He found two towels tied together and hung over the doorknob to hide the keyhole. In the chamber pot he found traces of the plaster of Paris from which the bomb had been made. In a suitcase he found another piece of fishline exactly like the piece he had found at the governor's gate two hours after the explosion." The sheriff, who was notified immediately, located a check to Orchard's trunk at the railroad depot; when it was opened the searching party discovered a quantity of the explosive that had been used in the Steunenberg bomb, a full set of burglars' tools and changes of clothing which would enable Orchard to assume the apparel of any walk of life.

The clerk at the bar of the Saratoga thought Orchard wanted to get caught. "He impressed me as being a smart Irishman who hungered for notoriety. I saw him in the hotel after the murder occurred. He seemed to be courting recognition, and I thought at the time that he was maneuvering to have suspicion directed against him." Orchard had left himself so wide open that for several days the newspapers refused to take him seriously, claiming that he was only a front for the real murderer whom he was helping to make his getaway. Nor does Orchard in his confession throw much light on this subject:

"I cannot tell what came across me. I had some plaster-Paris and some chloride of potash and some sugar in my room, also some little bottles and screw eyes, and I knew there might be some little crumbs of dynamite scattered around on the floor. I intended to clean the carpet and throw this stuff that might look suspicious away, and I had plenty of time."

However, if Orchard wanted to be arrested he appeared in no hurry. The following morning, January first, he walked unsolicited into a meeting of the Citizens' Committee taking place in the Commercial Bank, over which Sheriff Moseley was presiding. "I understand I am under suspicion," he said. "I should like to clear myself." So calm and assured was Orchard, so sincere and genuine in manner, "so obviously the whole-souled guy who wouldn't hurt anybody," that in spite of the overwhelming evidence piled up against him the committee was convinced of his innocence and let him go.

It was not until late that afternoon that Sheriff Moseley arrested Orchard and lodged him in the Caldwell jail. Orchard's good humor was not perturbed; he appeared unconcerned and sang in his cell and announced that there would be a lawyer to defend him as soon as it became known that he had been arrested. At Steunenberg's funeral the following day, the most impressive ever seen in Idaho, Senator Borah said wisely, "In the midst of this awful tragedy let us strive to be just. This crime, when fastened upon its author, will place him beyond the pale of human forgiveness or pity. Let us not believe it is the crime of any class or any portion of our citizens or that it finds sympathy with anyone other than the actual perpetrator."

But Borah was too late. The ever-vigilant General Sherman Bell of Colorado had beat him to the punch. The day before the funeral, when he had heard of the arrest, Bell predicted in the Denver *Republican* that Orchard would confess his guilt and tell who were his accomplices.

"I think we shall convince Harry Orchard of the wisdom of such a course," said the general.

The newspapers of Colorado, Montana and Washington filled columns with editorials that Steunenberg had been murdered by the Western Federation of Miners. Private detectives hired from the Thiele agency of Spokane, which supplied the mineowners with labor spies, non-union workers and armed deputies, cried, "Conspiracy to murder!" a cry echoed by the mineowners and officials of Colorado and reprinted in the Idaho *Daily Statesman* for home consumption.

Still the people of Idaho resisted the pressure being put upon them to drag the federation into a murder conspiracy. The state was mostly inhabited by peaceful farmers and small merchants who had no connection with the distant mines and who wanted to forget the outbreaks of 1899. They were anxious to bring Orchard to trial and convict this crime against the highest office of their state; they were a quiet, peaceful people who shrank back from starting or participating in a class war. For the eighteen days that Harry Orchard remained in the jail in Caldwell even those who said the murder had grown out of the Coeur d'Alene bull-pen days quickly added, "but it was the act of someone who was injured and nursed his grievance through the years."

Then on the twelfth of January someone convinced the ruling officers of Idaho that they should put James McParland, head of the Denver office of the Pinkertons, in charge of the investigation. He promptly set out for Boise to tell the state of Idaho who had killed their ex-governor.

"My God!" groaned Clarence Darrow.

5

Exactly one week after the *Statesman* announced that the Pinkertons had become Idaho's official detectives, and three days after McParland reached Caldwell, Harry Orchard was moved to the state penitentiary in Boise. The law provides that a prisoner may be moved to the penitentiary only if he is in imminent danger, yet the day before, when District Attorney Van Duyn of Canyon County was asked whether Orchard would be left in Caldwell, he had replied, "I cannot see where he would be safer in Boise. Sheriff Nichols has him well guarded." Sheriff Nichols had added, "It's up to me to say whether Orchard can be brought to Boise for safekeeping, and my answer has been 'no' emphatically several times. I will not consent to the man's being taken away from my county." The next morning, when the sheriff relinquished his prisoner, he was red faced and embarrassed. "I was firm in my belief that nothing could change my mind," he told the twitting newspaper reporters, "but the matter was put to me in an entirely different light. The reason for the removal will be made public in good time."

That good time did not take place for thirteen days, thirteen days of a very odd silence on the part of the *Statesman*, thought Darrow as he fingered through the pages and could find no reference to the Steunenberg murder. For ten of these thirteen days Orchard was held in solitary confinement in condemned men's row, with no human being permitted to see him or talk to him or communicate with him. That this maneuver was commanded by McParland is admitted by as implacable a foe of the federation as Charles Steunenberg, for Harry Orchard was no stranger to McParland. Orchard had worked as an informer and spy against his own union, drawing pay from the Mine Owners' Association. McParland was accustomed to dealing with informers; he knew that any man who will turn against his comrades for pay will make the most profitable bargain he can get. But first he had to be softened up by ten days of silence and loneliness, ten days of being frightened in a dark death cell, terrorized by the realization that the legal processes of Idaho had broken down, that he might easily rot out his life in this cell without ever coming to trial.

"The McParland-Pinkerton war with the Federation was a rough affair, and a book might be filled with it and hardly get past the earliest rounds of vituperation," writes the family biographer of the Pinkertons.

For eighteen years, ever since the inception of the federation, McParland had been retained by the Mine Owners' Association to fight the big union; before that he had been employed to destroy the young locals that were struggling to come into existence in Colorado. For more than twenty years, ever since he had been transferred to Denver after breaking up the Molly Maguires, the mineowners had been McParland's chief employer, often his sole employer. He had been paid millions of dollars to provide strikebreakers; to provide the equivalent of the Pennsylvania Coal and Iron police; to keep every local union infested with labor spies, men with names like Sirango, Crane, Conibear, spies in peacetime who were paid by the Pinkerton office to go into the mining fields disguised as workers: saboteurs who joined the unions, worked themselves into office by their ability and willingness to do clerical chores and from this vantage point supplied the mine and smelter operators with discharge lists, with information on every aim of the union; disrupted the unity of the men by causing factional strife; confused the records and squandered the funds; forced senseless strikes at times when the employers were in a position to win—as Sirango has boasted of having accomplished in the Coeur d'Alene. McParland's task of fastening the guilt for the killing of Steunenberg would be paid for not only by Idaho, but by the Denver office of the Pinkerton agency as well.

At the end of ten days Orchard was taken out of solitary and led to a pleasant room where Warden Whitney introduced him to McParland and then withdrew, an act which left no doubt in Orchard's mind but that McParland represented Idaho and was authorized to make a deal for the state. In his published *Autobiography* Orchard gives a one-paragraph picture of this first meeting, which for Darrow illuminated the whole story:

"He started in on my belief in the hereafter and spoke of what an awful thing it was to live and die a sinful life and that every man ought to repent for his sins and that there was no sin that God would not forgive. He spoke of King David being a murderer, and also the Apostle Paul. He also told me of some cases where men had turned state's evidence and that when the state had used them for a witness they did not or could not prosecute them. He said that men might be thousands of miles away from where a murder took place and be guilty of that murder and be charged with conspiracy and that the man who committed the murder was not as guilty as the conspirators. *He further said he was satisfied I had only been used as a tool, and he was sure the Western Federation of Miners was behind this,* that they had carried on their work with a high hand but that their foundation had begun to crumble."

Luncheon was served to the two men. It was the first good food that Orchard had tasted for ten horrible days. During the afternoon McParland read to him from the Bible—and told him the story of Kelly the Bum who had taken part in thirteen atrocious murders but who, persuaded by McParland to turn state's evidence, had been given a thousand dollars and permitted to leave the country. At the end of the day Orchard was returned to his solitary cell.

It was McParland's next task to make respectable a man who had begun his career of crime by short-weighting the farmers who brought milk to his Canadian cheese factory; who burned down the factory to collect the insurance; who abandoned his wife and six-months-old daughter to run away with another man's wife; who married a third woman without bothering to divorce his first wife, spent the money she had inherited from her husband and deserted her when she had become so destitute that she had to take in washing; who had stolen from his miner roommate the possessions of his trunk; who had robbed mines of their ore; who burned down a saloon for a hundred dollars so the owner could collect his insurance; who had plotted to kidnap the child of a former partner, to rob streetcar conductors, to sweat gold coins; a man who for years had roamed the West, living off the kit of burglars' tools found in his trunk in Caldwell; who had shot and killed a drunken man in a dark street; who admitted nearly every foul crime on the agenda. McParland had to get rid of this moral leper, whose only code for twenty years had been to live as comfortably and excitingly as he could without doing an hour of work, and replace him with another Harry Orchard who would be as credible and acceptable as this pathological liar was incredible and unacceptable. Without this Orchard's confession implicating the Western Federation of Miners would be worthless.

6

There was only one way to perform this miracle: a religious conversion so complete that the man's soul would be reborn. Then when Darrow would cry out in his towering rage, "How can anyone believe a word uttered by this self-confessed perjurer, kidnaper, thief, firebug and murderer?" the prosecution could answer, "Ah, but you are referring to the old Harry Orchard. This is the new Harry Orchard, who has found God." For Darrow the most strangulating moment of the series of bitter trials came when Prosecutor James Hawley told the jury:

"Orchard is everything despicable in a man save in one regard: he will tell the truth!"

During the succeeding days Orchard was brought to McParland's sanctum, where he intermingled passages from the Bible with tales of how men who had turned state's evidence had become national heroes. The *Statesman* relates the inside story, which, like Orchard's confession, revealed more for the historic record than it intended:

"McParland resolved to use his own personal energies in persuading Orchard to make a confession. This was slow work indeed, but the sagacity of the detective, his great ability of reading human nature, *his will power working over that of the prisoner, at last acquired the desired results. Orchard gradually became as clay in the hands of the detective.* At last one day Orchard met his visitor with an expression upon his face that told the detective as plainly as words that the man was about to confess.

"'You have something to tell me?' asked the detective.

"'I am ready to make a full confession. I am asking no leniency. My lonely imprisonment will drive me crazy if I do not confess. My conscience will not permit me to keep the guilty secrets. If ever a man suffered the torments of hell, I am that man. I can only hope that God in His infinite mercy will heed my prayers. I have been a wicked man. I want to tell.'"

On the day they broke the news of the confession Orchard cried in the headline of the *Statesman*, which had up until this time reviled him as a heinous murderer: "My only hope is to save my soul from hell!" Its lead column reported, "With tears rolling down his cheeks, with bowed head and thoughts of his early religious training, Harry Orchard broke down and made a full confession. It is believed that every word spoken by the conscience-stricken man is true. In fact, investigations made have proved conclusively that Orchard told the truth."

Orchard's confession is one of the most confounding ever made. He accused the officers of the federation of hiring him not only to kill Governor Steunenberg, but to murder Governor Peabody, General Sherman Bell, Supreme Court justices, mineowners, mine superintendents, private detectives; of plotting every unexplained mine explosion, including the Independence Depot explosion, fire, accident and death that had taken place in the Northwest since the blowing up of the Bunker Hill mine in 1899. Although Prosecutor Hawley swore that when the federation wanted Steunenberg murdered they had naturally turned to "their arch-killer Orchard" for the job, Orchard himself admitted that after spending years of time and thousands of federation dollars to bump off their foes, with the exception of Steunenberg, the condemned men were walking the streets hale and hearty, never having been hit by a pea-shooter.

"If I had been one of the federation officials," snorted Darrow, "and this bungler had been working for me, I would have fired him on the grounds of incompetence!"

It is an insecurity which threatens the entire juridical basis of justice for a state to offer promises of immunity to a criminal who will turn state's evidence, yet no man ever collected his rewards on earth, or in heaven, more instantaneously. Borah had said at Steunenberg's funeral, "This crime, when fastened upon its author, will place him beyond the pale of human forgiveness." But Borah was wrong, and when he agreed to take part in the prosecution he helped prove himself wrong. The state provided Orchard with whatever small sums of money he requested. Clothing was bought for him, new suits, shirts, collars, ties, shoes. He enjoyed frequent visits from Governor Gooding; within a short time the governor was calling him "Harry," and Orchard was calling Borah "Bill"; when Governor Gooding took him to Boise for luncheon at the best restaurant in town Judge Wood became so outraged, he was on the verge of citing the governor for contempt. Never again was Orchard confined in a cell. Never again was he kept inside the penitentiary. He was moved into a little bungalow outside the walls and fed from the guards' table. "He will be well fed and provided with reading matter and such luxuries as are deemed advisable to let him have," promised Warden Whitney. The nation was treated to a spectacle in which a man who only a few days before had been loathed as the most unspeakable scoundrel and lunatic in the history of the state became by the simple signature of one of his many aliases a hero and petted darling, to whom papers from the big cities of the East were brought every day so that he might feast on his picture and read the glowing accounts of his regeneration.

A clue as to what Orchard confidently expected was revealed when he was ordered to appear before Judge Wood for sentence. James Hawley, being away at the time and consequently unable to appear as Orchard's counsel, instructed his son Jesse to tell Orchard to plead "not guilty."

"But how can I do that when I am guilty?" asked Orchard.

"The people of Idaho will never convict you," replied Jesse.

"But I didn't confess for immunity," said Orchard. "I confessed to set myself straight with God. What do you think I ought to do?"

"I think you ought to swing for it, Harry."

"But why? I've helped the state all I can."

"Yes, but justice must be satisfied. And since you have found God it is better for you to die now, when there is no chance for you to backslide or lose your Christianity."

"No, no," protested Orchard. "I want to go out into the world and atone for my sins!"

It was by no means the first time that Clarence Darrow had to cry out, "Who will prosecute the prosecution?" In the long, flat silence that followed his question he perceived the answer: no one would prosecute the prosecution—except himself. Somehow that had become his main job; he would indict the indictors before a jury not of twelve men, but of a hundred million of his countrymen. Only before the bar of public opinion could their conspiracy be prosecuted.

7

Extradition papers were immediately drawn up in Boise against Charles H. Moyer, president of the federation; William D. Haywood, secretary-treasurer, and George Pettibone, who had formerly been active in the miners' union but now ran a supply store in Denver. Not even Orchard had claimed that these three men had ever been in Caldwell, yet since extradition could only be sought if they were fugitives from justice, Idaho made this consciously fraudulent claim. The officials of Idaho then conspired with the officials of Colorado to remove the three men.

"On the night of February 17, 1906, Moyer, I and George Pettibone were arrested," writes William Haywood. "Moyer at the depot where he was on his way to visit the Smelterman's Union at Iola, Pettibone at his home and myself at a rooming house near the office. About eleven-thirty there was a knock at the door. I got up and asked who was there. A voice replied:

" 'I want to see you, Bill.' I opened the door, when I saw a deputy whom I knew. He said:

" 'I want you to come with me.' I asked him why.

"He said, 'I can't tell you now, but you must come.' We went down and got into a carriage. I asked him where we were going. He told me, 'To the county jail.'

" 'If you are arresting me,' I said, 'why didn't you come with a warrant?'

" 'I have no warrant,' he replied.

"They put me in one of the Federal cells. A few minutes later the sheriff came around. I asked him what it all meant. He said:

" 'They're going to take you to Idaho. They've got you mixed up in the Steunenberg murder.'

" 'Are we to have no chance at all? You can't arrest a man without a warrant and transport him to another state without extradition papers.'

" 'It looks as though that's what they're prepared to do,' he admitted.

"About five in the morning I was taken with Moyer and Pettibone into the office. There were a lot of strange men there. We drove along quiet streets, each of us in a separate carriage with three guards. A train was ready and waiting. We were going at terrific speed. The train took on coal and water at small stations and stopped at none of the larger towns along the route. When we arrived at Boise we were again put into separate conveyances. We drove to the penitentiary. There was a sign over the gate, 'Admittance, Twenty-five Cents,' but I was admitted without charge. We were then put in murderers' row in the death house."

When the papers reported the methods by means of which Moyer, Haywood and Pettibone had been brought into Idaho the clerk of the court in which the men were to be tried exclaimed to one of the leading lawyers of Boise:

"That's pretty highhanded methods!"

"What's the difference," grinned the lawyer, "as long as we've got them?"

The difference, decided Darrow, was that by setting this precedent any man whom a partisan group wished to convict in a trial by passion could be kidnaped by a conspiring of the officers temporarily in charge of the state's legal machinery. When these illegal processes finally victimized the lawyer who had smilingly asked, "What's the difference?"—as it eventually would in some form or other once the legal structure of the country was kicked overboard —he would see the difference—and from his jail cell he would howl for his rights.

Judge James F. Ailshie of the Idaho Supreme Court, to whom the defense appealed for a redress against the kidnaping, called Darrow "an enemy of the people" for defending Haywood and Pettibone. "Yes, it is true that Idaho kidnaped those men," said the judge outside his court, "and committed an illegal act in so doing. The state of Colorado had every right to arrest the Idaho officers and convict them." The judge was having his little joke: the Colorado officers had been accessories to the kidnaping and so were not in a position to prosecute. In his Supreme Court decision, in which Moyer, Haywood and Pettibone were refused the right to return to Colorado and be given a public hearing on Orchard's charges, Judge Ailshie wrote:

"The fact that a wrong has been committed against a prisoner in the manner or method pursued in subjecting his person to the jurisdiction of a state, against the laws of which he is charged with having transgressed, can constitute no legal or just reason why he should not answer the charge against him when brought before the proper tribunal. The commission of an offense in his arrest does not expiate the offense with which he is charged."

The case went to the Supreme Court of the United States, but Darrow was no longer so naïve as he had been in 1894, when he had expected the Supreme Court to keep Eugene Debs out of the prison. He had been studying the decisions of the Supreme Court since that time, and he had come to the conclusion that the majority of justices handed down decisions aimed to preserve the rights of property over the rights of persons, an opinion which the Supreme Court did little to controvert when it declared unconstitutional child-labor laws and minimum-wage laws. Nor did the Supreme Court disappoint him; stroking themselves with the dead hand of the past, they decided eight to one that nothing was amiss in the state of Idaho.

"No obligation was imposed upon the agent of Idaho to so time the arrest of the petitioner and so conduct his deportation from Colorado as to afford him a convenient opportunity before some judicial tribunal in Colorado, to test the question whether he was a fugitive from justice." Only Justice McKenna dissented, and while America would continue to produce Justice McKennas, thought Darrow, there was some fighting chance for democracy to survive. "Kidnaping is a crime, pure and simple," wrote Justice McKenna. "All the officers of the law are supposed to be on guard against it. But how is it when the law becomes the kidnaper, when the officers of the law, using its forms and exerting its power, become abductors? The foundation of extradition between the states is that the accused should be a fugitive from justice from the demanding state, and he may challenge the fact by habeas corpus immediately upon his arrest."

8

The prosecution was so arrogant that it did not bother to save face even before the outside world. Though Warden Whitney had promised to provide Orchard with whatever luxuries he could, the electric bulbs were taken out of the cells of Moyer, Haywood and Pettibone and candles substituted. The warden said, "Our power plant of late has not been able to provide all the lights, and the change was necessarily made." When the prisoners wanted to buy warm socks and flannel shirts to protect themselves against the cold the warden would not make the purchases; they were confined to their cells because the warden said he had no authority to allow them exercise. They were denied the right to talk to each other; they were denied the right to send letters without having them censored or to receive letters without having them read; they were denied access to newspapers, magazines, books or any other contact with the outside world. They were denied the right to have visitors unless permits were signed by the governor and Prosecutor Hawley. When all four of the prisoners were taken to Caldwell for the preliminary hearings the three union men were locked in the jail, but McParland protested that the place was too small for Orchard, who was then escorted to the Saratoga Hotel to pass the night. By a curious twist the only room available for Orchard was number nineteen.

"I wonder if he found any use for his trusty chamber pot?" mused Darrow.

When a complaint was raised by the defense against the methods being used on men whom the American law declared "innocent until proven guilty," Hawley expostulated, "It is very plain why all this howl is being made. It is the object of the defense to prejudice the minds of all persons possible. They are trying to queer the chance of getting a jury by claiming persecution."

As a well-trained criminal lawyer Darrow plunged into the basic problem of the case: what would the federation gain from killing Steunenberg? What motive could they have for the crime? This was furnished in five short paragraphs in Orchard's confession:

"Moyer said that he thought it would have a good effect if we could bump Steunenberg off and then write letters to Peabody, Sherman Bell and some others that had been trying to crush the federation and tell them that they, too, would get what Governor Steunenberg got; that we had not forgotten them and never would forget them, and the only way they would escape would be to die. Haywood said we would go back to Paterson, New Jersey, and send these letters from there and write them in such a way that they would think it was some of those foreign anarchists that had sent them, and if we got Steunenberg, after letting him go so long, then they would think sure that we never forgot anyone who had persecuted us. Pettibone said this would be all right. Moyer told me to get what money I would need from Haywood. Haywood gave me two hundred and forty dollars and said he hoped I would succeed in getting Steunenberg."

The provocation for Idaho's kidnaping-and-murder charge against the three officers of the federation is based on these five sentences. Yet the simplest analysis of their content shows them to be an invention. Charles Moyer was a highly intelligent and capable executive of the caliber of Eugene Debs, Thomas I. Kidd and John Mitchell; he believed in the power of organization and unity to better the lot of his forty thousand members and their families. He constantly preached against the use of force as a decapitating boomerang for organized labor. Could this man have been so colossally stupid as to suggest that they kill Steunenberg and then send letters to their other enemies, promising them the same horrible death, when the receipt of the very first of such letters would literally convict them of the murder of Steunenberg? There were no labor disputes in Idaho, nor had there been any serious differences since the riots of 1899. The federation was exhausted from the beating it had taken from Peabody and Bell's militia. After Steunenberg's history in the Coeur d'Alene the union leaders would be instantly implicated by its enemies. Their organization would be vilified, their scant resources shattered; they would lose the sympathy and support of the public; their bargaining power with the employers would be hamstrung; their lawsuits in the Colorado courts would be injured; their years of heartbreaking labor and sacrifice to build hospitals, accident and death-insurance funds, to educate their members, to reduce the seventy-hour week to the forty-eight-hour week, to raise wages above the subsistence level, would all be thrown down the hopper.

What could have been Haywood's idea in saying that they would go back to Paterson and make the threatening letters look as though they came from foreign anarchists? If the letters were to terrorize their enemies those letters would have to come from the federation, not from foreign anarchists who lived two thousand miles away. If Peabody and Bell had walked the streets unmolested during the bloodiest class war in America why should they be frightened by threatening letters from foreign anarchists?—or from anyone else?

No, Steunenberg could do them no harm alive; his death could do them no good.

9

Before he left Chicago Darrow had met Senator Dubois of Idaho and asked him whom he should employ as associate counsel in Boise.

"Give me your blueprints and specifications," replied Dubois.

"I must have a good lawyer, one with a good reputation in the community, one who is prominent but who hasn't been identified with labor unions."

Dubois ran over a list of Boise lawyers, but of each he commented, "No, you wouldn't want him. No, that one won't do. . . ."

"Isn't there any lawyer in Boise who will fill my particulars?"

"Yes, I know exactly the man to fill the bill, but he's a very high-grade man, and I don't think he'll take the job. His name is Edgar Wilson."

When Darrow reached Boise he checked in at the Idanha Hotel, then went immediately to see Edgar Wilson to offer him the job. When news of this got about, Boise rose in arms: business firms that had been employing Wilson told him he would never get any more of their work; civic organizations threatened that he would be committing political and legal suicide; family friends implored Mrs Wilson not to let her husband associate with those murderers; they would be ostracized if he did—lose their friends, be driven out of Boise. The situation was complicated by the fact that Fremont Wood, who had been Wilson's law partner for twenty-five years, was to be the presiding judge.

Edgar Wilson was a fifth-generation American. He went to Judge Wood.

"Would it embarrass you if I took this case?" he asked.

"No, it won't embarrass me," replied the judge. "If you think it's right to take it, go ahead and take it."

Wilson returned to Darrow and accepted the association. The one-acre Wilson estate on the edge of town, with its thousands of beautiful flowers, became for Ruby and Clarence an oasis in the sagebrush desert of hatred and vituperation in which they perforce spent their next two years. Darrow liked the Wilsons at once; that afternoon as they were driving home he got out with them at their house.

"Why, Clarence, where are you going?" asked Ruby.

"I'm going in with the Wilsons for dinner," replied Darrow.

"Sure," laughed Mrs Wilson, "come along; we'll share with you."

Later, when Darrow found himself in the prisoner's dock, in his hour of desperation and defeat, when all the people he had fought for and championed fell away from him: the labor unions, the socialists, the radicals, the intellectuals, the vast throng of middle-class admirers and camp followers; when the world had abandoned him the Wilsons were still standing by.

"Laura Wilson," said Darrow, clasping her hand, "you compromised yourself to befriend us."

"There is no such thing as compromising yourself for a friend," replied Mrs Wilson.

Yet Edgar Wilson had had his legal and personal life blasted because he worked with Darrow. He was accused of having taken a thirty-thousand-dollar fee to use his influence on Judge Wood, and Wood, who earned himself a place in history by achieving a fair and impartial trial amidst the hysteria of the blood lust, was defeated for re-election by a green young Democrat in traditionally Republican country. Sometime afterward Judge Wood asked a lawyer friend:

"In what way was I censorable?"

"You were censorable for being a damn fool. You should have sworn in Edgar Wilson, then adjourned court and asked the governor to appoint another judge."

"But why? I wasn't afraid of my own honesty."

"It was a question of what people would think."

The reception Darrow received in Boise would have poisoned a less hardy man, one less inured to this kind of universal condemnation, this all-pervading hatred; he would have shriveled under it, become ill, been forced to flee. When he walked the streets, when he went into public buildings, when he entered restaurants, he found icy faces of loathing turned upon him or passionately burning eyes of aversion and contempt.

"He is defending the killers," said Boise, "so he must be in league with the killers."

It was the old Kinsman days all over again, except that this time the solid wall of animosity turned toward him was not in play: there would be no Virginia reel or square dances when the debate was over. For Boise, which had tried so valiantly to remain calm and fair after the shocking murder, was now saddled with a vindictive series of class-war trials which would breed endless dissention and strife, write black pages on the slate of the seventeen-year-old state, spend a half million dollars of its hard-earned money and so exhaust its treasury that before the trials were over they would have to issue paper warranties to provide them with funds. Their state officials, leading attorneys and leading newspaper had told the people that Moyer, Haywood and Pettibone were guilty of killing Governor Steunenberg; ninety per cent of the citizens wanted the three men hung as fast as possible.

"I was still convinced of Haywood's guilt after the trial," says a Caldwell lawyer, "but then, I was convinced before the trial."

Hysteria gripped Boise. Reports circulated that "every home in Ada and Canyon counties had suffered intimidation from federation men who went from door to door posing as book agents and insurance men who would talk to the housewives. Sooner or later the conversation would get around to the trial:

" 'I hear you have a big trial coming up.'

" 'Yes.'

" 'Well, you want to pray your husband doesn't get on that jury. I've watched the Western Federation of Miners in Colorado, and when a juryman convicted a union man that juryman was always killed afterward.' "

One attorney would not permit his wife to open the door of his office for fear a bomb would go off; he always insisted upon opening it himself. The *Statesman* continued to print such inflammatory articles against the federation that Judge Wood had to order it to stop trying the case out of court or he would never be able to find an unprejudiced jury in Ada County. Rumors swept the town that Darrow had posted marksmen on Table Mountain behind the penitentiary who were going to pick off Orchard as he left the prison and then get Hawley and Borah. Hawley sent word to the defense that:

"The second man to be shot will be Clarence Darrow!"

The city became overrun with detectives. Nobody knew for whom they were working. "One of the detectives was an offensive fellow, potbellied, who went around contacting everybody and insulting everybody," relates one lawyer. "He came to my office and offered me twenty-five dollars a day for the simple task of witnessing signatures for a change of venue. When I refused to work for the union he snarled, 'The federation will get you for this.' It was not until 1912 that I learned from my law partner, who had been prosecuting attorney for Canyon County, that this C. O. Johnson had been employed by the Mine Owners' Association to pose as a federation detective. My partner showed me the dossier in which my reactions to the bait of twenty-five dollars a day had been recorded. If I had accepted that employment I would never again have been permitted to practice law in Caldwell."

The *Capitol News* ran articles demanding that the lists of men working for the state and the salaries they received be published. When by repeated hammerings they became successful in this campaign Charles Steunenberg charged, "The *Capitol News* has been reached. We had to fire some of our best undercover men."

One or two detectives shadowed Darrow night and day; often these detectives were shadowed by detectives. His home was watched at night while he slept; detectives watched his house while he was away; his wife was trailed. His wires were tapped, his mail opened, his notes and reports stolen, his telegrams read: a complete system of espionage.

Yet in the midst of the suspicion and hatred the Darrows found a few friends. Mr and Mrs K. I. Perky, who were among Boise's liberals, invited the Darrows to stay at their home until they could find a place of their own. Boise was scandalized; Mrs Charles Steunenberg went to her friend to protest.

"Darrow has a good mind," exclaimed Mrs Steunenberg, "but it is perverted. No ethical man would take such a case."

When Mrs Perky only smiled tolerantly Mrs Steunenberg continued:

"But what about his morals?"

"His morals are his own," replied Mrs Perky.

Darrow writes, "When I landed at Boise about the first person I met was Billy Cavenaugh. His face beamed with a broad smile as he came toward me, extending his hand. He was a stonecutter employed on a building I was passing and had thrown down his tools to come down and give me a warm handclasp and rejoice over my arrival in town." Every night Billy Cavenaugh waited for him to finish his work downtown, no matter how late it might be, and walked home with him as his bodyguard. When Darrow was too exhausted from a sixteen-hour siege to fall asleep, Cavenaugh would give his charge an alcohol rubdown with his powerful stonecutter's hands.

After a time the Darrows found a furnished bungalow on the outskirts of town, just three blocks from the Wilsons. There was a rose garden, a bright green lawn and an apple tree. Ruby, who had somewhat wistfully stored her new furniture from the flat on Sheridan Road, moved in their few pieces of luggage and set up housekeeping.

"This is fine," murmured Darrow. "On Sunday mornings I shall loll under this apple tree and read the funnies."

But he never got to read the paper under his apple tree of a Sunday morning. Idaho rang in another extradition, another confession and another charge of murder, a charge of murder which he had to go into the icy regions of northern Idaho to defend, not once, but twice, an effort which very nearly cost him his life.

10

The prosecution realized how difficult it would be to convict the federation officers on Orchard's testimony alone. Orchard had named Jack Simpkins, a member of the executive board of the federation, as his confederate in Caldwell, but since Simpkins had disappeared so completely that not even the Pinkertons could locate him, they compromised on Steve Adams, whom Orchard had declared to have been an accomplice in the blowing up of the Independence Depot.

Steve Adams was working on the hundred and sixty acres he had homesteaded near Baker City, Oregon, when he was arrested by Thiele, head of the private-detective agency in Spokane, and by Brown, the sheriff of the county. "Adams wanted to know what the trouble was, and they said he was charged with the murder of ex-Governor Steunenberg. The next morning Adams said he wouldn't go any further until he had seen a lawyer. Sheriff Brown had been talking to Thiele and said to Adams, 'Steve, they don't think you are implicated in the Steunenberg murder. They don't want you for that, but as a witness, and if you go down and help them corroborate their stories you will come out all right and not be prosecuted.'"

"Adams was never brought before a magistrate or a judge," charged Darrow. "He was never indicted by a grand jury. He was not charged with a crime committed. He was not taken to the jail in Caldwell, as the law demanded he should if charged with a crime in that county, but straight to the penitentiary in Ada County, and there placed in the same cell with Harry Orchard. For five days Orchard worked on Adams, telling him of the horrible things the state would do to him if he didn't corroborate Orchard's confession and of all the good things that would happen if he did. The only person Adams was allowed to see during those five days was Warden Whitney, who told him that he would hang if he didn't help them. In the meanwhile Adams' lawyer, Moore, had come to Boise and seen the governor. At the end of the five days Moore reported to Adams that the governor had said that Adams would hang higher than Haman unless he corroborated Orchard but that if he did this the governor had promised faithfully that he could get out of Idaho, and Moore had been given a hundred dollars to go to Colorado to see the governor of that state to get him to make the same promise."

The morning after Moore's visit Adams was taken to the same room in which Orchard had made his confession; James McParland was waiting there, his Bible on his knee. "During this first interview McParland told Steve that he had enough evidence to hang him many times, that they would hang him and he would never leave there alive unless he helped the state. He said he knew Adams was the tool of the worst set of sons of bitches alive in the United States and begged him to corroborate the story of Harry Orchard and said that if he did he would soon go back to his home in Oregon with his wife and children; if he wouldn't he would either be hung in Idaho or taken back to Cripple Creek and hung by law or mob."

The following morning Adams saw McParland again, to hear tales from the Bible of the biblical murderers who had been forgiven, the story of Kelly the Bum, his thousand dollars and his freedom. He had been given the choice between hanging and going free; he had no money or friends in Idaho; Adams signed a confession corroborating Orchard on a number of crimes against property purportedly hired by the federation—though in no way implicating either himself or the federation officers in the Steunenberg murder, the crime for which he had been extradited. He was instantly taken out of his cell "and placed in a sunny room in the hospital." His wife and children were brought from Oregon, and the family was set up in a bungalow outside the penitentiary walls. Three meals a day were brought in from the guards' table; Harry Orchard became their boarder. Once again the officialdom of Boise journeyed out to the penitentiary to make calls: Senator Borah, James Hawley,

Governor Gooding, who dandled the youngest Adams baby on his knee.

From the fraudulently drawn extradition to the happy family reunion in the Idaho bungalow Darrow was able to point out ten successive illegalities. Yet with the Adams confession in his pocket Governor Gooding might be proved to be right when he exulted, "Those federation officers will never get out of Idaho alive." Orchard's confession would put the noose around their necks; Adams' confession would spring the trap. Somehow he must persuade Adams to repudiate his confession. But how accomplish this difficult end when absolutely no one except the prosecution was permitted to talk to him?

That night Darrow slipped away from the detectives who were trailing him and took the train for Oregon to locate Adams' uncle. It was a long journey, the last hours of which he spent on foot in the mountains. When at last he located the cabin he was tired and thirsty. He knocked on the door.

"Are you Mr Lillard, Steve Adams' uncle?" he asked. "I'm Clarence Darrow, the attorney who is defending Moyer, Hay——"

"You leave Steve alone," cried Lillard. "If you don't they'll hang him. What chance has the poor boy got, all the way off in Idaho? They promised they'd hang him, and now they got a confession."

"Those threats are pure intimidation, Mr Lillard. Idaho nor anyone else can hang Steve on a confession obtained through the illegal devices of fear or hope of reward."

"You go on away," cried Lillard. "I'm not taking any chances getting Steve hung just to help your defense."

"All right, I'll go," replied Darrow quietly, "but before I do would you mind giving me a drink of water? I've been tramping most of the day."

"Well, I guess it won't do no harm to get you a glass of water."

When he returned with the drink Darrow dropped down on the steps to mop his brow and chat quietly of how good spring water was, of the beauty of the Oregon woods and the imperishable character of mountains—the hidden wealth they contained, the lives of the men who labored to take that wealth from the ground, the work of the unions to pull the men up from the mile-deep pits of twelve-hour days, dollar-sixty-five wages and sudden death, the part played by the Pinkerton labor spies to crush the unions so the men could be forced back to the twelve-hour day, the starvation wage, the sudden death. After an hour he rose, extended his hand and smiled a slow, warming, lovable smile.

"Thank you for your hospitality, Mr Lillard. I guess I'd better be getting back to Boise and my work."

As he turned away Lillard called, with a puzzled expression on his face, "Wait a minute!" Darrow turned around. "You say they can't hang my nephew if he repudiates that confession?"

"They haven't a chance in the world."

"Well—Steve's got no right to peach on his fellows just to save himself. If you promise to get Senator Stone of Mississippi to defend him I'll go see Steve and tell him to fight."

A few days later Lillard arrived in Boise. Not knowing his mission, the warden let him see his nephew. Assured by the first person he had been permitted to see, aside from the prosecution, that Idaho could not hang him as blithely as they had promised, Adams repudiated his confession. The next morning Darrow demanded of the court a writ of habeas corpus which would force the state to show cause for holding Steve Adams in jail. The prosecution was promptly ordered to release him—but not before it had arranged with the sheriff of Shoshone County to be at the gate to handcuff Adams and take him three hundred miles north to Wallace, where he would be tried for the murder of a claim jumper whom he admitted having killed in the catchall confession. The Idaho authorities had known about this alleged killing for six months; they had known about it when they laid out the money with which to bring Mrs Adams and the children to Boise, when they had laughed and joked with Steve and called him their friend. That night, preparing to leave for Wallace, Darrow told Steve's uncle Lillard:

"Now don't you worry about this. I'm arranging to have Senator Stone defend Steve."

"Don't bother," replied Lillard. "I've been inquiring around and I guess you'll do."

11

But when Darrow reached Wallace he was refused permission to consult with his client. He cooled his heels outside the jail while McParland sat in Adams' cell, telling him over and over again, "I am your friend. I am here to help save you if you will do as I say. If you do as the lawyers tell you, when you stand with a rope around your neck you will be sorry. But it will be too late." Angry as he was, Darrow had to smile to himself as he read in the paper that Mrs Adams, having grown accustomed to the bounteous hospitality of Idaho, complained to reporters that "she had been treated shamefully by the deputies at the county jail, that she had not been allowed to visit her husband and that the food given him was very poor."

The prosecution was resolved to get a conviction in the Fred Tyler murder. Moyer, Haywood and Pettibone had been languishing in their jail cells for over a year now, but not even the combined efforts of Darrow and Richardson could force the state to bring the accused ones to trial. First the prosecution would try for the Tyler conviction to hold as a club over Adams' head and make him re-endorse his confession. Consequently the entire troupe, playing before a world-wide audience, packed up its props, sets and costumes and moved up to Wallace for an out-of-town tryout. James Hawley played the lead for the prosecution, a prime piece of indiscretion; if the state were interested solely in convicting Adams for the alleged killing of a claim jumper whose doubtful remains had been discovered in the woods by land prospectors some two years before and thrown none too reverently into a potter's field grave without the formality of an investigation, why was the busy and highly paid Mr Hawley superseding the elected county prosecutor? The tiny mountain town of Wallace was skeptical and a little put out at being used. For Darrow it was a distinct relief to find the people friendly and cordial; he even lectured to them in the evenings.

The facts in the Fred Tyler incident were indigenous to the snow-covered mountains of northern Idaho. Pioneers came in to homestead sixty acres of forested land; by backbreaking labor in the warm summer months they made clearings and built log cabins from the felled trees. In the winter months the men and their families would move to other parts of the state to work in the mines or the mills and save enough money to further develop their homesteads when spring came. While they were away freebooters would be employed to move into the cabins, lay claim to the properties and sell them to the companies, which would then cut down the trees. These claim jumpers were looked upon with the same loathing in the Northwest as were the early horse thieves in the Southwest and often were dispatched in much the same summary fashion. Only a few days prior to the alleged killing of Fred Tyler a committee of homesteaders in the Marble Creek district had knocked off two claim jumpers; the chairman of the committee had been questioned briefly by the sheriff and released. The spectators were more curious than interested as the prosecution opened its case.

"The case of the prosecution which charges Steve Adams with this particular offense will rest upon the confessions and admissions of the defendant himself, confessions made in a free and offhand manner and without any unusual inducement. The confessions of the defendant will show that after the deceased, Fred Tyler, left the cabin of his neighbor he was met upon the trail by the defendant and two other individuals, that these persons were armed, that they took him into custody by force, that they took him into the cabin of Jack Simpkins, I think, and kept him there during the night. I am not sure whether they spent the entire night in conversation. The next morning quite early, whether it was before breakfast or after breakfast I am not sure—I am not sure whether they gave him his breakfast or not—they took him up on the side of a little mountain there and shot him with a rifle, without any defense being made on the part of the deceased or anything of the kind."

"Surely," murmured Darrow, "not before giving him his breakfast?"

The prosecution was then forced to spend most of its time proving that the bones the prospectors had found were those of Fred Tyler, for no one knew for sure that Tyler was dead; he had simply disappeared. Dressing Mrs Tyler in heavy black mourning clothes, they brought her into court to identify her son from a swollen knucklebone injured by a baseball and from a few strands of hair that had been found upon a piece of bark. They were also hard pressed to show what motive Adams could have had for killing Tyler. He was not a homesteader in the region; he was only there visiting Jack Simpkins, whose claim someone, probably these poor bones, had been trying to jump. Even if the dead man had been successful in acquiring Simpkins' claim, why should Adams commit murder? To please a friend who was perfectly capable of shooting the claim jumper himself?

Why then did Adams confess to killing Tyler? Assuming that this dead man was Tyler and that Simpkins had killed him, Adams may have seen him do it or been told about it. He may have related the story to Orchard, who in turn conveyed it to McParland. The Pinkerton, wishing to implicate as many federation men as possible, had written the story into the Orchard confession. Once Adams had been locked up Orchard might have assured him that when he became a ward of the state the little murder story could do him no harm. Or Adams may have been telling the truth when he admitted the Tyler killing.

For Darrow the guilt or innocence of Adams seemed of far less importance than the guilt or innocence of the state; he fought the case on that basis. "Whether Steve Adams is guilty of murdering an unknown citizen is a matter of small consequence because these isolated acts of violence leave no impression on the state. Tomorrow somebody else will be murdered; next week, another; and yet the state will go on; the law will be preserved. But if the law can be violated, if the officers of the law can take a citizen without charge and without trial, if they can place him in the penitentiary and then turn him over to the tender mercies of every vagabond detective who seeks to entrap him, then you will not maintain the honor of the state which is meant to protect the liberty and life of its citizens from despots and malefactors. It is infinitely more important to know whether this confession was honestly secured than to know whether any man was murdered.

"This prosecution from the beginning to end is a humbug and a fraud. There is not one jot of honesty, not the least bit of integrity, in it. We say this without any regard as to whether this man is innocent or guilty of the crime with which you are charging him; he is not being tried for that today. These powerful interests which are back of this case are not interested in Steve Adams. They look upon this ignorant common workingman as simply a pawn in the game they are playing. They are not going to hang him, whatever this jury may do. They would use his conviction to try to get him back into their hands where he was before.

"It is a remarkable case; it is unprecedented in the annals of criminal prosecution. It is not for him, an humble, almost unknown workman, that all the machinery of the state has been set in motion and all the mineowners of the West have been called to their aid. It is because back of all this there is a great issue of which this is but the beginning. Because out in the world is a great fight, a fight between capital and labor, of which this is but a manifestation up here in the hills. You know it; I know it; they know it. There is not a man so blind, there is not a person so prejudiced or bigoted, to believe that all this effort is being put forth to punish an unknown man for the murder of an unknown man.

"Sometime the employers will learn, sometime we will learn, that hatred begets hatred, that you cannot cure conditions with policemen and penitentiaries, with jails and scaffolds. Sometime they will learn, sometime we will learn, that every man you butcher, whether with a gun or a dagger or with a club or upon the scaffold, only adds to the hatred and prejudice of the other side. Sometime these bitter passions will pass away."

When the jury of farmers and ranchers took their first ballot they stood seven to five for acquittal. Two days later the vote was the same, for no man had changed any other man's mind. The judge dismissed the jury but refused to let Adams out on bail.

From the flimsiness of the prosecution's case this hung jury was as stinging a defeat as Darrow ever suffered. Technically it was a victory: the prosecution could delay no longer; they would have to try Moyer, Haywood and Pettibone on Orchard's confession alone.

12

The first break in the conspiracy case Darrow had made for himself when he convinced Lillard that Idaho could not hang Steve Adams; the second break was handed to him by an overzealous prosecution.

From the jury panel selected many men declared that "they could not convict a defendant on the evidence of Orchard, the accomplice." Before sending out the sheriff with additional venires the prosecution moved to remedy the unfortunate situation by buttressing Orchard's credibility. Representatives of the New York *Times, Sun* and *World*, the Boston *Globe*, the Denver *News, Post* and *Republican*, the Cleveland *Press*, the Butte *Evening News*, the Chicago *Record*, the Idaho *Statesman*, newspapermen and writers from such syndicates as the Associated Press, Scripps-McRae and Hearst chains were taken by Governor Gooding in penitentiary rigs to interview Harry Orchard.

"Warden Whitney explained that Orchard had consented to be interviewed but that no question must be asked relating to any feature of the case." Not Orchard the murderer, but Orchard the celebrity had consented to be interviewed!

The following morning's *Statesman* glowed with eulogies of Orchard the reformed Christian. Judge Wood writes, "The statements were carried in heavy type under large headlines, calculated to call immediate attention of everyone even casually reading the paper." O. K. Davis of the New York *Times* gave the *Statesman* a personal interview in which he said that "Orchard conveyed a strong impression of sincerity." A. E. Thomas of the New York *Sun* allowed the *Statesman* to quote him to the effect that "whatever he has said or done since his confinement began has been done or said voluntarily and without coercion or inducements; he gave his word in my hearing. I believe his statements implicitly, not because I know anything of his credibility, but because the man is convincing." Judge Wood continues, "I have always thought, and I still think, that a grave mistake was made in these publications. My first thought was that the authors were guilty of a most flagrant contempt of court. The court was so impressed with the injustice and unfairness of these publications that it . . . referred the matter to the district attorney of Ada County to make a thorough investigation." He summoned James Hawley, who swore in court that the interviews had been given without his knowledge or consent.

Up until this time neither the mineowners nor the Idaho prosecution had dared to use Orchard's confession to its fullest advantage since every revelation of the details enabled the defense to assemble controverting witnesses. Darrow had been able to ascertain such a small part of the confession that his defense, even while he was examining jurors, was shaky and perilous. Now the Idaho officials allowed Orchard's confession, which he admitted he had been rewriting and revising with his collaborator McParland for a year and a half, to run in *McClure's* magazine.

As a result of the release of the confession the hysteria that had largely been confined to Boise spread throughout the country. When the police of big cities used force to break up protest meetings the *Statesman* exulted, "San Francisco is to be congratulated on the fact that its police tore down the red flags and cracked the heads of some of the worthless creatures assembled to participate in such a disgraceful attack on the law." Maxim Gorky, who had come to America with his common-law wife, was ejected from his hotel in New York because he sent a sympathetic telegram to the accused men, was refused other accommodations and driven from the country on the grounds of moral turpitude. President Theodore Roosevelt, who had refused to disapprove of General Sherman Bell's insurrection in Colorado, called Moyer, Haywood and Pettibone "undesirable citizens." Tens of thousands of workingmen in every section of America promptly broke out with badges on their shirts and coat lapels which read:

I Am an Undesirable Citizen!

Eugene Debs, who had been converted to socialism by the imprisonment from which Darrow had been unable to save him in 1894, committed one of the few indiscreet acts of a long and valuable life:

"Arise ye slaves!" he cried in a manifesto. "This charge is a ghastly lie, a criminal calumny, and is only an excuse to murder men who are too rigidly honest to betray their trust. Nearly twenty years ago the capitalist tyrants put some innocent men to death for standing up for labor—but there have been twenty years of revolutionary education and organization since that Haymarket tragedy, and if an attempt is made to repeat it there will be a revolution, and I will do all in my power to precipitate it." He then threatened to lead an army of workingmen into Idaho if they executed Moyer, Haywood and Pettibone, to which an upstate editor replied, "Let 'em come. We'll meet 'em at the border with guns!"

Revulsion swept the middle classes of the nation, doing the cause of labor inestimable harm—as the prosecution had known it would. But with the enemy's guns fully exposed Darrow at last knew the strength of the enemy. Large sums of money, as much as five thousand dollars apiece from local unions, had been pouring in for the defense; he used this money to employ hundreds of investigators to run down every statement in the Orchard confession, to find and interview people all over the West, to issue appeals to every man or woman who had ever known Orchard to check their memories against his dates, places and actions to see if they had any information that would help the defense. If this release of the confession gave Darrow a fighting chance to save his three clients from hanging, that was a price the mine owners appeared willing to pay: they were playing for larger stakes.

13

The little town of Boise became jammed with strangers who at times seemed to outnumber the residents: detectives, miners, operators, labor organizers, liberals and radicals, newspaper and magazine writers, politicians, observers of all shades of opinion. Heading a long list of prosecutors, most of whom had been hired for the case and whom the Idaho law allowed to be paid out of funds contributed by outside corporations—an officer of the mineowners declared they had raised a million dollars for a prosecution fund—were William Borah and James Hawley. Both of these men had gained their first prominence by acting as special prosecutors in the Coeur d'Alene in 1892; this was to be the same show, with only a slight change in the cast.

"When is Borah coming into the case?" Governor Gooding, who was feuding with Borah, had demanded of Charles Steunenberg shortly after the Orchard confession.

Charles Steunenberg relayed this message to Borah, who replied angrily, "I'll get in just as soon as the governor clears the way for me to get in, and he knows it!"

William E. Borah had come into Idaho from Illinois in 1891 as a young man of twenty-six, while the territory, too, was still young; he had earned his living by defending petty thieves and other minor criminals. His first major opportunity was afforded him when he was called in as special prosecutor in the Coeur d'Alene in 1892; his prosecution of the labor leaders, including George Pettibone, who were accused of dynamiting the Frisco Mill, was not only forceful but spectacular. Part of the defense resting on the assertion that the workers could not have remained on top of a freight train if it had been going at the alleged speed, Borah ordered out a freight train, climbed onto the roof and hung on before the eyes of the transported court. He won his case against the workers; from it he also won state-wide fame. From here he gravitated to the counseling of the Northwest lumber interests, doing so well that he had been able to put a hundred and fifty thousand dollars in cash into a lockbox. He had just been appointed by the state legislature to the United States Senate and had no real place in the prosecution, for his presence there made it appear as though the Senate were part of the prosecution; yet he had been eager from the very beginning to maintain his position as the first citizen of Idaho in the international spotlight.

The brunt of the prosecution was in the hands of James Hawley, a six-foot-two giant with a walrus mustache who had read law while working in the mining camps and had developed a rough frontier eloquence. Appointed one of the state's first circuit judges, he had ridden over the mountains on horseback, his lawbooks in the pack bags. When a man was convicted he would handcuff the culprit to himself and ride him down to the penitentiary in Boise. It was he who as far back as 1893 had suggested the idea of a federation to the struggling local unions and drawn up their first constitution. It was because of this ambidexterity that Borah paid him what Boise judged to be the highest compliment ever paid to an Idaho lawyer:

"Jim Hawley has defended more men and got them acquitted and prosecuted more men and got them convicted than any lawyer in America."

The defense counsel included Darrow, Richardson, Edgar Wilson, John Nugent, who was the attorney for the Silver City local, and Fred Miller, a member of a Seattle firm which had defended the federation in the Coeur d'Alene. It was understood that Richardson was to handle most of the cross-examination, that Darrow would guide the defense and make the final appeal.

The night before the trial was to open Darrow went into the jail to have a conference with the man for whose life he was to be responsible. He knew that Big Bill Haywood had been acting up, that he had quarreled with Moyer and Pettibone, who were no longer talking to him. Darrow was saddened to find the cell torn by silent dissensions. Big Bill sprang up to meet him at the door and to clasp his hand, for Darrow had been one of his childhood gods; he had followed the older man's speeches and articles with the intensest of interest. They made a memorable picture standing there in the dim light of the naked yellow bulb, America's strongest voice for tolerance and her strongest voice for war. Darrow, who was uncertain about so much in life, had a tendency to duck his head into his shoulders and shrink his size so others wouldn't think him bigger than they; Haywood, who was positive about nearly everything, had a tendency to tilt his chin into the air and swell up his chest so that people would think him even bigger than he was.

The two sat on the edge of Big Bill's bunk. Darrow knew that as crucial as any other aspect of the trial was the need to convince Haywood that he must not try to precipitate a revolution from the witness stand; that he must be quiet, restrained and conservative; that he must reason like a trade unionist rather than a socialist, not only to keep from endangering his own life, but so that he would not pull down Moyer, Pettibone and the federation in his roaring wake. He smiled to himself when he recalled his scene with John Mitchell in the hotel room in Philadelphia the night before the final appeal to the Coal Commission.

The man whom the state had selected to hang first was just as big, just as strong and just as tough as his prosecutor, Jim Hawley. Big Bill Haywood had been chosen not only because they thought they had the strongest case against him, but because he was one of the most outspokenly militant leaders in the union movement and an active member of the Socialist party. Honest, fearless, smart, incorruptible except by his own flaring emotions, he was an advocate of force and violence as a means of achieving the workingman's revolution, loathing the college professor-preacher-intellectual type of socialist as a wordmonger and armchair theorist; the workers had to take with their fists and their guns what belonged to them, what they had rightfully earned. He was a one-eyed son of the poor who had come out of the mines at Silver City and believed in smacking the other fellow first when the other fellow began swinging his fist. During one of the Colorado strikes, while Haywood, Moyer and another chap were walking down the streets of Denver:

"We met a gang of deputy sheriffs, headed by O'Neill, the young nephew of the captain of the Denver police. They all wore badges. Moyer sarcastically remarked, 'Pretty badges!'

"'Don't you like them?' O'Neill said sharply.

" 'Indeed I do,' replied Moyer. 'I'd like to have one for my dog.'

"One of them struck him squarely between the eyes. The man must have had on brass knuckles. As Moyer fell his head struck the stone threshold and he lay quivering. The captain's nephew whipped out a big six-shooter, swung at McDonald and struck him across the forehead, lifting his scalp about three inches. I then had the whole bunch to deal with. One of them struck me on the head with a gun. I dropped on my knees off the curb of the sidewalk and drew my revolver. The captain's nephew was rushing in to give me another blow; I shot him three times in quick succession."

"The Civil War of 1864?" asked Darrow. "No, the Class War of 1904."

A strong picture of Haywood was presented in *McClure's* at this time. "Haywood is a powerfully built man, built with the physical strength of an ox. He has a big head and a square jaw. Risen 'from the bowels of the earth' this man has become a sort of religious zealot, and socialism is his religion. He is a type of man not unfamiliar now in America, equipped with a good brain, who has come up struggling and fighting, giving blows and taking them, who, knowing deeply the wrongs of his class, sees nothing beyond. Take a character like this, hard, tough, warped, and give him a final touch of idealism, and you have a leader who will bend his people to his own beliefs. We do not expect to find such a leader patient of obstacles, nor farsighted, nor politic, nor withholding a blow when there is the power to inflict a blow."

To all of which Haywood would have replied, "I ought to know about blows: I went to school to the Mine Owners' Association!"

No philosophy could have been more repugnant to Darrow's pacifist temperament than Big Bill Haywood's belief in revolution by force, yet they stood side by side in court as comrades in the most important case the infant twentieth century had yet projected. Such are the sequence patterns of history that both men had been started on the divergent journeys which brought them together in this Boise courtroom, the defender reviled no less than the defended, by the execution of the anarchists for the alleged throwing of the Haymarket bomb. The execution of Parsons, Fischer, Engel and Spies had started Darrow on his lifelong crusade against capital punishment and against the persecution of honest men for their work for the underdog. These executions and the imprisonment of Neebe, Schwab and Fielden had started Haywood on his career of revolution by force.

To more closely knit the pattern, Oscar Neebe, the only one of the three men pardoned by Governor Altgeld ever to come out of voluntary retirement, did so to speak at a mass meeting protesting the conspiracy against Big Bill Haywood.

14

After many days of questioning, because both sides had exhausted their challenges, a jury of independent ranchers was accepted, including one man who had been a close personal friend of Steunenberg's. The quarters for the officials in the case were so small that Darrow, Richardson, Wilson, Nugent, Miller, Borah, Hawley, Van Duyn, Haywood, Moyer, Pettibone and Haywood's mother, crippled wife and daughter all sat so close to each other in a circle facing the judge and jury that anyone could lean out and touch his neighbor. The jury sat facing the circle, with its back to the judge, and Haywood was so close to the end juror, he felt that although they never exchanged a word they came to be devoted friends. From the first to the last day the little courtroom was jammed with spectators; because it was hot June weather the doors and windows were thrown open, and the crowds assembled on the courthouse lawn could hear portions of the testimony.

In spite of the closeness and intimacy, more ill will was generated than in any case Darrow had experienced. Hawley opened the hostilities by claiming they would "show that the leaders of this organization have been responsible not only for the death of Steunenberg but scores of others, besides," and that they would convict the defendants of all the violence that had happened in the Northwest mining regions in the past decade. Darrow jumped up for the first of a thousand spirited and bitter clashes with Hawley, demanding of the court that Hawley be ordered to stick to the murder of Steunenberg—an order which Hawley disregarded for the eighty vituperative days of the trial.

The prosecution promptly skyrocketed to the climax of their case: Harry Orchard was brought in to confess in open court. The most widely publicized man in America during his fling at fame, thousands of spectators lined the streets, jammed the hallways and thronged into the courtroom to catch a glimpse of him. He was placed upon the witness stand, and the great moment of the trial had arrived. Hawley led him gently through his confession, one so sordid and disgusting that the country was again revolted and, being revolted, saw no reason to doubt its accuracy. Orchard confessed to lighting one of the fuses which blew up the Bunker Hill mill; to setting a bomb in the Vindicator mine which killed two foremen; to blowing up the Independence Depot, which killed thirteen men; to the attempted killings of Governor Peabody, General Bell, Colorado judges Goddard and Gabbert and, almost parenthetically, the murder of Steunenberg. Mixed in with the alleged federation crimes were a hundred other crimes committed for himself on his time off.

So convincing was his manner that Professor Hugo Muensterberg, the Harvard psychologist who came out to hear him, declared in a Boston paper that Orchard was unquestionably telling the truth. Hawley's son reports:

"When Orchard was first arrested I hated the son of a bitch; I never saw such a bestial face. But at the trial you could see Orchard's soul through his eyes; the conversion was so complete."

George Kibbe Turner, the *McClure* editor who spent two weeks with Orchard, helping him prepare his articles for the magazine, was convinced because "only a man with the imagination of a Defoe could make up the stories he tells—and Orchard's mind is absolutely devoid of imagination. He has turned from a career of hideous crime to an unqualified devotion to truth." Nor was it easy to distinguish the part from the whole: the relating of the details of his long string of personal crimes during the twenty years before he ever heard of a labor union not only made credible his later stories of the crimes of the federation but laid the necessary character base for their plausibility.

Each afternoon Orchard was taken by the warden to Hawley's office, where he had conferences with Hawley, Borah and Gooding and then slept on Hawley's leather couch; each morning McParland came to the office for a session with his protégé before he went into court. It took Orchard three days to tell his story. It was almost airtight. The geography of the mining region was given so accurately that those who knew the country recognized it; the timing on dates of explosions and the havoc they wrought were so accurate that those who had seen, heard or read reports of the explosions recognized the authenticity of the descriptions; his occasional criticisms of the militia and the government made him appear an unbiased witness; his willingness to confess personal crimes gave him the appearance of the true repentant, and his accurate knowledge of where his victims were at specific dates convinced others that he had been an agent for murder. What no one was able to tell was how much of Orchard's story was based on McParland's Pinkerton files.

Was Orchard telling the truth? Was his conversion genuine?

One noon recess, when Orchard was lunching at Hawley's office, he met Charles P. McCarthy, young assistant to Senator Borah.

When McCarthy asked him how he could have committed all the horrible crimes to which he was confessing Orchard replied:

"When I was a young man in Colorado I thought there was a war. The government and militia were controlled by the mine-owners. I felt we were justified in using dynamite because it was the only weapon I could use. They sent me down to kill Steunenberg. Then they caught me and put me in a cell in solitary confine-ment. It was then I realized it wasn't a war; it was just revenge. They say that McParland got a confession out of me; *without wishing to detract from Mr McParland's accomplishment, I would have talked to a child if he had come into my cell.*"

This single unrehearsed answer, given seventeen months after his conversion, contains one bald-faced lie, one deception and one connivance. When Orchard claimed he committed the crimes because he thought he was in a class war he omitted the arson, perjury, fraud, bigamy, thievery, kidnaping and murder which he had also admitted having committed before he ever became a miner! When he says, "They put me in a cell in solitary confine-ment, and it was then I realized it wasn't a war; it was just revenge," he commits a deception in that he gives no reason for reaching this sudden and revolutionary conclusion except that he had been caught, was frightened and had been offered the bargain from which he was every day profiting handsomely. When he uses the phrase, "without wishing to detract from Mr McParland's accomplish-ment," he reveals the same conniving mind that had connived all the vicious crimes from his earliest youth. Would a man honestly converted have thought in terms of McParland's accomplishment? Would he not have thought of God's accomplishment in perform-ing the conversion? Would a man who had found God been so smoothly and glibly solicitous not to offend or detract from his benefactor, Mr McParland?

Was Orchard's conversion genuine? When he was applying for a pardon he said, "Now, I know there is a devil, but I also know that there is a God. God represents love and all the beautiful attributes that flow from that little word. The devil represents hate and all the cruel and inhuman things that hate engenders. The difference between me today and when I committed those cruel crimes is that God in his love and mercy *invited me to come over to His side.*"

He had worked as a strong-arm man for the federation when they made it profitable; he had worked for the Mine Owners' Asso-ciation as an informer when they made it profitable; he had worked on the side of saloonkeepers who wanted their buildings burned down when the saloon men had made it profitable, and he had stolen his roommate's few possessions when that had seemed profitable. Would Orchard go over on God's side if it could be made to appear profitable? If he could earn his life by helping to hang three other men when he had confessed to killing certain of his victims for as little as fifty dollars?

Charles Koelsche, who, as one of the prosecuting attorneys, ordered the arrest of Dr McGee because the physician testified that Orchard was a liar and perjurer, tells that, "I was in Jim Hawley's office when Orchard was brought there at lunch time during the trial. Governor Peabody of Colorado walked in. Orchard saw him and began blubbering like a baby. When he finally gained control of himself he said, 'You can't know how good it is to see your face alive, when I might have encompassed its death.'" Koelsche adds, "That had to be the truth, or Orchard was the greatest actor that ever lived."

He had abandoned his wife and six-months-old daughter, left them without any means of support and never sent them a dollar of help in all the years, yet when he writes his confession he says, "There was a dear little girl born to us that spring, and thus my dear little wife was no longer able to look after the cheese making as she formerly had. I rented a nice house in town shortly after our dear little girl was born—but my dear wife would often complain and plead with me to stay home." All these terms of endearment come within four consecutive sentences; are they the words of a genuine repentant, or are they the words of a sycophant and professional hypocrite wallowing in his highly profitable sentimentality?

Was Orchard's conversion genuine? When challenging its sincerity Darrow was accused of being an atheist, an infidel, an enemy of Christianity, who would not accept the possibility of conversion. He replied, "If Harry Orchard has religion now, I hope I may never get it. Before Orchard got religion he was bad enough, but it remained to religion to make him totally depraved. What does religion mean? It means love; it means charity; it means kindliness. If he had got religion it ought to be charity and kindness and forgiveness to other men whose lives are like his. Would you have any confidence in religion if a man was as cruel, as heartless, as he was before? Take Orchard. He was acquainted with Moyer, Haywood and Pettibone. He had worked himself into the confidence of Pettibone. He had been invited to his house. He had eaten at his table. He had slept in his bed. He was his friend. I ask you whether there was the least look of pity, the least sign of regret, the least

feeling of sorrow, when this man sought to hand over his friends to
the executioners. I want you to say whether religion has changed
the nature of this wretch, and I should expect if any of you were
interested in religion you would say he hadn't got it. You would
have to say that to keep from giving up your own."

15

That night Darrow tossed on his sleepless bed, tormented by the
shattering riddle behind the nightmare:

Why did Orchard kill Steunenberg? For whom—if anybody?
There were equal amounts of evidence that he had been hired
by the Mine Owners' Association or the Western Federation of
Miners, though the evidence in both instances was slight. He said
the federation had given him two hundred and forty dollars in
August and had given him nothing since, yet in his travel and
bounteous living he had spent over a thousand dollars. Who had
provided him with the money? He had always been a free-lance
speculator; it was possible that he heard wild talk at the Pinkerton
or federation headquarters and figured that if he stirred up trouble
by killing Steunenberg, either or both sides would pay him. The
newspapers had called him a professional killer, though his behavior had been that of a bungling amateur. He may have done it
for some disgruntled miner or merchant of the Coeur d'Alene
bull-pen days, or he may have been hired by some local union
executive like Jack Simpkins, who was a gorilla and troublemaker,
working outside the knowledge of the federation. It was possible
that he killed Steunenberg as revenge for costing him his one-
sixteenth interest in the Hercules mine, which he had deserted at
the time of the Coeur d'Alene trouble, but it was not probable. He
may have been hired by the cattlemen of Idaho who hated Steunenberg for his sheep activities or by lumber interests operating similar
land grabs. Or it may have been an act of a diseased brain without
motive or prompting other than that it would bring him notoriety,
fulfill his need for activity and self-expression, for suspense and
accomplishment. He had lived a long life of crime with complete
immunity and was confident that nothing serious could happen to
him for still another crime. There would always be a way out for
a resourceful mind.

And indeed nearly everyone had plumb forgot that he had murdered their Governor Steunenberg. After the trials Orchard became
foreman of the penitentiary shoeshop, making trips to Portland
and Chicago to buy machinery. For twenty years James Hawley

worked every means to get him pardoned. As late as 1922, when the Pardon Board was again to consider his case, the ever-vigilant Charles Steunenberg demanded the right to be heard on the appointed day. The board held a closed and secret meeting the night before, at which Orchard's pardon was at last granted. The next morning Steunenberg wrote an article denouncing this act, and the people of Canyon County threatened to shut up their shops and come into Boise en masse to stop the board.

Failing in their efforts to get him out of the penitentiary, Hawley and Gooding did all they could to make his life an easy one. "Orchard has never been in the penitentiary," says Mrs Charles Steunenberg; "he has always been their pet and darling, a privileged character." Charles Steunenberg relates, "The penitentiary outfitted a room for Orchard and paid for the electricity used. Private parties gave him the money with which to buy machinery; the state permitted him to use convict labor for his own private enterprise in which he manufactured shoes for prominent people in Idaho and rolled up a cash reserve of ten thousand dollars."

An investigation of the Boise penitentiary records reveals no clue of what Orchard paid his convict labor, if anything. Charles Steunenberg continues, "In 1911, when I was in Denver, McParland took me to lunch and held forth for an hour and a half on king's evidence and how in England the men who turned state's evidence were always freed. He wanted me to promise to work for Orchard's freedom."

In 1940, at seventy-three, Orchard is still fat and sleek, oily eyed and unctuous. He tells visitors to the chicken farm which he keeps for the penitentiary that he "just can't bring himself to kill a chicken." To anyone wanting to clear the historic record on the crime Orchard cries petulantly, "The trouble with you writers is that you never come here to write about me. You always want to use me to write about somebody else!"

16

Because Richardson had earned the title of the greatest cross-examiner of the Northwest Darrow had agreed when he entered the defense of Moyer, Haywood and Pettibone that Richardson should cross-examine Orchard. As a result of this agreement the defense suffered its only serious setback, one so severe that Richardson was released by the federation after the Haywood trial. For a solid week he shot questions at Orchard in an attempt to make him contradict himself; he matched his brains, his skill, his training, against the confessor, yet not once did Orchard fall into an important contradiction. So magnificent was his memory that once when Richardson read back some of his testimony from the day before Orchard interrupted to say that two words had been left out by the court reporter and insisted upon putting them in.

Great portions of the country were convinced by Orchard's invulnerability under fire. Day after day the *Statesman* told how Richardson had failed to shake Orchard, what a magnificent witness Orchard was, how true and clear and honest, while Richardson's methods were called "blundering, disastrous, stumbling, clumsy. Richardson is a bungler; he is damaging his own case; his fellow lawyers squirm under his methods. Orchard is determined, courageous, pert, resolute."

While it was true that Darrow squirmed some under his colleague's efforts, he perceived that Richardson had turned up material under cross-examination which would be important in settling the case. *Orchard admitted that he had previously committed perjury in court; that he had confessed before to crimes which he had never committed; that he had first met Moyer, Haywood and Pettibone when he had been sent to Denver by the mineowners' detectives to spy upon the federation.* In any other instance this would have been sufficient to throw Orchard and the indictments out of court.

Up to this point the case against Haywood had been based on four charges. Orchard said, "Haywood wanted to get ex-Governor Steunenberg. Haywood gave me two hundred and forty dollars and said he hoped I would succeed in getting Steunenberg." When the Colorado papers were implicating the federation in the murder Haywood had wired to the local union at Silver City, from which he had risen to office, "Press dispatches indicate that there is another conspiracy to connect the Western Federation of Miners with grave crimes. Several persons in Caldwell have been arrested in pursuance of the conspiracy. Have Mr Nugent take up the defense of any member of the organization so that, if innocent, he may be discharged." For this purpose Haywood offered to put up fifteen hundred dollars, but the Silver City local telegraphed back that it wanted no part of Harry Orchard, his crimes or his defense. Because of his concern over Orchard it was assumed that Haywood was employing him. It was also admitted by Haywood that in 1904 he had hired Orchard as a gunman to protect Moyer, who was going into the militia-infested Telluride region. When Haywood asked him if he had a gun Orchard took off his overcoat, unbuttoned his coat and vest and held open his trousers to show a long-barreled pistol.

"That's fine," commented Haywood acidly; "you'll have to get undressed to take out that thing." Moyer was arrested the moment he set foot in Telluride, before Orchard had had a chance to unbutton his pants.

Actually Hawley was trying Haywood on the crimes committed by the federation in the Coeur d'Alene in 1899, at which time Haywood was working as a miner in Silver City.

The prosecution spent from June fourteenth to June twenty-second leading a long line of witnesses to the stand, all of whom had been found and brought to Boise by the Pinkertons to prove that Orchard had committed many crimes of violence, that he had been acquainted with Haywood and, therefore, must have been commissioned to commit these crimes by Haywood. Hawley worked over the witnesses to prove that Orchard was telling the truth about other crimes he had committed and consequently must be telling the truth about the Steunenberg crime. Not one witness could testify that he had any evidence that Haywood had hired Orchard to kill Steunenberg.

When the prosecution finished presenting its case Darrow instructed Edgar Wilson to rise and ask Judge Wood to "give to the jury an advisory instruction for a verdict of not guilty on the ground that under the statute there was no corroborating evidence of Orchard's testimony sufficient to justify a conviction." Thereupon arose the greatest irony of the case: Judge Wood, wanting to instruct the jury to throw the case out of court, was afraid to do so because it was his former partner, Edgar Wilson, who had made the motion! Judge Wood writes, "As I then viewed and have ever since viewed the actual situation as presented by that motion, there was very little legal corroboration upon which a verdict of guilty could be justified, and when the court came to a consideration of the matter the appearance of Mr Wilson in the case was thrust upon the court as an almost controlling factor. Had Edgar Wilson been absent from the case as attorney for the defendants, the decision of the court on the motion for advisory verdict might have been different and the trials thereby terminated!"

It was a good thing for the fifty-year-old heart of Clarence Darrow, who had hired Edgar Wilson to aid in the defense, that he could not know why Judge Wood had refused his motion.

17

Darrow proceeded vigorously with his case, bringing eighty-seven witnesses to the stand to testify that in some one important detail Orchard was lying, that he had manufactured either the crime or his part in it, that he was not where he had said he was on certain dates, that often he had been very far distant and that it was not reasonable that he should be hired as an assassin by the federation officers when they had excellent basis to suspect that he was working as a detective for the mineowners. Five witnesses claimed to have heard him make threats against the life of Governor Steunenberg because of the loss of his interest in the now-valuable Hercules mine, when he had to flee the Coeur d'Alene after Steunenberg had called in the Federal troops in 1899.

Some of these witnesses were union men and union officers who doubtless would have agreed to perjure themselves to save their leader; others among them might have committed perjury for cash. But among the eighty-seven witnesses who testified that Orchard was a liar and perjurer were men and women from every walk of life: doctors, engineers, former mineowners and superintendents, state officers, the former attorney general of Colorado, businessmen, army officers, housewives, women in business. All of these reputable citizens could not have been lying and Orchard alone telling the truth.

Darrow was therefore cast into the deepest gloom when Hawley cried in court, "Wherever Orchard has been contradicted in his testimony it has been by a person interested as a party to this conspiracy or by a person whose testimony has absolutely been proved to be false." In his next move Hawley descended to one of the lowest levels ever reached in an American court. When Dr McGee, who conducted a string of hospitals in northern Idaho, who was considered to be a good doctor, prosperous and well loved in his country, testified that Orchard had lied when he claimed to have blown up a certain mine because he was with the doctor several hundred miles away on the day the explosion occurred, Hawley called Dr McGee's evidence "the hallucination of a disordered mind" and ordered the doctor arrested for perjury. McGee was arrested in his home, to which he had returned after giving his evidence. It is illuminating that this device had been most effectively used by McParland in the Molly Maguire prosecutions as the biographer of the Mollies testifies:

"A highly significant result of the trial for the murder of Yost was the prosecution for perjury of four witnesses in that trial. They—including two women—pleaded not guilty, were convicted and sentenced within a few days—receiving one- to three-year sentences. With witnesses disposed of thus summarily, friends of subsequent defendants were reluctant to testify in a manner contradicting one of the commonwealth witnesses, particularly if he were a detective or a member of the Coal and Iron police."

Dr McGee was arraigned on a perjury charge. The sole witness against him was—Harry Orchard! Released by the judge, McGee was indicted a second time; after the Haywood and Pettibone trials the prosecution was still attempting to press its charges.

Staggered by this kind of procedure, Darrow suffered frequent bouts of depression.

"I'm through with the law, Rube," he would grouse to his wife as he lay in her arms and let his hot, tired head be stroked by her relaxing fingers. "This is going to be our last case. We'll retire when it's over. That Black Mountain mine can support us from now on. We'll travel the world; we'll live in New York, London, Paris, Shanghai. I'll have all the leisure I need to write my books and stories."

Or he would go into the big cell occupied by the three prisoners to dejectedly smoke a cigarette with them.

"Cheer up, Clarence," said Pettibone; "we are the ones who are going to hang."

Pettibone was the only one who seemed to be enjoying the trial, but then, he had been through it before. Charged with participating in the blowup of the Frisco Mill in the Coeur d'Alene in 1892, he had been convicted in Idaho, only to have the conviction thrown out by the United States Supreme Court. Except for his ingrown hatred of mineowners, Pettibone was a kindly man with a child's love of explosives. One day when Orchard was telling of using some of "Pettibone's dope," a fire-spreading chemical which Pettibone had invented, Pettibone said laughingly to the clerk of the court, "Great stuff, that. A man could have a lot of fun with it. You ought to get some for the Fourth of July."

But Darrow's depression was not caused solely by the methods of the prosecution. It was caused in the main by a conflict within himself, a conflict which would grow with the years. For he gradually had come to the realization that he did not like Big Bill Haywood, that he did not approve of him, that Haywood's methods, unless curbed, would go a long way toward destroying the labor movement. Haywood believed in force and had used force; Darrow became certain that he was guilty of many acts of violence against mine property. Though Haywood gave an excellent account of himself on the witness stand, was quiet, sincere and moderate, in his cell he uttered such fierce bellicosity that even his two comrades turned from him and would no longer talk to him. Often he said, "I'd like to blast every mineowner out of the state of Colorado," and it was clear that he would if he could. Darrow was convinced that Haywood was completely innocent in the Steunenberg killing, which fact, he reasoned, would embitter him even more and send him on to greater acts of violence in the hopes of awakening a revolution by force. Darrow not only did not approve of such methods, but he did not like to be in the position of defending a man who believed in them.

His distress was caused by the realization that his career as a labor defender had taken a turn downward: he was defending a man who, though not guilty as charged, was guilty of other crimes in the same spirit: crimes against property rather than persons, crimes well provoked, but nonetheless crimes which would bring mass bloodshed and destruction if continued. By defending this man it would appear that he had always favored violence, that the unions he had defended in the past had been guilty of it. His defense of Haywood could only weaken the effect of all his past defenses and campaigns of education; could only cripple him in his future defense of labor, the cause he loved most in all the world. He was distressed by the inescapable knowledge that other officers and members of the federation also had been guilty of acts of destruction, acts which in part had brought down upon them the retaliation and further terror of the mineowners. He wanted labor to be right, always right, so that he could fight for it and defend it with all his heart. He did not want his defense of workingmen weakened by the knowledge that they had been guilty of anything worse than wanting to better the lot of themselves and their families. Yet he did no wishful thinking; as ever he was a sentimental realist:

"I do not mean to say the workingman has always been right. I believe in him; I work for him; I have fought for him; I have given him such ability as I had; I have given him all my energy; I have given him every pulse beat of my heart because I believe in his cause. I know he is sometimes wrong; I know he is sometimes cruel and sometimes corrupt; I know that he is often unreasonable and unjust. No bitter contest in the world was ever fought by an army which was always right; no bitter contest in the world was ever fought by an army that was always wrong. I know while they have committed errors and done wrong, I know that in this contest the poor are right, eternally right. I know that the world and the ages are working for them."

During his bouts with melancholia he turned with ever-growing gratitude to his wife, who kept herself aloof from the melee of black passions. Ruby worked in her garden, scrubbed incessantly to combat the dust blown in on the desert winds, kept the house always cool and neat and filled with flowers: a calm, restful haven. When Darrow closed his front door behind him he could shut out the noisome and bickering world.

But he must not be fainthearted at this crucial moment; he must not allow his disapproval of Big Bill Haywood to imperil the cause of unionism. He must not allow the forces of wealth and reaction to gain a victory and a hanging on these trumped-up, fraudulent charges. If Haywood were convicted as a murderer labor would be convicted as a murderer; the precedent would be set for hanging any and all labor leaders on any and all crooked, illegal charges. Justice would be destroyed; the state and its courts and legal system would be taken over by the controllers of industry; the democracy of the people would be paralyzed. He must carry on the course he had begun in the Debs trial of 1894, reveal to the world the brutality and greed and senselessness of an acquisitive society, lay bare the need for a more co-operative commonwealth. His voice must be the voice of peace, the voice of hope, the voice of faith, the voice of the future.

18

For almost eighty days Darrow battled with Hawley, and gargantuan battles they were, for both men knew how to fling epithets when they thought epithets effective. Judge Wood's daughter, who sat through the trial, says, "The whole procedure sounded as though it were taking place in an insane asylum." Though a stranger wandering into the Haywood trial would have felt impelled to cry, "Either the lawyers for the prosecution or the lawyers for the defense are the worst gang of liars, scoundrels and perjurers that ever violated the sanctity of an American courtroom," such is not necessarily the case. Each side was convinced that it was right; that is both the privilege and obligation of the lawyer and is, perhaps, one reason why the American judicial system, though its machinery has sometimes squeaked and groaned and gone out of whack, has survived to dispense an approximation of justice.

Hawley's summation was nearly solid invective against the federation and based on the assumption that every word Orchard spoke was absolute truth. "There is some mysterious but powerful influence back of this confession," said Hawley, to which Darrow murmured, "Hear, hear!" Senator Borah's summary showed equal conviction that the accused were guilty but was couched in moderate terms.

When Darrow rose to make his final plea it was a blistering mid-

July day. Since it was impossible to wear a coat in that heat he walked up and down before the jury box in his shirt sleeves and suspenders, sometimes with his thumbs locked into the suspender where it buttoned to the pants, at others holding the suspenders stretched back under his armpits; it was a picture for which he was to become famous. Haywood writes, "When Darrow rose to address the jury he stood big and broad-shouldered, dressed in slouchy gray, a wisp of hair down over his forehead, his glasses in his hand, clasped by the nosepiece. When he spoke he was sometimes intense, his great voice rumbling, his left hand shoved deep in his left pocket, his right arm uplifted. Again he would take a pleading attitude; his voice would become gentle and very quiet. At times he would approach the jury almost on tiptoe."

"There was a marked contrast between the audiences during Senator Borah's argument and mine," writes Darrow. "While I was speaking the courtroom was packed and the lawn swarming with workingmen, socialists and radicals, with idealists and dreamers from every section of America. Each felt that in this case his personal cause had its day in court and a spokesman who understood his life and sympathized with his needs. Mr Borah finished his argument in an evening session on a Saturday night. The courtroom was packed with the elite of Boise and all the state. All of them were dressed as though attending a social event, which indeed it was. The common people had been given their opportunity in the afternoon. The courtroom had been thoroughly aired, if not fumigated, during the recess. The elect now had their turn."

Darrow spoke to the jury for eleven hours. The words he said would fill a two-hundred-page book of normal print. The speech, even more so than the one he had made to the Anthracite Commission four years before, is astounding in its organization and its mastery of every detail that had been elicited in the seventy-six days of examination: for not once did he consult his notes or papers. He carried it in his head: the character of each witness and what he had contributed to the case, what he had sustained or admitted under cross-examination, the history of the mining regions for two decades and their design of violence, the complete genesis of Harry Orchard and his credibility, the history of conspiracy, the history of the labor movement, the history of the operators' oppressions and their use of force, the importance of this trial in the future making of the civilized world, the fundamental issues involved over and above the life of one William Haywood.

"Mr Haywood is not my greatest concern. Other men have died before him. Wherever men have looked upward and onward, worked for the poor and the weak, they have been sacrificed. They have met their deaths, and he can meet his. But, you shortsighted men of the prosecution, you men of the Mine Owners' Association, you people who would cure hatred with hatred, you who think you can crush out the feelings and the hopes and the aspirations of men by tying a noose around his neck, you who are seeking to kill him, not because it is Haywood but because he represents a class, don't be so blind; don't be so foolish as to believe you can strangle the Western Federation of Miners when you tie a rope around his neck. If at the behest of this mob you should kill Bill Haywood, he is mortal; he will die, but I want to say that a million men will grab up the banner of labor at the open grave where Haywood lays it down, and in spite of prisons or scaffold or fire, in spite of prosecution or jury or courts, these men of willing hands will carry it on to victory in the end."

He spent several hours dissecting the soul and brain of Harry Orchard as if with a scalpel; the world writhed to think that any member of the human race could be capable of such abominations. "I sometimes wonder whether here in Idaho or anywhere in the country a man can be placed on trial and lawyers seriously ask to take the life of a human being upon the testimony of Harry Orchard. For God's sake, what sort of a community exists up here in the state of Idaho that sane men should ask it? Need I come here from Chicago to defend the honor of your state? If twelve jurors could take away the life of a human being because a man like Orchard pointed his finger at him to save his own life, then I would say that human life would be safer in the hands of Harry Orchard than in the hands of a jury that would do it. A man who would believe Orchard against Moyer would strike a blow against his own manhood and against the manhood of all men.

"There is no way to give Moyer, Haywood and Pettibone back the eighteen months they have spent in the Boise jail. These are all parts of the premium one gets and has always received for his services to his fellow men. For the world is the same now that it always was, and if a man is so insane that he wants to go out and work for the poor and oppressed and the despised, for the men who do not own the tools, the newspapers, the courts, the machinery and organization of society, these are the wages that he receives today and which he has received since the time the first foolish man commenced to agitate for the uplifting and the upbuilding of the human race.

"I speak for the poor, for the weak, for the weary, for that long line of men who, in darkness and despair, have borne the labors of the human race. Their eyes are upon you twelve men of Idaho tonight. If you kill Haywood your act will be applauded by many. In the railroad offices of our great cities men will applaud your names. If you decree his death, amongst the spiders of Wall Street will go up paeans of praise for these twelve good men and true. In every bank in the world, where men hate Haywood because he fights for the poor and against the accursed system upon which the favored live and grow rich and fat—from all those you will receive blessings and unstinted praise. But if your verdict should be 'not guilty' in this case, there are still those who will reverently bow their heads and thank these twelve men for the life and reputation you have saved. Out on our broad prairies where men toil with their hands, out on the wide ocean where men are tossed and buffeted on the waves, through our mills and factories and down deep under the earth, thousands of men and of women and children—men who labor, men who suffer, women and children weary with care and toil—these men and these women and these children will kneel tonight and ask their God to guide your hearts."

Early in his plea he made a strange prophecy of the tragic circumstances in which he was to find himself five short years later. "Suppose one of you twelve men were taken from your farm, charged with murder, not to be tried in a community where you lived, not to be tried by farmers who knew you and your way of life, that you were to be taken to Chicago, taken to New York, to be dropped into a great and unfamiliar city whose men do not think the thoughts that you think, whose people do not lead the lives that you lead, and expected there, over fifteen hundred miles from home and friends, to make your defense, and then suppose you were charged with a crime which every member of that community regarded as a crime against the sanctity of his own state—then you could appreciate the condition in which we find ourselves today and could understand the handicap that has been placed upon us from the beginning of this case."

The book of Darrow's talk to the Boise jury has never been published, though Harry Orchard's confession has been. Read today in the back files of newspapers and magazines, it sounds as though a truly great writer had sat at his desk for many months to pour out this magnificent appeal, so beautiful is the language, so richly lyrical and cadenced, so varied in mood, so pungent the sarcasm juxtaposed to tenderness and pity for man's struggle, so stirring in its passion for life and justice to the poor, the people. For Darrow achieved greatness as a writer only when he was on his feet, his brain working at white heat, appealing not for the life of one man, but of all humanity. In those final hours in Boise he was as great as his cause; no man can be greater.

19

Although Judge Wood had refused to allow Darrow to charge the Mine Owners' Association and the state of Colorado with conspiracy against the federation, his conducting of the trial had kept it at all times fair, impartial and legal. He had not had the heart to instruct the jury to dismiss the case earlier in the proceedings, but in his long and detailed instructions he continued to reiterate the demands of the law before a verdict of guilty could be reached.

"The law views with distrust the testimony of an accomplice on account of the motive he may have when by so doing he may secure immunity for his own participation in the crime charged. Although the jury may believe that the testimony of an accomplice is true, still the jury could not convict the defendant upon such testimony unless they further find that the testimony of the accomplice is corroborated by other and independent evidence." After pointing out to the jury that the corroborating evidence had to connect Haywood with the crime as charged and not with crimes that had gone before, Judge Wood concluded, "The court instructs the jury that if you believe from the evidence that the witness, Harry Orchard, was induced or influenced to become a witness and testify in this case by any promises of immunity from prosecution or punishment, then the jury should take such facts into consideration in determining the weight which ought to be given to testimony so obtained. Such testimony should be received by the jury with caution and scrutinized with great care."

As the jury retired to its room a newspaper reporter leaned over to Darrow and said, "Well, it takes twelve."

"No," replied Darrow in exhaustion, "it only takes one."

The report quickly spread about town that Darrow was despondent, that the best he was hoping for was a hung jury. The faith of the Boise residents that Haywood would be convicted, which had never wavered throughout the trial, now rose to a positive conviction.

Darrow and Ruby went home about ten o'clock, but she could not get him to go to bed. He kept wandering about the house disconsolately, chain-smoking cigarettes. Despite his ideological differences with Haywood, a human life was at stake; the life of the federation and organized labor was at stake, and, most important of all, the legal structure of America was at stake. Every atom of his brain and spirit was in that hot, stuffy jury room through the interminable hours of the night, hours during which he never sat down, never stopped his silent pacing, smoking, worrying.

Just before five in the morning an eavesdropper on the lawn outside the jury room heard the jury take a poll and the foreman announce a vote of eleven to one. He conveyed his scoop to the newspaper, which was on the street in a very few minutes with an extra crying that the jury stood eleven to one for conviction.

"Boise rose up in joy," relates Mrs Edgar Wilson. "The women came out in their finest clothing and jewelry; the men were attired in their gayest suits and ties. The workingmen, the liberals, the poor, disappeared from the streets to make way for the throngs that laughed and sang and cried out to each other as they surged up and down as though it were New Year's Eve. They were all waiting for that last stubborn juryman to listen to reason, and then they would be ready for the big barbecue and picnic, a celebration that would have lasted for days and been unprecedented in Idaho history."

When the newsboy shouting with his extras passed the Darrow house Clarence bought a copy and read the news. The best he could hope for now was that the one juror would hold out against all odds and hang the jury. During the next hour he tasted bitter dregs of disillusionment, despair and defeat. At six-thirty, when he was summoned by a deputy because the jury had reached its verdict, he knew it could only mean one thing: the last juror had given in. He hurried through the streets, racked with cramps. The courtroom was deserted, for no one had been notified of the jury's decision except the attorneys. Richardson, Wilson and Nugent were there, and Hawley and Van Duyn. Borah was missing. First Haywood was brought up from his cell, then the jury was led into its box.

"Have you reached your verdict?" asked Judge Wood.

"We have, your honor."

"And what is that verdict?"

"Not guilty!"

There was a flash of silence, then Haywood broke into a tremendous smile. Tears came to Darrow's eyes as he sat limply, collapsed on his hard chair. The jurymen all suddenly relaxed, some with smiles on their faces, others with tears in their eyes. Darrow shook hands with Haywood, then rose and went to the jury to clasp each of their hands. From the foreman he learned there had never been any danger of conviction. The first ballot had stood eight for not guilty, two for guilty and two not voting. The fourth ballot had stood at ten for acquittal, one for conviction, one not voting. At three-thirty in the morning they had taken the fifth ballot, which had remained the same, so they agreed to get a little sleep. At five o'clock they balloted again, and the count now stood eleven to one for acquittal. This was the count the eavesdropper had heard; it is illuminative of the mind of Boise that, having heard this eleven-to-one count, the eavesdropper could only assume it was for conviction.

The crucial juryman, Samuel D. Gilman, said, "The eleven-to-one vote left me all alone. Then they worked on me. I told them to let me think it over, and finally I concluded it would not be right to hold out any longer. It was the consensus of the opinion as soon as we got into the jury room that we could not find the defendant guilty in the face of the instructions of the court."

Juryman S. F. Russell stated, "Haywood was not shown to be guilty. If the defense had not put in any evidence after the state closed its case, the verdict would have been the same."

The holiday-making Boiseans, who had been forming their opinions of the trial from the editorials of the *Statesman*, were stunned. They refused to believe that such an incredible thing had happened. "They quickly disappeared from the streets, cheated of their holiday," reports Mrs Wilson, "and in their place came the miners, the working people, the liberals, the poor, who laughed and cried and hugged their neighbors and felt as though the world had been saved."

It was eight o'clock before Darrow stepped again into the hot, bright sunlight of the Boise morning. A tremendous throng was gathered to hail him, to embrace him, to shout out his name. They caught him on their shoulders and carried him down the street. He saw Borah standing in a doorway, alone, abandoned in his hour of defeat.

"Poor Borah," murmured Darrow; "now we must do something for him."

It was three in the afternoon before the crowd released him to go to the victory breakfast at the Perky house. By that time the repercussions had begun. Judge Wood was publicly charged with throwing the case to his former partner. Borah was accused of throwing the case for fear of losing the labor vote. Darrow was accused of bribing jurors. Bailiff McGinty was accused of taking six thousand dollars to let the jurymen be reached. Jurors were accused of becoming suddenly rich. The federation was accused of packing the courtroom to intimidate the jurors. The good citizens of Boise gave every dishonest, illegal and scandalous reason for the acquittal that inflamed minds could conjure up. Few Boiseans then, or now, would concede that the jury had been honestly and genuinely convinced that Haywood had not been proven guilty. The manifestations of this class war in miniature spread through-out the country. The New York *Sun*, voice of Wall Street and big business, said editorially, "A 'reasonable doubt' apparently saved Haywood in spite of the network of corroborative evidence which Senator Borah wove around the defendant with as much fairness as skill and in spite of the vicious appeal to class prejudice which Clarence Darrow made to the jury." The liberal New York *World* said, "The verdict of the jury undoubtedly represents the opinion of a great majority of unprejudiced persons who followed the news-paper reports of the trial. The state failed to prove its case."

In spite of their fine teamwork Darrow and Richardson came to the parting of the ways. Darrow said, "Mr Richardson was very hard to get along with. He was egotistical, arrogant and exceed-ingly jealous. We could never travel double again." Richardson said, "Darrow was headstrong, heedless and nearsighted when the interests of the clients was being considered. His great fault was that he was a socialist and was inclined to put the interests of the party ahead of the interests of the men on trial for their lives."

Since Richardson and John Mitchell made the identical accusa-tion, only four years apart, the feeling must have been well grounded; yet Richardson missed the cause and motive of Darrow's radicalism. He was not a socialist member; he cared little for the party; he had denied Eugene Debs permission to come to Boise to report the trial for *The Appeal to Reason* on the grounds that he didn't want the added burden of having to acquit socialism as well as the defendants. It was only that when he marshaled the facts on the brutality, greed and endless oppression exercised by combina-tions of wealth against the working people who helped produce that wealth, he felt forced to the inescapable conclusion that only under a co-operative state could enduring peace and plenty be found. He could not think solely of one man and the particular charge. He had to plead for the acquittal of all humanity, for the understanding and compassion which would prevent similar conflict. Again he was the teacher pleading for tolerance, for the broader view, for a chance for humanity to live in security. He wanted to acquit Haywood, but he also wanted to break the pattern of enmity, violence and retribution.

The miners of the Northwest declared a holiday and staged gi-gantic parades. Haywood was offered fantastic sums to lecture throughout the country and was proposed as the next candidate for President on the socialist ticket. Moyer was promptly released on bail and went back to Denver to resume his duties as the head of the federation. Exhausted physically and emotionally, sure that the state would drop the remaining charges now that it had lost its strongest case, Clarence and Ruby Darrow returned to Chicago to pick up the threads of their life and their law.

20

He had been home only a few days when he received a telegram from his colleagues to return at once; Idaho was going to prosecute Steve Adams again in another attempt to gain a conviction with which to force him to testify against Pettibone. He took the next train out, the first of many trains which were to carry him across the ensuing months from doctor to doctor, from hospital to hospital, from court to court, in an agonizing journey, for no sooner had he reached Boise than he went down with influenza and "developed a violent pain in the left ear. The physician came to the opinion that I had received some infection and was in grave danger of it developing into a case of mastoiditis. The pain rapidly grew intense. It became impossible for me to get any sleep without opiates. I sent for Dr Hudgel in the dead of night; he said I had better make ready to go suddenly to California or Chicago for expert treatment and that in the meantime I should not take another case.

"I knew he was right, but what could I do? Adams had turned his back on the state largely through his confidence in me. I had told him I would try his case. If through my failure he should be put to death I could never forgive myself. I knew I was seriously risking my own life to save his—but no one but a lawyer can understand what a sense of responsibility one may feel toward a client."

The same edition of the newspaper which announced Darrow's removal from the Idanha Hotel to the St Alphonsus Hospital told of the opening of the Federal government's trial against Senator Borah for acting as Frank Steunenberg's attorney in the land deals. But Darrow did not die, and Borah was not convicted; both lived to do good work and to become devoted friends.

The second Steve Adams case was about to open in Rathdrum in northern Idaho, to which obscure spot the state had secured a change of venue. With the aid of Mrs Darrow, the doctor and two nurses, Clarence managed to get out of his hospital bed, dress and be moved to the railroad station. Here Dr Hudgel handed him a bag of medical equipment and some stern orders: the eardrum was to be kept open; it was to be irrigated every few hours; all of the equipment was to be sterilized each time it was used.

The train trip to Rathdrum was long and arduous, for they had to go the roundabout way through Washington and make several changes. The first night out most of their time was spent in the dining car, where Ruby could keep water boiling in the kitchen; the next day she had to purchase pots, boil her water over a coal stove and perform her ministrations in a cold and dirty depot. Coupled with the skull-cracking pain was the even less endurable uncertainty of what had gone wrong with his head, the knowledge that any instant the strange malady might shatter something in his brain and kill him before he had a chance to murmur his good-bys. The agonies that he endured remained fresh in his memory to his dying day.

When at length they reached Spokane and the specialist to whom they had been recommended had completed his examination, he, too, confessed himself baffled: it looked as though it were a mastoid, but until the swelling appeared behind the ear they could not be certain, and they surely could not operate. He, too, ordered Darrow into a hospital, for it had been his experience that such infections generated fever, and unless that fever was discovered and checked at once it proved fatal. He repeated Dr Hudgel's admonition in no uncertain terms that he was risking his life by going into the Adams case, that he could take no responsibility for him if he left Spokane.

Within the hour the Darrows were once again on a train, "for if Adams lost it meant his death or his surrender to the state, which would further imperil the lives of Moyer and Pettibone." The Spokane specialist had been sound in his judgment, but he had figured without one factor in Darrow's life: Ruby, who, no less than Clarence, was a fighter with a stout heart and tender hands.

"We were in Rathdrum for two months, two months of agony. There was scarcely a moment in court when I was not in pain. At night I would try to get some sleep with the aid of a hot rubber bag which had to be reheated from hour to hour and which was constantly and devotedly attended to by Mrs Darrow. When the pain was unbearable we had to resort to the hypodermic. I could not possibly guess how many times she went to the kitchen with its coal stove to keep the kettle boiling, refill the bag, prepare the apparatus for injecting the codine and then irrigate the ear. She filed the needle points to the slimmest of hairs with the finest emery paper; the instrument had to be boiled, the needle and the table-spoon that held the needle while it was being sterilized, as well as the liquid and the codine; the outfit assembled with sterilized gauze so that no fresh infection would be added. I believe Mrs Darrow suffered as much as I did over this treatment."

The second Adams trial was a replica of the first. The jury voted ten to two for acquittal; since nothing could persuade the men holding for guilty to change their minds, the judge dismissed them. Adams was once again taken to the penitentiary. Darrow, more ill than ever through the added strain of the trial, left for Portland to receive treatment with violet rays, then went on to San Francisco, where the doctors were still unable to explain his malady or provide him with either relief or mental assurances.

Pettibone was called for trial. Now it was the San Francisco doctor who told Darrow it would be fatal if he went to Boise; Pettibone replied that it would be fatal for him if he didn't. The two days on the train, with their constant hypodermics and irrigations, were endless nightmares of semideath. When he was taken from the train to the St Alphonsus Hospital in Boise, the Chicago papers sent newsmen to get his dying statement. Obituary notices were prepared throughout the country. However, Clarence had always been an ornery critter; he didn't want to die; he wanted to defend George Pettibone. On the opening day of the trial he was able to rise from the bed; the sisters at the hospital had given him magnificent care or he might not have been able to get up.

The main difference between the Haywood and Pettibone cases was that instead of cross-examining Orchard after he once again went through his confession, Darrow gently encouraged him to enlarge upon his personal crimes against his friends, particularly of how he had played on the floor with the child of his former partner, all the while planning how best to kidnap the boy and hold him for ransom. The jury turned from Orchard as from the carcass of a dead animal.

That was very nearly the last that he could give. He collapsed completely. Even Pettibone suggested he had better withdraw from the case. The next morning he was carried into court in a wheel chair, white faced, thin and stricken, to make his last whispered appeal to the jury. That evening the doctor ordered him to California, even though admitting that there was small chance of his surviving the thirty-six-hour train trip. Billy Cavenaugh, the stonecutter who had acted as his bodyguard, boarded the train on his own idea and his own money; between Mrs Darrow and Cavenaugh Clarence reached Los Angeles alive, to be sped in the waiting ambulance to the California Hospital where a conclave of physicians was held—but they didn't know what to do.

21

After seven days of constant and shattering pain a telegram was received that Pettibone had been acquitted; Moyer had been discharged, and the whole ghoulish affair was over. The good news made him feel strong enough to move into a little apartment on the top of Angel's Flight, where he had a view of the city and the mountains beyond, and for whole minutes at a time he could forget that he didn't know whether he would be alive when next the clock turned around.

They lived in the apartment for three weeks, three weeks of unrelenting pain. When there was no change in the condition behind his ear and the doctors continued to be baffled, he decided he might as well be miserable at home. Ruby packed their luggage, and late one afternoon they took a cab down to the station. No sooner had he bought his tickets than he felt the swelling behind the ear which the doctors had been anticipating for five months. He dashed to the California Hospital, where he was operated upon at once and the "freak mastoid" drained.

His many months of illness had depleted his strength. For days life hung on the slenderest thread. He could not talk; he could have no visitors; Ruby set up a twenty-four-hour vigil outside his door. Since he would eat nothing that had been prepared for him, the hospital authorities broke their ironclad rule and permitted her to go into their kitchen at any hour of the day or night to prepare the food she thought might tempt him. The little he was able to swallow could not be digested because of his shattered nerves.

For many weeks a financial panic had been sweeping through the United States; banks closed and investments were wiped out. From Gardner, Illinois, Lutz commenced to wire frantically that Darrow would have to sign certain papers in order that they might pull out of their Black Mountain gold mine. Telegrams, special-delivery letters, hysterical messages of all kinds continued to pour in, showing that his savings were being wiped out, that other investors also were being ruined, that only his signature could enable them to unload and save themselves from bankruptcy.

The doctors had warned Ruby that shock would kill him. She stuck the messages under the mattress of the couch on which she slept while Darrow slept. At last there came a telegram saying that it would be impossible to keep Mr Lutz from committing suicide unless Darrow boarded a train for Chicago at once. No longer wishing to take the responsibility in the matter, she showed the telegrams to the doctors, who assured her that she would be sacrificing her husband.

"So it amounts to saying that, for Mr Darrow, it's your money or your life?"

"We are sure that it's so, Mrs Darrow."

"We'll let the money go and save his life, of course."

After several weeks, when he had regained his strength and was judged able to leave the hospital, Ruby and the doctors told him as gently as they could that his investment was gone, that the Black Mountain gold mine was no more. Darrow jumped out of bed, broke away from the grasp of the doctors who were trying to keep him quiet and charged like a bull across the room.

"Do you realize what you've done to me?" he cried at his wife. "You've thrown away my life savings, my dream of retiring. Now I'll have to begin all over again—be a slave to that irksome law work—we'll never be able to travel the world, write all those books! I'll never forgive you for this—never, never!"

But he did, husband-like, when he learned that she had probably saved his life by letting his money go.

It was now two years since he had left Chicago to defend the federation. The union funds had been so depleted by the four trials that they could not pay him the fee they had agreed upon. He had his railroad tickets, enough money to pay his hospital bill and to return home, but that was all. He could not meet his doctor bills.

The first day he got back to Chicago he went down to his office, his head bandaged, only one eye peeping out. For seven weeks he had to wear that bandage, in his office and in court, but no one commented upon it or thought it strange: for everyone knew that Clarence Darrow had returned from the wars.

CHAPTER VIII

This Is War!

SEEKING a quiet neighborhood where her husband might recover his strength and serenity of mind, Ruby searched along the South Shore until she found a top flat of a six-story building called The Hunter, on the Midway, which overlooked the University of Chicago, Jackson Park, with its Japanese bridge and pagoda, and Lake Michigan. "It was built by a man who forgot that neither he nor his building would be everlasting," says Ruby, "so every inch of the inside was solid oak. The nine rooms were exceedingly large, with high ceilings and high and wide windows; even the kitchen was wide enough for a small banquet hall, a very great inconvenience. There were five windows across the front, every one affording beautiful views of lake, park, trees, lawn and unbroken distances." Clarence was delighted with its spaciousness and the sense of being above the tumult of Chicago life, but he declined to sign a lease.

"We'll have to take it on a month-to-month basis, Rube, because I'm not sure enough about my income. We're between ten and fifteen thousand dollars in debt."

Ruby took their furniture out of its two-year storage vault, recovered some of the pieces, then spent four days and nights in fitting the front room with the red carpet from the Sheridan Road apartment. She put flatirons on the gas stove and with them burned red dye into the carpet to brighten it. She then ransacked the furniture marts until she found an oversized brass bed in which big-boned Clarence could roam comfortably, placing it in "the large bow windows across the south end, looking out over five beautiful maple trees and miles beyond, over other people's yards, lawns and trees. What breezes, what sunlight, what space and privacy and quiet there was." There were also windows facing east and west, so he could watch the sun rise or set from his big brass bed. "There were seven pillows of many sizes," adds Ruby, "downy and refreshing, to bank back of himself as he pleased and back of me, too, when reading aloud together."

For a year and a half she cooked, scrubbed the nine-room flat, washed the household and personal linen, never spending a cent on anything but food. At the end of that time the Darrows had paid all debts. Only then did Ruby yield and hire a maid. Only then did Clarence sign a lease, a lease which was to run for thirty years, which was to see the rent rise from seventy-five to two hundred and fifty dollars a month as the district became popular and fashionable, drop slowly again to seventy-five dollars as the neighborhood ran its life circle and disintegrated; a lease which was to leave Darrow undisturbed while styles in housing changed and the big flats beneath him were remodeled into six apartments each; a lease which was to terminate only when he died in his roomy brass bed in the bow window at the age of eighty.

What he liked most about his new home was its proximity to the University of Chicago, where so many of the professors were old friends who liked to drop in for an evening of hearty talk over pipefuls of tobacco. He knocked out the walls connecting the front bedroom, living room and dining room to make one big ell-shaped library, thirty-three feet by twenty-five feet across the front, overlooking the Midway, and an additional twenty feet deep into the ell. The available walls were lined solidly with shelves to house his thousands of heterogeneous volumes. The room now being large enough to hold a considerable group comfortably, he took into his home the Evolution Club, of which he had been the guiding light and which had been meeting around town at various halls. The meetings were held once a week; young and enthusiastic instructors from the university gave courses in biology, archaeology, anthropology, paleontology, sociology, comparative religion. Sitting in one of Darrow's favorite wicker rockers in front of the fireplace, they lectured for an hour, then defended their science for another three hours while Darrow, rocking in the opposite wicker chair, guided the discussion with a deft hand, and the members munched on Ruby's sandwiches and wet their whistles with sour Italian wine.

When a young astronomy instructor arrived to open his course Darrow drew a chuckle by musing sardonically, "Now, Professor, don't try to tell us anything about what's happening down here on this earth; we know all about that; just tell us what's happening up in those stars."

These evenings became the most pleasant of his lifetime: visiting professors and philosophers, European writers and scientists, when they learned that the Midway library was the most exciting intellectual workshop in Chicago, came to dine with the Darrows and address the club. The instructors taught, and the members, who now numbered a hundred of the most vigorous minds in Chicago, learned, because the subjects were vital and important, because it was good to be alive in a world where knowledge was going forward, making constant encroachments against the darkness of ignorance and prejudice.

"When I think of Clarence Darrow," says Robert M. Hutchins, president of the University of Chicago, "I see a tall, majestic man debating with our faculty members, opposing their views, defending their rights, holding long, quizzical, deliberate conversations with them in the dark red library of his apartment on East Sixtieth Street, plumbing and challenging them, taking their measure."

"Cruelty is the child of ignorance," wrote Darrow to a friend during this period, "and someday men will stop judging and condemning each other. I am really more interested in this than anything else; I wish I could make the world kinder and more humane than it is."

It was this abstention from judgment, this refusal to condemn on the standard codes of good and evil, that made him a fire to which chilled human beings came to warm their hands and hearts. To the men and women who were struggling against a fear psychosis in a confused and competitive world, living in constant dread of a slip or a mistake, an accident or a failure, of somehow breaking down, not making the grade, of being judged and found wanting, he seemed a tiny spark of the godhead that saw everything, understood and never condemned. When the day's work was done his office would become crowded with young lawyers who wanted to talk to him, to get the feel of him, to grasp what it was that made this sprawling, drawling, inelegant, plain-faced and plain-mannered fellow a whole man in a sea of fractional human beings. They did not come to him because he was an omniscient casebook or crafty technician, for they knew by now that "he practiced law by ear"; they came because they felt what George Jean Nathan so well described in one word: he had "size."

Hundreds of the near great from every walk of life filed through his office, seeking advice or just a friendly word: Elbert Hubbard, Jane Addams, Senator Pettigrew, William Jennings Bryan, Herbert

Bigelow, Harold Ickes, Hamlin Garland, Kenneth Harris, Joseph Medill Patterson, John M. Holmes, William Allen White, Sam Jones, socialist mayor of Toledo, Mayor Tom Johnson, who inaugurated municipal railway service in Cleveland. Youngsters from all over the Midwest pushed open his door to ask his opinion of the law, whether it was a good profession, one they should enter. He discouraged them mildly and, when they were on their way out, handed them a copy of one of his lawbooks, such as Chitty on *Common Law Pleading*.

It became increasingly difficult for him to make any progress when walking on the streets of Chicago; so many friends, acquaintances and strangers alike wanted to stop him for a little chat. Once when he was late for court and an associate chided him for letting himself be waylaid by an unknown admirer, he replied, "Oh, but he was such a nice fellow." T. V. Smith reports, sometime later, that when he escorted Darrow to a meeting of the Democratic convention it took them two hours to cover the few blocks between the Illinois Central Station and the convention hall. "It wasn't a walk," says Smith, "it was a reception." People stood about in clusters to share a few words, to be enveloped, if for only an instant, in that healing smile. It was not so much that he had become a celebrity as that he had become a public property.

An amusing picture of Darrow as his fellow Chicagoans saw him walking their streets in 1907 was published in the St Louis *Mirror*: "A man of more than average height, with well-rounded limbs and body, a deep chest which droops into a general bearing of relaxation while the whole frame ambles along carelessly with the toes kicked up in the process of walking: movements that range from the slowness of contemplation to the mercurial quickness of sudden recollection of something forgotten, now necessary to be done at once; on the broad shoulders a round head, delicate at the back, but marked in front by an oppressively full brow which overarches the face like a crag; underneath the brow, eyes of gooseberry size and color, which roam restlessly or else assume a fixed expression as though looking through a stone wall or into the secrets of fate: a sallow, leatherlike complexion hanging loosely over the cheeks and jaws and shot through with heavy lines; lips that seem purple in contrast with the sallowness of the face; a varying expression, at times lowering into saturnine sorrowfulness while the wrinkles in the crag forehead rush together like sentinels and the gooseberry eyes sink deeper into the cavernous sockets; at others, mirroring the man's nature as his face melts into smiles and is wreathed in irresistible charm."

People hearing him lecture found it an exhilarating experience. "There was first his unerring judgment in selecting a great and vital theme, something that had vexed and puzzled the great thinkers of all times," recalls one of them. "Following this was the capacity of intellectual penetration which enabled him to grasp and then reveal the inner soul of his subject. While most men lost themselves in a labyrinth of preliminaries and technicalities, Darrow entered by the great gateway and walked calmly down the center aisle." It was this ability to walk calmly down the center aisle which enabled him, in the courtroom as well as the lecture hall, to achieve perspective for his listeners: slowly the walls of the room grew indistinct; the outer walls of the building began to fade; boundaries of state and nation, race and creed, fell away; prejudices and passions dissolved until the listeners were out in the wide world, seeing whole and timelessly as historian or internationalist.

The odd part of his heartening effect upon people was that he rarely had anything heartening to say about the world's conduct. He was no optimist who encouraged folks by telling them that everything would come out all right; the best he could convey was that the mess was not their fault. "How will things come out? I guess they just won't come out. Men have been hating each other, robbing and oppressing and killing each other for countless centuries; I see little on the horizon to indicate that they won't continue to do so for centuries to come." In a letter to a reporter for a labor paper he wrote:

"There are a lot of myths which make the human race cruel and barbarous and unkind. Good and Evil, Sin and Crime, Free Will and the like delusions made to excuse God for damning men and to excuse men for crucifying each other. Sunday I am to debate on the subject 'Is Civilization a Failure?' It ought to be easy to show. How anyone can think anything else I cannot conceive. I don't know why I do these things. I never convert anyone and don't want to. I am getting more and more convinced that if anyone has any 'dope' they ought to keep it. Chicago is now on a mad hunt for criminals; the big ones are after the little ones. People are getting more cruel all the time, more insistent that they shall have their way. I wish I was either younger or older. If I was younger I should go to the South Seas; if I was older I shouldn't care so much."

Hamlin Garland comments on this schizophrenic split between his Tolstoyan spirituality and Voltarian cynicism. "Darrow and his young wife were living in a new flat over near Jackson Park, and there we dined with them in 1907. I found him quite as grave and even more bitter than his writing indicated. He talks with much of the same acrid humor. He read to us some short stories called *The Law's Delay*, which were intolerably gloomy and savage but powerful. He impressed me as a man of enormous reserve powers, but his mind is uncultivated and undisciplined. As an advocate he weakens his cause by extreme expression. His uncompromising honesty of purpose and his aggressive cynicism make him repellent to many; hence he is to me a lonely figure. In all that he writes, in all that he says, he insists relentlessly on the folly and injustice of human society. His writing is too bitter in quality, too pessimistic in outlook, to succeed, but it has in it a protest which it is well to consider."

Darrow's indirect answer to Garland was not given until twenty years later, when he wrote an introduction for a new edition of Voltaire called *The Best of All Possible Worlds*. "Voltaire's works abound in cynical statements. He seemed to approach the world with a sneer, but often it is a protective covering against the pain and anguish suffered by the man who feels the sorrows of the world. Of course he joked and laughed and sneered in his deepest miseries. When haunted by the profoundest tragedies that move the sensitive man he wore his mocking grin and cynic's smile, but his tireless brain, his constant energy, even his mocking grin, have done much to rid the world of the cruelty and intolerance that has blasted the lives and destroyed the hopes of millions of human beings since man came upon the earth."

Lieutenant Commander L. H. C. Johnson observes, "While Darrow's keen sense of humor and knowledge of world affairs made him very popular with the men, he was a riot with the women. I took him to a birthday party, and when it came time for us to go I couldn't find the chief. I finally found him on the porch, sitting in a low chair, surrounded by at least twenty women of all ages. I almost had to insult the females to get him home." Now that he had passed fifty his interest in women had subsided a bit, but he never lost his connoisseur's eye; when he was returning home from a lecture the porter informed him that Miss Cissie Patterson, of the publishing family, had her private car attached to the train and had asked him to breakfast with her. When Darrow rejoined his wife in Chicago "he mischievously asked me why in the world I didn't wear slinky, satiny, thin, clinging bright green pajamas and pink velvet and things a fellow could see through and get a thrill from —and, oh yes, the kind of slippers that have no heels or toes and have continuously to be pushed back on the feet."

The lawyers who thronged to his office tried to get him to talk about his past cases and triumphs, but he could never be persuaded to discuss them. When someone asked him whether Big Bill Haywood had been innocent or guilty he replied, "By Jove, I forgot to ask him." George Leisure relates, "Clarence Darrow was the most modest man I have ever known. You scarcely ever heard him use the pronoun I. I never heard him tell anything he personally did in a courtroom, although he delighted in telling of occurrences in which other lawyers had been able to do brilliant work and distinguish themselves." A number of years later, when a group of friends tendered him a birthday banquet and celebrities from every walk of American life made eulogizing speeches about him, "the religionists trying to prove him to be deeply religious, the scientists claiming him to be a scientist, the judges and lawyers pulling for their ranks, Darrow got up slowly and said in the oh-so-deceptive drawl:

" 'I'm the one all this talk's been about. I always thought I was a hell of a fellow, but now I'm sure of it.' "

2

The firm of Darrow, Masters and Wilson was doing only fair to middling, for Darrow's two-year absence had cost them many of their profitable accounts, and the depression of 1907 had slowed down all business. Darrow, who had been their main business getter, found that his shattering illness and operation had taken their toll: he suffered recurrent spells of fatigue and general malaise that depleted his strength. The lines deepened in his face, making him look more than his fifty years. When the newspaper photographers laughingly offered to retouch the pictures he replied, "Don't wash out the lines, boys. I worked too hard to earn them." Partly because of this lessening of vigor, but also because he had seen so much bitterness and heartbreak in courtrooms, he began urging his clients to:

"Make a settlement. Give a little to get a little. Stay out of court. Court consumes your time, your money and your energy. Take less than you think you ought to have; you'll come out ahead that way."

He gave this advice to people who had damage claims against companies, to private individuals and business concerns that were hell-bent to sue each other, to unions that had claims against their employers and employers who had claims against their workers. "Make a settlement," he told them, and his clients followed his advice. He spent less of his time in courtrooms, earned less money;

his clients never got quite as much as they thought they were entitled to, but they were spared the rigors of a trial. Both sides having compromised and shaken hands on their bargain, the ill will and passions that were generated by a public conflict were avoided. This was the way Tolstoy would have done his job had he been practicing law in an industrial city.

Though his partners did not complain they were not too pleased with this change in the chief. "Darrow was sometimes too anxious to make a settlement," says Francis Wilson. "This was in part due to his convalescence and his natural laziness, though of course it was also partly due to his long experience with litigation."

His growing reluctance to squander hours in the courtroom sometimes embarrassed his office. Once when he failed to show up at the Ashland Block in time to make a ten o'clock trial William Carlin was driven to tell the court that Mr Darrow was ill.

"That's strange," observed the court; "we rode down with him this morning on the Illinois Central train."

Another time, when he was in Indianapolis debating "Is There a Hereafter?" an associate "was forced into trial in Darrow's place. It was a personal-injury suit, and the question was one of assumed risk. The condition of the premises was important for the purpose of showing whether the plaintiff knew of the hazard. In the afternoon Darrow came into town and continued the trial. During the morning session his associate had described to the court the premises and put on a witness for the purpose of proving the condition. Darrow had evidently forgotten the facts while contemplating the hereafter, for the rest of the afternoon was spent by the court and the jurors in correcting him. Everybody seemed interested in steering him along the right course; the jurors and the court were helpful rather than antagonistic."

Within another year he had built up one of the most diversified practices in Chicago. William Randolph Hearst brought back the accounts of the *American* and *Examiner;* the International Harvester Company consulted him on their taxation problems; he was adviser to the Teachers' Federation of Labor; the Shuberts came to him with their theatrical complications, and in their wake came the actors Richard Carle and Grant Mitchell, who were involved in a dispute with George M. Cohan and Sam Harris. Mayor Dunne offered him the post of corporation counsel and, when he passed it on to his friend, James Hamilton Lewis, appointed him special counsel for the city in traction matters at ten thousand dollars a year. The firemen's union and switchmen's union retained him to present their case before a Federal board; the employees of the

Kellogg Switchboard Company employed him to appeal all the way to the Supreme Court the conviction of certain of their members for picketing the plant in the face of an injunction that had been issued by a trial court; Bernarr MacFadden engaged him to represent his physical-culture school. The most famous case of the period that he turned down was that of Cassie Chadwick, who claimed to be the illegitimate daughter of Andrew Carnegie. Darrow made one trip to Cleveland to investigate "a certain lockbox which was purported to contain a will or trust involving many millions of dollars" to which Miss Chadwick claimed she was entitled, but in the end, though the lady spent two weeks in Chicago importuning him, he refused to become involved in the litigation.

By 1908 there began a rush of labor cases in which Clarence was pleased to find himself acting not so much as lawyer as arbitrator. Since he was one of the few men in Chicago whom both labor and employers would trust, he was selected by both sides to settle disputes between the National Brick Company and their brickmakers, the newspaper owners and the typographical union, the brewers and their bottlers, the clothing manufacturers and their cutters. He sat at the head of big conference tables, never permitting the employers to range themselves on one side of the table and the employees on the other, as though they were separate entities and conflicting interests, but persuading them to sit next to each other, to rub elbows, tell a little joke, smoke each other's cigarettes, to come to know each other and perhaps even like each other. Then from his position at the head of the table he brought to bear his gentleness and humor, his warmth and understanding, until the antagonistic slabs of ice in the hearts of the contestants were melted, and he shamed them into being just a little kinder, just a little more generous and sympathetic human beings than they could ordinarily achieve. In each instance a strike was averted; the loss of profits and wages was averted; both sides accepted a compromise solution and lived up to the terms of the agreement for the period of time agreed upon.

As business picked up Ruby began spending money to disprove the canard that Darrow slept in his clothes. She had his black satin ties made to order by Marshall Field, his hats custom made by Knox, a degree wider in the brim and a degree higher in the crown than the largest hat in stock, his silk shirts cut to order so "there would be no yawning effect down the buttonhole pleats in front," his handkerchiefs cut oversized and initialed, his suits designed by the best tailors in Chicago from materials she picked out herself. For the opening of one important trial she gave him a manicure and pedicure the night before, then sent him to court with every stitch on him brand new, looking as though he had just stepped out of a Bond Street window. When the afternoon papers reached the Midway she was flabbergasted to read a report that Darrow had been dressed in his usual rumpled gray suit and soiled cotton shirt. Her housekeeper was so outraged she ran to the laundry bin and began flinging out silk shirts, crying:

"There, that ought to show them! He doesn't have a cotton shirt to his name. He wears nothing but silk shirts!"

With the money coming in once again, he decided to invest his savings so that he might within a few years be able to retire and achieve his one remaining personal ambition: to write a long novel. The most promising idea on the market at the moment was a new machine which was expected to produce gas cheaper than the regular coal-gas or water-gas plants. Darrow and a group of his friends bought the patent rights from a bond-selling organization for ten thousand dollars, which included an option on the gas plants of Ottawa, Illinois and Greeley, Colorado.

"The gas-making machine was impractical," relates Paul, "and no money was left to handle the plants. It was up to me to look over the two option deals and guess which one could be handled with the money that could be put up and whether it looked as if anything could be paid back. Ottawa had recently lost some of its industries, so I guessed on Greeley, which was in the center of irrigated farming country. The town was growing, so it meant building a new gas plant and putting in an average of a mile of new mains every year for twenty years. It took most of the money I could get from Father and his friends for ten years and a lesser amount for the balance of the time."

Paul's management of the Greeley gasworks made it a valuable property. When the plant was sold in 1928 Darrow found himself for the first time in his life a rich man. Though Paul had not been able to work up any interest in his father's law business, that had not prevented him from keeping his eyes open while walking through the offices. When he left for Greeley he robbed the firm of Darrow, Masters and Wilson of a lovely dark-haired, fair-skinned, blue-eyed girl by the name of Lillian Anderson. Once again Paul's judgment proved sound; he enjoyed a fine married life, and Lillian Darrow presented her father-in-law with three granddaughters who were to bring him a good deal of joy, in particular the youngest, Mary.

And so the weeks and months passed, and the first decade of the new century. The time he earned by staying out of court he employed to write short stories and articles, the most widely known of which was his deep-cutting and brilliant essay, "The Open Shop," which was circulated in the big cities where unions were trying to bring workingmen into their organization. Twenty thousand copies had been distributed among the workers of Los Angeles during the industrial warfare that preceded the explosion of the Los Angeles Times Building; it was his authorship of this pamphlet which proved to be the determining factor in his defending of the McNamara brothers, a decision which was to wreck his career and drastically alter the external pattern of his life.

3

To the flat on the Midway came Samuel Gompers, president and founder of the American Federation of Labor. He was in a state of agitation, for he was about to break a pledge made to Darrow by the executive board after the Boise trials: that they would never again ask him to defend a labor-murder case. Gompers paced the library so distractedly that sometimes he disappeared into the ell, and only his voice could be heard. Darrow knew that he had reason to be upset, for one of the most crushing blows in the history of the American Federation of Labor had befallen him. John J. McNamara, secretary of the International Bridge and Structural Iron Workers, and his brother, James B., had just been arrested for the dynamiting of the Los Angeles *Times* and for the murder of the twenty men who had been killed in the resulting fire. Nor was that all: the McNamaras and their union were charged with committing more than a hundred dynamitings between 1906 and 1911, of blowing up bridges, aqueducts, powerhouses, theaters, steel buildings, in every major city in America. The Los Angeles *Times* swore it would hang the McNamaras on the scaffold of San Quentin and that no force on earth could stop it.

"No force except you, Clarence," said Gompers, stopping before the fireplace where Darrow was crouched disconsolately in his wicker chair.

At first glance it looked amazingly like a replica of the Moyer, Haywood and Pettibone affair. There had been a state of war between the National Erectors' Association and the Structural Iron Workers' Union since 1906, when all concerns using steel in their structures had combined and pledged themselves to maintain the open shop. The William J. Burns Detective Agency had been employed by the erectors to trail union men and garner evidence against them; in April of 1911 James B. McNamara and Ortie Mc-

Manigal were arrested in Detroit on charges of safeblowing, were moved without warrants to Chicago, where they were held captive in a police sergeant's house until extradition papers could arrive from Los Angeles.

After four days of being held incommunicado McManigal had confessed to numerous dynamitings. In the pamphlet containing the story, called *Ortie McManigal's Own Story of the National Dynamite Plot*, the frontispiece was not a picture of Ortie, the hapless author, but of William J. Burns. In it the uneducated McManigal purportedly had written, "Hindsight is a splendid quality, but how fine it would be if we could reverse its action. I did not realize then that unionism is a serious menace, not only to the existing government, with its glorious and patriotic traditions, but as a menace to all government and all liberty of the individual or even of the masses."

It would have required an even greater miracle than the regeneration of Harry Orchard for Ortie McManigal to have formulated those pontifical sentences. Since one finds the precise phrases and hundreds of their counterparts in Burns's autobiography, *The Masked War*, there can be little doubt of their authorship. Once again some member of the prosecution had been so confident of success that he had not even bothered to save face; once again it seemed clear that the opposition was not merely out to get McNamara and McManigal or to destroy an individual union. This time the war would be waged on a national front.

James B. McNamara had been handcuffed and bundled onto a train for California without an opportunity to fight his extradition in Illinois. Since McManigal had named as the brains and boss of the dynamitings John J. McNamara, he, too, was arrested, in his office in Indianapolis, and shipped out to Los Angeles by such a fraudulent conspiracy that both William J. Burns and Joseph Ford, assistant district attorney of Los Angeles, were subsequently indicted by the Indianapolis grand jury.

"History repeats itself," mused Darrow; "that's one of the things that's wrong with history."

The war over steel had begun many years before. When the industry was in its infancy Andrew Carnegie had kept a personal contact with his men, paid them fair wages, recognized their union and compromised his differences. In 1891 the Amalgamated Iron and Steel Workers' Union had been one of the strongest in the country, yet Carnegie's company had earned a net profit of almost two million dollars. Then in 1892 there came a gigantic merger of coal-and-iron lands and steel ovens. Darrow had learned in the Pennsylvania coal fields that mergers, cartels and trusts unfailingly acted as combinations against labor; the larger and more powerful the merger, the wider and more powerful the opposition to labor. Since it was in the natural and inescapable law of industry to combine for purposes of efficiency and economy, to control supply, processing and marketing, so was it equally inevitable that labor wars would extend to ever-widening fronts.

Yet so great had been the influence of one man, that this need not have been immediately true of the steel combine if Carnegie had seen fit to remain at its head. Instead he retired to his estate in Scotland, leaving the industry in charge of H. C. Frick who, like Pullman, was a mechanical and production genius without humanitarian ethics. More as a token of his power and policy than as a money saver, for steel investments were returning handsome dividends, Frick reduced wages during his first meeting with the union. When after a series of conferences he refused to come up to what the men considered a living scale, they struck.

Frick hired strikebreakers, ordered three hundred armed Pinkertons to come to Homestead and guard his new workers. When the strikers heard of the move they armed themselves, organized on a military basis, with companies and commanders and prepared to resist what they considered an invasion. They fired on the Pinkertons; the Pinkertons fired back; several men were killed on both sides—and the state militia was ordered to Homestead to protect the mills and the strikebreakers who were working them. By winter the union funds had run out; the families were growing hungry and cold and threadbare. The mills were running at full blast; the strikers saw that they had been crushed. Dispirited, broken, the men deserted their organization and went back to work on the best terms they could get as non-union men.

For thirteen years there was quiet in the steel industry while labor put in its seventy-two-hour-per-week stint at reduced wages and Frick zoomed the profits to forty millions a year. The discovery of the Mesaba iron range in northern Minnesota had so reduced the cost of making steel that the face of America was being renovated: cities of skyscrapers were beginning to rise; steel rails were pushing railroads to new borders; gigantic bridges, aqueducts, industrial plants, were being built of this safe and durable and light material. And along with the skyscrapers and bridges a new class of workmen had come into existence, the structural-steel worker: a crack mechanic, as tough as the material he handled, tireless, fearless, undaunted by the most insuperable obstacles, a master craftsman rebuilding the architecture of the nation. They built a strong union, the International Association of Bridge and Structural Iron Workers, which worked at peace with their employers as long as the companies remained comparatively small and independent. But it was an era of mergers: in 1905 the American Bridge Company was formed of firms throughout the country with contracts to build bridges, dams, and the like. The following year this was expanded into the National Erectors' Association, which embraced nearly every firm building with steel. Those firms that formerly had been independent and friendly with the union were obliged to participate in the general policy of the association. The structural-steel workers and the structural-steel builders soon split on the rock that was to cause succeeding decades of wrangling and bloodshed and over which the ultimate battle would be fought: the open shop.

4

Clarence Darrow had spoken for the workingmen of America when he had written, "In reality the open shop only means the open door through which the union man goes out and the non-union man comes in to take his place. The open shop furnishes, and always has furnished, the best possible means of destroying the organization of the men. The closed shops are the only sure protection for the trade agreements and the defense of the individual. The master naturally discharges those who have been most active in the union, who interfere the most with his business, who are ever agitating for higher wages, better conditions and shorter hours. He naturally employs those who are most complaisant, those who cannot afford to lose their jobs, those whom he can bring to be dependent on his will. The open shop means uncertainties, anxieties; it is a constant menace to the union man's interest. He understands that his job is dependent upon his lack of interest in the union; men who belong to the unions and accept their responsibilities cannot be persuaded to pay dues and make sacrifices for the benefit of the non-union men who work by their sides and who are always the first to claim and receive the benefits of every struggle made by the union, benefits they receive without danger, without labor and without cost. To prevent trade unionism from being conquered in detail, to keep its members from being thrown out through the open door, to maintain the best conditions in shop and mill and factory and strive for others better still, to save the workman from long hours of toil, all these need the effort of every union man, and without the right to protect themselves in a closed shop by refusing to work with those whose weakness or stupidity make them unfaithful to their class, trade unionism cannot hold that which it has won, still less go forward to greater victories."

He was thus the most literate and powerful proponent of the closed shop in America; since the McNamaras had been working through the years for the closed shop and anything they might have done against the Erectors' Association was done in their struggle against the open shop, that made Clarence Darrow the inevitable champion of the arrested McNamaras.

So Gompers told him. But Darrow refused to take the case.

His reasons were many and valid. The two hate-laden, fever-fraught years of the Western Federation of Miners cases had almost killed him. He was still by no means well or strong. He was now fifty-four years old and a little tired; he was convinced that younger men should conduct the case, men who had their full strength and vigor. He knew something of Los Angeles, which the workingmen of the country called "the scabbiest town on earth." If the Boise cases had been bitter and venom-laden, they would seem like a Sunday-school picnic compared with the vitriol bath in which he would be immersed in Los Angeles. The McNamaras had twenty indictments against them, one for each of the men killed in the *Times* fire; it would take him at least a year to try the first case, and if he earned an acquittal on that he would have to try the other nineteen cases.

When he had returned from Boise he had promised Ruby that he would take on no more labor trials. Ruby had threatened that if he broke his promise she would refuse to accompany him; that would stop him, for Clarence had become dependent upon his wife and would not consent to being separated from her. He loved his home on the Midway; he was getting along well with his practice; he would be able to retire soon to write his long novel.

He said no, he would not take the case. But Sam Gompers refused to take no for an answer. The entire country, labor and capital alike, had assumed it would be "Clarence Darrow for the defense." Unions from every city in America wrote to tell him how happy they were that he was to defend, because he would show up the conspiracy and save the McNamaras; letters arrived from plumbers in Schenectady, brickmasons of Duluth, carpenters of New Orleans, needleworkers in New York, lumbermen of Seattle, coal miners of Scranton, streetcar conductors of San Francisco, each enclosing a dollar bill, assuring him they would stand behind him in his defense. A major labor case without Darrow; that was unthinkable!

He spent the next few days in an unhappy state of mind. Ruby made it clear that she thought it suicidal for him to take the case. Masters and Wilson opposed his going with every argument at their command, even vowing to dissolve the partnership. When the executive board of the American Federation of Labor begged him to attend a meeting in Washington he could not turn them down. They offered him a fifty-thousand-dollar fee; they offered a two-hundred-thousand-dollar defense fund, to spend as he saw fit, without an accounting; they offered him the complete loyalty and backing of their press, of their millions of members. Still he refused.

On the following Sunday afternoon Gompers came again to the flat on the Midway, accompanied by some of the strongest voices in American labor. For hours they were quartered in the library, while Ruby waited with sickening anxiety in their bedroom.

Ed Nockels said, "The whole world is expecting you to defend the boys; if you refuse you convict them before they come to trial."

Gompers said, "You will go down in history as a traitor to the great cause you have so faithfully championed and defended if now, in their greatest hour of need, you refuse to take charge of the McNamara case."

"After many hours Dee came to me in the back," relates Ruby, "wearily, sadly, taking my hand and conducting me to a seat beside him, to break to me the news that he was asking me to break my pledge. He did not seem exactly afraid that I would refuse to do as he asked; he had never asked me anything that I had even hesitated about; he explained that the men in the front room were saying that he would go down in history as a traitor to his cause. He asked me to lift my pledge and promise to go along to Los Angeles. I did not add to his dismay and dread of the situation; I offered no objections to having him do as he deemed necessary and best."

"I felt I had done my share of fighting," writes Darrow of this moment of decision. "It was not easy to combat the powerful forces of society in the courts, as I had been doing for so many years, and I was now weary of battling against public opinion. I had fought through so many conflicts that I felt the need of rest from such strenuous work. The very name of Los Angeles was associated with so much misery and suffering that the thought of going back to that place and its painful memories seemed like a foreboding that I could not quiet. Yet hard as it was to give them my yes, it would have been harder to say no."

Masters and Wilson dissolved their partnership. "It would be the international limelight again," said Wilson, "a lure he couldn't resist. And there was always the chance of winning that fifty thousand dollars quickly, in a few months, so that he could retire to write his novel."

Darrow formed a nonactive partnership with a junior in the office, Jacob L. Bailey, so that his name should not disappear from the Chicago legal register while he was away.

Ruby covered her furniture with sheets and towels, packed their bags. "It may be imagined with what dread and distress we went West," she relates. "Enough had been brought out by the prosecution fine-combing for facts and by the relentless newspapers to show what a web of dangers and disasters awaited us. No one had any inkling about the truth, just how the explosion had occurred, what the motive was, who was most, or least, responsible; nothing could be sifted and weighed until it could be investigated in Los Angeles. Mr Darrow had never even heard of the McNamaras, had no idea what sort they were, what personalities he would find, what mental make-up. He had not the first or faintest reason for judging whether they were guilty. The situation frightened and bewildered him as nothing ever had in my acquaintance with him, and he would have given almost anything to escape giving himself over to that job. But it was a matter of honor now; he could not have borne the cry against him as a traitor to the cause."

"It was with heavy hearts that Mrs Darrow and I drove to the Chicago and North Western station," writes Darrow, "and boarded the train for Los Angeles."

5

Darrow went straight from the station to the county jail to meet his clients. He was pleased to find the McNamara brothers clean cut, intelligent, with a quiet and gentle manner. James B., who was twenty-eight, was lean of face and figure, had an amused, bright gleam in his eye and a poetic, almost mystical strain. His brother John J., the secretary of the union, was a year younger; he was broader of face and figure, with a touch of Irish melancholy in his eyes; he had come up from the ranks of labor, had given himself a legal education, was quiet spoken but intense.

He did not ask the brothers whether they were innocent or guilty as charged. "I've heard Mr Darrow say that he placed little value on the statements of clients," tells Mrs Darrow, "that he could do better work if he was allowed to presume his clients innocent."

It was easy to assume the McNamaras innocent because of their straightforward and honest manner. Fletcher Bowron, a reporter for the *Record*, who later became reform mayor of Los Angeles, says, "I talked to the boys frequently in the jail. From their appearance and way of speaking it would have been difficult to think them guilty. I thought they were innocent." Nor did the Mc-Namaras leave many in doubt. When Sam Gompers came to Los Angeles John J. took his hand and said, "I want to assure you that we are innocent of the crime with which we are charged."

That afternoon Darrow went with Job Harriman, who had had charge of the case until Darrow's arrival, to the charred hull of the Times Building, standing on the exact spot in ink alley where the explosion had taken place. Here Harriman re-created the scene for his chief:

Early in the morning of October first, after the editorial staff had put the paper to bed and gone home for the night, there had been an explosion in the roofed-over alley in which barrels of ink were unloaded from the drays and stored until they were needed for the presses. This explosion was followed immediately by a second, which was either the gas main or leaking gas blowing up. One whole wall of the stone building was blown out. The ink in the barrels caught fire at once, and within four minutes the entire building was a sheet of flames, the fire eating up the wooden floors that had not collapsed under the weight of their machinery in the second explosion. There were in the building some twenty telegraph operators, linotype operators, printers, machinists, compositors, pressmen, but the intensity of the fire made rescue work impossible. Those who had not crashed to the basement with their heavy machinery had fought their way through the fierce flames to the windows and doors. Those who jumped to the pavement below were killed; the others were sucked back by the flames, their stricken faces vanishing into the red curtain behind them.

Los Angeles had been awakened by the force of the explosions and the clang of the fire wagons. Within an hour thousands of people were standing opposite the burning building, many of them in their night clothes, fighting with the police to break their lines, to try to help in some sort of rescue. But it was to no avail: twenty men were killed in one of the most gruesome tragedies in American civilian life.

By dawn, while the firemen were still plying their hoses on the flames, a one-sheet edition of the *Times* hit the streets, having been printed in an auxiliary pressroom. An eight-column streamer read: Unionist Bomb Wrecks the Times. Harry Chandler, son-in-law of the owner, Harrison Gray Otis, and the managing editor, wrote, "The Times Building was destroyed this morning by the enemies of industrial freedom. The elements that conspired to perpetrate this horror must not be permitted to pursue their awful campaign of intimidation and terror." The men who had been killed were called "victims of the foulest plot of foul Union Labor Ruffians."

The next day Otis cried in his paper, "O you anarchic scum, you cowardly murderers, you leeches upon honest labor, you midnight assassins, you whose hands are dripping with the innocent blood of your victims, you against whom the wails of poor widows and the cries of fatherless children are ascending to the Great White Throne, go look at the ruins wherein are buried the calcined remains of those whom you murdered. . . ."

"But how could he make those charges?" demanded Darrow of Harriman, "when the firemen were still poking around in the ruins and no one could know what caused the explosion?"

"Ah," replied Job Harriman, "you don't know Harrison Gray Otis."

6

Few conflicts in American life are sudden or inexplicable: they have their roots deep in the past. This trial that brought Darrow to Los Angeles in 1911 had its beginnings in 1890, when the four local newspapers threatened a twenty-per-cent cut and the union typographers struck rather than take the reduction in wages. Within three days the *Tribune* and *Express* had settled their differences with the men; by the end of the third month the typographers were back at work on the *Herald*. This left only the *Times* men on strike; they were eager to compromise in order to go back to work. The decision rested in one man's hands, Harrison Gray Otis, a former union printer who had taken part in fifteen Civil War battles and had come out with a captain's commission in his pocket and a taste for warfare in his mouth. The pattern of life in southern California would be formulated by Captain Harrison Gray Otis's blunderbuss.

Between the Civil War and his purchase of an interest in the *Times* in 1882 Otis was a government hanger-on, constantly importuning for appointments. Failing to land the job of collector of the Port of San Diego, on which he had set his heart, he bought a fourth interest in the weekly *Times*, which was slowly dying of attrition in the mud-baked metropolis of eleven thousand souls. By the end of four years, when the first land boom descended upon southern California, Otis had bought out his associates for trifling sums; people poured in; money poured in; the *Times* became a daily; Otis began buying up tracts of land—and was on his way to becoming a multimillionaire and arbiter of American civilization.

"Otis was a large, aggressive man with a walrus mustache, a goatee and a warlike demeanor, resembling Buffalo Bill and General Custer," writes Morrow Mayo in his excellent book *Los Angeles*. "The military bee buzzed in his bonnet. He called his home in Los Angeles The Bivouac, and when the boom was at its height he built a new plant for the *Times*, which resembled a medieval fortress, with battlements, sentry boxes, surmounted by a screaming eagle. He was a natural warrior and not a man to be crossed. He was a holy terror in his newspaper plant; his natural voice was that of a game warden roaring at seal poachers."

Reporters on the *Times* accused Otis of never getting past the third reader, but they underestimated his functional intelligence for getting a specific job done. No man in all American history, not even in the blackest days of the War between the States, could touch Otis for range, power and intensity of vituperation, while a *schimpflexikon* of the abuse that Otis and the *Times* heaped upon the heads of workers, unions, liberals, progressives and the co-operative movements from 1890 to 1940 would constitute a confounding document. President Theodore Roosevelt wrote about him in the *Outlook* magazine: "He is a consistent enemy of every movement for social and economic betterment, a consistent enemy of men in California who have dared to stand against corruption and in favor of honesty. The attitude of General Otis in his paper affords a curious instance of the anarchy of soul which comes to a man who in conscienceless fashion deifies property at the expense of human rights. The *Times* has again and again showed itself to be such an enemy of good citizenship, honest, decent government and every effective effort to secure fair play for the workingman and-woman as any anarchist could show itself."

Otis declared that no man who had gone on strike could ever work for the *Times* again, that no union member would ever be employed by him in any capacity. Having embarked upon this road, there was no turning back; every step he took plunged him deeper into strife, and the continued strife only convinced him further that he was right. When he imported non-union printers from Kansas City in 1890 he set the tone for the long contest by writing, "These men came to Los Angeles much as the first settlers of New England came from the old country to escape religious intolerance and to gain personal freedom to worship as they saw fit. Like their hardy, selected forebears, these liberty-loving Los Angeles immigrants were pioneers who laid the foundation for the future growth of their adopted land." In 1929, when summing up in a supplement called *The Forty Years' War*, Harry Chandler carried on his father-in-law's tradition by writing, "It has been war, war in which many lives have been lost, millions of dollars of property destroyed, other millions lost through suspension of production. The cost to the city has been great, yet its profits infinitely greater."

There were other costs which the *Times* did not see fit to mention. "Outside pressure was exerted upon the Los Angeles police," writes Jerome Hopkins in *Our Lawless Police*, "by a dominant financial group, fanatically antilabor, which utilized the police as an adjunct to its open-shop industrial policies. Very early the Los Angeles police ceased to distinguish between economic dissenters, strikers, pickets and the criminal. This line of activity, kept alive by hysterical propaganda, has passed through successive phases: assistance in strikebreaking, espionage upon labor-union organizations, suppression of free speech, unlawful beatings, false arrest, brutality with arrest, unlawful detention, incommunicado and the third degree."

To Otis all this was another Civil War; it was his bounden duty to crush the Rebels. Battle was breath in his nostril. When his Civil War II began his cohorts promoted him from captain to general, and he was known as General Otis to the end of his days.

"It is somehow absurd but nevertheless true," laments Mayo, "that for forty years the smiling, booming sunshine City of the Angels has been the bloodiest arena in the Western world!"

By the decision of this one man Los Angeles became immersed in a half century of bloodshed, violence, hatred, class war, oppression, injustice and a destruction of civil liberties which was to turn it into the low spot of American culture and democracy.

7

The incalculable tragedy behind the Otis decision was that its tentacles soon spread to make this war a national affair. While Darrow was fighting for the American Railway Union in 1894 the groundwork for his present battle in 1911 was being laid, for in the midst of the railroad fight Otis called a meeting of the town's bankers, manufacturers and merchants, to form an organization called the Merchants and Manufacturers. Those businessmen who fought against being drawn into such an organization found their credit cut off at the banks; their customers were kept out of their shops; they found it difficult to sell their products anywhere in the country!

The San Francisco *Bulletin* wrote, "The Merchants and Manufacturers' Association has one confession of faith, one creed: 'We will employ no union man.' The M. and M. has also one command: 'You shall employ no union man.' The penalty for disobedience to this command is financial coercion, boycott and ruin. 'You hire union men and we'll put you out of business,' says the M. and M., and the businessman knows that the oracle speaks. 'You declare an eight-hour day and we'll stop your credit at the banks,' and the M. and M. does what it says. The M. and M. sandwich man does not walk up and down the streets. He walks boldly into the front door and puts his ultimatum on paper. The merchant who disobeys the M. and M. command runs into something which robs him of his business, hampers him in securing raw material for manufacture, holds up his payment for work when it is completed and frightens him out of speech to rebel."

The large flow of workingmen, attracted by the advertisements of all-year sunshine, flowers and beauty, found themselves at the mercy of the employers. The hours went as high as fourteen a day; wages fell to a new low. All workingmen had to pay dues to the M. and M. If anyone protested he was promptly fired, black-listed, put out of his house, run out of the country. This was Otis's "American Plan" for Industrial Freedom.

The unions were harried and weak, but they never gave up trying. While the *Times* called them cutthroats, assassins, robbers, thieves, rascals, lunatics, anarchists, sluggers, ruffians, swine, they kept plugging for shorter hours, better wages, striking whenever they could: teamsters, carpenters, plasterers, laundry workers, brewery workers, dozens of strikes, hundreds of strikes, bitter strikes filled with smashed heads. *Always the unions lost!* "This is war!" cried Otis from the *Times*, and the Merchants and Manufacturers gave no quarter.

For San Francisco, four hundred miles north, the strongest union city in America, and where wages were thirty per cent higher, the chaos of Los Angeles created a danger; the workers were afraid their wage would be pulled down to the Los Angeles level; the employers were afraid lest their low-wage competitors underbid them and take away their contracts. Realizing that Los Angeles constituted an infection area for the entire country, the American Federation of Labor in its 1910 convention voted to establish a unified labor council in Los Angeles and to fight the open-shop issue to a conclusion. Such powerful labor leaders in San Francisco as Tom Mooney, "Pinhead" McCarthy, O. A. Tveitmoe and Anton Johannsen were sent down to Los Angeles to serve as General Staff.

Since the ironworkers were the toughest fighters and had a strong national organization behind them, the San Francisco leaders used them as a spearhead of the attack. A new scale of wages was asked for; when it was refused fifteen hundred men walked out of such big plants as the Llewellyn and Baker Iron Works. Strikebreakers were hauled in from the Midwest; strong-arm squads were summoned from San Francisco to meet them. Deputies beat up the strikers; the strikers beat up the non-union workers; the police beat up the pickets. Blood flowed in a dozen different parts of the city.

General Otis mounted a small cannon on the running board of his car and dashed about the city to direct his police and special deputies. In his editorials he screamed, "It is full time to deal with these labor-union wolves in such prompt and drastic fashion as will induce them to transfer their lawlessness to some other locality. Their instincts are criminal, and they are ready for arson, riot, robbery and murder!" His hysteria rose to such heights in promising Angelenos that their city was about to be bombed off the face of the earth that a considerable portion of the citizens thought he ought to be clapped in a madhouse. At the peak of the insanity Senator Hiram Johnson hired the auditorium to cry out:

"In the city of San Francisco we have drunk to the very dregs of infamy; we have had vile officials; we have had rotten newspapers. But we have nothing so vile, nothing so low, nothing so debased, nothing so infamous, in San Francisco as Harrison Gray Otis. He sits there in senile dementia with gangrened heart and rotting brain, grimacing at every reform, chattering impotently at all things that are decent, frothing, fuming, violently gibbering, going down to his grave in snarling infamy. He is one thing that all California looks at when, in looking at southern California, they see anything that is disgraceful, depraved, corrupt, crooked and putrescent—that is Harrison Gray Otis."

This was the city, this was the opposition, this was the intrastate conflict, this the hysteria multiplied to infinity by the deaths of twenty innocent men, into which Clarence Darrow plunged when he stepped off his train in sunny southern California.

8

By the end of two weeks Darrow was settled in a comfortable flat on the high hill of Bonnie Brae and had assembled a brilliant legal staff. For his mastery of California law he chose Le Compte Davis, member of a Kentucky family who had come to California in the hopes of cheating death of another consumption victim. Davis had been assistant district attorney, had prosecuted labor for unruly conduct, was known to be a conservative and had an unimpeachable reputation. Next in line Darrow selected Joseph Scott, the leading Catholic attorney of the community, whose presence in the case would swing sentiment toward the Irish Catholic McNamaras. Another wise choice was that of Judge McNutt, former Supreme Court justice of Indiana, who was known to be favorable to labor.

Job Harriman was the fifth member and the expert on the California labor background. A little past forty, Harriman had been sent to California to die of tuberculosis but had lived instead to become the leading socialist of the district. He was a bright, eager man, a theorist and idealist who made a good educator but who had failed as an administrator in charge of a socialist-utopia community. Harriman was later accused by Edward Cantrell, a fellow socialist whom Harriman was instrumental in having expelled from the party for causing factional strife, of having known beforehand that the *Times* was to be bombed. After his expulsion Cantrell went unsolicited to the *Times*, the archenemy of his enemies in the party, and gave them an article in which he told of being in San Luis Obispo for a lecture the night the *Times* was blown up and of having Harriman appear at his hotel for no apparent reason. The next morning, when Harriman read of the twenty deaths, reports Cantrell, he became overwrought and almost hysterical. From these two deductions, that Harriman had joined him in San Luis Obispo merely to establish an alibi and that he had become overwrought when he read of the deaths, Cantrell went before the grand jury to accuse Harriman of complicity in the Los Angeles dynamiting conspiracy. Cantrell, a retired clergyman, was an honest man, but his unconscious motive was revenge against the men who had expelled and hence discredited him. No scrap of evidence ever implicated Harriman in foreknowledge of the explosion; Le Compte Davis, who was unsympathetic to both labor and socialism, voiced the opinion of everyone who knew Harriman when he said:

"Not all the angels in heaven or all the devils in hell could ever convince me that Job Harriman knew anything about the conniving and dynamiting. You had only to be with him for a few minutes to know that he was a good and honest and peaceable man."

Darrow rented the major portion of a floor of the Higgins Building on the corner of Second and Main streets, with offices adjoining those of Harriman. He then moved in desks, chairs, filing cabinets, typewriters, secretaries, a publicity man and a staff of investigators under the direction of John Harrington. Harrington had been for many years an investigator for the Chicago Surface Lines, until he lost his job through insubordination. Since Darrow had always thought him a good investigator and needed someone in Los Angeles whom he felt he could trust, he brought Harrington to Los Angeles to head his local detective staff. Darrow both liked Harrington and felt sorry for him; since he was without an acquaintance in Los Angeles, the Darrows took him and his little daughter into their home.

The first great obstacle was the Ortie McManigal confession. Before he had left Chicago Darrow had had Harrington bring to his home on the Midway Mrs McManigal and McManigal's uncle, George Behm. Having been successful in getting Lillard, Steve Adams' uncle, to persuade Adams to repudiate his confession, he saw no reason why he should not try to get Uncle George Behm to persuade McManigal to repudiate, particularly since he "promised to defend McManigal if they had forced him to make that confession." Mrs Ortie McManigal was convinced that her husband had made the confession under fear and threats.

"Mr Darrow asked me if I was a union man," related George Behm. "I told him I was. He asked me if I was in sympathy with the labor movement and the McNamara case, and I told him I was as far as I know about it."

" 'Are you willing to go out there and see what you can do with your nephew in regard to changing his testimony?'

" 'Well, I can't hardly leave home. I have to put in my crop.'

" 'All right, you lay off and go home and put in your crop. Get your help to carry on the farm while you are gone.' "

He had paid the expenses for the farm hand and given Behm, Mrs McManigal and her little boy enough money to get out to Los Angeles. But Behm was having no luck with his nephew. He told Darrow that "Ortie refuses to recall his confession. He says he is better off in jail than out on the streets where someone would be liable to blow his head off." Darrow sent Behm back to the jail again and again, but nothing could move McManigal, who finally cried in exasperation, "You will have to cut it out, Uncle George, for I won't talk about it at all. I have got my mind made up to tell the truth." And that was the last word he would speak about the McNamara case.

It looked to the defense as though the prosecution's case was to be based solely on the McManigal confession. If Darrow could prove that it had been written by William J. Burns, who had been holding Ortie captive at the time, he could free the McNamaras: for although McManigal had admitted placing charges of dynamite under bridges and aqueducts, always at the order of the union secretary, John J. McNamara, he had sworn that he had not been in Los Angeles or had anything to do with the *Times* explosion. Darrow employed almost a hundred investigators who combed the country to check up on McManigal, to see if he had been where he said he had been, to determine just what had caused the explosions in the various cities and whether McManigal could have had anything to do with them, to find people who knew McManigal and might contradict any part of the confession. He also sent out an investigating staff under Harrington to learn what had caused the *Times* explosion, to find the men who had complained of leaking gas in the plant the very night of the accident. He ordered a complete model of the Times Building made, with all interior fittings, which he planned to blow up in court to prove that only gas could have caused the tragedy; he engaged expert technicians to experiment with gas explosions and their results. He hadn't wanted to take the case, but now that he was in it he gave to his clients every last ounce of his energy and resourceful mind.

Once his investigation had started in earnest there began a campaign of espionage and counterespionage. When reports came in from his Eastern investigators Darrow found that the information was in the possession of the district attorney by the following day. He made connections with a deputy in the district attorney's office who informed him that one of his secretaries was a Burns detective and was making copies of everything that came into the office. Darrow put this deputy on his pay roll; he was daily to report back the information Darrow's secretary had passed on to the district attorney! Darrow, Tveitmoe and Johannsen, the two San Francisco labor leaders, concocted a secret code based on the pagination of Webster's dictionary; Joseph Ford, the assistant district attorney and private attorney for William J. Burns, selected Burns men to get themselves hired as investigators for Darrow and decipher the code. The manager of Burns's Los Angeles office came to Darrow in a secret conference and offered to sell him copies of all of Burns's reports, pay rolls and books. When Darrow learned that the district attorney's investigators were also scouring the East to get corroboration of the McManigal confession he hired several of the Burns men who were working for the district attorney to report back to him everything the district attorney's investigators had found in the East. Before long some of the private detectives were drawing three separate salaries, passing around their information in a daisy chain; Darrow, Fredericks, the prosecuting attorney, and Ford knew what each other had had for breakfast.

If the situation had musical-comedy aspects the trickery assumed dangerous proportions. Defense witnesses and relatives of the accused men were so hounded by night and day that they lost their jobs, their homes, were put out of their hotels and boardinghouses. Defense employees were shadowed, threatened, bribed, kidnaped. Anyone helpful to the defense was hauled before Fredericks' grand jury and threatened with indictment unless he retracted. Darrow's telegrams were stolen, his account books copied, his telephone conversations taken on hidden dictaphones. Once when his investigators unearthed a witness whom he considered valuable he moved him to a small hotel and told him to keep out of circulation. The following morning his spy in the district attorney's office informed him that the district attorney's spy in his office had learned of the man's value to the defense. The witness had then been kidnaped from his hotel and was being held prisoner in a barn in Culver City. Dr Atwater, a Los Angeles dentist, tells that "that night I drove Darrow in my buggy to Culver City. We left the buggy a safe distance from the designated barn, approached it quietly and saw two deputies stationed in front. We went around to the back, tunneled under the wall and found our witness lying on a pile of hay in a drugged or semiconscious condition. We pushed and dragged him under the wall, carried him to the buggy and got him away."

Dirty and stupid business for Clarence Darrow to be engaging in? War is dirty and stupid business.

9

The pressure of work left Clarence little time for social life, but once a week he and Ruby would go to a party given in their honor by Joseph Scott in Pasadena or by the Le Compte Davises for the cream of the Los Angeles intellectuals. He did not care greatly for big and formal parties; he preferred informal chin fests with cronies who loved books and thought that talking about literature was as important a pleasure as there was in life. His friend Fay Lewis came out from Rockford to stand by his side; Billy Cavenaugh, the stonecutter, who was working in Los Angeles as a policeman, gave him alcohol rubs several nights a week; an old pal from the Chicago *Inter-Ocean* by the name of James H. Griffes, who was publishing a little magazine in Los Angeles called the *Everyman*, ran a series of his articles on everything from Robert Burns's poetry to prison reform and acquainted him with southern California artists and writers.

Best of all he liked a little group of new acquaintances who never discussed the McNamaras nor law courts: Gerson, a young and sensitive physician; Reynold E. Blight, a young member of the Board of Education with a penchant for books, and Edward M. Williams, who liked to discuss philosophy. Once a week the four couples met at one of their homes for dinner, and then Darrow would settle in an armchair and read for an hour, mostly from Israel Zangwill and Tolstoy. When he had read something particularly pleasurable he would shyly lift his eyes above the book and look at his friends with a sparkling smile. These evenings so rested him and took his mind off his affairs that Ruby gave frequent little supper parties for them. He delivered only one lecture, at the Philharmonic Auditorium, where Blight reports that "he held twenty-four hundred people in thralldom just telling stories about Tolstoy. There was no flamboyance or purple passages in his talk; it was the simplicity, directness and clarity of what he said that held his audience."

As the scorching summer heat came on Darrow slowly became depressed and then dejected: his investigators could find no evidence to controvert the Ortie McManigal confession, no evidence to show that the McNamaras had not been guilty of the violence charged. Worse yet, the district attorney's investigators were sending in mountainous piles of proof to sustain McManigal. When McManigal told how they had bought dynamite from a certain well digger that well digger was found and identified James B. McNamara as one of the men who had bought it. When McManigal told of registering at a certain hotel just before the setting of a blast, there was J. B.'s signature on the register and people to identify him from his picture. When McManigal told of renting a house to store the explosives there was the landlord to identify J. B. One day, when his spy in the district attorney's office brought him a copy of a particularly damaging piece of evidence against J. B., Darrow walked into his cell and cried:

"My God, you left a trail behind you a mile wide!"

McNamara did not answer.

That night Clarence spent some wretched hours, torn by the most basic of his inner conflicts. "I never believed in violence on either side; I don't believe in the violence of war; I don't believe in the violence that everywhere abounds on earth. I know who is responsible for this struggle: it is the men who have reached out their hands and taken possession of all the wealth in the world; it is that paralyzing hand of wealth which has reached out and destroyed all the opportunities of the poor. The acts of the poor are protests against their wrongs; yet I don't believe in the violence of the poor and the weak, who think they can obtain their rights by fighting the rich and the strong." Harry Orchard had accused Moyer, Haywood and Pettibone with a hundred crimes, most of which had been uncommitted; McManigal had accused the McNamaras of a hundred crimes, all of which had been committed, most of which the prosecution could prove! True, the McNamaras were not yet charged with these other and distant crimes; they were charged with the bombing of the Times Building, which did not appear to have been bombed at all and on which no implicity for the Mc-Namaras had been found. But how quick people would be to assume that if they had committed a hundred other bombings and the *Times* had been their archenemy, therefore, they must also have bombed the *Times*. It would only be circumstantial evidence, and it was difficult to hang men on circumstantial evidence; but if he managed the miracle of an acquittal the brothers and the officers of the ironworkers' union would be indicted in every major city in America for the property bombings.

In the dark hours of the dark night he became ill with a despair which was rarely to leave him, night or day, for two years; a despair whose seeds had been sown in the days when he had come to understand that in defending Big Bill Hayward he was defending a philosophy of force. Part of his illness in Idaho had been due to this conflict of loyalties within himself, perhaps enough of it to turn an ordinary mastoid into the freak mastoid which had trebled his suffering. When he had returned to Chicago it had been not only his physical malaise that had converted him to the doctrine of settlement, for he had always believed in peaceful compromise—whenever he could find any peace. The Haywood case had brought him to grips with what he had always known, that in any conflict of force both sides were wrong and both sides must lose; in the unlikely event that either side should win a victory it could only mean that the war would have to start again. Every aspect of the Mc-Namara case confirmed him in this judgment.

If he defended these practitioners of violence, would not the country be entitled to assume that since he defended sabotage, force, crimes against property, he must necessarily condone the use of dynamite and violence? That he defended labor leaders, guilty or innocent? Would not his defense of dynamiters eventually convict the labor groups and leaders he had previously defended? Would not his presence in future cases stigmatize his clients as having been guilty of using force? Would not all his years of pleading for the broader view, for tolerance and sympathy, for co-operation and understanding between apparently conflicting interests, be undone? By portraying the barbarities on both sides of the class war he had been able to establish a kind of justification for force, but he did not want to become an apostle of force, confirm other firebrands in their belief that they could solve their problems by any number of crimes and any amount of violence, that they could never be brought to bay. How could he who had militantly in book and lecture preached for peace earn an acquittal for the philosophy of force, enstrengthen it to continue until it brought the industrial world down in flames?

Every American was entitled to a defense and a defender, the very best he could hire, yet Clarence Darrow was heartsick at the thought of betraying his own instincts and teachings.

He could not abandon the McNamaras now, he knew. Nor did he pass judgment against them for what they had done. They had been childish and misguided to imagine that they could conquer a billion-dollar industry by random explosions; he thought they had been blind not to see over the years between 1906 and 1911 that they were getting nowhere with their violence; that they must eventually be caught and do infinite damage to the union movement. Yet he understood their motivations. They were guilty of standing up and fighting in a war which they believed had been forced upon them by the National Erectors' Association. They had worked and sacrificed for years to establish their union, and now their efforts would be wiped out; they would become puppets of the steel trust. The only property the union man owned was his skill with his hands. He said:

"All right, we'll keep this a war of property. If you blast our property we'll blast yours. So long as you don't slug or club our men we won't hurt your men. You want to make our membership in a union so costly to us that we'll abandon our union; all right, then we'll make your membership in the erectors' union so costly to you that you will abandon your union."

They had kept their word; in all the explosions no man had ever been injured. In one instance where a watchman would have been hurt because his sentry box was close to the scene of the explosion, they had gone to the trouble and danger of setting off a small charge a distance away so that the watchman would run to investigate and not be hurt by the major explosion. He knew the McNamaras would cry:

"They had all the money, all the power. What else was left open to us? What else could we do? We had no way to fight them in terms of peace. If we did nothing we were licked, destroyed. We had to use force; it was the only weapon left to us. We had to fight the devil with fire!"

What could he answer them? Should he quote Matthew, "Resist not evil, but whosoever shall smite thee on thy right cheek, turn to him the other, also"?

He suffered an agony of mind over the trap in which he was

caught. He had a suspicion that if Le Compte Davis, Joseph Scott and Judge McNutt were to learn of the overwhelming guilt of the McNamaras in past dynamitings they would feel obliged to with- draw, an act which would convict his clients before they came to trial. Job Harriman, he felt, had known all along, but he did not discuss the piling evidence with him. What made his burden heavy was that labor throughout the country was still passionately convinced that the McNamaras were innocent of any dynamiting or other criminal acts; its press wrote flaming articles against the injustice in Los Angeles. May Day of 1911 was called McNamaras' Day; demonstrations were held in every major city of America at which tens of thousands voiced their protests against the frame-up. Twenty thousand men paraded in Los Angeles carrying banners which read, DOWN WITH OTIS! REGISTER YOUR PROTEST AGAINST THE McNAMARA FRAME-UP! Every union in the country was con- tributing funds; thousands of letters poured into the office in the Higgins Building from workmen who wanted to assure him of their loyalty and contribute a further bit from their savings.

He felt like a man with a rumbling volcano in his pocket, trying to hold back the eruption with his naked hand.

10

Early in the summer a strong socialist movement had begun in Los Angeles to offset the *Times* and the Merchants' and Manufacturers' Association. Eugene Debs was circulating forty thousand copies of his *Appeal to Reason* each week, and the paper was being read avidly as an antidote to the *Times*. Job Harriman was nominated for mayor; a strong ticket was put into the field. Alexander Irvine, a clergyman who had been stripped of his pulpit in New Haven for preaching Christian socialism, was sent out by national headquarters to conduct the campaign. Socialism was on the upswing in America; many socialist congressmen and legislators had already been elected; several cities had socialist mayors, while others were going into the new campaign with excellent prospects. Considering the heat and hysteria of the moment, the socialist platform was moderate: though it demanded the ultimate replacement of the capitalist system it was willing to settle in the meanwhile for woman suffrage, more schools, social centers, public beaches and plunges, public hospitals and em- ployment bureaus, civil service, an eight-hour law, municipal owner- ship of such ultilities as city railways, telephone, icehouse, cement plant. If the socialists could win in Los Angeles it would assure a sympathetic trial for the McNamaras.

In addition to everything else that was being charged against him Darrow was now accused of starting the socialist campaign to take over the city, and of financing its campaign out of McNamara defense funds. He had not started the socialist campaign; there had always been a strong movement in southern California; neither had he contributed more than a few hundred dollars for its literature, but once it was under way he gave it every aid he could, lecturing on those nights when he could break away from his work. Big Bill Haywood came to exhort large gatherings on the blessings of socialism and to swear that the McNamaras had been framed just as he had been in Idaho. Educational pamphlets were distributed by the tens of thousands; Harriman, who was an intelligent man of about forty, with thick, well-ordered hair, honest eyes and strong features, went about lecturing to the effect that "the labor unions are the only organized expression of the wageworker's interest within the present system of production, and they can no more be disbanded or crushed out of existence than can the wageworker himself cease to work for wages."

Thus were the McNamara defense and the socialist campaign inextricably interwoven.

The primaries would be held in October, and from the intensity of socialist interest in the city it appeared that the vote would be close, for the Good Government League of the Merchants and Manufacturers had been exposed in a series of land frauds and manipulations. The election would come in December; Darrow asked Judge Bordwell to set the opening of the McNamara case over until December. Bordwell decreed instead that the case should open on the eleventh of October.

On the day before the trial was to begin Sam Gompers addressed fifteen thousand labor sympathizers in Philadelphia, who shouted in unison their belief of the McNamara innocence. Seventeen thousand people paraded the streets with banners which read: "Down, Down with Detective Burns, the Kidnaper!" The *Times* rebutted with "Socialism is not anarchy, but it is a halfway house on the road to anarchy. It would prove the inevitable precursor of a condition of lawlessness, of robbery, of riot and murder. Carry Los Angeles for socialism? Carry it for business stagnation, abandoned industries, smokeless chimneys, bankruptcy, ruined homes, chaos of civil government. Carry it for hell!"

This was the temper of the country; this was the temper of Los Angeles when Darrow walked into Judge Bordwell's court on October 11, 1911, to begin his defense. People the world over gazed lovingly at his picture in the newspapers, assured each other that he would get the boys off, that he would expose the frame-up, that he would win another great victory for labor and the common people.

But Clarence Darrow walked into the courtroom a beaten man. He had learned that the McNamaras were guilty as charged.

11

In the summer of 1910 three men had gone to the Hercules Powder Plant on San Francisco Bay, represented themselves as businessmen from Folsom, California, and ordered a quantity of eighty-per-cent nitrogelatin, a rarely used explosive, for the avowed purpose of blasting boulders and tree stumps. A few days later they had rented a motorboat called the Peerless, painted another name over the first, picked up their explosive, carried it across the bay to a wharf in San Francisco, where they had loaded it onto a wagon and carted it to an empty house rented for the purpose. The three men were David Caplan, a San Francisco labor leader, Matt Schmidt, a young and brilliant engineer who had been traveling with James B. McNamara, constructing time bombs for his explosions, and James B. McNamara. All three were identified by the Hercules Powder employees, by the owners of the Peerless, by the landlord of the empty house, by people who had seen the wagon pulled through the streets of San Francisco. The district attorney's office claimed that the day after the *Times* explosion two suitcases had been found, one near Otis's house, one near the house of the secretary of the M. and M., containing time mechanisms made by Schmidt and sticks of the eighty-per-cent nitrogelatin which Hercules men identified as the explosive purchased by J. B. McNamara, Caplan and Schmidt.

And Darrow realized that his journey along the downward trail, which had begun when he defended Big Bill Haywood, who was innocent as charged but guilty of crimes of violence against mine property, had at last brought him into the swamps of defending men who were guilty as charged. It was no good to tell himself that the McNamaras were guilty of dynamiting but not of murder; that they had not intended to kill anyone but only to frighten Otis; that they certainly would never hurt their fellow workingmen, and that if Otis had not indulged in the negligence of letting gas escape in his building no one would have been hurt. Men who dealt in violence must ultimately have caused disaster: he knew too well that the McNamaras were morally responsible for the deaths of the twenty *Times* employees.

This day was one of his blackest, yet even in his despair he did not condemn the McNamaras. They had done what they thought was right; they had been fighting for labor; they had worked for the cause and not for personal profit or aggrandizement. He himself had been instrumental in showing them that they must battle the open shop. They had fought with the only weapons at hand. He could not abandon them, not even in his mind, yet the knowledge of the indictment that would be brought against labor made him ill. What a field day Otis, the Merchants and Manufacturers, the National Erectors' Association, the Steel Trust would have! And what could he do to stop them?

To further harrow him he found that James B. McNamara and young men like Matt Schmidt, who had started as labor's martyrs, had grown flushed with success because they had operated for years without being caught. In the early days they had lived carefully, had worked cautiously, but their victories had made them contemptuous of both the law and their opponents. Without knowing it they had become enamored of the life itself, the excitement, the suspense, the danger of hiding out in swamps and bulrushes through the night, the fascination of the flight, the pursuit; all the nefarious thrills of the life of crime that ensnares the young and emotionally unstable.

Over and above the excitements there had been the pleasures of the irregular life: freedom from routine, from constant supervision, from responsibilities of the family and the home, the zest of the nomadic life, the constant travel with its changes of scenery, its new faces and cities and ways of life. The men had been paid two hundred dollars an explosion, in addition to certain expenses; they had lived irregularly; they had lived well, and slowly they had become unable to resist the subtle encroachments upon character that result from such an existence. They fell into the habit of acquiring new women in each successive town, of necessity posing as something they were not: concealing, dissembling, lying and finally of drinking, in their enforced idleness, in their excitement, in the letdown after the tension of placing the bomb and hearing it explode. They had started out as soldiers in a war and not as evildoers; nor were their deteriorations in character known to them; that was why they had grown bolder, defiant, careless. And that was why the McNamaras were now in jail after being responsible for the deaths of twenty innocent workmen. That was why their union would now be wrecked and every union man in the world injured.

J. B. McNamara says, "On the night of September 30, 1910, at 5.45 P.M., I placed in ink alley, a portion of the Times Building, a suitcase containing sixteen sticks of eighty-per-cent dynamite, set to explode at one o'clock in the morning. It was my intention to injure the building and scare the owners. I did not intend to take the life of anyone. I sincerely regret that these unfortunate men lost their lives; if the giving of my life would bring them back I would freely give it."

Slumped behind his desk in the Higgins Building, feeling confused and torn, Darrow asked himself two questions:

"How can I defend the McNamaras? How can they be defended?"

He shambled slowly over to the jail, had the guard admit him to the McNamara cell and sat on a bunk between his two clients. He had sat in many cells with many clients, but for him this was the most hopeless meeting of all. . . .

"Why did you do it?" he asked hoarsely of no one in particular. There was a long silence, during which J. B.'s face looked long and thin and solemn. His feverish eyes gleamed.

"There was a labor parade," he answered in a hoarse, impersonal tone, as though talking to himself. "The police beat up some of the boys. The next morning the *Times* praised those cops for their heroic work. It was more than I could stand."

It was a reason. . . . But to Darrow it was little consolation; he knew with a terrible surety that these two men, warm live flesh that touched him on either side, both under thirty, would be convicted, would be walked up to the scaffold at San Quentin, the ropes adjusted about their necks, the traps sprung beneath their feet, their necks broken in the noose.

The passage of the years, the burden of suffering and of death he had seen, had not made him hard shelled, had not blunted his almost pathological empathy. And of all the brutalizing acts he had encountered, there was none he found more degrading or more injurious to the spiritual fabric of the people as a whole than the taking of a life by the state.

"That capital punishment is horrible and cruel is the reason for its existence," he wrote in *Crime, Its Causes and Treatment*, the book in which he paid his debt to John P. Altgeld and carried forward Altgeld's teachings. "That men should be taught not to take life is the purpose of judicial killings. But the spectacle of the state taking life must tend to cheapen it. Frequent executions dull the sensibilities toward the taking of life. This makes it easier for men to kill and increases murders, which in turn increase hangings, which in turn increase murders, and so on, around the vicious circle."

He believed passionately in the sanctity of human life; if the state could take human life for revenge or punishment, why could

:t not take it for a thousand other reasons? If every last iota of life was not made sacred, how could the preciousness of life, and hence the human race, be maintained?

Mrs Edgar Wilson, who was now living in Los Angeles, saw him riding home on the streetcar that night. He did not see her. Mrs Wilson says that he slumped down into a corner, looking haggard and mortally ill, only the shell of the man she had known in Boise. Fletcher Bowron, who went up to his office every morning to find if there was any news, saw at once that something crucial had happened to Darrow; his fire was gone; his confidence was gone; his concentration, singleness and clarity of purpose, his grip on the organization of his job, had disintegrated. He was confused, helpless, terror-stricken.

He didn't know where to turn or what to do.

12

It was during this period that certain questionable acts began to happen around defense headquarters. One of the most damaging witnesses against J. B. McNamara was Diekleman, a Los Angeles hotel clerk who had registered J. B. McNamara as J. B. Bryce a few days before the *Times* explosion. Diekleman had in the meanwhile joined the Harvey restaurant system and been transferred to Albuquerque, New Mexico. The prosecution knew at all times where he was because it kept Burns operatives surrounding him. One day Burt Hamerstrom, Ruby's itinerant-journalist brother, turned up at Diekleman's restaurant in Albuquerque, introduced himself as Mr Higgins (name of the building in which Darrow had his defense offices) and said:

"We are trying our best to save that man. He is innocent. Don't you think it would be right for you to consider the least doubt there is and be on our side?"

"I don't think there is any doubt," replied Diekleman.

"Now you are a valuable witness to us, and whatever your price is we will give it to you. Do you know Rector's Restaurant in Chicago?"

"Yes."

"Well, I think Mr Darrow is interested in that. How would you like to be assistant manager there?"

Diekleman refused to leave Albuquerque. Hamerstrom came back several times, offering railroad fare to Chicago and thirty dollars a week for expense money until the trial was over and a round-trip ticket to Los Angeles. When Diekleman still refused Hamerstrom assumed that he didn't want to leave his girl friend behind and offered to pay her expenses too. Diekleman agreed, accepted a railroad ticket and left for Chicago on September 19, 1911. The morning he arrived in Chicago he had a meeting with Hamerstrom and Ed Nockels, then wired the district attorney's office in Los Angeles where he was and returned to Albuquerque on the afternoon train. It was a fiasco which was to cause Darrow a deal of trouble, as did the wild ride of Mrs Dave Caplan.

Mrs Caplan's husband was now a fugitive from justice, for he was one of the three men who had bought the nitrogelatin from the Hercules Powder Plant, and it was his wagon in which the explosive had been hauled from the Embarcadero to the empty house he had rented. When Mrs Caplan was served with a subpoena and told that she would remain under subpoena from October eleventh on, Tveitmoe and Johannsen hired a limousine and chauffeur, picked up Mrs Caplan and had her driven for two nights to Reno, Nevada. The next day Johannsen accompanied her on a train to Chicago.

With the passage of the weary and disheartening days, only one good thing happened for the defense: Job Harriman won the primary runoff by a whopping vote. It was clear to everyone that he would defeat Alexander in the final election. There would still be the same district attorneys, Fredericks and Ford, the same *Times* and Merchants' and Manufacturers' Association, the same Erectors' Association in the East, which was paying Otis to keep up his fight; but at least the city government would be in friendly hands. The election would be a protest vote against the M. and M., a vote of confidence in liberalism, unionism—and, incidentally, in the McNamaras. The election of a socialist government in Los Angeles could not help but have an effect upon the jury.

For therein would lie the solution of this case: the jury.

When the first venire lists were drawn Darrow engaged a man by the name of Bert Franklin to set up an agency which would investigate all prospective jurors. For the five years previous Franklin had been a deputy investigator for the United States marshal's office in Los Angeles; before that he had been for four years in charge of the criminal investigations under Captain Fredericks, before that had been a guard in the Los Angeles jail. He was recommended to Darrow by Job Harriman and Le Compte Davis. Franklin opened an office, engaged a crew of private detectives and set to work.

"Mr Darrow said he wanted to find out the apparent age, religion, nationality, of every prospective juror, what their feelings were toward union labor, their feelings and opinions regarding the *Times* explosion, their opinion as to whether the McNamaras were guilty or not guilty of the crime with which they were charged, their financial condition, their property, the bank at which they did business."

The prosecution had a similar investigating staff. As soon as the lists were drawn each side would make a copy of the names, and the investigators would dash out of the courtroom to get to the potential juryman first to investigate him and bring back a report. Each day as his investigators brought in their reports Franklin took them to the Higgins Building and placed them on Darrow's desk. As Darrow looked over each summary Franklin suggested, "Challenge him when he is called up; he is antagonistic to labor. Accept the next fellow; he is a liberal. Get rid of that next one fast; his brother is a member of the M. and M." When the trial opened on October eleventh Darrow would go into court with Franklin's reports and suggestions to use as a basis for questioning prospective jurors. The only difficulty was that everyone whom Darrow would consider acceptable would be thrown out by the prosecution, and everyone the prosecution wanted would be promptly dismissed by Darrow. So complete was their system of checks that over three hundred jurors would be examined before six men could be found who were acceptable to both sides.

On the sixth of October Franklin went to the home of Robert Bain, an elderly carpenter whom he had known for twenty years and who was about to be drawn for jury duty. Although a workman himself, Bain was known to the prosecution to be hostile to the unions and hence would be acceptable to them. When no one answered his ring at the Bain house Franklin went next door, left his card with the neighbor and asked her to please tell Bain to telephone him at his office. Later that day he went back and found Mrs Bain at home. Franklin relates his conversation with Mrs Bain:

"I told her that I would like to have Bob on the McNamara jury, that I was in a position to pay him five hundred dollars down and two thousand when he had voted for an acquittal for McNamara.

"'Well,' she said, 'you know that Bob is a very honest man.'

"'Yes, Mrs Bain, I realize that. I have always felt so.'

"'But that sounds good to me. I would like to have Bob consider it.'"

That night Franklin returned to the Bain house. "I asked him what he thought about the matter, and he said he raised some objection when his wife spoke about it but that she had convinced him that it was to the interest of both of them to accept the proposition, as he was getting old and that it would only be a matter of two or three years until he would have to quit his labors. I asked him his financial condition. He told me he had but very little money and that he was paying for his place. I then asked him if he would accept five hundred in cash with the promise of two thousand more after he had voted for acquittal. He said that he would. I first asked that the curtains be drawn, then took four hundred dollars from my pocket and gave it to him. He asked me what assurance he would have of getting the balance of the money, and I told him that we would be compelled to pay the money; if we didn't he could report it. He agreed, and then I left."

Franklin handed his employer a satisfactory report on Robert Bain. Bain was called into court and accepted by both sides as a juryman, the first to be seated.

The days spun themselves out as Darrow thrashed in his mind to find a tenable means of defense. He asked Judge Bordwell for a postponement, but it was refused. He caused every conceivable delay, sometimes for good reason, sometimes for bad. Judge Bordwell seemed hostile; Darrow asked for a change of judge. Bordwell refused to eliminate himself. The people in the courtroom observed that he questioned for hours and days prospective jurors, even when it was obvious that he would dismiss them—killing time, earning the postponement the judge had refused him, waiting for the break or development that would enable him to prepare a telling defense. He continued to carry the burden alone: to the world the McNamaras were still proclaiming their innocence; Gompers and Debs were declaring them innocent; the great mass of workers were declaring them innocent. His defense associates might have gleaned that portions of the McManigal confession were true, but neither Davis, Scott nor Judge McNutt had access to his private files; they could not know that the McNamaras were guilty as charged. And he was afraid to tell them.

In the third week of October another juror was selected, in the fourth week two more, in the first week of November a fifth. It was on the fourth of November that Bert Franklin made another important trip, this time to the small ranch of George Lockwood, near Covina. Lockwood, who was past sixty, had spent most of his life working for the police and district attorney's office as policeman, deputy, investigator, guard in the jail with Bert Franklin under Captain White.

"George," said Franklin, "I want to talk to you confidentially. May I do so?"

"Yes, Bert."

"This is a matter of the strictest confidence, and it might lead to complications. I consider you are my friend, and I know that under no circumstances will you repeat anything that is said to you without my permission."

"Bert, under no circumstances will I do anything that will cast any reflections on you."

"Did you know I was working for the defense in the McNamara case?"

"No, but I am glad to hear you are employed."

"George, you and I are getting old, and both of us have worked very hard and accumulated very little, and I think the time has come when you and I should use our brains a little more and our feet and hands less."

"Yes, Bert, I agree with you."

"George, I have a proposition to make to you whereby you can make some money and be of material assistance to myself at the same time."

"All right, Bert, spit it out."

"Did you know that your name was on the prospective list of jurors that might be called at a future date?"

"No, I didn't."

"In the case that you are drawn, upon proper arrangements would you vote for a verdict of acquittal in the McNamara case?"

"Well, I don't know."

"Take your time and think it over, and if you see your way clear I can give you five hundred dollars in cash, and at the end of the case I will give you two thousand more."

"Bert, that is a matter I would want to think over."

While Lockwood was thinking over the deal offered to him by his former associate, before his name was drawn from the county lists, Lincoln Steffens, in his early years one of America's most penetrating muckrakers and fearless researchers into big business's corruption of government, arrived in Los Angeles and went to see his old friend, Clarence Darrow. Thereupon the McNamara case took on a new dimension.

13

In his popular magazine articles and in such books as *The Sham of the Cities*, *The Struggle for Self-Government*, Lincoln Steffens had been, along with Henry Demarest Lloyd, author of *Wealth against Commonwealth*, among the first to demonstrate that a political democracy has difficulty surviving under an industrial oligarchy. During the months of Darrow's preparation for the McNamara trial Steffens had been abroad seeking material with which to muckrake England and Europe. Certain that the McNamaras were guilty and having been converted to the stand of Kier Hardie, the British labor leader, that "labor has done it, and capital and the world should learn why," he conceived the plan of selling New York newspaper editors on the idea of sending him to Los Angeles to show why labor was guilty and what lay behind their acts of violence. The editors were so astounded to find a labor sympathizer convicting his men before their trial, they gave him the assignment.

Steffens immediately asked Darrow for permission to see the McNamara brothers. Not knowing his mission, Darrow gave his approval. Though the brothers did not know Steffens they greeted him warmly as a friend of labor. He then told the boys that he wanted to write a series of articles called "Justifiable Dynamiting," in which he would reveal to the world why labor had been forced into violence. While the McNamaras sat in shocked silence Steffens continued:

"It's a doubtful experiment and a risk for you, but it's got to be done sometime. Why not now? Why not help me dig up on the side, while the legal case is going on, the case of Labor against Capital as a parallel, as a background to the case of California versus the McNamaras? I might be able to show why you turned to dynamite."

John J. McNamara asked sardonically, "Have you seen Darrow about this?" Steffens reports James as saying, "If you could do what you propose I'd be willing to hang," then continuing to his brother, "It's for this that we have been working, Joe, to force attention to the actual conditions of labor. He means to go and get the actual cases of black-listing that have made it impossible for discharged men to ever get work. Why wouldn't I risk my life to get that told? It's what I've been risking my life for right along."

Elated, Steffens walked briskly back to Darrow's office to make the most extraordinary proposal ever made to a lawyer who had clients to defend against a murder charge. A cold sweat broke out on Darrow's brow. He told Steffens to forget it and dismissed him —but he himself was not able to forget it. If Steffens was so positive that the men were guilty, must not others be equally sure about it? If it was as plain as that to people who had no access to the mass of evidence accumulating in his file, what chance would he stand in a courtroom? If, as Ruby says, he was frightened and bewildered when coming out on the train, he was now plunged into a shattering hopelessness. Every avenue of escape was blocked. He could not withdraw from the case now; that would hamstring his clients. Though sufficiently ill to be admitted to any hospital, he could not sneak out that way.

At odd moments he would think he saw some hope, some chance, then he would realize that it was wishful thinking. His moods changed so swiftly that Steffens reported of him, "At three o'clock he is a hero for courage, nerve and calm judgment, but at three-fifteen he may be a coward for fear, collapse and panicky mentality. He is more of a poet than a fighting attorney; his power and his weakness is in the highly sensitive, emotional nature which sets his seeing mind in motion in that loafing body." When someone brought Darrow further bad news, Steffens says, "His face was ashen; he could hardly walk; he was scared weak and did not recover for an hour. He said, 'I can't stand it to have a man I am defending hanged. I can't stand it.' "

That Saturday, November nineteenth, E. W. Scripps invited Darrow and Steffens to spend the week end with him at his ranch, Miramar, near San Diego. Scripps, like Hearst, had founded a chain of newspapers and a great fortune upon liberalism and the cause of the American masses. An astute student and merciless thinker, his grounding in sociology had given him a genuine sympathy for the labor movement. He met Darrow and Steffens at the station but, because Darrow looked fagged and forlorn, steered the conversation away from the McNamara case. However, Darrow could think and talk of nothing else; that night as they sat in the patio after dinner he outlined to Scripps the strength of the evidence that had come in against the structural-iron workers. Scripps rose, went into his study and emerged with the manuscript of an article he had just written for his papers, an article in which he explained and justified labor's use of force and dynamite.

" 'We, the employers, have every other weapon,' " he read to Darrow; " 'we have the jobs to give or withhold; the capital to spend, or not spend, for production, for wages, for ourselves; we have the press to state our case and suppress theirs; we have the Bar and the Bench, the legislature, the governor, the police and the militia. Labor has nothing but violence and mob force.' "

Darrow remained silent, thinking, "That's all true, but how does it help me? My boys are charged with murder." Then Scripps made an observation which stopped the wheels from churning in Darrow's head. After three months he was to reach his first decision.

"Workingmen should have the same belligerent rights in labor controversies," observed Scripps, "that nations have in warfare. There has been war between the erectors and the ironworkers; all right, the war is over now; the defeated side should be granted the rights of a belligerent under international law."

Darrow looked beyond the flower-filled patio to the deep night sky. "I wish the people of Los Angeles could see it that way," he murmured. "I believe it would be to the best interests of the community and also right and just to get rid of this case without shedding any human blood. I wish we could make a settlement."

14

The next night Darrow and Steffens took the sleeper back to Los Angeles; while they breakfasted at the Van Nuys Hotel Steffens asked, "Did you mean it when you said you wanted to make a settlement?"

"Yes, but I don't believe it will be possible to bring such a thing about. The feeling is too bitter, and the people are not in a reasoning state of mind."

"I think I can convince the businessmen of Los Angeles," said Steffens, hardly able to contain his excitement, "that it would be better all around to avoid the passions of a trial and to accept a plea of guilty from James B. McNamara."

"I am perfectly willing you should do it, but if you see anybody you must make it very plain that it does not come from me or from our side, for if it should get out to the community that we are making overtures it will make it that much more difficult to defend the men and save their lives."

"I will take it up on my account, and if any proposition comes it will come to you, not from you."

"I must caution you to use great care. At all events there will be no use to try to get a settlement unless the *Times* people are in favor of it, as it was their building that was destroyed."

That night Steffens returned to Darrow to tell him that he had seen some of the local politicians and businessmen and "that they believed the matter could be put through to permit James B. McNamara to plead guilty, receive a life sentence and end all other prosecutions in Los Angeles." Steffens was afire as he outlined to Darrow how he was going to bring love and brotherhood to Los Angeles, how everyone would forgive everyone else and become friends, and there would be no more labor troubles in Los Angeles. Darrow believed none of this nonsense; he knew his adversaries too well, yet he was eager for the settlement to be arranged.

"I told Steffens that if such a thing could be done it would take a great burden off me, and I thought it would be a good thing both for labor and capital, especially for the defendants and the city of Los Angeles. I did not have confidence enough to present it to any of my associates at the time or even to my clients, although I felt that I knew what they would think about it."

The next morning, November twenty-second, when Le Compte Davis walked into court he was met by District Attorney Fredericks, Otis's protégé who had been elected to his position by the *Times*.

"Why don't you get those boys to plead guilty and quit your horseplay?" demanded Fredericks.

Taken aback, Davis replied, "I was not hired for that purpose."

"You know you're going to do it; a committee has been consulted about it, and I have been approached."

When Darrow reached court and saw the expression on Davis' face he promptly explained the Steffens' mission and his reasons for wanting to make a settlement: the prosecution had a great mass of evidence to produce and every day was bringing people into court to look at James B. McNamara and identify him; the defense had no contradictory evidence to offer, nor could they let James B. testify on his own behalf; he wouldn't be able to stand up under cross-examination. The trial would be a rout.

"Is J. B. willing to plead guilty?" asked Davis.

"I haven't talked to him yet, but I think I can make him see the reasonableness of it. You are a good friend of Captain Fredericks; will you go to him and work out a settlement?"

"I don't think we have any right to do it without consulting organized labor," replied Davis. "The American Federation of Labor is my employer in this case, and I won't do anything until I have their approval."

"Well, Gompers and all the other boys are at the convention in Atlanta. I wired for them to send someone out here. They ought to be here very soon, but if they are not it is up to us to act when the time comes anyway."

"As far as I'm concerned, I don't believe it's right," insisted Davis. "The money to defend the men has been furnished by labor, and it will ruin you with labor if you do this without consulting them."

"The money was furnished by organized labor," answered Darrow, "but these two men are our clients, and nobody can possibly give us money that can in any way influence us in an action that is due our clients. As far as I am concerned, I have no right to consider myself; all I have to consider are these two men, and if they think it best and we think it best, we should act, whatever the consequences are."

That afternoon Darrow wired Fremont Older, crusading editor of the San Francisco *Call* and one of the most respected men on the

Pacific coast, to come to Los Angeles for an important conference. Older arrived in Los Angeles the following morning, November twenty-third; over the luncheon table Darrow detailed the situation to his old friend and asked for approval of the plan. Older, who had thought the boys to be innocent as charged, or at least to have a fighting chance in court, was too stunned to answer. After a time he managed:

"Well, Clarence, you know best—if you think it's the thing to do. . . . It will be misunderstood by a large number of laboring men who never believed that dynamite was placed in the Times Building—but I'll do what I can to make them understand. I suppose you know what this will do to you with organized labor?"

"Yes, I know—but the lives of my clients come first. The Mc· Namaras have a right to know that their case looks bad, that they will probably hang. I won't advise them to plead guilty; I will merely tell them their case looks hopeless. They have the right to choose, to save their own lives."

That same evening Ed Nockels arrived from Chicago, listened to Darrow's presentation of the case and agreed that a settlement was the best way out. Darrow sent Nockels to see Le Compte Davis.

"Are you empowered to speak for the American Federation of Labor?" demanded Davis.

"Yes."

"Very well, I'll undertake to settle with Captain Fredericks."

The next morning, November twenty-fourth, Davis went to see Captain Fredericks, and Darrow went to see his clients. They listened attentively while he showed them why they had no chance; that a plea of guilty on the part of James would be the best way out, not only for themselves but for their union and their friends. He assured them that he would work to have John J. freed entirely; that he would insist that James be allowed to plead without giving a detailed confession which would implicate other men; that he would secure from the state a promise not to pursue or bring to trial Dave Caplan or Matt Schmidt; in short, that they be granted an honorable surrender.

"John, who had done more of the consulting with us than the other," writes Darrow, "said without hesitation that it ought to be disposed of, and he believed organized labor would come to understand it if they didn't at once. He thought there was little chance to save James's life without it, which was the controlling interest with him, and that his own case was also very dangerous. James from the first was willing to plead guilty and take a life sentence but not willing for John to plead guilty at all."

In the meanwhile a Merchants' and Manufacturers' Association committee had received Steffens' proposal with interest. The mayoralty election was only a few weeks off; Job Harriman's plurality assured him of winning. They did not want to give up their trial, but they saw a way to kill socialism in southern California for at least a generation: they would let James B. McNamara plead guilty—provided he did it before Election Day! The confession of guilt would wreck Harriman's chances. Harry Chandler, Otis's son-in-law, thought this was a wise plan, but Otis was adamant: they had the evidence to destroy unionism, and he wasn't going to rest until every last shred of it was brought out in trial and publicized to the world.

Le Compte Davis went to see Otis on the morning of November twenty-fifth. "Take the bird while you've got it in your hand, General," he said. "By his plea of guilty McNamara will give you a complete victory and prove that everything you have been claiming is right. If you take a chance and force them into trial, lightning might strike; an accident might happen; they might get off."

Otis grumbled, barked, swore, "I want those sons of bitches to hang!" and finally agreed—but not until he showed Davis a telegram from the National Erectors' Association, which was helping to finance the prosecution, in which the erectors said that John J., the directing mind behind the dynamiting, was the one they really wanted and that they would accept no settlement unless he also pleaded guilty and received at least a ten-year sentence.

For Darrow the need to accept punishment for John J. and to plead the McNamaras guilty in time to wreck the socialist campaign was a heavy defeat. Since James B. had never been a structural-iron worker or a member of their union, his activities could somehow be interpreted as happening outside the sanction of the body of workers. But John J. was the directing secretary; when he pleaded guilty he thereupon pleaded his union guilty. Further, to sacrifice the Socialist party and their vigorous campaign on the eve of a stunning and nationally important victory was not only to deal his friends a deathblow, but to do it by means of a stab in the back: for Job Harriman, who had been too busy campaigning to take much part in the preparation of the McNamara defense, had not been informed of the plans to make a settlement; Darrow had not told him for fear he would refuse to sacrifice the Socialist party and the election for the McNamaras.

It was a nasty price to have to pay, but it was obvious to Darrow that he could have his settlement on no other terms. He consoled himself by thinking that if socialism were as truly a historical imperative as its adherents claimed it was, it did not need to ride into office and power on the coattails of guilty men.

15

On the afternoon of Saturday, November twenty-fifth, Darrow took Le Compte Davis, Judge McNutt and Lincoln Steffens with him to the jail to impart the bad news to the brothers. James refused to plead guilty if his brother had to plead with him, and no amount of reasoning on Darrow's part would change the older brother's mind. He sent Davis back to Captain Fredericks to see if the district attorney would reconsider and let John off. The following morning, Sunday, November twenty-sixth, the group reassembled in the jail. John J. had been thinking things over during the night.

"It's all right," he said; "I'll take ten years. Anything to save Jim's life."

"It's not all right," repeated James. "I won't let them send Joe to prison. Besides, his pleading guilty will have a bad effect on labor. It will have a pretty serious effect on you too, Mr Darrow."

"You needn't bother about that part of it," grunted Darrow. "Neither do I think that labor has any right to be consulted about a lawyer's duty. I don't think you should sacrifice your lives when something better can be done." But James would not be persuaded.

Darrow says, "I was anxious to have it closed up as soon as possible; if they did not plead before the election we could never get the district attorney to accept the plea; it was getting to be a great burden, and I did not want anything to happen that could prevent the settlement."

He took John J. aside and talked the matter over with him. John said that his brother's consent wasn't necessary; he would save James's life without it: he was not on trial at the moment, and as soon as Darrow pleaded James guilty, he, John, would come into court and accept some sentence, as light a one as possible, but ten years if that was the best he could do.

16

This same Sunday, November twenty-sixth, while Darrow was bringing the settlement to a head in the county jail, his chief investigator, Bert Franklin, was on his way out to the George Lockwood ranch.

"George, haven't you been served yet?" Franklin asked.

"No."

"Well, your name was drawn yesterday, and you will be served between now and tomorrow morning. There will be four thousand in it for you, and I want you to have that money."

"Bert, if I go into this I don't want no mistake about the money."

"There won't be any trouble at all. Captain White will be custodian of the money. We both know him, and he is straight; the money will be perfectly safe in his hands, and he will turn it over to you when the trial is over."

"When the trial is over," protested Lockwood; "why, there might be no one know anything about the balance of the money."

"I can't see any way out of it but Captain White."

That night Franklin went to see Captain White, former head of the Los Angeles jail under whom both he and Lockwood had served as guards but who was now running a jewelry store. Franklin told White of his plan to bribe Lockwood.

"My God, Franklin," exclaimed White, "I wouldn't trust Lockwood as far as I could throw a bull by the tail!"

"Captain," said Franklin, "I believe that George Lockwood is the kind of a man that if he gives his word he will do a certain thing, he will do it."

"If you are satisfied," the captain replied, "why, other people should be."

Franklin then offered to pay White a hundred dollars for his trouble if he would act as intermediary and hold the thirty-five hundred dollars' balance until Lockwood voted for an acquittal. Captain White agreed.

The following morning, Monday, Davis came to Darrow's office to report that he had had a final conference with District Attorney Fredericks and that the settlement would go through on the terms agreed upon in the jail the night before: a life sentence for James, with the possibility of commutation, and ten years for John, who could be freed at the end of seven years for good behavior. Darrow then asked Judge McNutt, Davis and Steffens if they fully approved the plan. Everyone agreed that it was the best way out.

Darrow left for his flat on Bonnie Brae, and, like a fever-racked man who has passed his crisis, slept soundly for the first time in months.

17

While Darrow slept Bert Franklin was hard at work. That morning he had received a telephone call from Lockwood to come out to the ranch.

"Shall I bring the Big Fellow along?" asked Franklin.

"Yes."

When Franklin reached the Lockwood ranch that evening it was well covered by detectives from the district attorney's office. Lockwood led Franklin out to the barn, where a stenographer was planted to take down the conversation, and asked:

"Where is Darrow?"

"Why, George, did you think Darrow was coming?"

"Yes, that is what I understood."

"Well, you was mistaken; I intended to bring Captain White, but he didn't wish to come."

Lockwood expected to be paid his five hundred dollars that night, but Franklin didn't have the money on him. He said, "George, be at the corner of Third and Los Angeles streets tomorrow morning at nine, and I will see you there at that time." He then returned to Captain White's house, where he made arrangements for the captain to meet him at the corner of Third and Main streets the following morning at eight forty-five, where he would give him four thousand dollars in cash, five hundred of which White was to turn over to Lockwood.

The next morning Darrow rose early. Ruby gave him a manicure and cut some of the hair off the back of his head. Happy to see that he was looking better, she laid out a fresh linen suit and a clean white shirt and tie. After a light breakfast he strolled the two blocks to the car line; since there was no car in sight he walked through Echo Park as far as the aqueduct, the warm November sun lighting his face. At the aqueduct he boarded the car, rode to the terminal at Second and Hill streets and walked to his office. He arrived at his usual eight-thirty, sat down to his desk and dug into the work of clearing up his accounts.

In the meanwhile Bert Franklin was meeting Captain White on the corner of Second and Main streets.

"Good morning, Captain," said Franklin. "I have the money."

"This is a poor place to hand it to me," grumbled White. "We'd better go into this saloon."

They went into the saloon, had a drink at the bar, then Franklin handed Captain White a thousand-dollar bill and six five-hundred-dollar bills. The two men left the saloon together, but once on the sidewalk Franklin left White and walked ahead of him to the corner of Third and Los Angeles streets. Here he met Sam Browne, captain of the Los Angeles detectives, with Detective Campbell following him. Franklin exchanged greetings with Detective Browne, slipped down a side street, came back through an alley and entered a saloon on the corner of Third and Los Angeles, where he could watch White pass the money to Lockwood. While Franklin slipped down the alley Detectives Browne and Campbell went up to the second floor of a rooming house where they, too, could watch White pass the money to Lockwood.

A third detective by the name of Home, who had also been trailing Franklin, entered the saloon after him. He saw that Franklin was behind the red swinging doors of the toilet, the open doors making it possible for him to recognize Franklin from the knees down. When Franklin came out of the toilet Detective Home hid himself by turning his face toward the wall behind an icebox, which was some twelve feet away from the toilet. Franklin walked out of the saloon, looked around and came back in. This time a fourth detective, Dana Ong, followed him in, walked up to the bar beside Franklin and ordered a drink. After downing his drink Franklin walked to the swinging doors and looked over the top, as though searching for someone. He returned to the bar, had another drink, walked again to the swinging doors to peer out. Detective Ong followed him to the door to look over his shoulder. They both saw Lockwood come up Los Angeles Street and Captain White cross over to meet him. The two men shook hands.

"What is new?" asked Lockwood.

"Nothing, except a mutual friend of ours has entrusted me with some money to be paid to you on certain conditions. Are you ready to receive it?"

"How much money, and what are the conditions?"

"I am to hand you five hundred dollars and hold three thousand for you until such time as a verdict of not guilty is rendered or the jury hung in the McNamara case."

"It don't go. There was thirty-five hundred to be held, not three thousand. Where is Franklin?"

"He just went away from here."

"Well, it don't go at all, because there was to be four thousand."

"Possibly there is in this roll. I haven't had time to examine it."

"Well, go in that store and examine it."

"I ain't got no business in that store. I'll walk up the street a bit and look."

White walked up the block a ways, turned toward the store windows and counted the money. Then he returned, saying, "There is thirty-five hundred dollars in the roll aside from the five hundred I am to hand you."

"All right, I am ready."

White handed Lockwood a five-hundred-dollar bill, showing him the other bills as he did so.

"I think the passing of a five-hundred-dollar bill on a proposition of this kind is decidedly out of the way," complained Lockwood. "It ought to have been in twos or fives. It's all wrong in a case of this kind; how could a fellow go to work disposing of a five-hundred-dollar bill under these circumstances?"

Before White had a chance to reply a fifth detective, Detective Allison, came down the street on his motorcycle, stopping close to Lockwood and White. Just as he stopped Lockwood dropped his five-hundred-dollar bill to the sidewalk. As he stooped to pick it up Franklin, who was watching from behind the saloon doors, pushed his way out and joined Lockwood and White. After the exchange of a few sentences Franklin looked up, saw Detective Home watching him from behind the saloon doors, turned slightly and saw Detectives Browne and Campbell coming toward him.

"Don't look around," he said to Lockwood. "Let's get out of the way."

Franklin and Lockwood then walked down Third Street, away from the two detectives on foot, but in the direction from which the motorcycle detective had come a moment before. White trailed behind them.

When Franklin and Lockwood had walked half a block down Third Street they saw Clarence Darrow on the opposite side of the street. Darrow saw them and crossed the street. Just as he was about to put a foot up on the sidewalk Detective Browne stepped between Darrow and Franklin, pushed Franklin back sharply and said:

"Don't talk to this man, Mr Darrow. He's under arrest."

To Franklin he said, "Bert, I want you."

"What for?" asked Franklin.

"You've been a detective long enough to know what for. You know what you've been doing."

Darrow stood in silence, staring at the two men.

18

"The first thing that entered my mind," says Darrow, "was as to whether it would be possible to carry out the settlement, and if not, whether it would be possible to save these men's lives. I was shocked and broken up over it."

Steffens came into Darrow's office to ask, "Is this going to interfere with the settlement?"

"Not as far as I am concerned. What about your committee of businessmen?"

"I don't see why it should make any difference to them," replied

Steffens. "Suppose they should think that you or any of the rest of the lawyers were connected with this: then what?"

"If that question is raised I want you to tell them that under no circumstances am I to be considered in this matter; if there is any man who thinks that I or any lawyer in this case had anything to do with the bribery, you tell them that there will be no bargaining on that case, that they can take care of that when the time comes. All we are proposing to settle is the McNamara case."

"This is quixotic. Why not get rid of them all at once?"

"No. I never in my life let my own affairs interfere with my clients, and I never will. You go and carry that message to the committee."

Wednesday morning and afternoon was spent in a series of conferences between the lawyers, the businessmen, the district attorney and Otis. By nightfall the district attorney's office had agreed to let the settlement go through, but the two McNamaras would have to plead guilty together. That would make it impossible for Joseph to plead after James had been sentenced. Darrow knew that it would be another difficult struggle with James. On Thursday morning, Thanksgiving, he again assembled his staff at the jail: Davis, Scott, McNutt—and Steffens, who brought the report that industrial warfare was over in Los Angeles: after the McNamaras were sentenced there would be a meeting between capital and labor at which the hatchet would be buried, all differences dissolved.

Darrow again reviewed the case for the McNamaras, showing them the hopelessness of their situation. James was unmoved: he would not permit his brother to go to prison. Each lawyer in turn presented his arguments in favor of the brothers pleading together; he fought them all. It was not until midafternoon, when they had all been defeated and it looked to Darrow as though they would have to go through with the trial, that Davis took a new tack.

"Jim," he said quietly, "I think you're right, and we've been wrong. It's best that you hang. It'll be better for labor."

J. B. stared at him without speaking.

"It's better that your brother hang too," continued Davis. "Then labor will have two martyrs instead of only one."

J. B. straightened suddenly, his body rigid, his face tense.

"Is that the way it looks to you?" he demanded. "That they'll hang Joe too?"

"That's the way it looks to me."

J. B. threw himself face down on his bunk and cried brokenly for a quarter of an hour. Darrow and the others sat huddled into themselves, trying not to see or hear or weep. Then J. B. raised himself on one elbow, pushed the tears off his eyes with the palm of his hand and said quietly:

"All right. I'm licked."

The next morning at the opening of court Darrow and Davis went into Judge Bordwell's chambers to tell him that the Mc-Namaras had agreed to the terms; that they would plead guilty that morning.

"Ten years isn't enough for John J. McNamara," said Judge Bordwell. "He'll have to take fifteen."

Darrow had no authority to accept fifteen years for John; though he knew that the prosecution was laying it on now that they had the upper hand, he had no recourse but to hasten back to the jail and tell the brothers the additional bad news. Having resigned themselves to the idea of prison, the brothers had little spirit left. They agreed. Darrow rushed back to Judge Bordwell to tell him that John would take fifteen years. Judge Bordwell ordered the two men brought into court at two o'clock.

The arrangements had been so closely guarded that only those in the conference circle knew they had been going on. The city was overwrought because of the trial, the election and the torrents of abuse being unleashed on both sides. Thousands of people walked the streets wearing buttons that read: McNamaras Not Guilty! Vote for Harriman! The majority were passionately convinced that the McNamaras had been framed, that Darrow would excoriate the Otis-*Times*, Merchants and Manufacturers clique, that the trial would be a complete vindication not only for the McNamaras but for organized labor—and the people would be freed from their bondage.

That very morning, as he had every morning, Darrow found hundreds of letters on his desk, most of them containing money for the defense, all stoutly avowing their loyalty and faith in the Mc-Namaras' innocence. All over America Thanksgiving meetings had been held to voice support of the McNamaras; the labor councils of nearly every major city: New York, Boston, Philadelphia, Chicago, Pittsburgh, Cleveland, San Francisco, were planning gigantic demonstrations "to protest against the dastardly frame-up, to force the capitalist class to release the McNamaras."

At two o'clock on the afternoon of December 1, 1911, Clarence Darrow had his two clients brought into the courtroom. The newspaper reporters, who had been sitting around bored during the questioning of prospective jurors, sat up in wonderment when they saw John J., for he was not on trial, and it was the first time he had been in court.

When the court opened District Attorney Fredericks rose and said in a low, undramatic tone, "Your honor, the defense wishes to address the court."

With that he sat down. Darrow nodded to Davis, whom he had decided was the closest to the court and the best man to speak. Davis rose and said without inflection, "May it please the court, our clients wish to change their plea from not guilty to guilty."

The announcement fell with a flat, sickening thud. Spectators turned to look at each other in befuddlement, wondering if they had heard aright. No one spoke.

Suddenly, as the import of the astounding twist in the case reached the consciousness of the people, "there was a psychic explosion" that was heard around the world. The reporters were the first to recover their power of action; they dashed, sprawling over each other, for their telephones. Some of the spectators wept; others stood shakily on their feet, their faces white and shrunken. A clamor went up; men rushed into the court from the corridors to learn if the news were true; fist fights started; the room filled with a bewildered, questioning, pushing, screaming, mauling crowd. Within a very few moments the extras were on the streets with the biggest headlines in their history: McNamaras Plead Guilty, but the people of Los Angeles refused to believe: they had belonged to a cause; they had been fighting for a cause; they were strong, resolute; they had an army; they would fight unto the death. And now, suddenly, without warning, without explanation, their army, their strength, their cause, had collapsed.

Judge Bordwell instructed the McNamaras to be brought into court for sentencing on the morning of Election Day, then adjourned court. For an hour the crowd milled about, constantly renewing itself, trying to find out if this heresy were true, to learn who was responsible for the debacle. The district attorney, the court officers, left; Darrow's defense attorneys left; slowly the crowd exhausted itself, dispersed and emptied the big room. Darkness fell. Darrow, who had been sitting slumped in his chair during the storm, his eyes closed wearily, tried to rise. He could not. He sat there in the gloom, aching, miserable, alone.

19

It was the most disastrous day for labor in American history, and Clarence Darrow was responsible for it.

Should he have pleaded the McNamaras guilty?

Two lives had been spared from almost certain hanging. He had obstructed the prosecution from exploiting the full force of its case, forestalled the putting into evidence of material which would have been used against union officials in San Francisco and Indianapolis. He had saved millions of peaceful workingmen from implicating themselves further in the fate of men who had betrayed the American Federation of Labor's pronouncement on peaceable methods; quieted a scandal which could reflect no possible credit on the ironworkers, the details of which would have revolted and alienated great sections of the American public. The country could now say, "The McNamaras are guilty; they have admitted their guilt and gone to prison; they are paying the penalty; let's forget about it and go back to work and our normal way of life." A year, two years, three years, would not be spent in whipping up passions, making accusations, spreading factionalism and warfare so wide and so deep that it might never be rooted out of American life. He had saved the union workers hundreds of thousands of dollars that would have been wasted in a futile defense; avoided a bitter and bloody class-war trial; prevented the horrifying precedent of having labor leaders hanged for their part in it; enabled the city to travel more quickly the road toward peace and co-operation.

He knew that if he had tried the case with all his force he might have brought in a hung jury. But could he have brought all his force to bear? No one knew better than he that his greatest effectiveness, not only before judge and jury, but before the country as a whole, had grown out of his burning honesty and conviction that his clients were innocent. Great and epochal phrases had poured from his lips, phrases that had helped to reshape the minds of men and the life of his country; but how would they have sounded from the lips of a man who knew that he was being dishonest, who in his heart repudiated his own clients? He would be a mountebank and a hypocrite; his insincerity would show in every expression of his face, and he would convince no one.

He might have fought for a verdict of second-degree murder, exploded his miniature model of the Times Building, brought in experts to swear that the escaping gas had caused the huge explosion and the twenty deaths; yet he knew that it would be a feeble gesture at best, that with twenty men dead no jury would take into account the lack of intent to kill. Perhaps he could have appealed the convictions, used up years of time in the hope that passions would cool and his clients would be spared. But he knew, too, that the appeals could not save the lives of the men once they had been convicted in open court by a jury, and the constant appeals only would have continued to spread the details of their guilt and the ill will in the community.

Perhaps he could have let them hang and become labor martyrs. But he could not see the cause of labor building on false premises. If labor had to have martyrs, let them be innocent men. He could not have brought himself to making of the trial a campaign of education, when anything he might have said would have inflamed the hotheads in the movement to further violence, with everything in his nature crying out against the approval of violence. The National Erectors' Association has said, "This is war!" Otis had cried in the *Times*, "This is war!" War was cruel, destructive, brutal, senseless, and until it was banished from the face of the earth all barbarities would not only be condoned but approved, if they led to victory. He despaired of such methods, not only because they caused class war, destruction, bitterness and ineradicable ill will between men, but because they were shortsighted and futile, serving only one purpose: to perpetuate the struggle.

"I know I could have tried the McNamara case," said Darrow, "and that a large class of the working people of America would honestly have believed, if these men had been hanged, that they were not guilty. I could have done this and saved myself. I could have made money if I had done this—if I had wanted to get money in that way. But I know if they had hanged these men it would have settled in the hearts of a great mass of men a hatred so deep, so profound, that it would never die away."

He shook his hot and weary head as he recalled how John Mitchell had accused him of wanting to make a plea for socialism instead of better wages and hours for the miners; how Edmund Richardson had charged him, in Boise, with putting the interests of the Socialist party before those of Haywood, Moyer and Pettibone. Now the cycle had been completed: he would be charged by the socialists with sacrificing the party to save his clients.

Sitting alone in the darkness on the field of battle where he had surrendered his cause and his people to momentary defeat, he was completely convinced that he had done right. To the end of his days he never faltered in this belief. Yet after fighting for labor for twenty years, bringing them by his brilliance, devotion and fearlessness many miles along the saber-studded road to civilization, he had now been the indirect instrument of causing them great harm. Labor would never forget—he knew that—and would never forgive him. He had known that his career as a labor defender was finished the day he had learned that he was defending guilty men; labor would now put the seal upon his judgment.

Once again he tried to rise from his seat but could not. From out of the darkness came a friend to help him up. He walked slowly down the long aisle of the courtroom. When he reached the steps of the courthouse he looked down and saw a throng gathered there, waiting for him, standing in stark and sinister silence. In the flickering light of the gas lamps he could see the Harriman and McNamara badges littering the lawn and the gutters.

He shook off his helpful friend, straightened his shoulders and walked slowly down the stairs, his eyes straight ahead but unseeing. A murmur rose to greet him, a murmur which grew in intensity as he came closer. When he reached the sidewalk the crowd closed in: workers, union officials, socialists, liberals, intellectuals, men and women for whom he had spent his years fighting. From the outskirts someone called him a name: an evil name. Close by a man spat in his face. The crowd pushed in closer, surrounding him, pressed against him, heaping their frustration, their defeat, their humiliation, upon him in sordid imprecations. He was hemmed in so close now he could not move. Billy Cavenaugh pushed through the mob, caught Darrow by the sleeve and cried above the tumult:

"Come with me!"

Darrow gazed at the ring of dark faces about him.

"No, Billy, I shall go down the street with the crowd. I have walked with them to the courthouse when they cheered me, and I shall go back the way I came."

He took a step forward. A wall of sullen faces peered into his. He took another step—and the front line fell back. The crowd parted. He walked through it, cleanly, alone. As he went down the street, the crowd at his heels, one cry came out of the night·

"Traitor! Traitor!"

CHAPTER IX

Prisoner's Dock

By MORNING the full force of the storm had descended upon the McNamaras and their attorney for the defense, Clarence Darrow.

With tears in his eyes and the hand that held the paper trembling, Sam Gompers cried, "I am astounded! If all this is true, my credulity has been imposed upon. We have had the gravest assurances that these men are innocent. We have discouraged acts like these. We are patriotic and peace-loving men. Those two men must have been crazy. It is an act that I condemn with all the force that is in me." So outraged was he that in his autobiography, *Seventy Years of Life and Labor*, he completely omitted mention of labor's greatest legal defender, in spite of Darrow's monumental work for the American Federation of Labor.

Harry Orchard "could not conceal his joy. 'This seems providential on the jump,' he told reporters. 'This confession will convince many who bitterly condemn me that I took the right course when I made a clean breast of my connection with the crimes charged against the Western Federation of Miners.'"

Hundreds of local unions hastened to jump off the McNamara band wagon, each local issuing its own renunciatory proclamation to the press. The president of the Oregon State Federation of Labor said, "Organized labor as a whole was not to blame for the dynamiting of the *Times*, but organized labor as a whole will have to suffer. We are completely stunned. We cannot conceive how any man could be so foolish as to do this thing to which they have confessed. We certainly resent their misleading their union brothers into faith in them when they are guilty."

305

The socialists repudiated the McNamaras as being trade unionists; the trade unionists repudiated them as being anarchists; the
anarchists repudiated them as being terrorists. The sinking ship
was deserted as fast as possible, the survivors pausing only long
enough to yank off their cap, spit over their shoulder and cry,
"Not in my family!" Only Big Bill Haywood stood stanchily by,
reiterating, "I'm with the McNamaras and always will be. You can't
view the class struggle through the eyes of capitalist-made laws."

On election morning, December 5, 1911, Darrow brought his
clients before Judge Bordwell. Lincoln Steffens had had a chat
with the judge and had reported to Darrow that Bordwell would
handle the McNamaras gently and say nothing further to array
class against class. When Darrow stood before the bench between
the two brothers and heard the judge call them "murderers at
heart," his skin blanched and he wrung his handkerchief in his
hands.

In the midst of the lashing he understood that every promise
made in the settlement would be broken. Caplan and Schmidt
were to be hunted for five years, captured and convicted in Los
Angeles; the evidence that had been gathered against the Mc-
Namaras would be paraded before the public, not so much to convict Caplan and Schmidt as to get into the public record the material
that had been suppressed when the McNamaras pleaded guilty.
Ninety per cent of the Schmidt trial would deal with J. B. Mc-
Namara and not Schmidt, so that when Schmidt met McNamara
in the yard of San Quentin the first thing he could say was:
"They tried you and convicted me!"

As soon as the McNamaras were hustled off to prison Los Angeles
went to the polls to administer its defeat to the socialists. Job
Harriman, who had learned about the settlement in the headlines of
the afternoon papers of December first, did not show up at his
campaign headquarters until the voting was over and darkness
had fallen.

"Where have you been?" demanded Alexander Irvine.

"I couldn't come here," replied Harriman; "they were going
to shoot me in the morning."

"That would have been a good place to shoot you. It would have
won us the election."

The finality with which the McNamaras were dismissed included
their chief counselor, Clarence Darrow. He was now accused of
aiding and abetting a conspiracy whereby labor had been deceived
into supporting the dynamiters and thus injured. In spite of labor's

renunciation he issued a statement in which he took sole responsibility for what had happened. "I have known for months that our fight was hopeless. I never would have consented to their pleading guilty if I had thought there was a chance left. It was intimated to us that we must act promptly; there was danger that what was being considered would get out and make settlement impossible. We were responsible to our clients alone."

He had known when he saw the indisputable proof of the Mc-Namaras' guilt before him on his desk that he had reached the end of his journey as a labor lawyer; labor now confirmed his decision by casting him off.

It was seventeen years since the day he had made his choice behind the counsel's desk of the Chicago and North Western Railway and taken the long walk down the hall to tell President Hughitt that he was giving up his secure, remunerative job to defend Eugene Debs and the American Railway Union. A man who cherished peace, he had ever since been in the center of incessant strife; a man who advocated tolerance, he had spent most of these years in internecine war; a man who believed that the world could survive only if based on good will, he had seen more ill will, rancor and bitterness than anyone of his age. Yes, it had been a stormy route since that moment in the library of the governor's mansion in Springfield when Altgeld had told him, "Clarence, if you want to get a clear picture of what will happen to you if you defend labor leaders and fight for social justice, just watch the flood of invective that will be poured on my head in tomorrow's papers for protesting this clear and inexcusable violation of the Constitution." Yet neither his years nor his battles had been altogether in vain: the millions of men and women who worked with their hands to earn their daily bread had had the hard-biting economic shackles about their ankles and wrists eased the tiniest bit because Clarence Darrow had raised his voice in their defense. Altgeld would approve of his seventeen years.

2

The last of his papers had been sorted and filed, the desks nearly cleared, when Le Compte Davis called at the Higgins Building to see him.

"I'm certain that Bert Franklin is innocent," he said. "His wife came to see me last night. We can't abandon him. We've got to put up his ten-thousand-dollar bond."

When Darrow remained silent Davis continued, "I recommended

Franklin to you, and I'll stand responsible for him. Franklin won't jump bail, but if he does I'll make good the ten thousand."

Darrow hesitated for a moment longer; he knew that if he went bond for Franklin he implicated himself in anything that Franklin might have done; then he wrote out the check for ten thousand dollars against the McNamara defense account.

After Davis had closed the door behind him Darrow sat hunched and motionless at his desk. From the trail Franklin had blazed in his bribing operations and from his willingness to have the Lockwood money passed on a detective-infested corner, it appeared that he had wanted to be caught. And if he had wanted to be caught it could only have been part of his orders. Darrow's wide-ranging thoughts told him that it was possible that the San Francisco labor leaders had given Franklin four thousand dollars with which to bribe jurors, that if they had been willing to sanction the use of dynamite they would not shrink from bribing jurors. It was also possible that the Indianapolis ironworkers' officials, who were afraid that a conviction in the McNamara case would be injurious to their own cases in the Midwest, would attempt to bribe jurors. Yet how was it conceivable that any of the labor men would use Franklin for this purpose when they knew that Bert Franklin had been a district-attorney investigator for years, that he was being watched by Burns's operatives, that any slip would cause serious damage to himself and to the McNamaras?

Clarence lighted a fresh cigarette off the butt of the last, then crushed the old one with a vigorous gesture of dismissal. Then whose money was it? Whose machinations could this scheme be except William J. Burns? And if Burns had ordered Franklin to get himself caught, not only in attempts to bribe prospective jurors, but in the actual passage of the bills on an open street corner, then surely Burns could not want Bert Franklin. Surely he must be after bigger game!

He sat at his desk in the now-quiet and -deserted suite, letting his thoughts flow freely so that he might fit the parts into a pattern, while Le Compte Davis went to the courthouse, put up the bail and had Franklin released. Franklin went immediately to see Tom Johnson, a lawyer.

"You are friendly with the district attorney, aren't you?" Franklin asked.

"Yes."

"Will you go see Joe Ford and request him that if he will postpone my case and give me an opportunity to find a certain party with whom I had several meetings prior to my arrest but whom I have been unable to find, that if I can find that dark-complected man—there will be something doing; I will find the party who gave me the money with which the bribery was committed?"

Tom Johnson went to Ford but soon returned to tell Franklin that "Ford refuses to continue the case; he takes no stock in this cock-and-bull story about being furnished the money by a man you didn't know; he is securing new evidence every day, and in a short time he will have sufficient evidence to send Darrow to the penitentiary."

"Neither Davis nor Darrow gave me money to bribe jurors," replied Franklin quickly, "and they know nothing about it. I would be a goddamned liar if I said they did. I know I am expected to say that Darrow did it."

Within a week of his arrest Franklin met with Darrow and Davis in Darrow's office.

"Ford sent word to me that if I know anything about any of the local lawyers," declared Franklin, "to forget about it. Ford says the only one they want to get is Darrow."

Clarence looked up sharply. He had been expecting this blow to fall; it had been in the air.

"But why are they so anxious to get me?" he flared. "Why are they more anxious to get me than—than Job Harriman, for instance?"

"I don't know, Mr Darrow, but I told them that you never gave me a corrupt dollar."

Nor was it to Clarence alone that Franklin uttered such protestations. He was walking down the street when he saw two acquaintances, John Drain, a contractor and former superintendent of streets, and Frank Dominguez, an attorney who had never met Darrow, chatting in front of the Waldorf Saloon.

"You're not ashamed to have a drink with me, are you?" asked Franklin.

The men said they were not ashamed and went into the saloon. After a moment or two the conversation drifted around to the jury bribery. Frank Dominguez said:

"I can't believe that an attorney of Mr Darrow's eminence and standing in the profession would be guilty of anything of that kind; it is absolutely inconceivable to me that a man of Darrow's character and reputation as a man of honor would be guilty of such a thing."

"I don't believe it either," agreed Drain. "I think he is too smart for that."

"I never received a dishonest dollar from Mr Darrow," replied

Franklin. "He never knew anything connected with this matter. He is too good a man to do anything of that kind. He is the most kindhearted, generous and the best man I have ever known in my life and would not stand for any corruption or dirty work."

Drain reports, "This conversation occurred in a loud tone of voice on Franklin's part and could readily be heard by everyone around. Thereupon a man whom I did not know came over. took Franklin by the sleeve and pulled him away."

A few nights later Franklin attended a meeting of the Forester Lodge, where he saw an old friend by the name of Hood, a dairyman.

"You are a damned fool, Franklin," said Hood; "why didn't you just take that money and put it down in your jeans and just simply forget about it and tell them it was all fixed and not take a chance of going behind bars?"

"I was being watched too closely," he replied; "the man who gave me the money for the bribery was a stranger to me; he stood only thirty feet from me when I passed the money. I think he came from the East or San Francisco. I never saw him again."

He was arraigned for his preliminary hearing. On his way into the court he met D. M. Willard, press telegrapher for the Associated Press, who was chatting with the Associated Press reporter. Franklin joined them. "I can't talk about my case until it comes up for trial," he announced, "except one thing: Mr Darrow knows nothing about this affair, and you can make that as broad as you like."

He then went into the courtroom, where a group of reporters were sitting at the press table. After an exchange of greetings he turned to Carl White of the *Express*: "If anyone says I used Mr Darrow's name in connection with the bribery he is a damned liar. Mr Darrow is innocent of any connection with this case."

To Harry Jones of the *Tribune* he added, "I may be guilty of all I am charged with, but I am not a damn fool; I certainly am not going to drag an innocent man into this thing." To J. L. Barnard, a reporter for the *Express*, he concluded, "Anybody says that Darrow gave me a cent to bribe a juror is a goddamned liar."

The Christmas holidays of 1911 passed bleakly for Clarence and Ruby. Rumor continued to fill the air. Though the district attorney's office was still saying in the newspapers that they had nothing on him, reports reached him constantly of the pressure being put upon Franklin to "confess that it was Darrow or go to San Quentin." He made no attempt to conceal the gravity of the situation from his wife. She did her best to lighten his heart by putting

up a small Christmas tree and inviting a few of his friends to a
turkey dinner. The Peede family invited them to go horseback
riding in the mountains of Tujunga Canyon, giving Clarence an
old white horse on which he jogged along slowly, drinking in the
beauty of the hills. He wanted to go home and resume his old life,
but he knew that he dared not give the opposition the chance
to smear him with extradition from Illinois.

Meanwhile the intrigues kept swirling about his head. Suspecting
that he would have trouble securing work in Los Angeles, Bert
Franklin went to the beach town of Venice to see if he could open
a private-detective agency there. He met with F. D. Stineman,
owner of the Decatur Hotel, and Jordan Watt, who had been city
clerk of Venice for sixteen years, and Peter Pirotte, a policeman.
They had a drink at the hotel, where Franklin told them:

"If Mr Darrow would give up certain evidence he has against
Gompers he would be let off. Gompers is the man they want, because Gompers is head of the union, and Burns wants to break
the union up. They want to get Darrow because he has been defending the unions and is a prominent man on their side. Outside parties
furnished me with the money, a 'Frisco man; Darrow never gave
me any money to fix jurors or anything of the kind."

Then Franklin had two long, secret sessions with the Executive
Board of the Merchants' and Manufacturers' Association; the picture
thereupon changed for Clarence Darrow.

Within a couple of days Franklin joined Stineman, Watt and
Pirotte for lunch, again to press Pirotte into opening a private
agency with him.

"But what about that trouble you're in?" asked Pirotte.

"Oh, I am going to get out of that all right," murmured Franklin.
"The D.A. doesn't want me; they want Darrow."

Walking into a haberdashery store, Franklin confided to the
manager, Joseph Musgove, "I can't afford to spend much money
because I am under a serious charge and stand a chance of going to
the penitentiary. But I have many friends in town and I'm playing my
cards; before I will go to the pen I will put it on somebody else."

By the middle of January Darrow had terminated his business
in Los Angeles, sent an accounting of the defense expenditures to
the American Federation of Labor, closed his offices in the Higgins
Building. There was nothing more to keep him in Los Angeles;
he was longing to get out of the hostile atmosphere, to return to
his home and books and friends and practice. Yet he knew that he
could not leave, that any move on his part would be interpreted as
flight.

By the end of January Franklin came up for trial. He pleaded guilty and was fined the precise four thousand dollars that had been taken from Captain White and Lockwood on the morning of the arrest. The city of Los Angeles came into possession of the bribe money, and Captain Fredericks called for a meeting of the grand jury.

On January twenty-ninth, while Bert Franklin stood testifying before the grand jury, Clarence Darrow secluded himself in the offices of Earl Rogers, an attorney whom he had engaged to defend him if he should be indicted. At three-thirty in the afternoon a message was brought to him that he was wanted by the grand jury. He hurried to court with Rogers and Judge McNutt.

The proceedings were short and drastic. The foreman rose to inform him that he had been indicted on two charges: of subornation of perjury, of attempting to bribe Robert Bain and George Lockwood, that he would have to stand trial on these charges. Bail was set at twenty thousand dollars. Mrs Le Compte Davis furnished bond for half of the amount; Young, of the beach town of Playa del Rey, the other half. The photographers made him pose again and again; he was now more of a celebrity than he had ever been as a simple defense counsel.

In spite of an inner dread Clarence had been hoping that somehow the members of the grand jury would not believe him capable of these criminal acts. Their indictment came to him as a fresh blow. When the interviewers flocked around him he sat for several moments, "his broad shoulders stooping, his seamed and lined features showing evidence of strain and illness."

"What have you to say about all this, Mr Darrow?"

He straightened up and managed a small smile.

"Just what I have said from the beginning, and that is that I know nothing of this bribery charge, know nothing of any attempt to approach prospective jurors and knew absolutely nothing of this thing at all until Franklin was arrested."

The next day he issued a formal statement, aimed at his sympathizers throughout the world. "I am innocent of the charges that have been brought against me, and I hope that you will withhold judgment until I am given an opportunity to establish that fact. The charges that have been brought against me are too serious to treat lightly. Doubtless the district attorney's office believes that there was evidence to warrant the advice that it gave the grand jury, but in the end it will be shown that a grave error and injustice has been perpetrated."

3

He needed legal brains to defend him. His thirty-five years in the law had taught him that he had better get the very best that money could buy. That was why his mind had turned at once to Earl Rogers. Rogers was one of the cleverest criminal lawyers in the country; his penchant was freeing murderers. He had a sharp, fast, resourceful, pyrotechnic brain, a good deal sharper, faster and more resourceful than Darrow's. When he was sober, which was perhaps a third of his waking hours, he was almost impossible to beat. Tall, magnificently proportioned, with a full head of graying hair, roguishly handsome features, beautifully expressive eyes and a stirring voice, a dandy who dressed in the height of fashion, Earl Rogers had all of the requirements of a matinee idol. That was in effect what he had become, for he used the courtroom as a theater, staged every trial as though it were a play in which he were the leading actor. For him the law was not a system of balance, protection and justice upon which the civilization of the Western world was founded; it was a game to play for high stakes, an adversary to be outwitted, a set of props against which he could display his talents and golden personality.

In the legal profession Earl Rogers was at the polar extremity from Clarence Darrow. He used his penetrating brain mostly for antisocial purposes. There was no client too venal for him to lavish his inexhaustible gifts upon. Once when he had tricked a jury into freeing a procurer who had murdered his wife, Rogers brushed aside his client's thanks with: "Get away from me, you slimy pimp, you know you're guilty as hell!" Yet he was terribly proud of this victory. In the days before legal ethics were solidly established Rogers brought fits of apoplexy upon judges and prosecutors by the manner in which he juggled testimony, stole or switched incriminating exhibits, engaged in torrential acts of passion, anger, ecstasy, hysteria, to confuse the issue, divert the attention of the jury and jim up the prosecutor's case.

Darrow knew all this; he knew that it was a wry twist of fate that made it necessary for him to engage a clever and conscienceless rascal; yet when he took Ruby to the small town of Hanford to watch Rogers try a case and saw the manner in which he dominated the court, the skill with which he had prepared and then conducted his case, they both agreed that they had no alternative but to engage him. It was an ironic twist that made it possible: Rogers had been engaged by the state to track down the evidence in the McNamara case and had been largely instrumental in tacking the purchase of the nitrogelatin onto McNamara, Caplan and Schmidt.

"If the state can honorably employ Rogers," Clarence told Ruby, "then so can we."

Rogers was enormously set up at being selected. "I've been slipping somewhat," he told friends, "and I need Darrow almost as much as he needs me. Selecting me to defend the nation's acknowledged premier criminal lawyer will eventually place me in Darrow's class."

For his defense staff Darrow also chose Horace Appel, an eccentric who was not overly fond of shaving or changing his linen but who was an expert on the admissibility of evidence. A youngster in the office of Rogers, by the name of Jerry Geisler, was given the job of looking up the law.

Clarence was at once under heavy expense. He had collected in advance only a small part of the fifty-thousand-dollar fee agreed upon by the federation, and a considerable portion of what he had received he had used for living expenses. He had several thousand dollars in the Los Angeles bank, but he knew that this would be a long siege, that he would need every dollar of his savings. Ruby moved them out of their comfortable flat on Bonnie Brae to a small apartment with a roll-away bed in the dining room, reducing their expenses to a hundred dollars a month. When Darrow visited a friend's house and was led in to dinner he asked:

"Francis, is this the dining room?"

"Yes."

"Well then, where is the bed?"

The weary weeks of February and March dragged past while the district attorney used the Burns agency to gather evidence. Clarence had little to do; his defense was simple. The strain of waiting in idleness, the cloud under which his name had fallen, the feeling of impotence in the face of the combination against him, served to make him nervous and overwrought. He tried again and again to have the case called for trial. When interviewers sought him out he said:

"I am innocent. I am ready. I most welcome the beginning of the trial, for it will mean my vindication. I am anxious to get home to Chicago among my friends."

He had plenty of leisure to read, even to write, but he possessed neither the mind nor the patience for them. He became thin and ill. Over and over he would mumble:

"What a hell of a trap I'm in!"

Ruby, striving valiantly to keep his spirits up, went to their friend Dr Gerson, and cried, "Doctor, help him. He's walking the floor!"

And at last Clarence Darrow, who had started with fewer illusions about the human race than any of his contemporaries, found himself stripped of that ultimate illusion without which no man can carry on: that there was any hope or reason left for living. The world was a vile place in which greed and injustice had always triumphed and would continue to triumph—what was the sense of struggling further?—nothing could straighten out the vicious mess; his efforts had been futile; nothing would be left of his name or character or work; he was fatigued with life and the world; he had had enough; he was through. . . .

In his despondency during the interminable days of April he began to drink, he who rarely had taken more than two drinks at a sitting. Dr Gerson became alarmed and tried to stop him. Earl Rogers interfered.

"Oh, let him alone, Doc. The liquor is good for him at a time like this."

Finally on May fifteenth the trial opened. Captain Fredericks fired the opening shot by telling the *Examiner*, "The evidence against Darrow is convincing; it is just as convincing as the evidence in the McNamara case." The *Times* revealed its journalistic attitude by stating, "Every effort will be made to prevent a recurrence of the scenes prior to the McNamara confession, when a permanent juror in the trial admitted receiving bribe money."

Clarence said, "I feel bully physically. Mentally I am also in excellent shape." But his appearance belied his protestations. The *Herald* reported that "his face was haggard, and the muscles of his cheeks twitched unceasingly, while the lines around his eyes and mouth told of nights of sleeplessness and worry."

Ruby had dressed that morning in a simple dress of a thin, dark material and a sailor hat trimmed with green ribbon. When she appeared at the door of the courtroom "she shrank visibly even at the effort of walking through the courtroom to the seat within the railing reserved for her." However, she took a grip on herself, smiled and walked through the stares of the spectators. She sat down beside Clarence and put her hand lightly in his; when the proceedings began her smile gave way to tears.

Judge Hutton, a young, good-looking man with a gentle smile and manner, called:

"The People against Clarence Darrow."

Rogers rose and said, "Ready, your honor."

Then he looked down and saw that the outstanding criminal lawyer of America had not realized that he must rise to hear the charge against him.

4

Rogers put his hand on Darrow's shoulder; only then did the older man rise.

"Clarence Darrow, is that your true name?" asked Assistant District Attorney Joe Ford.

"It is," replied Darrow, then turned to glance reassuringly at Ruby. She smiled back at him with more courage than she felt, for this man who stood before her was only a fraction of the attorney she had watched in action these many years. At this, the most crucial moment in his career, "his voice appeared to have lost its resonancy and piercing caliber, and his manner in worming from the talesmen the facts concerning their home, surroundings, associations, was considerably different from that shown during the Mc-Namara case. His arrest upon the bribery charge appeared to have left its indelible imprint upon him." The best he could manage was:

"You are a transfer man?"

"Yes."

"You appreciate my position, don't you?"

"I think so."

"Knowing my position, you would not let bias or prejudice enter your mind against me, would you?"

"I would not."

"Well, I am charged with a serious crime. It means everything to me to have men of fair mind on this jury, and I don't think you would mislead me concerning your fairness."

"Certainly not."

However, if Darrow were being feeble in his questioning, if he were appealing for fairness rather than ascertaining for himself whether it was there, District Attorneys Fredericks and Ford also were having a difficult time. Dozens of talesmen had to be dismissed because they made the outright statement that Clarence Darrow would never stoop to bribery, while an even larger number said that Darrow would never be so stupid as to order the passing of a bribe on one of the busiest corners of the city and then go down to that corner to make sure the bribe had been passed.

"Mr Mullchaney," asked Fredericks of a white-haired Irishman, "did you ever meet this defendant?"

"No."

"Did you ever hear him speak?"

"No."

"Did you ever read any of his books?"

"I read one."

"Which one?"

The Rights and Wrongs of Ireland."

"What do you think of him?"

"He is a fine man!" answered Mullchaney.

When the spectators laughed Fredericks turned to the court to exclaim, "I request of the court that these demonstrations of feeling and emotion among the spectators cease. Laughter has no place in these proceedings."

By May twenty-fourth a jury consisting mainly of ranchers and orange growers from outlying towns and one or two businessmen was agreed upon.

In his opening speech Fredericks set the tone of the trial by accusing Darrow of being a director of a wholesale bribery plot, by calling him such foul names that Rogers sprang to his feet to accuse Fredericks of misconduct. Clarence had been hoping that his honorable record of thirty-five years before the Bar would have earned for him at least a quiet and courteous trial; he was stricken by Fredericks' outburst. The *Herald* reporter observed that "both Mr and Mrs Darrow were stunned by the withering remarks of the prosecutor. Darrow fumbled and toyed with a cigarette paper, and his face was flushed from chin to forehead."

The following day saw another explosion in the courtroom. An officer of the National Erectors' Association had given an interview to the *Examiner* in which he said, "I shall convict Darrow with my dictaphone." This line was printed in large banners at the head of the interview and the Hearst paper so exhibited in store windows along the jurors' line of travel from the hotel to the courtroom, they could not help but see it. Again Rogers charged misconduct; the jury was sent out of court; hours were spent while Darrow and Rogers tried to learn how and why the National Erectors' Association had become part of the prosecution.

The case of *The People* vs. *Clarence Darrow* took ninety days to try; the testimony and disputes between the lawyers over the admissibility of evidence fills eighty-nine volumes, comprising five thousand pages. Within the course of the days nine private detectives came forward to accuse Darrow of various things, but only one man accused him of the crime with which he was charged. Bert Franklin confessed:

"I told Mr Darrow I thought I could talk to Mr Lockwood, that he was a man in whom I had the utmost confidence, a man of character, and I thought Mr Lockwood's friendship for me would be such if he didn't wish to accept the proposal as offered to him, he would tell me so, and that would be the end of the matter."

Though Darrow was being tried solely on the charge of bribing Lockwood, Franklin accused him of ordering the bribing of five other prospective jurors, the most important of whom was Robert Bain. "I told Mr Darrow that I knew Mr Bain, that I thought Mr Bain would be a poor juryman for the McNamaras, that I thought he was prejudiced against union labor. He then asked me what I thought about Bain. I asked him if he wished me to see Bain along that line, and he said yes and asked me if I thought I could get him. I told him I thought I could, that Mr Bain was the kind of a man if he didn't want to go in that way he would come out and tell me so, and that would be all there would be to it. Darrow said, 'All right, I will give you a check for a thousand dollars.' He turned to his desk, wrote the check and handed it to me."

When Franklin told the court that he had asked Darrow "if he wished me to see Bain along that line," he inferred that there had been a previous conversation in which Darrow had discussed with him the bribing of jurors. Yet Franklin never referred to or re-created this earlier conversation, nor did the district attorney bring it into evidence; its happening is never introduced in the trial.

Of the other four men whom it was claimed Darrow wanted bribed, the third was Guy Yonkin, who ran a cigar store on the corner near the jail and courthouse and whose father had served under Captain White with Franklin and Lockwood. Franklin told Yonkin that he could make it worth his while to serve on the McNamara jury, and Yonkin replied that "he was not that kind of a man." The fourth man was Frank R. Smith, who stated that Franklin came to his house in Covina and offered him four thousand dollars if he would serve on the jury and vote for acquittal. Smith said, "There ain't no use to talk to me 'cuz you haven't got enough money to buy me." The fifth prospective juror was A. J. Krueger, who had been fined three hundred dollars by Captain Fredericks for running a blind pig. Franklin testified that he told Darrow that Krueger would not be acceptable to the prosecution because of his character and the grudge he would bear against Fredericks, but Darrow replied:

"Go give him five hundred dollars anyway."

The testimony of Franklin about the sixth prospective juror was the most illuminating in the case, not only as to fact but as to Franklin's character and motives. Darrow leaned forward in his seat as Rogers rose to cross-examine the witness. During some of the more incredible Harry Orchard testimony in Boise he had cried out, "Sometimes I think I am dreaming in this case." The words again came to his lips as he listened to Bert Franklin's convolutions. Earl Rogers' biographers were not exaggerating when they said of him in *Take the Witness* that Earl Rogers reached his peak as a criminal lawyer during this trial.

"When you got in sight of John S. Underwood's place of business you knew it was an ironworks, didn't you, by the sight of it?" asked Rogers.

"I don't remember whether I knew it. I did when I got inside," replied Franklin.

"That was before you said anything to Underwood about acting as a juror in the McNamara case?"

"Yes sir."

"After you had found that he was in the iron trades did you ask him if he had any strike on?"

"He told me he had one on."

"Was that before you approached him on the subject of acting as a juror in the McNamara case?"

"I think so."

"After he told you that he had a strike on and you saw that he was in the iron business, you mean to say you went on and approached him about accepting a bribe and acting as a juror?"

"Yes sir."

Darrow looked over toward the jury box and saw several of the jurors smile; he, too, smiled a tiny smile, the first since he had risen to answer the charge against him.

"After you had made an ironworker a proposition to serve on the jury," sneered Rogers, "what did he say?"

"He told me he would not go into anything of that kind under the circumstances, that he could not afford anything of that kind, that he was friendly to Mr Ford—they both belonged to the same church—and he would not do anything to hurt Joe Ford."

"How long had you known Johnny Underwood?"

"About twenty-two years."

"If you were really in earnest in trying to bribe Underwood and not trying to get up a play or performance, why did you congratulate Underwood on the stand he had taken?"

"Because I am always glad to meet an honest man."

"You went up to bribe him, believing him to be an upright man and an honest man and a man of integrity?"

"I never had any reason to believe that Johnny Underwood was anything but a splendid citizen."

"For that reason you went up to bribe him?"

"No, because he was a friend of mine and, being a liberal man, I thought I could talk to him."

The cross-examination having shown him up as either a liar and a knave or a fool, Franklin backed down and admitted that Darrow had not known anything of the attempted bribery of Underwood, Yonkin, Smith or Krueger, that he had not told Darrow before he had approached these men; nor had he told him that he had failed to secure them. He inferred instead that Darrow had simply given him carte blanche to bribe all the prospective jurors he thought necessary. The fact that he had just testified that Darrow had told him to "Go give Krueger five hundred dollars anyway" did not appear to worry him.

As Franklin's final contribution Captain Fredericks, also an able courtroom tactician, led him to tell the events of the morning of November twenty-eighth. This was the moment that the courtroom had been waiting for. At last it would hear how Darrow had gone to the street corner to watch the bribe being passed. Franklin set himself squarely in his seat in the witness box as he proceeded to tell his story.

"I met Mr Darrow about eight-forty in his office in the Higgins Building," said Bert Franklin.

"Who else was present?"

"Mr Darrow and myself were the only ones present. I asked Mr Darrow if he had gotten the money; that I had made arrangements to meet Captain White at Third and Main streets at eight forty-five. He said that he had not at that time received the money but that he would ring Job Harriman up and find out what time he would be in the office with the money. He then took up the phone and rang up someone unknown to me. After hanging up he said, 'Job will be here in ten minutes.' In about five minutes Mr Harriman came into the office of Mr Darrow with his overcoat over his left arm and walked with Mr Darrow into the room immediately adjoining. In about ten seconds Mr Darrow came out and handed me a roll of bills. I left the office, went to the elevator, looked to see how much money there was in the roll. There was four thousand dollars, one thousand-dollar bill and six five hundreds. I then went down in the elevator—handed the bribe money to Captain White . . ."

Several weeks were spent by the district attorney in proving what no one denied: that Franklin had actually passed bribe money. The Bains were brought to the witness stand, the Lockwoods, the detectives who had been on his ranch, the chauffeur who had driven

Franklin out, Captain White, the detectives who had followed the crime in action. All of the briberies and attempted briberies were re-enacted in full detail in an attempt to prove that Franklin had passed the bribes, and since Franklin was employed by Darrow, he must have passed the bribes at his employer's command.

Darrow had taken small part in the cross-examination of the witnesses. For the most part he had listened closely. For him the most disabusing turn of the trial was the defection of John Harrington, whom he had brought to Los Angeles as an investigator because of his need for someone loyal and whom he had taken into his home. Up until the last night before the Darrows were to move to the less expensive apartment Ruby had selected, Harrington and his daughter had had supper in the Darrow home. The following morning Harrington demanded fifteen thousand dollars from his employer as compensation for his services, not as an investigator, but as a lawyer. "I'm entitled to what the other defense lawyers got!" he cried.

When Darrow told him that he had no such money to pay him, nor any reason for so doing, Harrington went to the district attorney's office to report that he, too, knew about Darrow's wish to bribe prospective jurors. Once again Earl Rogers in his cross-examination proved the tenuousness of the testimony.

"Mr Harrington, you say Mr Darrow told you he got ten thousand dollars at Tveitmoe's bank at San Francisco and showed you the roll of bills?"

"Yes sir, showed me a roll of bills."

"Just out of the spirit of bravado, to show you he had a roll of bills?"

"I think it was more buffoonery."

"He told you he had a roll of bills to buy jurors with, in a spirit of buffoonery? What do you mean by buffoonery?"

"Just showing how smart he was."

"That he had ten thousand dollars to bribe jurors and show you how smart he was, a kind of joke?"

"I didn't regard it as a joke."

"You mean to say Mr Darrow showed you a roll of bills and told you he was going to bribe jurors with it?"

"He didn't use the word bribe; he used the word reach."

"Was there any reason why he should tell you he was going to reach jurors with a roll of bills?"

"I didn't know but what he might want me to do it. Feeling me out on it."

"Did he suggest to you that you should do it?"

"No sir. I put a damper on that right away. I told him it would be foolish to attempt such a thing; it would be his ruin. Then he said, 'I guess you're right. I won't try it.' "

This was the case against Darrow. Of the million words spilled during the presentation, perhaps six hundred of Franklin's had a direct bearing on the Lockwood bribery charge. A trial that should have been concluded in a week, as protested by the Eastern papers, stretched on to two weeks, three weeks, a month, two months, three months. . . . The mountains of evidence elicited dealt with everything except the guilt of Darrow in ordering Franklin to bribe Lockwood.

5

Though the trial was kept in the white heat of the international spotlight and was given sensational space on the front pages of most of the newspapers, Darrow knew that whole sections of society were indifferent to its outcome: the mass of working people did not care whether he was acquitted or convicted; they had lost interest in Clarence Darrow. The socialists, anarchists, radicals of all descriptions, also sloughed him off; he was no longer their man; they would not waste their energy fighting for him. The great middle class of liberal educators, churchmen, doctors, lawyers, journalists, were confused and perplexed; the circumstance of his pleading the McNamaras guilty two days after the arrest of Franklin, his chief investigator, looked suspicious. If he had sacrificed the McNamaras to save his own hide, as some of the hostile papers were saying he had, then they did not care what happened to him.

Here and there friends stood stanchly by; scattered individuals who had loved him for his good works these many years protested stoutly, "Darrow wouldn't do a thing like that. Give him a chance to prove his innocence." Yet some of those who loved him best believed him guilty as charged. Sweet Billy Cavenaugh, when giving him a rubdown one night, broke out with, "Mr Darrow, why did you have to go on down to that corner and let yourself get caught? Why didn't you send me; you know you could trust me, and I would have watched Franklin for you."

Clarence felt sick to his stomach to think that Billy, who trusted him implicitly to do the right thing, had convicted him without even waiting to hear the evidence. He tried to formulate an answer in his mind: "Billy, you have known me a long while—how can you——?" But no words would come; how could he protest to an accuser who had instantly assumed him to be guilty?

A few nights later, when he was at the Severance Club chatting with a group of intimates, Dr Gerson commented:

"None of your friends blame you for what you did, Clarence. If you are guilty, what of it? You had to fight the devil with fire."

This, he knew, was loyalty in its broadest sense; yet it was a loyalty that broke his heart, not only because his closest friends could believe him guilty of a criminal act, but because they could assume him guilty of so wantonly stupid and suicidally destructive an act. His breath died in his chest; he hung his head and closed out from his eyes the picture of his friends who were going to be loyal to him to the bitter end.

"My God," he groaned, "I am as fitted for passing a bribe as a Methodist minister is to be a bartender."

A few days later Mrs Fremont Older informed him that Senator Hiram Johnson had accused him, in front of Senator Borah, of having bribed jurors in the Haywood case.

"No, Darrow didn't bribe those jurors," Senator Borah replied; "he frightened them to death."

Though it was good to know that the man he had defeated in Idaho was affirming his integrity, Darrow was stunned that Senator Johnson, bitter enemy of Otis, who had gotten himself elected on a liberal ticket, should be spreading the gossip that it was his regular and established practice to bribe jurors!

If some of his dearest friends and others on whose side he had been working for decades were openly convicting him, what chance did he have of ever clearing his name, of coming out of this scandal whole and clean?

With his friends and comrades abandoning him outside the courtroom and murderous vituperation being heaped upon him inside, Clarence Darrow sank to the lowest ebb of revulsion and world disgust. The fight no longer seemed worth waging. Rogers' biographers report that "time after time Rogers railed at him under his breath because of the drooping chin, the fear-stricken eyes that so clearly told of his trepidation. At times he was absolutely without hope, and only the rough prodding of the Los Angeles lawyer could make him realize that he was providing for the jury a portrait of guilt."

At last Clarence Darrow perceived that his own attorney believed him guilty. Instead of extinguishing entirely his will to be saved, this knowledge awakened in him anger and indignation. Up to this point he had done very little of the cross-examining, sensing that it would have an adverse effect upon the jury; but at this point he decided he would take a stronger hand in his own defense.

He had been holding long meetings with Rogers after court each afternoon, sessions in which the two men, always antagonistic, quarreled over tactics. Though Rogers had accused Darrow of presenting a picture of guilt as he sat glued to his chair, he now in his jealousy refused to allow his client to rise to his feet or share in his own defense.

"Earl wouldn't let any man in his office get credit for anything," says Mrs Rogers, while his daughter, Adele Rogers St John, adds, "He was the most jealous man in the whole world."

Darrow's determination and strength mounted slowly; he insisted upon helping to try the case. Rogers thereupon rushed out of the office and got drunk. He stayed drunk for two days, while the court wondered where he was. When he returned from his binge and his wife asked him where he had been, instead of answering the question, he muttered, "Oh, that son of a bitch has been up to his old tricks again," from which Mrs Rogers deduced that Darrow had been trying to bribe members of his own jury.

Rogers' absence from court did Clarence a deal of good; while cross-examining Burns and several of the other private detectives, while again thinking on his feet, his blood began to circulate more rapidly, his confidence to come back; he grew certain that he would win.

Rogers re-entered the case, but their differences continued. Trouble between the Darrows and Rogerses had started at once and was never to end. Early in their acquaintanceship Mrs Rogers had invited the Darrows for dinner, and Ruby had telephoned to say, "I trust you won't be offended, but Mr Darrow doesn't eat chicken. I thought it would be better to tell you, because everyone serves it to him."

Mrs Rogers, a brainy woman but a purist, had been deeply offended at this breach of etiquette. At dinner she had seated Darrow at her right and noticed wax in his ear. "I never liked Darrow," she maintains. "He always had a hangdog look. He was one of the dirtiest men I ever saw; his nails were dirty; his ears were dirty." When she noticed in court that Ruby was wearing white cotton gloves with the finger tips darned she was confirmed in her dislike for Mrs Darrow, whom she accused of putting on a show of poverty. Now a new and serious difference arose: a difference over money. Rogers was a prodigious spender; it was never possible for him to get enough cash. Darrow's few thousands had been melting rapidly with the paying of court costs, three lawyers and investigators to investigate the Burns investigators. He was far too quickly reaching the point where he would be without funds and without the means of earning a dollar. By the end of July Rogers was refusing to go into court each morning until Darrow had given him additional cash.

"Earl never got any part of his fee from Darrow," says Mrs Rogers, "except maybe running expenses. They were always pleading poverty, right on the verge of starvation. It got so I couldn't pay our bills at the stores."

Ruby says, "Earl Rogers came to us every morning and blackmailed us. If we didn't give him money he said he wouldn't go into court that day."

Each night, when Rogers was in his cups, he would confide to friends that he had little respect for Darrow's ability as a lawyer, attributing his success mainly to wide publicity and his wonderful gift in delivering emotional appeals to juries; each morning Clarence would dig down into his pocket for a roll of bills. Each morning he and Earl Rogers would walk arm in arm into court and, along with Horace Appel, present such a brilliant defense that the outside world never knew of their quarrels.

6

When the heat of June came on Ruby found an apartment in Ocean Park overlooking the ocean, for which they paid thirty dollars a month. Each day, dressed in a gown of some dark, thin material and the sailor hat with the green ribbon, she rode into town with her husband. Through the endless hours of wrangling and accusation she sat next to Clarence, always managing a comforting word when he turned to her. Her fierce loyalty, her confident and courteous manner above the strife about her, soon won the respect and then the love of the newspapermen. Before long every news story carried its eulogizing paragraph about Ruby.

After the long session in court she would ride back to Ocean Park, draw Clarence's bath, lay out clean linen for him and, when he emerged refreshed, ask, "What would you like for dinner tonight? A cold salad? Or a steak?" She would then shop, prepare dinner, wash the dishes, straighten the apartment, press a linen suit for him to wear the next day and get to sleep long after midnight.

By the middle of July Ruby suffered a nervous breakdown, not from fatigue, but from the violence in the courtroom.

As the Los Angeles papers were frequently commenting, it was the most violent trial in the history of southern California. Apart from the vicious name calling and conniving, physically the lawyers were forever at each other's throat. Several times all four of the lawyers were fined by Judge Hutton for abusing each other. At one point Fredericks became so enraged at Appel that he picked up an inkwell to hurl at his opponent; Rogers grabbed him but in so doing cut his hand on the glass. Another time Joe Ford picked up the inkwell to hurl it at Rogers. Once when Rogers was given the privilege of paying a fifty-dollar fine for contempt of court or going to jail, he refused to pay the fine or go to jail, had himself released on a writ of habeas corpus. Rogers and William J. Burns came to blows as Rogers accused Burns of calling him a son of a bitch, of coming into court with a gun and a sword cane. Judge Hutton fined them both twenty-five dollars; Rogers borrowed the money from his young assistant, Geisler, muttering that it was worth it. Hardly an hour went by without an uproar; even Darrow found it impossible to stay aloof.

Judge Hutton presided over this torrential maelstrom, an angel of patience. A Christian Scientist, he wanted harmony to prevail; he believed that the truth would emerge, not from this abuse but from a kind of legal harmony in which both sides did their best work but gave fair play. Most judges suffering the insolence that he endured would have fined all four of the lawyers into bankruptcy. Judge Hutton so deprecated the flare-ups, quarrels and outbursts of passion that he went himself to the newspaper editors and asked them to please devote less space to the quarrels between the lawyers and more space to the serious aspects of the trial.

"These outbursts are only the sparks that fly up in any busy workshop," he said.

If the quarreling and violence sent Ruby to bed with a breakdown and Judge Hutton to the papers with a plea for less sensationalism, it also gave a bad time to the twelve jurors who were to decide whether Clarence Darrow was to go to the penitentiary. Hours and days were spent by them locked in their jury room, while the lawyers fought it out before the judge.

Judge Hutton had done everything he could to make the life of the jurors bearable. The top floor of the Hotel Trenton had been reserved for the twelve men, with the partitioning walls broken down to make it a complete suite. There was a social room with a piano, cards, checkers, chess, all the magazines and newspapers—with the material on the Darrow trial cut out. One Sunday Judge Hutton invited the jury to his home in Santa Monica for a swim and dinner. He gave standing orders that every Sunday they were to be taken either to the ball game at Washington Park or for an automobile ride over Topanga Canyon to the beach. But no juror was left alone for more than a minute during the ninety-two days of the trial, not even when he went up on the roof to play soft ball. The outside doors of the suite were locked at night, deputies holding the keys and guards remaining on watch in the hallways until it was time to move the men in a body to the Hollenbeck Hotel for breakfast. Always the jurors ate their meals at one big table with three deputies interspersed to chaperon the conversation. All incoming and outgoing mail was censored, all telephone calls listened to by a deputy; when one juror hurt his hip and called for an osteopath a deputy stood over them to watch the treatment; when another juror went to his dentist on a Saturday afternoon his deputy stood over the drill.

Every Saturday afternoon the men would be loaded into cars which would take them home. The first stop was at San Gabriel at the home of Snyder, then on to Monrovia to the home of Williams, then to Moore's house at Duarte. At each stop the juror would kiss his wife, hand over his bundle of soiled linen in return for a package of fresh linen, discuss pressing family business for fifteen minutes, treat his fellows to a glass of orange juice or lemonade, kiss his wife again and be off.

"It was like ninety-two days in jail," says Manley Williams, foreman of the jury.

Having spent weeks demonstrating that a bribery had taken place, the prosecution launched into its broad-scale attack on Darrow's character to prove that he was capable of the crime with which he was charged, that he was a lawyer without principle or scruple who would employ illegal or criminal methods to win a case. Fredericks and Ford re-enacted in the fullest detail the removal of Diekleman from Albuquerque, the removal of Mrs Caplan from California to Chicago, the bringing of Ortie McManigal's wife, child and uncle to Los Angeles.

Darrow was able to demonstrate that it was entirely legal to use four hundred dollars to bring McManigal's family to Los Angeles, particularly since Mrs McManigal had said in Chicago that she did not believe her husband to be guilty, that the statements Burns had given out were not true, that Ortie had been bulldozed, given a third degree and had made his confession under threat, intimidation and promises.

Dozens of witnesses were brought to the stand to retrace Mrs Caplan's automobile ride from the Santa Cruz Mountains to Reno after she had been subpoenaed, the district attorney accusing Darrow of thus illegally removing a witness. Darrow went on the stand to swear that he had not ordered the removal of Mrs Caplan. He was followed by Anton Johannsen, who testified that Darrow had known nothing about the removal of Mrs Caplan, that he had taken her out of the state to free her from hounding by the Burns operatives. The truth probably was that Darrow had not ordered Mrs Caplan's removal but had known about it and been unable to stop Johannsen; the San Francisco labor leaders had interfered continually in the preparation of the McNamara case.

Diekleman's removal from Albuquerque was also fully staged with many witnesses. Darrow's defense was that he wanted to get Diekleman out of the influence of the Burns detectives who were surrounding him in Albuquerque; that since Diekleman had been offered a job in a public restaurant in Chicago he had not been concealed, and since Diekleman had been given a round-trip ticket to Los Angeles, it could not be claimed he was being kept away from the trial. His removal was not illegal, though Darrow's hope that once he got Diekleman away from the Burns men and into his own sphere of influence Diekleman would become sympathetic to his cause and refuse to identify J. B. McNamara was doubtless unethical. In the five thousand pages of testimony it is the only unethical act proved against him.

The district attorney put on three Burns detectives to tell how Darrow had attempted to buy their information. Guy Bittinger was the star of this troupe. A former saloonkeeper and policeman, Bittinger had been one of the Burns detectives who had arrested J. B. McNamara and Ortie McManigal in Detroit. When he had been introduced to Darrow in Chicago he had said that J. B. McNamara had offered him thirty thousand dollars for his release and, when refused, J. B. had continued, "If you don't take that money Clarence Darrow will take it. I have the American Federation of Labor behind me, and it will be impossible to convict me."

Bittinger now testified that Darrow had thought this testimony so damaging he had offered Bittinger five thousand dollars not to swear to it in an affidavit. Bittinger says he refused because five thousand dollars was not enough and was then reproved by the friend who had introduced him to Darrow because "you should be friendly with Darrow; he threw money around like it was water up in Idaho."

Arriving in Los Angeles, Bittinger continued, he went immediately to Darrow to tell him that he had twenty-seven hotel registers with the J. B. Bryce or McNamara signature on them. He reports Darrow as saying: "Couldn't you arrange for a couple of my boys to hit you over the head and take them away from you?"

Bittinger replied that he would let him know, whereupon he claimed Darrow promised to pay him a thousand dollars the next morning and that when they met at the bar of the Alexandria Hotel the following morning Darrow said, "I've got that money for you."

"I don't want to take it here," said Bittinger.

"Do it open and aboveboard," replied Darrow. "Suppose you are being watched? I know you in Chicago and you know me, and we have a right to meet and talk and have a drink. Suppose some of the Burns men are around, what of it? The bolder you do it the less they will think of it."

This type of testimony went on for hour after hour, week after week, until finally Juror Golding demanded of the court if he might ask the witness a question. The permission granted, he turned to Bittinger.

"Do you know," queried Juror Golding, "what the charge is against Mr Darrow?"

It was a question which people all over the country who had been reading the daily accounts of the trial were beginning to ask themselves and, in the asking, slowly—very slowly—edged back toward faith in the accused man.

7

Nine private detectives, Franklin, Harrington and seven Burns men, had attacked his character. An alien in a foreign city, Darrow wrote to Edgar Lee Masters, requesting him to go to the lawyers, judges and city officials of Chicago and take depositions to the effect that he was not a scoundrel but a man of good character.

Within a few days the depositions started coming in: "I have known Clarence Darrow for twenty years; he is a man of complete honesty and integrity." "I have watched Clarence Darrow practice law for twenty-five years; he has the highest possible regard for the ethics of his profession." "I have been acquainted with Clarence Darrow for thirty years; his conduct, both personal and professional, has always been above reproach." "I have known Clarence Darrow for thirty-five years; I do not see how he could so suddenly violate his background and character."

Having spent weeks blackening Darrow's character, Captain Fredericks tried to keep these testimonials from being read to the jury on the grounds that they had nothing to do with the case on hand! When Judge Hutton admitted them into evidence Clarence smiled wanly.

June exhausted itself and then July. Ruby recovered her strength and once again took her place by her husband's side. Their friends, Gerson and Blight, persuaded them to join the Severance Club which met every other Saturday night for dinner at Al Levy's restaurant or the Westminster Hotel. Here Darrow lectured on nonresistance and spent hours with friends who were visiting in Los Angeles from other parts of the country. Once or twice a week they went to dinner at the house of Peede, the editor of *Everyman*. Francis Griffes Peede relates, "We lived in a Swiss-chalet affair high in the hills, and usually on such nights as I looked out the dining-room window I would see Father, the Darrows and half the courtroom following. It meant flying down the hill to the grocery store for more cans of corned beef, one of Clarence's favorites, and potatoes to take care of the mob. After dinner everyone stayed in the dining room and talked until two o'clock about single tax, capital punishment, the Bill of Rights, with Father and Clarence holding forth on 'Free Will versus Determinism.'"

The prosecution having finished presenting its case, it was time for the Darrow defense to begin. Rogers first elicited from Bert Franklin the information that the day before he was to be let out of his job in the United States marshal's office he had gone to Joe Ford and asked for work.

"What kind of work do you want?" asked Ford.

"I'll do anything," replied Franklin.

And the very next day he had called on Job Harriman to tell him he would like to work for the defense. Within the next two days he also saw Le Compte Davis and Joseph Scott, telling them how much he would like to work for the defense.

Rogers pointed out that in each instance where Franklin had reported Darrow as telling him to pass a bribe no one else had been present at the meeting. Many persons were on hand, however, when Franklin went to pass his bribes.

"Mr Franklin," said Rogers, "will you tell the jury which it was, whether you was careless and incompetent and was lacking in judgment, was so lacking in good sense as to take people out on bribery expeditions, leaving a trail painted down the middle of the street behind you on every occasion, taking a woman on a bribery expedition whose name you didn't even know, or whether as a matter of fact you were trying to get caught under an arrangement? You endeavored to get corroborating evidence by somebody everywhere you went, by speaking to somebody immediately before you went there, didn't you?"

"If I had been trying to do so," replied Franklin, "I could not have succeeded any better, apparently."

"How is it that a smart detective like you, with your years of experience, could make such a perfect case?"

"According to your statement, I am not very smart, and I will admit it too."

The defense tackled the triple pass of money on the morning of November twenty-eighth. Franklin had testified that he offered Captain White a hundred dollars to act as intermediary, but Captain White categorically denied this; he stated that he hadn't done it for money but had served as an accessory before the fact and committed a felony merely to help an old friend—then admitted that he had not seen Franklin for two years. Captain White further admitted that although he had been arrested and taken to the district attorney's office, once he had handed over the thirty-five hundred dollars he had been holding he was released, never put under bail, never charged with a crime, never indicted, never tried—all this in spite of the fact that, under California law, he was as guilty as Franklin. Nor did the prosecution try to save face by claiming that White had been acting under orders from the district attorney.

Franklin had claimed that when he came out of the toilet of the saloon he had not been able to see Detective Home hiding behind the icebox twelve feet away. The manager of the saloon came into court to testify that this was impossible, and the entire court, judge and jury alike, made the trip down the street to the saloon to see if it were possible.

Then came the series of confounding witnesses against Bert Franklin. John Drain and Frank Dominguez told from the witness stand the story of Franklin's loud protestations of Darrow's innocence. Franklin called these two men liars and perjurers. Hood told of his conversation with Franklin at the Forester meeting, when Franklin described the stranger who had given him the bribe money. Franklin called his brother Forester a liar and a perjurer. F. L. Stineman, Jordan Watt and Peter Pirotte recounted the discussions with Franklin in Venice and Los Angeles, in which he had said he was going to get out of his trouble because the district attorney wanted Darrow. Franklin called Stineman, Watt and Pirotte liars and perjurers.

Joseph Musgove, who had been manager of the haberdashery store in which Franklin had shopped but was now a lawyer, told of Franklin's boast that before he would go to the pen he would put it on somebody else. Franklin called Musgove a liar and perjurer. The four newspapermen, Carl White, D. M. Willard, Harry Jones and J. L. Barnard all went on the stand to repeat Franklin's heated assertions that "anybody says Darrow gave me a cent to bribe a juror is a goddamned liar." Franklin called them liars and perjurers.

Job Harriman denied from the stand that he had even been in

Darrow's office the morning of the twenty-eighth, let alone given him four thousand dollars. Franklin called Harriman a liar and a perjurer. Frank Wolfe, former managing editor of the Los Angeles *Herald*, testified that he had met Darrow on the streetcar on the morning of Franklin's arrest, gone with him to his office and talked to him there until a telephone call had summoned Darrow to socialist headquarters. Franklin called Wolfe a liar and a perjurer.

It was becoming increasingly obvious that someone in the case was a liar and perjurer. The question was: Who? The scoreboard read: Bert Franklin versus Drain, Dominguez, Hood, Stineman, Watt, Pirotte, Musgove, White, Willard, Jones, Barnard, Harriman, Wolfe, Le Compte Davis and Tom Johnson, Franklin's own attorney, who was subpoenaed by the defense and testified only after Judge Hutton had forced him to, and given evidence for which Franklin called him a liar and a perjurer.

John Harrington was quickly dispensed with: Fletcher Bowron testified that Harrington had told him he knew absolutely nothing against Mr Darrow, that he knew of no corruption or bribery. Harrington and Franklin had sworn that they had met only three times since Franklin's arrest, but two secretaries in Darrow's office and the manager of the building said they had seen the two men together every day for weeks. It was also brought out that since Harrington had left the Darrow roof he had been living with Guy Bittinger and two other of the Burns detectives.

There were only two things more for the defense to tackle, then it could close its case. Lincoln Steffens, Le Compte Davis and Fremont Older took the stand to tell the story of the settlement that had been arranged prior to the morning Franklin had given the bribe money to Captain White. For eighty-seven packed pages of pleading Captain Fredericks strove to keep the Fremont Older testimony out of the evidence. Judge Hutton admitted Older's testimony as material, relevant and competent.

Breathing a deep sigh of relief, Darrow ran his crumpled handkerchief over his brow and lumbered to his feet for the most critical, colorful and dramatic clash of the trial: between himself and his accuser, Bert Franklin. Darrow framed his questions so that the whole world, and not Franklin alone, would have to answer them.

"You say that on October fifth I suggested to you that we had better take care of the jury and the next day said it was time to get to work on Bain and gave you a check for a thousand dollars for this purpose. Then why is the check I gave you dated on October fourth? If I was sending you out to bribe a prospective juror would I give you a check that could be traced back or would I give you cash? If I wanted prospective jurors bribed would I send you out, my chief investigator whose every move was being watched by Burns operatives, or would I have imported a stranger for the dirty work? Would I send you on this bribery expedition when I knew that you had worked for Captain Fredericks and the district attorney's office for years and would try to go back to work there when the McNamara case was over? If I gave you four thousand dollars on the morning of November twenty-eighth to bribe Lockwood and you didn't tell me where the bribe was to be passed, how would I know where to go to check on you? If I knew you were passing a bribe there would I let myself be seen in the vicinity? Would I have crossed the street to talk to you, after the bribe had been passed, when I saw Detective Browne walking right behind you? If I had ordered that whole arrangement would I pick one of the busiest corners in the city?

"If you told me that the district attorney would never accept Krueger why did I tell you to give him five hundred dollars anyway? Why would I send you out to bribe John Underwood, owner of an ironworks, whose employees were on strike? If you were bribing these men without my specific knowledge how could I find enough millions of dollars to give you carte blanche to bribe the hundred upon hundreds of men on the venire lists? Would I be such a fool as to try to bribe hundreds of men, any one of whom could have wrecked my life and the lives of my clients?

"If you were trying to pass a bribe for me why did you allow it to be passed when you had seen four detectives following and watching you? Why did you lie about not seeing Detective Home or not knowing Detective Ong? Why did you take witnesses with you on every bribery expedition? Why did you try to bribe the owner of an ironworks, whom you knew would instantly report the attempt to the Merchants and Manufacturers and to the district attorney? The district attorney claims the bribe was passed with marked bills; then when could they have been marked, if you say that Harriman brought them to my office from his safe-deposit vault? Were not those markings put on the bills by the Burns detectives before they were handed to you on the morning of November twenty-eighth?

"You testified that when you asked me if the bribe money could be traced I replied, 'No, I got it straight from Gompers.' Knowing the intensity of the steel trust's hatred for Gompers and unionism, would I have so blithely and callously betrayed the cause for which I have given my heart's blood for twenty-five years, put their fate in the hands of a private detective whom I had known for only three months? You testified that when Job Harriman brought me the four thousand dollars' bribe money and you solicitously asked me if there wasn't a record kept at the safe-deposit department where Harriman had withdrawn the money, I replied, 'You don't need to worry about that part of it, because Mr Harriman took five hundred dollars of the money he got at the same time and paid off a mortgage, so that he could account for being at the safe-deposit department that morning.' Was that Clarence Darrow talking? Since when have I become so lip-loose, so wantonly garrulous? If I were participating in a crime would I wreck Mr Harriman's only possible defense, destroy so blithely the life and good works of a fine labor lawyer and the man who was slated to be the next mayor of Los Angeles? Why do you have to call twenty-five of the most reputable citizens of southern California liars and perjurers? Or are all these things details in a gigantic conspiracy to destroy as many of labor's leaders and defenders as possible? Or is your entire testimony against me the price the district attorney made you pay to keep yourself out of prison?"

The world could not answer those questions any more than Franklin, twitching and squirming on the stand, could answer them. And the people who knew Clarence Darrow, by his life and by his works, said, "No. It is impossible. Clarence Darrow did not do this thing. He is innocent."

8

The final pleas were begun August twelfth by Assistant District Attorney Joe Ford, a forceful young man, a scholar, with one of the best libraries in California on Irish folkways and literature and oriental philosophies. Politically ambitious, Ford hoped by the power of his closing plea to win Captain Fredericks' position as district attorney at the next election. One of the jurors commented, "Ford wrote out his speech, learned it by heart, then dressed up in his Sunday best and invited all his friends to come to court to hear him. But he laid it on too heavy; he was too bitter. He was vicious and venomous; I hated him; I couldn't bear to look at him."

He called Darrow a coward; accused him of corrupting some of the best men in the city, among them Le Compte Davis; called his entire testimony perjured; accused him of sacrificing John J. McNamara in order to save himself; described Darrow's conduct in that case as viler than that of Judas or Benedict Arnold. He also told the jury that since Darrow had written that there was no such thing as crime, he had encouraged such misguided wretches as

James B. McNamara to kill innocent men; that therefore it was Clarence Darrow rather than James B. McNamara who was guilty, not only of the *Times* explosion and the murder of twenty men, but also of the dozens of explosions that had been caused by the dynamiters.

"It is one of the misfortunes of the American Bar," cried Ford, "that some criminal lawyers practice subornation and perjury and use bribery to win their cases. There is really no difference between the men inside the jail and those outside with men like the defendant employed to fight the case."

From Ford's diatribe Clarence Darrow emerged as one of the arch criminals in history, a shade or two worse than Harry Orchard. During his long attack Clarence sat at the attorney's table, carefully studying the faces of the jurors.

That night he and Earl Rogers had their last quarrel. It had been agreed when Rogers was engaged that Darrow would make the final plea to the jury. Rogers now balked; he did not think Darrow was capable of making a good plea; he did not wish to take a back seat and let Darrow wind up the case; he did not wish to relinquish the spotlight. Darrow agreed to let him make a brief final appeal along with Horace Appel. Both men accused the district attorney's office of conspiracy, tearing Ford limb from limb, even as he had drawn and quartered Darrow.

Then in a few simple sentences Rogers stated the crux of the case: "Will you tell me how any sane, sensible man who knows anything about the law business—and this defendant has been at it for thirty-five years—could make himself go to a detective and say to him: 'Just buy all the jurors you want. I put my whole life, my whole reputation, I put everything I have into your hands. I trust you absolutely. I never knew you until two or three months ago and I don't know very much about you now, but there you are; go to it!' "

On August fourteenth Darrow rose to his feet to defend his good name. The Los Angeles *Record* cried in headlines: THOUSANDS FIGHT TO HEAR DARROW. "More than one thousand spectators who had fought and struggled with bailiffs in a narrow corridor for two hours listened as the defendant slowly rose and advanced to the jury box. A thousand others had fought and struggled to get in, only to be disappointed. Hundreds of people were crowded into a space of ten feet, and a thousand more pressed in on them in a wild effort to gain entrance to the courtroom. The bailiff shut the doors in the faces of the crowd. Women fainted and men gasped for breath. . . . Reserves were called from the sheriff's office to quell the crowd, and clubs had to be drawn before it could be handled. Finally the mob surged into the room and filled all the standing space."

They had come to hear America's greatest pleader plead for himself: for a day and a half they heard pour from his lips words that came out of his blood and guts. While cross-examining the Burns men he had appeared weak and uncertain, and Rogers had accused him of being fainthearted—when he had been brokenhearted. But that was over now; as finally he rose to make the ultimate plea for an end to the rottenness and corruption, hating and killing, with which the Western world was infested, he was once again the attorney for the defense.

In his organization of the material, the interweaving of the minute details of evidence, the dissection of character and credibility of the witnesses, he rose to the power he had always displayed; his lashing of what he called "the criminal interests of the country" that usurp and pervert government, that carry on gigantic swindles in their account books and stock manipulations, that rob and bleed the public by extortionate price fixings, was the most passionate and ringing he had ever made. In it he made the plea of which he had deprived himself in the McNamara case.

He thrust his hands deep in his coat pockets and began to speak in a low voice, "Gentlemen of the jury, I am a stranger in a strange land, two thousand miles away from home and friends. I think I can say that no one in my native town would have made to any jury any such statement as was made of me by the district attorney in opening this case. I will venture to say he could not afterward have found a companion except among detectives and crooks and sneaks in the city where I live if he had dared to open his mouth in the infamous way that he did in this case.

"What am I on trial for? I am not on trial for having sought to bribe a man named Lockwood. I am on trial because I have been a lover of the poor, a friend of the oppressed, because I have stood for labor all these years and have brought down upon my head the wrath of the criminal interests in this country. That is the reason I have been pursued by as cruel a gang as ever followed a man. Will you tell me why the Erectors' Association and the Steel Trust are interested in this case way out here in Los Angeles?

"I have committed one crime which I cannot be forgiven. . . . I have stood for the weak and the poor. I have stood for the men who toil. Therefore, I have stood against them, and now this is their chance. I have lived my life and I have fought my battles, not against the weak and the poor—anybody can do that—but against power, injustice, against oppression. Now let me show you the villainy and infamy of the prosecution which reeks from beginning to end with crime and corruption and with bloodlessness and heartlessness to the last degree. I have practiced law a good long time and I tell you I never saw or heard of a case where any American jury convicted anybody upon such testimony as that of Franklin and Harrington, and I don't expect to live long enough to find that sort of jury.

"By all my training, inclination and habit I am about the last person in all this world who could have possibly undertaken jury bribing. Mine was a position which needed to be guarded most carefully, as these events have shown. If you think I would pick out a place half a block from my office and send a man with money in his hand in broad daylight to go down on the street corner to pass four thousand dollars, if you think I did that, gentlemen, why, find me guilty. I certainly belong in some state institution.

"Gentlemen, don't ever think that your own life or liberty is safe, that your own family is secure; don't ever think that any human being is safe when under evidence like this and circumstances like these I, with some influence and some respect and some money, am brought here and placed in the shadow of the penitentiary.

"Show me, in all their watching and their spying, show me, with all the money they have spent, with all the efforts of the strong and the powerful to get me—show me in all these long, weary months where one honest man has raised his voice to testify against me. Just one. Just one. And are you ready, gentlemen, in this day and generation, to take away the name and liberty of a human being upon the testimony of rogues, informers, crooks, vagabonds, immunity hunters and detectives? If so, I don't want to live; I don't want to live in a world where such men can cause the undoing of an American citizen."

He spent hours dissecting the prosecution's case, bringing up from his omnivorous memory point after point of the evidence against him, weighing it carefully and placing it in its proper perspective.

He retraced the struggles between the Steel Trust and the workers; he said, "I would have walked from Chicago across the Rocky Mountains and over the long, dreary desert to lay my hand upon the shoulder of J. B. McNamara and tell him not to place dynamite in the Times Building. I have loved peace all my life. I have taught it all my life. I believe that love does more than hatred. I believe that both sides have gone about the settlement of these difficulties in the wrong way. The acts of the one have caused the acts of the other, and I blame neither. Men are not perfect; they had an imperfect origin and they are imperfect today, and the long struggle of the human race from darkness to comparative civilization has been filled with clash and discord and murder and war and violence and wrong, and it will be for years and years to come. But ever we are going onward and upward toward the sunshine, where the hatred and war and cruelty and violence of the world will disappear."

"It was a good argument," Darrow said later. "I have listened to great arguments and have made many arguments myself and consider that my judgment on this subject is sound."

9

In his instructions to the jury Judge Hutton threw out two thirds of the trial, two thirds of the evidence and two thirds of the ninety days of battle when he instructed the jury that "the defendant is not on trial here for kidnaping Mrs Caplan, nor for the removal of Diekleman from Albuquerque, nor for the payment of money to Bittinger."

He put his finger on the most perplexing aspect of the case: if Darrow were innocent, who was guilty? but made no attempt to solve this problem and instructed the jury that "it is not the duty of the defendant to prove who, if anyone, furnished the money to Franklin for the purpose of bribing the juror."

He instructed the jury to acquit Darrow if they believed a conspiracy had been entered into by the three former policemen, Franklin, Lockwood and White, to fasten the alleged crime on the defendant.

"The defendant has a right to claim that the whole charge against him is a conspiracy, that it is a trumped-up charge and that there is no truth in it whatever, and you are instructed that in the absence of any evidence in the case tending to show beyond a reasonable doubt that the defendant actually committed the offense, you have a right to take into consideration whether or not the circumstances and evidence establish the fact that there was a conspiracy on the part of Franklin, White and Lockwood to act so that it might appear that a crime had been committed, for the purpose of charging the defendant or connecting him with the crime."

Then Darrow must have been plunged backward four years to the spasms that were Boise, for Judge Hutton used the identical words that had been used by Judge Wood in his instructions to the

Haywood jury: "You are instructed that a conviction cannot be had on the testimony of an accomplice unless he is corroborated by other evidence which in itself, and without the aid of the testimony of the accomplice, tends to connect the defendant with the commission of the offense. The law absolutely prohibits the conviction in a criminal case upon the uncorroborated testimony of an accomplice, although the jury may believe the testimony of the accomplice to be entirely true."

Abruptly the judge stopped. A bailiff gave a signal; the jury rose and marched out of its box. Judge Hutton left the bench. No one else stirred. Darrow sat clasping the hand of his wife, bruising her knuckles by his intensity. The defense lawyers sat across from the prosecution lawyers, silent, their eyes down. The spectators were motionless; there was hardly a breath or a movement in the room. It was not only that people did not speak; neither did they think nor hope nor feel. It was a hiatus, a moment out of life, out of consciousness, so numb was everyone with fear.

The jury was taken out at nine-twenty in the morning, for Judge Hutton, ill from the overwork and violence of the trial, had used only twenty minutes to deliver his instructions. At nine-fifty there was a buzz from the jury room which announced that the jury wanted to return. No one of the two thousand persons jammed into the courtroom had moved when the jury went out; they now looked at each other in amazement.

"What does it mean?" whispered Ruby.

"Maybe they want some instructions," replied Clarence.

But the jurymen were grinning broadly as they filed into their box. Judge Hutton took his place on the bench amid the deathlike silence.

"Your pleasure?" he asked.

"A verdict," replied Foreman Williams.

"Read it," ordered Judge Hutton.

"Not guilty!" cried Foreman Williams.

Darrow jumped to his feet and kissed his wife. Judge Hutton rushed down from the bench, embraced him and cried, "There are millions of people throughout the land today who will cry 'Hallelujah!' "

The Los Angeles *Herald* tells that "the scene immediately following the reading of the verdict was one of the most remarkable that has ever been witnessed in a courtroom of the West. Darrow rushed over to the jury box where he was received with open arms. Jurors Dunbar, Golding and Dingman embraced him. Other jurors forced their way into the circle to shake the hand and pat affectionately the shoulder of the man they had freed. The spectators, the majority of whom were women, fought their way past the bailiffs to the jury box; some were weeping, others smiling, as they poured forth their congratulations. Some in their eagerness made the mistake of choosing members of the district attorney's staff. Rogers was slapped on the back and shoulders until he was forced to stand against the wall in self-defense. For two hours neither Mr nor Mrs Darrow left the courtroom. Besieged by friends, they held a reception, and men and women on the streets, learning of the news, thronged into the room."

Juryman Williams relates, "We reached our decision on the first ballot. The testimony given by informers was never taken into consideration, nor were they or their evidence discussed. Darrow did not furnish the bribe money. Of this I am convinced. But I do believe some other man did, and I think it is up to the district attorney to find that man."

"No, I don't feel like crying," said Ruby. "I just feel like giving twelve rousing cheers for the jury—and I could embrace every one of them." She did embrace several of them as they came forward to congratulate her.

Darrow said, "It has been a long, hard ordeal and, of course, I have a great sense of relief. None of those who knew me ever believed that I was corrupt, and their encouragement and faith has been my greatest help."

10

But his troubles were far from over. He was now indicted for the Bain bribery. If the motion for the second trial had been asked of Judge Hutton he probably would have thrown it out of court and Clarence would have been free to return home, vindicated; but Hutton was ill and exhausted, and another judge bound Darrow over on the grounds that he could not know what material the district attorney had against Darrow in the Bain case.

Profoundly embittered now by what the wife of the assistant district attorney, Ford, always called "the Darrow persecutions," Clarence underwent the agony of more months of anxiety and depression. Nor did it cheer him to see how little effort the prosecution was making to save its own face, giving Lockwood a job in the information booth of the Hall of Records, a job he was to hold until he was ninety; refusing to charge, indict or try Captain White for his acknowledged implicity in the crime; learning that Bert Franklin stopped Juror Golding on the street and murmured *sotto voce*, "I just wanted you to know that the D.A. made me wash their dirty linen." What comfort were these things when his money was gone, his strength shattered by his great effort, when he was still under indictment for being a criminal?

So broke now that he could no longer maintain the Midway flat, Ruby requested friends in Chicago to sublet it. The rentees stayed for two months, paid no rent and walked out, leaving the apartment in a sorry state. As a final blow, and in order to enable history to live up to its reputation for repeating itself, their last investment was lost in a bankruptcy.

Yet even in the deepest gloom there came a few lights. A literary club of San Francisco affirmed its faith in him by inviting him north to lecture on Tolstoy. And as an even more important token of confidence the Chicago labor counsel urged him to come back, if only for a few days, to select a jury in the Shea case. Shea was the head of a teamsters' union who had been arrested in a rough strike in 1911; Darrow had undertaken his defense, only to be released to the McNamaras when they were arrested. Shea had been tried and convicted, but the judgment had been set aside. The Teamsters' Union did not care that Darrow was still under indictment for bribing jurors; they asked him to come East, and he did, spending a week of feverish work, avoiding his old friends and acquaintances and returning to Los Angeles the moment the last juror was selected. The money he earned enabled him to meet his own court costs, and the not-guilty decision handed down by the jury he had picked sparked up his energy and courage.

Earl Rogers and Horace Appel withdrew from the second trial; Clarence retained young Jerry Geisler to help him with the law and an elderly attorney by the name of Powers to assist with the admissibility of evidence. He knew that the brunt of the trial would be upon his shoulders; he felt entirely equal to the task.

The attack by Fredericks and Ford was even more vitriolic than it had been in the first case. Since the Bain bribe had been passed on October sixth, six weeks before the settlement arrangements had begun, Darrow was deprived of this important factor in his defense. As he had sensed when hiring another lawyer to defend him in the first trial, it did not sit well with the jury when he left the lawyers' table to take the stand as a witness, when he rose as the attorney to object to evidence; it was difficult for the jurors to separate his functions. He felt the hostility of three or four of the jurors whom he came to believe were part of Fredericks' professional jury servers, for he had not been able to afford investigators to check on the veniremen.

In his final plea, instead of solely defending himself against the charge of bribery, he again defended the McNamaras for what they had done on their side of the class war. Between his first and second trial a number of the Indianapolis officers had been convicted and sent to prison; he defended them, too, in a fierce attack upon the exploitation of the American trusts.

Entering the jury room, the jury voted eight to four for conviction. After three days of deliberation they reported that they could never agree and were dismissed.

Ford and Fredericks were not yet through. They threatened a third trial. This persistence to "get him" drained him of his physical and spiritual strength. He didn't have ten dollars to his name; he was terribly in debt; he was tired, discouraged, ill; he did not feel he could endure another trial. And then came a telegram from a complete stranger which read:

HOT SPRINGS, ARK., MARCH 13, 1913

HON. CLARENCE DARROW
LOS ANGELES, CALIFORNIA

I NOTICE FROM THE DAYS PAPERS THAT YOU HAVE EXHAUSTED YOUR LAST DOLLAR IN YOUR DEFENSE STOP YOU HAVE SPENT YOUR WHOLE LIFE TRYING TO SEE THAT THE POOR GOT A SHOW NOW YOU SHALL HAVE EVERY CHANCE THE LAW AFFORDS TO PROVE YOUR INNOCENCE STOP IF YOU WILL WIRE ME THE AMOUNT YOU REQUIRE I WILL SEND IT TO YOU

FRED D. GARDNER

Darrow wired back:

YOUR KINDNESS IS SO GREAT I CAN HARDLY UNDERSTAND IT STOP MY CONDITION IS ABOUT AS YOU STATE STOP IT WAS SERIOUSLY HANDICAPPED IN LAST FIGHT STOP DONT KNOW YOUR CIRCUM-STANCES AND WHETHER I OUGHT TO LET YOU DO SO MUCH STOP AT LEAST IT SHOULD NOT BE KNOWN UNTIL ALL IS OVER OR IT WOULD ADD TO EXPENSES STOP WIRE ME MORE FULLY AS TO HOW MUCH HARDSHIP IT WOULD BE TO YOU

C. S. DARROW

The following day he received an answer.

MAILING CHECK TODAY STOP WILL SEND MORE IF NECESSARY STOP CHEER UP TAKE HEART AND PROVE TO THE WORLD THAT YOU ARE INNOCENT STOP A MAN OF YOUR GREAT CAPACITY MUST NOT BE LOST TO THE POOR OF THIS NATION ON ACCOUNT OF LACK OF FEW PALTRY DOLLARS TO MAKE A LEGITIMATE DEFENSE

FRED D. GARDNER

In a few days a check arrived for a thousand dollars, accompanied by a second check from Mrs Gardner, who sent two hundred dollars out of her private savings account.

Frederick Gardner had gone to St Louis at the age of sixteen. Looking for a job, he had seen a "Boy Wanted" sign in the window of a casket factory, had taken the job and become the owner of the plant by the time he was twenty-one. The particularly beautiful part of his gift to Darrow, a man he had never met, was that Gardner, who later became governor of the state of Missouri, had had considerable labor difficulties in his casket factory and was by no means sympathetic to the unions.

The generous gesture revived Clarence. He further was cheered when he learned that the attorney general of the United States had publicly accused William J. Burns of having bribed jurors in a Washington case and had succeeded in obtaining a pardon for the man convicted because of Burns's subornation of perjury, and by the fact that William J. Burns had had his licence to practice as a private detective revoked in several states.

Within a few days the district attorney's office dismissed further charges against him, and he was free to return to his home in Chicago after more than two years of misery in a city where he had never known anything but misery.

In the library of his home on the Midway Darrow gathered together some of his first editions to sell to the secondhand book stores so that he could have money with which to buy food. As he trudged down the street with his beloved books under his arm he knew only one thing, but he knew that for sure; he was through with the law.

CHAPTER X

In Defense of the Indefensible

IT WAS NO LONGER difficult for him to walk down the street. A few friends stopped him, shook hands, told him how glad they were to have him back, how happy they were that he had been exonerated, but for the most part the people of Chicago were hurt and resentful. They felt that he had been responsible for injuring the city's name, that if he had not been guilty of a crime he had been guilty of the prime indiscretion of falling into trouble. Though the general run of folks believed him innocent of the bribery, the more cynical said, "You know how it is—where there's smoke there's bound to be fire. Even if he didn't pass the bribe he probably knew it was being done." And Clarence Darrow saw confirmed the fear he had felt when he sat in the Los Angeles courtroom and heard Joe Ford accuse him of being worse than Benedict Arnold or Judas Iscariot: if you fling mud at a fence some stains will remain after the mud has dried and fallen off.

The only ones to rise to his defense were his blood brothers in the profession, the liberal and idealistic attorneys of the state who carried on a general practice, defended unpopular causes, gave their services to the poor and unfortunate as often as they could and sustained the profession of law with honest hearts and high minds. Edward Maher, a friend of Darrow's, came to him with the suggestion that "a banquet be given by the Lawyers' Association of Illinois in honor of his return to Chicago." Darrow was touched by the display of loyalty and hurt by the intuition that his confreres felt the display to be necessary. A committee was formed to "put over" the banquet—from time to time Clarence would inquire, a trifle wistfully, how the sale of the tickets was going.

It was fortunate for his proper love of self that he had already renounced the practice of the law, for immediately it became evident that Chicago had renounced him as a lawyer. Though the newspapers told of his return, though he traversed the business circles, though he went for a few days to the office of Darrow and Bailey to clean up his papers and dissolve the firm, no one of his former clients, corporation or individual, whom he had served successfully over the years, came to him and said, "Clarence, we're sure glad you're back. We've got a deal we want you to handle. . . . We would like you to arrange . . . There's a suit . . ." He needed only a few days to learn that no one wanted his services, that individuals and corporations alike were afraid of prejudicing their interests by having as their representative a man who had just come through two criminal trials.

He was not too unhappy, for he had long wanted to be finished with the arduous requirements of the law, to be free to write and lecture. He closed the office door behind him for the last time, boarded an Illinois Central train. When he reached home he found Ruby in the library, on her hands and knees, burning fresh red dye into the carpet; she had spent the intervening days scrubbing the flat and making it livable after their two-year absence. He dropped into a wicker rocker and sat for a few moments with his chin on his chest.

"Well, Rube," he murmured, "it kinda looks like our lawyering days are over."

Ruby picked up another hot iron and went on burning dye into the carpet.

Though he had a good many thousands of dollars invested in Paul's gas plant in Greeley, he not only could not get his money out but had to keep investing more in order to protect what he had already put into it. There was only one way he could earn a living now, from lecturing. If his troubles would keep away audiences as they had law clients he would indeed be in a bad way. Determined to make a quick test of his standing, he arranged with one of the Chicago lecture managers to engage the Garrick Theater for a lecture on Nietzsche. The Chautauqua managers of the Midwest had always liked him and found him a good drawing card; when they met for their annual convention in Chicago they invited him to dinner with them at the States Restaurant. Clarence sat at the head of the long table and talked during the dinner hour; the managers were delighted to find that his misfortunes had neither hardened nor embittered him. Sitting next to him was a young woman by the name of Caroline McCartney, who participated in the rapid-fire discussion. Toward the end of the dinner Darrow turned to Professor Foster and said, "This girl thinks as we do; I don't know about the rest of them."

He took two tickets from his vest pocket and said to Miss Mc-Cartney, "I'm going to lecture at the Garrick Theater, and I'm going to give you a couple of tickets." Then he added hastily, "But please don't take them just because I'm offering them to you."

Caroline McCartney, who was to become one of his most enthusiastic lecture managers, went to the Garrick a few nights later, as did several thousand other Chicagoans, men and women from scattered segments of the city life who still loved him and who gave him a tremendous ovation as he came out on the platform. Inspirited by their vote of confidence, he delivered one of his most delightful lectures, as a result of which the Chautauqua managers drew up a schedule for forty appearances, and the Walt Whitman Club invited him to be chairman of their annual banquet, a gesture which helped greatly in his repatriation.

He should have been pleased at the successful turn of events. But he was not. For years he had wanted to retire so that he might be free to write, study, teach, but he had wanted to retire voluntarily, with money put aside for travel and leisure and peace of mind. It had never been his intention to retire because he somehow had failed, been forced out. He knew the dangers of becoming an itinerant preacher, baggy in the pants and baggy in the windpipe, talking not because he had something burning or beautiful to say, but hollowly, to earn his bread. He had never intended to turn to lecturing as a means of earning a livelihood.

2

In 1894 a short, squat, bristly-eyebrowed Russian immigrant by the name of Peter Sissman, who had just finished his law course and with whom Darrow had become acquainted at socialist meetings, had asked Darrow to be taken into his office. Sissman could bring the firm no business; he had a thick accent and was not particularly personable, but Darrow had liked the boy's spirit and, as he had told Ethel McClasky when hiring her, "We radicals should patronize each other." He had taken Sissman into his office and trained him. Now, almost twenty years later, Sissman found his opportunity to repay the debt. When someone told him that Clarence Darrow had given up the practice of law Sissman went to Darrow and exclaimed:

"You must not. If you remain in Chicago and don't open your office it is a tacit admission of guilt."

"No, Peter. I'm through with the law," replied Darrow.

"If you give up your profession now," insisted Sissman, "you will end in a few years as a broken-down book agent."

"But I have no practice."

"It will take no time for you to build it up again."

Darrow shook his head, thanked Peter Sissman for his kindness.

In the months that followed whenever a lawyer would say to Sissman, "We hear Darrow has quit the law," Sissman would reply, "He must not. He must start over again. I would be overjoyed to start with him if he would want me."

It did not take long for this sentiment to reach Darrow. One afternoon he telephoned Sissman and invited him to the Midway for dinner. Over their cigarettes and coffee Darrow said:

"Peter, I hear you would be willing to join up with me."

"Of course I would be willing," replied Sissman brusquely. "I would be happy, but I'm not sure it would be advisable for you. I have only a small Jewish practice, a small office business. I can't bring you anything."

"You think kindly of me," answered Darrow.

"Ah!" murmured Sissman.

"I am not sure I can earn anything," continued Darrow.

"You must make an announcement that you are back," said Sissman.

"How do you propose we do it?"

"We must keep Bailey in the firm name. Darrow and Sissman is impossible."

"You give me courage, Peter," observed Darrow, "courage I would never have to start it alone."

Sissman opened a joint bank account, dug down into his savings and spent a couple of hundred dollars for a desk, chair and carpet for an office for his new partner. But the weeks passed, and the months passed, and no one brought their legal problems or troubles to Clarence Darrow, not even the poor, who would have to ask for his services for nothing. He continued to go out on his Chautauqua lectures, which earned him from one to three hundred dollars apiece. Each time he returned from a lecture he would go into Sissman's office and ask:

"Haven't you anything for me to do?"

"Mr Darrow," exclaimed Sissman, "can I ask you to sit down and examine an abstract of title? That's not the work for you. You must wait until important things come in."

At the end of three months Darrow asked, "Peter, have we any money in the bank?"

"Yes, there are a couple of hundred dollars you can take."

"Well," murmured Darrow, "this is the first time I ever had a partner who brought in the business and made money for me."

Then, exactly like the young graduate sitting in his office waiting for the first case to walk in and give him his chance, Darrow listened to Mildred Sperry asking him to defend her against the charge of perjuring herself for her employer, an insurance agent who had burned a building. He won an acquittal and vindication for the girl even while acknowledging her guilt. The case started him on the long road back, earned him two hundred and fifty dollars. He next was given a bankruptcy to handle, which earned him twenty-five hundred dollars. When Police Chief Healy was indicted for malfeasance of office Darrow agreed to defend him and was paid a thousand-dollar retainer fee.

When Darrow and Sissman had formed their partnership Darrow had said, "As to fees, I think we better start even."

"That wouldn't be fair to you," Sissman had replied.

"We better start even," Darrow had insisted. "If I don't uphold my end I won't take my share."

This total of thirty-seven hundred and fifty dollars represented his legal earnings for the first year; when Sissman split the income of the firm he found that he had made a few hundred dollars less than he had the year before, when he had been by himself.

The passing of time slowly healed the wounds in Chicago's pride. The people in the streets saw his shaggy figure go by, saw him smile and wave to friends, heard his drawling, kindly, musical voice, and their faith in Clarence Darrow, first citizen of Chicago, resurged. The Biology Club met again in his home; groups all over the city asked him to speak to their membership; cases began to straggle in. Each victory brought two new clients in its wake. As the cases increased in importance the fees began to rise. He would walk into Sissman's office, pull from his pocket a roll of bills and checks with which he had been paid, anywhere from five hundred to five thousand dollars, toss the money on Sissman's desk and say:

"Here you are, Peter; deposit it."

The only time he ever mentioned money was when he would go into Sissman's room and ask, "Peter, how does the treasury look?" And Sissman would write him a check. Every once in a while Sissman would hand him a statement and say, "Don't you want to examine the books? Don't you want to see what we made on what?"

"What's the use of two of us doing that work?" he would reply. "You're taking care of it fine."

By the end of the second year Sissman saw that he had made several thousand dollars more than he had ever earned alone. He took his account books into his partner's office.

"Mr Darrow," he said, "I think you are beginning to get the worst of this."

"What do you propose, Peter?" smiled Darrow.

"In the future I think sixty-forty would be fair."

"All right"—he nodded—"we'll do it that way."

Very little of his corporation and civil clientele returned, but by 1915 criminal cases began flooding into his office. Never in his thirty-eight years of practice had Clarence Darrow thought of himself primarily as a criminal lawyer. Yet he was enough of a poker player to know that a man must play the cards the way they fall. Men accused of crimes were the only ones who sought his services? Very well then, he would be a criminal lawyer. Never had he gone seeking for causes; he was too old and too wise to start now; if ever the day should come when a cause needed him it would find him and rout him out from under the deepest, most meaningless of courtroom procedure.

3

Once again it was Clarence Darrow for the defense. Every type of case came to him, and he took them all, all except those of the habitual criminals. He gave his clients the best he had in him. The habitual criminal he turned down, no matter how large the sum of money put on his desk; he felt he could do nothing for him.

Terry Druggan, son of a poor family, had stolen an automobile and asked Clarence to defend him. When the day came for the trial Druggan, who was out on bail, did not show up. Darrow managed to get a continuance, then went out to find Druggan, whom he was defending without pay.

"Terry, what do you mean by not being in court?" he demanded.

"Well, Mr Darrow," replied Druggan, "I just didn't want to be there when they were passing out the time."

Darrow won an acquittal for the boy, then said to him, "I've given you your chance; now you go straight. If you ever get into this kind of trouble again don't come back to me."

Before long Druggan had become one of Chicago's big brewers and, without Darrow's knowledge, engaged the firm of Darrow and Sissman to handle his business. One day he bumped into Darrow in the anteroom.

"What are you doing here?" demanded Darrow sternly.

"Oh, I'm in the civil department now, Mr Darrow," replied Druggan, edging away.

"Well, see that you stay there," cautioned Darrow. "If you ever get over into my department again you'll be there when they're passing out the time."

Many murder cases were brought to him, and he defended wherever he thought the crime had been a result of poverty, circumstance, passion or insanity. In some instances he secured an acquittal; in others he saved his client from hanging by earning him a life sentence. In one case a Greek choked his landlord to death for "screwing up the rents." The man asked Darrow to defend him, placed five thousand dollars in cash upon his desk. Darrow did some preliminary investigating, entered a defense, then saw that the case was hopeless and advised his client to plead guilty and accept a life sentence.

"I'm paying you five thousand dollars to get me off," replied the Greek, "not to send me to jail."

Darrow returned the five thousand dollars. The man went to another lawyer, was convicted and executed.

His real pleasure during these months came from earning another chance for folks who, by a combination of circumstances, had fallen into trouble, fundamentally good people who would lead well-behaved lives once again if they could escape the state's prison. In this defense he found his justification. Because he felt a genuine sympathy for these people, because he understood the intricate network of causations behind their acts, but above all because he was an infinitely resourceful and versatile attorney, he won nearly all his cases.

In the case which he dubbed "the early bird gets the barrel" two elderly peddlers, who bought empty barrels from one department of the packing plants for ten cents, then sold them back to a different department of the plant for twenty-five cents, were accused of conspiring with the foreman of the plant to get credit for more barrels than they turned in. The loot ran to several thousand dollars. The packers had hidden an auditor behind the barrels to get the correct check, and this auditor now brought long sheets of figures into court. These sheets could have been objected to when introduced into evidence because they were copies rather than originals, but when the judge asked, "Do you object, Mr Darrow?" Clarence

looked up from a book he had started reading with great interest
and replied, "Oh no, no, I haven't any objections."

He hadn't known why he suddenly had picked up a book that had
nothing whatever to do with the case and begun reading furiously;
he hadn't known why he made the judge bring his attention to the
objection that could have been made; he hadn't known why he had
disdained to make that objection. He had moved instinctively; he
had had a prescience that the case would break about this point.
At the noon recess, when the jury was riding down in the elevator
to get its lunch, one juror was overheard to say to another, "From
the way Darrow didn't object, I think the prosecution must be
trying to hide something." This tidbit was mentioned to Darrow.
When he rose to make his plea he spoke of the meagerness of the
peddlers' lives, of the necessities they had bought for their families
with the extra money, of the temptations that had been put in their
way, of how hard on them it would be if at their late stage of life,
when they had never been in trouble before, they were put in prison.

"That is," he added, "assuming they have been guilty of defrauding the packing plant. Now let's see if they were. There were a
bunch of figures introduced into evidence, and that was all the prosecution had to rely on. Now I can prove anything in the world by
figures, then turn right around and disprove it by the same figures.
I don't know what they hoped to cover up by this long list of
figures, but it seems to me they're trying to keep something from
you. You'll have to figure it out for yourselves."

The jurors returned in a few minutes with a verdict of not guilty.
On the way back to his office Darrow chuckled as he said, "I hope
I never have to try an easy one."

Again, when defending a newspaper against a libel suit, he was opposed by Francis Walker, a brilliant and dynamic Irish lawyer, who
was a dangerous opponent in a trial. The case was open and shut;
the only question was how much; Darrow offered a substantial
figure in settlement, which Walker refused. When it came time to
plead before the jury the impending battle between Darrow and
Walker packed the courthouse. While a junior associate from
Walker's office was arguing a point of law, Walker, who was to
plead after Darrow had finished, began walking up and down in the
back of the courtroom, marshaling his argument and whipping
himself into a passion for its delivery. When Walker's clerk had
finished Darrow rose, cast an appraising eye at Walker and said,
"Your honor, we'll waive argument," which also stopped Walker
from making his final plea. Walker threw up his hands and cried
from the back of the courtroom:

"Clarence, you wouldn't do that to me, would you?"

Darrow roared with laughter. The judge and jury joined him. When the jury returned it brought in a judgment for a figure less than that Darrow had offered in settlement before the opening of the trial.

The case in which he thought he did his most astute work during this period was the Eastland case. The Eastland, a lake steamer, was lying at anchor in the Chicago River at the Clark Street Bridge one summer morning, loaded with women and children who were going on an excursion to Michigan. Most of the passengers were standing on the side of the ship next to the dock, talking to friends and relatives, when suddenly the ship tipped downward on its heavy side and sank into the water. Hundreds of women and children were drowned instantly in one of the worst civil tragedies in American history. The genuine and terrible need to blame someone was so great that, in spite of the fact that the Eastland had recently been inspected and approved by both city and Federal inspectors, the captain was indicted for criminal negligence. Darrow was summoned to Grand Rapids, Michigan, the home of Captain John Erickson, to defend him.

The prosecution put upon the witness stand a university professor who described for the jury the building of the boat from the laying of the keel to the applying of the last coat of paint. When this world authority on ship construction was turned over to Darrow for cross-examination the Grand Rapids attorneys associated with him insisted that he break down the damaging testimony. "No, no," replied Darrow, "I shall build him up." Then with his magnificent ability to assimilate technical information, he led the professor through the mechanics of shipbuilding from the beginning of time, plying him with complex and technical questions for days on end until the judge, the jury and the witnesses were not only exhausted but outraged at him for so inconsiderately wasting their time. When the professor had completed his testimony on the mechanics of ship construction and operation, a good part of which had been unintelligible to the jury, Darrow asked simply:

"Professor, is there anyone else in the world beside yourself who knows everything there is to know about ship construction?"

"Only one other man," replied the professor without a trace of false modesty. "He lives in Scotland."

"Then," demanded Darrow of the jury, "if there are only two men on the face of the globe who know everything there is to know about ships, how could it be possible that the poor captain of a lake steamer could know what was wrong with the Eastland?"

It was this question that led the jury to acquit Captain Erickson. In cases where he didn't have a prayer he waited for the break in the case. In one instance the son of a state examiner had sold the questions for a dental examination to some students and accepted checks in payment. Every time one of the checks was introduced into evidence George Francis, one of his juniors, would shrink and mutter, "God, how can we beat them now?" Then the state put on the stand a witness who had confessed to buying the questions.

"Yes, I confessed," he cried unexpectedly. "I was routed out of bed at midnight, taken down to a dark jail and thrown in with two thugs who, I was told, were policemen. They pushed me around and threatened me and abused me for hours, until I would have confessed to anything just to get away from them."

This outburst changed the aspect of the case. Darrow murmured to Francis, "Well, George, if they put on one more witness like that you'll start forgetting about those damned checks, won't you?" George forgot about them; so did the jury.

"If no break came," said one of his junior partners, "Darrow would take what they offered and explain it away."

As he continued to win case after case that had looked impossible the state's assistant attorneys angled to be matched against him, sitting up nights to prepare their material, because if they could beat Darrow their reputation would be made. Few of them did, and Darrow's masterful cross-examination was often the reason why. It became increasingly clear that the success of his cross-examination was also due to his prescience, his sixth sense, by means of which he divined those things the witness so determinedly was concealing behind his words. In the Lundin cases, which took almost two years to try and earned him forty thousand dollars in fees, his cross-examination of one of the men accusing Lundin of grafting in the purchase of school supplies "stunned the judge, the jury, the press and the spectators. He left the witness in a state of panic, little short of hysteria, with a cross-examination which satisfied the people that Lundin's prosecution was political in origin."

So impressed was the Chicago *Tribune* that it printed its first friendly words about Clarence Darrow in the three decades since he had come to the big city from Ashtabula: "Darrow's cross-examination was the most masterly ever heard in a Chicago courtroom."

4

He was just another criminal lawyer, and yet he was something more. Now that he again was successful, with his name in the papers, the poor came back to his office, crowding his anteroom, bringing their troubles and griefs. He did not hold it against them that they, too, had abandoned him in his dark hours; that was another facet of human nature that one had to understand. He took their cases and once again was spending half his time defending people without compensation. He defended friendless and penniless men accused of murder whom he felt a sensation-mongering press had already convicted and hung for the crime. He constantly took care of unfortunate Negroes who had fallen into trouble and who could not get a white lawyer. He defended people from whose malefactions the public turned away in abhorrence, men so loathed and reviled, so completely abandoned by the human race that they could find no other defender. He would go before judges, juries, the press and the public and try to trace the long chain of circumstances that had led up to this crime, plead for understanding and mercy.

"I do not know anyone who does not need mercy. This weary old world goes on, begetting, with birth and with living and with death; and all of it is blind from the beginning to the end. I do not know what made him do this act, but I do know there is a reason for it. I know that any one of an infinite number of causes reaching back to the beginning might be working out in his mind. If there were such a thing as justice it could only be administered by those who knew the inmost thoughts of the man to whom they were meting it out. Aye, who knew the father and mother and the grandparents and the infinite number of people back of him; who knew the origin of every cell that went into the body; who could understand the structure and how it acted; who could tell how the emotions that sway the human being affected that particular frail piece of clay. It means that you must appraise every influence that moves them, the civilization where they live and all society which enters into the making of the child or the man. If you can do it— if you can do it you are wise, and with wisdom goes mercy."

Many people considered it antisocial of him to have pleaded for Healy, a public malefactor; felt that by pleading for the freedom of guilty men he made it easier for others to loot the public. Healy was the elderly chief of police of Chicago, now suffering from locomotorataxia, paralyzed and partly blind. He had been part of a corrupt political machine, giving protection to grafters and underworld interests, making himself a sizable fortune. A reform administration secured enough evidence against him to convict him in any courtroom, but when Darrow went before the jury he pleaded that it would be cruel to send an old and sick man to prison; that it could help no one to put him behind bars; that Healy had been dishonorably expelled from the police force, he and his family disgraced; that that was sufficient punishment; that the state should not be cruel or vindictive. It was a plea which he honestly and genuinely felt and which earned an acquittal for Healy.

Peter Sissman gives a trenchant portrait of his partner at the time of the Healy trial. "Darrow impressed on juries that it was not always easy to distinguish between right and wrong, particularly for historical purposes. His skepticism was so genuine that he imbued the juries with it. He would defend anyone who was in trouble, even a capitalist against a labor racketeer. He was consistent in this human philosophy of defense, which forced him into contradictions in his sociological philosophy. He was not committed to any party or permanent creed; that was his greatness and tragedy both. That was why he was essentially a free man, not bound by doctrines; but it is also why he was inconsistent and sometimes antisocial. Though his motivations were different, he sometimes used the same methods as cheap criminal lawyers. It would be all right for other lawyers to do these things; it is part of their job, but Darrow was a fighter for the people; he had a social duty which he sometimes abused to defend individuals in trouble. To call every crook in trouble an 'underdog' was sentimental nonsense, even though Christ would have approved it highly. Darrow was a Christian anarchist; that was the reason he never fulfilled himself; he had no consistent life plan or design; he just drifted along from case to case and year to year. He was a behaviorist. He said, 'No matter what system we will be under men will be essentially beastly. All a fellow can do is preach charity rather than forgiveness, to be tolerant because we will all eventually do something wrong, and what I mean by charity is love.'"

In an article called "Darrow at the Defense Table" a Chicago lawyer who had watched him in action writes: "In a tight place Darrow would shrug his shoulders and talk to the jury somewhat like this:

"'Maybe. Perhaps. You can't tell. It all depends. Neither you nor I know. Why take a chance? Give the accused the benefit of the doubt.

"'Suppose the defendant did err. What could you expect from the environment he grew up in? Was he really responsible?

"'Would you have acted differently than the defendant under the circumstances? Is he to be imprisoned because he did the natural thing you would have done, were you in his place?

"'The question is not how the provocation would affect you or how it would affect someone else. The question for you to determine is "How did it affect the defendant with his particular mental, moral and physical make-up?" Nobody is all good or all bad. Criminal! That word is loosely used. Many are out of jail who should be in it, and many imprisoned should be on the street.'

"The state was interested in only the bad things the accused had done. Darrow would ask, 'What about his good deeds?' The state would dwell upon the victim of the crime. Darrow would draw a picture of the members of the defendant's family affected by the verdict. The state would emphasize the jury's sworn duty to convict if the facts proved guilt. Darrow would stress the jury's solemn duty to understand the defender."

"Maybe. Perhaps. You can't tell. It all depends. Why take a chance?"

He had returned to Chicago under a cloud; at the age of fifty-six he had had to start all over again; he had come up the hard way, taking those cases with which he felt a genuine sympathy. Yet by 1917 he had once again so thoroughly manifested his integrity that few who had relations with him any longer believed he had been guilty in Los Angeles. After only four years he could tell one of his juniors to call any attorney, prosecutor, judge or businessman in Chicago and say that something would be done; his word was accepted as final; they knew it would be done precisely as he had said it would. By the end of the fourth year the firm of Darrow and Sissman had taken in thirty thousand dollars, and Clarence Darrow was called "the outstanding criminal lawyer of the country."

He had completed his comeback.

5

There now began for Clarence Darrow one of the most tumultuous decades ever vouchsafed to a practicing attorney, a period of spirited activity to crown an already crowded life, a period in which he created a pattern of defense which was to mark him as one of the most courageous and persuasive pleaders of history, a period in which he was never once to be on the popular side, in which he was frequently defeated and yet, in the broader sense, nearly always triumphed. The lines in his face deepened; his hair thinned; his shoulders hunched, but the fighting gleam in his eye never dimmed. He began his great stretch in 1917 in defense of the conscientious objectors.

During the early years of the World War he had been an ardent pacifist, but by 1917, like most of the American pacifists (with the exception of his friend, Eugene Debs, who was to go to Atlanta Penitentiary for opposing the entry of the United States into the war), he regretfully had been swept to the conclusion that it was no longer sensible to be pacifistic. For two years he had maintained that America must remain neutral, but by the time the SS Lusitania had been sunk and he had been shown a number of German atrocity pictures, he, too, was saying in interviews that America must join up to destroy the "Beast of Berlin."

Yet when the first conscientious objectors were arrested for refusing to participate in the draft, when the entire country turned against them as something loathsome and undeserving of any kind of defense, he rushed to their side. When they were accused of not being willing to fight because they were cowards rather than because they had ethical scruples, he tried to show the country that it took more moral stamina to brave the contempt and revilement of one's contemporaries than to face an enemy's guns. But he knew that the issue was far broader in its scope; the issue was whether or not in a democracy young men could be forced to bear arms and to kill, particularly when their religion forbade it. If these young men had a right to their religion, which the Constitution guaranteed them, then how could any specific act passed by the Congress make them go contrary to the teachings of that religion? Could a democracy be strong enough to grant to these objectors the right to their objections? Would this granting of a minority right weaken or strengthen the fabric of a democracy?

The smallness of the number involved was a help to his plea for tolerance, even though that tolerance might appear to run contrary to the immediate interests of the country at large; yet he knew that the number of persons involved had nothing whatever to do with the principles involved. If these few hundred objectors should grow to a few thousand and then to a few hundred thousand, would they still have the right to object, to remain out of the army, out of the war? Who was to determine at precisely what numerical point a constitutional right had to be abrogated for fear that not only the Constitution but the country that guaranteed it would be crushed by an enemy?

Since he himself had long opposed America's entry into the war, he was able to understand why other persons might still oppose that entry, might still feel that this war was just another European fracas, that it held no threat to America or American democracy, that the United States had no function in it. But once the country had entered the conflict, was it not imperative that it strain itself to the utmost so that its position in a hostile and sanguinary world might not be weakened? What would happen if the country were invaded; would the conscientious objectors still have the right to refuse to bear arms in defense of their homes and the homes of their neighbors? To a country caught in the flush of its first major war against a European power, Darrow's contention that a man had a right to refuse to bear arms even when his homeland was invaded came as a blow which alienated large sections of people, many of whom slowly had been won back to him. As late as May 1925 the Richmond, Virginia, *News Leader* was to speak of "the Clarence Darrow who was so hated during the war."

"If a man's religion tells him he must not kill," maintained Clarence as he looked straight at his audience from the lecture platform, "then he cannot kill even to defend himself and his home. It is better that he be killed himself and have his family killed than that he kill another fellow being. This may appear like suicidal nonsense to the ninety-nine per cent of us who do not agree with it, but if their religion tells them that their God wills it so, then we have to grant them the right to follow the will of their God. That is what democracy means. It would be more injurious to the structure of our country to deny them this right than to deny ourselves the use of their arms in conflict." If this were true of those who objected on religious grounds, it also had to apply to those who based their objections on moral, ethical or humanitarian grounds.

Then in the spring of 1918 the government of England decided that there was need further to consolidate and strengthen American sympathy for the British. They cast about to learn which American best understood the mass of his countrymen and to whose voice the greatest number of American people would listen sympathetically. They chose Clarence Darrow.

From the moment he closed behind him the door of his flat in the Midway until he returned to that front door some four months later he was the guest of Great Britain. He was wined and dined in London; he met the great and near great. H. G. Wells who, when asked by an interviewer how he had enjoyed his stay in America, had replied, "Well, I met Clarence Darrow!" introduced him to England's literary figures. He was thrilled because Frazier, author of his beloved *Golden Bough*, treated him as an equal; he discussed the McNamara case with Kier Hardie; he discussed labor, socialism and conservatism with the best minds in England; then he went to France and Belgium to watch the war in action. But search as he would for the atrocities allegedly committed by the German soldiers, he could find none, nor evidence that any had been committed outside the offices of the British Propaganda Bureau. When he was tendered an official farewell in London by representatives of the government he did not tell them that their efforts had been in vain, that the sights he had seen had made him once again profoundly pacifistic.

He returned to Chicago in October, where he made only one speech. The meeting was held in a torrential downpour, which led him to remark that it was only fitting the meeting should be held in the Baptist Church. To an audience expecting a fight talk peppered with tales of German horrors Darrow instead made a standing offer of one thousand dollars to anyone who could bring forward evidence of a French or Belgian child whose hand had been cut off.

"I had gone over hating the German warriors because they had been press-agented as the most horrible, bloodthirsty soldiers, committing fiendish atrocities. But I found that the German soldiers are like all other young boys forced to go to war: round-faced, innocent, bewildered, not understanding what it was for—excepting to obey orders or be court-martialed—dreading and fearing, fighting against their will, hoping that the hideous thing would soon be over and they might return to normal life."

A few days later the Armistice was signed, rescuing him from the painful dilemma of wanting to help England because America had to win its war but being congenitally unable to further the British propaganda. The only lasting effect of his trip to war-torn Europe was that now, in addition to believing that the conscientious objectors had a right to object, he also thought they might be right in their objections. If everyone refused to kill, who would carry on the wars? The supermen, the generals, the politicians?

6

Upon his return from Europe he plunged into the first of a series of conflicts over radicals which for the next four years, as the war hysterias would give way to the even more dangerous postwar hysterias, kept his a voice crying in the wilderness. Starting with his plea for the rights of the conscientious objectors, Clarence Darrow was to become the greatest band wagon in America: millions who would jump off, abandon him in one fight, call him a traitor, a radical, a lunatic, would climb aboard again when his next case was one with which, for some reason inherent in their own backgrounds and temperaments, they could sympathize; those who had stoutly supported him during his pleas for the conscientious objectors, eulogizing him as a true Christian, a defender of democracy, an authentic hero, would, when he defended other rebels, label him an anarchist, a chaos maker, a menace to organized society. What Sissman had termed Darrow's greatest weakness, that he had no cause, no party, no doctrine, no direction, only identification with all human suffering, now sent him rushing to all parts of his country, became his greatest strength.

"In a democracy the best people to rule," said Darrow, "are those who believe in human liberties more than the causes they are wed to."

In his unending defense of human liberties he fulfilled the function of the lifeguard on the beach. He did not interfere with the people who were splashing about in the water; he made no effort to teach them to swim, to be champions. He said, "If they are enjoying themselves let them alone." But as soon as someone was in trouble and cried for help Clarence Darrow made a flying leap for the surf.

The one regret of his professional life was that he had come to Chicago from Ashtabula a few months too late to assist in the defense of the Haymarket anarchists. Now in the crucial case of *The State of Wisconsin* vs. *Peter Bianchi, Mary Nardini, et al.*, he was given another chance to speak his piece; for here, thirty years after the four Haymarket anarchists had been executed, was another anarchist case, which the state of Wisconsin based squarely upon the Haymarket precedent in order to secure a conviction of all eleven of the defendants. The Haymarket anarchists had been convicted on the ground that "he who inflames people's minds and induces them by violent means to accomplish an illegal object is himself a rioter, though he takes no part in the riot." The eleven Italians of Milwaukee had been convicted, not of throwing the bomb which blew up a police station and killed several officers, but of having in their possession more than a hundred pamphlets, magazines and newspapers which set forth the political virtues of anarchism.

The eleven Italians had already spent one year of a twenty-five-year sentence in the state penitentiary when they asked Darrow to appeal their case. Before leaving for Milwaukee, where the original trial had been held, Darrow began reading in the almost unintelligible translations that had been made for the court of the Italian anarchist literature, jotting down those sentences which seemed to express the crux of their belief: "The governments commit as many crimes as they prevent. The governments feign a desire to want to put a remedy to the evils of the workingman, but how could they put a remedy to it if they are the principal cause of these evils? The capitalists gain without any punishment and use the workers or else starve them; the financiers steal with a free hand. At the least sign

of discontent of the workingmen the government interferes with
its soldiers, with its policemen, with its paid judges, and oppresses
the oppressed. The government is the servant of the bourgeoisie, the
enemy of the workingman, the starver of the people, the pestilence
of society."

The fact that these ten men and one woman in the Wisconsin
penitentiary were aliens, that they had made no attempt to become
American citizens, that they spoke no English, that their public
conduct proved them to be emotionally unbalanced, made no difference in the fundamental issue involved: that if America was to
survive as a free land it had to be a country where men could be
so completely free that they could believe in any erroneous, even
crackpot, opinion and be guaranteed the right of expression of that
opinion. So long as they did not actually violate the existing criminal
code they must be protected in their rights by the hundred million
citizens who would thus be protecting their own rights. It was true
that these people were not citizens of the United States, but so long
as they were not deported, so long as they were allowed to remain
in this country, the least of them was entitled to the same rights the
greatest American was entitled to. These childish, hysterical malcon-
tents, who could never become an integral part of American life,
were the last people in the world who had any claim to protection,
yet to Darrow they seemed the first to need protection: if he
could erect a defense for those who least seemed to warrant it, that
defense would be the stronger for those who warranted it the more.
If he could make a valid defense of the indefensible, then the
defensible would be certain of a sound defense.

Darrow took Sissman with him to Milwaukee, where they dug
deeper into the case of the anarchists. They learned that August
Juliani, connected with the Methodist Church of Milwaukee, had
gone with some of his Italian congregation, on a Sunday afternoon
in the summer of 1917, to the corner of Bishop and Potter avenues
in the center of an Italian district. As their band played "Columbia"
a crowd of about a hundred gathered. Juliani then "started to talk
patriotically about the war, the draft and the registering in Italian."
One of the Italian spectators cried out, "I don't believe in God; I
don't believe in priests; I don't believe what you are saying." Another cried, "We don't believe in this war," while a third said, "We
don't believe in any government; Wilson is a pig; the American
flag is a rag, and this country is a jail." The other members of the
little clique echoed, "You bet; you bet!"

The following Sunday afternoon Juliani led his group to the
same corner, where a similar disturbance broke up his meeting. On

the third Sunday he asked for police protection. Four detectives went along with him. The meeting started peacefully, but after a few minutes the dissenters left their clubhouse a block away, marched on the meeting and again started a row. Paul Wieler, one of the detectives, called out, "If you don't like this crowd move on. They have a permit." When the man he was addressing refused to move the detective began to search him. Someone opened fire with a revolver. Others returned the fire. Two anarchists were killed; two of the detectives were injured. Eleven anarchists were taken into custody.

Then in November a bomb was placed in the Central Police Station which exploded and caused the death of ten persons, including two of the detectives who had made the arrests on the corner of Bishop and Potter avenues. The eleven defendants held in the jail under charges of assault with deadly weapons had the charge against them raised to conspiracy to commit murder. The trial was rushed, a change of venue denied, even though the populace was violently inflamed against all Italians. District Attorney Zabel, who had been elected on the socialist ticket, charged that anyone having anarchist literature in his possession was equally guilty of the bomb outrage and, as in the Haymarket case, guilty even if the actual perpetrator of the bombing never was found. He read to the jury inflammatory passages from the translated Italian tracts, and the jury had convicted all eleven of the defendants, giving them sentences of twenty-five years each—not for throwing the bomb, not for having ordered the bomb to be thrown, not for knowing who had thrown the bomb, but for being anarchists whose published literature appeared to favor the throwing of bombs.

"These people have a right to believe in the philosophic idea that they can free themselves by force," cried Darrow. "It is only when it can be proved that they have used force to injure people, when they have run counter to the criminal code, that they can be prosecuted. There is no such crime as a crime of thought; there are only crimes of action. It is bad taste for guests in a country to call that country a jail; it is bad taste to call its President a pig, but these are errors of judgment rather than transgressions against the legal structure. If we wish to keep speech free, to keep criticism open and alive, we have to tolerate even such criticisms as these, distasteful as they may be to us."

In his brief to the Supreme Court of Wisconsin Darrow, with the help of Sissman, who made his most brilliant effort in this case, set out to demonstrate that the eleven anarchists had had a trial by passion; that because of an inflamed press and countryside the jury had been prejudiced; that the district attorney's reading of the inflammatory sections of the anarchist literature had deranged the trial; that the presiding judge had shown prejudice and passion in imposing a uniform twenty-five-year sentence without any attempt to vary the sentence according to the degree of participation; that the anarchist literature had nothing to do with the crime with which the defendants originally were charged; that a shocking confusion had been created in that the defendants, ostensibly being tried for shooting the detectives on the corner of Bishop and Potter avenues, were in actuality tried for a conspiracy to explode the bomb that had killed the police officers, and lastly, that no conspiracy or specific intent to assault the detectives had emerged from the evidence.

The appeal was granted. Nine of the defendants who had had no firearms in their possession at the time of the arrest were acquitted in a new and dispassionate trial. The two men who had been carrying guns were convicted of assault. Darrow boarded a train for Madison to call on the governor of Wisconsin. "A grave injustice has been done to these nine innocent persons who had to spend a year in the penitentiary," he pleaded. "The best way we can show our disapproval of these trials by passion and Wisconsin's repudiation of such methods is for you to pardon the two men who have just been convicted."

The governor pardoned them.

7

Though he was fast approaching sixty-five, neither his astuteness nor capacity for work was dimming. "Darrow didn't pay much attention to the technicalities of the law," one of his new partners, William Holly, remarks. "He worked on facts. He was a very hard worker, one of the hardest workers I've ever known. He would eat a hearty breakfast and then wouldn't eat again until he was finished with his day's labors, even if it took until midnight." Like the lawyers who had worked with him in the past, Sissman says of him, "Darrow was endowed with a remarkable memory, was a quick observer and could retain without outside aids. Whether it was arguing a motion or the main case, there was hardly a point that could be used that escaped him. Once when I filed a demurrer for a non-profit organization I prepared a long notation. Darrow glanced at my notes for a couple of minutes, then walked to court and talked for a solid hour, logically and legally, remembering every point in the notation. If I had taken two weeks to write and memorize the talk I couldn't have done it as well. The demurrer was sustained."

As the business of Darrow and Sissman grew Darrow had found it expedient to enlarge the firm. He took in George Popham to help with the criminal work and William Holly to assist with the civil cases. Holly was young, intelligent, fine looking, sympathetic; Clarence came to love him almost as a son. "He is wise and kindly and dear to me," said Darrow. Holly went frequently with his chief to the Midway for dinner, where they spent "companionable evenings together, discussing the ignorance and inhumanity of the world, the men that they admired and approved, those whom they disagreed with and disliked."

He was not so fortunate in his choice of George Popham, who had been an assistant state's attorney and who was recommended to him by a member of his family. Popham had been in the office only a short time when he had forged a will for a woman client. The opposing attorney had called Sissman to tell him that the will was forged, but Sissman was unable to believe such a charge, nor did he want to bother Darrow with the accusation. When Darrow went into court "the scandal broke over the forged will, and Clarence was sick about it." Upon returning from court Popham called George Francis into his office, showed him a revolver in his desk drawer and said, "You have to testify in my behalf or I'll blow my brains out."

When Francis went to Darrow's office to report the scene to his chief Darrow barked, "You go back and tell Popham that's the best thing he can do but not to do it in the office; he's made enough mess around here."

"That's pretty hard, Mr Darrow," replied Francis. "I don't believe I can tell him that."

"You don't have to be afraid to tell him," grunted Darrow. "I've had a hundred in here threatening to do that; when they talk about it they never do it."

He once again was earning from twenty-five to thirty thousand dollars a year. Each summer he went to Greeley to vacation with Paul and his three granddaughters. His apartment on the Midway continued to be one of the most pleasant intellectual centers in Chicago; the Biology Club still met there once a week; nearly every evening saw Clarence surrounded by old and new friends with whom he would read and philosophize. Ruby took flawless care of him, too good care, Clarence complained, for often she was more like a nurse than a wife. She no longer permitted him to eat what he wanted or when he wanted; he had to eat what was good for him, though he might detest the stuff, and eat it at regular hours, though he might not be hungry. She told him what clothes he must wear, wher. he must change them, when he must take his medicine, when he must bathe, when he must rest, when he must sleep, when he must get up, which friends he could have around him and which he could not. There was rarely an instant spent in her company that he was free from her watchful eye, taking orders which were designed to protect his health and preserve his strength but which in effect distressed him, made him cranky and uneasy.

A man who loved personal freedom above all things, he began to grouse that he had no freedom in his own home. This had sent him off to Europe alone when England had invited him; led to his taking more business and lecture trips than perhaps were necessary. "You know how a hen is with one chick," he once growled when Ruby forced him at a big dinner party to drink some soup, for she was not as solicitous of his need for the illusion of independence. When William Carlin found him opening the office at eight o'clock in the morning instead of his usual eight-thirty he asked Mr Darrow why he had come down so early.

"Are you married, Willum?" asked Darrow.

"You know I am not, sir."

"Well, when you are you may be getting down earlier than this."

He understood that the confining influences arose from Ruby's love for him, from her tremendous and unused vitality, from her need to be important to him, to keep him healthy and alive; for the most part his grumbling was good natured and resigned. Their only serious trouble in thirty-three years of successful marriage arose over claim jumpers, for as Ruby had occasion to learn, American women did not always respect vested interests or property rights when it came to marriage or a desirable male. Age made little difference in Clarence Darrow; he never burned out: at thirty, forty, fifty, sixty and seventy women loved him. This was difficult for Ruby to endure, but what made it more difficult was that a number of them decided they would replace her, become the third and last Mrs Clarence Darrow. There had been one during the Los Angeles trials to add to her troubles, a clever and talented woman who was convinced that Clarence was misunderstood by his wife, or at least that Ruby undervalued him, and that she would make a far finer mate. She had caused Ruby hours of anguish, for Clarence was all she had in life; she had abandoned her journalism and other contacts, had made her husband her sole interest, and she loved him idolatrously; the thought of another woman cutting her out was wormwood and poison.

Now that Clarence was back on his feet, was again a celebrity, surrounded by crowds wherever he went, the claim jumpers again surged forward. When her husband was pursued by adoring women, as he often was, instead of enjoying the fact that she was Mrs Clarence Darrow, that she had the vantage position, that she had the man they apparently wanted, instead of being the queen of the roost, Ruby became racked with suspicions, fears, doubts, jealousies. Clarence found these suspicions and jealousies intolerable, though he was by no means completely innocent of bringing them on: he was not by nature a one-woman man; he enjoyed the company and especially the adoration of attractive women; he enjoyed matching wits against them, savoring of their female humor and logic; he liked feeding his ego with their admiration. Nor is it unthinkable that upon occasion he might have been above a little adultery.

One of the reasons he had married Ruby instead of X was that he had found unbearable X's incessant spying, observing, questioning and accusations. As Ruby, now unhappy and miserable with her fear of losing him to some scheming woman, wept and made scenes, he became angry, upset, off balance. He took more freedom from her than he actually wanted or needed, especially when she refused to invite to their home one of his friends of whom she had become suspicious. There were weeks of estrangement: Ruby wrung her hands; he was harsh in demanding that he be let alone, that he be granted some measure of independence, some slight illusion of freedom to come and go as he willed.

But the bad days passed, and the bad weeks. He had never loved anyone but Ruby since he had married her, had never entertained for an instant the thought of giving her up; he knew that she was as fine a woman as he could find, and he told her so. After a time she came to see that she had nothing serious to fear. She quieted; he quieted. He explained; she explained. She apologized; he apologized. And like most soundly based marriages, they went on their way together; their relationship had perhaps another dimension because it had been troubled, because they had made each other suffer, because they had understood and forgiven.

8

War years are bad ones for a man with a lust for justice. Even though the United States had not been attacked and was in no conceivable danger, the nation was caught in a paroxysm of fear which suspended all judgment and paralyzed the legal apparatus. Under the Espionage Act of 1917 and the Sedition Act of 1918 almost two thousand American citizens, including editors, clergymen, educators, had been sent to prison for terms of ten to twenty years for declaring that America did not belong in the war, for offering evidence that the manufacturers of war supplies were looting the public funds of billions of dollars, for suggesting improvement or change in governmental tactics, for criticizing an act of the Congress or a departmental bureau. Several thousand other native-born Americans were clubbed, horsewhipped, tarred and feathered, beaten with an iron cat-o'-nine-tails for declining to buy Liberty bonds or subscribe to the Red Cross, for challenging the operation of the draft, for promoting a World Peace League, for making "disloyal" comments in their own homes. Meetings of university students, of Bible students, of socialists, pacifists and irate farmers were broken up by enraged mobs of self-appointed "espionage agents." Judges and juries alike were caught up in the dementia, and the country suffered its most complete suspension of civil liberties since the War between the States.

Darrow had been convinced that it was necessary to advocate America's entry into the war; he had then been forced to observe in a state of agony and impotence the legal maelstrom which the war caused. In a country where "public officials and the press were encouraging the people to mob, whip, shoot, jail or kill all dissenters," where men and women were imprisoned without trial, defense was impossible even for a man who had made defense his lifework. He would have had to be not merely one pleader, but an army of pleaders, and then his multiple voice would not have been heard, for any attempt to defend the men and women accused of impeding the conduct of the war brought increased violence and bloodshed.

But cruel, senseless and oppressive as were these "gag laws," he had felt that they were the perhaps not unexpected pus sacs generated by a nation in the high fever of international conflict. When the war was over and peace had been declared, when "our boys had come home," the infections would slowly subside. What he had not been prepared for were the even more severe postwar hysterias which were to rack the country with a series of bitter prosecutions when the war between the nations gave way to a civil war between the classes. Against these latter excesses Darrow did not feel impotent, for they were waged on his field of battle, the public courtroom. Against them he raised his voice in some of the finest pleading of his age. Never was good pleading more sorely needed.

The success of the communist revolution in Russia had immediate and drastic repercussions in the United States. By 1919 the situation had developed on three fronts: American troops had been sent to Siberia to help the White Russians overthrow the Bolsheviki. The extremists among the American socialists had split off from their party to form the Communist Labor party with an avowal that "the present is the period of the dissolution and collapse of world capitalism; unless capitalism is replaced by the rule of the working class world civilization will collapse; the working class must organize and train itself for the capture of the world state; the Communist Labor party of the United States declares itself in full harmony with the revolutionary working-class parties of all countries and stands by the principle stated by the Third International formed at Moscow." Congress passed the Overthrow Act, which made it unlawful for any person "openly to advocate by word of mouth or writing the reformation or overthrow by violence or any other unlawful means of the representative form of government now secured to the citizens of the United States; to publish, issue or knowingly sell any book, paper, document or other written or printed matter which advocated crime and violence as a means of accomplishing the reformation or overthrow of the Constitution; to organize, aid in the organization of or become a member of any society or association, the object of which is to overthrow the government."

Small communist nuclei were formed in American cities. On November 29, 1918, William Bross Lloyd, son of Henry Demarest Lloyd, author of *Wealth against Commonwealth*, drove down State Street in Chicago, an American flag and a huge red flag flying from his car. A crowd gathered about his car, shouting, "Take that down!" Lloyd refused. A policeman tore down the red flag and hauled Lloyd off to jail. Asked why he also flew the American flag on his car, he replied that he did it as a matter of courtesy, that if he could not fly the red flag here he would go to Russia. A few weeks later, on January 12, 1919, he addressed a mass meeting at Convention Hall in Milwaukee. "Comrades," he said, "I am mighty glad you are all here but I am not so terribly proud of you at that. You have let a bunch of plutocrats and lawyers run this country instead of the workingman. What we want is preparedness. We want to organize so if you want every socialist in Milwaukee at a certain place at a certain time, with a rifle or a bad egg in his hand, he will be there. You want to get rifles, machine guns, field artillery and the ammunition for it; you want to get dynamite. Dynamite the doors of the banks to get the money for the revolution!"

Attorney General A. Mitchell Palmer, in charge of the enforcement of the Overthrow Act, cried, "Like a prairie fire, the blaze of revolution is sweeping over every American institution of law and order. It is eating its way into the homes of the American workman; its sharp tongues of revolutionary heat are licking the altars of the churches, leaping into the belfry of the school bell, crawling into the sacred corners of American homes, seeking to replace marriage vows with libertine laws, burning up the foundations of society. There can be no nice distinctions drawn between the theoretical ideas of the radicals and their actual violations of our national law. The government is in jeopardy!"

He then sent out his Department of Justice agents to perpetrate what Darrow felt to be one of the most sustained series of illegal acts ever authorized by a high government official. Thousands of innocent persons, most of them foreign-born, were rounded up in mass raids, blackjacked, knocked down, kicked, third-degreed and tortured, imprisoned without warrants, held for weeks and months incommunicado, without trials, their property destroyed, their jobs taken from them, their life in the New World shattered.

Clarence Darrow spent his days and nights rescuing bewildered, frightened men and women from prison cells. "My God," he cried, "these Palmer raids are as bad as the atrocities committed by the czar's Cheka. In suppressing this movement which Palmer alleges is about to overthrow the United States government by force and violence, our attorney general has himself very neatly managed to overthrow our form of government by force and violence. This reign of terror is the sort of thing that caused the Russian Revolution; if the American patriots and businessmen really want a bloody uprising in the United States, Attorney General Palmer and the Department of Justice have found the best possible means of achieving it."

It remained for the town of Rockford to afford him the opportunity to state legally the case for the revolutionist to the American people. When some of his stanchest supporters demanded to know how he could defend these indefensibles he uttered the credo on which his life had been built:

"I am defending this case for two reasons. The first is that I have seldom known a case where I believed so heartily that I am right. The second is because when I entered the practice of my profession years ago I determined that there never should be a case, however unpopular or whatever the feeling, that I would refuse to do my duty and defend that case; and I can honestly say that I have kept the faith; that I have never turned my back upon any defendant, no matter what the charge; when the cry is the loudest the defendant needs the lawyer most; when every man has turned against him the law provides that he should have a lawyer, one who can not only be his lawyer but his friend, and I have done that."

He and Ruby left for Rockwood, a factory town of sixty-five thousand people, ninety miles from Chicago, where they were made comfortable in the home of Fay Lewis. He found the community suffering from the same hysteria that he had encountered in Boise at the time of the Big Bill Haywood trial and in Los Angeles when he had arrived to defend the McNamara brothers. Men were meeting on the streets and exclaiming as they shook hands, "Well, now we'll be rid of these agitators for good. Very meritorious work on the part of the authorities. So they got the Reds! The damned traitors! We'll send them over the road."

Four Department of Justice agents had swooped down upon the home of Arthur Person, a glass beveler who had come from Sweden at the age of fifteen and who for twenty years had worked in Rockford factories. Person had three children, a wife who was ill, a home he was paying off on monthly installments, an interest in socialism and a score of friends who declared him to be honest, square, peaceable and law abiding. When the Communist Labor party was formed in Chicago Person was asked to join by Dr Oleson, an old-line Rockford socialist who had once been elected to public office in the city and who was attending Person's wife. Person was made secretary of a Rockford branch, held several open meetings in his home. When the raiding party invaded the house they found a collection of dusty socialist pamphlets in his attic, a membership list of seven persons, thirty cents in the treasury, a brown notebook with a notation of a six-dollar bill for a hall and a speaker, which they were unable to pay, and a red-colored pamphlet containing the Communist Labor party's platform. While being third-degreed by his captors in the automobile that was carrying him to jail Person admitted that "I believe in a government for the working people, of the working people."

When Darrow learned that an important part of the state's case against Person was to be based on this comment he exclaimed, "Why, that is almost the exact language Abraham Lincoln used! Lincoln would be under indictment here, too, if he were living now and could talk."

A number of other raids were committed until ten workingmen and the wife of a prominent businessman were lodged in the jail. Darrow had many friends among the liberals and socialists of Rockford; they turned to him at once for the defense.

The hostility against him was intense, but he gave no sign that he saw it or that it bothered him, any more than he had to the Saturday-night debate audiences in Kinsman. He went on his soft, kindly, persuasive way, using every device he could think of to buck up the town's frightened liberals so that he would have enough public opinion behind him to guarantee a fair trial. On the erstwhile liberal editor of the town paper, who was afraid that if he dared print material about the constitutional rights of the imprisoned he would lose his advertising, Darrow used an old-fashioned dodge: "I've been told that there are a few honest-to-God people in this town, but I was afraid that it might be another case of a town without a single outstanding man in it who understands what's going on in the world. It's a relief to know I'm wrong. Of course you and I know that these radicals have a lot to learn. Liberals like you and me, we're the only ones who have got the courage to let both sides to a controversy have their say. Well, old-fashioned liberals like us have got to see fair play in a case like this. We know what this country will be like if the owners of industry are going to be allowed to chuck everyone who disagrees with them into jail."

The state's attorney agreed to try Arthur Person only and let the result of this trial determine the fate of his fellow members. The charge was advocating the change and overthrow of the government, and he revolved his prosecution about the red-covered platform of the party, picking out such highly combustible words as "revolution," "conquest," "capture," "dictate," "overthrow," "mass action," "collapse of civilization," attempting to show that men who read and approved of such terms would not hesitate to use illegal methods to destroy the existing form of the American government. With the town of Rockford in attendance and a corps of reporters gathered to flash the news to all parts of the country, the state's attorney tried to prove that any criticism of the government was treachery to that government and must be punishable as such.

Darrow had tried to keep the red pamphlet out of the evidence, but the judge had admitted it. Now his answer was simple and direct; he told the state's attorney and the judge, the jury and the country at large, "If you want to get rid of every socialist, of every communist, of every trade unionist, of every agitator, there is one way to do it, and that is to cure the ills of society. You can't do it by building jails; you can't make jails big enough or penalties hard enough to cure discontent by strangling it to death. No revolution is possible, no great discontent is possible, unless down below it all is some underlying cause for this discontent; men are naturally obedient, too almighty obedient."

He would have liked to spend his time flaying the state of Illinois which had put a war-scare statute on its books. Yet there the statute was, and he must be careful lest Arthur Person and his comrades go to Joliet penitentiary: as always he reasoned that first he had to earn an acquittal for his client, after which he could attack the law.

An eyewitness tells that when the judge turned to the chief counsel for the defense "Darrow hitched himself to his feet, walked slowly across the narrow space that separated him from the railing of the raised platform on which the jury sat and looked at the twelve men in a keen and friendly way, not in the least like a man about to make a speech. They had all heard a great deal about him as a spellbinder who would so twist and turn the truth that the first thing they knew he'd be having them turned completely around. Now they were disarmed by his casual, informal manner, his way of looking at them over his glasses like a country schoolteacher. He had a voice better adapted to shouting than the state's attorney. It resounded threateningly through the room. Then he dropped it abruptly in humorous appreciation of his own histrionics and resumed his lazy confidential drawl, which the audience were obliged to strain to hear."

He built his defense upon his conviction that Arthur Person, the simple workingmen who were indicted with him and the thousands of workingmen throughout the country who had joined the Communist Labor party, thinking it to be a sort of reanimated Socialist party which might help them to get a little more wages, to get a little quicker redress of the workingman's grievances, did not and could not understand the implications of the confused language of the communist platform.

For Darrow the essence of the case was contained in his opening appeal. "What could we think of a jury who would deprive a man of his freedom because he does just what every other human being in the world is trying to do; tries to get enough of his fellow men to see things as he sees them, that he may change laws and institutions so that the workers will have a better chance? Now Person may be wild and crazy; I don't know. I am not here to try another man's views; I am not here for that, and neither are you. It may be that there isn't a single plank in that platform that I believe, and there may not be a single article of faith in the Lutheran Creed that I believe or in the Catholic Creed or any other creed ever made by man; but, gentlemen, unless I will stand for the right of every man on earth to accept his own religious faith and his own political creed and his own ideas, whether I believe in them or not, unless I will do that, I am a very poor American. I would be a very poor citizen and I would belong to that class of bigots who in almost every age have piled the fagots around their fellow men and burned them to cinders because of difference of faith."

He leaned heavily on sarcasm to pierce the prosecution's case. "The state's attorney is engaged in the common occupation of seeing red. These men are guilty because their platform is printed on red paper. The trouble with the officers in this case is that they would like to change the common blood until there would be no red-blooded men in America, no red-blooded men who would dare stand up in America. I don't know what malign and deadly influence can overhang a state's attorney's office that they can bring in an indictment like this. But I know that the enemies of this Republic are not the workingmen who give their lives and strength and their blood in the interests of wealth, these workers out of whose lives is spun the gold that makes the arrogance and the greed of America. I believe that since the world began the men who do the work have had much less than they should have, and I am glad to see an effort amongst the working people to get more. I wouldn't want to take that hope and inspiration from them, because when you take that away a man is dead."

When he had tried his first important case, that of Eugene Debs and the American Railway Union, he had evolved the technique of defense by offense. He found that this technique would serve him equally well in Rockford.

"I am engaged in the difficult task of trying to preserve a Constitution instead of destroying it, and I am seeking to save for the people of this country such liberties as they have left. It is hard for me to realize that men of power and some intellect would seek to terrorize men and women into obedience to their opinions. We wiggled along for a hundred and fifty years without this Espionage Law, and we did pretty well. Where did it come from? It came from the people who would strangle criticism; it came from the people who would place their limits upon your brain and mine, and if we give them their way in this world, every man, if he would be safe, should wear a padlock on his lips and only take it off to feed himself and lock it up after he gets through. No man would dare speak above a whisper; no man would feel himself safe to belong to an organization, whether it was for American freedom, Russian freedom, Irish freedom or any freedom, because the word 'freedom' is the most dangerous word that the English language knows. The time will come very soon when America will be ashamed of her cowardly attempt to send men to jail under laws of this kind; ashamed of the suppression of freedom of thought and freedom of speech which is making a madhouse of a once-free land."

It had been his hope that the American way of life would prove that the employer and the employed might work together in com-

mon trust and common prosperity, that there was no need for so
rich and resourceful a country ever to be ravaged by class war.
Yet as he continued to work against the bitterness and hatred of
the Rockford prosecution he was forced to acknowledge that the
proceeding was a manifestation of class war. With all his strength
and persuasiveness he yearned to prove that this was class war, to
show the people that they deluded themselves and perpetuated the
war by calling it other and false names and that once they had
recognized that this was class war they would understand that
they must declare a truce, that they must grant a just peace, that
they must make permanent a fair distribution of wealth to keep
either side from destroying the other.

"The danger to this country is not from the workingman," he
repeated over and over. "It is from those who worship no God but
greed; it is from those who are so blind and devoted to their idol
of gold that they would destroy the Constitution of the United
States, would destroy freedom of speech and the freedom of the
press. That would paralyze the human brain; that would awe the
human mind; that would threaten with jail and imprisonment every
man who dares think, who dares hope, and I trust there will never
come to me a time in my life, no matter what the reward might
be, when I will hesitate to lend such strength and such courage and
such power as nature gave me to the defense of the weak or the
poor, of those who spin in darkness that other men may be clothed.

"Gentlemen, it is wonderful, the power of greed; I have fought
this battle for many years in my own way; I have tried to do it
kindly. I have never condemned the individual man. I recognize
that the captains of industry are made of the same stuff that I am.
I know that this mad fever has possession of them and they brook
nothing that stands between them and their gold. I know that they
would destroy liberty that property might live.

"The world has just been through a great war. The world has
been crazy, all of us. I hate to think that we went through it all
for nothing. I have been one of those dreamers who has felt that
from the fire and the smoke and the ashes of the battlefield of
Europe there might arise a fairer, a better, a juster civilization than
this world has ever known; that out of the infinite sufferings of
the human race men might grow kinder and more humane and give
a better chance to the common man. I have still not lost faith that
the poor and oppressed all over the earth will have a chance to
try and better their conditions. But money, wealth, greedily as ever,
learning nothing by all the sorrow of the world, said, 'No, all of our
privileges must remain; nothing shall be gained by the war for all

the blood that has been shed, and whenever a man dares to raise his voice for new conditions or for a better world we will send him to jail.'

"Arthur Person is obscure; he is unknown; he is poor; he has worked all his life, but his case is one that reaches down to the foundation of your freedom and mine. If twelve men should say that they could take a man like him and send him to prison and destroy his home, a man who is guiltless of crime and whose only stain is that he loved his fellow men; if twelve men like you should say that they would take him from his home and send him to Joliet and confine him behind prison walls, you should hang this court-house in crape and drape your city hall with black and wear sack-cloth and ashes until his term expires."

The jury apparently had no desire to wear sackcloth and ashes: they brought in a verdict of not guilty, though it was never made clear whether Person was innocent of intending to overthrow the government by force and violence, of knowing what the Commu-nist Labor party platform was all about, of transgressing against a law which had no right to be on the statute books of a democracy.

Darrow was elated because he imagined that in the Arthur Person victory he had dealt a deathblow to Attorney General Palmer, established a precedent which would throw out indictments held over the heads of other victims of the Department of Justice raids.

His optimism was short lived: he was summoned to return at once to Chicago to defend the sixteen communists who had been arrested with William Bross Lloyd.

9

He saw at once that this case went beyond the problem of the workingman who did not understand the implications of com-munism, for the Chicago clique was composed of native-born Americans, well educated, several of them with wealth and social position. William Bross Lloyd's father, Henry Demarest, had married a daughter of the McCormicks, but he and his wife and children had been dispossessed by his father-in-law because he had worked for the pardoning of the Haymarket anarchists. Apparently the grandfather had relented, for "the record shows that William Bross Lloyd is a man with considerable property and that he regu-larly employs a manager for his estate and financial matters. He maintains an office and an office force in the Tribune Building in Chicago. He is surrounded with luxuries in his home in Win-netka."

The Chicago group was made up largely of intellectuals, men

who did not work with their hands for a living but who were in the forefront of the radical movement, trying to give it the voice and expression which they decided the uneducated working-man could not find. Despite the fact that they had repudiated control from Moscow by refusing to join with the Russian Communist party, their members looked constantly to Russia for their ideology and direction. It was intellectuals like William Bross Lloyd who organized the Communist Labor party in America, who financed it, directed it, wrote its literature and attempted to convert to its economic philosophy the mass of American working people. This was to be a case of the agitator, the organizer, rather than the workingman. Unlike Person and the Rockford workingmen, Lloyd and his fellows had openly called for the use of force and dynamite.

So vociferous had been the street meetings held by his Chicago clients that the charge against them was "conspiracy to overthrow the government." It would not be sufficient for him to point out that although these men had advocated force they never actually committed an act of force; that they had been guilty only of the crime of talk; that once they used force or dynamite their action would violate the criminal code and the perpetrators then could be dealt with; that it was implicit in the character of a democracy that it had to be patient, put up with harsh and antagonistic words; that in cases of this nature the jingle, "Sticks and stones may break my bones, but words will never hurt me," was particularly true; that the structure of American life was not so weak that it could be blown down by the first gust of wind. No; the Overthrow Act had made it possible for his clients to be arrested and imprisoned before they had performed an act of violence, and the state's attorney had only to prove that any one of the group had an "intent" to overthrow the government, and the entire local would go to prison.

Upon what basis then was he to make his defense, his plea for tolerance? He could base it only upon the principle that these citizens had a right to preach the overthrow of their own government because the Constitution guaranteed them the freedoms of speech, press and assembly and that these rights were implicit in a democracy. He would admit to the court that his clients well knew what they were doing but that they had a right to heresy, economic and political as well as religious. He knew that such a defense not only would be courageous, but foolhardy. But if he could achieve an acquittal on the solid basis of American revolutionary precedent, there could be no further prosecutions.

Once again he was to play the role of the thorn in the side.

When the prosecution argued that it was men like Lloyd and his associates who had been responsible for the bloodshed and destruction of the Russian Revolution he defended that revolution by portraying vividly the czarist oppressions and barbarous cruelties during the centuries preceding the uprising. "Russia has been the last word in tyranny in Europe for more than a thousand years, a government of despotism tempered by assassination, where all the brave and the liberty-loving people have been killed or sent to Siberia." When the prosecution accused his men of scheming to achieve their ends by means other than the ballot he defended the right to collective action outside the polls. When the prosecution charged that his clients were attacking the Constitution he quoted from Charles A. Beard's *Economic Interpretation of the Constitution* to show how the Constitution had originally been drawn to protect property rights above personal rights and had constantly to be amended to include such personal rights as would enable a republic to function.

His name and character had been reviled, yet all that had gone before was but a gentle zephyr compared with the tornado that was unleashed when Clarence Darrow defended the right of the working people to take control of their own country. As always throughout his career, he was accused of believing in and advocating the theories of the people he was defending. Few would believe him when he said that he was merely acting as a mechanism of defense.

"Why should not the workingman make a conquest of the power of the state?" he asked. "No organization could believe in the conquest of the power of the state unless it believed in the state. Is there any more reason why the workingman should not make the conquest of the state than any other part of society? Every political party in America is trying to do it and are doing it. The Republican party is now very busy making the conquest of the power of the state and doing everything it can think of that they may make the conquest of power. My clients' policy is just like the policy of everyone else, excepting this, they think they would use it for the benefit of the workingman. Perhaps even if these men did make the conquest of the power of the state their dreams would not come true; I cannot tell, but they have a right to try; they have a right to think; they have a right to proselyte; they have the right to their opinion and to make their opinion heard. This is what I plead for, and I am not interested in whether their opinions are right or wrong. If they are wrong the American people under free discussion can find the wrong, and if by any chance these opinions shall convert the United States, then the United States needs converting.

"I do not know whether socialism or communism will work or not. I do know that the present system does not work; that it is a crazy quilt that allows no man to be really honest, that allows no man to be unselfish, that allows no man to live without sacrificing his fellow man. I know that it makes men greedy and selfish and mean. I know that it stifles every good motive in man. I know that under the present system no one on earth can be as good as he would be. I know that capitalism does not work and never can work.

"Gentlemen, I cannot tell whether this scheme will work, but it is what they believe. They have the same right to their belief under the laws of this country as you have to yours, and all of you told me over and over again that you would protect the right of another man the same as you would protect your own rights.

"I know that freedom produces wealth, and then wealth destroys freedom. I know that the nation that is not watchful of its liberty will lose it. I know that the individual that will not stand for his rights will have no rights, and I believe the first duty of every American citizen is to protect himself and his country in all the liberties we have and all that we can get.

"You can only protect your liberties in this world by protecting the other man's freedom. You can only be free if I am free. The same thing that would get me may be used to get you, and the government that is not strong enough to protect all its citizens ought not to live upon the face of this earth."

It was a good speech, as Darrow would have said. It reverberated around the world. Always juries had gone with him, but this time he had gone too far. In order to accept his philosophy they would have had to undergo a revolution in their own minds which would have been more radical than the one advocated by William Bross Lloyd and his fellow radicals. It was impossible for them to make any final decision in this issue; they sentenced all sixteen of his clients to the penitentiary for one- to two-year terms, a comparatively light sentence, considering the rights that Darrow had demanded for them. Some of his friends were astonished that the jury did not turn around and ask for an indictment of counsel for the defense.

He appealed the case to the Illinois Supreme Court, which upheld the decision of the lower court. This made Darrow a little sad. However, he was cheered by the lone dissenting voice of Justice Carter, who insisted upon writing into the record, "Under the constitution of 1870, governing freedom of speech, this Overthrow Statute of 1919 should be considered so vague and general and so clearly against the American doctrine of freedom of speech as to be held unconstitutional."

As Darrow had commented when a single justice of the United States Supreme Court had ruled against the kidnaping of Moyer, Haywood and Pettibone, "There is always one man to state the case for freedom. That's all we need, one."

CHAPTER XI

Even the Rich Have Rights!

THE DARROWS were fast asleep in the early-morning hours of June 2, 1924, when they were startled "by a frightening ringing of the front doorbell, as though the place were afire."

"I hastened out of bed," says Mrs Darrow, "and while I sped through the long hall to the front of the apartment the bell kept ringing frantically. When I threw open the front door I found myself confronted by four men who seemed like masked desperados, clutching at their upturned coat collars. They forced themselves forward and demanded, 'We've got to see Clarence Darrow! Is he here?'

"'Mr Darrow is asleep. He isn't well—he should not be disturbed.'"

The four men insisted upon seeing Darrow and dashed into his bedroom. The leader of the group, Richard Loeb's uncle, flung his arms about Darrow's shoulders, exclaiming, "Thank heavens you are here! No one else can save us. If you had been away we would have been ruined. You must save our two boys!"

Darrow had known the Loeb family for many years; he had watched the arrest of Richard Loeb and Nathan Leopold, Jr, for the murder of fourteen-year-old Robert Franks with sickened amazement. "But they are not guilty. You have your nephews, the Bachrach brothers, defending them; their innocence should not be difficult to prove."

"No, no!" cried the uncle, distraught. "Dickie and Babe confessed this afternoon."

Darrow pulled himself up slowly in the big brass bed, unable for the moment to believe that the two boys, both sons of million-aires, brilliant students who had been the youngest to be graduated from the Universities of Michigan and Chicago, could have com-mitted the shocking murder. The grief-stricken faces of the four men who surrounded his bed told him that the story was true. After a long moment of silence he murmured hoarsely, "Then what can I do?"

"Save their lives! Get them a life sentence instead of a death sentence. That's all we ask of you."

"That's all you ask," whispered the sixty-seven-year-old attorney, more to himself than to his intruders. "Millions of people will demand their deaths, and all you ask is that I save their lives."

Loeb fell on his knees beside the bed. "But you will do it!" he cried. "Money's no object. We'll pay you anything you ask. Only for God's sake, don't let them be hung. You have saved a hundred others. Why won't you save them?"

Darrow sat propped against the brass rungs, his eyes closed, his big head sunk on his chest, remembering an incident that had happened only a few nights before. He had been lecturing on the inequalities of the law when a young radical had popped out with, "Mr Darrow, since the capitalist law is designed to protect the rich and privileged, don't you think you have wasted your forty-five years in the courts?"

"Why don't you ask the hundred and two men whose lives I have saved?" queried Darrow succinctly.

Therein, despite his advancing years, the rheumatism and neu-ralgia that were harassing him, his fatigue, disillusion and pessimism over mankind's ability ever to raise itself from its animal heritage and create a peaceful and brotherly order, lay his compensation: he had saved one hundred and two lives, kept one hundred and two human beings from being executed by the state.

He had fought for many causes in his day, some more tenable and worthy than others, but his great and permanent crusade had been against capital punishment. Always he had worked with the idea in mind that if he could set a movement on foot which would one day, in some distant century, put an end to legalized killings, his efforts and hardships and sufferings and abuse would have been worth while. Not so long ago in England more than a hundred crimes, many of them minor, had been punishable by death; in the early days of America many offenses, including witchcraft, had been punishable by death. Now only one crime remained which evoked this vestigial relic of barbarism.

All killings by the state were murder in the first degree. Since one could not reform an offender by executing him they were acts of revenge. His half century in the courts had convinced him that, like all acts of revenge, the executions did not act as a deterrent to further killings, but instead tended to cheapen human life, break down the barriers of its indestructibility at the hands of man.

"Everyone who advocates capital punishment is really ashamed of the practice for which he is responsible. Instead of urging public executions, the most advanced and sensitive who believe in killing by the state are now advocating that even the newspapers should not publish the details and that the killing should be done in darkness and silence. In that event no one would be deterred by the cruelty of the state. If men regarded the murderer as one who acted from some all-sufficient cause and who was simply an instrument in an endless sequence of cause and effect, would anyone say he should be put to death?"

It was assumed by many that killers must be executed for fear that they might one day, twenty or thirty years later, be pardoned. So much the better, thought Darrow; let the following generation re-evaluate the crime, come to judge it in the light of deeper scientific knowledge, of greater understanding. When the fear and the hatred and the hysteria engendered by the crime had passed, subsequent doctors, judges and juries might be able to look upon the killer as a man who had acted from a complex set of impulses, over few of which he had any control. Giving the succeeding generations the right of review could only breed mercy; could the quality of mercy injure a social organism?

Could he defend Loeb and Leopold for this murder? Would he not once again bring down on his head the wrath of the mob, the hatred and vituperation of the pack? Would he not once again be called an anarchist, an enemy of society, a chaos breeder? He knew what a hue and cry would be raised over any defense; the public was too wrought up and frightened by the ghoulishness of the murder to draw the fine distinction between a defense of the crime and a defense of the hapless ones who had perpetrated it. He knew that once again he would be running alone, against the field.

He was getting tired; did he wish to plunge into the midst of another bloody and vituperative maelstrom, one which would rob him of his little energy? Could he again endure the hatreds, the abuse, the ostracism, that must inevitably result? He was no longer a sixteen-year-old-boy in Kinsman debating with the light of battle in his eye; he was rapidly approaching threescore and ten. He had endured the bitterness and revilement of the crowd as much as any public figure of his day. Did he have the strength and courage to take still another beating?

Yet how could he stand aside while nineteen-year-old Nathan Leopold, Jr, and eighteen-year-old Richard Loeb were executed by the state? Could he abandon his fight against capital punishment merely because these particular defendants might appear indefensible? How could one set of human beings justify taking another human being's life?

If he could convince the public that Loeb and Leopold were two defective human machines which had somewhere broken down because of heredity or the pressure of external environment, if he could save their lives when all the world wanted them exterminated, might not he deal a deathblow to capital punishment? While the state was trying Loeb and Leopold he could try capital punishment. His book, *Crime, Its Cause and Treatment*, which he had recently published, had been neglected and unread, but if he defended Loeb and Leopold he would have the ears of the world; he could teach its inhabitants everything that was in his book. Perhaps it was fateful that this symptomatic case had come along while he was still alive, for in it he could recapitulate his teachings, state the complete and ultimate case for the abolition of capital punishment, for a saner, more just, more scientific treatment of the criminal.

Crime, Its Cause and Treatment was the most valuable and revolutionary book he had yet written; in it he had stated the essence of his belief: the machine that is every man is completely formed by the time it slips from its mother's womb, but once its inherent boundaries had been proscribed, the actual fate or pattern of this human machine was determined by the circumstances in which it found itself set up in the external world. Under this philosophy there was no room for free will: a man acted according to the equipment with which he had been endowed and in accordance with the surroundings into which he had been plunged. If, then, there was no free will, there could be no praise or blame; no man was alone responsible for his acts: his ancestors were responsible, and the state of society in which he lived was responsible, and to punish a man for having a brain, a spirit, a character, a set of action impulses that had been determined for him by powers beyond his control, was stupid, wasteful, cruel and barbaric. The papers were screaming that there was absolutely no reason for this fiendish murder by Loeb and Leopold, that it could be traced to no intelligible causes. Yet Darrow knew that there were thousands of tiny and intricate reasons behind the crime, all of them woven into the character and environment of the killers, and that the causes would be intelligible once the world could be made to understand all of the contributing factors that had made these two human machines go haywire.

Crime, Its Cause and Treatment had once again caused him to be accused of criminal anarchism on the grounds that he had apologized for the criminal, justified him by a mechanistic philosophy of life. It was this philosophy with which he had defended thousands of human beings. It was the philosophy with which he would defend Richard Loeb and Nathan Leopold.

For this decision, made in the dead of night by an old and tired and disillusioned man, young Leopold was to write to him with a scrawling pencil across cheap note paper, "Is it courage for a man who, after forty-six years of untiring effort, had built up one of the greatest reputations for forensic ability to stake that entire reputation upon a seemingly impossible case? Suppose that man has defended countless murderers against overwhelming odds and has never suffered a hanging verdict. Suppose further that he is sixty-seven years old and that during an energetic life, devoted always to the weaker side, the poor and the friendless, suppose this man has accumulated sufficient means for all his needs and has built a 'monument more enduring than brass.' Now this man jeopardizes a reputation of fifty years' standing and risks it upon a seemingly impossible case. It is a case which has been heralded far and wide and which has been decided by the unreasoning mob long before it reached a court of law! Why does he do it? He does it for the sake of his principles. Is this bravery? By God, if it isn't, then the definition of bravery ought to be revised. Nay, it is more than bravery; it is heroism."

Darrow climbed wearily out of bed, dressed, went downstairs with the four men, entered the Loeb limousine and headed for the county jail.

2

He sat quietly in the back seat while the four men talked explosively at him. He was not listening to them; he was listening to his own voices reminding him that he had always emphasized poverty as the cause of crime.

Nathan F. Leopold, Jr, and Richard A. Loeb had been raised in the fashionable South Shore section of Chicago. Leopold's father was a retired millionaire box manufacturer, while Loeb's father was the multimillionaire vice-president of Sears, Roebuck and Company. The Loeb estate at Charlevoix, Michigan, was set in the midst of hundreds of acres of magnificently wooded country. The two boys were raised amidst great wealth from their early childhood, with governesses, chauffeurs and the soft, luxurious appurtenances that can be bought by millionaires. Loeb had an allowance of two hundred and fifty dollars a month, with three thousand dollars in the bank under his own name and a standing order from his father to the family secretary that "Dickie" was to be given a check for any sum of money at any time without question. Though Leopold was given only half as large a monthly allowance, he had the family chauffeur to drive him, his own car, charge accounts in the big stores and could have any amount of money for which he asked.

Darrow knew the adage, "You can't convict a million dollars." That was what people would be saying over their breakfast tables in the morning. And would not the public be entitled to say if he undertook the defense, "That old rascal, Clarence Darrow! When his clients are poor he cries about poverty to get them off, blames society and the state and the economic structure. But just let him get a chance to earn a whopping fee by defending millionaires and watch how fast he forgets about crime as a result of poverty." Would he not be giving himself the lie, controverting the good work he and his predecessor, John P. Altgeld, had accomplished in teaching the world about the economic base of crime?

Yet as the car sped through the darkness along the lake and Darrow began listening to the men beside him who were attempting to explain the crime in terms of the boys' backgrounds, he realized that this crime not only sustained his theories of criminology but gave them another dimension. Excessive wealth had been the real protagonist in this murder; the same accumulation of money had corrupted Loeb and Leopold that had corrupted by its unavailability the young boys of the Chicago slums who had gone wrong. The Loeb-Leopold murder was the reverse of the shield.

Nathan Leopold, Jr, was the more interesting and brilliant of the two boys; the numerous illnesses in his psyche were largely responsible for the murder of Robert Franks, even though Loeb was the one who desired, planned and executed the killing. Young Leopold was adored by his parents, who called him "Babe." In turn the boy worshiped his mother, whom he called "my sainted mother." From earliest childhood he had been hypersensitive: the barest affront or imagined slight was enough to wound him deeply, cause him mental anguish. Abnormally shy of girls, his parents sought to correct this lack of poise by sending him to a girls' school in charge of his governess, who took him there every morning and brought him home every afternoon. The ignominy of being the only boy in a girls' school turned him the more against the opposite sex, created psychic wounds from which he never fully recovered.

Young Leopold was suffering from glandular irregularities and disorders which were having an effect not only upon his body but upon his mind, that group word for the interfunctions of the brain, the nervous system and the glandular structure that go to make up a complete being. Medical examinations showed that he had had an overactive and diseased thyroid which led to an early sex development. The doctors also found that he had a disorder of the nervous control of the blood vessels, that he suffered from a retrogression of the pineal glands, which had already calcified at the age of nineteen, and that he suffered from an adrenal insufficiency.

This glandular composition inevitably had its effect on Leopold's appearance and consequently on his attitude toward the world. He was small in stature, had prominent eyes, coarse hair, was round-shouldered, flat-footed, with a protuberant abdomen. The glandular disturbances which caused him to suffer from blood disorders, muscular fatigue, low temperature, low blood pressure, low metabolism and anemia depressed him, made him moody as his energy waxed and waned, made him the victim of physical afflictions or inadequacies which determined his personality. These inadequacies, coupled with the fact that he judged himself physically unattractive, gave him a severe inferiority complex, an inferiority complex which made him an easy victim to a superiority complex engendered by his father's great wealth. His father had taught him and demonstrated to him that wealth controls the world, that anything he desired could be bought. When he wanted to hunt birds in the park and it was out of season his father's wealth had secured him a special permit; when he was caught fishing out of season his father not only paid the fines but replaced the equipment that had been taken from Leopold and his friends. Neither the father nor the mother made any attempt to teach the boy that his wealth involved responsibilities and obligations to the society that had created it. On the contrary, they showed him by example that through his wealth he was superior to all other people, that he was not bound by the same laws that bound the herd. Young Leopold grew up with the idea that he was beyond responsibility because he was beyond the need to earn money, that all his life he could do precisely what he wished because he would always have the money with which to buy that wish.

Thus he suffered constantly from the conflict between his physical heritage and the environment into which he had been born:

nis physical inheritance brought him pathological inferiority; his environment brought him pathological superiority. From his earliest childhood the boy was a schizophrenic, caught between the blades of his complexes, his conduct pattern never able to be whole or unified because it was constantly cut to shreds by the incessantly working blades of the giant scissors. The youngster did not know why he was constantly churned and torn, why he was so introspective, why he shunned people and preferred to be by himself.

The outstanding characteristic of Nathan Leopold, the one which overshadowed everything else, was his precocity. By the age of eighteen he had completed his course at the University of Chicago, the youngest ever to be graduated from that institution. In addition to the brilliant work he did in class he was widely read in philosophy, metaphysics, literature and science; he read for the pleasure of learning, was able to retain and correlate astounding amounts of these mature and difficult subjects. He was an expert ornithologist, made frequent trips into the country in pursuit of specimens, had a first-rate amateur museum in his home, wrote papers on the subject and was highly thought of by professionals in the field.

This precocity was also a manifestation of the nerve and glandular structure which determined his physical aspect. For the practical purposes of making his life a happy one, his precocity had done him more harm than good: in the lower grades the children had shunned him as the white-headed boy and teacher's pet, while later in his college years he was too much younger than his fellows to form friendships on the basis of equality. He was never popular; he was never well liked; he had almost no friends. This failure of other young people to like him caused him profound agony, an agony so intolerable that he decided to defeat it by escape, escape from the external world into the realms of the intellect where he could be a master, where he would no longer have feelings, where he would be safe from slights, hurts and emotional pains. The death of his mother increased the intensity of this resolve; further, it turned him against God and religion for taking away so needlessly and senselessly the good woman whom he had loved above all others.

By the time he was fourteen he encountered the superman philosophy of Nietzsche. Equipped to understand this philosophy intellectually, while at the same time too immature to digest or grasp its social implications, young Leopold garnered the idea that there were some few men born who were so much wiser and more gifted than all other men that they could rule the world. Everything they did was right for the reason that they had chosen to do it;

they need have no thought or consideration for the feelings of others, for the lower breeds of humans had been put upon the earth merely for the superman to lead and do with what he would. This philosophy gave direction to his escape: behind its golden portals he could shut out the manifold agonies of maladjusted youth, conquer his inferiority complex and find surcease from his introversion.

At that moment there was introduced into the Leopold household a governess who committed sexual malpractices on the boy, taught him also to commit sexual malpractices of a cunilingual nature. Several years of exposure to this perversion made any approach to a normal sexual relationship extremely difficult, completed Nathan's maladjustment. Nathan Leopold, Jr, developed an obsession which was the bastard offspring of a coalescing of his father's great wealth, the disturbance of his endocrine glands (one of which may have been pouring an abundance of female secretions into his blood stream), the Nietzschean philosophy and his exposure to the governess. He did not want to become a superman at all; he wanted to become a superwoman, a superwife, the female slave of the superman above him, a voluntary and joyous slave who served out of the overwhelming love which he bore for the superman.

"He became obsessed with the idea of becoming a slave to some big, handsome, powerful king. He would be the abject one who would carry out the orders of the ruler and, if necessary, bear punishment in his stead."

In this state of mind he met Richard Loeb, tall, athletically built, with a beautiful face, alert, sparkling eyes, a brilliant mind, a hard ego and an indomitable will. Young Leopold had found his superman; he fell in love.

In speaking of his worship for Loeb, young Leopold said, "I can illustrate it to you by saying that I felt myself less than the dust beneath his feet. I am jealous of the food and drink that he takes because I cannot come as close to him as does the food and drink."

Babe, who never performed sexual acts with any other boy, implored Dickie Loeb to have relations with him. Loeb, who had been seeking eagerly for several years for a crony who would carry out his orders in committing crimes, decided that he had found the perfect mate in Leopold to help him plan and execute these crimes. He agreed to a homosexual relationship with Leopold, if Leopold would agree to a crime relationship with him. Leopold consented unquestioningly, and the compact was formed.

3

Richard Loeb was a good-looking boy; the defense physicians had been able to find nothing wrong with him, yet his fraternity brothers reported seeing him faint as many as three times while at school. In spite of his father's millions, the numerous cars, the huge gymnasium at Charlevoix, the horses, the boats, the woods and lakes, the countless servants, Dickie Loeb also had had an unhappy childhood. He frequently thought of suicide and seemed to have a will toward self-destruction. The causes may have arisen from the normally painful process of coming through adolescence, the religious differences of his parents, from the same nervous disturbance which caused the fainting spells, from the dislocative effect of great wealth upon an emotionally unstable child.

Loeb, too, blamed his downfall upon a governess, under whose control he remained for a number of years. Miss S. was an intelligent woman and a strict disciplinarian who loved young Dickie and wanted to make of him a fine, disciplined and well-educated man. She kept him long hours at his studies, was ever vigilant, made him read books in which he had no interest. Young Dickie liked to read cowboy stories and detective stories, was irked by the routine of duty imposed upon him. A bright and resourceful lad, he soon found that the easiest way to avoid the work was not to come into conflict with his governess over it but to trick her into thinking that the work had been done. He lied; he cheated; he dissembled; he deceived. Always he was clever enough to get away with it. This brought him double pleasure, for now he not only could indulge in his omnivorous reading of crime stories, but he could also congratulate himself on his cleverness. As the years passed he grew to enjoy deception for its own sake, ever sought for newer and more ingenious methods of achieving an object while concealing his intent. The boy had such a beautiful manner, seemed so honest and frank and open and lovable to those who met him, that they would not have believed him capable of duplicity. The youngster got such a thrill out of fooling people that he soon was telling lies, cheating and deceiving solely for the pleasure of the accomplishment.

Dickie, like Leopold, had a brilliant and retentive mind. He was graduated from the University of Michigan at seventeen, the youngest to be graduated. However, by the time he had reached college his psychotic personality was already well developed. One of his fraternity brothers tells of him, "Loeb spoke in a jerky manner, would argue on valueless points, pop into a room instead of walking in, smoke rapidly and nervously, then pop out again. He was regarded as childish. It was my duty to appoint seniors as mentors for freshmen, but I did not appoint Loeb because his judgment and conduct were not considered sufficiently wise to guide a freshman." While at the University of Michigan Loeb amused himself by pilfering from his fraternity brothers; he always enjoyed a theft the more if he could watch the victim's discomfort.

For several years before he met Leopold he had been reading almost nothing but crime stories; he had become obsessed with the idea that he could become a master criminal. This phantasm was in part developed to combat the influence of his suicidal tendencies, but more, was the result of the overwhelming wealth of the Loebs which engendered in Dickie the feeling that he was already a master because a millionaire, that the rules which applied to ordinary people did not apply to him. He believed himself so brilliant that he could never make a mistake in committing a crime, hence could never be caught; even if he were caught, his father's millions could buy him off.

Leopold was fourteen and Loeb thirteen when they entered their pact; for the next four years they contented themselves with such minor crimes as breaking windshields, starting small fires and petty thefts, such as a typewriter from Loeb's fraternity at Ann Arbor. All the while they were reading about crime and laying various plans for the commission of the perfect crime. Their relationship was a stormy one; both boys threatened to kill the other on numerous occasions. Although Leopold looked up to Loeb as the king and superman, he was actually the stronger of the two, just as the adoring wife is often the stronger in a marriage. He was stronger, more brilliant and far more psychotic. Darrow realized the extent of his psychopathy when he read a letter written by Leopold to Loeb when Leopold was only seventeen.

"When you came to my home this afternoon I expected either to break friendship with you or attempt to kill you unless you told me why you acted as you did yesterday. I am going to add a little more in an effort to explain my system of a Nietzschean philosophy with regard to you. It may not have occurred to you why a mere mistake in judgment on your part should be treated as a crime, when on the part of another it should not be so considered. Here are the reasons. In formulating a superman, he is, on account of certain superior qualities inherent in him, exempted from the ordinary laws which govern ordinary men. He is not liable for anything he may do, except for the one crime that it is possible for him to commit—to make a mistake. Now obviously any code which conferred upon an individual privileges without also putting on him extraordinary responsibility would be unfair and bad. Therefore, an *Übermensch* is held to have committed a crime every time he errs in judgment—a mistake excusable in others."

In the spring of 1924 Loeb and Leopold were idle and looking for amusement. Leopold had passed his entrance examinations for the law school at Harvard, which he was planning to enter in the fall after he returned from a tour of Europe. Loeb was also planning to enter a law school in the fall. Both boys sensed that they were reaching the end of their relationship. Loeb, dissatisfied with the petty crimes of arson and thievery, longed to commit the great crime of the age, one which would go down in history as the perfect crime. Leopold had no desire to commit a murder, but for four years the boys had been pointing toward their perfect crime, discussing and planning it, day in and day out, until it was too late for him to withdraw.

That was why Bobby Franks lay in the morgue with his head bashed in; that was why Loeb and Leopold were behind prison bars; that was why Clarence Darrow was now speeding through the dark streets of Chicago at three in the morning.

4

The jailor flatly refused to allow Darrow to see the boys. "I have my orders from State's Attorney Crowe," he said. "No one is to talk to them."

All attempts to secure permission from Crowe over the telephone being futile, there was nothing for Clarence to do but wait for morning. The five men climbed back into the car and drove to his office. Here Loeb's uncle wrote out a check for ten thousand dollars, the first act in a tragicomedy which was to alienate large portions of the public from Darrow and cause greater misunderstanding of his philosophy and intent than any single factor in his stormy career.

Before nine in the morning Darrow was at State's Attorney Crowe's office, demanding that the two boys be bound over to the sheriff and sent to the county jail, where they would be free to confer with their relatives and attorneys. Up to this time Crowe had been holding them as his personal prisoners in a room in the Hotel La Salle and in the city jail, where his psychiatrists were examining them in an effort to secure evidence on their sanity. Crowe refused to release the boys. Darrow haled him before Judge Caverly to fight it out.

"I realize these boys have rights," said Crowe, "and if the court will give me until two o'clock I will turn them over to their families and attorneys for as long a conference as they want."

"Now there's an extraordinary statement," exclaimed Darrow. "These boys are minors; they have rights."

"A cold-blooded, vicious murder has been committed," retorted Crowe, "and these boys have confessed to it."

"Another most astounding statement," said Darrow. "It matters not how cold-blooded the murder was; there is but one place for them to be held, in the county jail, in the custody of the sheriff. That question is not debatable, and the matter of an indictment has nothing to do with it."

Judge Caverly agreed with him, ordered the boys to be taken at once to the county jail. Within the hour Darrow was closeted with his two young clients, both of whom were immensely pleased and flattered to have defending them America's leading criminal lawyer. Loeb said to him, "Mr Darrow, your slightest wish will be law to me." Leopold said, "Anyone, Mr Darrow, who had the slightest grain of intelligence could not help but be impressed, almost overpowered, by the unfathomable depth of your own intellect. This one attribute of man has always appealed to me more strongly than any other, and since you happen to possess more of it than any other man whom I have had the pleasure of meeting, this alone would cause me to bow down in abject hero worship. It would be an inconsistent 'superman' indeed who did not reverence his superior."

Darrow saw that his first task would be to bring the two boys together again, for no sooner had they been caught than they had begun quarreling. Though the police had seen at once that Leopold was the softer of the two, they had also concluded that Loeb was the weaker. Though both boys had been grilled incessantly for twenty-four hours Leopold had kept up his high spirits and brightness of reply. Loeb had fainted, broken down and confessed. When Leopold learned that his king, his superman, his adored husband, had confessed, he exclaimed in disgust, "Tell Loeb I am surprised he was so weak as to confess in the first place and that I was surprised when he was so weak as to faint under the strain. He's just a weakling after all."

The first real sign that Loeb was breaking down, not merely in confessing, but in his inner spirit, was when he denied having done the actual killing of Bobby Franks. "I drove the car," said Loeb. "Leopold sat in back and hit Bobby over the head with the chisel." When photographers asked him to pose in the back of the murder car he refused, saying that he had driven the car and that he would have his picture taken only at the wheel. This reluctance to admit the actual killing was the only sign of remorse Loeb was ever to show publicly; later he confessed to one of Darrow's psychiatrists that he had struck the blow. To his mother and father he wrote from his jail cell a few days after he was caught:

DEAREST MOMPSIE AND POPSIE: *This thing is all too terrible. I have thought and thought about it, and even now I do not seem to be able to understand it. I just cannot seem to figure out how it all came about. Of one thing I am certain, tho—and that is that I have no one to blame but myself. I am afraid that you two may try and put the blame upon your own shoulders, and I know that I alone am to blame. I never was frank with you—Mompsie and Popsie dear—and had you suspected anything and came and talked to me I would undoubtedly have denied everything and gone on just the same. Dr Glueck says that I was bent on destroying myself, and I believe he was right. I seem to have discarded all the finer things out of my life! Mompsie and Popsie dear—it may seem terrible, but in one way it is almost providential that I was caught, going on that way, confiding in no one—there is no telling how far I might have gone. This way at best I have a long prison sentence staring at me, but I am hopeful that someday I shall be free again and I really and truly think that I shall be able to do some good and at least live a much better life than I would have been able to otherwise.*

I realize that there is always a chance of the death penalty. However, I am not worried and I assure you that although I know I never lived the part—I do know that should I have to pay the penalty, that I at least will die as becomes the son of such a wonderful father and mother as I know now more than ever that I have.

What I wanted to tell you is that I am not really so hardhearted as I am appearing. Of course, dearest ones, I am afraid that my heart is not what it should be, else how could I have done what I did?

DICK

Although Loeb also had written to his mother, "Mompsie dear, in regard to coming down for the trial, it could not possibly do any good, and altho I should love to see you, I feel that it would only bring more sorrow to you and that we must all think of Dad first and foremost," for Darrow one of the more sorrowful twists of the tragedy was that Loeb's parents never came to visit him in jail. He at last went to the Loeb home and pleaded with the mother, "If you don't show mercy to your own son by at least visiting him in jail, how can you expect the judge to show mercy?" Mrs Loeb then called to see her son, but the father never attended a hearing, never again mentioned his son's name or allowed it to be mentioned in his presence.

When Leopold heard that Loeb had accused him of wielding the chisel "his face contracted in a spasm of passion as he vented his spleen against his former friend, the one who, he now believes, would sacrifice him in the hope that he might win exoneration." Just a moment before he had been kidding Chief Hughes by telling him that Caesar had married an Irishwoman, because "In the nineteenth chapter, fourth paragraph, you can read that he married a woman of the name of Bridget, and that, Chief, is a good Irish name, isn't it?" When he learned that Loeb had accused him of the slaying he cried bitterly, "Tell Loeb for me that it makes no difference which of us did the actual killing. Tell him that he should not forget that my repugnance to violence is such that I could not have killed Robert. Tell him that my one regret is that I find him so weak as to accuse me and that I know the reason. He thinks that by proving me the actual slayer he will eventually go free. Tell him that I know the law and that I am merely amused by his flourishings. We are both principals in the first degree, and—there is no forgiveness!"

Darrow knew that any further quarreling between the boys would seriously injure their defense. He talked to them quietly and earnestly for several hours. At the end of this time Loeb sang out, "We're both in for the same ride, Babe, so we might as well ride together."

Leopold turned around and looked straight into the eyes of Loeb. "Yes, Dickie, we have quarreled before and made up; now we are at the homestretch of the greatest gauntlet we will ever have to run. It is right that we should go along together."

Now that he had the two boys friendly again, Darrow asked them to retrace the crime for him, leaving out not the slightest detail, so that he might be in full possession of the facts that had already been assembled by the prosecution.

The plan to commit a murder had not been sufficient to satisfy Loeb; he also had wanted to commit a kidnaping and collect ransom money. In this way they would be committing the most difficult and complicated of all combinations of crimes, and while the world was searching for the victim, whom it did not know to be already dead, they could be holding the ransom bills and gloating over the success of their accomplishment.

Their first task had been to select a victim. Since neither had any physical courage they planned to kidnap a small boy. They considered in turn abducting Loeb's younger brother, then the grandson of Julius Rosenwald, then a chum by the name of Richard Rubel. They abandoned the idea of killing the brother because in the hour of trouble Dickie would not be able to get away from his family to collect the ransom money; they abandoned the idea of kidnaping Rosenwald's grandson because as Rosenwald was president of Sears, Roebuck and Company, it might hurt the family business; and they abandoned the idea of young Rubel because they had heard his father was a tightwad and in all probability would not come across with the cash.

They decided to set a date for their crime and let circumstances name the victim. Leopold wrote a melodramatic ransom letter on the typewriter they had stolen six months before from Loeb's fraternity house. They opened a bank account under a false name to finance their operations and established credit at a rent-a-car company. Then they began making trips on a Michigan Central train and throwing a package off the observation platform to establish a safe spot for collecting the ransom.

On the twenty-first of May the boys rented a sedan, bought a chisel, a rope and hydrochloric acid. Their plan was to strangle their victim, with each of the boys pulling one end of the rope so they would be equally responsible. Then they drove to the exclusive Harvard Preparatory School just across the street from the Leopold home. They spied a likely victim in the yard, but when this boy suddenly ran away they settled upon fourteen-year-old Robert Franks, a cousin of Loeb's, whom they enticed into the car under the pretext of discussing a new tennis racket.

In the broad daylight of a well-traveled Chicago street, only a few feet from Leopold's home, Loeb brought his chisel down on the head of the Franks boy. Blood spurted, and he fell unconscious. Loeb pulled the boy onto the floor of the back seat, struck him over the head with the chisel three times more, then wrapped his body in Leopold's lap robe.

Leopold groaned, "O God! I didn't know it would be like this."

They then headed their car through Jackson Park, came out on the Midway and drove for some twenty miles through crowded streets, surrounded on every side by automobiles, streetcars and pedestrians. Knowing that they would have to wait until darkness before they could safely dispose of the body, they stopped at a little restaurant for a sandwich, then drove down the road toward Hammond. At a desolate spot they parked their car, carried the body of young Franks some two hundred feet to a culvert by the side of the Pennsylvania Railroad tracks. They stripped the boy of his clothing, after which Leopold shoved him into the culvert, where they figured he would not be discovered for years. They put young Franks' clothing in the car and started back for town. Not wanting his family to worry about him, Leopold telephoned home to tell them he would be late. The boys stopped at a restaurant for their dinner, then drove to the Loeb house, where they stuffed Franks' clothing into a furnace and burned it. Young Franks' shoes, the buckle from his belt, his jewelry and the bloodstained lap robe they buried in the country, then returned to the Leopold house to wash the bloodstains off the floor of the car.

At midnight Loeb addressed his ransom letter to the Frankses' house while Leopold telephoned to say, "Your boy has been kidnaped. He is safe. Don't worry. Instructions will follow later." They mailed the ransom letter special delivery. The following morning they drove to the Illinois Central depot, where Loeb bought the same ticket he had bought so many times for his ransom-money junkets. He went to the observation car and put into the telegram slot of the stationery desk a letter telling Franks' father the exact spot near the Champion factory where he was to throw his packet of money.

Leopold in the meanwhile telephoned the father, instructing him to take the Yellow Cab that would be at his door and drive to a certain drugstore, where he would receive further orders by telephone. He then ordered a Yellow Cab to go to the Frankses' house. Loeb got off the train, rejoined Leopold in the depot; they next drove slowly uptown, giving Mr Franks sufficient time to reach the designated drugstore. When their watches told them that Mr Franks would have barely enough time to catch the train they telephoned the drugstore to tell him where he must look for further instructions. That task done, they would drive out to the spot near the Champion factory and wait for their ransom money to be thrown from the observation platform. If the train were even one minute late they would drive away, for that would mean that Mr Franks had communicated with the police.

But something had gone wrong: Mr Franks was not at the drugstore when they telephoned. They telephoned twice, three times, until they saw that it was now too late; the father would no longer have time to make the train. Wondering what they must do next to collect their ransom money and thus complete their perfect crime, they stepped out into the street. Staring them in the face were newspaper extras with huge headlines announcing that Bobby Franks' body had been found. A workman on a maintenance crew had seen a bare foot sticking out of the culvert and had summoned the police. Within a very few hours another member of the maintenance crew picked up a pair of horn-rimmed spectacles not far from the culvert. A Chicago optical firm identified the special rims, giving the police the names of three persons who had them. At their first call they found a woman with her glasses on her nose; on the second call they found that the man was in Europe; on their third call Nathan Leopold, Jr, who knew that the officials were in possession of a pair of horn-rimmed spectacles, went to the door to find the police looking for him. Loeb, who had spent the intervening hours feverishly discussing the crime, helping newspapermen locate the drugstore where Mr Franks was to have received his final instructions, was with Leopold when the police arrived. Both boys were taken to the Hotel La Salle where Crowe was waiting. Leopold admitted the glasses were his but maintained that he had frequently gone to the murder spot on his ornithological expeditions and must have lost them there a few Sundays before.

"Do you think you should be released?" he was asked.

"No, it would be criminal on the part of the police to let me go now, on account of the glasses. I thought all along that the glasses were the best clue for the police to follow, never thinking they were mine. I didn't know I had lost them, but now I am sure I did and was on one of my many bird trips to that vicinity. I think the last time I was there was on the Sunday preceding the Franks murder."

Leopold's alibi, which he and Loeb had agreed upon after the killing, was that on the evening of the kidnaping he and Dickie had taken two girls riding in Lincoln Park in his car.

After Leopold had stuffed young Franks' body into the culvert he had called to Loeb to pick up his coat and bring it to the car. The glasses, which Leopold very seldom used or carried with him, fell out of the pocket when Loeb picked up the coat. At that instant the perfect crime had begun to disintegrate; when the Leopold chauffeur told the police that Nathan's car had been in the garage on the afternoon and evening of the murder and that the next morning he had seen the two boys trying to wash red stains off the floor of a strange car, the perfect crime, and Loeb along with it, collapsed.

By noon, when Darrow took leave of his two clients and went into the warm June sunshine, the extras were already on the street, heralding his entrance into the case. He had known the night before, riding downtown in the Loeb limousine, that people would be resentful, but he was unprepared for the avalanche of protest that broke over his head. Though Chicago had suffered many venal crimes in its turbulent history, the fate of Bobby Franks sickened, frightened and stunned every family. The Franks boy had been so young and small and innocent, so brutally murdered, that nearly every mother and father of Chicago felt they had lost a son under the most heartbreaking of circumstances. A heavy pall of gloom and anxiety hung over the city. Most Chicagoans wanted Loeb and Leopold hanged instantly as object lessons, so that other children would be safe. When they learned that Clarence Darrow was going to defend the two murderers their indignation rose to a blazing intensity that he had never before savored even in the bitterest of his class-war cases. It was immediately concluded that he would plead the boys not guilty because of insanity, have them committed to an asylum, where they would live for a few years in comfort on their fathers' millions, and then be freed. Knowing his reputation, his powers, the city became convulsed with fear that he might get them off. Sweet and gentle elderly ladies were to desecrate Darrow's memory after his death for what they considered his defense of the murder itself.

W. R. Kellogg, a newspaper owner of Nebraska and a dear friend of Darrow's, says, "More of his followers renounced Darrow because of his defense of Loeb and Leopold than for any other case in his entire history. Very few of his stanchest friends stood by. Lawyers said, 'He is disgracing the criminal lawyers of the country,' while criminals said, 'If this Darrow can get Loeb and Leopold off we can commit any crime we like; all we have to do is to get Darrow to defend us, and we'll beat the rap.' The practice of criminal law in America fell into its greatest disfavor and disrepute in decades."

The fact that the country felt Loeb and Leopold should have no defense once they had confessed was only part of the people's objection to Darrow's entering the case; they knew that the combined wealth of the Loeb and Leopold families was between fifteen and twenty million dollars. The country as a whole, including the laboring and poorer classes for whom Darrow had given so much of his time without compensation, jumped to the bitter decision that Clarence Darrow had agreed to defend these two indefensibles in order to earn the single largest fee that had ever been earned in the history of American criminal law. The rumor started at once that "Darrow is to get a million dollars."

When reporters stopped Darrow and Loeb's uncle on the steps of the courthouse that afternoon one of them said, "It's true, isn't it, Mr Darrow, that you are to receive a million-dollar fee for defending Loeb and Leopold?" Darrow, hearing this rumor for the first time, simply gaped in astonishment, but Loeb only smiled a knowing smile. The story was broadcast throughout the land that Darrow was to receive a million dollars.

Folks said, "Darrow has sold out. He finally got his price and turned traitor—but who can blame him for a cool million bucks? If those were poor boys they'd be hung on the spot. Darrow is a hypocrite; all his life he's screamed that crime is the result of poverty, but when it's the sons of millionaires that commit a horrible murder he turns his back on his teachings and grabs the chance to defend them for the dough he can get."

The following afternoon when Ruby went to her favorite department store to buy a new dress to wear at the trial and picked out one of her usual inexpensive models, the saleslady said, "Oh, Mrs Darrow, you don't want that cheap little dress. You'll want something more expensive now that your husband is earning a million dollars for one case." This scene was repeated in several of the stores; for the next three months Mrs Darrow had to give up going to her usual shops and trade in places where she was unknown. In order to completely conceal her identity she had the packages sent to the Midway flat in the name of Marie Thompson, her maid.

Realizing at once that this rumor would injure his defense, Darrow issued a flat denial that he was to receive any such sum of money. "No sum has been agreed upon," he stated, "or even discussed. We will have the Bar Association determine the fee at the end of the trial in order that it shall be fair to everyone."

No one believed him.

5

While the fury was raging about him Darrow was trying to think his way through an almost impossible situation. There was only one thing of which he was certain. These two boys whom he had taken under his wing and for whose lives he alone would be responsible were mentally ill. They had been mentally ill for a number of years. After their arrest and confession their illness had accelerated rather than subsided.

"The killing was an experiment," Leopold had told him. "It is just as easy to justify such a death as it is to justify an entomologist in killing a beetle on a pin." He had asked for all the newspapers and gloated over his picture on the front page. "It is unusual for one to see his name adorning the front pages," he observed. "But I suppose that is the only way that I shall ever be able to break into print."

Loeb stuck his chin high in the air and declared, "This thing will be the making of me. I'll spend a few years in jail and I'll be released. I'll come out to a new life."

Surely anyone could see that these boys were mentally ill, thought Darrow. Then why should the state want to hang them? They would not hang two boys who had committed irrational acts while in an epileptic seizure or the ravages of a physical fever. He must save the lives of these two boys, and he must save Chicago from indulging itself in another of its recurrent blood lusts.

But how to save them? If he declared them not guilty because insane he would have to try the case before a jury, a jury which could not escape the hysteria and pressure being put upon it from the outside, which would be caught up in a trial by passion, which would declare that because the boys had brilliant minds, were able to think fast and talk fast, because they were millionaires' sons who had had every opportunity, they must be sane and hence responsible for their acts and hence executed for the benefit and protection of society.

"I know perfectly well," he observed, "that where responsibility is divided by twelve it is easy to say: 'Away with him!'"

No, even he could not risk a jury trial. He could not risk failing to prove the boys insane within the legal framework of that term. He had far better plead them guilty and throw them upon the mercy of the court.

"We did plead guilty before your honor," he was to admit during the trial, "because we were afraid to submit our cause to a jury. I have found that experience with life tempers one's emotions and makes him more understanding of his fellow man. I am aware that as one grows older he is less critical; he is inclined to make some allowance for his fellow man. I am aware that a court has more experience, more judgment and more kindliness than a jury. Your honor, if these boys hang, you must do it. You can never explain that the rest overpowered you. It must be by your own deliberate, cool, premeditated act. It was not a kindness to you. We placed this responsibility on your shoulders because we were mindful of the rights of our clients, and we were mindful of the unhappy families who have done no wrong."

But what right had he to ask for mercy from the court? What defense could he contrive which would persuade a judge to have mercy on killers who had shown no mercy? Well, there was only one possible defense, the inevitable defense: the boys were mentally diseased and hence were not responsible for their acts. He knew that mental illness had never been allowed as a defense in American courts; men were either sane or insane, one hundred per cent or nothing, with no shadings or gradations allowed in between. But this kind of reasoning was barbaric and ignorant, out of line with everything that medical science and psychiatry had evolved. He would have to demonstrate to the court that mental illness was a mitigation, and therein would lie a great opportunity.

From his decades of association and friendship with criminals he knew that a majority of them were either emotionally unbalanced or mentally ill. Over the years he had come to the point of view that the punishment meted out to a miscreant should be based not on the crime itself, but on the degree and curability of the mental illness of the offender. Prisons should become curative institutions for the mentally ill, just as hospitals were curative institutions for the physically ill. If an individual who had committed a major crime could be completely cured by psychiatrical treatment of the illness that had caused the crime, he should be returned to his family and society when it was entirely safe to do so. However, if another man committed only a minor crime but it was found that there was no way to cure his mental illness, even after years of scientific and medical treatment, then that man should be kept away from society all the days of his life. This would be true justice; this would be the civilized way to treat individuals who run afoul of the legal structure.

Not guilty because mentally ill! How many trespasses this would cover in a difficult and complex world! Mental illness, the halfway house between sanity and insanity, the house in which lived so many folk, in which transpired so much maladjustment and frustration, so much unhappiness and desperation, in which were committed so many seemingly incomprehensible acts. The world did not blame or punish people who became physically ill; then why should they blame people who became mentally ill when that mental illness was contributed to so largely by physical factors: nerves, glands, secretions, chemical composition. Only two years before he had written a chapter for *Crime, Its Cause and Treatment* called "Responsibility for Crime," which stated his biological attitude, the scientific attitude of understanding with which from his earliest days he had tried to replace the God-religion-moralistic creed of condemnation and punishment. To an astounding degree the chapter applied to and explained the Loeb-Leopold crime.

"It is only lately that we are beginning to find out anything about the origin and nature of man," he had written. "Laws have come down to us from old customs and folkways based on primitive ideas of man's origin, capacity and responsibility. It has been generally assumed that man was created different from all the rest of animal life; that man alone was endowed with a soul and with the power to tell good from evil, and that in the beginning man was perfect but yielded to temptation and since then has been the subject of an everlasting contest between the powers of light and the powers of darkness for the possession of his soul; that man not only knew good from evil, but was endowed with 'free will' and had the power to choose between good and evil; that when he did wrong he deliberately chose to do so out of an abandoned and malignant heart, and that all men alike were endowed with this power, and all alike were responsible for their acts.

"The old indictments charged that 'John Smith, being a wicked, malicious and evil-disposed person, not having the fear of God before his eyes but being moved and seduced by the instigation of the devil, etc.' It followed, of course, that John Smith should be punished or made to suffer, for he had purposely brought all the evil on himself. The old idea is still the foundation of the world's judgment of men in court and out. Of course this idea leaves no room for mercy and understanding. Neither does it leave any chance to give the criminal the proper treatment for his defects, which might permit him to lead a normal life.

"As a matter of fact, every scientific man knows that the origin of life is quite different from this and that no sane treatment of crime can follow this assumption of man's origin and nature; that the result of this foundation is almost infinite injustice and cruelty to a large and constantly growing number of men and women, and that it tends to endless injury and evil to society. This conception of man and of the treatment of crime and criminals by the courts is no better nor more scientific than was the old-time doctors' treatment of physical ailments by magic, incantations and sorcery.

"The origin and development of all animal life is the same. All children have the same origin, the same development and the same pattern, yet no two are alike. The size of the body, real and potential, the size and fineness of the brain, the delicacy and sensitiveness of the nervous system, the innate instincts upon which conduct mainly rests, the emotions which control action and which flow from the structure, is all hidden in the original cell, hidden in the germ or seed from which it sprang.

"The laws of growth and development which govern organic

matter do not except man. Life begins with the cell and evolves according to pattern. If the cell is that of a human being it will be black or white, male or female, tall or short, intelligent or stupid, sensitive or stolid; it will develop a large or a small brain, a fine or a poor one, a sensitive nervous system or a defective one. That the baby had nothing to do with its equipment will readily be admitted by everyone. All of his actions both as a child and as a man are induced by stimulation from without. To the end of his days he receives impressions and stores them; all of these impressions are more or less imperfectly received, imperfectly conveyed and imperfectly registered. However, he is obliged to use the machine he has.

"Stimulated by these impressions, certain secretions are instantly emptied from the ductless glands into the blood, which, acting like fuel in an engine, generate more power in the machine, fill it with anger or fear and prepare it to respond to the directions to fight or to flee or to any type of action incident to the machine. It is only within a few years that biologists have had any idea of the use of these ductless glands or of their importance in the function of life. Very often these glands are diseased, and always they are more or less imperfect; but, in whatever condition they are, the machine responds to their flow.

"That man is the product of heredity and environment and that he acts as his machine responds to outside stimuli and nothing else seem amply proven by the evolution and history of man. Man's every action is caused by motive. Whether his action is wise or unwise the motive was at least strong enough to move him. If two or more motives pulled in opposite directions he could not have acted from the weakest but must have obeyed the strongest. This is not a universe where acts result from chance. Law is everywhere. Every process of nature and life is a continuous sequence of cause and effect. There is a cause for the eternal revolution of the earth around the sun, for the succession of seedtime and harvest, for growth and decay and for the thoughts and actions of man.

"Before any progress can be made in dealing with crime the world must fully realize that crime is only a part of conduct; that each act, criminal or otherwise, follows a cause; that given the same conditions the same result will follow forever and ever; that all punishment for the purpose of causing suffering or growing out of hatred is cruel and antisocial; that, however much society may feel the need of confining the criminal, it must first of all understand that the act had an all-sufficient cause for which the individual was in no way responsible and must find the cause of his conduct and, so far as possible, remove the cause."

Before the Loeb-Leopold trial Clarence Darrow was modestly famous; through this trial he was to become immeasurably notorious. While his defense could be important for the furthering of the science of criminology, it could not have the far-reaching social implications of his important appeals for labor and civil rights; yet it was the case for which he was to receive the greatest amount of publicity and through which he was to become known in remote parts of the world which had not troubled to report his activities in sectional strife. Because of the weirdness of the crime, the wealth of the participants, the fascination with which people are drawn to the death appeal of a murder, he was to remain best known by the general public for the Loeb-Leopold case. This did not displease him; the gods with one of their occasional kindnesses had given him the opportunity to bring his work against capital punishment into focus.

6

Keeping his defense plans secret, he made his first moves to quiet the public outcry against the two boys. He sent men to mingle in the crowds in the Loop and ask people whether they thought Loeb and Leopold should hang. Sixty per cent of those questioned said, "Yes." He then had the fathers of Loeb and Leopold issue a letter to the press saying that there would be no attempt to free the boys, only to prove them insane, and that they would agree to have Darrow's fee set by the Bar Association. After the newspapers had printed this letter the men went back to the Loop to ask the same question and found that sixty per cent of the people were now willing to accept life imprisonment for the culprits.

Darrow found himself caught up in a fever of preparation, surrounding himself with books on psychiatry and endocrinology. "During that concentrated stretch during the hot summer," says Ruby, "while Mr Darrow was getting ready for the trial of the boys, there was never a letup from conferences and preparations and huddles with witnesses and acquaintances. Mr Darrow had no leisure and no privacy and no rest from the day-and-night sessions; we were routed out of bed at all hours of the night; they would come ringing and bursting in upon us with fresh rumors, with bright ideas to discuss, with strangers to meet and to talk with, not infrequently remaining until daylight. On Sunday our large apartment was jammed with people so that five or six confidential and separate conferences were in progress behind closed doors and partitions, extending into the bathrooms. The back of the flat as well as the front sections, and even the maid's quarters, housed a group safeguarding themselves against being discovered or overheard. Rarely did they allow Mr Darrow a chance to snatch some sleep and rest so that he could be equal to the morrow."

There was a convention of American psychiatrists meeting in Philadelphia at the time. Darrow sent Ben Bachrach there to hire the best men he could find. Bachrach engaged, among a number of others, Dr Benjamin Glueck, former psychiatrist at Sing Sing Prison; Dr William A. White, director of St Elizabeth's Government Hospital at Washington, D.C.; Dr William J. Healy, head of the Judge Baker Foundation for Psychiatric Research in Boston, Massachusetts; Dr Harold S. Hulbert, Chicago neurologist. All of these men had done extensive research and had published authoritative books in their field. They came to Chicago when their convention was over and began to diagnose the young slayers. Loeb and Leopold enjoyed these psychiatrical interviews. Leopold insisted that he didn't care what happened to him during the trial so long as he was allowed to maintain his dignity; that he would not mind going to prison for life, just so long as he could take a complete scrapbook of clippings with him. Loeb recited the gruesome details of the crime matter-of-factly, showing neither remorse, regret nor compassion.

On July 21, 1924, Darrow astounded the state's attorney and the country by pleading his boys guilty. "We dislike to throw this burden upon this court or any court," he said, "but we feel that we must. We ask that the court permit us to offer evidence as to the mental condition of these young men to show the degree of responsibility that they had. We wish to offer this evidence in mitigation of the punishment."

The state's attorney objected on the grounds that since Darrow had pleaded the boys guilty he could not at the same time try to prove their insanity. Judge Caverly declared he would listen to the evidence in mitigation. When either side would object to medical testimony which seemed obscure or irrelevant he would rule, "I want to give you all the leeway I can. I want to get all the doctors' testimony about the boys if I can. There is no jury here, and I'd like to be advised as fully as possible."

Darrow reached the courtroom shortly after ten o'clock on the morning of July twenty-third, to find thousands of people jamming the sidewalk and street trying to get in. He had had to battle his way through excited mobs before, but he had never seen anything to compare with this. It looked as though every last soul in Chicago wanted to witness the hearing which was to remain throughout the years the most talked-of and unforgettable trial in the history of Chicago's crime. When he at last had succeeded in shouldering his way into the courtroom he was pleased to find that with the exception of the young girls who had managed to worm their way in to get a look at handsome Dickie Loeb, most of the spectators' seats were occupied by outstanding lawyers and judges of the Midwest, some of whom had traveled as much as a thousand miles to hear what they considered would be one of the most interesting and dramatic trials of their age.

When State's Attorney Crowe arrived Darrow rose, said, "Hello, Bob," and shook hands warmly. Crowe pumped Darrow's hand as he exclaimed, "Hello, Clarence!" Though these two men would lash each other unmercifully during the trial as part of their job, they were to remain friends afterward, just as Clarence remained friends with most of the prosecutors—Fredericks and Ford excepted—with whom he clashed in courtrooms.

Loeb and Leopold were then brought in, both fastidiously dressed and barbered. When one of the reporters commented that they had taken a great deal of care regarding their appearance Loeb replied "Of course, this is our show. The public must not be cheated." He flirted with the pretty girls throughout the hearing. Leopold commented, "With our looks and Darrow's brains we'll get along all right." He maintained that he had considerable interest in observing himself as a murderer. Both boys enjoyed themselves so thoroughly that Darrow perceived they had been successful in accomplishing the end for which they had set out: they had achieved immortality by committing the perfect crime: a crime so perfectly without motive or justification that their names would never be forgotten. From the expressions on their bright, shining faces Darrow saw that they were neither displeased nor unhappy over their bargain with immortality.

Chicago was at its greatest fever heat at this beginning moment of the hearing; the rest of the country was excited and tense. Millions of people discussed the trial, argued whether the boys would be hanged or not, wagered hundreds of thousands of dollars on the outcome, as though it were a World Series or a prize fight. The newspapers of the country were dominated for days on end with the Loeb-Leopold news: for their brief span the murderers were America's two most important personages.

The struggle over the lives of Richard Loeb and Nathan Leopold revolved about two battle cries:

"Mitigation is a defense!" reiterated Darrow.

"The real defense in this case," replied Crowe, "is Clarence Dardow's dangerous philosophy of life!"

In this instance Darrow's dangerous philosophy of life was his belief in psychiatry, the study of man's mental and neurological disturbances and their effect on conduct. Prior to the World War of 1914–18 psychiatry had been both neglected and ridiculed as a curative branch of medicine. Its practitioners had been called "nut doctors." Those suffering from mental and nervous disturbances were sent to insane asylums or sanatoriums or were endured at home by long-suffering families. But when thousands of American soldiers returned shell-shocked and suffering from obscure mental disturbances, when the generation that grew up during the war and postwar hysterias found itself with a high number of disrupted conduct patterns, psychiatry came into its own. With this critical problem on its hands both the people and the government of the United States said to its psychiatrists, "Help us! You say you can cure these people just as other doctors cure typhus or tuberculosis. Then take our war veterans, take our young men and women who are veterans of moral and ideological revolutions at home, and give them back their emotional balance. Restore their mental health so that they can return to their jobs and their families and lead normal lives."

The psychiatrists had done magnificent work; they had achieved thousands of cures; the practice of their craft had at last become respected and respectable and taken its proper place in the practice of medicine. But the general public still distrusted psychiatrists, or alienists, as they most often were called, when they went into court to testify about the sanity of an offender, for apparently these men managed to find medical justification for whichever side was paying their fee, or at least they were not hired unless they agreed with those who did the hiring.

Darrow had said at the opening of the case that he would not try to prove his boys insane but only mentally diseased. The country asked itself, "What is the real difference between the two?" State's Attorney Crowe bawled, "They denied that their clients are insane and are now spending tens of thousands of dollars to get them off on the grounds of insanity." He cried out against one alienist, "When the learned doctor who has been employed to find out just how crazy these two fellows were got on the stand he was probably instructed, 'Just make them crazy enough so they won't hang, but don't make them crazy enough to make it necessary to put this up to twelve men, because twelve men are not going to be fooled by your twaddle. Just make them insane enough so it will make a mitigating circumstance that we can submit to the court.'" Over and over the state asked with sarcasm, "Just how insane can a sane man be without being so insane that he needs a jury to determine just how insane he is?"

Darrow now led his defense psychiatrists through their testimony in such a clear and simple fashion that the lay public was able to understand most of what went on in the Chicago courtroom, digesting their first comprehensive course in mental illness as a base for crime.

Dr Bernard Glueck of Sing Sing, whom Loeb maintained was the only psychiatrist who understood him, said about Dickie Loeb, "I was amazed at the absolute absence of any signs of normal feeling. Loeb is suffering from a disordered personality; the nature of this disorder is primarily in a profound pathological discord between his intellectual and emotional life. We might designate it as a split personality. This boy, while capable of orienting himself intellectually, is quite incapable of endowing these surroundings with an adequate emotion."

Dr William Healy said of Leopold, "To my mind this crime is the result of diseased motivation—that is, in its planning and commission. It was possible only because Leopold had these abnormal mental trends with the typical feelings and ideas of a paranoiac personality. He needed these feelings and ideas supplemented by what Loeb could give him. There is no reason why he should not have committed the crime with his diseased notion. Anything he wanted to do was right, even kidnaping and murder. There was no place for sympathy and feeling to play any normal part. He had an established pathological personality before he met Loeb, but probably his activities would have taken other directions except for this chance association. He is right; the world is wrong. There has been a tremendous subordination of many normal feelings and emotions to this excessively developed conception of himself as a superior individual, and he has reacted in a most abnormal way in regard to the whole crime. Leopold shows little disgust at jail surroundings. His main concern seems to be whether or not the reporters say the right thing about him."

Dr W. A. White testified that both Loeb and Leopold had an infantile emotional make-up and hence were not normal, that Loeb had confessed that he had lived his life out and had come to its logical conclusion. "I do not believe the Franks homicide can be explained without an understanding of the relation between Loeb and Leopold." He, too, maintained that Leopold would not have

entered it alone, because he had no criminalistic tendencies. Loeb
would never have gone as far as he did without Leopold to give
him that final push."

Speaking somewhat satirically, the New York *Times* characterized
Darrow's defense at this point as "a killing in response to an irresistible mandate of two coincidentally insane impulses."

After a number of days of testimony on "diseased motivation,"
"paranoiac and pathological personalities," "dual life," "abnormal
needs," "nervous instability," "subordination of normal feelings
and emotions," "profound disorder of judgment," "continuation of
childhood fantasies into mature life," "split personality," and "pathological discord between intellectual and emotional life," Darrow
led the doctors through their evidence on the endocrine glands,
the pathology of internal gland secretions and their effect upon
the nervous system. Crowe fought him stubbornly all the way,
putting on the stand doctors to testify that "the general status
of knowledge concerning the endocrine glands might almost 'be
compared to the interior of Africa before Stanley went there.'
There are many definite facts known, but they are scattered,
disordered, unrelated." Alvin Sellers, in his reportorial book on the
Loeb-Leopold case, says, "Dr H. S. Hulbert and Dr Karl M. Bow-
man submitted a report which covered several thousand type-
written pages. It included physical, neurological, educational, social
and mental studies and included researches in the physical chemistry
and in the glandular constitution of the defendants." The evidence
offered by the other psychiatrists amounted to several thousand
pages more.

Each day the excitement in Chicago rose higher; each morning
at dawn throngs appeared in the street to find places in the courtroom. The more extreme sensation mongers were disappointed,
however, when the testimony on the homosexual relations between
the boys was taken behind the closed doors of the judge's chamber.
The amounts of money wagered on the outcome of the hearing
climbed into the millions. Sob sisters poured out their hearts in
sticky black ink. Students in law schools argued the fine points of
the case. Leading jurists throughout the country published their
opinions on the legal status of the culprits. Criminologists had a
field day lecturing up and down the length of the land. Loeb and
Leopold received quantities of fan mail. One open-faced post card,
addressed to "Loeb-Leopold murderers, County Jail," read, "Don't
worry, boys, money and a slick lawyer can fix anything in America."

There was sitting in a cell in the county jail, waiting to be
hanged in only six weeks' time for the murder of a policeman, a

nineteen-year-old boy by the name of Bernard Grant, son of a poor man, who had been forced out to work at fourteen. The predicament of young Grant did more to injure Darrow's chances to save the lives of his clients than anything that was to happen in the courtroom. The newspapers and the public at large cried, "Have we one law for the rich and another for the poor? If Grant must hang, why should not Loeb and Leopold hang? Grant's crime was far less vicious and dangerous than Loeb's and Leopold's, for it was unpremeditated." With Grant's impending execution hanging over the courtroom, Darrow could only say unofficially, "It would be as wrong to hang Grant as these two young boys. We must save Grant's life. We must save the lives of all minors who commit murders."

As with most of his important trials, this one took place in the intense heat of summer. Cartoons of him "strumming his galluses" appeared in every paper, giving to the country its most clearly limned portrait: a man in shirt sleeves and suspenders, pacing the courtroom, his thumbs holding the suspenders under his armpits, his big round shoulders hunched forward, a now-thinning wisp of hair hanging down over his eyes, his face lined and seamed, his eyes dark and brooding and hurt: the picture of a plain man, a man who knew the sufferings of others, who said, "I may hate the sin but never the sinner."

7

The defense having done its best to show reason for mitigation, the prosecution then began its attempt to show aggravation. State's Attorney Crowe based his case on three points: first, the boys were entirely sane; second, their motivation for kidnaping the Franks boy had been the ten thousand dollars in ransom which they needed to pay their gambling debts, and third, that they had abused him homosexually and then had been forced to kill him to cover their attack.

As many alienists took the stand to declare Loeb and Leopold sane and responsible as had testified that the boys were mentally ill and irresponsible. Dr Hugh T. Patrick claimed that he found no evidence of mental disease in the boys, that they were not without emotional reactions. Dr Harold D. Singer stated that a paranoiac personality did not necessarily mean a diseased mind. Dr William O. Krohn testified that the boys had both health and integrity of memory, that they were perfectly oriented as to time, space and social relations. Loeb and Leopold sat with stolid, unchanging faces as they heard the witnesses proclaim them sane. Leopold rested his elbows on a chair arm and cushioned his chin with his hand. Loeb, hands in his lap, stared at the witness. Occasionally they held whispered conversations.

Darrow's outbursts at the testimony were frequent and savage, not only because the accusations of sanity hurt his clients but because he believed these doctors represented a past age of psychiatrical medicine, which considered no one insane unless he were a raving maniac. He spent hours and days cross-examining the prosecution's physicians in an attempt to bring not only to Judge Caverly but to the country at large a conception of the new and crucially important science of psychology, which was revealing hundreds of subtle forms of unbalance which fell short of insanity.

"Doctor Church," he asked of a prosecution psychiatrist who testified that after close observation he found no evidence of mental disease in either defendant, "what do you mean by an emotion?"

"Emotion is a play of feeling," replied Dr Church.

"There is a difference between the part of the human anatomy which produces emotion and the mind, which is supposed to be the seat of reason, isn't there?"

"I don't know of any such difference," answered Dr Church. "No one has emotion unless he intellectually perceives it."

"You are assuming that mind is the product of brain action?"

"Yes, I believe it."

"The mind is probably a product of the whole organism, isn't it?" pressed Darrow.

"No, I don't think so."

"Is there anything in the mind excepting the manifestation of the physical organization?"

"Practically not."

"When is the most trying age in a young man?"

"At the age of puberty and adolescence."

"Then comes a change of emotional life, doesn't it, as a rule?"

"Yes sir."

"Then if ever, with the young man or the young woman, they are the most apt to jump out of or leave the habits that have been inculcated in them to keep in a given path and break over on account of new feelings or emotions, are they not?"

"They are."

"And it is the most prolific time for insanity with youth, is it not?"

"Yes."

Darrow paused for a moment and then asked pointedly:

"A diseased mind functions in fantasies often, doesn't it?"

"I presume it does."

"And the individual is ruled by fantasies as well as realities often, is he not?"

"Not until they attain the delusional stage."

"As a broad general rule, a daydream and a night dream are both reflections of mental life?"

"Nothing can occur in fantasy or in a night dream that has not in some way come to the experience of the individual."

"If you would know all a man's dreams, or a boy's dreams, and fantasies and hopes and ideals, you would know something about the boy, would you not?"

"You would know the boy's character."

For almost a month the battle raged between expert and cross-examiner, till nerves were frayed. Epithets flew between Crowe and Darrow. Crowe accused Darrow of defending the boys only for the large fee involved. He accused him of preaching doctrines of anarchy, saying that if Judge Caverly put his official seal of approval upon Darrow's anarchy "a greater blow has been struck to our institutions than by a hundred, aye a thousand murders."

Darrow retaliated by calling Crowe a "hanging" state's attorney. When Crowe said that the greater part of the defense psychiatrists' testimony made him laugh Darrow countered with, "Yes, you would laugh at anything, except possibly a hanging, and I think maybe you would laugh at the hanging of these boys." Crowe retorted, "We have heard considerable about split personalities in this case. I was somewhat surprised to find that my old friend, who has acted as counsel and nursemaid in this case for two babes who were wandering in dreamland, also was possessed of a split personality. I had heard so much of the milk of human kindness that ran out in streams from his large heart that I was surprised to know he had so much poison in his system also."

As in most American criminal cases, the taking of testimony was only the preliminary to the joining of the issue which would result from the final pleas of counsel and would settle the fate of the boys. Assistant State's Attorneys Thomas Marshall and Joseph P. Savage made the first pleas for the state, offering into evidence cases in which boys, seventeen, eighteen and nineteen, had been hung in Cook County. State's Attorney Crowe made a strong and able plea in which he maintained, "The law says in extreme circumstances death shall be the penalty. If I were in the legislature I might vote against such a law. I don't know. But as a judge I have no right to put aside that law. I have no right to defeat the will of the people, as expressed by the legislature of Illinois. I have no right to be a judicial anarchist, even if Clarence Darrow is an anarchistic advocate." He then went on to say, "Darrow says that hanging does not stop murder. I think he is mistaken," and attempted to prove that public executions had always lessened the number of murders committed in Chicago, just as all punishment deterred others from committing crimes.

He repeated his theory that the Franks boy had been kidnaped for the sake of the ransom money, that the testimony about the glandular structure and secretions was unscientific, that the king-and-slave fantasy was "a pure figment of the imagination of the defense," that the two clever killers had fooled and deluded the psychiatrists, that the psychiatrists were quacks, that the murder was planned logically and sanely by two young boys with criminal instincts, and that "there is nothing the matter with them mentally. The only fault is the trouble with their moral sense, and that is not a defense in a criminal case." He endeavored to show that the age of the boys did not lessen their responsibility. "Mr Darrow is a student of criminology; he has written a book on it and he says the criminal age, the time when crimes are committed, is between the ages of sixteen and twenty-four. Your honor and I know that the average age is twenty-two. If we are going to punish crime and by the punishment stop it, and the criminal age is between seventeen and twenty-four, how can we punish if the age is a defense?"

"Indeed," murmured Darrow. "How can you?"

Crowe caused an explosion by emphasizing certain testimony that had been given to the effect that Leopold had claimed he would get off because the case would be tried before a "friendly judge." Judge Caverly called the "friendly judge" suggestion a "cowardly and dastardly assault upon the integrity of this court. This court will not be intimidated by anybody at any time or place, so long as he occupies this position."

The state's attorney then concluded his plea by charging, as had so many prosecutors before him, that Clarence Darrow was responsible for the crime being tried. He went back to Darrow's speech before the prisoners at Joliet to demonstrate Darrow's anarchism by quoting him as saying, "I do not believe in the least in crime. I do not believe that there is any sort of distinction between the real moral condition in and out of jail. The people here can no more help being here than the people outside can avoid being outside. I do not believe people are in jail because they deserve to be. They are in jail simply because they cannot avoid it on account of circumstances which are entirely beyond their control and for which they are in no way responsible."

He called on Judge Caverly not to succumb to Darrow's anarchism but to do his duty, protect the state and pass upon the boys the death sentence.

On the day Darrow was to make his final plea the New York *Times* reported that "people stormed the courtroom; women fainted in the mob that came to hear him." He spoke for three days; many of those who listened thought it the finest single plea of his life for love, mercy and tolerance, even greater than his appeal before the Anthracite Coal Commission two decades before. After his first day of pleading the newspaper reporters were to name him the Old Lion. It was a name he was to retain to the end of his days.

"When the public is interested and demands a punishment it thinks of only one punishment, and that is death; when the public speaks as one man it thinks only of killing. I have heard in the last six weeks nothing but the cry for blood. I have heard from the office of the state's attorney only ugly hate. I have seen a court urged almost to the point of threats to hang two boys, in the face of science, in the face of experience and all the better and more humane thought of the age.

"Ninety unfortunate human beings have been hanged by the neck until dead in the city of Chicago in our history. We would not have civilization except for those ninety that were hanged, and if we cannot make it ninety-two we will have to shut up shop. Some ninety human beings have been hanged in the history of Chicago, and of these only four have been hanged on the plea of guilty. I know that in the last ten years three hundred and forty people have been indicted for murder in the city of Chicago and have pleaded guilty, and only one has been hanged! And my friend who is prosecuting this case deserves the honor of that hanging while he was on the bench. But his victim was forty years old. Of ninety men hanged in Illinois since its beginning, not one person under twenty-three was ever hanged upon a plea of guilty—not one.

"They say we come here with a preposterous plea for mercy. When did any plea for mercy become preposterous in any tribunal in all the universe? Mr Savage tells this court that if these boys are hanged there will be no more boys like these. Mr Savage is an optimist. If these two boys die on the scaffold, which I can never bring myself to imagine, if they do die on the scaffold the details of this will be spread over the world. Every newspaper in the United States will carry a full account. Every newspaper of Chicago will be filled with the gruesome details. It will enter every home and every family. Will it make men better or make men worse? How many will be colder and crueler for it? How many will enjoy the details? And you cannot enjoy human suffering without being affected for the worse. What influence will it have upon the millions of men who will read it? What influence will it have upon the millions of women who will read it, more sensitive, more impressionable, than men? What influence will it have upon the infinite number of children who will devour its details as Dickie Loeb has enjoyed reading detective stories?

"Do I need to argue to your honor that cruelty only breeds cruelty; that hatred only causes hatred; that if there is any way to soften this human heart, which is hard enough at its best, if there is any way to kill evil and hatred and all that goes with it, it is not through evil and hatred and cruelty? It is through charity, love and understanding. How often do people need to be told this? Look back at the world. There is not a philosopher, not a religious leader, not a creed, that has not taught it.

"I am not pleading so much for these boys as I am for the infinite number of others to follow, those who perhaps cannot be as well defended as these have been, those who may go down in the tempest without aid. It is of them I am thinking and for them I am begging of this court not to turn backward toward the barbarous and cruel past."

Throughout the trial Loeb and Leopold had been calm and composed. Leopold had taken notes as though he were in a classroom; both boys had smiled and laughed frequently during the proceedings. While State's Attorneys Crowe, Savage and Marshall had depicted them as the vilest humans ever to crawl on the face of the earth the boys had kept a perfect composure, regarding their assailants with curiosity. But when Clarence Darrow pictured the tragedy and suffering that had befallen the three families because of their crime Richard Loeb and Nathan Leopold, Jr, became two desperately frightened and sorrowful little boys. The New York *Times* reports, "The appeal proved too much for the self-control of the culprits. Throughout most of the afternoon they sat tense. Loeb followed every word of the lawyer. Leopold grew pale beneath his customary ruddy flush, and when Darrow's eloquence pictured disgrace to the families, the grief of mothers, the sorrow of fathers, the blasted hopes for the boys themselves, Loeb flicked tears from his cheeks and Leopold stumbled from the courtroom with bowed head. So overcome was the latter that he struck blindly against a partition of the narrow entrance to the 'bull pen.' The impact drove him sideways, but he did not raise his head. With extended arms he plowed past the bailiffs and fairly plunged into the elevator that was waiting to convey him to the approach of Cook County's Bridge of Sighs."

On the last day of his plea Darrow's voice faltered frequently, sometimes becoming so faint that it could hardly be heard; yet every syllable was clear in the terrible silence of the Chicago courtroom. Judge Caverly leaned forward, resting his chin on his clasped hands, his eyes riveted on the speaker.

"Crime has its cause. Perhaps all crimes do not have the same cause, but they all have some cause. And people today are seeking to find out the cause. Scientists are studying it; criminologists are investigating it, but we lawyers go on and on and on, punishing and hanging and thinking that by general terror we can stamp out crime.

"If a doctor were called on to treat typhoid fever he would probably try to find out what kind of milk or water the patient drank and perhaps clean out the well so that no one else could get typhoid from the same source. But if a lawyer were called on to treat a typhoid patient he would give him thirty days in jail, and then he would think that nobody else would ever dare to take typhoid. If the patient got well in fifteen days he would be kept until his time was up; if the disease was worse at the end of thirty days the patient would be released because his time was out.

"I do not know how much salvage there is in these two boys. I hate to say it in their presence, but what is there to look forward to? I do not know but what your honor would be merciful if you tied a rope around their necks and let them die; merciful to them, but not merciful to civilization and not merciful to those who would be left behind.

"We placed our fate in the hands of a trained court, thinking that he would be more mindful and considerate than a jury. I cannot say how people feel. I have stood here for three months as one might stand at the ocean, trying to sweep back the tide. I hope the seas are subsiding and the wind is falling, and I believe they are, but I wish to make no false pretense to this court. The easy thing and the popular thing to do is to hang my clients. I know it. Men and women who do not think will applaud. The cruel and thoughtless will approve. It will be easy today, but in Chicago and reaching out over the length and breadth of the land, more and more fathers and mothers, the humane, the kind and the hopeful, who are gaining an understanding and asking questions not only about these poor boys but about their own—these will join in no acclaim at the death of my clients. These would ask that the shedding of blood be stopped and that the normal feelings of man resume their sway.

"But, your honor, what they shall ask may not count. I know the easy way. I know your honor stands between the future and the past. I know the future is with me and what I stand for here; not merely for the lives of these two unfortunate lads, but for all boys and all girls, for all of the young and, as far as possible, for all of the old. I am pleading for life, understanding, charity, kindness and the infinite mercy that considers all. I am pleading that we overcome cruelty with kindness and hatred with love. I know the future is on my side. You may hang these boys; you may hang them by the neck until they are dead. But in doing it you will turn your face toward the past. In doing it you are making it harder for every other boy who in ignorance and darkness must grope his way through the mazes which only childhood knows."

It was four in the afternoon when Clarence Darrow finished his plea. He closed it with a verse from Omar Khayyám, which the Chicago newspapers said should be his epitaph:

> *"So be it written in the Book of Love,*
> *I do not care about that book above;*
> *Erase my name or write it as you will,*
> *So I be written in the Book of Love."*

The Chicago *Herald-Examiner* told that "there was scarcely any telling where his voice had finished and where silence had begun. Silence lasted a minute, two minutes. His own eyes, dimmed by years of serving the accused, the oppressed, the weak, were not the only ones that held tears."

8

Two weeks were to go by while Judge Caverly studied the testimony and prepared his decision. Two weeks of impatient waiting on the part of the country, of downright agony for Clarence Darrow. He returned to his office, tried to work, but the Loeb-Leopold case had thrown his firm into chaos. For two interminable weeks he lived from hour to hour, breaking out in cold sweats during the day, awakening a dozen times during the night—while Judge Caverly received anonymous letters threatening his life if he did not sentence the boys to hang, and Loeb and Leopold received crank letters telling them that they would be killed on the way to prison if the judge failed to impose the death penalty. When the newspapers editorialized on the need for Judge Caverly to sentence the boys to hang, Darrow cried out more in anguish than in anger:

"If these boys hang the United States might well vote murder indictments against the unjudicial agencies, many of them far removed from this court, who are trying to fix public opinion. It is not a question of the sanity or insanity of the two defendants that is at issue. It's a question of the insanity of the methods by which certain forces are seeking to direct public opinion to bloodshed without permitting the world to consider, impartially, the finding of the alienists."

On September tenth, the day upon which Judge Caverly had announced he would read his decision, Darrow closeted himself in his office and began pacing first back and forth, circling the desk in one direction, then in the other. When one of his partners went into the room he found the blinds drawn, the room thick with smoke, Darrow chain-puffing cigarettes, standing limp and exhausted, with as distraught and stricken and helpless a look on his face as though it were his own two sons who stood in imminent danger of hearing themselves condemned to die on the scaffold.

At last word reached him that Judge Caverly was ready. Every-one involved in the trial assembled in the courtroom. The Chicago *Evening American* reported that, "the judge read his decision in a calm, low voice, while the two boys sat motionless in their chairs before him. Clarence Darrow, who made the supreme plea of his life to save them, rocked gently backward and forward in his tilted chair."

Judge Caverly first announced that in view of the profound and unusual interest that the case had aroused throughout the world, he considered it his duty to state the reasons which led him to his conclusion.

"The court is willing to recognize," said the judge, "that the careful analysis made of the life history of the defendants and of their present mental, emotional and ethical condition has been of extreme interest and is a valuable contribution to criminology."

He then read his decision: "The court is willing to meet his responsibilities. It would have been the path of least resistance to impose the extreme penalty of the law. In choosing imprisonment instead of death the court is moved chiefly by the consideration of the age of the defendants. This determination appears to be in accordance with the progress of criminal law all over the world and with the dictates of enlightened humanity. The records of Illinois show only two cases of minors who were put to death by legal process—to which number the court does not feel inclined to make an addition.

"Life imprisonment may not, at the moment, strike the public imagination as forcibly as would death by hanging, but to the offenders, particularly of the type they are, the prolonged suffering of years of confinement may well be the severer form of retribution and expiation."

A reporter for the Chicago Evening *American* gives a touching picture of the finale of this great hearing. "As the judge delivered his sentence Leopold listened unblinkingly. Loeb winked his eyes, and a terrified look crept into them. Judge Caverly finished. Nobody said a word. The courtroom was silent as death. Nobody seemed to know what to do. Then the bailiffs tugged at the boys, and Dickie rose, the puzzled, frightened look still on his face; Nathan, the ironhearted philosopher, jumped up, and the march from the courtroom, with its social contact to the bleakness of a lifetime behind prison walls, began. Before he went he shook hands with Clarence Darrow, a smile of thanks on his face. Dickie just stood still with that pathetic look on his countenance. Then everybody crowded around the defense attorneys and about the relatives of the boys. There were smiles on the faces of all of them—even on the grief-worn face of Nathan Leopold, Sr."

Within a few moments Loeb and Leopold were on their way to Joliet, Loeb to be cut to death after a few years by a fellow prisoner, Leopold to establish a brilliant educational system for incarcerated men.

Darrow's happiness over the forward-looking decision of Judge Caverly was cut sharply by the adverse criticism of a large section of the American public and press. The Minneapolis *Star* said, "It was difficult indeed to find an excuse for not sending these vicious degenerates to the gallows, we will admit. But in view of the circumstances any excuse would have stood the test of analysis better than that of youth." The Washington *Evening Star* commented, "No recommendation by the court can safeguard against a release of these utterly worthless persons by executive action. In that fact lies the reason for the feeling of disappointment and of indignation caused by the imposition of the life sentence."

However, the verdict was a great triumph for the Old Lion, and above all it was a triumph for mercy and understanding and love.

9

He tried to pick up the threads of his normal practice. The ten-thousand-dollar retainer fee that Loeb had given him that first hysterical night had been spent on court costs, psychiatrists and office expenses. Since the entire Darrow office had been concentrating on the case, the firm was now several thousand dollars behind in its efforts to save the boys' lives. Neither of the two fathers made any mention of paying Darrow for his services. The weeks went by; several months went by; still no attempt was made to meet the obligation or to ascertain what Darrow's fee might be.

At the end of four months, when he had received no word from either of them, Darrow wrote a polite note to Loeb. The letter was ignored. So disgusted with this conduct was Judge Harry Fisher, a friend of Darrow's and an officer of the Bar Association, that he asked Darrow to let the Bar Association both name and collect his fee.

"No," said Clarence, "I don't want to make any trouble. I'll write to Loeb again asking for my money."

At the end of six months he sent another letter to Loeb, suggesting that he come into the office and discuss a settlement. One full month later Dickie Loeb's uncle came into the office and remarked breezily, "You know, Clarence, the world is full of eminent lawyers who would have paid a fortune for the chance to distinguish themselves in this case."

Sick at heart, Clarence could only think, "This is not the same man who fell on his knees by my bedside and begged me to save the boys' lives."

"A hundred thousand dollars is all we can pay in this case, Clarence," continued Loeb. "From that I'll have to deduct the ten thousand dollars I already paid you." He then reached a hand into his pocket, pulled out three checks and handed one to Darrow. "I've broken this up three ways," he said. "A third for each of the Bachrach brothers and a third for you. Here's your check for thirty thousand dollars—now if you will just sign this release."

Ruby reports that "Dee came home that night feeling pretty bad. He said, 'Rube, I hope you won't disapprove of what I've done.'"

" 'I don't very often. What have you done?' "

Darrow told her the story, then said, "I took the check and signed the release. What else could I do? I didn't take that case to make money. I hoped to establish a precedent that boys in their teens should not be held accountable for their acts. I can't go in now and fight for more money or the world will think that's what I took the case for."

"But Judge Fisher telephoned again this afternoon—the Bar Association——"

Darrow shook his head sadly.

"No, Rube," he murmured. "I couldn't let it be said that I haggled about the price. I've said that I wasn't doing it for the big fee the world expected would be paid to me. I have to be true to my ideals."

should not be held accountable for their acts. I can't go in now
and fight for more money or the world will think that's what I
took the case for."

"But Judge Fisher telephoned again this afternoon—the Bar Association—"

CHAPTER XII

"Your Old Man's a Monkey!"

N<small>OW</small> <small>APPROACHING</small> <small>SEVENTY</small>, Clarence Darrow decided that he
would slowly ease himself toward retirement. He and Ruby took
a trip to Europe. This European vacation had been made possible
by the one "gravy" case of his career. Harold McCormick, son
of the founder of the McCormick Harvesting Machinery Company, was having difficulties in securing a divorce from Mrs Edith
Rockefeller McCormick, third daughter of John D. Rockefeller.
"Of the two lawyers handling my case," says McCormick, "John
D. Wilson was an aristocrat; the other was a nabob. When I became convinced that these two attorneys were hurting me in the
eyes of the public I decided I would call into the case a democrat
and a humanitarian. I had always admired Clarence Darrow as one
of the great men of his time, with a wonderful soul, and I felt
that if he came into the case on my side the public would no longer
think it was a contest between millionaire families. When I told
Wilson that I wanted Darrow brought into the case he exploded
with, 'Why, I wouldn't associate with Clarence Darrow!'

"I finally convinced him that if he knew Darrow he would
respect him. Wilson replied, 'All right, Harold, I'll take your word;
I'll meet him and we'll talk it over.' Mr Darrow was so kind,
sympathetic, patient and gentle with Mrs McCormick that our
complications dissolved and Mrs McCormick settled amiably."

For these few meetings Darrow had received a fee of twenty-
five thousand dollars. His face wore a strange and quizzical expression as he fingered the check, an expression similar to the one
Ruby was to detect there a year later when the Darrows were

entertained on the yacht of Samuel Untermeyer, a New York attorney who had made millions from his practice. Untermeyer had pinned a corsage of orchids onto Ruby's frock as she came aboard from Miami, orchids which he had sent on from his private nurseries every day of the week. As Darrow gazed a little forlornly at Ruby's spray of orchids he muttered, "Hummph, maybe I should have been practicing corporation law all these years. Then I could-a had a yacht and fresh orchids for you every day."

"What would you do with a yacht?" asked Ruby.

As had been true all through his life, he still derived his most constant pleasure from lecturing, debating and writing. Mostly he liked to debate on religion; he enjoyed it so much that his intimates believed him to have deep religious promptings. While in Cannes he went frequently to watch the fishermen hauling in the catch in their nets. He said, "There are Peter and John and all the men who were associated with Christ." However, these promptings did not relax his native irreverence. While they had been wandering through Palestine an Arabian boatman had offered to take them to the spot where Jesus had walked upon the waters.

"How much will you charge for rowing us over?" he asked.

"Fifteen dollars," replied the boatman.

"No wonder Jesus walked," murmured Darrow.

Despite the fact that he was constantly attacking the intellectual base of organized religion, his friends declared him to be the most religious man they had ever known, one of the few true Christians alive in America. Liberal clergymen who debated against him on the platform or answered his articles in the press were particularly fond of saying, "Here is a man who lives by Christ's teachings." Once when he had completed an evening lecture to the students of Harvard a Congregational minister commented to the students, "No one was ever a greater worker for the good of mankind and for God than Clarence Darrow." Another time, when debating Dr Shirley Case of the University of Chicago on the subject, "Has Christianity Failed?" "Doctor Case said that Clarence Darrow himself was an argument against the failure of Christianity, for he lived as close to the Golden Rule of Jesus as anyone he had ever known."

Clarence's friend and physician of forty years' standing, Dr Leeming of Chicago, says, "Darrow exemplified the Christian life. I never knew him to do anything mean or wrong." John Haynes Holmes, minister of the Community Church of New York, wrote more elaborately of him, "Darrow was sharp of tongue, ironic in thought and speech, a pessimist and unbeliever, but he had a heart which could exclude no man from its sympathy. In his own life he demonstrated the reality of the religion which he denied. This world was to him a mad and cruel world. There was no sense nor sanity in it. Especially was there no pity. But men needed pity, just because they were living helplessly in such a world. And this pity Darrow himself proposed to supply. Thereupon appeared in action such a piteous heart as mankind has seldom known. There were no limits to Darrow's compassion. It reached everywhere, touched every life. The underdog was his especial friend, the downtrodden and oppressed his brethren, the outcast and wretched and despised his loved ones. Not since Saint Francis walked this earth has the world seen such mercy clad in human flesh. Not since Jesus himself has there been such an exemplar of the gospel of 'unto this last.' If religion is love, as it surely is, then Clarence Darrow was one of the most religious men who ever lived and his pessimism a purer wellspring of the spirit than all the founts of faith."

During his forty years of work for the poor, the underdog, the defenseless, he received letters from every part of the world in which strangers would say, "God bless you, Mr Darrow; you are a true Christian."

Though he was a confirmed materialist, though he debated over the country against the immortality of the human soul, he had an unquenchable thirst for knowledge on immortality. As he grew older this searching was never very far from the fore part of his mind; there were times when he seemed obsessed by the idea. Once when he was dining with Rabbi Goldman in Chicago he stopped in the midst of Mrs Goldman's pot roast to discourse on the improbability of a God or a life after death. Rabbi Goldman's eleven-year-old daughter listened gravely, then replied, "Mr Darrow, Mother gave me a box of beautiful beads for my birthday, and when I dropped the box the beads rolled all over the floor because they had not been strung. We need God to string together all the different parts of life."

Darrow smiled as he replied, "I won't argue with this younger generation. I'll stick to the older generation; they're easier."

Rabbi Goldman says of him, "He was the intuitive man rather than the profound man; he was a human thinker rather than a learned thinker. He declared himself to be a pessimist, yet he couldn't have loved life and human beings as much as he did without being an optimist. There was a great deal of the Old Testament in him: a great emphasis on the sanctity of the individual, the value of human life, the value of justice."

Professor A. Eustace Haydon, authority on comparative religions at the University of Chicago, confirmed Rabbi Goldman's estimate. "Darrow's pessimism was an inverted optimism. He would prove that life was not worth living, then he would turn around and prove it was worth living by doing things for people." A Chicago journalist, with whom Darrow had collaborated on a book against prohibition, says, "Darrow had a great Christian charity, without tolerance for what he believed to be Christian superstitions and the theological absurdities."

He had a tremendous lust for life, yet he came about as close to living according to the Sermon on the Mount as could any man trying to earn his way in a competitive world. He was a man with all the faults, shortcomings and inadequacies of a man, but he was a civilized human being in that he could not endure to see his fellow human beings suffer.

His quarrel had never been with religion itself but with those creeds which turned their backs on education and science; his quarrel with these forms of worship was on the ground that they operated against the welfare of their own people. For forty years now he had been carrying on this fight against those sects which kept knowledge away from their members, which told human beings precisely what they might think and at that point erected unscalable stone walls, sects which battled all findings of science which appeared to controvert their dogma. For the Christian ethic he had love and admiration, but he had only disgust for those branches of religion which circumscribed the human brain, set boundaries to its activities, limited its growth and direction, pre-scribed what it might think, feel and believe, kept the brain from crying out, "I am free! I am unafraid! I am unbounded and un-limited! I go wherever the truth may lead me." He flayed against those faiths which discouraged the processes of unbiased, vigorous, fearless thinking and which consequently made defective the brain; which not only cut off part of its potential power but cramped and restricted and enslaved it. He believed with all his heart that if ever man was to become free his brain must be utterly free to lead him to that freedom, for no one could free man but man himself, and he could never accomplish this tremendous task without exerting himself to the utmost through the days and the centuries, without having the full power of his brain, without making it an ever-stronger, bolder and more resourceful machine to serve him.

He was a Christian by example and precept, but by intellect he was an agnostic. He was no atheist, as was so commonly charged against him, though he often used the atheist press and pulpit to combat what he judged to be the more baneful influences of rigid dogma. He never became an atheist because he knew it was as difficult to prove "There is no God" as "There is a God."

Time and again clergymen exclaimed, "I know I ought to hate Clarence Darrow for his sacrilegious beliefs, but when I am with him I love him."

No man in America was better prepared by background or temperament to meet the challenge of William Jennings Bryan and the Fundamentalists. For him the saying that the postman always rings twice was true; just as the Loeb-Leopold case had given him the recapitulatory opportunity against capital punishment, so now the Scopes Evolution Case was to afford him the opportunity to bring into an international focus his campaign against the oppression, bigotry and ignorance fostered by an intellectually hamstrung church. The newspapers were to call it America's most amazing trial.

2

The Scopes Evolution Case in Dayton, Tennessee, did not spring up whole and unexpected; the forces had been gathering on either side, the battle swelling for several years. In the early summer of 1923 Bryan and Darrow fought the early skirmishes which were to lead directly to the contest in Dayton which so shocked, amused and revolted the civilized world.

For some time William Jennings Bryan had been quarreling in the press with university professors, offering a hundred dollars in cash to any one of them who would sign an affidavit to the effect that he was personally descended from an ape. He had launched an attack against science which the Chicago *Tribune* published. Darrow had replied in a letter to the *Tribune*, whose editor considered it of sufficient news value to give it the number-two column of the front page.

"I was very much interested in Mr Bryan's letter to the *Tribune* and in your editorial reply," Darrow said. "I have likewise followed Mr Bryan's efforts to shut out the teaching of science from the public schools and his questionnaires to various college professors who believe in evolution and still profess Christianity. Likewise a few questions to Mr Bryan and the Fundamentalists, if fairly answered, might serve the interests of reaching the truth—all of this assuming that the truth is desirable. For this reason I think it would be helpful if Mr Bryan would answer the following questions." He then posed fifty questions at Bryan in an attempt to find out whether Bryan thought the biblical account of the creation of the earth and of life literally true or a poetic allegory.

Bryan replied, "I decline to turn aside to enter into controversy with those who reject the Bible as Mr Darrow does."

Two years later he was to answer all fifty of the questions from the witness stand in the courthouse in Dayton in a shattering scene which proved to be the tragic fulfillment of a tragic career. When the legal aspects of the case had been fought to a temporary conclusion, when both sides had belabored the rights of a sovereign people to pass any legislation it saw fit, when the question of whether the Anti-Evolution Law violated the constitution of Tennessee or the Constitution of the United States had been hopelessly obscured, it was these fifty questions which suddenly flashed the trial into focus, turned defeat into victory, discredited the Anti-Evolution Bill and dealt a deathblow to Fundamentalism.

Strong movements were already under way in fifteen states to enact anti-evolution laws. The state of Kentucky had escaped from such a law by a majority of one vote in its legislature. Darrow feared that if Bryan and his cohorts were permitted to carry on their work unopposed they would soon have the Bible Belt of the Solid South caught in a Fundamentalist dictatorship. Nor had Bryan any intention of stopping at the Mason-Dixon line. His avowed purpose was to carry the fight into the North and the West until he had secured anti-evolution bills in two thirds of the states and could get an anti-evolution amendment added to the United States Constitution. Bills to stop the use of government funds for ethnological research had already been drawn and would be introduced at the next session of the Congress. "The purpose of the movement," commented the Chattanooga *Daily Times*, "is to bar the Smithsonian Institute from investigating as to the origin of man and to have Congress accept the Bible theory of the genesis of the human family."

In America there had been effected such a complete separation of Church and State that no religious instruction was allowed in the public schools. The Fundamentalists were now determined to pass laws which would prohibit the teaching in public schools of all subjects which conflicted in any detail with the particulars of their own religion. Did biology and zoology conflict with the biblical story of the creation of the world and man? So much the worse for biology and zoology! Did geology conflict; did anthropology conflict? So much the worse for geology and anthropology. Hidden beneath the anti-evolution movement was an attempt to bring the state under the control of the Church, William Jennings Bryan's church.

Nor was Darrow one of those who thought this aim impossible

of attainment. Had not these almost identical forces put over prohibition on an unwilling public? Had they not bullied legislators,
connived, cried, kicked, yelled, screamed and finally succeeded?
He subscribed wholeheartedly to the sentiments of the journalist
who wrote, "According to Mr Bryan, the Fundamentalist party
will not be satisfied with writing a defense of the code into state
after state; it must be written into the Federal Constitution itself.
Journalists laugh. But they are the same journalists who laughed
when these same people, not satisfied with capturing state after
state for prohibition, began to talk of an Eighteenth Amendment."

He felt that the issue had to be joined, that Bryan and his
World's Fundamental Association had to be stopped, not in their
own belief or practice of Fundamentalism, but in trying to force
their religion upon the rest of the country. Ever since Charles
Darwin's earliest promulgation of his theories of evolution certain
churches had been fighting them bitterly, ridiculing them, commanding their members to abstain from studying the perfidious
doctrines on the pain of excommunication, denying the results of
research, calling the scientists and the educators tricksters, dupes,
atheists, liars, instruments of evil and destruction. But for the most
part, the battle for education and enlightenment in America had
been well won; even the universities in the Bible Belt had excellent
science departments, where the studies of those subjects which contributed further to knowledge of evolution went on fearlessly and
brilliantly. America had thought that the issue was dead; it had
forgotten that as long as mankind inhabits this earth, no issue, no
matter how cruel, stupid, vicious, or destructive, is ever dead.

And, indeed, in the state of Tennessee an anti-evolution bill had
already been drafted, passed through the house and senate, signed
by the governor, decreed as the law of their land. John T. Scopes,
science teacher and athletic coach of the Rhea County High School,
had been arrested for violating the Anti-Evolution Law.

3

When Darrow entered Dayton on the afternoon of July eighth
he found the town decked out as though for a carnival. The road
leading in from Chattanooga had been lined with signs which read,
"Sweethearts, Come to Jesus," "You Need God in Your Business,"
"Where Will You Spend Eternity?" Across Main Street were strung
colorful banners and flags. Newly constructed hot-dog stands,
lemonade stands and sandwich stands lined the sidewalks. Most of
the shops had comic posters depicting monkeys and coconuts pasted

in their windows. J. R. Darwin's Everything-to-Wear Store had put out a huge flag which read, "DARWIN IS RIGHT—inside." The Anti-Evolution League had taken over a whole building, in front of which they set up bookstalls to sell Bryan's books and their featured volume, *Hell and the High School*. One circus man who had brought two chimpanzees to testify for the prosecution rented a store on Main Street and set them up as a side show. Preachers of a hundred different sects, most of them untutored men who had graduated from some Bible institute of the Deep South, came to Dayton to transform the town into a giant revivalist meeting; they preached on the street corners, set up their tents on the outskirts of town, night and day exhorted the passers-by to repent and come to Jesus. At the more populous street corners "blind, wandering dervishes from the remote hills played their fiddles and chanted gospel hymns through their noses." The Holy Rollers chose Dayton for their annual revival meeting; each night along the riverbank they writhed and rolled on the ground in ecstatic spasms of religious emotionalism. These goings on resulted in the inevitable comment in the newspapers that the people of Dayton were making monkeys of themselves.

By the time Darrow reached Dayton the village already had been overrun by two different groups: on the one hand the hundreds of newspapermen, photographers, editors, radio and telegraph operators, educators, scientists, atheists, liberals, radicals, who thronged there during their summer vacation to see their side win a great victory and whose presence so filled the hotels and boardinghouses that the private homes rented out rooms. On the other, the farmers of the surrounding countryside, the marginal-subsistence families from the hills, the unemployed coal miners, the itinerants and mendicants of all types, most of them Fundamentalists who came to see their side win a great victory and who slept in wagons, rickety cars, in tents and on the ground under the trees. When the trial opened the Daytonians were in a minority in their own town; nor were the reporters always meticulous in distinguishing between the residents and their visitors. The article that Frank R. Kent wrote in *The New Republic* was true of Dayton at the time of the trial but not an accurate portrait at any time before or after Dayton's critical moment in the sun.

"Religion, basic Bible religion, is the big thing in this country—the religion of the camp meetings and of the queer, violent acrobatic sects, creeds and faiths, all based on literal Bible beliefs. The whole region is saturated with religion. Nine tenths of the people are steeped in it. It *is* their mode of recreation as well as their means of redemption, their single emotional outlet, the one relief from the deadly drabness of cut-off existence. It is a literal fact that, so far as the great bulk of the people are concerned, a religion, the rigidity of which it is difficult to exaggerate, absorbs all the thought they have aside from their work. In Dayton religion takes the place of golf, bridge, music, art, literature, the theater, dancing, clubs. Take religion away, and the desolation and distress would be pitiable to contemplate."

Aside from the carnival aspect, Clarence found Dayton to be an. attractive and prosperous village of two thousand inhabitants, located in the scenic Cumberland Mountains. The town had many beautiful homes, two banks, a hoisery mill, a canning factory, a crate factory, a blast furnace of the Cumberland Coal and Iron Company. The surrounding country yielded good crops of strawberries, tobacco, wheat, soy beans, clover. Main Street, whose most imposing feature was the comfortable Hotel Aqua, was lined with brick and wooden buildings and open Model T Fords.

He met a number of enlightened and liberal people in the community. There was a progressive Readers' Club, which tried to keep abreast of current thought by reading the new publications and which founded the Dayton Library. At the other extreme he encountered an illiberal group, fanatics who wanted to control the thinking and feeling of the rest of the country. In between were the majority of Daytonians, many of whom had graduated from high school and whose children often went away to college. Dayton was intensely religious; its two thousand residents supported nine churches. Even the most educated would stand around in little knots until past midnight, discussing such theological questions as whether Jesus lived to save mankind or died to save mankind. But as far as Darrow could determine, no one in Dayton, intellectual or fanatic, had ever taken a child out of school because he didn't like something that was being taught. Dayton believed in the creation of man as revealed in Genesis, was frankly skeptical about evolution but had done nothing to deserve the ridicule, contempt and contumely that was now to be heaped upon its head when the town was taken over by forces outside its control.

Dayton businessmen originally had encouraged the idea of a trial because they had hoped to put Dayton on the map and capture a permanent tourist trade. They printed a handsome pamphlet called *Why Dayton—Of All Places?* illustrated with pictures of the town and its main industries. The booklet asked, "Why not Dayton? Permit her to tell in faltering voice but, nevertheless, with the ring of sincerity, why this bowl in the Cumberland holds, 'logically, fundamentally and evolutionarily,' the amphitheater for a world's comedy or tragedy, whichever viewpoint the spectators may choose." Dayton's leading newspaperwoman says, "There was some hope that persons of means might find Dayton attractive enough to cast their lots here. The people seemed to be enthusiastic over the legal and literary talent descending in their midst because of the trial." But the members of the Progressive Dayton Club came to realize that they had a serious trial on their hands and not a highly profitable farce; the monkey posters were taken down, their plans to present "monkey medals" to the participants abandoned.

The chamber of commerce tendered Clarence a banquet at which time he was given the honorary title of Colonel. The same group also had given Bryan a banquet a few days before, at which he had appeared in "a prodigious white pith helmet which gave him the air of a polo player from the neck up." Bryan had announced that the trial would be "a duel to the death." Colonel Darrow retorted, "We will smother Mr Bryan's influence under a mountain of scientific testimony."

Three months before the arrest of Scopes, William Jennings Bryan had delivered a lecture in Nashville called "Is the Bible True?" Though he had not practiced law for thirty-six years, he offered his services to head the prosecution of Scopes, an offer which the hundreds of thousands of people throughout the South who had heard him lecture on the literal verity of the Bible demanded be accepted. At this moment Darrow was also in the South, speaking on "The Sane Treatment of Crime" before the Annual Convention of the American Psychiatric Association in Richmond, Virginia. The occasion was a great honor, for he was the first lawyer to be invited to make the annual address in the eighty years of the association's history. On the evening of May 13, 1925, he was introduced at the Mosque to an alert audience of five thousand doctors, lawyers, clergymen, educators, businessmen and their wives. Taking his cue from the religion-versus-science turmoil going on about him, he contested the "divine-inflatus" conception of man's nature by a biological attack best described as a "divine de-flatus." "For an hour or more he kept the audience on its toes. He spoke practically without notes, showed a knowledge of biology, psychology and law, spiced with wonderful bits of humor and sly cynicism."

He enjoyed himself thoroughly; Dr James K. Hall reports, "Darrow's coming to Richmond shook up the serenity of the city and loosened the opinions of some of us psychiatrists. It was a great day for American psychiatry. Clarence Darrow impressed me as an honest, fearless, humble man, passionately anxious to find the truth

and to live by it. In spite of his unorthodox speech I thought him
deeply religious."

The following day he was taken by Dr Beverly Tucker, together
with Dr Hall and the novelist, James Branch Cabell, for a drive
through the surrounding country. That morning the newspapers had
announced that William Jennings Bryan was going to prosecute
John Scopes in Dayton, Tennessee. Clarence was deeply agitated.

"We all enjoyed Mr Darrow's conversation so much," Dr Tucker
says, "that I do not think he had a chance to see the country. He told
us that he was interested in the arrest of Scopes and that he had
just heard that Mr Bryan was going to prosecute Scopes. Then in a
rather wistful way he said, 'I would like to meet Bryan in this case;
I believe I could down him. I would be willing to do it without
charging Scopes any fee.' I said, 'Mr Darrow, why don't you offer
his attorneys your services on that basis?' He replied, 'I think that
would be rather sticking my neck out.' However, when we arrived
back in Richmond I told him that there was a telegraph office in
the Jefferson Hotel lobby if he wished to offer his services in the
Scopes case. 'I believe I shall do it,' he said. We went to the telegraph office from which he sent the telegram."

"For the first, the last, the only time in my life," says Darrow, "I
volunteered my services in a case. I did this because I really wanted
to take part in it."

The week before, when he had been in New York, he had discussed the anti-evolution trial with Arthur Garfield Hays and Dudley Field Malone of the Civil Liberties Union; the three men had
decided that it would be better for the controversy to be handled
by Tennessee attorneys. The entrance of Bryan into the case had
shifted its focus from law to religion; if Bryan had not become involved in the prosecution Darrow would never have become counsel
for the defense.

4

He returned immediately to New York to debate with Will
Durant on "Progress." Under the caption DARROW SORROWS FOR
BRYAN AND ALL IGNORANT BIGOTS, the New York *World* reported
him as laying the blame for the Anti-Evolution Bill on the shoulders
of William Jennings Bryan. "Mr Bryan's mind was set by his ancestors, and it has remained set. The sorrow is that it was set to believe that man must not think for himself, that he must study only
what his ancestors studied, that one may not teach or study what
he wishes." When these comments were published in Tennessee
the following day State Representative John Washington Butler

was deeply offended. "I alone am responsible for the Anti-Evolution Bill," said Mr Butler. "Mr Darrow is wrong in claiming that William Jennings Bryan had anything to do with it."

John Washington Butler was a moderately prosperous farmer who raised corn, tobacco, wheat, on his hundred-and-twenty-acre farm. A thickset man with a rugged face and a sincere manner, he had in his youth taught school for five years during the winter, when no farming could be done. In 1922 a visiting preacher from Nashville had told from the pulpit of Butler's Primitive Baptist Church the story of a young woman who had gone to the university and returned home believing that, instead of God creating man, he was descended from a lower order of animals. This sermon set Butler to worrying; he was a devout man who had raised his five children on the letter of the King James Bible. He knew that evolution was being taught in the Tennessee high schools; it seemed to him neither fair nor just that the public schools, which were run on the taxes paid by surrounding farms, should undermine the religion that had been planted in the young while at home.

That year Butler ran for representative of his district; one of the main planks of his platform was the advocacy of a law prohibiting the teaching of evolution in the Tennessee schools. "Ninety-nine people out of a hundred in my district thought just as I did. I say ninety-nine out of a hundred because there may be some hold different, but so far as I know, there isn't a one in the whole district that thinks evolution of man can be the way the scientists tell it. On the morning I was forty-nine I was thinking what to do on my birthday, and I said to myself, 'Well, the first thing, I'll get that law off my mind.' I wrote it out after breakfast at home just like I wanted it. I had the stenographer up at the capitol type it for me, and that's the way the law stands now, just the way I first wrote it."

The Tennessee house of representatives passed the bill with a seventy-five-to-five vote. The legislators later said that they had passed the buck to the senate, thinking the senate would kill the bill. The senate, however, passed it twenty-four to six, with two men rising to their feet to speak against it. The senators later avowed that they had passed the bill, thinking that the governor would veto it. The governor signed it on March 21, 1925, remarking that it would never be enforced. The Nashville *Southern Agriculturist* declared, "We should feel ourselves faithless to the children of Tennessee and to the other states in which similar laws are threatened if we did not protest against it." It was the restlessness of the thirty-one-year manager of the Cumberland Coal and Iron Company which brought the act into immediate focus.

George Rappelyea was raised on Third Avenue in New York City; as a boy he sold newspapers at the Times Square entrance to the subway. He studied geology at college for a short time, wandered South on a geological exploring trip, located the main vein of the Cumberland Coal and Iron Company which had disappeared at a fault, a feat for which he was made manager of the mine. "He was an untidy little person with rather ill-tended teeth," writes Mrs Haldeman-Julius. "His dark brown eyes behind horn-rimmed spectacles are fine and alert. His mind is essentially a scientific one, clear, disciplined; his mental integrity and intrinsic sincerity are obvious."

Rappelyea's distaste for Fundamentalism had become acute on the day he went into the mountains to attend the funeral of an eight-year-old boy who had been crushed between two coal cars. "This here boy," said the Fundamentalist preacher, standing by the little coffin and directly before the weeping parents, " 'cause his pappy and mammy didn't get him baptized, is now awrithin' in the flames of hell." When Rappelyea protested the preacher said with dignity, "Mr Rappelyea, you can boss the men in the mine, but you've got to keep your hands off'n our religion."

"But that isn't religion; that's horrible superstition!"

"Hit's our religion," said the preacher, "and we're going to stick by hit."

"Well, a few days later," said Rappelyea, "I heard that this same bunch, the Fundamentalists, had passed that Anti-Evolution Law, and I made up my mind I'd show them up to the world. Everybody said to calm down and forget it, but I couldn't."

When the Anti-Evolution Bill had been passed John T. Scopes had gone to his principal and shown him that Hunter's *Civic Biology*, which had been the standard textbook in all Tennessee high schools for five years, violated the law. The principal had decided that since school would be out in a few weeks it would be wiser to make no changes or comments but to carry on his teaching as he had before. Scopes reported this scene to his friend Rappelyea, reading to him the pages from *Civic Biology* which taught that man was descended from a lower order of animals. Rappelyea had seen an announcement that the American Civil Liberties Union of New York City had declared itself ready to back any schoolteacher who would test the law. That night he wrote to the Civil Liberties Union asking if they would finance a defense if he could arrange a test case in Dayton. Arthur Garfield Hays, guiding genius of the organization which tried to provide legal protection for every form of American freedom, guaranteed not only the expenses of the defense, but offered a thousand-dollar fee to each of the prosecuting attorneys as well.

Late in the afternoon of May fifth Rappelyea went to Robinson's drugstore, which served as the community center and meeting place for the town, and had a nickel lemonade with his cronies at the circular ice-cream table. Three of Dayton's lawyers dropped in after their day's work. A heated discussion arose over the validity of the Anti-Evolution Law.

"Johnny," said Rappelyea to Scopes as he came in for a soda, "Johnny, you're going to be arrested."

"What for?" asked Johnny mildly. He was a modest boy, one of the best-liked members of the community, particularly among the students, though some of the more rigorous churchgoers had been heard to criticize him because he smoked cigarettes and danced.

"For violating the Tennessee Anti-Evolution Bill. For teaching that man is descended from a lower order of animals."

While towheaded, bespectacled John Scopes sipped his soda Rappelyea continued earnestly, "The American Civil Liberties Union has promised to defend you."

"All right," replied Scopes quietly, "I'll stand as a test case."

Rappelyea went for the sheriff, swearing out a warrant for the arrest of John T. Scopes. A deputy came to Robinson's drugstore to arrest him. Four days later the Rhea County grand jury met and indicted him for violating the Anti-Evolution Law.

Rappelyea conceived the romantic idea of reopening The Mansion, an imposing home on the outskirts of Dayton that had been abandoned several years before. It was shaded by huge trees, was far enough out to give seclusion and was the only house in the vicinity large enough to accommodate the group of attorneys and experts who were expected to testify. The fact that the plumbing system did not work, that there was no water in the pipes for washing or shaving, no facilities in the kitchen with which to cook, did not deter Rappelyea. He moved in a few beds, a table and some chairs and awaited the coming of his guests. One visitor commented, "This is Rappelyea's show; he is the impresario and is inordinately fond of his artists."

Darrow slept only one night in the abandoned mansion. The next day Ruby arrived and, as though by magic, one of the bankers of the town transported his family to the foothills in order that the Darrows might move into their home and be comfortable. Since the town was flooded with strangers, foodstuffs were extremely difficult to buy, particularly milk and butter, and it was next to impossible to secure any ice. That week end the Darrows went to the mountains to escape the lacerating heat; when they returned they found that their neighbor, Mr Wilbur, had filled their icebox "with ice, milk, cream and butter, and even a choice cantaloupe for Monday breakfast."

"The attitude of the townspeople toward us was especially kindly," says Mrs Darrow, "despite the differences of our beliefs. No one ever displayed the least sign of discourtesy, except perhaps Mr and Mrs Bryan. I was not introduced to them, and I am not aware that they ever had any intention to be rude to me, but certainly they glanced the other way any time we were at all near each other."

Early on Friday morning of July tenth Clarence and Ruby left their borrowed home and walked to the Rhea County Courthouse, a large brick building with a belfry, surrounded by a neat lawn and half concealed in a grove of elm, oak, poplar and sweet-gum trees. As Darrow entered the courtyard he saw a huge banner which read, "Read Your Bible Daily for One Week"; a signpost near the entrance of the courthouse door read, "Be a Sweet Angel." The green sward was jammed with vendors of pennants, toy monkeys, hot dogs and lemonade, with barefoot preachers holding prayer meetings and exhorting the milling spectators at the top of their lungs. An observer wrote, "One was hard put to it on the tenth of July to know whether Dayton was holding a camp meeting, a Chautauqua, a street fair, a carnival or a belated Fourth of July celebration. Literally, it was drunk on religious excitement."

Though it was early in the morning, a blazing sun beat down upon the sward and the courthouse. Darrow climbed the flight of stairs to the courtroom, which seated more than seven hundred people but which now held another three hundred standees. He pushed his way through the already sweltering spectators, past the tables at which were assembled a larger number of journalists than had met and worked on any assignment since the Washington Arms Conference. Microphones had been set up to carry the trial to the nation, the first broadcast of its kind. French, German and English correspondents were present to cable each day's story to their European papers.

Everyone was in shirt sleeves, with the sleeves rolled up and the collar open at the throat; in this crowd Darrow somehow appeared well dressed, for he had replaced his usual black string necktie with a white string necktie which he declined to take off and had on a pair of dashing purple suspenders; it was probably the first time in his forty-five years of practice that he was among the best-dressed members of the court, though he could not compete with Dudley Field Malone, who continued to wear his coat during the worst of the brutal heat.

At the defense table sat Clarence Darrow, Arthur Garfield Hays, Dudley Field Malone and John Randolph Neal of Tennessee, a former judge and the leading constitutional lawyer of the state, who had represented the American Civil Liberties Union in the past. Neal was in actual charge but preferred to remain in the background to handle the constitutional problems and let his widely publicized colleagues occupy the limelight in the controversy between religion and science. Malone was a handsome, debonairly dressed, silver-tongued pleader who had no brief for the theory of evolution but who, as Darrow observed of him, "put his allegiance on a higher ground." Arthur Garfield Hays, short, stocky, with a strong face, was an excellent and necessary counterbalance to the eloquent Darrow: in addition to his courage and years of devotion to the unpopular cause of civil liberties, he was an expert on the technical aspects of the law and always insisted upon "keeping the record straight."

Opposite these four men at the prosecution's table sat William Jennings Bryan and his son, former Attorney General Ben McKenzie and his son, Attorney General Stewart and the Hicks brothers of Nashville. The judge was John Raulston, an attorney of Dayton.

Bryan announced, "The trial uncovers an attack for a generation on revealed religion. A successful attack would destroy the Bible and with it revealed religion. If evolution wins Christianity goes." Darrow retorted, "Scopes isn't on trial; civilization is on trial. The prosecution is opening the doors for a reign of bigotry equal to anything in the Middle Ages. No man's belief will be safe if they win."

Judge Raulston banged his gavel. The monkey trial was on.

5

The Reverend Mr Cartwright uttered a long prayer which was in effect a judgment for the prosecution. "We are conscious, our Father, that Thou art the source of our wisdom and of our power. We are incapable of thinking pure thoughts or performing righteous deeds unaided by Thee and Thy divine spirit. With the consciousness of our weakness and our frailty and our ignorance, we come to Thee this morning, our divine Father, that we may seek from Thee that wisdom to so transact the business of this court in such a way and manner as that Thy name may be honored and glorified among men."

The first row between the attorneys was symptomatic of the

geographic nature of the controversy. Judge Raulston announced, "We are glad to welcome the foreign lawyers for both the state and the defendant." The defense looked at each other quizzically but said nothing until former Attorney General McKenzie claimed the Anti-Evolution Law to be so clear it could be understood by a sixteen-year-old Tennessean, but "if these gentlemen have any laws in the great metropolitan city of New York that conflict with it or in the great white city of the Northwest . . ." Then they objected to geographic distinctions being drawn, since they were present as American citizens. Judge Raulston, who was a courteous man, albeit a trifle bombastic in speech, sought to pour oil on the troubled waters by replying, "I want you gentlemen from New York or any other foreign state to always remember that you are our guests and that we accord you the same privileges and rights and courtesies that we do any other lawyer." The defense subsided resignedly.

Scopes originally having been indicted in unseemly haste, Attorney General Stewart asked that a new indictment be brought against the defendant. The grand jury was summoned. Judge Raulston read to them Section One of the Anti-Evolution Law. "Be it enacted by the general assembly of the state of Tennessee that it shall be unlawful for any teacher in any of the universities, normals and all other public schools of the state, which are supported in whole or in part by the public-school funds of the state, to teach any theory that denies the story of the divine creation of man as taught in the Bible and to teach instead that man has descended from a lower order of animals."

Since the act made it illegal to teach any theory that denied the divine creation of man as taught in the Bible, Judge Raulston picked up his well-worn copy of the Bible, read the first twenty-three sections of Genesis and then pronounced slowly:

> "25: And God made the beast of the earth after his kind, and cattle after their kind, and everything that creepeth upon the earth after his kind: and God saw that it was good.
> 26: And God said, Let us make man in our image, after our likeness: and let them have domination over the fish of the sea, and over the fowl of the air, and over the cattle, and over all the earth, and over every creeping thing that creepeth upon the earth.
> 27: So God created man in His own image, in the image of God created He him; male and female created He them."

The grand jury promptly returned a new indictment against John T. Scopes.

Since the veniremen thought that service in the jury box would afford them a grandstand seat for the proceedings, few declined to serve. Darrow took charge of the examination, but he questioned the prospective jurors only mildly; those selected were middle-aged farmers, eleven of whom were inveterate churchgoers. One juror who admitted he could neither read nor write was accepted by both sides because it was said of him that "he can think and has got quick ears."

After this first session on Friday court was adjourned until Monday to permit the defense attorneys who had assembled from different cities to chart their program of defense and to work with the scientists, educators and clergymen who had come to Dayton to explain evolution and to attribute its workings to God. There were a number of hectic sessions around the table in The Mansion, but by Sunday afternoon Darrow was well enough satisfied to leave his confreres and drive into Chattanooga to lecture on Tolstoy to the Young Men's Hebrew Association.

Court convened on Monday morning. The crowd had changed somewhat in character; the overall-and-gingham-clad farmers had given way to the native Daytonians dressed in their best. The day was devoted to the technical aspects of the law, to its constitutionality, for the defense first appealed to Judge Raulston to quash the indictment against John Scopes. The jury was sent out of the courtroom during these arguments. Several days were to elapse before they were allowed back in.

John Neal pleaded that the Anti-Evolution Law was unconstitutional because the title of the law was misleading and did not include everything that was in the body of the law; that it violated the part of the Tennessee constitution which provided that "knowledge, learning and virtue being essential to the preservation of republican institutions, and the diffusion of the opportunities and advantages of education throughout the different portions of the state being highly conducive to the promotion of this end, it shall be the duty of the general assembly in all future periods of this government to cherish literature and science"; that it further violated the constitution of Tennessee which provided that "all men have a natural and indefeasible right to worship Almighty God according to the dictates of their own conscience." Arthur Garfield Hays asked that the indictment be thrown out of court because the Anti-Evolution Law unreasonably extended the police powers of the state and was a restriction on the powers of the individual. Dudley Field Malone asked that it be quashed on the grounds that the law imposed upon the people of Tennessee a particular religious opinion from a particular religious book.

When Darrow came into the courtroom after the noon recess to climax the pleading, he told his friends that he was going to take off his gloves and give the enemy the whole works. The New York *Times* reported, "There was a craning of necks, for Mr Darrow is of intense interest hereabout. He is known as 'the infidel,' and the crowd gazed curiously at the bent figure with the seamed brown face and the great head. He was in his shirt sleeves, his purple suspenders standing out against his shirt, which had a little tear at the left elbow. He would stoop and brood a minute, hunching his shoulders almost up to his ears, and then they would drop; his head would shoot forward and his lower lip protrude as he hurled some bitter word at his opponents. Or he would stand swaying sideways at the hips, balancing himself, while words came slowly from his lips, and then launch himself, a thunderbolt of indignation, words streaming from him in a torrent of denunciation."

In his opening Darrow declared the Anti-Evolution Act to be as "brazen and as bold an attempt to destroy learning as was ever made in the Middle Ages." He turned to William Jennings Bryan, who had thus far sat in humid silence, fanning his face with a palm fan, and declared in unequivocal terms that Bryan was the one responsible for this "foolish, mischievous and wicked act." The spectators gasped to hear their champion labeled foolish, mischievous and wicked: Darrow could feel the familiar wall of resentment rise against him. This resentment became almost tactile when he demonstrated that he had rightly been named an infidel by maintaining, "The state of Tennessee, under an honest and fair interpretation of the constitution, has no more right to teach the Bible as the divine book than that the Koran is one, or the book of Mormons or the book of Confucius or the Buddha or the Essays of Emerson or any one of the ten thousand books to which human souls have gone for consolation and aid in their troubles.

"I know there are millions of people in the world who derive consolation in their times of trouble and solace in times of distress from the Bible. I would be pretty near the last one in the world to do anything to take it away. I feel just exactly the same toward every religious creed of every human being who lives. If anybody finds anything in this life that brings them consolation and health and happiness I think they ought to have it. I haven't any fault to find with them at all. But the Bible is not one book. The Bible is made up of sixty-six books written over a period of about one thousand years, some of them very early and some of them comparatively late. It is a book primarily of religion and morals. It is not a book of science. Never was and was never meant to be."

He believed that the things he had to say in these few hours of pleading might be among the most important of his lifetime. For this reason he was not content to plead merely for the right to heresy; he wanted his argument to be based solidly on the law, for if the law of a land will not maintain a man's intellectual freedom the people of a country never will. He went to great pains to review the legal and technical reasons why the statute was untenable: that the law was so indefinite and uncertain that no citizen could obey it or court enforce it and that it was entirely possible, since science only illuminated the poetic observations of Genesis, to both violate the law and obey it at the same time; that the constitution of Tennessee, which was patterned after the one written by Thomas Jefferson, maintained that no act should ever be passed which would interfere with religious liberty.

"They make it a crime to know more than I know. They publish a law to inhibit learning. This law says that it shall be a criminal offense to teach in the public schools any account of the origin of man that is in conflict with the divine account that is in the Bible. It makes the Bible the yardstick to measure every man's intelligence and to measure every man's learning. Are your mathematics good? Turn to I Elijah ii. Is your philosophy good? See II Samuel iii. Is your chemistry good? See Deuteronomy iii 6, or anything that tells about brimstone. Every bit of knowledge that the mind has must be submitted to a religious test."

As Darrow stood before Judge Raulston, his thumbs locked in his suspenders, the native Tennesseans wondered how a man who looked and acted so much like a farmer could utter such heretical beliefs. "If today you can take a thing like evolution and make it a crime to teach it in the public schools, tomorrow you can make it a crime to teach it in the private schools. And the next year you can make it a crime to teach it in the church. And the next session you may ban books and the newspapers. Soon you may set Catholic against Protestant and Protestant against Protestant and try to foist your own religion upon the mind of man. If you can do one you can do the other. Ignorance and fanaticism is ever busy and needs feeding. Always it is feeding and gloating for more. After a while, your honor, it is setting man against man and creed against creed until with flying banners and beating drums we are marching backward to the glorious ages of the sixteenth century when bigots lighted fagots to burn the man who dared to bring any intelligence and enlightenment and culture to the human mind."

One of the journalists wrote of Darrow at this instant, "In one of his great leisurely shrugs, in which his whole torso participates, he can put more contempt, more combativeness, more of a sense of reserve power, than anyone else can express in a dozen gestures."

The crowd paid him respectful but shocked attention. One spectator exclaimed, "They ought to put him out!" His friends surrounded him, shaking his hand and congratulating him on his fine speech for intellectual liberty. When Ruby approached, the group of admirers separated respectfully to allow the wife to embrace and congratulate her husband.

"Clarence," said Ruby, pointing at the tear in his shirt through which his elbow was now protruding, "don't you think you'd better put on another shirt?"

"Well, Ruby," smiled Darrow, "don't you think it's too hot today for two shirts?"

As he walked along Main Street toward the Hotel Aqua several Daytonians who had disagreed with the thesis of his talk said when passing him, "A wonderful speech, Mr Darrow." One Daytonian stepped up to grasp his hand and say, "Mr Darrow, if I could have heard you before I would never have spoken of you as I have in the past."

"That's all right; that's all right," he replied, touched almost to the point of tears. He did not hear the two women behind him mutter, "The damned infidel!"

Ben McKenzie, who had battled hard against the legal arguments of Neal, Hays and Malone, got out of his Ford when Darrow came along, threw an arm affectionately about him and said in a husky voice, "It was the greatest speech I have ever heard in my life on any subject." Darrow returned his embrace so warmly that McKenzie was to say in court the next day that between him and Mr Darrow it had been love at first sight. "It's mighty kind of you to say that," murmured Darrow.

Feeling pleased with themselves, the defense attorneys met for dinner in the dining room of the Hotel Aqua. They had settled down to a serious discussion of the next day's technique when Bryan appeared, laden with bundles of celery, radishes and other vegetables which he had just bought in the local market. Bryan disdained to glance at the defense table but walked to his own, handed the bundles to his waitress and asked her to prepare and serve them along with his dinner. Bryan in full sail, with the huge bundles of vegetables under his arm and the pith helmet on his head, caused the defense sloop to sheer.

6

The following morning, July fourteenth, Darrow exploded a series of bombs in the Dayton courtroom; he objected to the trial being opened each morning with a long prayer by a Fundamentalist preacher. "I don't object to the jury or anyone else praying in secret or in private," he commented. "But I do object to the turning of this courtroom into a meetinghouse in the trial of this case. This case is a conflict between science and religion, and no attempt should be made by means of prayer to influence the deliberation and consideration by the jury of the facts in this case."

A whistling sound of shock swept through the audience; Darrow turned from addressing Judge Raulston to stand facing down his critics. Catching him thus in a still picture, a reporter of the Chattanooga *Daily Times* wrote, "The Chicago lawyer knows he is a second Ajax defying the lightning; he knows that hot curses are being heaped upon his aged head and stooping shoulders, but he stands and has his say." Then, using almost the identical words uttered by Dr Beverly Tucker of Richmond at the close of the psychiatrists' convention, the *Times* reporter concluded, "Dayton will never be the same until Darrow leaves. Even then it may be marked for life."

Though it was not the custom in Tennessee to open court with a prayer, Judge Raulston was a deeply religious man; he had always opened court with a prayer if there were a clergyman present. Darrow's request hurt him even more than it astonished him. He felt that every Tennessean in the courtroom desired the day's proceedings to be opened with a prayer; he denied Darrow's request but asked the Reverend Dr Charles Francis Potter of the West Side Unitarian Church of New York, a defense witness, to say the prayer the following morning, a compromise which succeeded in satisfying neither side.

The flare had no sooner died down than Darrow lighted another. That morning Attorney General Stewart publicly had labeled him not only an agnostic, but an infidel. Darrow was not unprepared for this attack; when he first had offered his services to the Civil Liberties Union certain members had objected to his entrance into the case on the grounds that he was an agnostic and that "the struggle in Tennessee must be between Christianity and Fundamentalism, not religion versus agnosticism." Philip Kinsley in the Chicago *Tribune* had reported one of the Dayton prosecutors as saying, "All we have to do is to get the fact that Mr Darrow is an atheist and does not believe in the Bible across to the jury, and his case is lost. He will not get to first base here; the jurors will merely yawn. They will listen to no one but Bryan." But Dayton had become so upset at the report that it might lose Clarence Darrow that the residents had planned a mass meeting to protest the ban being put upon him. John Scopes had saved the day by rushing to the defense of his defender. "Yes, I consider Mr Darrow an agnostic, but as such that would not prejudice any fair-minded juror. I call myself an agnostic, but I am devoutly religious in my own way."

Darrow now admitted Stewart's right to call him an agnostic: "I do not consider it an insult, but rather a compliment, to be called an agnostic. I do not pretend to know where many ignorant men are sure." However, he was outraged at being called an infidel by an officer of the state of Tennessee. He spent a heated fifteen minutes trying to show the court that to peoples of other religions, in other lands, the good Christians sitting in the Dayton courtroom were regarded as infidels. Judge Raulston reprimanded Attorney General Stewart, ruling that religious criticism should join geographic deprecation in being banned from the prosecution's remarks.

On the courthouse lawn the jury sat cooling its heels, as well as its brow, for as long as arguments were being carried on as to whether the indictment should be quashed, the jurors had to be excluded from the courtroom. On the afternoon of July fifteenth, almost a week after the opening of the trial, Judge Raulston read his opinion, refusing to throw the case out of court.

Everyone had known he would refuse to quash the indictment, yet Darrow was made thoroughly and bitterly angry by the decision in a way in which he had never before become angry in a trial, not even when the final verdict had gone against him. Only the night before he had said to a group of Daytonians, "I have never judged any man. I have had sympathy for all. I have done my best to understand the manifold conditions that surround and control each human life. You know it is said, 'Judge not, that ye be not judged.' I do not judge a man; I defend him."

Yet he did not defend Judge Raulston's bias, nor did he consider the background and conditions that had led to the judge's decision: the fact that John Raulston had been born in a little cove in the mountains called Fiery Gizzard, that his mother, a devoutly religious woman, had led him on muleback over the hills to school each day and read the Bible to him each night, that he had come out of the primitive hill life of Tennessee, a conscientious and honest man who was seen with a Bible under his arm as often as a lawbook and who was called "part priest, part judge." From his years of study he undoubtedly knew that it would have been as congenitally impossible for John Raulston to disavow the Anti-Evolution Law as it would have been for Clarence Darrow to approve it. Judge Raulston was to say as late as 1940, "The people of Tennessee are profoundly fundamental in their religious beliefs, that is, they do not trace their origin to the lower order of animals but attribute their existence to the divine creation and were in full accord with the provisions of the statute and with the position taken by Mr Bryan and his associates in the trial of this case." The Tennessee legislature had passed the act almost unanimously; the governor had signed it; a Federal judge in Knoxville had refused to issue an injunction against it. How then could he have expected a small-town trial judge of the criminal court, who agreed wholeheartedly with the law, to set the law aside?

Darrow's nature was intensely emotional; his emotions often ruled his head. His head had told him that Judge Raulston would force Scopes to go to trial, but his heart had led him to hope for a miracle, that a little man sitting on a bench in a little town in the Tennessee hills would rise to great heights of nobility, cry out to the world that man's brain must be forever kept free.

He left the courtroom greatly depressed. As he passed the Hotel Aqua someone handed him a telegram from San Francisco which read: HAVE FOUND THE MISSING LINK—WIRE INSTRUCTIONS. He laughed and was relieved; as long as there was humor left in America its people were safe.

The next morning the jury at last was allowed to take its place in the jury box. The trial of John T. Scopes was to start. Dudley Field Malone first stated that to convict Scopes the prosecution had to prove that Scopes not only taught the theory of evolution but that he at the same time denied the theory of creation as set forth in the Bible. He attempted to convince the jury that there was more than one theory of creation set forth in the Bible and that these were conflicting, that while there was a conflict between evolution and the Old Testament there was no conflict between evolution and Christianity and, lastly, that science did not claim, as the prosecution continued to reiterate, that man had sprung from monkeys. Hays equaled the high standard of pleading set by Darrow and Malone when he discoursed on the history of the Bible, tracing its development from the original manuscripts in Hebrew, Aramaic and Greek and pointing out the difficulties of translation.

Stewart and McKenzie for the prosecution argued spiritedly that the sovereign state of Tennessee had the right to pass any law it wished and to refuse to teach anything in its public schools which it saw fit. Fourteen-year-old Howard Morgan, son of the banker who had given up his home to the Darrows, was put on the stand to testify what he had been taught about evolution by Scopes. Young Morgan said that Scopes had taught him, "The earth was once a hot, molten mass, too hot for plant or animal life to exist upon it; in the sea the earth cooled off; there was a little germ of one-cell organism formed, and this organism kept evolving until it got to be a pretty good-sized animal and then came on to be a land animal, and it kept on evolving, and from this was man, and that man was just another mammal."

McKenzie evolved the best gag of the prosecution when he summed up this testimony by saying, "God issued some sort of protoplasm or soft dishrag and put it in the ocean and said, 'Old Boy, if you wait around about six thousand years I will make something out of you.' "

The courthouse continued to be jammed with spectators, many of whom arrived at dawn with their lunch boxes. On this first day that the jury was allowed to be present a number of the spectators rose at the noon hour to go for some lunch but, when they saw the mob of people waiting to take their places, dashed back to their seats and went without food. Again and again the thousand pairs of eyes in the courtroom were turned on William Jennings Bryan, but Bryan sat cooling himself with his fan. The faithful were neither frightened nor impatient; they knew that in his own good time Bryan would speak.

Against the charge that Scopes had taught certain elementals of evolution Darrow had no intention of entering a defense. His defense was to be that there was possible more than one interpretation of the biblical creation; that although Scopes might have violated the Fundamentalist idea of biblical interpretation he had by no means gone contrary to the biblical theory of creation held by millions of other Christians; that a teacher could demonstrate to his pupils that man had evolved over a period of hundreds of thousands of years, from an infinite variety of lower organisms, and by no means violate the story of Genesis.

The defense had assembled in Dayton an illustrious group of biologists, zoologists, geologists, anthropologists, educators, clergymen and Bible experts who were prepared to go on the stand and relate with facts and figures, charts and graphs, the story of the birth and growth of the earth and mankind, to testify that this process of evolving through which every living thing had gone was the precise one which the story of Genesis retold in poetic form. For Darrow this was to be the great and important part of the proceedings; with millions of people caught up in the bizarre excitement of the trial, with the press reporting every word from Dayton on its front pages under arresting headlines, there would be an opportunity almost unparalleled in mass education, an opportunity to illuminate the findings and attitudes of science for those people who had never had an opportunity to encounter these strides forward in man's learning of the truth about himself and his world.

But the prosecution thought otherwise; they had not the slightest intention of allowing Darrow, Hays and Malone to use the Tennessee courtroom for the purpose of spreading their heresies. The Fundamentalists of Tennessee said that evolution violated the story of creation as told in the Bible; therefore, anything the expert witnesses might have to say about birds and bugs would be immaterial, irrelevant and incompetent. Judge Raulston refused to rule against the admissibility of such evidence until he had heard some of it. Once again the jury was banished, and Darrow put on the stand the first and only defense witness to be called, Dr Maynard M. Metcalf, a zoologist from Johns Hopkins University. Dr Metcalf defined organic evolution as a theory which bound together the findings of the geologists, zoologists and anthropologists; he traced the earliest forms of flora and fauna, sketched briefly the development of man as a primate.

Acrimony once again broke out, for Attorney General Stewart made another personal attack on Darrow. "Mr Darrow is the greatest criminal lawyer in America today. His courtesy is noticeable; his ability is known, and it is a shame in my mind, in the sight of a great God, that a mentality like his has strayed so far from the natural goal that it should follow—great God, the good that a man of his ability could have done if he had aligned himself with the forces of right instead of aligning himself with that which strikes its fangs at the very bosom of Christianity."

Hearty "Amens" came from the spectators.

Darrow wheeled and glared.

The case cut too deeply into his vitals for him to remain calm and judicial, particularly since the greater portion of the trial was being held outside the bounds of law or judicial procedure. No case had ever moved him as did this attack on education. He was terrified at the thought of what would happen to the United States and its people if these Fundamentalists who were pressing so hard against him in the courtroom, fighting his every word and gesture, cheering every sentiment of his opponent, should gain control of the country, the way the Prohibitionists had gained control. In virtually every case of his almost half century of practice he had known that there were two sides; no matter how relentlessly he had fought his opponents, he had been able to understand them and their point of view. This was the first case in his career in which he was profoundly convinced that there were not two sides, but only one; that the Fundamentalists were an insidious potential for destruction; that there was no tolerant word that could be said for their intolerance, not even when he realized that their intolerance and primitive religion had arisen from the devastating poverty growing out of the Civil War, which had left the South little to go on but its belief in God. So passionately did he feel about it that there were moments when it threw him.

It was the first case in which Clarence Darrow had proffered his services; it was the first case in which he quarreled with the judge in open court until he was held for contempt; in which he was to lose his temper with the spectators in the courtroom. In his microscopic dissection of Harry Orchard he had found a moment to pause and say that he did not condemn Orchard, who could not help being what he was; now he was for the first time to be merciless to the point of cruelty to his leading adversary, William Jennings Bryan.

With the jury still banished, Bryan at last rose to his feet; he would permit no more of this "pseudoscientific" material to be interjected into the trial. His shirt collar was tucked under, his sleeves rolled up, his mouth pulled taut and thin, and there was a fighting gleam in his eye. The courtroom became hushed and still; Tennesseans fixed their eyes upon their spokesman with great love and trust. Like Darrow, Bryan, too, considered this a magnificent opportunity for mass education, a God-inspired command to lead a wandering and confused people back to the bosom of the Lord.

Darrow had watched with growing uneasiness how Bryan, stripped of political influence and eased out of the Democratic inner circles, had turned to religion as a career, as a means of reestablishing his power and importance. He did not find it strange that Bryan should devote his full energies to religion as a means of expression. He had always thought that Bryan should have been a preacher; even the "Cross of Gold" speech which had earned him the Democratic nomination in 1896 had been more of a religious harangue than a political or economic one, as the title indicated.

William Jennings Bryan based his Fundamentalism on his oft-repeated statement that "I am more interested in the rock of ages than in the age of rocks." To this mentality and approach to life Clarence Darrow was the complete antithesis; for fifty years he had been fascinated by the ever-ramifying study of evolution, a working theory binding together the factual material that had been unearthed by the sciences. "I had been reared by my father on books of science," he wrote. "Huxley's books had been household guests with us for years, and we had all of Darwin's as fast as they were published. Such books as Tyler's *Primitive Culture*, Lyell's *Geology*, Draper, Winwood Reade, Buckle, Tyndall and Spencer also were on my father's shelves and later were on mine, and most of them I had read. They had long been my companions."

He felt that Bryan preaching in the Chautauqua Circle on "The Prince of Peace" could do no harm, but Bryan working with an inexhaustible energy to organize the Southern states into a solid anti-evolution block could accomplish an irreparable harm, for in William Jennings Bryan the Fundamentalists had found their perfect leader.

7

In one respect Clarence Darrow and William Jennings Bryan had achieved a similar greatness. Bryan called himself a commoner; he named his weekly magazine *The Commoner;* he fought always for the poor, the disinherited. Few men fought for the common people; that was why millions of Americans loved him; that was why they had looked up to him for guidance, were confident that he would never betray them because he could never be bought. He had fought for the income tax as a method of leveling wealth when the income tax was being condemned as vicious, radical and destructive. He had worked for international peace; he preached peace on earth, good will to men. So completely had Bryan been for the common people against the money powers of Wall Street that the New York *Tribune* had charged after the 1896 campaign that he belonged to the tradition of Altgeld and Debs.

But Bryan had a sluggish and shallow mind. He was sketchily educated, knew nothing of the arts except that an occasional painting, piece of music or line of literature could be used to illumine a religious principle. He had a native wit, the ability to turn a phrase neatly, but he was too lazy to study, to broaden, deepen or sharpen his mind, to pursue facts and figures with which to put his humanitarian convictions on a solid base. He was possessed by the conviction that he was the most important man of his times, sent to earth directly by the Heavenly Father. "I have always been right," asserted William Jennings Bryan, and he believed it, for how could he be wrong if his every movement was being directed by God? He exclaimed that he did not mind so much with whom he laid down so long as he was clad in the armor of a righteous cause. Never once in his life did he believe that his cause was not righteous. On the lecture platform millions of words poured forth from his enormous mouth, couched in the rolling, majestic prose of the King James Bible, which he read unceasingly, for his outstanding gift lay in his vocal chords; he was an overpowering orator; only Henry Ward Beecher had a voice more moving and mesmeric than his.

A hypnotic purveyor of a vague Christian humanitarianism, Bryan never learned anything of the practical affairs of administration or the ways of the world. Though he had failed three times to get himself elected as President of the United States, in 1896, 1900 and 1908, his influence had secured the Democratic nomination for Woodrow Wilson in 1912. Partly out of gratitude, partly because he knew Bryan still had widespread popularity among the Democratic voters, Wilson named him secretary of state. As secretary of state, Bryan displayed such abysmal ignorance of international affairs that he dumfounded the American ambassadors and threw the department into confusion. He set into motion a spoils system for "deserving Democrats" which threatened to disrupt half the governmental service. Of the meaning of legislation, of the economic background and basis of such modernizing of government as the Federal Reserve Act, he could understand nothing. The best men in the administration talked at him night and day to find that his mind was closed and barred by an iron door behind which nestled only his stock phrases and set speeches.

Colonel House said of him, "I do not believe that anyone ever succeeded in changing his mind. He feels that his ideas are God given and are not susceptible to the mutability of those of the ordinary human being." David Huston remarked, "I discovered that one could drive a prairie schooner through any part of his argument and never scrape against a fact or a sound statement."

Bryan protested against the appointment of Dr Charles W. Eliot as ambassador to China on the grounds that "Eliot was a Unitarian and did not believe in the divinity of Christ, and the new Chinese civilization was founded upon the Christian movement." He spent his hours at his desk sending out autographed cards to Americans, asking them to sign their name above his and thus take the temperance pledge. He further made of his office an object of ridicule throughout the world by insisting upon appearing between vaudeville acts at Chautauqua revival meetings. After a little more than two years he had resigned from his office, to the relief of everyone, because he could not approve President Wilson's policy, which he thought was driving the United States into war. Once war was declared, he offered to enlist in the army as a private—at the age of sixty-five.

A fanatical worker for temperance in the drinking of liquors, he had told President Wilson that he would accept the position of secretary of state, "only if I do not have to serve intoxicating liquors in the course of my duties." However, according to the statement of the man who traveled with him on his presidential campaigns, "few more intemperate men ever lived. Sloan Gordon remembers one huge breakfast eaten by Bryan on a Virginia plantation in 1900. First a large cantaloupe. Then two quail followed by Virginia ham and a half-dozen eggs. After that a full plate of batter-cakes swimming in butter and a second helping of the same. In addition, there were many cups of coffee and fried potatoes and side dishes of various kinds before he left the table, ready to begin a day of speechmaking on temperance."

His outstanding virtue was that he was a good man. An associate commented, "When Bryan attempted to debate he entangled himself and his listeners in a mass of illogical and irrelevant material. His intentions were honest, but he was wrong."

That, thought Darrow, should be Bryan's epitaph: his intentions were honest, but he was wrong.

During the past few years Bryan had been dealing in Florida real estate and had earned for himself well over a million dollars. He continued his preaching, particularly to the crowds in the parks at Miami, but both his influence and his powers were waning. In spite of his advancing years, in spite of his disappointment and frustration, his ego flamed with the same intensity as it had in his youth. He had tried unceasingly to wedge himself into an office, to have Florida elect him to the United States Senate, to be elected moderator of the Presbyterian Church, which had just refused his command to pass an anti-evolution resolution. No one wanted to listen to him except the Fundamentalists of the Bible Belt.

Very well then, if God had reduced his vineyard to the Fundamentalists, then God must have a purpose; God must have meant for him to conquer the world through Fundamentalism. At last he began devoting all his time to preaching Fundamentalism in the South, traveling across mountains and prairies and swamps to harangue, exhort, plead and command that his followers work unceasingly to have their state legislatures pass anti-evolution laws. He hoped to turn Fundamentalism into a political movement of which he would be the head; though he did not hope to get himself elected as President of the United States on a Fundamentalist ticket, he was confident that garbed in this righteous cause he this time could become so powerful that he could dictate the choice of President, congressman, governor; control the school, the university, the press.

He now raised both arms in a pontifical gesture, converting the Dayton courtroom spectators into a congregation. "My friends——" he said. "I beg your pardon, if the court please, I have been so in the habit of talking to an audience instead of a court that I will sometimes say 'my friends,' although I happen to know not all of them are my friends."

When the laughter subsided he continued. "If the people of Tennessee were to go into a state like New York, the one from which this impulse comes to resist this law, and tried to convince the people that a law they had passed ought not to be enforced, don't you think it would be resented as impertinence? The people of this state knew what they were doing when they passed the law, and they knew the dangers of the doctrine, knew that they did not want it taught to their children. It isn't proper to bring experts in here to try to defeat the purpose of the people of this state by trying to show that what they denounce and outlaw is a beautiful thing that everybody ought to believe in."

The courtroom clapped. Not satisfied with this solid argument, Bryan humorously attacked the evolution testimony of Dr Metcalf. Though his barbs steadily drew laughter, they were based on a tangential reasoning by means of which he avoided the point at issue. He drew a laugh by saying that, judging by some of the people he had met, there must be more than thirty-five thousand varieties of sponges. He got another by saying that he would quote the number of animal breeds in round numbers even though he didn't think the animals bred in round numbers. He drew not only laughter but applause by saying, "Then we have mammals, thirty-five hundred of them in a little circular diagram, with man also in the circle, and try to find man! They were teaching your children that man was a mammal, and so indistinguishable among other mammals that they leave him there with thirty-four hundred and ninety-nine other mammals." He earned further chuckles by commenting on how hard it was to shut up man in a little circle with all these animals that have an odor that extends beyond their circumference. But his loudest laugh was gained when he lamented satirically that the evolutionists wouldn't even let us descend from American monkeys, only from European monkeys.

The Fundamentalists were delighted with their champion; their confidence rose, for they felt that Bryan was annihilating the evolutionists by making fools of them. They listened with rapt eagerness while he maintained that evolution was not a theory but only a hypothesis, that since the evolutionists could not agree among themselves on the origin of the species, since important changes had been made since Darwin first promulgated his findings, evolution was, therefore, an incoherent mass of conjecture and guesswork with neither a scientific nor factual base.

He then delivered the long-awaited sermon on the immutability of revealed religion. "The Bible is the word of God; the Bible is the only expression of man's hope of salvation. The Bible, the record of the Son of God, the Saviour of the world, born of the Virgin Mary, crucified and risen again. That Bible is not going to be driven out of this court by experts who come hundreds of miles to testify that they can reconcile evolution with its ancestor in the jungle, with man made by God in His image, man put here for purposes as a part of the divine plan."

There were loud "Amens" from the back of the courtroom. Darrow cried, "I want those 'Amens' to be put in the record."

Encouraged by the response, Bryan rose to a higher pitch and reached his climax. "Your honor asked me whether evolution has anything to do with the principle of the virgin birth. Yes, because this principle of evolution disputes the miracles, there is no place for the miracles in this train of evolution, and the Old Testament and the New are filled with miracles. If this doctrine is true this logic eliminates every mystery in the Old Testament and the New and eliminates everything supernatural, and that means they eliminate the virgin birth—that means they eliminate the resurrection of the body—that means they eliminate the doctrine of atonement and that they believe man has been rising all the time, that man never fell, that when the Saviour came there was not any reason for His coming; there was no reason why He should not go as soon as He could, that He was born of Joseph or some other corespondent and that He lies in His grave; and when the Christians of this state have tied their hands and said, 'We will not take advantage of our power to teach religion to children by teachers paid by us,' these people come in from the outside of the state and force upon the people of this state and upon the children of the taxpayers of this state a doctrine that refutes not only their belief in God but their belief in a Saviour and belief in heaven and takes from them every moral standard that the Bible gives us."

There was thunderous applause. The crowds swarmed around Bryan, shaking his hand, thumping him on the back, thanking him with tears in their eyes. Darrow turned in his chair to ask of Arthur Garfield Hays, sitting just behind him, "Can it be possible that this trial is taking place in the twentieth century?"

8

The attorneys for the defense walked out of the courthouse glaze-eyed and bewildered. If Judge Raulston should agree with Bryan, forbid the scientific witnesses to testify, the trial would be over. The defense would be defeated.

The only one who cheered them up was Representative Butler, who had written the Anti-Evolution Law. "The Judge ought to give 'em a chance to tell what evolution is," said Butler. "Course we got 'em licked anyhow, but I believe in being fair and square and American. Besides, I'd like to know what evolution is myself." Butler had thought that his Bible was the first and only Bible ever written; when someone had told him that the King James version of the Bible was not the only version the poor man was overcome.

The next morning the court assembled to hear Judge Raulston rule to exclude the experts and their testimony. He based his ruling on the claim that neither religion nor evolution was on trial, that Scopes was on trial for violating a specific Tennessee law.

Some of the newspapermen, in particular H. L. Mencken, were so convinced that the ruling ended the case that they packed up and went home. Robbed of his last shred of defense by what he considered a prejudiced verdict, Darrow went icy with anger. When Judge Raulston attempted to interject humor into his ruling by saying, "I desire to suggest that I believe evolutionists should at least show man the consideration to substitute the word 'ascend' for 'descend,'" his anger exploded.

"The state of Tennessee doesn't rule the world yet," he snapped. "With the hope of enlightening the court as a whole I want to say that the scientists probably will not correct the words 'descent of man,' and I want to explain what descent means as starting with a low form of life and finally reaching man."

"We all have dictionaries," said Attorney General Stewart.

"I don't think the court has one," rejoined Darrow.

When he asked for the rest of the day to draw up certain papers which the defense wished to present to the court and the judge asked why it would take the rest of the day, Darrow replied, "I do not understand why every request of the defense is overruled."

"I hope you do not mean to reflect on the court?" asked Judge Raulston.

"Well," drawled Darrow, "your honor has the right to hope."

"I have a right to do something else," said the judge.

"All right, all right," murmured Darrow.

The next morning the Chattanooga *News* cried in its headline: RAULSTON BANS DEFENSE EXPERTS; DARROW INSULTS COURT.

On Monday Judge Raulston cited him for contempt of court. "Men may become prominent," said Judge Raulston from the bench, "but they should never feel themselves superior to the law or to justice. He who would hurl contempt into the records of my court insults and outrages the good people of one of the greatest states of the Union." He thereupon ordered Darrow to appear before him the following morning to answer the citation and required him to post a lawful bond for five thousand dollars.

"What is the bond, your honor?" gasped Darrow.

"Five thousand dollars," repeated Judge Raulston.

"I do not have to put it up this morning?"

"Not until the papers are served upon you."

"Now I do not know whether I can get anybody, your honor." Frank Spurlock of Chattanooga went bond. The hearing proceeded for another hour while Darrow calmed himself. He then pulled himself up from his reclining position in the chair and fingered the thin lock of hair back from his eyes. He had placed himself at a disadvantage. Apologizing to the court, he said, "I have been practicing law for forty-seven years, and I have been most of the time in court. I have had many a case where I have had to do what I have been doing here, fighting the public opinion of the people in the community where I was trying the case. I never yet have in all my time had any criticism by the court for anything I have done in court. I haven't the slightest fault to find with the court. Personally I don't think it constitutes a contempt, but I am quite certain that the remark should not have been made and the court could not help taking notice of it, and I am sorry that I made it ever since I got the time to read it, and I want to apologize to the court for it."

He got his biggest hand of the trial on this apology. Judge Raulston forgave him by saying, "My friends, and Colonel Darrow, the Man that I believe came into the world to save man from sin, the Man that died on the cross that man might be redeemed, taught that it was godly to forgive, and were it not for the forgiving nature of Himself I would fear for man. The Saviour died on the cross pleading with God for the men who crucified Him. I believe in that Christ. I believe in these principles. I accept Colonel Darrow's apology. I feel that I am justified in speaking for the people of the great state that I represent when I say to him that we forgive him and we forget it and we commend him to go back home and learn in his heart the words of the Man who said, 'If you thirst, come unto Me and I will give thee life.' "

The next morning Judge Raulston ordered the trial to be transferred to the courthouse lawn because the throngs in the courtroom, with their laughter and applause and demonstrations, were weakening the floor, and there was danger of its collapsing. The judge, jury, and counsel were seated on the raised platform used by the preachers of the town, from which Bryan had delivered an address the Sunday before. Just below the platform tables were set out for the newspaper-, telegraph and radio men. The rough benches which covered almost the entire lawn were quickly filled with five thousand spectators, sweltering under the midsummer sun, but far cooler than they had been in the stuffy courtroom. For the defense this was to be a move from the enclosed areas of technical law to the open air of free discussion and the solid earth of reason.

And once again Darrow caused an uproar; he demanded that the huge sign saying READ YOUR BIBLE, which was attached to the side of the building not more than ten feet from where the jury was to sit, be taken down because it was prejudicial to the interests of the defendant. Ben McKenzie sprang to his feet to voice the sentiments of the Tennesseans in the audience when he said, "It is their defense that they do not deny the Bible, that they expect to introduce proof to make it harmonize. Why should we remove the sign cautioning the people to read the word of God, just to satisfy the others in the case?" His son added, "I have never seen the time in the history of this country when any man should be afraid to be reminded of the fact that he should read his Bible, and if they represent a force that is aligned with the devil and his satellites——"

The accusation that Darrow, Hays and Malone were aligned with the devil caused a furor. Bryan entered the fray to cry, "If their arguments are sound and sincere, that the Bible can be construed so as to recognize evolution, I cannot see why READ YOUR BIBLE would necessarily mean partiality to our side. However, Paul said, 'If eating meat maketh my brother to offend, I shall eat no meat while the world lasts.' If leaving that up there during the trial makes our brother to offend, I would take it down during the trial."

Darrow agreed to let the READ YOUR BIBLE stay where it was, provided the defense could put up a banner of equal size right beside it, which would read, READ YOUR EVOLUTION.

Judge Raulston ordered the sign removed from the courthouse wall. The jury which again had been excluded during this fracas was brought in hopping mad because they had been sent out to twiddle their thumbs during nine tenths of the trial and had missed the fun. They were ready to acquit Scopes of any and all charges to get even with the court.

It was an old Darrow stratagem of putting the prosecution on the defense, which not only kept the hearing alive but turned the tide of victory. Since the court would not permit him to put scientific witnesses on the stand to build up evolution and the defense of his client, the only recourse he had left was to put the prosecution on the stand and try to break down the literal interpretation of the Bible. He asked William Jennings Bryan if he would be willing to go on the stand to testify as an expert on the Bible. Bryan assented most happily, and the Scopes monkey trial took on another dimension, providing the American people with what the New York *Times* described as the most amazing court scene in Anglo-Saxon history.

Bryan took his seat on the hard, spindle-legged pedestal, began fanning himself and faced his inquisitor. Darrow hesitated for a moment before beginning.

"You have given considerable study to the Bible, haven't you, Mr Bryan?" he asked quietly.

"Yes, I have," replied Bryan. "I have studied the Bible for about fifty years."

"Do you claim that everything in the Bible should be literally interpreted?"

"I believe everything in the Bible should be accepted as it is given there; some of the Bible is given illustratively. For instance: 'Ye are the salt of the earth.' I would not insist that man was actually salt or that he had flesh of salt, but it is used in the sense of salt as saving God's people."

"When you read that the whale swallowed Jonah, how do you literally interpret that?"

"When I read that a big fish swallowed Jonah, I believe it, and I believe in a God who can make a whale and can make a man and make them both do what he pleases. One miracle is just as easy to believe as another."

"You mean just as hard?" smiled Darrow.

"It is hard to believe for you, but easy for me," replied Bryan.

After a brief flare-up by Stewart on the grounds that Darrow's questions were argumentative Darrow continued. "Do you believe Joshua made the sun stand still?" he asked Bryan.

"I believe what the Bible says," answered Bryan doggedly.

"I suppose you mean that the earth stood still?"

"I don't know. I am talking about the Bible now. I accept the Bible absolutely."

"Do you believe at that time the entire sun went around the earth?"

"No, I believe the earth goes around the sun."

"Do you believe that the men who wrote it thought that the day could be lengthened or that the sun could be stopped?"

"I believe what they wrote was inspired by the Almighty, and He may have used language that could be understood at that time—instead of language that could not be understood until Darrow was born."

There was laughter and applause in the courtyard. Bryan beamed. Darrow stood quietly by, expressionless.

"Now, Mr Bryan, have you ever pondered what would have happened to the earth if it stood still suddenly?"

"No."

"Don't you know it would have been converted into a molten mass of matter?"

"You testify to that when you get on the stand; I will give you a chance."

"You believe the story of the flood to be a literal interpretation?" Darrow now asked.

"Yes sir," replied Bryan.

"When was that flood?"

"I would not attempt to fix the day."

"But what do you think that the Bible itself says? Don't you know how it was arrived at?"

"I never made a calculation."

"What do you think?"

"I do not think about things I don't think about."

"Do you think about things you do think about?"

"Well, sometimes."

Once again there was laughter in the courtyard, but this time it was derisive laughter turned against William Jennings Bryan. He did not like it. He turned to glare at the spectators. Russell D. Owen reports that "Bryan was calmly contemptuous of this intellectual upstart as he answered the first questions, but he became restless under Darrow's relentless prodding and finally lost all control of his temper." When Attorney General Stewart objected to Darrow's cross-examining his own witness Bryan replied, "These gentlemen did not come here to try this case. They came here to try revealed religion. I am here to defend it, and they can ask me any questions they please."

This answer drew sharp applause. Darrow commented acidly, "Great applause from the bleachers."

"From those whom you call yokels," declared Bryan.

"I never called them yokels."

"That is the ignorance of Tennessee, the bigotry," mocked Bryan.

"You mean who are applauding you?" grinned Darrow.

"Those are the people whom you insult."

"You insult every man of science and learning in the world because he does not believe in your fool religion!" retorted Darrow.

Judge Raulston grew red in the face. It looked for a moment as though Darrow would once again be cited for contempt. Stewart put up a strong plea to have the examination stopped, to have Bryan removed from the stand. The court replied, "To stop it now would not be just to Mr Bryan."

Darrow took a deep breath before going on.

"How long ago was the flood, Mr Bryan?"

"Two thousand three hundred and forty-eight years B.C."

"You believe that all the living things that were not contained in the ark were destroyed?"

"I think the fish may have lived."

"Don't you know there are any number of civilizations that are traced back to more than five thousand years?"

"I am not satisfied by any evidence that I have seen."

"You believe that every civilization on the earth and every living thing, except possibly the fishes, were wiped out by the flood?"

"At that time."

"You have never had any interest in the age of the various races and peoples and civilizations and animals that exist upon the earth today?"

"I have never felt a great deal of interest in the effort that has been made to dispute the Bible by the speculations of men or the investigations of men."

"And you never have investigated to find out how long man has been on the earth?"

"I have never found it necessary."

"Don't you know that the ancient civilizations of China are six thousand or seven thousand years old, at the very least?"

"No, but they would not run back beyond the creation, according to the Bible, six thousand years."

"You don't know how old they are; is that right?" repeated Darrow.

"I don't know how old they are," answered Bryan, "but probably you do. I think you would give the preference to anybody who opposed the Bible."

"Well, you are welcome to your opinion. Have you any idea how old the Egyptian civilization is?"

"No."

"Mr Bryan, you don't know whether any other religion ever gave a similar account of the destruction of the earth by the flood?"

"The Christian religion has satisfied me, and I have never felt it necessary to look up some competing religions."

"Do you know how old the Confucian religion is?"

"I can't give you the exact date of it."

"Do you know how old the religion of Zoroaster is?"

"No sir."

"What about the religion of Confucius or Buddha? Do you regard them as competitive?"

"No, I think they are very inferior. Would you like for me to tell you what I know about it?"

"No. Do you know anything about how many people there were in Egypt thirty-five hundred years ago or how many people there were in China five thousand years ago?"

"No."

"Have you ever tried to find out?"

"No sir; you are the first man I ever heard of that has been interested in it."

"Mr Bryan, am I the first man you ever heard of who has been interested in the age of human societies and primitive man?"

"You are the first man I ever heard speak of the number of people at those different periods."

"Where have you lived all your life?"

"Not near you."

The audience again broke into laughter and applause. Darrow lost his composure, turned to the crowd and barked, "Why don't you cheer?" After a moment, when the spectators had become quiet again, he continued, "Did you ever read a book on primitive man? Like Tyler's *Primitive Culture*, or Boas, or any of the great authorities?"

"I don't think I have read the ones you have mentioned."

"Have you read any?"

"Well, I have read a little from time to time. But I didn't pursue it because I didn't know I was to be called as a witness."

"You have never in all your life made any attempt to find out about the other peoples of the earth—how old their civilizations are, how long they have existed on the earth—have you?"

"No sir, I have been so well satisfied with the Christian religion that I have spent no time trying to find arguments against it. I have all the information I want to live by and to die by."

Darrow paused for a moment. "Do you think the earth was made in six days?"

"Not six days of twenty-four hours."

"Doesn't the Bible say so?"

"No sir."

"Mr Bryan, do you believe that the first woman was Eve?"

"Yes."

"Do you believe she was literally made out of Adam's rib?"

"I do."

"Did you ever discover where Cain got his wife?"

"No sir; I leave the agnostics to hunt for her."

"Do you think the sun was made on the fourth day?"

"Yes."

"And they had evening and morning without the sun?"

"I am simply saying it is a period."

"The creation might have been going on for a long time?"

"It might have continued for millions of years."

"Yes. All right." Darrow waited a long moment to allow this admission to sink in. "Do you believe the story of the temptation of Eve by the serpent?" he continued.

"I will believe just what the Bible says. Read the Bible and I will answer."

"All right, I will do that. 'And I will put enmity between thee and the woman and between thy seed and her seed; it shall bruise thy head and thou shalt bruise his heel. Unto the woman he said, "I will greatly multiply thy sorrow and thy conception; in sorrow thou shalt bring forth children; and thy desire shall be to thy husband, and he shall rule over thee."' That is right, is it?"

"I accept it as it is."

"And God said to the serpent, 'Because thou hast done this, thou art cursed above all cattle, and above every beast of the field; upon thy belly shalt thou go and dust shalt thou eat all the days of thy life.' Do you think that is why the serpent is compelled to crawl upon its belly?"

"I believe that."

"Have you any idea how the snake went before that time?"

"No sir."

"Do you know whether he walked on his tail or not?"

"No sir. I have no way to know."

This answer brought a laugh, one with more derision than humor in it, the kind Bryan did not like. He flushed, turned to the judge. "Your honor, I think I can shorten this testimony. The only purpose Mr Darrow has is to slur at the Bible, but I will answer his questions, I shall answer them at once. I want the world to know that this man, who does not believe in a God, is trying to use a court in Tennessee——"

"I object to your statement," exploded Darrow. "I am exempting you on your fool ideas that no intelligent Christian on earth believes."

Judge Raulston was heartily sick of the rows. He ordered court adjourned before another one could break out. A group gathered about Darrow, shaking his hand and congratulating him. As he left the yard a throng followed him. Looking back, he saw Bryan standing with only one friend by his side. He had taken a terrible licking; the Bible had not suffered, but William Jennings Bryan had. He had been exposed as an ignoramus with a childlike mind. But Darrow felt neither triumphant nor happy; he remembered too well the day he had walked out of the Los Angeles courtroom after pleading the McNamaras guilty, when only one man had stood by him, when the crowd had turned against him as even now it turned against its own champion and spokesman.

In the press of the nation Bryan took an even worse beating, particularly from the columnists.

Bugs Baer released his acidulous humor on the father-and-son combination. "There are now two William Jennings Bryans. When Darrow walked into the courtroom this morning he saw a pair of Bryans perched in two practically empty chairs. The jury's verdict was that there were two Bryans, with no extenuating circumstances. Junior is a splendid orator of the hip-and-elbow type that mistakes a gesture for an argument and a loud voice for reason."

Will Rogers tried to be humorous about the incident but ended by being in deadly earnest. "Now personally, I like Bill, but when he says that he will make this his life's issue and take it up through all the various courts and finally endeavor to get it into the Constitution of the United States and make a political and presidential issue out of it, he is wrong. More wrong than he has ever been before. These other things he was wrong on didn't do much harm, but now he is going to try to drag something that pertains to the Bible into a political campaign. He can't ever do that. He might make Tennessee the side show of America, but he can't make a street carnival of the whole United States."

The next morning Judge Raulston ruled that Bryan could not go back on the stand. that everything he had said the day before had to be stricken from the evidence. The order to strike Bryan's testimony from the record was a blow to the visiting attorneys in that it took away their last basis for defense, and yet it was at the same time their only victory. Had Bryan been successful in defending the Fundamentalist conception of the Bible he doubtless would have been permitted to return to the stand; Judge Raulston's ruling could only be an admission of rout, defeat.

The trial was over. The jury was brought in. Darrow asked that they agree on a verdict of guilty in order that the case might be appealed to the Tennessee Supreme Court. Sullenly the jury obeyed Darrow's request and Judge Raulston's instructions; they declared Scopes guilty. The judge fined him a hundred dollars, then made a closing address. "It sometimes takes courage to search diligently for a truth that may destroy our preconceived notions and ideas. It sometimes takes courage to declare a truth or stand for an act that is in controvention to the public sentiment. A man who is big enough to search for the truth and find it and declare it in the face of all opposition is a big man."

Darrow thought this a fine and noble sentiment; he wished it had been manifested a little earlier in the trial.

9

The hot-dog and lemonade stands disappeared from the streets of Dayton. The anti-evolution headquarters took down its bookstalls. The visiting religious sects struck their tents and went home. The flags, the banners, the streamers and monkey pennants were removed from the streets, and Dayton went back to its quiet, peaceful life. A reporter for the Knoxville *Sentinel* chanted its requiem: "A lonesome quietness seemed to hover over the little Tennessee village. The only visitors to the courthouse were now and then some who had attended the trial and left some of their belongings in the courtroom. At the regular hour at which court had been called on previous mornings Sue Hicks, one of the attorneys for the prosecution, went strolling in the yard, walking casually up the steps. But instead of being watched by a crowd of eager spectators he was passed unnoticed by a group of barefoot boys playing around the entrance."

The Darrows left with friends for the Smoky Mountains to cool off and enjoy a rest. Bryan remained in Dayton, preparing for publication the closing speech to the jury which he had not been permitted to make in court, one of the most abstruse, confused and unintelligible documents of its times. On Sunday morning he spoke in a near-by town, telling his audience of his plans for a national campaign to force all schools to teach evolution as a theory instead of a fact and to see that all teachers who taught evolution as a fact were made to resign. On the drive back to Dayton he had a serious discussion with his wife in which he agreed that although he must continue his fight against evolution he must be careful not to encroach upon individual religious beliefs, because this would be intolerance.

Back in Dayton, in spite of the intense midday heat, he ate one of his enormous dinners. He then lay down to take a nap and died in his sleep.

Clarence and Ruby were hiking across a summit of the Smoky Mountains when the word of Bryan's death was brought to them. They returned to Dayton. When reporters said to him, "People down here believe that Bryan died of a broken heart because of your questioning," Darrow shrugged his shoulders and murmured in a voice so soft that the reporters could not hear him, "Broken heart nothing; he died of a busted belly." Aloud he said, "His death is a great loss to the American people."

It was almost a year later that the appeal was heard by the Supreme Court of Tennessee. In his argument Darrow recapitulated his philosophy of the freedom of the human mind. Though the hearing in Nashville was more dignified than had been the one in Dayton, the same passions and prejudice were displayed, with audiences thronging the statehouse, jamming the court, indulging in wild bursts of applause.

The Tennessee Supreme Court reversed the decision of the Dayton court on the technicality that Judge Raulston, instead of the jury, had fixed the amount of the fine, a politic evasion. Two of the justices held that the Anti-Evolution Law was constitutional; a third held that it was constitutional but had nothing to do with the Scopes case. One justice declared the law to be unconstitutional. "Always there is one man!" murmured Darrow. "Amen!"

The Scopes case had won another conquest for freedom: Bryan and his Fundamentalist dogma had been discredited; the literal interpretation of the Bible had been weakened; the Bryan University in Dayton, which had been projected to teach Fundamentalism, had progressed as far as a deep hole in the ground, in which state it remained. The high-school students of Tennessee were reading about evolution; the scientific approach to the understanding of man's inheritance had gained impetus; Judge Raulston had agreed to read Darwin's *Origin of the Species* and *Descent of Man*. The scientists who had worked on the case expressed to Darrow their "genuine respect for his ability, high purposes, integrity, moral sensitiveness and idealism."

Yet for Clarence Darrow the most meaningful aftermath of the trial was that a dance was given in his honor by the young people of Dayton. This tiny uprising seemed to him as though it might be a good omen.

CHAPTER XIII

Road to Glory

H<small>E LOVED</small> to go for long drives through the Wisconsin woods during the fall to look at the blaze of changing colors. He and Ruby made frequent trips with the Dwight McKays; before starting each would put an equal amount of cash in a money "poke" which they would then kick around the back seat of the car and have to search for frantically whenever they wished to buy something.

"Clarence didn't want people to cater to him," say the McKays; "he just wanted people to like him. He never criticized, never talked against anyone. He preferred our rattletrap where we shared everything fifty-fifty to being taken out in a Rolls-Royce. Once he drove out to Colorado in a terrible old Ford just because he liked the owners. If he enjoyed something he wanted to go all over it again to show his friends. On our driving trips we found that the whole world knew him, the great and humble alike, and in turn he was completely adjustable to all classes of people, particularly to children." Darrow was fond of the three McKay youngsters; frequently in the evening he would go to their home just to play with them. He would pretend to be reading from *The Book House* but instead would be making up the stories as he went along. When the children grew older and wanted to join their parents the McKays suggested that they shouldn't go on any more trips together because "someone else's kids are not like one's own."

"The first thing we do wrong," replied Darrow plaintively, "we'll get out and take the train home."

On long trips he liked to sing hymns and camp-meeting songs, frequently beguiling the McKays with "Onward, Christian Soldiers" or "Jesus, Lover of My Soul." When he wasn't feeling up to snuff he would eat apples and cheese out of his pocket. On one trip the seat of his pants wore so thin they could see his underwear through them. Once they all drove up to Flint to watch Clarence defend a woman who had shot her boy friend. "When we reached the town," says Mrs McKay, "Clarence couldn't remember the woman's name. We had to pump the local policeman in order to find out who his client was. When we registered at the hotel we had a riot because Clarence couldn't find his money; we hunted all over for it for an hour, only to find that Ruby had pinned it to the inside of his watch pocket."

Mrs McKay was a Catholic and, like his innumerable Catholic friends in Chicago, was always selling him chances for one of the church benefits. Finally he exclaimed, "I'm not going to buy any more of your lottery tickets until I can take a chance on a whole church." Among the Catholic priests he had many warm and devoted friends, particularly Father Barett, of Lowell, and Father Brummer. To a strange woman on a train who had listened to one of his discussions and suddenly asked, "Pardon me, Mr Darrow, but are you a Catholic?" he replied, "No, but if I were going to belong to any church I would belong to the Catholic Church; if I were buying life insurance I would buy it in a mutual company and not a stock company."

He bought his first automobile early in 1925, learning to drive it forward, but since he could not contrive to back it up he did not get much use out of it. He took numerous car trips into Minnesota with his newspaper friend, W. R. Kellogg, who says, "Darrow liked scenery and nature; he liked wilderness, game life, wild life. He loved to study the habits of insects in the woods at night; he had read extensively on the subject. He approved government reservations for the preservation of wild life, commenting on the fact that there were reservations for animals but not for humans. I was constantly amazed at the wide range of his interests; when we were driving through the wheat fields of North Dakota, discussing agrarian problems, he asked me what the freight charge was on a bushel of wheat from North Dakota to Minneapolis, the exact same question that had been asked me by Colonel Robert Ingersoll thirty years before, when I drove him through the same territory. Once when we were driving through the Black Hills of South Dakota we stopped at nightfall at Rapid City. As soon as people heard that Clarence Darrow was in town he was besieged by requests to give a lecture that night. The folks had only an hour or so to spread the news around the countryside, but by eight o'clock the hall was full. When he walked onto the platform Clarence looked like a human penguin with his hands behind him under his coat, but his personality was electric; electricity emanated from his physical body as well as from his mental equipment.

"Darrow had an active mind, restlessly investigating the facts and the truth. He reached the highest levels I ever knew personally of any man, yet his character was an enigma. He wanted people to be happy; he thought that was the goal of human life, but when he looked at the world he became pessimistic. People felt he had a wider and deeper conception of his subject and of his fellow man than anyone else, yet at the same time they knew he was like a small child because he was so simple and natural and uninhibited. In spite of his simple and honest and lovable character he excited the antagonism, the antipathy and the aversion of millions of people."

Further illuminating the enigma of Clarence Darrow, Peter Sissman says, "The really great souls somehow become tangled up in their thinking by their constant search for an answer to the riddles of life and of the universe. I consider Darrow a really great soul. He undoubtedly had the spark of genius, and he was a very acute thinker, but he would not resign himself to limit his thinking to what Spencer terms the knowable. In *Anathema* Leonid Andreyev pictures the struggle of a man like Darrow, seeking release from the prison wall of obscurity, attempting to scale it and perishing in the struggle."

Though Darrow may have been perishing in the struggle, he was a long time at it and was enjoying the process. Through the years Ruby continued to make his life pleasant in the flat on the Midway, a task in which she was aided by a fortunate choice in a helper. Marie Thompson was a young Frenchwoman, vigorous, intelligent, fun-loving, with an even disposition. She had been studying music at South Bend. "I told Mrs Darrow that I would come in as a companion and housekeeper," says Marie, "but that I wouldn't go in as a maid. I expected just to help them for a while and then continue with my music."

Marie cooked the meals, kept the house clean, helped Ruby burn red dye into the living-room carpet, traveled with them on many of their trips about the country. Marie was a Catholic; Clarence liked to twit her on ecclesiastical subjects. She catered to his idiosyncrasies about food, cooking Hubbard squash, old-fashioned red kidney beans, corn bread, corned beef, tongue, ham.

roast beef and lemon-cream pie, zealously eschewing spinach. As the years passed and she remained faithful and helpful, the Darrows came to feel that she was part of the family; Marie enlivened many an hour with her keen wit and laughter.

"I went out a lot," says Marie, "so Mr Darrow would ask me what I had heard about certain men or issues in the news, because he wanted to know what other people were thinking. I had lost my parents very early, and Mr Darrow was like a father to me. He was milk of human kindness. He was a family man; everything went along peaceful in the house. You could go to him with your troubles, and he was always so gracious. He never turned anyone away. He was occasionally irritable at what had happened in town, but we nearly always had lovely times. I liked being on the job, doing things for Mr Darrow; I felt he was entitled to it because he did so much for others."

He had spent the balance of the summer after the Scopes case lecturing to large crowds in Kansas City, St Louis and Denver. Whatever his announced subject, the experts in that field came to listen; even Al Capone, the liquor racketeer, came to hear him speak on prohibition in a Negro church in Chicago. Shortly after Darrow had returned from Dayton he had been called to the telephone. After listening a while he said, "Why, no. Do you think I would do such a damned-fool thing as that?" and hung up the receiver, exasperated. Asked what the trouble was, he replied, "Why, that damned-fool manager over at the vaudeville house has a trained ape, and he wants me to have my picture taken with the ape and he hasn't even got the ape's consent!"

He had been trying to retire from the practice of law since the Pettibone case in Boise in 1907. By 1926 he again had determined to take no more cases in which national conflict, intersectional strife, prejudice and passion played a part; he would watch from the side lines as younger and more vigorous men took up the cudgels. Practically every cause to which he had devoted himself had flashed into focus, giving him the opportunity to state his ultimate case. The sole labor of love which had not yet been afforded him was the chance to recapitulate the plight of the American Negro; he hoped to carry on his work in their behalf through writing and lecturing. Then, because it was an imperative of his life's design to resolve the causes with which he had been identified, in the city of Detroit, Michigan, race riots and mob violence culminated in the arrest of eleven Negroes on a charge of murder. He returned to New York in September, where he was visiting with Arthur Garfield Hays, when a committee from the National Association for the Advancement of Colored People called to urge him to undertake the defense of the family and friends of Dr Ossian Sweet.

"We found Clarence in bed with all his clothes on," relates Arthur Spingarn. "He had been told that one colored man and two white men would come to see him." Spingarn, who had dark hair and a swarthy complexion, related the facts of the Sweet case to Darrow. When he had finished Darrow said sympathetically:

"Yes, I know full well the difficulties faced by your race."

"I'm sorry, Mr Darrow," replied Spingarn, "but I'm not a Negro."

Darrow turned to Charles Studin, another member of the committee, and said, "Well, you understand what I mean."

"I am not colored either," replied Studin.

Darrow looked at the third man, who had blond hair and blue eyes. "I would not make that mistake with you," he said.

"I am a Negro," replied Walter White, secretary of the National Association for the Advancement of Colored People.

Darrow jumped out of bed. "That settles it," he cried. "I'll take the case."

2

When Clarence was five years of age John Brown had come to Kinsman to confer with Amirus Darrow about the Underground Railroad. John Brown had put his hand on the boy's head and said, "The Negro has too few friends; you and I must never desert him." Darrow had followed this command, not out of a sense of duty, but out of love. He said, "When it comes to human beings, I am color blind; to me people are not simply white or black; they are all freckled." He had delivered to colored audiences throughout the country one of the most glowing lectures in his repertoire, a eulogy of John Brown, "whose love of the slave was a part of that fire that, through the long and dreary night, kindles a divine spark in the minds of earth's noble souls." He had traveled from Chicago to Washington, D.C., to lecture for a week in the classrooms of the Howard University School of Law, a Negro school, and on Sunday had addressed the entire student body in the chapel. While refusing to join hundreds of worthwhile organizations that had solicited his membership, he had been a member of the National Association for the Advancement of Colored People since its inception, contributing liberally of his time and money, writing articles for the Negro press, lecturing to their groups, helping them to form trade schools, colleges and labor unions, trying always to secure for them the rights guaranteed by the Federal government but ignored by the individual states. He had defended penniless Negroes in court, attended Negro churches; his friends among the colored people were frequently in his home. Ruby had worked by his side for tolerance and the eradication of racial prejudice.

Once when they had gone South to lecture at Tuskegee they were met at the station by a number of fine-looking, uniformed students of the college. Clarence was ushered into a large car at the front of the procession. When someone guided Ruby toward the same car she explained that she would be pleased to let as many as possible occupy the car in which her husband would ride and that she would ride with some of the others. The colored students exchanged glances, then explained stumblingly that it was forbidden by local law for a white woman to ride with a colored man.

"What might happen?" she asked.

"We might be arrested, heavily fined; we men might be imprisoned."

"We're all going to get into this rear car together," decreed Ruby. "I'd be glad to offer myself as one protesting against such unconstitutional and illegal action against the equality of American citizens. I'd like nothing better than to have our procedure interfered with. We have an attorney in the front car that could handle the situation." They were not arrested.

Clarence and Ruby were honorary members of the Four Hundred Club of colored women in Harlem, to which they took such friends as Lillian Gish and George Jean Nathan. W. E. B. Du Bois, the Negro editor, says, "Being a Negro and rather tense in my feelings, I was drawn to Clarence Darrow because he was absolutely lacking in racial consciousness and because of the broad catholicity of his knowledge and tastes. He was one of the few white folk with whom I felt quite free to discuss matters of race and class which usually I would not bring up." Darrow's favorite colored story was about a freed man in the South who was asked: "Sam, how are you getting on?" "Well, not doing so well." "Don't get food so regular as you used to?" "No suh!" "Don't have nobody to look after you?" "No suh, that is a fact." "Well, Sam, weren't you better off in slavery?" "Well, I tells you, suh, it's like this: there's a sort of looseness about this here freedom that I likes!" Du Bois recalls, "I can see Darrow in his loose-fitting clothes chuckling over this story. The 'looseness' of freedom was something that appealed to him."

On the twelfth of October Darrow arrived in Detroit to secure a brief postponement and to assemble the facts in the Sweet case; he found them indigenous to the industrial growth of the city. In 1910, before the automobile industry had developed, there were only six thousand Negroes in Detroit. The expansion of the factories having created a demand for labor which could not be supplied by local markets, the manufacturers set up employment bureaus in various parts of the country, importing workers to Detroit in great numbers. The chief source of supply was the poor white and the Negro of the Southern states, where wages were low, labor mobile. By 1925 the Negro population in Detroit had increased to sixty thousand, yet they were still confined to the three small wards that had been apportioned to them in 1910. Rents were exorbitant; most of the buildings violated the health and safety laws. Since the Negro population was earning around seventy-five thousand dollars a day in wages, it was inevitable that there should be a constant immigration of colored doctors, dentists, lawyers, teachers, clergymen, businessmen and entertainers. Many of these could afford to buy good homes. As fewer residences became available in the Negro section, they looked for them outside the colored boundaries. This had happened in many American cities, the Negroes reaching out in several directions from their central district, absorbing further living quarters, generally without financial loss to those who either sold to the Negroes at higher prices than they could get from the whites or kept possession of their property and rented to the Negroes at high rentals.

However, many of Detroit's workers had brought with them from the South their anti-Negro prejudice. The police force had taken on a good many Southerners who did not doff their color prejudice when they donned the uniform of the city. During the war there had been a resurgence of the Ku Klux Klan, taking such strong root among the Southerners in Detroit that by 1925 it had gained control over portions of the political machine. When the more affluent colored people began seeking homes outside of their limited neighborhood the Ku Klux Klan organized neighborhood-improvement associations to keep them from either owning or renting property within these districts. Its propaganda campaign spread fear and distrust of the Negro among the native residents. The Detroit police instituted a reign of terror, shooting dead on the streets between forty and fifty colored men. The mayor issued a statement in which he begged the public to see that the riots "do not grow into a condition which will be a lasting stain on the reputation of Detroit as a law-abiding community." No investigation was made of the killings.

In early June of 1925 Dr Ossian Sweet, an attractive young Negro, one of the most brilliant of Detroit's colored population, purchased for eighteen thousand five hundred dollars a two-story brick house in a foreign-born workingman's section. He anticipated no trouble when buying the house, partly because the husband of the white woman who owned it was a Negro (albeit so light in coloring that the neighborhood was never sure of his race) and because the house was only a few blocks from the white district in which Mrs Sweet, the cultivated, well-educated daughter of a Negro musician, had been raised. Yet there were signs on the horizon that portended trouble. Only three months before, a colored woman with a five-weeks-old baby had purchased a home on Merrill Street, in a white neighborhood; a crowd of whites had gathered and stoned it. The next day the woman resolutely had had the windows repaired. The threatening mob again gathered in front of the house. This time she fired over their heads with a shotgun. The crowd ran, but a white neighbor swore out a warrant for her arrest. In April a mob of whites attacked the home of another Negro who had moved a short distance out of the colored section. Dr Turner, highly respected physician and surgeon, was mobbed, his possessions smashed. Negro families who had lived for years in peace and friendliness with their white neighbors were threatened and warned to move back to the colored wards.

During the following weeks Dr Sweet saw three more families driven from their homes. He also knew that a Waterworks Park Improvement Association had been formed in his own neighborhood shortly after he had purchased his home on the corner of Charlevoix and Garland, and that at a meeting of this association held on the school grounds opposite his newly acquired property a crowd of six hundred people gathered to hear a speech by the incendiary who had led the mob which drove Dr Turner from his home. The woman from whom Dr Sweet had purchased his house but who had not yet moved out of it received a telephone call after the meeting of the association, telling her that the assemblage agreed to "co-operate in enforcement of existing property restrictions; that if Doctor Sweet moved in she would be killed, the house blown up." She cried to Sweet, "My God, since the other doctor has allowed them to run him out it looks like they will run everybody out!"

Ossian Sweet knew what these people meant by "co-operation in enforcement." It became obvious that he could not move into his new home without encountering serious trouble. He had already

made the down payment of thirty-five hundred dollars, the total
of his savings. If he gave up this house, took his loss, what was
he to do then? He still had to have a home for himself and his
family, and there was no home available in the colored district.
If he did not move into this house, which he now owned, where
would he move? Over and above the personal problem there was
the problem of his race. If he, too, allowed a mob to keep him
out of his own home by threats of force and violence, would he
not be setting a precedent which would victimize his fellow Negro
throughout the land, make his lot harder than ever, keep him
forever penned within the slums of inadequate quarters? Could
he let himself down? Could he let his people down?

The answer to the problem emerged from the character of the
man. Ossian Sweet had been born in Orlando, Florida. He had
worked his way through Wilberforce Academy in Ohio and the
medical school of Howard University in Washington, D.C. Equipped
with a first-rate brain and an indomitable resolution to "rise in
the world and make a great deal of money," he paid his tuition by
firing furnaces, shoveling snow, waiting on table and serving at
parties. In 1921 he opened an office in the colored section of
Detroit, where he was immediately successful. The following year
he had married Gladys Mitchell. After two years of practice they
had put together sufficient savings for a trip to Europe. Ossian
worked in the hospitals of Vienna for six months, studying gyne-
cology and pediatrics, then went to Paris where he worked under
Madame Curie of the Curie Institute. Upon returning to Detroit
the Sweet family lived with Gladys' parents until the spring of
1925, when they had accumulated thirty-five hundred dollars, and
Gladys Sweet went looking for a home. "I had in mind only two
things," said Mrs Sweet; "first to find a house that was in itself
desirable and, second, to find one that would be within our pocket-
book. I wanted a pretty home, and it made no difference to me
whether it was in a white neighborhood or a colored neighborhood.
Only I couldn't find such a house in the colored neighborhood."

Dr Sweet decided that he must not only move into his new home at
all costs but that he must defend it against mob violence. He notified
the Detroit police that he was going to move in on September
eighth. At ten-thirty in the morning, under police guard, he arrived with two small vans of furniture, a supply of food and a
case containing ten guns and almost four hundred rounds of ammunition. Dr and Mrs Sweet, who had left their baby with its
grandparents, were joined by two of Ossian's brothers, Dr Otis
Sweet, a dentist, and Henry, a student at Wilberforce College.

With them went a chauffeur, a chum of Henry's and another friend. Two colored women decorators came in later in the afternoon to assist Mrs Sweet.

Through the neighborhood spread the news that the Negroes had moved in. That evening large numbers of people walked up and down in front of the house. The decorators were too frightened at the aspect of the loiterers to leave. The next day Dr and Mrs Sweet did some shopping downtown, returning home late in the afternoon. They were joined by three friends from the Liberty Life Insurance office. When night fell a crowd began assembling across the street and in the schoolyard. As the laborers came home from work the mob swelled, until it consisted of about four hundred people. Mrs Sweet remained in the kitchen preparing dinner; the men pulled down the blinds, kept the front room dark. Ten policemen walked up and down in front of the Sweet home. Traffic was blocked off by other officers for three blocks around, but cars and taxicabs kept driving up and discharging passengers.

The mob was in a quarrelsome mood. They began throwing stones at the house. "Somebody went to the window," said Dr Ossian Sweet, "and I heard him remark, 'People—the people!' I ran out to the kitchen where my wife was. There were several lights burning. I turned them out and opened the door. I heard someone yell, 'Go and raise hell in front! I'm going back!' After getting a gun I ran upstairs. Stones were hitting the house intermittently."

Dr Sweet threw himself on his bed and lay quivering while the history of his race flashed through his mind, the beatings, the hangings, the burnings, the cruelty and terror that had been inflicted upon the black people by the white. He was in an agony of fear and uncertainty: Should he surrender, put his family into the protection of the police? . . . flee his new home . . . or should he fight it out? . . . sacrifice the lives of the ten people in the house. . . . Should he give the order to fire?

A stone hurtled through the bedroom window, splashing the doctor with broken glass. He jumped up in a paroxysm of terror, ran downstairs. "Pandemonium broke loose," he said. "Everyone was running from room to room. There was a general uproar. Somebody yelled, 'There's someone coming.' They said, 'That's your brother!' A car had pulled up to the curb. My brother and Mr Davis got out. The mob yelled, 'Here's niggers. Get them! Get them!' As they rushed in a mob surged forward. It looked like a human sea. Stones kept coming faster."

Suddenly a shot was fired. Six of the Negroes inside the house fired their guns. One man across the street fell dead. Another was injured. The police instantly thronged into the dark house, turned on the lights, pulled up the shades, arrested the ten Negroes and Mrs Sweet. They were charged with murder. Once again, as in the Arthur Person case in Rockford and in the Peter Bianchi, Mary Nardini case of Milwaukee, it was the state against ten men and one woman; the state against Clarence Darrow for the defense.

3

No set of circumstances in all of his experience moved him to such depths of pity as he felt for these unfortunate Negroes, whom he had always considered to be the underdog under the underdog. Nor did he feel that the Negroes would be the only ones to suffer from this invasion of a man's home, on the sanctity of which much of Anglo-Saxon law was based. As he had told a colored audience twenty-five years before, when the white man was cruel and contemptible to the black man he injured and debased himself far more than he did his victim. For a half century now he had been preaching that hatred created hatred, that violence begot violence. Today it was the Negro who was suffering. Who would be tomorrow's victim of this transgression of human rights and dignity? And how was he to prevent mob violence in Detroit from convicting these eleven human beings and sending them to prison? How could he win their freedom when Detroit was determined to convict?

"A kind of hysteria swept over the city," says Mrs Josephine Gomon, a prominent civic leader. "The law-and-order leaders and organizations demanded that these Negroes be made an example. The presiding judge was reluctant to take any action. It was the custom to rotate the office of presiding judge, and it was Frank Murphy's turn next to assume those duties. He told me that no action would be taken until he was presiding. 'Every judge on this bench is afraid to touch the case. They think it's dynamite. They don't realize that this is the opportunity of a lifetime to demonstrate sincere liberalism and judicial integrity at a time when liberalism is coming into its own.'" As soon as Judge Murphy took his seat he released Mrs Sweet on bail, an act which met with disfavor.

For Darrow it would once again be a case tried in a court of law but in which almost no law would be involved; as with the Scopes trial, for him it would be a social case, a racial case, a citizenship case. He learned that the prosecution was formulating its attack on two lines: first, that race prejudice had nothing whatever to do with the affair, that the fact that the indicted ones were Negroes did not alter the situation; second, that there had been no mob in front of the Sweet home, no violence had been threatened or performed, that the Sweets were in no conceivable danger and hence the shots fired were unwarranted, unjustified and constituted first-degree murder. The only important point of law over which he had to concern himself was, what constituted a "mob"? It was to be his task to prove to the jury that there had been a hostile gathering in front of the Sweet house, in sufficient number to justify the Sweets in believing that they had to protect their home against violence. But from beginning to end it was to be a trial by prejudice, race prejudice.

He spent three weeks in selecting his jury; he did more than select a jury; he gave the jurors a three weeks' education in the history of the Negro, the only group of people in the country that had been forced into American life. He portrayed feelingly the tragedy of the American Negro imprisoned always in the psychic wilderness of inferiority, relegated to menial and debasing labor, kept in fear, ignorance and poverty. Two Detroit schoolteachers, strangers to Ruby Darrow, telephoned her one night at the Book-Cadillac Hotel to ask if, since they wanted to hear Mr Darrow present his viewpoint on race prejudice, she couldn't get them seats in the courtroom. Mrs Darrow gave one of them her own seat and made arrangements for the other. The two women enjoyed the forenoon session so much, they begged to be allowed to return for the afternoon session.

"I explained that I was having James Weldon Johnson, head of the National Association for the Advancement of Colored People, as my guest for luncheon in the basement cafeteria of the courthouse," says Ruby, "and if they cared to join us we could all go back to court together. The two women were speechless; they didn't see how they could allow it to be said that they had sat with a colored person at a meal, the feeling in Detroit being so high and they teachers in the public school. The woman who had done the telephoning, the wife of the superintendent of the largest school, said their very livelihood depended on their preserving their standing. I asked them to meet Mr Johnson and then decide whether they would be my guests with him. They were won by Mr Johnson's personality and his achievements. As a result of this meeting Bernice Powels founded clubs for colored boys and girls and has worked toward making the Detroit schools accept colored students on an equal basis with the whites."

A reporter for the Detroit *Free Press* was to say, "When I was assigned to cover the trial I had the average prejudice against Negroes. Now as I look back over the trial which ended a week ago I am lonesome for some of the Negroes I met. The thought comes to call them up or, better still, go to see them. I want to know them better, go into their homes, meet their children and grandparents. I give Clarence Darrow credit for destroying my race hatred. He opened up a new and interesting vista for me."

His examination was confined to one main tack: "Are you prejudiced against the Negro? Do you consider him as an equal and as a fellow American? Do you like him? Do you believe in him? Do you believe you could give him as fair and square a deal as you would a white man? Will you make every effort to keep prejudice out of your hearts?" At the end of three weeks of brutally hard questioning, after exhausting his panel of two hundred men, he came to the conclusion that he at least had twelve men who, if they were prejudiced against the Negro, carried that prejudice so deep in their minds they did not know it was there. As the jury was taking its oath Darrow turned to Mrs Gomon and said: "The case is won or lost now. The rest is window dressing."

The window dressing proved to be highly dramatic and revealing. The prosecution put on the stand seventy-one witnesses, most of whom lived in the neighborhood of the Sweet house, to testify that although they individually had been close to the Sweet home on the night of the disturbance, they had seen no crowds and had not seen each other. Under Darrow's relentless cross-examination they writhed and stumbled through explanations of having been at the corner of Garland and Charlevoix that evening to locate errant wives, daughters, sons. In spite of the fact that he was able to make the explanation appear ludicrous, to demonstrate their intense racial prejudice, they held fiercely to their story: there had been no unusual gathering in front of the Sweet house on the night of the shooting; the Sweets had been in no danger. The policemen who had been sent to guard the Sweets while they moved into their home testified that although they had blocked off traffic that night, they had seen no unusual crowds across from the Sweet house. In 1941 Prosecutor Toms says,

"There were probably more people around the Sweet house than the people's witnesses testified to and less than the defendant's witnesses testified. At any rate, there were enough to frighten (and justifiably so) a group of nervous, apprehensive Negroes who anticipated trouble. I am sure that the police had the situation

well in hand and that there was no immediate danger of the house
being stormed or any real riotous conduct. Undoubtedly the situation did not appear that peaceful and harmless to the colored
people in the house, and their conduct should probably not be
judged from a calm and unimpassioned point of view."

For the defense Darrow called to the stand only a few witnesses.
One man revealed the meeting of the Waterworks Park Improvement Association during which violence against Sweet was urged
if he moved into his newly bought home. A newspaper reporter
told that, passing close to the Sweet house on the night of the killing,
he had had his car routed away from the scene by a police officer,
had come back on foot and seen a crowd of between four and
five hundred people surrounding the Sweet house. Ray Lorenzo,
proprietor of a close-by automobile-accessory shop, estimated that
there were at least five hundred people in the schoolyard across
from the Sweet house on the night of the shooting. Mrs Mary
Spaulding testified that, while driving through the neighborhood
on the night of the shooting, she saw people gathered at the
corner as if for a meeting and testified that there were at least
five hundred.

In spite of the scene of passion that was being described the
trial was carried on in an aura of judicial calm, the like of which
Darrow had rarely experienced. Prosecutor Robert Toms tells,
"I was quite aware of Mr Darrow's capacity for invective and I
did not propose to lay myself open by matching barbs with him.
Accordingly I treated him throughout the trial with the utmost
reverence and deference. After a week of this he said to me, 'God
damn it, Toms, I can't get going. I am supposed to be mad at
you and I can't even pretend that I am.' He complained throughout the trial that my decent treatment of him was purely strategic
and that it was working a great hardship on him."

The second outstanding characteristic of the trial was the startling
contrast in the educational and cultural development of the white
neighbors of the Sweets, the Poles, Assyrians, Swedes and Germans, and of the Negro witnesses, including the Sweet family, who
testified for the defense. The white neighbors were laborers who
had had almost no schooling, spoke English badly and were not
only unread but uncultivated. The Negroes were largely college
graduates, and included doctors, dentists, teachers, clergymen,
lawyers, social-service workers, most of whom spoke well and
showed evidence of developed minds. For Darrow the irony of
the trial was that it was the Sweets who were lowering themselves
by moving into a house on the corner of Garland and Charlevoix.

Arthur Garfield Hays, who was associated with Darrow in the case, pleaded superbly and brought every technical point to its logical conclusion. Darrow didn't trouble himself over the technical aspects. Toms relates, "During the course of the trial a rather complex legal point was raised, and all the attorneys retired to the library to look it up. Darrow, however, remained seated in the courtroom. As I passed him he said, 'You go along and talk to Arthur Hays; I can't be annoyed with the goddamn books!' "

The first break in the case he earned for his clients by the intensity of his cross-examination. He cross-examined Alfred H. Andrew, who admitted he had attended a meeting of the Waterworks Park Improvement Association on the grounds of the Howe School before the riot. He also admitted that a visiting member of the Tireman Avenue Improvement Association was among the speakers.

"Did he tell you about any race-riot trouble they had in his neighborhood?" asked Darrow.

"Yes, he told us about a Negro named Doctor Turner, who had bought a house on Spokane Avenue."

"Did he say his organization made Turner leave?"

"Yes. He said that they wouldn't have Negroes in their neighborhood and that they would co-operate with us in keeping them out of ours."

"Did the crowd applaud him?"

"Yes."

"Did you applaud?"

"Yes."

"You feel that way now?"

"Yes, I haven't changed."

"You know a colored man has certain rights?"

"Yes, I was in favor of keeping the Sweets out by legal means."

"Did the speaker talk of legal means?"

"No, he was a radical. I myself do not believe in violence."

"Did anybody in that audience of five hundred or more people protest against the speaker's advocacy of violence?"

"I don't know."

A Mr Monet insisted that there were only a few people in the street on the night of the shooting but under Darrow's cross-examination admitted that he had joined the Waterworks Park Improvement Association to keep out Sweet and his family. The owner of a filling station near the Sweet house, who swore there was no particular crowd there on the fatal night, finally admitted that he had sold an unusual amount of gas during the hours in question. A young boy who admitted that there had been "a large crowd" opposite the Sweet home stopped short in his story, as though he had said something he shouldn't have. The police lieutenant in charge, who had ten officers with him in front of the Sweet house, denied that there had been any congregating or any disturbance, then admitted that he had run for reserves immediately the first shot had been fired. One ominous piece of evidence the prosecution was unable to explain away was the quantity of rocks picked up from the Sweet lawn on the morning after the shooting.

At one point in the trial Darrow had started to cross-examine a particularly vitriolic witness but, after merely asking her name, excused her. In view of the fact that she had given damaging testimony on direct examination Toms asked Darrow, "Why didn't you cross-examine Mrs Blank?" He answered, "Because I didn't know what she would say. I never ask a question unless I know beforehand what the answer will be."

The third outstanding characteristic of the trial was the changing nature of the spectators. When the trial opened the audience was largely composed of whites; only a few colored people had the courage to attend or were able to find places in the courtroom. However, as the trial progressed, as it became manifest that there was little or nothing involved for the whites but that on the other hand it was a matter of life and death for the American Negro, the colored spectators grew in number. By the time Darrow rose to his feet to make his final plea it was a plea he was making to a white jury and a colored world.

In addition to proving that a threatening mob was assembled before the Sweet house, which had already thrown stones and inflicted damage, he set out to prove that the bullet which had killed Leon Breiner could not have been fired from the Sweet house but had been fired by a policeman who admitted having "emptied his gun during the excitement."

He then illuminated the crux of the Sweet murder case. He called Dr Ossian Sweet to the stand to describe his state of mind on the night of September eighth with the milling crowd outside his home. Ossian Sweet told of the race riots he had seen in Washington, when colored men had been hunted through the streets by mobs; of the violence of the Chicago race riots; of the five Negroes who were shot to death in Rosewood when eighteen Negro homes and a Negro church were burned; of the four Johnson brothers of Arkansas, one a physician and another a dentist, who had been taken from a train and lynched; of Dr A. C. Jackson of Tulsa, whom the Mayo brothers had declared to be a first-rate surgeon and who was murdered by the police to whom he surrendered after trying to protect his home from a mob; of the three thousand Negroes who had been lynched within one generation, of the mobs that had burned, hung, shot and beaten his fellow Negroes to death.

Coming back to Detroit, Dr Sweet told of violence that had been exerted against colored people who had moved into homes in the white sections. His voice faltered as he related his vivid memory of what the mob had done to Dr Turner and his possessions. Dr Turner had bought a house on Spokane Avenue, in the northern part of Detroit. He had moved in under police guard, but his house had been broken into, the furniture smashed, the windows broken, the interior defaced, his shattered belongings thrown into a van which had been backed up to the front door. Sweet had seen the mob stone the colored couple as they fled. He commented, "Turner always had the greatest confidence in the word of white people; he felt that they belonged to a race superior to his own. Consequently when they wanted to enter his house to rob him it wasn't necessary to break down the door. It was far simpler to deceive him. One of the leaders simply knocked and, when Doctor Turner came to the door, said, 'Open, Turner, I'm your friend.' Turner believed him and opened the door. The next moment he was dough in the hands of the mob."

Referring to the night of the shooting, he said quietly, "When I opened the door and saw the mob I realized I was facing the same mob that had hounded my people through its entire history. In my mind I was pretty confident of what I was up against. I had my back against the wall. I was filled with a peculiar fear, the fear of one who knows the history of my race. I knew what mobs had done to my people before."

Said one reporter, "Without Clarence Darrow the ten Negro men and women in that house would have been in the penitentiary today. Through the medium of one of the defendants who took the stand, and in his pleas, Darrow traced the Negro up through the eons of his evolution, traced him in his whilom habitat along the Zambezi River, traced him through the Gethsemane of slavery, pictured him being tortured by the Simon Legrees of Puritanism, as the victim of mob vengeance, burning at the stake and finally emerging into the hope of a new day."

The trial lasted for almost seven weeks. In the evenings Clarence would rest himself by reading aloud to his friends from Newman Levy's *Opera Guyed*. Levy was brought to meet Darrow by James Weldon Johnson. Darrow asked Levy what he was working on. "A series of articles about shyster lawyers for the *Saturday Evening Post*," was the reply. "What do you mean by shyster lawyers?"

exclaimed Darrow angrily. "You mean poor devils who can't make a living? If we were in their condition we wouldn't be any better than they are." Then, afraid that his outburst might have hurt Levy's feelings, he apologized.

At the end of the seven weeks he made his final appeal. William Pickens of the National Association for the Advancement of Colored People says, "For the purposes of the defense Clarence Darrow had studied the Negro problem in all of its history and in all of its phases; he had read cases, programs, the stories of movements and the biographies of Negro men." Arthur Garfield Hays reports, "In his address to the jury Darrow showed his master hand. The ordinary lawyer collates facts, analyzes evidence and makes his appeal. There are few who use history, psychology and philosophy in order to show the real underlying facts. Darrow said to those men on the jury that if he had merely to appeal to reason he would have little doubt of the result but that the difficulty lay deeper. It arose from a prejudice which white men take in with their mother's milk. Darrow questioned whether it was possible for twelve white men, however they might try, to give a fair trial to a Negro."

"The Sweets spent their first night in their new home afraid to go to bed," observed Darrow. "The next night they spent in jail. Now the state wants them to spend the rest of their lives in the penitentiary. There are persons in the North and the South who say a black man is inferior to the white and should be controlled by the whites. There are also those who recognize his rights and say he should enjoy them. To me this case is a cross section of human history. It involves the future and the hope of some of us that the future shall be better than the past."

The jury was out for three days and three nights; the wrangling and quarreling was so violent that good parts of it could be heard through the courthouse. A considerable portion of the furniture in the jury room was broken; one juror lost twelve pounds. Judge Murphy, convinced that no verdict was possible, declared them a hung jury and ended the trial.

4

It was rarely vouchsafed to Clarence Darrow to go through an ordeal only once; most of his major cases he had had to try twice. If this pattern of repetition doubled his exhaustion it also doubled his opportunity to campaign for tolerance.

Prosecutor Toms decided to try young Henry Sweet alone, since Henry had admitted firing his gun. Toms went to great pains to gather testimony to the effect that the slain man had been stooping over, lighting his pipe, when the bullet had hit him and that for this reason it would have been entirely possible for the bullet to have come from the Sweet house. When the trial opened Darrow nullified Prosecutor Toms's efforts by admitting that Henry Sweet might have fired the shot, claiming that it was in defense of his life and his home.

The second trial was practically a replica of the first; the outstanding difference lay in Darrow's final plea. "I shall never forget that final plea to the jury," says Mrs Gomon. "He talked for eight hours. One could have heard a pin drop in the crowded courtroom. Everyone listened breathlessly, crowded so closely together that women fainted and could not fall. He went back through the pages of history and the progress of the human race to trace the development of fear and prejudice in human psychology. Sometimes his resonant, melodious voice sank to a whisper. Sometimes it rose in a roar of indignation. The collars of the jurors wilted. They sat tense, in the grip of strained contemplation of historic events and tragic happenings which he made real and present again before their very eyes.

"As Judge Murphy left the bench I met him just inside the door of his office. I had never seen him so moved. He took my hand and said, 'This is the greatest experience of my life. That was Clarence Darrow at his best. I will never hear anything like it again. He is the most Christlike man I have ever known.' "

His closing words in his last great international case of social urgency were more a defense of his own philosophy and of himself as a member of the human race than of Henry Sweet, the accused one, for once again he placed all of humanity in the prisoner's dock.

"I do not believe in the law of hate. I may not be true to my ideals always, but I believe in the law of love, and I believe you can do nothing with hatred. I would like to see a time when a man loves his fellow man and forgets his color or his creed. We will never be civilized until that time comes. I know the Negro race has a long road to go. I believe the life of the Negro race has been a life of tragedy, of injustice, of oppression. The law has made him equal, but man has not. And, after all, the last analysis is, what has man done? and not what has the law done? I know there is a long road ahead of him before he can take the place which I believe he should take. I know that before him there is suffering, sorrow, tribulation and death among the blacks and perhaps the whites. I am sorry. I would do what I could to avert it. I would advise patience; I would advise toleration; I would advise understanding; I would advise all of those things which are necessary for men who live together.

"What do you think is your duty in this case? I have watched day after day these black, tense faces that have crowded this court. These black faces that now are looking to you twelve whites, feeling that the hopes and fears of a race are in your keeping.

"This case is about to end, gentlemen. To them it is life. Not one of their color sits on this jury. Their fate is in the hands of twelve whites. Their eyes are fixed on you, and their hopes hang on your verdict.

"I ask you, on behalf of this defendant, on behalf of these helpless ones who turn to you, and more than that—on behalf of this great state and this great city which must face this problem and face it fairly—I ask you, in the name of progress and of the human race, to return a verdict of not guilty in this case."

His argument, published in pamphlet form by the National Association for the Advancement of Colored People, stands with his appeal to the Anthracite Coal Commission, with the plea to the jury in the Big Bill Haywood case, with the plea to Judge Caverly in the Loeb-Leopold case, as an outstanding document for peace and good will. In it he fulfilled John Brown's stricture made almost sixty-five years before, that "the Negro has too few friends; you and I must never desert him."

As the jury filed out Darrow indicated one of them and "smiled in that slow, quizzical way he had. 'That is the most stubborn man I have ever run up against. I didn't make any impression on him. His mind is made up, and I don't think anything could have changed him. I wonder if he is for or against us.'"

Later they learned that "when this juror went into the jury room he pulled a box of cigars and a book out of his pocket and announced to his fellow jurors, 'When you get ready to vote not guilty call on me. Until then I am not interested,' and proceeded to light a cigar and settle himself with his book."

George Murphy, brother of the presiding judge, relates, "It was very interesting to watch Mr Darrow after the jury had gone into the jury room for deliberations. While others wandered about and left the courtroom and came back in Mr Darrow never relaxed a moment in his vigilance."

At the end of three hours the jury sent word that it had reached a verdict. Judge Murphy took his place upon the bench; the jury filed in. The foreman announced, "Not guilty!" Dr Ossian Sweet thanked Darrow in the name of the twelve million American Negroes for this verdict which freed not only Henry Sweet and the other defendants but, in some small measure, the colored people.

George Murphy tells, "When the jury came in Darrow was seated
with his hands grasping the arms of the chair, his great body stooped
over, his head leaning forward, waiting to hear the verdict. When
the verdict of not guilty was rendered his great spirit almost seemed
to have left his body. He had given his all, body, mind and soul, to
the trial."

Darrow was unutterably weary from the long and impassioned
plea; he sank heavily into his chair. Prosecutor Toms, thinking that
he was about to faint, rushed to his side and put both arms around
him. Darrow's eyes twinkled as he looked up at Toms.

"Oh, I'm all right," he murmured. "I've heard that verdict before."

5

At last, following the Henry Sweet case in May of 1926, Clarence
Darrow decided that the only way to retire was to retire. He packed
up his papers, moved his beautiful black desk and chairs home to the
Midway. One of the rear bedrooms had been converted into a
study, and here, for the next decade, he devoted the major portion
of his time to writing articles for magazines. Continuing in his role
as the man on America's conscience, he entered the fray with his
sharp lance wherever he thought personal liberty and freedom were
being invaded.

In *Vanity Fair* he published a series of articles of which the
generic title was *Our Growing Tyranny;* he wrote extensively for
the *American Mercury* on biology and "boobology"; he wrote on
combatting crime for the *Forum* and on capital punishment for the
Forum and *Rotarian;* for the *Libertarian* he wrote on socialism. For
the *Saturday Evening Post* he wrote an article called *At Seventy
Two*, in which he said, "As a propagandist, I see no chance to grow
weary of life. I am interested in too many questions that concern the
existence and activity of the human race. I have more and more come
to the firm conviction that each life is simply a short individual
expression and that it soon sinks back into the great reservoir of
force, where memory and the individual consciousness are at an
end. I am not troubled by hopes and still less by fears. I have taken
life as it came, doing the best I could with its manifold phases, and
feel sure that I shall meet final dissolution without fear or serious
regret."

His articles were sharp, witty, fearless and discerning, but in only
one field did his work stand out with a passion and a fury that made

him worthy of his master in pamphleteering, Voltaire. As early as 1909 he had begun writing and lecturing against prohibition. In 1909 in New Bedford, Massachusetts, under the auspices of the New England Union Labor League, he delivered his first scathing talk against the proposed plan to prohibit the sale of liquor. He fought the passage of the Eighteenth Amendment with every weapon at hand; now, seeing the evils it had brought upon the country, he re-entered the struggle to help eradicate it from American life. He published frequent articles in *Collier's*, *Plain Talk*, *Vanity Fair* and the *American Mercury;* he lectured and debated on the subject from platforms in nearly every American city; having ample time to write, he published a book in collaboration with Victor S. Yarros called *The Prohibition Mania*, which was widely read and helped considerably in establishing the full case against prohibition by de-bunking the statistical charts in favor of prohibition published by Professor Irving Fisher.

His argument was not merely that prohibition did not work; that the nature of man being what it is, it could never work; that it in-creased rather than decreased drinking and drunkenness and was forcing upon people crude and often poisonous liquor; that it was breeding a new class of racketeer, gangster and criminal which was becoming a serious threat to the preservation of law and order. Though these things seemed to him to be of major importance, he based his attack against prohibition on the ground that it was a grievous invasion of personal liberty. He argued that a hundred mil-lion persons had had their lives circumscribed on the grounds that a few men and women had drunk to excess, that prohibition was a hang-over of Puritanism and, if tolerated by the American people, would set a precedent for the further encircling of human rights. Because he did not believe that the Eighteenth Amendment ever could be repealed, he advocated that Congress simply refuse to allo-cate funds for the enforcement of the Volstead Act; it was one of his few errors in social diagnosis.

In 1928 Paul sold the gas plant in Greeley. To Darrow his own share of the proceeds seemed a small fortune. He invested the entire sum in remunerative stocks and prepared to live out the rest of his life on his income.

He and Ruby went to Europe, where for a year they had a mag-nificent time traveling through the countries they loved, visiting with economists, writers, artists, sculptors, with old friends such as John A. Hobson, T. P. O'Connor, H. G. Wells, Charles Edward Russell Brand Whitlock, Somerset Maugham and Jo Davidson. They toured England, Scotland and Wales by car with W. R. Kellogg and found special pleasure in retracing the literary geography of England, rereading such books as *Lorna Doone* on the spot where the scene was laid. They spent happy months wandering through Switzerland and France as they had on their honeymoon, and again, as on their honeymoon, Clarence began a new book. He felt too old now to tackle the long novel he had been contemplating for twenty years; instead he started work on his autobiography. Ruby worked with him, often typing most of the night so that he might have fresh manuscript to read in the morning. He was to call the book *The Story of My Life,* though it might more accurately have been called *The Story of My Philosophy,* for his almost pathological modesty kept him from telling very much of his own participation in his important cases and causes. That he should have written the book at all was an out-of-character surprise for, when one of his associates had asked a few years before, "Mr Darrow, why don't you write the story of all your cases? It would make one of the greatest books in the world," he had flared, "That book will never be written!"

He wrote little else while in Europe, but he continued to send childlike letters to his granddaughter Mary, as he had through the years. Some of his playfulness would have made his English teacher from the academy in Kinsman turn over in her grave: "Eye take mi penn in hand two let U no that Eye am wel and hop U.R. the sam. I kant rite very mutch bekaus it is ten oklok an Eye must do sum worruk. Ur *Grand* Dad." Another time he would write to the twelve-year-old girl, "Dear Mary: Enclosed you will find five dollars. This is sent to you on condition that you shall buy nothing useful with it. Don't spend any of it for stockings or food or tuition. Don't send any of it to foreign missions; the heathens are bad enough as they are. Don't buy any books, at least none that are good and dull. You can buy Esquimaux pie, for that is unhealthy and will make you look sick and interesting. I don't know as I told you much about London; my hotel is near Trafalgar Square, where Lord Nelson fought a sea battel against the French. I have never yet found out how they fought a sea battel on Trafalgar Square, for there aint any water anywhere near it, but that was a long time ago, and maybee the water was there, or else they pumped it in so he could win the battle and get the monument. There is a Cleopatra Needle standing on the banks of the Thames; it is called an obelisk, but I don't know why, except that it looks like an obelisk. The only thing they use the Parliament Building for is a big clock up in the tower. The clock is mighty handy, for it strikes every fifteen minutes all night, so that when it wakes you up you can tell what time it is without turning on the light and looking at your watch. This is a mighty good plan, because if the clock didn't strike in the night you might go right on sleeping and never know what time it was until you woke up in the morning, and in that way you would lose a lot of time.

"I don't believe I will be home for Christmas. I feel as though I shouldn't go back to all that cold weather, so I am going to Cannes. I have figured it all out, and I find it wont cost me as much to go there until the first of March as it would to go back home and buy a lot of Christmas presents for use kids."

Then in November of 1929 the stock market crashed in New York City. Darrow returned to America to find himself almost penniless at the age of seventy-three, with a living to make. The loss of his money led him to plunge once again into a controversy which kept him both interested and excited and covered another mile along the endless road to brotherhood and unity.

6

He vowed that he would not try to go back into the law but would earn his living from writing and lecturing. An enterprising young lecture manager by the name of George Whitehead, who worked out of the Redfern Agency in Chicago, conceived the idea of staging four-way debates on religion. In the big cities of the Midwest he arranged with a Protestant clergyman, a prominent Catholic spokesman and a Jewish rabbi to meet with Clarence Darrow, the agnostic, on one platform, to present their varying views. Whitehead was an intelligent, lovable chap whom Darrow enjoyed; sometimes they would be out on the road together for weeks at a stretch. When they were taking the night train out of Chicago Darrow would put on a long white nightgown which he would stuff into his pants; Whitehead would call for him, and they would go down to the station together in a cab. Ruby always prepared two satchels filled with dozens of neat little boxes and envelopes, each labeled, one containing handkerchiefs, another his shoestring ties, another shoelaces, another needles and thread and buttons, another cookies, another fruit, another bottles of medicine. She had a standing arrangement with the Pullman Company to send back all the things he left behind him in the berth and smoking rooms. On their first night out, when the two men were undressing in the Pullman, Clarence had noticed Whitehead carefully watching over him, trying to get him to do all the things that Ruby had ordered. Finally he grumbled:

"If you're going to take such good care of me there's no reason for me to leave home." He complained to Whitehead that "Ruby takes too good care of me; apparently she believes that eternal vigilance is the price of a husband." Once when he went to New York alone the Spingarns found him greatly disturbed. He took out a shirt and begged Mrs Spingarn to duplicate it. The doctor had forbidden him to smoke; Ruby had allowed him to make the trip alone on a promise that he would not smoke, and he had burned a hole in the shirt.

"Why don't you just lose that shirt in the Pullman car?" asked Spingarn.

"You don't know Ruby," mourned Darrow.

The four-way debates on religion carried to an even higher pitch the excitement that had been generated by the Scopes case. For the first time in many a year purely religious discussion found itself headlined. Outside the Carnegie Music Hall in Pittsburgh a thousand people who were unable to buy tickets tried to break into the auditorium; the police had to be called to control them.

"The only fair way to arrange the order of speaking," said Whitehead, "was to have the four men draw lots from a hat. Since Darrow was always the oldest of the group and, in addition, a visitor in town, the three participants invariably paid him the courtesy of having him draw first. I couldn't have my star draw the number-one slip and open the show, so I always concealed the number-one slip under the hatband before Darrow dove in. I never told him about this little stunt; he would not have permitted me to do it if he had known."

On the morning of each debate Whitehead would arrange a breakfast at which the Protestant, the Catholic, the Jew and the agnostic would meet and discuss the program for that evening, with the photographers and newspapermen present. In Houston they signed a paper for a reporter on which the Protestant clergyman wrote, "God is love." The Catholic wrote, "Religion is love of God and fellow man." The Jew wrote, "I believe that Judaism is the best religion for the Jew, Christianity for the Christian, Mohammedanism for the Mohammedan, agnosticism for the agnostic." Darrow glanced at the three sentences, winked at the reporters and scribbled, "If the above sentiments really represent what religion is, then I shall stop debating." After each debate they gathered at the home of the Catholic or the rabbi to meet the cream of the town's intellects and to enjoy the best of food, drink and conversation. "Almost never did the Protestant clergyman give the party," commented Whitehead, "and almost never would he attend at someone else's home."

For several years they crisscrossed over the face of the nation, lecturing and debating in forums of religion in Washington, D.C., Baltimore, Cleveland, Pittsburgh, Minneapolis, St Paul, Columbus, Cincinnati, Chicago, St Louis, Louisville, Nashville, Boston, Hartford, New York City. "We covered the United States, North, South and East," relates Whitehead, "and Mr Darrow took a few special engagements in the Northwest, but he steadfastly refrained from intruding himself in California because of the unpleasantness at the ending of the McNamara case."

When he went to Pittsburgh to debate Judge Michael Musmanno on "Does Man Live Again?" the judge asked him, during their get-acquainted meeting at the hotel, "How do you feel about what must have been your most absorbing case, the case in which *you* were the defendant?"

"The sons of bitches," muttered Darrow. "They knew damn well I was innocent, but they knew also damn well that if they accused me there would be somebody to believe the accusation."

"On the platform," says Judge Musmanno, "he was utterly different from the man who had been conversing intimately with me a few minutes before. He was the antagonist, the fighter, the inexorable adversary. We clashed on a quotation from Voltaire. He questioned the authenticity of my quotation, and when I was able to find the quotation in a book on the table and presented it to him he still shrugged his shoulders to dispute the point. Here he was being the intellectual athlete, the consummate actor, the resourceful barrister. Even with the most damaging evidence being presented against his case he still shrugged his shoulders as if to say: 'Oh well, that doesn't amount to much.' Yet if I had failed to authenticate the quotation in question he would have pulverized me with scorn.

"At the conclusion of the speeches I was surprised at the sincere affection with which he grasped my hand, because I thought he was angry with me."

He received five hundred dollars for each debate, plus fifty dollars for expenses. At the close of the first debate in Cincinnati Whitehead had only a hundred and fifty dollars left for himself. When Darrow learned of this he said, "That's not enough; you forget the expense money and take a hundred dollars from my check in addition." Later they made an arrangement to share the profits, but in Pittsburgh, when he learned how much money had been taken in from standing room, he said to Whitehead, "Oh, my regular cut is enough for me. You keep the standing-room money." For one gigantic meeting in Orchestra Hall in Chicago Darrow's cut would have been seventeen hundred and fifty dollars. He insisted that this was too much, that his three opponents be given a bonus and that Professor Hayden be paid for serving as chairman. Says Whitehead, "Mr Darrow always leaned over backward to give men the best part of the deal. With rare exceptions we had capacity audiences. Mr Darrow enjoyed these meetings as much for the association with the local intellectuals as for the compensation."

He got a kick out of matching wits with his adversaries on the platform, but his interest lay in bringing religion into the open air and sunshine of free discussion. There was freedom of religious worship in America, but there was also a tendency on the part of the various religions to suspect, dislike and fear each other. He felt that if every man could be acquainted with every other man's religion, visit his church, understand his point of view, the fear, suspicion and dislike would melt away. Yet of the four men on the platform in each of the cities, the only one who was received with suspicion, fear and dislike was the agnostic among them.

"Eighty per cent of the audiences hated Darrow's point of view," reports Whitehead, "and came to the meeting to hear it demolished. Darrow violated all the rules of oratory, yet he watched his audience like a hawk. He would get under the hide of the religionists, but in the next moment he would say something nice, and they would have to like him. He could tell how far he could carry his audience, and he would spank them half to death, but he knew when he had to give them relief. Many came despising him, thinking him a devil with horns. They went away liking him and feeling sorry for him."

The intensity of the feeling against him throughout the Midwest is exemplified by George Whitehead's mother; Mrs Whitehead was delighted to have her son successful and to see him earning large sums of money, yet so profoundly did she hate Clarence Darrow's agnosticism that she would not permit his name to be mentioned in her presence.

During these years of writing, lecturing and debating on religion the world was constantly interested and informed as to the state of Clarence Darrow's soul. He received thousands of letters, some of them flailing him for his "paganism and godlessness," warning him that unless he repented he would be condemned to roast in hell-fire through all eternity; most of them were letters of tenderness and love, sympathizing with his plight in having lost God, telling him of the beauties and comforts of religion, relating the experience of having seen the light and having been redeemed, clasped to the bosom of their Maker.

Many of the letters were truly persuasive, but they did not succeed in converting him. As he said at the dinner table, "I don't like onion soup, but you go ahead and have some; I wouldn't force my prejudice on you." Yet stories constantly circulated about Clarence Darrow's conversion to one church or another. The most prevalent was that while in a hospital in Denver he had called for an Episcopal bishop and asked to be saved. He retorted, "I was visited in a hospital in Denver by an Episcopal bishop, Doctor Johnson. He was a good fellow. He filled up his pipe and lit it and we had a nice talk, in which neither of us mentioned religion. I was not that ill. And if I had been, I do not imagine the doctor would have bothered me about my soul. I still believe that when I die there will be nothing left over, neither heaven nor hell."

Another time, when he told a reporter in St Paul that he would be pleased to join the Humanist Society, "which was purely agnostic and anthropocentric, transferring man's loyalty and obligation from God to man," newspapers throughout the country ran articles under banners which read: DARROW JOINS RELIGIOUS SOCIETY. Because the Humanist Society was connected with the Unitarian Church of Minneapolis, he read in the press that "Clarence Darrow, long known as America's leading agnostic, has become a church member, it was confirmed today." John H. Dietrich, minister of the First Unitarian Church of Minneapolis, who was responsible for Darrow's having joined the Humanist Society, says, "This news created quite a sensation both among the religionists and the agnostics and disturbed Mr Darrow considerably." Darrow at once withdrew from the Humanist Society, disclaiming any knowledge of the fact that it had been connected with a church; nevertheless, newspapers continued to report, "Darrow got scared and joined the Church."

He countered the native ill feeling of his audiences by his humor. Once when debating on immortality he turned to inquire of the chairman how much time he had left for his speech. Before the presiding officer could answer he added, "I guess I haven't much time left if I don't believe in the hereafter." One of his opponents told an audience, "I am the master of my fate; I am the captain of my soul." Darrow retorted, "The captain of his soul? Why, he isn't even a deck hand on a raft!" To an audience in Cleveland he said, "I take it that a great many of you are religious people; I judge that by the way you applaud utterly irrelevant things." When asked by one of his opponents if, when he died, he didn't want to live eternally, he replied, "When I die all I ask is that there be some friends who will remember my weaknesses and forget my virtues."

Will Rogers cautioned Clarence's adversaries, "Don't anybody debate with Darrow. He will make a monkey out of any opponent. He hadn't been in Tennessee two weeks till he had the entire state jumping up on the backs of chairs, picking fleas off each other." When debating Albert Edward Wiggam in Cleveland Darrow said, "I am surprised and grieved to hear my friend say that rich men are the most intelligent. Imagine a man with brains spending his time making money! The best way to get money is to marry it." When the subject of marriage came up for discussion and one of his opponents asked, "Mr Darrow, don't you think that marriage could be described as a lottery?" he replied, "Yes, if only there were prizes." When he was accused of being an agnostic because he was a pessimist he retorted, "When a pessimist is disappointed he is happy. Optimists are easy to discourage; I've never seen anyone so despondent as an optimist who didn't get what he expected." To a young woman who happened in on the tail end of a discourse on international finance and asked him to restate his thesis, he replied, "Girl, that's a subject even men don't understand." During the Herbert Hoover-Al Smith campaign he observed, "Hoover, if elected, will do one thing that is almost incomprehensible to the human mind: he will make a great man out of Coolidge."

He debated frequently with Dr Clarence True Wilson on the Eighteenth Amendment. He and Wilson were sent to Canada together by *Collier's* magazine to gather material for a series of articles on prohibition. Darrow enjoyed the drive along the Hudson and the stopovers at Saratoga Springs and Lake George, but most of all he loved to twit the good doctor, who was an ardent religionist and prohibitionist. J. E. Joiner, who managed the trip, tells that Darrow worked crossword puzzles in the car, the newspaper completely covering the gearshift. "I have a mental picture of him working a puzzle, a straw sailor on his head, the brim of which was in various stages of gnawed dilapidation from rolling around on the floor of the car among the brake and clutch pedals, his glasses sitting on top of and pinning to his nose one of his long wisps of hair which the wind had blown. One afternoon his face lighted up in triumph as he filled in a four-letter word meaning 'a future state of punishment' and spelled it out: 'H-e-l-l. Doctor, there's one you could never have gotten.'" When they reached Toronto Dr Wilson was annoyed because the stores were closed and he couldn't make certain purchases. "Why, Doctor," exclaimed Darrow. "Aren't you aware that today is Sunday? I think I had better sing you a few hymns to put you in the proper frame of mind." And he sang them.

He was frequently getting other people's goat; only once did they visibly get his. He happened to be in Washington, D.C., when the Daughters of the American Revolution were holding a convention. One evening, while sitting in the lobby of the Mayflower Hotel, he learned that the D.A.R. had passed a resolution declaring him to be an undesirable citizen. As a group of the ladies passed before him, their sashes strung across their bosoms, he grumbled, "Daughters of the American Revolution! Humph! Undesirable citizen! Humph! I'm as much a rebel as their forefathers ever were!"

He would tell an audience, "I feel myself growing older, the machine failing, and I think, 'It won't last always. My next rest won't be for a while, but forever. Death is the only consolation.'" Then after the debate he would ask Whitehead, "Do I shock people too much when I ridicule the idea of a soul?"

Once when he was debating Professor Scott Nearing on the subject "Is Life Worth Fighting For?" in Symphony Hall in Boston, Nearing, who was arguing for the affirmative, defeated Darrow by a clever maneuver. Professor Nearing enumerated a list of the contributions Clarence Darrow had made to mankind, then, turning to Darrow, said, "What you have done bolsters my argument more than anything else." Darrow received a thunderous ovation.

7

And so the years passed pleasantly for the Old Lion. His autobiography was well received by both the critics and the public, fulfilling his hope that "someday I shall write a book where the royalties will pay for the copies I give away." When the autobiography was first released a woman journalist of Chicago called Ruby to tell her that Mr Darrow had no right to call his book an autobiography because he had told nothing whatever of his love life. When Clarence returned home that evening Ruby related the conversation to him, adding that the woman had insisted he could have done a whole chapter on his love life. "A whole chapter," grunted Darrow. "Why, I could do a whole library!" Catching Ruby's wifely stare, he apologized with "Well, maybe not a whole library, but at least a couple of best sellers."

With Professor Howard Parshley, a zoologist, he made a motion picture for Universal called *The Mystery of Life*, in which the spectators were beguiled by a sound track of his voice, telling in a rather hoarse tone the story of evolution. The recording was done in a studio in the Bronx. "I would write an ordinary scientific lecture to go with a section of the film," recounts Professor Parshley, "which Darrow would then translate into—as he said—bad English; that is, the vernacular. In all of our work together he manifested a rare combination of genuine modesty and irrepressible histrionics. I have never met any person who approached him in the power to attract inevitably the love and respect of others." The film played the major cities of America with moderate success.

Though he considered himself as out of the practice of law, he went back to the courts whenever he thought he could save a human life. He defended Greco and Carrillo, anti-Fascists who were accused of murdering two Italian Fascists parading in New York City. The sole connection between Greco, Carrillo and the killing was that Greco and Carrillo had opposed the Fascist movement in America. When Arthur Garfield Hays and a defense committee asked him to try to save the two boys he said, "I'm tired. I want to rest. I'm past seventy, and it's winter. I want to go away somewhere." Greco's brother burst into tears. Darrow turned to him. "All right, I'll take the case. For God's sake, stop crying." He won an acquittal for his clients.

Once he was discussing with Arthur Spingarn whether or not he should take a certain case which would require a lot of time and in which he would need a good deal of travel and maintenance expense. "What fee can the accused pay?" asked Darrow. "Oh, he has absolutely no money," replied Spingarn. "Well, that settles it," said Darrow. "I'll have to take the case." He paid the disbursements out of his own purse. Yet he could be exasperating about money matters: he would embarrass his friends by debating over a restaurant table whether he and Ruby should order two portions of a dish or share one between them. He always demanded his money's worth and "got sore as hell when anybody overcharged him or didn't give fair value." He had stingy moments, when he tried to save a few cents—and then gave twice the amount to the next mendicant he passed on the street. There were times when he appeared grasping and eager for money but, as in the Spingarn tale, a touching phrase or twist of a situation could immediately melt him.

Again, at his own expense, he went into Rockford to save the life of seventeen-year-old Russell McWilliams, son of a laboring family who had, while drunk on prohibition liquor, killed a street-car conductor in a holdup. McWilliams had pleaded guilty and, to everyone's astonishment, since only one minor ever had been executed on a plea of guilty in the history of Illinois, was sentenced to be electrocuted. The streetcar company kept constant pressure on the governor not to commute the sentence. Jessie Binford of Hull House recounts, "The case had a terrific appeal for Darrow because McWilliams had never had a chance; he was a product of poverty, a slender, tragic boy, hardly knowing what it was all about. The courtroom was filled with the poor and the working people of Rockford who had come, mute-eyed and mute-tongued, hoping that the boy of their class would be saved." Through Darrow's efforts the boy's sentence was commuted to life.

Another time a prisoner at the Northeastern Penitentiary asked his chaplain to persuade Darrow to look over the record of his case and help him secure a pardon. The chaplain relates, "Despite the fact that Mr Darrow had retired from active practice, he took many hours to go through the material and give the prisoner the benefit of his advice and assistance." Darrow secured the pardon; after a time the released prisoner set up a social-service agency dedicated to the task of rehabilitating paroled prisoners.

The only case from which he withdrew, even though he considered an injustice had been done, was that of the five Scottsboro boys, Negroes who were charged with the rape of a white woman. When he agreed to undertake the defense and prepared to leave for the South Arthur Garfield Hays had asked, "Why are you going so early? The trial doesn't start for several months." Darrow had replied, "Oh, I'm not going down for the trial. I'm going down to make friends." He soon withdrew, however, because "the case was controlled by the Communist party, who cared far less for the safety and well-being of those poor Negro boys than the exploitation of their own cause. If I could not be free and completely independent, without political ties, I would have none of it."

He had become a myth during his own time. Few people in America did not know his name and his face. No one of his day was more discussed, more loved and more hated; nor was he unaware of this split in the public affection for him. He had been invited to luncheon at H. L. Mencken's house in Baltimore and was climbing the flights of narrow, steep stairs, when Mencken called down to him, "Be careful, Clarence; if you fall and kill yourself in my house the public will crucify me."

"No, they won't," he sang back. "They'll canonize you."

George Whitehead's twelve-year-old daughter exclaimed after her first trip to Chicago, "I enjoyed Mr Darrow more than I did the Aquarium or the World's Fair." Whitehead comments, "Darrow didn't want anyone to think he had a sentimental side, but he had a hard time being tough. He liked all the attention, but he didn't like people to think he liked it." Frequently he would ask, "Am I as good as I was five years ago? Am I doing it as well?"

Nevertheless, he did not like attention centered on him when he was in public. Once when he was attending the theater Will Rogers came out to do his rope act and, while chatting with the audience, said, "I see my friend Clarence Darrow sittin' down there. Get up, Clarence, and let the folks have a look at you." Darrow rose briefly and received a big hand, but Rogers understood that he hadn't liked being singled out. Will chewed his gum for a moment, then murmured *sotto voce*, "Shucks, I should-a known better than to do that; I guess I just wanted to brag on the fact that I was a friend of his." Another time Rogers commented, "Clarence Darrow is the only freethinker the American people have allowed to live for seventy-three years."

He plugged along, sensing that his vigor was beginning to diminish, hoping that he could do still a little more work for tolerance before he died. H. L. Mencken wrote of him, "The marks of battle are all over his face. He has been through more wars than a whole regiment of Pershings. And most of them have been struggles to the death, without codes or quarter. Has he always won? Superficially, yes; actually, no. His cause seems lost among us. Nearly all the imbecilities that he has sought to lay live on. But they are not as safe as they used to be. Someday, let us hope, they will be put down. Whoever at last puts them down will owe half his bays to Clarence Darrow."

Charles A. Beard says, "To men and women who wore their hearts on their sleeves and paraded their virtues and omniscience Darrow was a 'cynic.' He gave months and months of his life to helping poor wretches in trouble, without compensation and without seeking any publicity for his unselfish action, and he did have little use for people who made public professions of goodness. But his alleged cynicism was really nothing more than calm irony—the irony of keen judgment which could not fail to take note of differences between men's professions of righteousness for public consumption and things they actually did. Yet Darrow was among the gentlest of persons. He could fight when he had to, but there was no rancor in his soul. He felt sorry for the world—its cruelties, its sufferings, the huge injustice of man to man. He would have wiped away its tears if he could and made the world a joyful and beautiful place in which to dwell. Despite his hilarity over the antics of his fellow creatures, he seemed to me to be grief incarnate in his solemn hours."

He rarely allowed his solemnity to show. He tried always to laugh a little at himself and the foibles of the world. When on his trips with Whitehead he liked to recite such poems as *My Love Works in a Greenhouse* and *The Romance of a Persian Kitty*. Once he insisted upon taking Whitehead to see a lake in the woods which he had thought so beautiful he had remembered it for twenty-five years.

Disappointed, he now murmured to Whitehead, "I'll tell you, when I saw that lake before I had a very pretty girl with me. Maybe that's why it looked so good." His most famous quip, which has since become an American classic, was, "I never wanted to see anybody die, but there are a few obituary notices I have read with pleasure."

He continued to have an answer for everything, one that was nearly always pungent and satiric, but given with such sweetness and good will that the other fellow could not take offense. A young law clerk whom he knew failed to pass his bar examination, taking it a second time six months later. When Darrow again saw the boy he asked, "Well, did you pass?" "Yes sir, I sure did," replied the young chap. Darrow murmured, "And now I suppose you'll want the standards raised." When someone used as an argument in favor of religion that business depressions brought people close to the Church, he replied, "So do funerals." When a lovely blonde who had attended one of his lectures asked distressedly, "Mr Darrow, isn't there anything you believe in?" he replied a trifle wistfully, "Yes, I used to believe in blondes."

Now that he had become the Old Lion his audacity was regarded as a privilege granted to the patriarch. He had become the Tom Paine of the twentieth century, fighting for the rights of man, the voice that spoke when other voices were hushed and still. He had become the Barb, the Shot in the Arm: when invited to speak at a dinner of the American newspaper publishers, he excluded the *Christian Science Monitor* and then flayed the publishers for not telling the truth, for kowtowing to their advertisers, for serving as propaganda sheets instead of newssheets. Invited to speak at an assemblage of motion-picture producers he cuffed them mercilessly for being in possession of a great medium and doing nothing with it, for excluding ninety per cent of the realities of life, for daring to speak out on nothing but love.

Though he had grown old his prescience had not dimmed. Once when he was debating a clergyman, his opponent read a paragraph from the New York *Times* which pretty well demolished Darrow's argument up to that point. Darrow had not been able to see the card from which his opponent was reading, but when it came time for his rebuttal he asked the clergyman for the card in question, then read to the audience a second paragraph from the New York *Times* which the clergyman's secretary had copied down by mistake. The second paragraph contradicted the first, sustained Darrow's theory and turned the laugh on his opponent. The clergyman could never understand how he had known that there was another and contradictory paragraph on that card.

At last there emerged an ironic twist to his work for free thought. By the time Clarence reached seventy-five many clergymen and religious students had already passed him by. Dr A. Eustace Haydon, Professor of Comparative Religion at the University of Chicago, claimed that, in the tradition of Ingersoll, he was attacking a conception of religion that already had been outworn; that he was "fighting a conception of God that first-rate minds had discarded; he was fighting an anthropomorphic God with white whiskers and a spear in his hand, sitting on a cloud someplace."

When he went to speak at the Meadville Theological School, from which his father had been the first student to be graduated, the Unitarian students found him a little old fashioned! "The men always enjoyed his trenchant criticism of religion and the ministry, and their discussions were fierce and hot, with no quarter given; however, I got the impression from their discussion that Mr Darrow did not realize how emancipated Unitarian ministers were of old theology and clericalism. In fact, in comparison with some of our humanists Mr Darrow seemed a bit conservative, and I think this rather annoyed him."

T. V. Smith of the University of Chicago debated him frequently on religion, using against Clarence the most modern and advanced theories of philosophy and metaphysics. "The first time I sprang this on him," says Smith, "he got up and said to the audience, 'If I had three weeks to think this over I might be able to answer it. As it is, I'll have to give my old lecture on free will.' After I had debated Darrow three times on this subject he finally leaned over in the cab one night, put his hand on my knee and said, 'You know, Professor, tonight for the first time I think I understand what you are saying, and there may be something in it after all.' "

8

In 1932, when Darrow was seventy-five, there was brought to him the last case in which he was to work in the glare of the international spotlight. In the city of Honolulu, Mrs Thalia Massie, wife of a lieutenant in the United States Navy, left a party at the Ala Wai Inn at midnight; the café was hot and smoky; Mrs Massie was upset over a quarrel she had just had with her husband; she decided to walk home alone. She turned onto the John Ena Road, a fairly well-lighted boulevard in the general direction of her home but which at its far end held a row of bungalows which the service men rented when they wanted women brought to them. Mrs Massie had gone only a short way up the road when a car containing two

Hawaiians, one Chinaman and two Japanese pulled up at the curb; they were apparently intent upon hijacking one of the native women on her way to the service bungalows, a practice that had been going on for a number of months. One of the Hawaiians and one of the Japanese jumped out and grabbed Mrs Massie. When she struggled with them Kahahawai, a famous Island athlete, slugged her with his fist and broke her jaw. They then threw her into the back seat of the car and drove down the Ala Moana Drive to an abandoned spot where the five men ravished her. Mrs Massie stumbled back to the road, was found by white motorists and taken to her home. She was immediately transferred to the hospital where, the following morning, she identified four of her assailants.

The relations between the mixed-breed population of Honolulu and the whites of the civilian population and army and navy settlements had always been delicate; the army and navy commanders had done everything in their power to keep the atmosphere peaceful and friendly. Now the resentment between the various groups flared up. The army and navy men were seriously disturbed; on the Island during the past year there had been some forty cases of attacks on native women that had necessitated hospital treatment. Since the service men had to leave their wives alone while they were at sea, this attack on the wife of an officer shocked and terrorized them. The smoldering ill will the natives felt against the whites manifested itself in large defense funds raised by the Hawaiian population for the two accused Hawaiians, by the Japanese colony for the two accused Japanese, the Chinese colony for the accused Chinaman, in the refusal of the largely native and mixed-breed police force to gather evidence against the five accused men, in the reluctance of the elected district attorney to prosecute, in the insistence that the junior assistant district attorney be assigned to try the case against the two best white attorneys on the Island. A widespread whispering campaign was waged against Mrs Massie in which her character was defamed, her reason for leaving the Ala Wai Inn attacked and a questionable motive attributed to her presence on the John Ena Road.

When the mixed-breed jury disagreed on the verdict and the four accused men were released on bail to engage in Island sports and resume their normal life, the ill feeling between the whites and the natives grew stronger. In an attempt to force a confession from one of the four men Lieutenant Massie severely beat one of the Japanese. He secured his confession, but the Japanese had a photograph taken which revealed the welts from the lashing on his back, and Massie's attorney informed him that such a confession, obtained through force, would be worthless. Lieutenant Massie and his wife's mother, Mrs Fortescue, aided by two sailors who acted out of loyalty to their superior officer, then kidnaped Kahahawai from in front of the courthouse by means of a fraudulent affidavit. They took him to Mrs Fortescue's bungalow, where it was claimed by Lieutenant Massie that while he was trying to get the Hawaiian to confess, in the face of a service revolver, he had gone temporarily insane and pulled the trigger, killing Kahahawai instantly when the Hawaiian had mumbled, "Yeah, we done it." The sailors wrapped his body in a piece of canvas which they found in the garage and, after Mrs Fortescue had pulled the blinds in the car, dumped it onto the floor of the back seat. Mrs Fortescue then started driving very fast for the cliffs of Koko Head, where they intended to throw the body into the sea. However, the police already knew about Kahahawai's disappearance; when they saw the drawn blinds of Mrs Fortescue's automobile they gave pursuit, and the four participants in the kidnaping and murder were arrested.

Though the attack upon Mrs Massie had caused consternation in army and navy circles, it had been paid but moderate attention on the mainland. The killing, the arrest and murder charge against Lieutenant Massie, Mrs Fortescue and the two sailors immediately became a *cause célèbre*, was made a major issue in Congress, was heralded on the front pages of newspapers as far away as Budapest. Since it was impossible to secure an all-white jury in Honolulu, the Massie and Fortescue attorneys were fearful of the results of the trial. It was not only that the four indicted ones had an excellent chance of spending the rest of their lives in what the naval commanding officer, Rear Admiral Yates Stirling, described as "a disgusting and revolting Hawaiian prison," but that such a sentence would cause civil war among the varying races, breeds and colors that had to live together.

The friends and relatives of the socially prominent Massie and Fortescue families insisted that the finest criminal lawyer to be found must be retained for their defense. They approached Clarence Darrow. He had been following the unfolding situation with interest but was taken completely by surprise when he was offered a fee of twenty-five thousand dollars to undertake the case.

"I wondered if I could stand the trip," he said, "and I was not certain that I could bear the daily routine beginning in court early each day and watching and catching all that goes on in the trial. I was not even sure that my mind would click with its old-time vigor."

He communicated his doubts to the Massie and Fortescue families; they would not accept his refusal. He went to see his friend Arthur

Spingarn, confiding to him that it was not the kind of case he liked, that he felt he ought not to be involved in it.

"I urged him to go for two reasons," relates Spingarn. "One, that he was tired and the trip to Hawaii would do him good and, two, that he needed the money so desperately, he was entitled to take on a case for money, just as other lawyers did, as against the thousands he had tried for nothing."

He accepted the Massie case. When asked after the trial why he had done so he replied, "I had never been to Honolulu and thought I should like to see the country. Besides, they said I was through as a lawyer, and I wanted to show them that a man in his seventies was keener than a younger person. In addition, Mrs Massie, as a psychological study, interested me and appealed to my sympathy." Having decided to undertake the defense, he telephoned to a stranger by the name of George Leisure, a Wall Street lawyer.

George Leisure relates, "One day the telephone rang and a voice said, 'Is this George Leisure?' I said, 'Yes.' He said, 'This is Clarence Darrow speaking.' I thought at first that it was one of my good friends inviting me out to lunch and using his name because he knew that I was an admirer of C. D. Since the voice sounded serious, however, I answered, 'Yes sir,' and listened. Mr Darrow then proceeded to say: 'I am about to try a case in Honolulu, and I have been told that you tried a case in Honolulu a year or so ago. I have nevei tried a case there and I thought that perhaps you would be willing to talk to me and tell me something of the nature of the procedure in that jurisdiction. If you could have lunch with me today I would appreciate it very much.'

"Some years before, while on a steamer going to Europe, I had read Ludwig's *Life of Napoleon*. Upon contemplating the book, I thought how interesting it would be to be able to sit down and talk personally with Napoleon about some of his campaigns. My mind then drifted to the great men of my own profession, and I resolved that when I got back from Europe I would one day go to Chicago and have just such a talk with Clarence Darrow. When I got back to New York the regular demands of courtroom practice kept me at my work, and I never had the opportunity of going to Chicago as I had planned. I now saw Mr Darrow for luncheon and not only had lunch with him but spent the entire afternoon with him, during which time I had precisely the kind of talk with him that I had thought it would be interesting to have had with Napoleon. He seemed surprised to know that I was familiar with many of his cases.

"When I left him at the close of the afternoon he said, 'I have been retired from practice for some time now, and I have not been regularly engaged in courtroom work for several years. I am also getting along in years and I would be very pleased to have a young man accompany me on this trip. I wonder if it would be possible for you to go to Honolulu with me?' Without even checking with my office I assured him that it was entirely possible and that I was prepared to leave at any time. Soon after that Mrs Leisure and I joined Mr and Mrs Darrow in Chicago, and we proceeded to Honolulu together." Clarence and Ruby came to love the Leisures, who proved to be devoted friends; they enjoyed their trip to the Islands and were enchanted with their beauty.

In Honolulu Darrow found that most of the legal work already had been done by his associates; he asked the court for a week's postponement in order to interview his clients and witnesses and gain a more complete knowledge of the facts. He found Lieutenant Massie and his wife Thalia to be fine-looking, sensitive young people caught in the grip of a tragedy which would never release them. Massie and his wife were, under the circumstances, quiet and self-possessed, but Thalia's mother, Mrs Fortescue, was a high-strung woman whom some of the Islanders believed to be responsible for the kidnaping. The navy men, solidly behind Massie, were grimly resolved that their brother officer should not go to prison. Darrow determined once again to plead mental illness, this time basing his case on an overwhelming provocation. He learned that the prosecution would be headed by the most successful pyrotechnical trial lawyer on the Islands; that Judge Davis, son of an outstanding Island lawyer who had come from New England, could be counted on to remain fair and impartial in the midst of the conflicting passions.

During his four thousand miles of travel Darrow had kept hoping that he would be able to get a majority of white men on the jury. When he finished his examinations and faced the men in the jury box he saw that they were all natives except two. "Even with these natives, however, Mr Darrow always extracted either a laugh or a smile from each juror before he accepted him, although at times the smile was drawn out almost by use of the corkscrew method. Mr Darrow would place his hands in the side pockets of his unpressed coat and, hunching his shoulders forward, make some friendly remark to the prospective juror which would bring forth the desired friendly contact." When he went into action on the first morning of the case Darrow was thrilled to find that his brain was working with its old-time precision and clarity. Though he had expert legal assistance always at his elbow, he tried most of the case himself. "Darrow, his coat hanging loosely about his bony frame, breathed kindliness and sympathy for all," says Rear Admiral Yates Stirling. "The courtroom seemed pervaded with this gentle, old voice. Its soothing effect upon that courtroom was miraculous to see. Slowly his voice was stamping out all bitterness."

He made no attempt to deny the killing, to keep any of the prosecution's material out of evidence, even when the facts were dubitable; neither did he deny that all four of the participants of the kidnaping were equally involved, even though the other three did not know that Lieutenant Massie might kill Kahahawai. The only legal fracas occurred when he attempted to introduce the facts of the rape as mitigation, as a basis for Massie's mental illness. The prosecution fought to keep the story out of the evidence, but Judge Davis ruled the story of the attack to be material and relevant. From the witness stand Mrs Massie recounted the details of the abduction, assault and ravishment, even to the need of having herself curetted because of pregnancy. Lieutenant Massie tried to picture for the jury his state of mind after the attack upon his wife.

Not since the Loeb-Leopold murder had the newspaper readers of the United States been so unified in their concentration on events happening in a courtroom. For the five weeks of the trial they argued the high points of the case, told what they would have done if they had been Lieutenant Massie or Mrs Fortescue or Mrs Massie, what they would do if they were on the jury. Great numbers of them felt that they had something personal involved and were wrought up by its implications. With the exception of those lawyers who insisted that the law could not be overthrown, no matter how extenuating the circumstances, the American people were vehement in their demand that the jury in Honolulu declare the four indicted ones not guilty.

If feeling on the mainland was intense, the Islanders were caught in the grip of the most dangerous fever that had seized its people since the American occupation. As many as five hundred people slept on the courthouse lawn each night, in order that they might get seats as soon as the doors opened. The feeling of the navy men ran so high that all shore leave had to be denied.

In his summation Darrow spoke to the jury for four hours. He pleaded in almost poetic terms of the need for good will on the Islands, for an end to racial antagonisms. He appealed to them in quiet, gentle terms to put an end to this terrible tragedy, which kept multiplying itself with every new development. But even as he spoke he realized that his words were failing. "When I gazed into those dark faces I could see the deep mysteries of the Orient were there. My ideas and words were not registering."

He closed his final argument, which was broadcast by radio to the mainland, by saying, "I would like to think that some time not too far away I might come back here with a consciousness that I had done my small part in bringing peace and justice to an island that today is racked and torn by internal strife. I place this case in your hands and ask you to be kind, understanding and considerate, both to the living and to the dead."

Judge Davis agreed with the attorneys on the mainland; in his instructions to the jury he stressed the implacable fact that no man can take the law into his own hands. In spite of these instructions Darrow and the other defense attorneys, as well as ninety-nine per cent of the people of the United States, were convinced that the jury could bring in nothing but a verdict of not guilty. After two days of anxious and puzzled waiting he was genuinely surprised to hear a verdict of manslaughter, with a recommendation for leniency. Judge Davis sentenced Massie, the two sailors and Mrs Fortescue to ten years' imprisonment.

The backwash of resentment from the mainland was intense. In the United States Senate the verdict was denounced from the floor; the House Territories Committee voted for a sweeping investigation of the government of Hawaii to see if changes weren't necessary. Members of both the House and the Senate demanded that the four convicted ones be pardoned instantly and outright; congressmen publicly condemned Governor Judd, Judge Davis and the jury. Within twenty-four hours the jurors began apologizing for their verdict, explaining that it was the judge's charge which had forced them to bring in a manslaughter decision.

Then something happened that had never before happened to Clarence Darrow in his fifty-four years of practice: the attorney general of Hawaii came to see him at his hotel to say that the prosecution was distressed with its victory! He further told him that any attempt to move Mrs Fortescue, Massie and the two sailors to the Hawaiian prison would cause serious trouble—that Governor Judd wanted to dispose of the case. Darrow could take a hint; he convoyed his four clients to the governor's office. Judd commuted their sentence to one hour; the four convicted persons sat with their defense attorney in the Old Palace for the hour, after which they were released. The commutation was roundly condemned in Congress, for without a full pardon, Massie, Mrs Fortescue and the two sailors had lost certain of their citizenship privileges, including the right to vote.

Nothing had been settled by the verdict or the commutation. Navy officials in Hawaii and the United States Congress demanded that the three remaining abductors once again be tried for the Massie outrage. Here Darrow performed the most valuable service of his journey. He persuaded the Massies and the navy men that enough harm already had been done, that another trial would only prolong the bitterness, that it would be far better for everyone concerned to drop the matter and let it be forgotten as soon as possible.

They listened to his counsel. A few days later the Darrows boarded ship to return to the mainland, taking with them Mr and Mrs Massie, Mrs Fortescue and the two sailors.

"I felt as we went away," said Darrow, "that we were leaving the Island more peaceful and happy than I had found it, for which I was very glad."

9

One night in January 1934 he sat up in a Pullman smoking compartment with Lowell B. Mason, an attorney of Washington, D.C., and Senator Gerald Nye of North Dakota, discussing the National Recovery Act, which had been in effect since July of 1933. On his trips to Washington during the past months he had been keenly aware of both the extent and the nature of the changes in American political economy that had taken place during his lifetime, changes so great as to constitute a revolution. In 1894, when he had fought in the American Railway Union strike, it had appeared to him that the national government was but another arm of industry and finance; in 1933 the newly elected Democrats appeared to be devoting the major portion of their efforts to getting people back to work at good wages and moderate hours, to the elimination of child labor, to making collective bargaining the law of the land—causes to which Clarence Darrow had given the love and vitality of his most fruitful years.

The N.R.A. was in the process of putting two million men back to work; wages had been raised throughout the country; hours had been shortened; children were being taken out of the factories and sent to school; labor unions had been given the backing with which to become an integral part of American life. Yet in the crucial need to rescue the people from the country's shattering depression, in the frantic scurryings of the tens of thousands of businessmen, lawyers, lobbyists and administrators who poured into Washington, in the haste, the hostility, the confusion and the need to compromise, errors were being made. From small businessmen all over the country there arose a cry. In order to peg prices in a falling market so that industry could re-employ men at higher wages, price-fixing clauses had been written into most of the newly created business codes, which were then administered by the industries themselves. This power to fix prices had placed advantages in the hands of the giant corporations and combinations; the small businessman, who did not have the capital to enlarge his plant to deal in volume business, to advertise and promote, could not compete at the higher price levels, nor could he get his share of contracts unless he belonged to the industrial combinations.

The complaints of these smaller businessmen had become so wide-spread that Senator Nye had demanded an impartial review board be set up to diagnose the shortcomings and injustices of the N.R.A. General Hugh S. Johnson, administrator of the N.R.A., and Donald Richberg, chief counsel, insisted that a proven liberal be named to head the board. Remembering the discussion in the Pullman smoking compartment, Senator Nye suggested that Clarence Darrow be made head of the Review Board. President Franklin D. Roosevelt, Senator Borah, General Johnson and Donald Richberg agreed that Darrow was the man for the job. Darrow undertook what he was quite certain would be a laborious and thankless task because he knew that in order to gain labor-and-wage concessions, the code authorities had permitted such of his old adversaries as the Iron and Steel Institute and the National Coal Association to set their own prices and then maintain them at a level which eliminated free trading.

He and Ruby moved to Washington, where he had Lowell B. Mason appointed as his legal adviser, secured the appointment of W. O. Thompson, his former partner from Chicago, and Robert S. Keebler, a Tennessee attorney who had been ostracized by the Nashville Bar Association because he had attacked the anti-evolution bill when it had been passed. He met with the balance of his Review Board, which was popularly to be known as the Darrow Board, to outline what he conceived to be their function in Washington. The board then marched en masse to the offices of General Johnson for instructions. After the amenities had been exchanged Darrow asked Johnson what he thought they ought to do.

"I have provided rooms for you here, right next to mine," replied Johnson. "Also clerical help and supplies. You do some investigating and let me know if the codes are all right."

"But supposing we find the codes are not all right?" inquired Darrow.

"Then you report to me," replied Johnson. "I am the big cheese here."

"I don't think we care to do that," replied Darrow slowly. "I expect we had better go see the President."

There was a moment of strained silence, then Darrow rose and led his troupe to the White House. President Roosevelt received them warmly. He said, "We believe it is a good thing for the country and democracy that we have appointed the N.R.A. Review Board. There are always those who will say that Big Business is ruling this country; you will not find this so under this administration. We believe that the N.R.A. codes have been drafted by men who know their business and who represent, fairly, all types of business, both big and small."

"Mr President," said Darrow quietly, "we are assembled here as a board of review. Before we accept the appointment we want it understood that we will be active and functioning. We want hearings, lots of them. We want testimony that will prove to us the N.R.A. codes have been fairly written. We are here to protect the interests of the small businessmen, and we do not propose to let them down. Now, Mr President, you are a man of your word. Do we have a free hand?"

"Mr Darrow, you have a free hand," replied the President. "Conduct your hearings, make your findings and give them to me within a specified time, with your recommendations."

Turning to his board members, Darrow said, "Gentlemen, we will begin work tomorrow morning. And when I said work, I mean work."

The next day President Roosevelt signed an executive order, making the Review Board responsible to him instead of Hugh S. Johnson. Refusing the adjoining offices offered to him by Johnson on the grounds that he did not want the public or the complainants to feel that he was in any way attached to the administrator or under his control, Darrow opened his first hearing in his hotel room at the Willard. As soon as it was learned that he would hear the complaints of small businessmen the room was flooded with letters, telegrams, telephone calls, personal visitors. Within a few days the Review Board had perforce expanded from the adjoining rooms of Darrow and Mason to four large rooms on the second floor of the Hotel Willard, then to fourteen offices in an uptown office building.

Because of his eagerness to listen to every businessman who thought he had been injured, the seventy-seven-year-old Darrow drove himself and his board mercilessly. Awakened in the middle of the night by a problem that had been presented at the day's hearing, he would think it out to a satisfactory conclusion and, at two or three in the morning, telephone Mason to give him orders. He worked the board for fourteen and sixteen hours a day, including Sundays. Mason comments, "His disregard for the lunch hour became so bad that I finally had to plead with him to adjourn at noon for the sake of the complainants, witnesses and lawyers whose crusading spirits couldn't overcome their hunger. It was comical how some of the other members hid behind Darrow by saying, 'Well, now, gentlemen, I think we should adjourn for a couple of hours; Mr Darrow is in need of a little rest.' Or one of the members who was deaf would say, 'Speak up, Mr Witness, you know Mr Darrow had a mastoid operation years ago, and he can't hear very well out of one ear.' "

During the four months that the Darrow Board was in existence it held fifty-seven public hearings, examined thirty-four codes, investigated three thousand complaints. Though Darrow invited the code-authority attorneys and deputy administrators to be present whenever their particular code was being attacked and to cross-examine the witness after he had completed his testimony, the impression got around Washington that he was hostile to the codes. Newspaper stories about a rift between Darrow and Johnson began spreading. On the only occasion that General Johnson ever saw Darrow alone he took him for a ride in his limousine. Sensing that a major battle would be fought in the back seat of the car, reporters assembled twenty-five strong in front of the Hotel Willard to await its return. When Darrow, who had forgotten to take a hat with him, stepped out of the limousine his head was well covered.

"I got the general's hat, boys," he told the reporters with a chuckle. He had also got the general's goat.

On April eighteenth the Darrow Board gave its chief a seventy-seventh birthday party. The Hotel Willard served its regular two-dollar-and-fifty-cent banquet dinner for a dollar and sent Clarence a bouquet of American Beauty roses. Witty Charles Edward Russell acted as toastmaster. The Darrows had a most enjoyable evening. In only one way did Clarence show his age. Mason persuaded him to see the moving picture of Greta Garbo as Queen Christina. Just as the queen was climbing into bed with the Spanish ambassador Darrow turned to Mason and said, "Lowell, I think Gerry Nye will be up at the room waiting to see us. I guess we had better go now." Mason complained that he had to go back alone the next day to find out what had happened to the queen.

If he was getting old he didn't seem frightened by the idea; as he was entering one of the Hotel Willard elevators an acquaintance called out, "Mr Darrow, how are you today? You lock a little tired.

Maybe you're like me—my spirit is strong, but the House in which it lives is feeling weak." He replied, "There is no spirit; when your House is gone, you are gone."

After three months of hearings and investigations he came to the conclusion that the National Recovery Administration, in its desire to help the workingman, had baited its hook with price protection and that the trusts had proceeded to swallow the bait, the hook, the line and the fisherman. One member of the Review Board says, "Darrow didn't like the spectacle of a regulatory system which seemed to have been seized by large industry with its effects pressed upon small business. He felt it was too large a price to pay for social betterment." Nor did he believe that the country should approve injustices in the codes in the name of labor progress; labor had been progressing solidly and steadily year after year, fighting its way toward collective bargaining and fair wages; though the N.R.A. had accelerated the pace, he did not like, and thought dangerous, the N.R.A.'s burdening of labor with the onus of monopolistic codes deemed necessary to the nation's recovery. To his board members he kept saying:

"You can't get to a pleasant place to be at unless you use pleasant methods to get there. When you are dealing with a human society the means is fully as important as the end. This compromise of handing big business a monopoly in order that they may give more work at higher wages will result in destroying all small and independent businesses in the country and will ultimately leave labor and the nation in the hands of a few overwhelming trusts."

At the end of three months Darrow submitted his first report to President Roosevelt. He permitted no word of its content to leak out. When the report was released to the press two weeks later it was accompanied by a terrific blast from General Johnson, defending the N.R.A. against Darrow's charges. Under the heading of "Tender-Hearted Cynic," *Newsweek* magazine wrote, "Another sign of the nation's upturn is that Clarence Darrow is on one of his peculiarly cool and deadly rampages again. As a foreman of a kind of governmental grand jury to tell the administration how the N.R.A. is working, he has brought in a report saying it's doing perfectly terribly. Last week Washington sat forward nervously to see how many holes that particular bomb would tear in New Deal pavements. Meantime Mr Darrow sat back, hitched his fingers in under his gallus straps and looked on with that amazing mixture of cynicism, compassion and incredibly brilliant intelligence that is his character."

In the following month Darrow submitted two more reports to the President in an attempt to outline revisions in the N.R.A. that would protect the small businessman without losing any of the gains that had been made for labor. These he released to the press at the same time that he sent them to the White House. President Roosevelt read both reports, was convinced by Darrow's evidence, appointed a Senate committee to study the recommendations.

Hugh Johnson was outraged; he "vigorously criticized all of its reports and demanded that the President remove its members, declaring them to be ill advised, prejudiced and engaged in special pleading." Both Johnson and Donald Richberg felt that Darrow had betrayed them, that they had made a mistake in thinking him a proven liberal. In spite of Johnson's objections most of the major recommendations of the Darrow Board were put into effect. Price fixing was eliminated from all new codes; the Federal Trade Commission was given the right to examine charges of oppressive practices by monopolies; price fixing was taken out of the service trades; labor controversies were placed in the hands of a special industrial-relations board; the N.R.A. power was taken out of the hands of Johnson, to be distributed through such branches of government as the attorney general's office and the secretary of the interior.

In March of 1935 Darrow appeared before the Senate Investigating Committee in Washington to give the final conclusions from the investigation.

"I had not been here very long," he told Senators Harrison, George, Barclay, Guffy, Cousins, La Follette and a number of others, "until I rather got the idea that the N.R.A. in effect made it easier for the people who had it all and made it harder for the people who did not have it. The outstanding opinion was that the N.R.A. was gotten up to help 'big business,' and they could not help big business very much unless they took the business away from the small fellows. I know something about big business, more than small business, and my sympathies are all with the small fellow. If there were not so much big business there would be more small business, much more, in my opinion. Big business has all of the advantage, and the N.R.A. very materially increased that advantage. Big business exists because they have got keen men at the head of it; they have got plenty of money, and they can advertise in the leading newspaper, fences and barns. They not only can, but do. Little business is supposed to pick up the crumbs that are left to fall from the rich man's table. They are made up of people with small capital. The concentration of wealth is going on, and it looks almost as if there were nothing to stop it. If we do not destroy it there will be nothing but masters and slaves left before we get much further along."

He complained against what he called "the economy of scarcity," which created high prices, and attacked the idea that there could be overproduction in a country where half the people were not enjoying a sufficient consumption of goods.

When Senator Lonergan asked, "Have you any ideas for improving the system of distribution as to the output of factory and farm?" Darrow replied:

"Yes, I have got a lot of them, but nobody listens to them."

"Do you think there is any substitute for economic laws?"

"I am not at all sure about economic laws," rejoined Darrow. "I do not think they are like the laws of gravity. I think we will find that most of them have been made by human beings and pretty human at that. The lords of creation think that the Almighty meant that they should be rich and the great mass of people should be poor. Men have got to do these things themselves, but men are awfully hardhearted. Kindliness comes from imagination, and very few people have any to waste. When they get so that they can put themselves in other people's places and suffer because they suffer, we will probably get rid of most of these inequalities, but whether they will ever get there, I do not know. I think that something like a socialistic system would be the only thing that would make anything like an equal distribution of wealth. What are all these machines made for if they are not made to help the human race to live a better life and an easier life, to have more pleasure and less pain? They have had their share of pain. I think it is possible that we will have a better situation a few hundred years from now. I hate to wait so long."

He was far from being in top form; he was tired. In addition he was torn by the same lacerating dilemmas that had Washington and the rest of the country sorely perplexed: how to cross nineteenth-century capitalism with twentieth-century socialism so as to retain the best qualities of both, kill off neither parent and breed a healthy, happy, lusty economic child, indigenous to the character of the people and the resources of the land, with a chance for survival in a hostile, changing world. To the majority of Americans the confusion arising from this problem in sociopolitical eugenics was a new kind of headache; to Darrow it was an old, old friend.

The Senate Investigating Committee was neither able nor willing to legislate Darrow's quasi socialism into existence, but it did co-operate in securing the passage of laws which helped to wipe out many of the injustices of the National Recovery Act.

In this last public appearance in which he was to voice a social philosophy for all the nation to hear and read Darrow put the small businessman in the anomalous position of having their champion plead for socialism at the same time that he was pleading for a fair capitalism. William Hard commented in *Survey-Graphic*, "Mr Darrow is in favor of the restoration of competition, and he is in favor of progress into socialization. Walter Lippmann cannot see how Mr Darrow can advocate both capitalistic competition and Russian communism. That is because Mr Lippmann is a logician. Mr Darrow is as wild as life."

10

Shortly after his appearance before the Senate Investigating Committee he began markedly to fail. Though his heart had been troubling him for a number of years, he paid himself scant attention, figuring that if he had lived to be seventy-eight without taking care of himself it was too late to mend his ways. His interest in the subjects for which he had always worked was of greater importance to him than the conservation of his waning energies. He continued to write his critical articles at the broad black desk he had brought home to his study and went out on the road to lecture under any and all weather conditions. Warden Lewis E. Lawes tells, "I was delivering a talk in Albany during a terrific rainstorm, but during the lecture I noticed Mr and Mrs Darrow entering the hall. In spite of the weather, they had taken the time between trains to come and hear me." When reporters came to him for interviews he continued to make as sharp and dramatic a charge as he could formulate against those forces which he considered destructive of the peaceful society.

Julian Street says, "If ever I saw a man whose character showed in his face, that man was Clarence Darrow. He had the face of a prophet. Nobody else looked in the least like him. He must have known that many people didn't understand him, that many regarded him as a devil's advocate, but he didn't care a hang. Placidly, magnificently, he went his way without regard to anything but his own sense of what was right."

He was still in there pitching, but the old arm was getting weak. By the time he reached seventy-eight Ruby had to persuade him to abandon the more arduous lecture tours, to write more sparingly at his desk. He would sit in his wicker chair before the fireplace or at the windows overlooking Jackson Park, the little Japanese bridges and pagodas on Lake Michigan. Opie Reid, author of *The Arkansas Traveler*, lived a few houses down the street; the two men spent amusing hours together, telling each other how the world would go to hell once they had departed from this earth.

He was almost seventy-nine when he wrote one of the most delightful and discerning articles of his journalistic career. Asked by *Esquire* magazine to contribute a piece on jury picking, he minted the accumulated wisdom of his fifty-eight years in the court-room into a very few paragraphs. Starting off by advising that one should always choose a man who laughs, because a juror who laughs hates to find anyone guilty, and to avoid wealthy men, because rich men will always convict—unless the defendant allegedly had violated the antitrust laws—he then dissected the influence of the various religions upon the character of the prospective juror. He advised that Methodists be accepted as jurymen because "their religious emotions can be transmuted into love and charity," but warned against taking Presbyterians because "they know right from wrong but seldom find anything right," and against Lutherans be-cause "they were almost always sure to convict." After counseling that one should never accept a prohibitionist under any circum-stance, he recommended that the best jurors for the defense were Catholics, Unitarians, Congregationalists, Universalists, Jews and agnostics.

The last words he was to write, which were found in his desk, scribbled in longhand on composition-book paper, were an epitome of his life. "The fact that my father was a heretic always put him on the defensive, and we children thought it was only right and loyal that we should defend his cause. Even in our little shop the neighbors learned that there was something going on and that my father was ever ready to meet all comers on the mysteries of life and death. During my youth I always listened, but my moral sup-port was with my father. I cannot remember that I ever had any doubt that he was right. The fact that most of the community were on the other side made him so much surer of his cause." It also had made Clarence, son of Amirus, surer of his cause.

On his seventy-ninth birthday he made a sentimental trip to Kins-man with George Whitehead, for he sensed that this would be his last chance. He visited his old friends, making pilgrimages to the spots he had loved best as a child, the schoolhouse where, on Friday nights during the fall and winter, he had gone with his brother Everett and his sister Mary to listen to the discussions of the literary club, the big barns where on Saturday nights he had debated. As he sat on the steps of the octagonal-shaped home the reporters gathered around to hear one of his famous blasts at some greed or stupidity current in the news. Clarence wasn't up to it. "The old man didn't have all his buttons," says one of the local Ohio reporters. "But we polished up his quotes. It was that way with Darrow."

He returned to Chicago to enter a hospital for a general diagnosis. There was little that could be done for him. Ruby took him home, put him to bed, called in three male nurses. Young and vigorous, Ruby was stricken at the thought that she and the world must soon lose Clarence Darrow. During the first few weeks of his seventy-ninth year she permitted friends to come and visit with him, but after a time she saw that this exhausted his strength, that he sometimes fell asleep on his guests, that his mind did not always work collectedly. She thereupon shut out all visitors.

In nice weather he had liked to walk for an hour along the Midway or through the University of Chicago campus, but as he grew weaker Ruby would not let him go out. His friends complained that he was being held a prisoner in the flat in the Midway; Darrow, too, complained that he would rather go about his normal way, do the things he liked and die a little sooner. When he felt too badly about being confined to the house she would wrap him up warmly and send him across the Midway to visit Professor T. V. Smith at the university. He would chat with Smith about philosophy and religion and the good old days. One day, thinking to amuse the Old Lion, Smith told him that he was going to put up three statuettes in his office: the first of Socrates, his ancient master, high up on the file; the second of Thomas Jefferson, his modern master, on a stand where he could see him face to face, and third, very close to hand, a statuette of the American gadfly, Clarence Darrow. Tears filled Darrow's eyes as he said, "Why, I didn't know you felt that way about me." Smith had been bantering; when he saw the tears in Darrow's eyes he knew that the rock that was Clarence Darrow had been shattered.

Clarence spent a slow, painful and ugly year dying; on his eightieth birthday he could give no interview which his newspaper friends might polish up.

He died on March 13, 1938, from almost eighty-one years of living.

11

A friend from Woodstock, Illinois, sent a mahogany casket as a gift. The funeral parlor on Sixty-third Street in Chicago was supposed to close at eleven at night but did not shut its doors for forty-eight hours. Not since the death of John P. Altgeld had so many people walked past a casket with tears in their eyes for their champion who had gone.

At all hours of the day and night people filed past to say their fare-wells: workingmen from the stockyards and steel mills in their overalls; scrubwomen in their Mother Hubbards; colored men with their lunch baskets under their arms; colored women with groups of wide-eyed little children who had been brought to see the white man who had fought for their race; the cold and frightened ones who had gone to him to warm their hands at his fire; the weak and confused and indeterminate ones who had been strength-ened by his boldness and resolution; the harassed, the unhappy, the mentally ill, whose plight he had tried to make intelligible; teachers, whose freedom he had broadened by his struggles; students, whose minds had been stimulated by his iconoclasm; lawyers, to whose trade he had given another dimension; clergymen, to whom he had revealed Christianity at work; those who came from no specific class or section; the indescribable ones who had spilled out their grief to him and whose worries had been lightened by his sympathy; the misfits whom he had defended and for whom he had pleaded in a harsh and cruel world; the labor leaders and union members whose organizations he had preserved under fire; the liberals, for whose middle-of-the-road navigation he had fought unceasingly for half a century; the radical for whose freedom of thought and speech he had endured the spleen of reaction; the long line of men accused of crime for whom he had earned another chance; those who had killed and who lived now only because this dead man had lived; the middle-class folk for whom he had been a rallying point, a debunker, an intellectual spark.

In the dark small hours the creatures of the night, the prostitutes, the bums, the addicts, the thieves, the derelicts; for forty-eight hours, mixed in with those who had come to pray for his soul, with those who had come to remember his friendship and his love, the underdog, the poor, the weak, the oppressed, the uncertain, the sick, the weary: all streamed past his coffin, all those who had needed a friend and had had no friend and to whom Clarence Darrow had been a friend.

Darrow had said, "Let Judge Holly speak at my funeral. He knows everything there is to know about me, and he has sense enough not to tell it."

Funeral services were held in Bond Chapel at the University of Chicago in a torrential downpour. Ruby remained at home, but it seemed as though the rest of Chicago had come. One man, about to enter the chapel, saw an old tramp, coatless, the water oozing from his shoes, come up the street and enter the chapel door. "You look as though you've come a long way," said the man. "Yes," replied the tramp; "I walked all the way from downtown." A large crowd that could not be accommodated inside stood outside in the rain to hear whatever they could of the services.

At the funeral of John P. Altgeld, Darrow had said, "In the great flood of human life that is spawned upon the earth it is not often that a man is born. John P. Altgeld was a soldier in the ever-lasting struggle of the human race for liberty and justice on the earth. Today we pay our last sad homage to the most devoted leader, the most abject slave, the fondest, wildest, dreamiest victim that ever gave his life to liberty's immortal cause."

Judge Holly said, "It is a magnificent thing that Clarence Darrow lived. The colored race will long remember him with grateful hearts for his heroic battles in their behalf. The man who toils with his hands, the poor and the unfortunate whom society hunted down, found him ever ready to devote his extraordinary talents in their behalf. He gave up a brilliant legal career, that would have made him one of the rich men of the country, to espouse the cause of labor. In Clarence Darrow's heart was infinite pity and mercy for the poor, the oppressed, the weak and the erring—all races, all colors, all creeds, all humankind. He made the way easier for many. He preached not doctrines, but love and pity, the only virtues that can make this world any better. Thousands of lives were made easier and happier because he lived. He looked out upon the earth and his heart was riven; his great abilities were given freely to the cause of human liberty and for the succor of the weak and the un-fortunate."

Ruby said, "Mr Darrow always maintained that he didn't care whether he went to heaven or hell because he has so many good friends in either place."

Clarence had asked that he be cremated. His son Paul, George Whitehead and the three nurses carried his ashes to the bridge crossing from the mainland of Jackson Park to the Wooded Island, from where they were scattered to the wind, the rain and the water. The owner of the funeral parlor would accept no pay, asking in-stead for a signed copy of *The Story of My Life*.

From all over the world the tributes poured in. The newspapers said, "What he did for America can never be forgotten." "No one was more reckless of the consequences of what he might say or do in defense of the defenseless."

Judge Frank Murphy called him one of the great spirits of our time. George Jean Nathan said, "One of my greatest and deepest admirations has gone from the world." Senator Lewis said, "His death removes one of the disciples of justice and charity." James Weldon Johnson said, "Clarence Darrow was one of the greatest of Americans, and as time passes the nobility of his character will stand out clearer and clearer in perspective, above misunderstanding, above bitterness, above calumny. I, and the members of my race, feel grateful for his courage and willingness to stand always as the champion of fair play and justice for the Negro." Arthur Garfield Hays said, "I paraphrase from words blazoned on the statue of Wendell C. Phillips in Boston: 'When the Muse of Time shall be asked to name the greatest of them all, she shall dip her pen into the sunlight and write across the clear blue sky—Voltaire—Paine—Ingersoll—Darrow.' "

The *Nation* said, "With the death of Clarence Darrow the nation loses the most colorful of the older generation of rebels. His achievment was to bring a measure of humanity into the law." The *Christian Century* said, "He had a profound concern for men; he pitied them and pitied most the ones most in need of a redress of bitter grievances. He wanted them to have liberty to think and work and live out their little lives in such joy as is possible for men."

Dr Harry Elmer Barnes wrote, "The death of Clarence Darrow brings to an end one of the most colorful and commendable careers in the whole of American biography. The permanent estimate of his career will probably lay most value upon the fact that he was the outstanding libertarian in American history since the days of Thomas Jefferson. Darrow's death marks the passage of one of the last great figures in the American liberal tradition."

He had been a propagandist for humanity. One clergyman said, "The three great Americans of our time are Luther Burbank, Thomas Edison and Clarence Darrow: Burbank because he helped release the forces of the earth; Edison because he helped release the forces of nature; Darrow because he helped release the forces of the human spirit."

A young student friend of Darrow's, writing about him as a classroom assignment, carved out the finest epitaph any man could deserve: "Freedom is a favorite word with Darrow. When he wished to express a favorable opinion of someone he would begin by saying, 'He is for freedom.' "

An admirer commented, "I'll bet he's confounding the heavenly courts, just as he did here."

If Darrow could have heard these tributes he would have ducked his head into his big shoulders, raised one eyebrow quizzically and drawled, "I'm the one all this talk's been about. I always thought I was a hell of a fellow, and now I'm sure of it."

And he would have smiled.

THE END

Sources

PROLOGUE

Page

2   Capitalization and employment of railways taken from *Railways, the Trusts, and the People,* by Frank Parsons, Equity Series, Philadelphia.

2   Material on Marvin Hughitt and the Chicago and North Western Railway offices was supplied by Cornelius Lynde and John R. Guilliams of Chicago, both of whom worked in the Chicago Northwestern offices at the same time as Darrow.

2   The quotation, "Help a great many people," is from Darrow's *The Story of My Life,* Scribner, N.Y.C., 1934, p. 57.
The conversation between Darrow and Hughitt was related by the Darrow family.

CHAPTER I

6   Much of the Amirus Darrow material, such as the episode in the second-hand bookstore and the family hearse, was related to the author by Paul Darrow.

8   All direct quotations about his father are taken from Clarence Darrow's *Farmington,* the story of his childhood.

10   The Boise incident about chicken was related to the author by Mrs Wilson.

10   All quotations from Jenny Darrow were given to the author in conversation.

11   Darrow's pictures of school are from *Farmington.*

12   The incident at the Nicholas Senn High School is related to the author by Lawrence Draymar, Lahaska, Pennsylvania.

13   The quotation on the Kinsman church is taken from *Farmington.*

14   The story of Darrow's Decoration Day speech is provided by Jenny Darrow.

15   Darrow's failure to paint the bottom of chairs is related by his son Paul, who has chairs with unpainted bottoms to prove his point.

Page

15 Charles A. Beard's story is contained in a letter to the author.

16 The story of Mary Darrow's lawsuit was related to the author by Paul Darrow.

16 The quotation about pie and cake is from *The Story of My Life*, p. 28.

17 The story of the Saturday-night debates and Darrow as a speaker of pieces was provided by Paul and Jenny Darrow.

18 "The law is a bum profession" was written in a letter by Darrow to Robert Gros of Palo Alto, California.

19 Quotations on the Fourth of July are from *Farmington*.

20 The story of Jessie Ohl and the Ohl family was related to the author by Jessie Ohl and her sister Belicent.

21,22 The tale of James Roberts was related to the author by Paul Darrow, as was Darrow's reaction to making twenty dollars in one day.

22 Darrow's description of the olden-day lawsuits is from *Farmington*.

23 Darrow's appeal to the farmer jury was related to the author by Paul Darrow.

24 Darrow tells the story of the Ashtabula house in *The Story of My Life*; it is supplemented by the imaginary Chicago case, related to the author by Paul Darrow.

24 Darrow's comments on Protestantism and Republicanism are from *The Story of My Life*, p. 33.

25 The quotation on the early power of Chicago is from the manuscript of "The Triumph of Justice," a short story by Darrow.

25 The poetic lines about Chicago are from Carl Sandburg's *Slabs of the Sunburned West*.

26 The racial description is from *Chicago*, by Charles E. Merriam.

27 Darrow tells the story of the Henry George Club in *The Story of My Life*.

29 The material on John Peter Altgeld is taken from *Altgeld of Illinois*, by Waldo R. Browne, which broke ground in 1924, and from *Eagle Forgotten*, by Harry Barnard, the definitive biography of Altgeld. Darrow's love for Altgeld is revealed in all his writings.

30 The quotation on the tariff is from "Free Trade or Protection," *Current Topics Magazine*, April 1894.

30 The portrait of Darrow lecturing on Tolstoy is contained in a letter to the author from Abram E. Adelman of Chicago.

31 Peter Sissman's description of Darrow on the lecture platform was given to the author in conversation.

31 Darrow's passing the hat for the Boers is told in a letter to the author from William B. Spencer of Los Angeles.

32 Darrow's speech to the Phineans was published in pamphlet form by Charles H. Kerr of Chicago, under the title of *The Rights and Wrongs of Ireland*.

32 The picture of Darrow fighting for streetcar seats is contained in a letter to the author from L. Andrew Larsen of Benton Harbor, Michigan.

32 Darrow tells the story of Mayor Cregier in *The Story of My Life*.

Sources

Page

33 The material on Darrow's activities as city counsel is contained in a series of letters to the author from Morris St. P. Thomas, Darrow's assistant in this job and later his law partner.

CHAPTER II

36 The joke on the Pennsylvania legislature is from *Railways, the Trusts, and the People,* by Frank Parsons.

37 The conduct of Federal Judges Grosscup and Woods and Assistant Attorney General Walker was revealed by Allen Nevins in his *Grover Cleveland.*

37 Material on George Pullman comes from *The Story of the Pullman Car,* by Joseph Husband, published by McClurg in Chicago.

40 The full story of the Pullman strike, as well as the character of the town of Pullman, is contained in The Chicago Strike, Senate Executive Documents, Vol. 2, No. 7, 53 Congress, 3rd Session, 1894–95.

46 Darrow's conversation with Governor Altgeld is reported in *Clarence Darrow,* by Charles Yale Harrison, Cape and Smith, N.Y.C., 1931.

48 The correspondence between President Cleveland and Governor Altgeld is available in both Altgeld biographies.

49 For the story of the American Railway Union strike see Senate Executive Documents, Vol. 2, No. 7, and the report of the adjutant general for Illinois, 1894–95.

51 The picture of Debs in prison is given in *Eugene V. Debs,* by McAlister Coleman, Greenburg, N.Y.C., 1931.

51 The story of the school debate on Debs is related in *Henry Demarest Lloyd,* by Caro Lloyd, G. P. Putnam Sons, N.Y.C., 1912.

55 The material on criminal conspiracy is taken from an article by F. B. Sayre, *Harvard Law Review,* Vol. 35, pp. 393–427; also from *The History of Conspiracy and Abuse of Legal Procedure,* by P. H. Winfield, and *Law of Criminal Conspiracies,* by R. S. Wright.

57 Darrow's description of the S. S. Gregory is from *The Story of My Life,* p. 65.

57 The description of Debs in the courtroom is from the Coleman biography.

64 For the decision of the United States Supreme Court see *In Re Debs, Petitioner—158 U.S. 565.*

CHAPTER III

67 The portrait of Darrow in his office was given to the author in conversation by William Carlin.

68 Darrow's inability to say "No" was related to the author by Peter Sissman.

68 Darrow's comment on everyone being welcome whether he had money or no was related to the author by Peter Sissman.

69 The story of Darrow and his personal-injury clients was related to the author by William Carlin.

69 The story of the five-hundred-dollar check was related to the author by William Carlin.

69 Darrow's work for widows and orphans was told to the author by Sidney Love of Chicago.

69 The story of the American Bar Association in Paris is related in a letter to the author from Mrs Ruby Darrow.

70 The portrait of Darrow by the junior partner is contained in a letter to Francis Wilson from Ralph R. Bradley.

71 The story of Darrow's acceptance of an unseen agreement was related to the author by Maurice Berkson, a Chicago lawyer.

72 The story of how Darrow always picked common people for jurors was related to the author by Ben Short, a Chicago lawyer.

72 Darrow's strictures on judges were related to the author by Peter Sissman.

72 The story of the elderly lady in the dining car was related to the author by Paul Darrow.

73 The story of the small-town sheriff was related to the author by Francis S. Wilson of the Illinois Supreme Court.

73 All stories about William Carlin were related to the author by Mr Carlin.

75 The story of Darrow signing fifty checks at once was related to the author by Ben Bachrach, Chicago lawyer.

75 The story of Darrow's refusal to count money was related to the author by Harold Mulks, a Chicago lawyer.

75 The debacle following the cleaning of Darrow's desk was related to the author by Francis S. Wilson.

76 The H. G. Wells story was told to the author by Ruby Darrow.

76 Darrow's enjoyment of poker was described to the author by Angus Roy Shannon, a Chicago lawyer.

76 Darrow's pleasure in logic and a new fact was described to the author by W. R. Kellogg of North Dakota.

78 The "down-with-the-rich" story was told to the author by Max Epstein, in whose home it occurred.

79 The Wilson quotations were given to the author in conversation.

79 The material "coming out pure Darrow" was told to the author by Angus Roy Shannon.

79 The shortcomings in Darrow's reading were recounted to the author by Peter Sissman.

79 The Dr Leeming story was related to the author in conversation by Dr Leeming and his wife.

80 Darrow poking fun at the socialists was revealed to the author by Peter Sissman.

81 The Hamlin Garland story is contained in a letter to the author from Ruby Darrow.

84 Jessie's reply to Darrow was told to the author by Jessie Darrow.

86 Darrow's reply to the dude newspapermen was told to the author by the Darrow family.

86 The story of Darrow's trip to Europe with the Barnums was told to the author by Gertrude Barnum.

87 The material on Collins, Goodrich, Darrow and Vincent is contained in a series of letters to the author from Morris St P. Thomas.

90 Darrow's complaint on who was going to feed him was related to the author by Peter Sissman.

90 Darrow's comments on the good lawyer and criminal law are from *The Story of My Life*, pp. 75–76.

91 The David Lilienthal story is contained in a letter to the author from Mr Lilienthal.

92 Darrow's arguments on criminology are quoted from his book, *Crime: Its Causes and Treatment*.

93 Darrow's attempt to free Mildred Sperry before conviction was related to the author in conversation by Francis Wilson and Paul Darrow; further material on the case is contained in Darrow's article on Governor Frank Lowden, *Scribner's Magazine*, April 1928.

94 Darrow's reaction to the attempted assassination of President Roosevelt is contained in a letter to the author from Rabbi Jerome Folkman of Grand Rapids, Michigan.

96 The story of Darrow's reading his anarchist paper in Rockford, Illinois, was related by Fay Lewis.

96 The material on the Haymarket riot is taken from Henry David's definitive work, *The History of the Haymarket Affair*, Farrar and Rinehart, 1936.

100 Altgeld's comments on Bryan are from *Eagle Forgotten*.

101 Darrow's relief upon not being elected to office is told in *The Story of My Life*.

101 Darrow's bicycle friendship with the colored tailor was related to the author by Paul Darrow.

101 Darrow's supporting of the Negro family is from *Clarence Darrow*, by Charles Yale Harrison.

102 The story of Darrow's chat with the colored waiter was related to the author in conversation by Mr and Mrs Dwight McKay of Chicago.

103 Darrow's comments on the purity of the Anglo-Saxon race are recounted in a letter to the author from Leon Nelson, Richmond, Virginia.

105 Senator Hammond's mudsill theory is stated in Bancroft's *History of California*.

107 Darrow's encountering a copy of his closing argument in Switzerland was related to the author by Mrs Ruby Darrow.

107 The material on the summation is taken from the *Woodworkers' Conspiracy Case*, by Clarence Darrow, the Campbell Printers, Chicago, 1900.

CHAPTER V

113 Darrow's life in the Langdon Apartments was described to the author in conversations and letters from Justice Francis S. Wilson of Illinois.

114 The Gertrude Barnum material was supplied to the author in conversations and letters; portions of it are from her unpublished autobiography and an unpublished article, "The Immortality of Clarence Darrow."

Page

116   The portrait of Miss Addams' failure is from Gertrude Barnum's unpublished autobiography.

117   The "no-conscious-seduction" remark was made by George A. Briggs of Los Angeles.

117   Darrow's relation to his son was portrayed to the author by Paul Darrow.

118   The story of Darrow's meeting and courtship of Ruby Hamerstrom was related to the author by Ruby Darrow and verified by John Gregg, Francis Wilson and other intimates of that period.

121   Darrow's tribute to Colonel Ingersoll was published in the Chicago *Inter-Ocean* and was made available by Eva Ingersoll Wakefield.

122   *The Atlantic Monthly* story was told to the author in conversation by Howard Vincent O'Brien of the Chicago *Daily News*.

122   The Polish story was related to the author in a letter from S. A. Bloch.

123   The quotations on Khayyam and Whitman are from Darrow's *A Persian Pearl, and Other Essays.*

124   Darrow's short stories had never been collected; the quotations used here are from the original manuscripts.

125   Altgeld's refusal to take a taxi was related to the author by William Carlin.

126   Darrow's walking alone beside Altgeld's hearse was told to the author by George A. Briggs.

126   Darrow's eulogy of Altgeld can be found at the back of *The Story of My Life* and was recently read into the Congressional Record by T. V. Smith, congressman from Illinois.

126   Darrow's name as anathema to Chicago businessmen was described to the author by Gertrude Barnum.

126   Darrow's telling his constituents not to vote for him is related in a letter to the author from Anton Johannsen of the Illinois Industrial Commission.

127   The quotation about the coal barons getting all the coal is from a speech made at Industrial Hall in Philadelphia, October 30, 1902.

128   Baer's contemptible-failure speech will be found in the Scranton *Times*, October 4, 1902.

129   The miners' ambulance is told about in the Scranton *Times*, November 20, 1902.

129   The story of the miner who lost his leg is told in the Wilkes-Barre *News*, December 11, 1902.

129   Dr Gibbon's story is told in the Scranton *Times*, November 20, 1902.

130   Mitchell's statement is quoted from his book *Organized Labor*, American Book and Bible House, Philadelphia, 1903.

131   The evidence on the composite man and the company store was brought out in a hearing before the commission. It is obtainable only in the back files of newspapers, the most complete of which is the Philadelphia *North American.*

132   Ex-superintendent Shea's testimony will be found in the Scranton *Times*, November 20, 1902.

Page

133 George Baer's worries over the college the miners should send their sons to will be found in his closing address to the commission, p. 9816 of the stenographic report.

133 Mrs Kate Burns's story was recounted in the Wilkes-Barre *News*.

135 The story of the Jeddo evictions will be found in the Philadelphia *North American*, January 27, 1903.

140 The New York *Evening Journal* article was printed on October 7, 1902.

140 Mrs John Lochner's letter appeared in the New York *Evening Journal*, October 7, 1902.

141 The tribute to the O'Neil brothers is from *The Story of My Life*.

141 The discommoding of the commissioners and the death of the Hungarian are reported in the Pittston *Gazette*, October 31, 1902.

145 The story of the miner who worked in the parlor vein will be found in the Wilkes-Barre *Daily News*, December 12, 1902.

146 President Fowler's speech against the unions was reported in a Pennsylvania newspaper (name obliterated), November 12, 1902.

146 The story of the Molly Maguires is told in *The Molly Maguire Riots*, by J. Walter Coleman, Garrett & Massie, Richmond, 1936.

147 The story of the founding of the Pinkerton agency will be found in *The Pinkertons*, by Richard W. Rowan, Little, Brown, 1931. This book is a family eulogy and ignores all social implications of the Pinkerton anti-labor work.

149 The estimate of Darrow and Mitchell as a combination is contained in a letter to the author from Richard J. Beamish, commissioner of the Pennsylvania Public Utility Commission.

149 Mitchell's interrogation of the sheriff is recounted in the Philadelphia *North American*, January 7, 1903.

150 General Gobin's "shoot to kill!" was reported in the Philadelphia *North American*, February 4, 1903.

150 Baer's claim that the unions were corrupting the children of America will be found in a transcript of the hearing; his reasons for not increasing wages will be found in his summary.

151 The story of the conflict between Darrow and Mitchell is related in a letter to the author from Richard J. Beamish.

152 Darrow was called a comet by Angus Roy Shannon, a Chicago lawyer.

152 The quotations from Wolverton, Baer and Darrow are taken from the United Mine Workers' transcript and from complete reports of the Philadelphia *North American*.

153 Darrow's waving aside the sheaf of notes is recounted in Harrison's story of Darrow.

155 The awards are briefed from the reports of the Anthracite Coal Strike Commission to President Theodore Roosevelt.

CHAPTER VI

159 The quotations on the legislature are from Darrow's *The Story of My Life*, Chapter 15.

Page

159   Thompson's reasons for leaving Darrow are given by William Carlin.

160   The description of Masters' apartment is taken from a letter to the author from Ruby Darrow.

160   The story of the Darrows' honeymoon through Europe is contained in a letter to the author from Ruby Darrow.

161   Darrow's habit of ordering beefsteak and potatoes for the crowd was related to the author by Gertrude Barnum.

161   All material by Ruby Darrow was given to the author in conversation and letters.

162   The "wall-of-ice" phrase is from Gertrude Barnum.

162   Darrow's comparison of marriage and a restaurant was supplied by George A. Briggs in conversation with the author.

163   The vivid description of Darrow is given in a letter to the author from Abram Adleman.

163   All material on Ethel Maclaskey was provided by Mrs Maclaskey in letters and conversation with the author.

163   The Mrs Simpson stories were related to the author by George Francis of Los Angeles.

164   Masters losing the personal-injury suit was related to the author by William Carlin.

164   The story of the doctor and his new hospital was related to the author by George Francis.

164   The Massie case story is contained in a letter to the author from Lieu-tenant Commander L. H. C. Johnson.

165   The massage-parlor story was told to the author by George Francis.

165   All material from George Leisure is contained in a letter to the author from Mr Leisure.

167   Darrow losing patience with the judge is related in a letter to the author from Fay Lewis, Rockford, Illinois.

167   Darrow's gripe about misspending his life in courtrooms is contained in a letter to Jim Tully from Mr Darrow.

167   Darrow's attitude toward the Yellow Kid was related to the author by George Francis.

167   Darrow's love of the spotlight and limelight was related to the author by Howard Vincent O'Brien.

168   Darrow's boast of keeping away from his father's carpenter shop was related to the author by George Whitehead.

168   Darrow's remark in Miami is reported in a letter to the author from John Beffel, Adrian, Michigan.

168   Both labor-meeting stories are contained in letters to the author from Fay Lewis.

169   The story about President Taft is contained in a letter to the author from Mrs R. Louis Gomon of Detroit.

169   The Cunard story is contained in a letter to the author from Charles Edward Russell.

169   The story of the college professor is told in a letter to the author from Fay Lewis.

Page

178   The Paul Darrow material was provided the author by Paul Darrow.

178   The interrogation of Paul as a political prospect was related to the author by Paul Douglas of the University of Chicago.

179   The Abner Smith story was related to the author by Paul Darrow and Francis Wilson.

180   Darrow's inability to charge what he was worth was told to the author by Francis Wilson.

180   The letter to Miss S. is in the Darrow collection of papers; in the letter he gives no name other than Miss S.

181   The story of the Black Mountain gold mine is contained in letters to the author from Ruby Darrow.

182   The story of the deed to the widow's house was related to the author by George Francis.

183   Darrow's law student calling him crooked is contained in a letter to the author from George Pople.

CHAPTER VII

186   The quotation on nonresistance is from *Resist Not Evil*, pp. 11 and 12.

186   The General Bell statement was reported by Ray Stannard Baker, *McClure's*, May 1904.

186   The statistics of 1902–04 are reported in *Current History*, August 1904.

187   Darrow's comments on the Constitution are from his final appeal in the Haywood case, published in *Wayland's Monthly*, October 1907.

187   The figures on the eight-hour amendment are from *The Independent*, June 1904.

188   The article from the *Army and Navy Journal* was quoted in *McClure's*, May 1904.

188   The picture of General Bell and his prisoners was portrayed by Ray Stannard Baker and Henry George, Jr.

189   Judge McClelland is quoted from *McClure's*, May 1904.

189   The Henry George, Jr, dispatch will be found in the New York *American*, June 12, 1904.

189   For the confession of Harry Orchard, see *The Confessions and Autobiography of Harry Orchard*, the McClure Company, New York, 1907.

190   The Sterling quotation will be found in the transcript of evidence, Haywood trial.

190   Dumping the union men into Kansas is told in *Current History*, August 1904.

190   The quotations from *The Arena* is in the August 1904 issue.

190   The Alliance quotations are from *Harper's Weekly*, January 10, 1904.

191   The story of the explosion was related to the author by members of the Steunenberg family and by old-time residents of Caldwell.

193   Judge Burch's statement about Steunenberg will be found in the Boise *Capitol News*, December 26, 1907.

194   The picture of Steunenberg in the Palace Hotel was related to the author in conversation by Henry Z. Johnson of Pasadena.

Page

194 Descriptions of the crowd around the Steunenberg home were given to the author by Ralph Scattergay and William Griffith of Caldwell.

194 Descriptions of Harry Orchard were given to the author by Scattergay and Griffith of Caldwell.

195 The Sheriff Mosely description of Orchard will be found in the Idaho *Daily Statesman*, January 2, 1906.

195 The bartender's comment will be found in the *Capitol News*, January 16, 1906.

196 The Orchard quotation is from his published confessions.

196 Orchard before the Citizens' Committee was described to the author by Charles Steunenberg.

196 Senator Borah's funeral oration will be found in the *Capitol News*, January 2, 1906.

197 The man who urged the hiring of James McParland is reported to the author by Charles Steunenberg to have been Judge Stockslager.

197 The quotations of Van Duyn and Sheriff Nichols will be found in the *Capitol News*, January 18 and 19, 1906.

198 The quotation on the McParland-Pinkerton war is from *The Pinkertons*, by Richard W. Rowan, Little, Brown, 1931.

198 Sirango's story will be found in *Silver Strike*, by William T. Stoll, Little, Brown, Boston, 1932.

200 Hawley's quotation is from his final appeal in the Haywood case.

200 The scene between Orchard and McParland is described in the *Statesman*, February 20, 1906.

201 The *Statesman's* belief in Orchard may be found in the issue of February 20, 1906.

201 The Judge Wood outrage was related to the author by the judge's daughter, Fayette Simpson, of Boise.

202 Warden Whitney's statement will be found in the *Statesman*, January 20, 1906.

202 The Jesse Hawley story was related to the author in conversation with Jesse Hawley.

203 The story of the arrest of Moyer, Haywood and Pettibone will be found in *Bill Haywood's Book*, International Publishers, 1929, pp. 192–93.

203 The highhanded-method story was related to the author by Otto Peterson, clerk of the court.

204 Judge Ailshie's opinions were expressed to the author in conversation; his court decision is 12 Idaho 250.

204 The U.S. Supreme Court decision is in 203 U.S. Rep. 192, 51 Law Edition, pp. 148–60.

207 The Senator Du Bois story was related to the author by Henry Z. Johnson, to whom it was told by Senator Du Bois.

208 The scene between Edgar Wilson and Judge Wood was related to the author by Mrs Edgar Wilson; it is also mentioned in Judge Wood's pamphlet called *Moyer, Haywood, Pettibone and Orchard*, Caxton Press, Caldwell, Idaho.

Sources

208 Darrow going to the Wilsons' for dinner was related to the author by Mrs Wilson.

208 The story of Judge Wood's being called a damn fool was related to the author by Henry Z. Johnson, of whom Judge Wood had asked his question.

209 The Caldwell lawyer was Ralph Scattergay, who made the comment to the author.

209 Intimidation on the part of the federation was related to the author by Ralph Scattergay.

209 Darrow posting marksmen was told to the author by Jesse Hawley.

210 The story of C. O. Johnson was related to the author by Ralph Scattergay.

210 Mrs Steunenberg's stories were related to the author in conversation.

210 The story of Billy Cavenaugh is told in Darrow's *The Story of My Life*.

211 Darrow's comment about the apple tree was told to the author by Ruby Darrow.

211 Darrow's indictment of the Idaho legal procedure will be found in the pamphlet, *Argument of Clarence Darrow in the Steve Adams Case*.

212 Adams' statement on what McParland told him was given to Darrow by Adams.

213 The Lillard story was related to the author by Paul Darrow.

214 McParland's last statements to Adams were related by Adams to Darrow.

214 Mrs Adams' complaint will be found in the *Statesman*, August 10, 1907.

215 The opening statement of the prosecution was reported in the *Daily Idaho Press*, Wallace, February 16, 1907.

217 Darrow's final plea in the Adams case is published in a pamphlet under that title.

218 The incident of the newspaper reporters and Harry Orchard is taken from Judge Wood's pamphlet on the trial.

220 The Borah-Gooding story was related to the author by Charles Steunenberg.

223 The picture of civil war in Colorado is given in Haywood's autobiography, p. 145.

225 The conversation of Orchard was described to the author by Jesse Hawley.

226 Orchard's reply to Charles P. McCarthy was related to the author by Charles McCarthy.

226 Orchard's story of going over to the side of God is reported in the *Statesman*.

227 The Koelsche story was related to the author by Judge Koelsche.

227 Darrow's comments on Orchard's religion will be found in his final plea to the jury.

229 The statements of Mr and Mrs Steunenberg were made to the author in Boise.

231 Judge Wood's wanting to throw the case out of court is told in his pamphlet on the case.

232 The Molly Maguire material is from *The Molly Maguire Riots*, by J. Walter Coleman, p. 136.

Page

233 Darrow's grouse to his wife was told to the author by Mrs Darrow.

233 Pettibone's comment on his chemical was related to the author by Otto Peterson.

234 Darrow's statement of why he loves workingmen is from his final plea in the Steve Adams case.

235 The comment of Judge Wood's daughter was made to the author in conversation.

236 Haywood's picture of Darrow is in Haywood's autobiography.

236 Darrow's picture of the courtroom is from *The Story of My Life*.

237 Darrow's final appeal to the jury will be found in *Wayland's Monthly*, October 1907.

240 Mrs Wilson's picture of Boise was made to the author in conversation.

241 Darrow's lament for Borah was told to the author by Mrs Darrow.

243 All pictures of Darrow's illness are from *The Story of My Life*, supplemented by material given to the author by Mrs Darrow.

246 The story of Darrow's financial troubles and the scenes in the hospital over them were described to the author in a series of letters from Ruby Darrow.

CHAPTER VIII

248 All information on the Midway flat is contained in a series of letters to the author from Ruby Darrow.

250 Robert Hutchin's quotation is from a letter to the author.

250 Darrow's comments on cruelty are contained in a letter to Mary Field.

251 The story of Chitty's *On Common Law Pleading* is contained in a letter to the author from Abram Adleman.

251 All T. V. Smith stories were related to the author in conversation by Mr Smith.

251 The portrait of Darrow in the St Louis *Mirror* was reproduced in *Current Literature*, August 1907, p. 158.

252 The description of Darrow as a lecturer is contained in an unsigned letter.

252 The letter to the labor reporter is to Mary Field.

252 The Hamlin Garland quotation is found in *Companions on the Trail*, p. 322.

253 Darrow's introduction to the Voltaire book is in the Vanguard Press Edition, 1929.

253 Lieutenant Commander Johnson's story was related to the author in a letter from Mr Johnson.

253 The Cissie Patterson story is contained in a letter to the author from Ruby Darrow.

254 The George Leisure material is contained in a letter to the author from Mr Leisure.

254 Darrow's reply at his banquet is related in a letter to the author from Francis Griffes Peede.

254 Darrow's predilection for making settlements was related to the author by Francis Wilson.

Sources

Page

255 The story of Darrow's failing to get to court and of his return from Indianapolis were related to the author by Francis S. Wilson and William Carlin.

256 Stories about keeping Darrow well dressed were furnished to the author by Ruby Darrow.

257 The story of the gas-producing machine and the plant in Greeley was related to the author by Paul Darrow.

258 The picture of Sam Gompers in the Midway flat was given to the author by Ruby Darrow.

259 *Ortie McManigal's Own Story of the National Dynamite Plot* was published in Los Angeles by the Neale Company.

259 *The Masked War* was published by Doran, New York, 1913.

261 Darrow's pamphlet on *The Open Shop* was published by Kerr in Chicago; the best of it is contained in an article in *The American Magazine* for September 1911.

263 The comments of Nockels and Gompers were reported to the author by Ruby Darrow, as was Darrow's request of his wife to be released from his pledge.

263 Darrow's comments on having done his share of the fighting are from *The Story of My Life*, pp. 173–75.

263 Wilson's gripe at Darrow was told to the author in conversation.

264 Mrs Darrow's picture of their distress as they went West is contained in a series of letters to the author from Ruby Darrow.

264 Darrow's never asking clients whether they were guilty is contained in a letter to the author from Ruby Darrow.

265 All Fletcher Bowron material was given to the author in conversation by Mayor Bowron.

265 McNamara assuring Gompers of his innocence is related in *Gompers' Seventy Years of Life and Labor*, Dutton, New York, 1925.

266 Much of the Otis portrait comes from *Los Angeles*, by Morrow Mayo, Knopf, New York, 1933.

270 Hiram Johnson's harangue against Otis is taken from *Revolution in Los Angeles*, by Alexander Irvine, Los Angeles, 1911, p. 84.

271 Cantrell's accusations against Harriman were related to the author by Cantrell.

271 The Davis estimate of Harriman was given to the author in conversation with Mr Davis.

272 The conversation between Darrow and George Behm will be found in the transcript of evidence in the Darrow trial, to be found in the Los Angeles Hall of Justice.

273 The hounding by the Burns detectives was related to the author by Katherine Schmidt, sister of Matt Schmidt.

273 Burns admitted from the witness stand that his office manager, Mills, offered to sell Darrow the records.

274 Darrow going to Culver City to recover a witness was related to the author in conversation by Dr Atwater.

Sources

Page

274   Darrow's social life in Los Angeles was described to the author by Ruby Darrow, Dr Gerson and Reynold Blight.

275   Darrow's exclamation about J. B. leaving a trail behind him was related to the author by J. B. McNamara.

275   Darrow's disbelief in violence is from his appeal to the jury on the second trial, published by the Golden Press, Los Angeles, and reprinted in *Everyman*, May 1913.

277   The McNamara attitude toward their war was given to the author in conversation and letters by J. B. and J. J. McNamara.

278   The socialist platform will be found in *Revolution in Los Angeles*, by Alexander Irvine.

280   The story of the purchase of the nitrogelatin will be found in the transcript of evidence of *The People* vs. *Matt Schmidt*, Los Angeles Hall of Justice. The story was also related to the author by Matt Schmidt.

281   A facsimile of the J. B. McNamara confession was published in the Los Angeles *Times*, October 1, 1929.

282   J. B. McNamara's reason for dynamiting the *Times* was related to the author by J. B. McNamara.

282   The quotation from *Crime, Its Causes and Treatments* is from the Watts and Co. edition, London, 1934, Chapter 23.

283   Mrs Wilson's picture of Darrow was given to the author in conversation by Mrs Wilson.

283   The conversation between Hamerstrom and Diekleman was told from the witness stand by Diekleman in the Darrow case.

284   Franklin's description of his work for Darrow is taken from his testimony in the Darrow trial.

285   Franklin's story of his bribing of Bain is contained in his testimony in the Darrow trial.

286   Franklin's story of his attempt to bribe Lockwood is taken from his testimony in the Darrow case.

288   For Steffens' statement of his role in the McNamara case, see his *Autobiography*. There can be no doubt but that Steffens blew up his own importance in this case to many times the size of its actuality.

289   The portrait of Darrow as a coward and hero is from the *Autobiography* of Lincoln Steffens, Harcourt Brace, New York, 1931.

289   The scene between Darrow, Scripps and Steffens is reported by both Darrow and Steffens.

290   The settlement conversation between Darrow and Steffens at the Van Nuys hotel was related by Darrow from the witness stand in his own case.

291   Le Compte Davis's part in the settlement was related to the author by Mr Davis.

292   The Fremont Older conversation was given from the witness stand by Mr Older and corroborated to the author by Mrs Older.

293   Davis's interview with Otis was related to the author by Davis.

293   Otis's profanity is quoted in *Take the Witness*, by Alfred Cohn and Joe Chisholm, Stokes, New York, 1934.

Sources

Page

295 Franklin's sessions with Lockwood and White were related from the witness stand in the Darrow case.

296 The story of the Franklin-White-Lockwood bribery was told by the three men in the Darrow trial.

298 Parts of the conversation between Darrow and Steffens are reported by both men in their autobiographies.

299 The story of J. B. McNamara's breakdown was related to the author by Mr Davis.

301 The "physic-explosion" phrase is from Harrison's book on Darrow.

303 Darrow's statement on how he could have tried the McNamara case is contained in his final plea to the jury in his own defense, Golden Press Edition, Los Angeles, p. 57.

304 Billy Cavenaugh's last kindness is told in Darrow's autobiography.

Chapter IX

305 Sam Gompers' statement will be found in the Los Angeles *Times*, December 2, 1911.

305 The Harry Orchard statement will be found in the Los Angeles *Examiner* for December 4, 1911.

305 The Oregon State Federation statement will be found in the Los Angeles *Times* for December 2, 1911.

306 The Big Bill Haywood statement will be found in the Los Angeles *Examiner*, December 5, 1912.

306 Judge Bordwell's sentence of the McNamaras will be found in the Los Angeles *Times*, December 6, 1911.

306 All evidence on Matt Schmidt and Dave Caplan will be found in the transcript of evidence in *The People* vs. *Matt Schmidt*, a copy of which will be found in the Los Angeles district attorney's records.

306 Schmidt's "They tried you and convicted me" was told to the author by J. B. McNamara.

306 The Irvine election story was told to the author by Irvine.

307 Darrow's statement will be found in the Los Angeles *Times* for January 30, 1912.

307 The Le Compte Davis story was related to the author by Mr Davis.

308 The Tom Johnson–Bert Franklin conversations are related by Johnson in the transcript of evidence in the Darrow trial in the Los Angeles Hall of Justice.

308 The meetings between Franklin, Darrow and Davis, between Franklin, Willard, Carl White, Harry Jones, John Drain, Frank Dominguez, Hood, F. L. Stineman, Jordan Watt, Peter Pirotte, Joseph Musgrove, are all to be found in the transcript of evidence.

311 The story of Darrow on the white horse is furnished by Francis Griffes Peede.

312 Darrow's statement about his indictment will be found in the Los Angeles papers of January 30 and 31, 1912.

Page

313 Much of Earl Rogers' material comes from his biography, *Take the Witness*, by Alfred Cohn and Joe Chisholm.

314 The roll-away-bed story is told in a letter to the author from Francis Peede.

315 The Dr Gerson story was told to the author in conversation by Dr Gerson.

315 The description of Darrow at the opening of his trial is from the Los Angeles *Herald*, May 17, 1912.

316 The Mullchaney story is contained in a letter to the author from Anton Johannsen.

317 Bert Franklin's testimony in the trial will be found to start in Vol. 4 of the transcript of evidence.

318 The Yonkin-Smith-Krueger testimony will be found on pp. 3616, 3685 and 3643 respectively in the transcript of evidence.

321 The John Harrington testimony begins on p. 2668.

323 Darrow at the Severance Club was told to the author by Reynold E. Blight.

323 The Hiram Johnson story was related to the author by Mrs Older.

324 Mrs Rogers' comments were made to the author in conversation.

325 Mrs Darrow's comment on Earl Rogers is contained in a letter to the author.

325 The story of the Darrows' home life is provided by Mrs Darrow and Mrs Edgar Wilson.

326 Judge Hutton's appeal to the jury will be found in the Los Angeles *Examiner*, July 4, 1912.

326 The personal life of the jurors was told to the author in conversations by Jurors Williams and Golding.

328 The Guy Bittinger testimony starts on p. 3269.

330 The quotation from Francis Peede is in a letter to the author.

330 Rogers' cross-examination of Franklin on leaving a trail behind him will be found on p. 693 of the transcript.

332 Fletcher Bowron material was given to the author in conversation by Mr Bowron.

334 The description of Joe Ford is given by Mrs Ford.

334 Juror Williams' comment on Ford's speech was given to the author in conversation.

335 Joe Ford's summation will be found in the Los Angeles *Times* for August 13, 1912.

335 The paragraph from Rogers' summation will be found in *Take the Witness*.

336 All material on Darrow's closing plea is taken from the account published in pamphlet form by the Golden Press, Los Angeles, 1912.

338 Judge Hutton's charge to the jury will be found in the Los Angeles *Times* for August 8, 1912.

339 The Los Angeles *Herald* story is given on August 17, 1912.

Page

340 Juror Williams' story will be found in the Los Angeles *Herald*, August 17, 1912.

342 Material on life of Frederick Gardner was provided in conversation with the author by Mrs Gardner.

CHAPTER X

345 Darrow at the meeting of the Chautauqua managers was told to the author by Caroline McCarthey.

347 The arrangement between Darrow and Sissman was related to the author by Sissman and corroborated by Francis Wilson and William Holly.

349 Terry Druggan's story was related to the author by Sissman and Francis.

350 The story of the Greek murderer was told to the author by Sissman.

350 The story of the early bird was related to the author by George Francis.

351 Darrow's handling of Francis Walker was related by George Francis.

352 Darrow's pride in his work in the Eastland case was related to the author by Paul Darrow.

354 Darrow's comments on everyone needing mercy are from his final plea in the Loeb–Leopold case.

355 Sissman's portrait of Darrow was given to the author in both conversation and letters.

355 The article, "Darrow at the Defense Table," is by Charles C. Arado, *Chicago Bar Record*, November 1940.

358 Darrow's trip to Europe as a guest of Great Britain was related to the author by Ruby and Paul Darrow.

360 Material on *The State of Wisconsin* vs. *Peter Bianchi, et al*, will be found in the Wisconsin Supreme Court records, August and October terms, 1918.

363 All William Holly stories were related to the author by Judge Holly.

364 Darrow's comments on William Holly are from his autobiography.

368 For the story of the formation of the Communist Labor party, see *I Confess*, by Benjamin Gitlow, Dutton, New York City, 1940.

368 For the story of Henry Demarest Lloyd, see the biography by Caro Lloyd, Putnam's, 1912.

369 Attorney General Palmer's article was published in *Forum* magazine, March 27, 1920.

369 Articles on the Palmer raids will be found in the *New Republic*, January 28, 1920; May 12, 1920; January 19, 1921, and in *The Nation*, June 12, 1920.

369 Darrow's avowed reason for defending the communists is stated in his *Argument in Defense of the Communists*, Charles H. Kerr and Company, Chicago, 1920.

370 Comments of the Rockford businessmen on the Reds are quoted from *The Trial of Helen McCleod*, a novel by Alice Beal Parsons, Funk and Wagnalls Company, New York, 1938. Mrs Parsons was the woman indicted with the other Rockford communists.

371 Darrow's appeal to the newspaper editor is from *The Trial of Helen Mc-Cleod*.

Page
372 The eyewitness who describes Darrow is Mrs Parsons.

372 Darrow's appeal to the Rockford jury was published in a pamphlet called *Address of Clarence Darrow in the Trial of Arthur Person*, Defense Committee, Communist Labor party of Illinois.

377 Darrow's final appeal for the Chicago communists was published in a pamphlet called *Argument in Defense of the Communists*, Charles H. Kerr, Chicago, 1920.

CHAPTER XI

380 All Ruby Darrow material was related to the author in conversation and in letters by Mrs Darrow.

382 The quotations on capital punishment are from *Crime, Its Cause and Treatment*.

384 The letter from Nathan Leopold, Jr, is in the Darrow collection.

390 Letters from Leopold to Loeb are reproduced in the Sellers book.

392 Quoted comments by Loeb and Leopold are taken from the psychiatrists' reports or newspaper interviews.

392 Leopold's statement about Loeb is from the Chicago *Herald Examiner*, June 2, 1924.

393 A copy of Loeb's letter to his parents is in the Darrow collection.

397 Leopold's reply to the officer about his release is from the New York *Times*, May 31, 1924.

398 W. R. Kellogg's comments on Darrow and the Loeb-Leopold case were given to the author in conversation.

400 Darrow's statement on choosing to submit his case to a judge rather than a jury will be found in his closing plea.

401 For a partial statement on Darrow's ideas on criminology see *Crime, Its Cause and Treatment*.

404 Darrow sending men to interview in the Loop was recounted to the author by George Francis.

405 Judge Caverly's statement appeared in the New York *Times*, August 17, 1924.

405 A partial report of the *Loeb-Leopold Case*, by Alvin V. Sellers, Classic Publishing Company, Brunswick, Georgia, 1926.

407 Crowe's outburst against the alienists will be found in his final plea to Judge Caverly, which was published in pamphlet form in Chicago. Further material was provided the author by Mr Crowe.

407 The legal battle between Crowe and Darrow is from the New York *Evening Journal*, June 4, 1924.

409 The editorial in the *Times* appeared in the July 18, 1924, issue.

411 Darrow's cross-examination of Dr Church will be found in the Sellers book, p. 34.

414 Darrow's final plea to Judge Caverly is published by the Haldeman-Julius Company, Girard, Kansas, 1926, B-20.

418 Darrow's demand that the United States vote murder indictments, etc., will be found in the New York *Times*, August 2, 1924.

Page

418 The picture of Darrow on the day Judge Caverly was to read his decision was provided the author by George Francis.

419 The quotations from the Minneapolis *Star* and the Washington *Evening Star* are taken from the *Literary Digest* of September 27, 1925.

420 The details of Darrow's fee were related to the author by Ruby Darrow and corroborated by Darrow's associates in Chicago.

CHAPTER XII

422 The Harold McCormick story was related to the author by Mr McCormick.

423 The Untermeyer story was related by Ruby Darrow.

423 The Arabian boatman story was related by Peter Sissman.

423 Dr Shirley Case's comments on Darrow are contained in a letter to the author from Mrs Alice Coyle, Berwyn, Illinois.

423 Dr Leeming's comments were made to the author in conversation.

423 The quotation from John Haynes Holmes is from *Unity* magazine, May 16, 1938.

424 The Rabbi Goldman story was related to the author by Dr Goldman.

424 The Professor Haydon comments were made to the author in conversation.

425 The Victor Yarros quotation is from *Unity* magazine, May 16, 1938.

426 Darrow's letter to Bryan will be found in the Chicago *Tribune*, July 4, 1923.

427 Bryan's answer was reported in the *Tribune* on the following day.

427 The quotation from the Chattanooga *Daily Times* will be found in the July 20, 1925, issue.

430 Descriptions of the townspeople were provided the author by Mrs Will Robeson of Dayton.

431 The description of Bryan as a polo player is from the Chattanooga *Daily Times* for July 8, 1925.

431 All material on Darrow and the American Psychiatric Association was provided by Dr James K. Hall and Dr Beverly R. Tucker of Richmond, Virginia.

432 The quotation from the New York *World* is in the May 18, 1925, issue.

433 Portraits of John Washington Butler are from the *Literary Digest* of July 25, 1925, and from *Clarence Darrow's Two Great Trials*, by Marcet Haldeman-Julius, Haldeman-Julius Company, Girard, Kansas, 1927.

433 The Nashville *Southern Agriculturist* quotation is from the *Literary Digest*, July 25, 1925.

434 The portrait of George Rappelyea is from *Clarence Darrow's Two Great Trials* and Charles Francis Potter's article in *Liberty*, September 28, 1935.

434 Rappelyea is described by Mrs Haldeman-Julius.

435 The kindness of Mr Wilbur is described by Darrow in his autobiography.

436 Mrs Darrow's comments on the townspeople are contained in a letter to the author.

Page

436 The picture of Dayton drunk on religious excitement is given by Mrs Haldeman-Julius.

437 All references to the actual material of the trial are taken from *The World's Most Famous Court Trial*, National Book Company, Cincinnati, 1925.

440 The New York *Times*' portrait of Darrow is in the July 14 issue.

442 The description of Darrow's eloquent shrugs is from Mrs Haldeman-Julius.

442 The picture of Darrow on the streets of Dayton after his speech is given in the Knoxville *News*, July 14, 1925.

442 Bryan with his bunches of vegetables is described by Mrs Darrow.

443 The Chattanooga *Daily Times*' comments are from the July 16 issue.

443 Philip Kinsley's article is from the Chicago *Tribune* of May 27, 1925.

444 Darrow's description of himself is from *Bryan and Darrow at Dayton*, edited by Leslie Henri Allen, Arthur Lee and Company, New York City, 1925.

445 The quotations from Judge Raulston are contained in letters to the author from Judge Raulston.

449 Darrow's description of his childhood books is from his autobiography.

449 The quotation from the New York *Tribune* on Bryan is from *Bryan*, by M. R. Werner, Harcourt Brace and Company, New York, 1929.

450 The quotations from Colonel House, David Huston and another of Bryan's intimates are from Werner's biography.

451 The quotation on Bryan's intemperance is from *E. W. Howes Monthly*, April 1926.

454 John Butler's comments on fair play are from Charles Francis Potter's article in *Liberty*, September 28, 1935.

463 The Knoxville *Sentinel* requiem is in the July 14, 1925, issue.

Chapter XIII

466 All stories about the Dwight McKays were related to the author by the McKay family.

467 The W. R. Kellogg stories were told to the author by Mr Kellogg.

468 The Peter Sissman quotation is contained in a letter to the author from Mr Sissman.

468 The Marie Thompson material was provided by Ruby Darrow and Miss Thompson.

469 The story of Darrow and the ape was related to the author by Charles E. Mason.

470 The Spingarn story is contained in a letter to the author from Mr Spingarn.

470 The John Brown story is told by Clarence True Wilson in *Unity*, May 16, 1938.

471 The Ruby Darrow story was related to the author by Mrs Darrow.

471 The W. E. B. Du Bois material is contained in a letter to the author from Mr Du Bois.

473 A good description of Gladys Mitchell Sweet will be found in Marcet Haldeman-Julius' *Clarence Darrow's Two Great Trials*, Haldeman-Julius Company, Girard, Kansas.

473 Mrs Smith's comments to Dr Sweet are told in Arthur Garfield Hays's *Let Freedom Ring*.

474 The quotation from Mrs Sweet will be found in the Haldeman-Julius pamphlet.

475 Dr Ossian Sweet told of his state of mind from the witness box.

476 The material from Mrs Josephine Gomon is contained in letters to the author.

477 The story of the two schoolteachers was related to the author by Mrs Darrow.

478 The *Free Press* reporter is Cash Asher; his comments are contained in the manuscript of an article sent to the Darrows.

478 The Prosecutor Toms story is contained in a letter to the author from Mr Toms.

480 The cross-examination of Alfred H. Andrew was reproduced in the Detroit *Sunday Times*, May 2, 1926.

482 Dr Sweet's comments on Dr Turner will be found in the Haldeman-Julius pamphlet.

482 The reporter is Cash Asher.

482 The Newman Levy anecdote is contained in a letter to the author from Arthur Spingarn.

483 The quotation from William Pickens is from a letter to the author from Mr Pickens.

485 Darrow's comment on the stubborn juror was related to the author by Mrs Gomon.

485 The George Murphy comments are contained in a letter to the author from Mr Murphy.

486 Darrow's reply to Toms is related by Mrs Gomon.

488 Darrow claiming his autobiography would never be written was related by George Francis.

488 Darrow's letters to his granddaughter were made available by Mary Darrow.

489 Much of the George Whitehead material was related to the author in conversation; some of it comes from published and unpublished manuscripts, comments and notes turned over to the author by Mr Whitehead.

490 The four comments on religion are from the Houston *Press*, March 12, 1931.

491 Judge Musmanno's material is contained in letters to the author.

493 Darrow's alleged joining of the Episcopal Church, and his answer to the charge was related to the author by Dr Sidney Tedesche.

493 Darrow's mix-up with the Humanist Society was related to the author by Dr John H. Dietrich, then head of the movement in Minneapolis.

Page

494 The picture of Darrow and Dr Wilson on their way to Canada was provided by J. E. Joiner.

495 The tale about Darrow's love life was related to the author by Mrs Darrow.

495 The material on *The Mystery of Life* is contained in a letter to the author from Professor Parshley.

496 The Jessie Binford story was related to the author by Miss Binford.

497 The story of the prisoner at Northwestern Penitentiary is contained in a letter to the author from Dr Charles Matinband, as is the reason that Darrow refused to defend the Scottsboro boys, which was substantiated by Arthur Garfield Hays.

498 H. L. Mencken's comments on Darrow will be found in *Vanity Fair*, March 1927.

498 Charles A. Beard's estimate of Darrow is contained in a letter to the author from Mr Beard.

499 The story of Darrow's prescience was related to the author by T. V. Smith.

500 Dr Haydon's comments on Darrow were given to the author in conversation.

500 Darrow's visits to the Meadville Theological School were recounted to the author by Charles Lyttle.

500 The best picture of the Massie case, albeit a bit prejudiced, will be found in *Sea Duty*, by Rear Admiral Yates Stirling.

502 Mrs Fortescue told her story in a series of articles in *Liberty*, July and August 1932.

502 Darrow's disinclination to take the Massie case is told in his autobiography.

503 The Spingarn story was related to the author by Mr Spingarn.

503 The George Leisure material is in letters to the author from Mr Leisure.

504 Darrow extracting a smile from the jurors was related by Mr Leisure.

504 A picture of the trial was given to the author by Commander L. H. C. Johnson.

507 Information on Darrow as the head of the Review Board was furnished to the author by Lowell B. Mason, Robert S. Keebler, John Schulman and J. Adin Mann, all members of the board.

508-9 The scenes between Darrow, Johnson and President Roosevelt were described to the author by J. Adin Mann.

510 The story of Darrow in the elevator was told by Mr Mason.

511 *News-Week*, May 19, 1934.

512 Darrow's comments before the Senate Investigating Committee will be found in Volume 1, Investigation of the N.R.A., Hearings before the Committee on Finance, U. S. Senate. Government Printing Office, Washington, 1935.

514 *Survey-Graphic*, July 1934.

514 Warden Lawes's story is contained in a letter to the author.

514 Julian's Street's comments are contained in a letter to the author from Mr Street.

Page

515 *Esquire*, May 1936.

516 The observation of the Ohio reporter is contained in a letter to the author from Willis Thornton.

518 Judge Holly's funeral oration was published in *Unity*, May 16, 1938.

518 The story of the owner of the funeral parlor is told by Ruby Darrow.

519 Justice Frank Murphy's comments, like those of George Jean Nathan and Senator Lewis, were messages to Mrs Darrow, reprinted in *Unity*, May 16, 1938.

519 James Weldon Johnson's comments are from "Clarence Darrow—As I Knew Him," *Unity*, May 16, 1938.

519 The Harry Elmer Barnes quotation is from his article in *Unity*, May 16, 1938.

519 Darrow confounding the heavenly courts is from Louis E. Mesam.

519 The young student was Francis Borrelli, who probably was quoting from "A Day with Clarence Darrow" in the Haldeman-Julius Monthly (1925) by John W. Gunn.

Selected Bibliography

Adamic, Louis, *Dynamite*, 1931.

Allen, Leslie Henri, *Bryan and Darrow at Dayton*, 1925.

Barnard, Harry, *Eagle Forgotten*, 1938.

Bates, Ernest Sutherland, *The Story of the Supreme Court*, 1936.

Black, Forrest Revere, *Ill-Starred Prohibition Cases*, 1931.

Bogen, Jules I., *The Anthracite Railroads*, 1927.

Borah, W. E., *Closing Argument in the Haywood Trial*, 1906.

Browne, Waldo R., *Altgeld of Illinois*, 1924.

Bruere, Robert W., *The Coming of Coal*, 1922.

Bryan, W. J., *Memoirs*, 1925.

Burns, William J., *The Masked War*, 1913.

Chambers, Walter, *Labor Unions and the Public*, 1931.

Clay, Samuel H., *Assassination of Ex-Governor Steunenberg*, 1907.

Cohn, Alfred and Chisholm, Joe, *Take the Witness*, 1934.

Coleman, J. Walter, *The Molly Maguire Riots*, 1936.

Coleman, McAlister, *Eugene V. Debs*, 1930.

Crandall, Allen, *The Man from Kinsman*, 1933.

Crowe, Robert E., *Final Appeal to Judge Caverly*, 1924.

Darrow, Clarence. Books: *A Persian Pearl*, 1899. *Resist Not Evil*, 1904. *An Eye for an Eye*, 1905. *Farmington*, 1905. *Crime, Its Cause and Treatment*, 1925. *The Prohibition Mania* (with Victor S. Yarros), 1927. *Infidels and Heretics* (with Walter Rice), 1927. *The Story of My Life*, 1932.

    Pamphlets: *The Rights and Wrongs of Ireland*, 1895. *A Persian Pearl and Other Essays*, 1897. *The Woodworkers' Conspiracy Case*, 1898. *Leo Tolstoi*, January 1902. *Argument for Steve Adams*, 1907. *Closing Argument in the Haywood Case*, October 1907. *Liberty vs. Prohibition*, 1908. *The Open Shop*, 1909. *Plea in His Own Defense*, August 1912. *Second Plea*, 1913. *War Prisoners*, 1919. *Argument in Defense of the Communists*, 1920. *Address in the Trial of Arthur Person*, 1920. *Capital Punishment Debate*, 1924. *Voltaire*, 1925. *Plea in Defense of Loeb and Leopold*, 1926. *Argument in the Case of Henry Sweet*, 1926. *Crime and the Alarmists*, 1926. *Why I Am an Agnostic*, 1929. *The Myth of the Soul*, 1929. *Capital Punishment. The War in Europe. Darrow-Starr Debate. Darrow-Foster Debate* (no dates given). *Does Man Live Again Debate*, 1936.

MAGAZINE ARTICLES: "Free Trade or Protection," *Current Topics*, April 1894. "Literary Style," *Tomorrow*, January 1905. "The Hold-up Man," *International Socialist Review*, February 1909. "Why Men Fight for the Closed Shop," *American*, September 1911. The *Everyman Magazine* series: "Address on John Brown," March 1913. Second Plea in His Own Defense, May 1913. "Address on Land and Labor," June 1913. "Crime and Criminals," August 1913. "Henry George," September–October 1913. "Industrial Conspiracies," November–December 1913. "Voltaire," January–February 1914. "Single Tax," August–September 1914. "On Europe's War," October–November 1914. "If Men Had Opportunity," January–February 1915. "Address to the Prisoners at Joliet," November 1915. Defines Non-resistance, December 1915. "An Appeal for the Despoiled," January 1916. "Robert Burns," February 1916. "Skeleton in the Closet," May 1916. "Land and People," October 1916. "Schopenhauer," *Liberal Review*, March 1917. "The Ordeal of Prohibition," *American Mercury*, August 1924. "Crime and Punishment" (with H. J. Bridges), *Century*, March 1925. "Salesmanship," *American Mercury*, August 1925. "The Edwardses and the Jukes," *American Mercury*, October 1925. "Where Are the Pre-War Radicals?" *Survey Graphic*, February 1926. "The Red Flag," *Libertarian*, March 1926. "The Eugenics Cult," *American Mercury*, June 1926. "Liberty, Equality, Fraternity," *Vanity Fair*, December 1926. "The Foreign Debt and America," *Vanity Fair*, February 1927. "Tyranny and the Volstead Act," *Vanity Fair*, March 1927. "What Is the Matter with the Farmer?" *Vanity Fair*, April 1927. "The War on Modern Science," *Modern World*, July 1927. "The Divorce Problem," *Vanity Fair*, August 1927. "Should Capital Punishment Be Retained?" (Debate), *Congressional Digest*, August–September 1927. "Name Your Poison," *Plain Talk*, October 1927. "Capital Punishment," New York *Herald Tribune*, January 1, 1928. "Our Growing Tyranny," *Vanity Fair*, February 1928. "The Lord's Day Alliance," *Plain Talk*, March 1928. "Frank Lowden, the Farmer's Friend," *Scribner's Magazine*, April 1928. "Prohibition Cowardice," *Vanity Fair*, September 1928. "Is Capital Punishment Right?" *Forum*, September 1928. "Why Was God So Hard on Women and Snakes?" *Haldeman-Julius Monthly*, September 1928. "The Myth of the Soul," *American Parade*, January–February–March 1929. "At Seventy-two," *Saturday Evening Post*, July 6, 1929. "Combating Crime," *Forum*, November 1929. "Lawful Liquor" (with Clarence True Wilson), *Collier's*, September 27, 1930. "Let No Man Therefore Judge You in Meat or in Drink," *Collier's*, October 11, 1930. "John Brown—He Who Struck the First Blow," *Abbott's Monthly*, November 1930. "The Religion of the American Negro" (Debate), *The Crisis*, June 1931. "Why the 18th Amendment Cannot Be Repealed," *Vanity Fair*, November 1931. "Who Knows Justice?" *Scribner's*, February 1932. "Punishment," *Rotarian*, November 1933. "The N.R.A. and Fair Competition," *Rotarian*, November 1934. "The Lord's Soldier Joshua and the Sun and the Moon," *Truth Seeker*, September 1935. "Attorney for the Defense," *Esquire*, May 1936. "Attorney for the Defense," *Legal Chatter*, July 1937. "Our Reactionary Tendency," (no dates given) *Kessinger's Mid-West Review*. "Conduct and Profession," *The Rubric*. (no dates given)

David, Henry, *The History of the Haymarket Affair*, 1936.
Foote, Mary Hallock, *Coeur d'Alene*, 1894.
Frankfurter, Felix, and
Greene, Nathan, *The Labor Injunction*, 1930.
Frey, John P., *The Labor Injunction*. (no date)
Garland, Hamlin, *Companions on the Trail*, 1931.

Gitlow, Benjamin, *I Confess*, 1940.
Gompers, Samuel, *Seventy Years of Life and Labor*, 1925.
Goodrich, Carter, *The Miners' Freedom*, 1925.
Haldeman-Julius, Marcet, *Clarence Darrow's Two Great Trials*, 1927.
Harrison, Charles Yale, *Clarence Darrow*, 1931.
Hays, Arthur Garfield, *Let Freedom Ring*, 1928.
Haywood, Bill, *Bill Haywood's Book*, 1929.
Husband, Joseph, *The Story of the Pullman Car*, 1917. *Investigation of the National Recovery Administration*, S. Res. 79, Hearings before the Senate Committee on Finance, 1935.
Irvine, Alexander, *Revolution in Los Angeles*, 1911.
Johnson, Claudius O., *Borah of Idaho*, 1936.
Karsner, David, *Talks with Debs in Terre Haute*, 1922.
Lewis, Oscar, *The Big Four*, 1938.
Lloyd, Caro, *Henry Demarest Lloyd*, 1912.
McManigal, Ortie, *Ortie McManigal's Own Story of the National Dynamite Plot*, 1913.
Masters, Edgar Lee, *Across Spoon River*, 1936.
Mayo, Morrow, *Los Angeles*, 1933.
Merriam, Charles E., *Chicago*, 1929.
Merriam, Brig. Gen. H. C., *Report of Miners' Riots in the State of Idaho*, 1899.
Mitchell, John, *Organized Labor*, 1903.
Myers, Gustavus, *History of the Supreme Court of the United States*, 1925.
Nathan, George Jean, *The Intimate Notebooks*, 1932.
Nevins, Allen, *Grover Cleveland*, 1932.
Orchard, Harry, *Confessions and Autobiography*, 1907.
Parsons, Alice Beal, *The Trial of Helen McCleod*, 1938.
Parsons, Frank, *Railways, the Trusts and the People*, 1906.
Radin, Max, *The Law and Mr. Smith*, 1938. *Report to the President on the Anthracite Coal Strike of May–October*, 1902.
Rodell, Fred, *Woe Unto You, Lawyers*, 1939.
Rowan, Richard W., *The Pinkertons*, 1931.
Sandburg, Carl, *Slabs of the Sunburned West*, 1922.
Sayre, F. B., *Harvard Law Review*, Vol. 35.
Sellers, Alvin V., *The Loeb-Leopold Case*, 1926. *Senate Executive Documents*, Vol. 2. No. 7–53 Congress, 3rd Session.
Shaw, Charles G., *The Low-Down*, 1928.
Sirango, Chas. A., *A Cowboy Detective*, 1912.
Steffens, Lincoln, *Autobiography*, 1931.
Stirling, Admiral Yates, *Sea Duty*, 1939.
Stoll, William T., *Silver Strike*, 1932. *Sunset Club Year Book*, 1893. *Tennessee Evolution Trial. Complete Report of Scopes Case at Dayton*, 1925.
Van Kleeck, Mary, *Miners and Management*, 1934.
Walsh, Rev. William J., *The United Mine Workers of America as an Economic and Social Force in the Anthracite Industry*.
Werner, M. R., *Bryan*, 1929.
Wood, Fremont, *Moyer, Haywood, Pettibone and Harry Orchard*, 1931.

MAGAZINE ARTICLES ABOUT CLARENCE DARROW

"A Dangerous Doctrine," *Golden Elk*, July 1907. "Who Is This Man Darrow?" *Current Literature*, August 1907. "Aftermath of the Haywood Trial," *Pandex*, September 1907. "Society Held Responsible for Crime," *Current Opinion*. May

1923. "Against the Death Penalty," by S. J. Duncan-Clark, *Success*, December 1924. "Darrow on Divorce," by Walter House, *Liberty*, January 16, 1926. "Clarence Darrow's Birthday Party," by J. G. Bennema, *International Engineer*, May 1927. "Our Own All-American Team," by George Ade, *Cosmopolitan*, May 1927. "Had Darrow Been a Journalist, by One Who Is," *Nation*, August 10, 1927. "The Big Minority Man," by George C. Whitehead, *Debunker*, May 1929. "An Evening with Clarence Darrow," *Etcetera*, September 1930. "The Case against Anti-Semitism," by Joseph Brainen, *Jewish Times*, April 24, 1931. "Editor's Uneasy Chair," *Vanity Fair*, November 1931. "Lincoln, the Politician," by Lloyd Lewis, *Chicagoan*, February 1932. "Clarence Darrow as He Is," by Charlotte Kinney, *Psychology*, August 1932. "The Study Table," by Nathan Essell, *Unity*, February 6, 1933. "In Memoriam," *Unity*, May 16, 1938. "Darrow, Friendly Enemy," by Clarence True Wilson, *Forum*, July 1938. "The Man Clarence Darrow," by Mary Bell Decker, *University Review*, Summer 1938. "Darrow at the Defense Table," by Charles C. Arado, *Chicago Bar Record*, November 1940.

Personal Contributors to This Biography

Leonard D. Abbott
Abram E. Adelman
Joseph Agor
Charles C. Arado
Dr H. Gale Atwater
Ben Bachrach
Walter Bachrach
James J. Barbour
Harry Barnard
Gertrude Barnum
Richard J. Beamish
Charles A. Beard
John Beffel
Elizabeth Bensberg
Maurice Berkson
Rose Berwald
Jessie Binford
Reynold Blight
S. A. Bloch
Francis Borrelli
Fletcher Bowron
Preston Bradley
Ralph R. Bradley
Lawrence Braymer
Frank E. Brennan
George A. Briggs
Lina Brooks
Mrs R. C. Bryant
Mrs A. Burton
George T. Bye
Edward Cantrell
William Carlin
Henry E. Colton
Edward L. Conwell
Mrs Alice Coyle

Robert E. Crowe
Jenny Darrow
Mr and Mrs Paul Darrow
Mary Darrow
Verna Darrow
Le Compte Davis
Albert Edward Day
Mary Bell Decker
Oscar De Priest
Robert Dienst
John H. Dietrich
Paul Douglas
Lawrence Draymar
W. E. B. Du Bois
Samuel Eichold
Max Epstein
Ben Farbstein
Arthur Davison Ficke
Rabbi Jerome Folkman
Mrs Joe Ford
George Francis
Frances Gaither
Mr and Mrs Frederic Gardner
Jerry Geisler
Dr T. Perceval Gerson
Elmer Gertz
Lillian Gish
Maurice Goldberg
Dr Morton Goldberg
Fred E. Golding
Rabbi Solomon Goldman
Mrs R. Lewis Gomon
John Gregg
William Griffith

Robert R. Gros
John R. Guilliams
Marcet Haldeman-Julius
Dr James K. Hall
William Hard
Jesse Hawley
Albert Eustace Haydon
Arthur Garfield Hays
Genevieve Forbes Herrick
William Holly
Robert Hunter
Robert M. Hutchins
Alexander Irvine
Anton Johannsen
Henry Z. Johnson
Commander L. H. C. Johnson
J. E. Joiner
Milton A. Kallis
Robert S. Keebler
W. R. Kellogg
Philip Kinsley
A. Kroch
Mrs Oliver Kuhn
A. F. La Marche
Corliss Lamont
L. Andrew Larson
Warden Lewis E. Lawes
D. A. Lawson
Dr and Mrs John Leeming
George Leisure
Fay Lewis
Joseph Lewis
David Lilienthal
Sidney Love
Cornelius Lynde
Charles Lyttle
Ethel Maclaskey
Claude A. Mahoney
J. Adin Mann
Rabbi Charles Mantinband
Charles E. Mason
Lowell B. Mason
Charles P. McCarthy
Caroline McCartney
Harold McCormick
Mr and Mrs Dwight McKay
J. B. McNamara
J. J. McNamara
H. L. Mencken
Louis E. Mesam
Judge Lester S. Moll
Harold Mulks
Judge George Murphy

Michael Musmanno
Leon Nelson
Walter M. Nelson
Ralph G. Newman
Howard Vincent O'Brien
Belicent Ohl
Jessie Ohl
Mrs Fremont Older
Marion Oliver
M. C. Otto
Howard M. Parshley
Alice Beal Parsons
Mary Field Parton
Francis Griffes Peede
Otto Peterson
Charles C. Pettijohn
William Pickens
George E. Pople
Adeline Lobdell Pynchon
William Raoul
Judge John T. Raulston
Mrs Will Robeson
Arthur Robinson
Mrs Earl Rogers
Charles Edward Russell
Ralph Scattergay
Katherine Schmidt
Matt Schmidt
John Schulman
Evelyn A. Seguin
Dr Max Seham
Angus Roy Shannon
David Shipman
Ben Short
Fayette Wood Simpson
Peter Sissman
George M. Smith
T. V. Smith
William B. Spencer
Arthur Spingarn
Mr and Mrs Charles Steunenberg
Rear Admiral Yates Stirling
Julian Street
Dr Ossian Sweet
Dr Sidney Tedesche
Dr J. J. Thomas
Morris St P. Thomas
Marie Thompson
Willis Thornton
Robert Toms
Jessie B. Trefethen
Dr Beverly R. Tucker
Jim Tully

O. M. Van Duyn
Eve Ingersoll Wakefield
Walter White
George Whitehead
Mr and Mrs Manley R. Williams

Clarence True Wilson
Mrs Edgar Wilson
Francis S. Wilson
Mrs Victor S. Yarros
Leo J. Zuber

INDEX